QUANTITY COOKING

QUANTITY COOKING

Thomas Mario

Senior Associate, Food Science
Associates, Inc.

Coordinator, Food Service Study,
Educational Facilities Laboratories
and New York City Board of Education

Instructor, Quantity Cooking, New
York City Board of Education

AVI PUBLISHING COMPANY, INC
Westport, Connecticut

Library of Congress Cataloging in Publication Data

Mario, Thomas.
    Quantity cooking.

    Includes index.
    1. Quantity cookery. I. Title.
TX820.M33   641.5'7   77-13466
ISBN 0-87055-236-8

Printed in the United States of America

Contents

Foreword

Managers as well as other members of restaurant staffs are keenly aware that in recent years important changes have taken place in the job organization of many kitchens. At one time a cook's title explained the daily duties. The fry cook fried, the roast cook roasted, and the broil cook broiled. Those who now work in the industry know that the once clear-cut assignments of workers behind the range have been noticeably modified in the past decade or two. New union contracts, schedules and working conditions, the introduction of labor-saving equipment and the use of preportioned meats and convenience foods have altered the picture. A roast cook who comes to work at noontime may be a fry cook during lunch, a roast cook in the afternoon and a broiler cook at dinner. But in the staffs of many of the finest large hotel and restaurant kitchens, you will still find cooks working at their traditional stations. These stations and training for them are the basis for this book, not in any attempt to roll back time and pursue the once rigid traditions of job duties, but to stress the fact that the work of these specialist cooks is the best possible map for the beginner exploring the art of quantity cooking. By focusing on the basic skills of sauce making, soup making, broiling, roasting, etc., one at a time, the student becomes adept at the vitally important job prototypes which, when mastered, open up his or her eventual ability to range through the vast field of cookery in all of its branches. Students and apprentices are often drawn to the culinary arts because they have been intrigued by novel dishes, foreign foods and attractive variations on old recipes. To such students I would offer the advice that music instructors give new talented students: Learn to play the scales first. Learn your etudes before you attempt a concerto. Once you begin to succeed in the traditional jobs in the kitchen, you will find that your zeal is actually stronger than when you first started, and that the upward climb is really easier than you may have expected.

I would like to express my cordial thanks to the following people who generously offered suggestions and advice: Mr. Arno Schmidt,

Executive Chef, the Waldorf-Astoria Hotel, New York City; Dr. Guy Livingston and Dr. Charlotte Chang, Food Science Associates, Dobbs Ferry, N.Y.; Mr. William Sultan, author of *Practical Baking* and former Chairman, Food Trades, Food and Maritime Trades High School, New York City. I am especially indebted to two present members of the staff of the same school who read the script and made valuable comments, Mr. Buron Abramowitz, Assistant Principal, and Mr. Armand Risbano in charge of the Cafeteria and Catering Department. Finally, I express my appreciation to Mrs. Jane Krantz who made the drawings for Chap. 2.

Thomas Mario

Long Beach, New York
May 1977

Glossary

The list below includes trade terms which students frequently encounter in the kitchen. It also includes brief descriptions of spices as well as meat and fish terminology with which newcomers in the field are often unfamiliar.

A la (Fr.)—Phrase meaning prepared according to a certain style or accompanied with certain garnishes

A la carte—Menu term for items each of which is individually priced and may be made to order rather than a complete meal, usually prepared in advance, listed at a set price

A la king—Dish of diced cooked chicken, sweet peppers and mushrooms in a *velouté* sauce (*see Velouté*)

A la mode—Prepared according to a particular fashion, frequently used for beef braised in a red wine gravy and for pie topped with ice cream

A l'anglaise (Fr.)—Phrase meaning literally "according to English style," often employed to describe a process of breading food prior to frying by dipping it successively in flour, eggs and bread crumbs; also applies to meat or poultry cooked in white stock or water

Additive—Substance added to a formula for processed food to enhance flavor, improve keeping quality or otherwise serve as a stabilizing element

Aftertaste—Flavor sensations remaining in mouth after food is eaten; an important factor in making quality judgments of raw or cooked foods

Aged beef—Applies generally to cuts used for steaks or roasts which, when raw, are kept under controlled refrigerator temperature and humidity for 2 to 3 weeks during which enzymatic action improves tenderness and changes flavor; because of weight loss during aging, beef thus treated costs more than unaged beef

Agneau (Fr.)—Lamb

Allemande (Fr.)—*Velouté* sauce enriched with cream and egg yolks

Allspice—Single spice, most of which comes from the island of Jamaica, resembling other spices such as nutmeg and cloves; in whole or ground form; used in meat dishes and desserts

Allumettes (Fr.)—Strips of deep-fried potatoes, between French fried and julienne in size; also very light pastry cut into strips and filled as appetizer

Amandine—Served with toasted or sautéd almonds cut into thin strips or slices

Anchovy—Very thin small fish, fillets of which are salted and packed in olive oil or salted and sold dried

Antipasto—Term literally meaning "before the meal," used to describe appetizers

Apprentice—In the culinary field, one working with an experienced cook or baker learning the trade; may be working as an apprentice while going to a specialized school

Apricot glaze—Thick strained mixture of cooked apricots and sugar spread on top of apples, fruit tarts, etc., to add a high gloss as well as flavor

Arrowroot—Starchy white powder of tropical American plant used for thickening delicate sauces, puddings, etc.

Artichoke—Vegetable of compact thistle-like leaves and "choke" or center portion which is discarded; base of artichoke known as artichoke bottom; may be fresh, frozen or canned in water or oil

Arugula—Delicate salad vegetable of loose small elongated leaves with piquant flavor; also known as raclette; frequently served in Italian restaurants

Aspic—Jelly of clear soup or stock used to bind or coat cold foods

Au (Fr.)—Word meaning "with," used in such phrases as *"au jus"* (with the natural gravy), *"au beurre"* (with butter), etc.

Au gratin—Phrase meaning with a brown crust often of grated cheese or bread crumbs

Au gratin pan—Pan with very shallow sides used in making au gratin dishes as well as for broiling or for brief exposure to oven heat to complete cooking

Avocado—Pear-shaped fruit with green or purplish skin, oily flesh and large seed; used mostly in salads or appetizers

Bain marie (Fr.)—Double boiler or steam table, a table with water pan partially filled with hot water maintained at a fixed temperature for keeping pots or pans of food hot during meal service; pots which fit into steam table are called *bain marie* pots which may also be used as double boilers for cooking such items as hollandaise sauce or other foods requiring gentle heat

Baking sheet—Large pans frequently 18 × 26 in. with very shallow sides to permit maximum exposure to oven heat; also called bun pans

Bard—To cover lean meat, poultry or game with thin sheets of fat, usually pork fat, to prevent excessive drying during cooking

Barley, pearl or pearled—Polished grains of a cereal widely used as an ingredient in soups

Baron—Leg and loin of lamb in one piece; in England term is used for a double sirloin of beef

Bartlett pear—Popular variety of pear with yellow skin and creamy sweet flesh; widely used in salads, fruit cocktails and desserts

Basil—Fresh herb with leaves 1/2 to 1 in. wide, frequently used in recipes with tomatoes or tomato products; widely used in dried form

Baste—To periodically spoon pan drippings or other liquids in pan over roast meat, poultry or game during cooking

Bâtonnets (Fr.)—Food cut into shape of small sticks

Batter—Mixture principally of egg, milk and flour; used to coat foods before frying, to make fritters or baked products such as muffins; batter may be thin enough to pour when used for coating other foods or for popovers or Yorkshire pudding; may be of thicker consistency for cakes; distinguished from much stiffer mixture or dough

Bay leaf—Oblong aromatic leaf of bay tree widely used in soups, sauces, etc.; frequently left whole and removed from food before serving

Béarnaise sauce—Sauce of melted butter and egg yolks, similar to hollandaise sauce but flavored with tarragon and *glace de viande*

Beat—To mix ingredients with rotating motion using spoon, flat paddle-shaped attachment in mixing machine or wire whip

Béchamel sauce—Common sauce of fat, flour and milk

Beef—Meat of steer or castrated male bovine; lower quality beef is taken from cows or bulls

Beignets (Fr.)—*See* Fritters

Beignets soufflés (Fr.)—Fritters made from a batter which is cooked before it is fried

Beurre (Fr.)—Butter

Beurre manié (Fr.)—Butter and flour kneaded to a smooth paste used for thickening sauces

Beurre noir (Fr.)—Butter heated until it turns brown

Bibb lettuce—Lettuce of small flat leaves with curly edges known for its delicate flavor

Bill of fare—Menu; term is less widely used nowadays than in former times

Bisque—Cream of a particular shellfish soup such as bisque of shrimp, bisque of lobster, etc.

Black peppercorn—Dried berry of pepper plant picked before maturity; during drying process, becomes wrinkled; used whole or ground

Blade bone—Flat bone in rib section of beef, pork or lamb removed before roasting

Blanch—To immerse or cook briefly in boiling water in order to remove surface impurities, to aid in removing skin or to facilitate later cooking; also to partially fry

Blanquette (Fr.)—Stew usually of veal in a creamy white gravy

Blaze—To flame spirits or wine in cooking

Blend—To combine a number of ingredients so that all are distributed smoothly, sometimes inseparably

Blender—Electric device with whirling blades for making purees and other mixtures; heavy-duty models are used in restaurant kitchens

Blue cheese—Blue-veined cheese made with a special mold similar to French Roquefort and Italian Gorgonzola

Bluefish—Fish with bluish green skin, silvery belly and pronounced lower jaw; flesh is gray or grayish brown; most commercial sizes range from 3/4 lb to 10 lb

Boeuf (Fr.)—Beef

Boil—To cook liquids, producing bubbles that rise to surface, agitating as they rise

Bolster—Section of cook's knife abutting handle

Bombe (Fr.)—Dessert in a molded form of ice cream of several flavors frequently including sherbet or mousse (*see* Mousse)

Bonne femme (Fr.)—Popular style of cooking fish fillets in a sauce of mushrooms, white wine, fish stock and cream; also a soup with diced potatoes or potato puree and leeks

Bordelaise (Fr.)—Name of a brown sauce made with shallots, red wine, marrow and parsley

Bosc pear—Fresh pear available in winter months, with long neck and brownish skin, used in fruit cocktails and salads

Boston lettuce—Lettuce of loose outer green leaves and yellow leaves inside; also known as Big Boston or butterhead

Bouillabaisse (Fr.)—Stew of assorted fresh fish including eel and shellfish, flavoring vegetables, tomatoes, water or fish stock, saffron and bread croutons

Bouillon—Consommé with pronounced beef flavor

Bouillon cup—China cup with two handles; may be used for both clear and thick soups

Bouquet garni—Herbs and spices sometimes with seasoning vegetables tied in a cloth bag of muslin or cheesecloth, attached to handle of pot; bag is removed after cooking is completed; also known as sachet or faggot; used in many soups and sauces

Bourguignonne (Fr.)—In the Burgundy style; especially a beef stew made with red wine (for which Burgundy is noted), mushrooms, salt pork and silver onions

Braise—To cook large pieces of meat by first browning and then cooking in a liquid until tender; loosely used to mean any cooking process in which foods give off their own juices without added liquid

Braisière (Fr.) or Brazier—Large cooking pot with short loop handles on two sides used for braising or stewing meat or poultry; may be round or rectangular

Bread—To cover food with flour, eggs, and bread crumbs before frying

Bread flour—Hard wheat flour with strong gluten which forms elastic strands when flour is mixed with water; desirable in bread and roll baking

Break—To lose emulsification; applied to sauces such as hollandaise or mayonnaise when ingredients separate, usually after standing

Brew—To extract flavor by infusion or otherwise, applied to making coffee or tea

Brisket—Breast, particularly of beef

Brochette—Skewer or spit made of metal or wood on which chunks of food are fastened before broiling

Broil—To cook by exposure to direct heat above or below food; to grill

Brook trout—Small freshwater fish usually less than 1 lb each, covered with small scales; may be brown trout or rainbow trout; latter generally bluish on top, silvery on sides with a line of pink along length of body; flesh of trout considered a special delicacy

Broth—Thin soup made from cooking meat, poultry or seafood in water

Brown stock—Liquid used as a base for brown sauces and brown stews, prepared by simmering in water previously browned meat, poultry and flavoring vegetables

Brunoise (Fr.)—Vegetables cut into extremely small dice usually used in soups

Buffet—Large, sometimes tiered, table in dining room on which are placed foods which may include courses of a meal from appetizers to desserts and beverages; often consists of decorated foods; frequently self-service

Buttercream—Mixture of butter, sugar, eggs and flavoring for icing cakes

Cacciatora (Ital.)—Literally "hunter style"; popular American version of chicken cacciatora is chicken stewed with tomatoes; as prepared in Italy, chicken is cooked with onions, garlic, anchovies, wine and vinegar

Cake flour—Soft wheat flour with much less gluten than bread flour, used in pastry department rather than by cooks behind range

Cala—Smoked lower end of pork shoulder

Calf—Young of cow, less than 1 year old; when less then 12 weeks old, meat is called veal; terms sometimes used interchangeably and inaccurately on menus

Canadian bacon—Boneless smoked pork loin, sliced thin, used as breakfast item

Canapé—Small appetizer on bread, toast, crackers, etc.; may be made of meat, poultry, seafood, cheese or eggs; usually served with drinks before meal

Capers—Small dark buds of caper bush, packed in vinegar or salt; used in sauces and salads

Capon—Castrated male chicken which grows to large size and yields tender flesh

Captain—Dining room employee working under headwaiter or maitre d'hotel, usually in charge of a group of waiters

Caramel—Burnt sugar

Caramel coloring—Burnt sugar in liquid used for coloring sauces; also used for coloring gravies, stews, etc.

Caramel sauce—Burnt sugar syrup used in desserts

Carbon steel knife—Knife made of steel which derives its principal strength and hardness from carbon as distinguished from stainless steel made from a different alloy

Carcass—Body of slaughtered animal excluding hide, head, internal organs and sometimes limbs; when applied to beef, means halves or sides, or quarters such as forequarter or hindquarter

Cartilage—Connective tissue of meat or poultry; also called gristle

Carving board—Board of wood or composition material used for carving meat, poultry, etc.; also used for other cutting procedures such as dicing, chopping, etc., and called cutting board

Casaba—Large round melon with furrowed rind and deep yellow skin when ripe; flesh is white

Caviar—Roe (eggs) or sturgeon or other fish, usually salted, packed in cans or jars, served as appetizer

Cayenne pepper—Very hot small pepper similar to chili pepper; usually ground; although the term is widely used by cooks, the spice trade has been substituting "red pepper" for cayenne on its labels

Celery salt—Mixture of ground celery seed and salt frequently used in seafood dishes

Celery seed—Taken from a plant related to parsley and not from table celery; used in cole slaw and in marinades

Cellulose—Constituent of cell walls of many foods including un-cooked cereal which must be made tender during cooking

Cèpes (Fr.)—Wild mushrooms with firm flesh and large cap, yellowish brown; often canned

Chafing dish—Device used in dining room for cooking food at table or reheating food; consists of pan with handle, container for hot water beneath pan and flame using alcohol or other fuel

Chantilly (Fr.)—Name given to a number of preparations which contain whipped cream

Cheesecloth—Coarse porous fabric, usually muslin, used for making bouquet garni and for straining some soups and sauces; also called tammy cloth

Chef—Term meaning, literally, head or chief of an organization or department, such as a kitchen.

Chervil—Herb related to parsley, with curly leaf and pronounced aroma, used in soups, stews, sauces, etc.; may be fresh or dried

Chicory—Salad green, sometimes called curly endive, with narrow curly leaves, slightly bitter in flavor; root of chicory roasted in processing plants and, in some homes and in some sections of country, added to coffee for flavor and color

Chiffonade (Fr.)—Salad materials or other vegetables cut into long thin strips; also a salad dressing with chopped hard egg and sweet peppers

Chili pepper—Very strong pungent pepper pod widely used in Mexican and Spanish cookery

Chili powder—Seasoning of ground dried chili peppers, cumin, coriander, garlic, oregano and other spices

China cap—Cone-shaped strainer of metal with long handle and hook for fastening on edge of pot; various size china caps are made in fine to coarse mesh

Chine bones—Backbone of pork loin usually removed before carving

Chives—Slender green herb with onion-like flavor, finely chopped for soups, salads, etc.

Chowder—Thick soup with vegetables always including potatoes; in the US mainly clam chowder or fish chowder

Chuck—Cut of beef from forepart of animal excluding shank and brisket; used for chopped beef, stews, braised dishes, etc.

Cider vinegar—Vinegar made from fermented apple juice

Cioppino—Fish stew featured in Italian restaurants made of a variety of fish, shellfish and red wine

Clam broth—Liquid derived from fresh clams by steaming them open or cooking in water

Clarify—To melt butter after which the foam on top and deposit on bottom are removed (clarified butter is sometimes called drawn butter); also to make thin soups clear by the use of egg whites and straining, removing the solids in suspension

Cleaver—Heavy utensil with sharp blade for chopping bones or other hard substances

Cloves—Dried reddish brown buds of clove tree with sweet pungent flavor, used whole in bouquet garni and in baking hams; ground cloves used in cake and pie preparation

Club sandwich—Double-decker sandwich with combinations of sliced meats, poultry, tomato, lettuce, etc.

Coagulate—To change from a fluid to a thickened state

Cocktail—In restaurants, an appetizer whose principal ingredient may be seafood, fruit, clam juice, tomato juice, etc.; in bars, a mixed drink of spirits and other liquids shaken with ice

Cod—Heavy-bodied fish of north Atlantic waters with large head, skin gray to grayish green or brown with brown spots; curving line paler than rest of body visible on sides; although fish reaches enormous sizes, most cod for restaurants runs from 6 to 12 lb; may be filleted or cut into steaks

Coddled eggs—Eggs in shell cooked in hot water removed from fire

Coffee decanter—Glass container in which coffee is made by vacuum brewing, or glass container for serving coffee

Coffee urn—Equipment for quantity brewing of coffee, in which boiling water is poured over coffee grounds and filtered through a cloth or paper

Coffee urn bag—Cloth for filtering coffee in urn, fitted with ring for holding bag in place

Colander—Wide strainer with coarse mesh for draining liquids from solid foods

Commis (Fr.)—Term for assistant to cook or waiter; frequently apprentice learning specialized skills

Compound butter—Softened butter mixed with another flavoring component which may be pureed or finely chopped; used in hors d'oeuvres, butter sauces for fish, meat, etc.

Consommé—Thin soup of meat stock with highly developed flavor, clarified and often garnished with rice, vegetables, etc.

Convection oven—Oven with fan which creates air currents of high velocity, increasing heat delivery to products and reducing cooking time

Coral roe—Cooked roe of female lobster

Coriander—Fragrant seed of coriander plant, usually ground, used in ground meat dishes including sausage, as well as in sauces and desserts

Corned beef—Fresh beef, usually brisket or rump, steeped in a saltwater solution until it acquires characteristic "cured" or pickled flavor; process produces meat of bright red color when cooked

Coupe (Fr.)—Term for ice cream dessert corresponding to American sundae; consists of ice cream or ices served with fruits, sweet sauces, whipped cream, etc.

Court bouillon—Vegetable stock with vinegar and spices, used mostly for cooking fish

Cover—Dining room term for a set of table articles including chinaware, silverware, glassware, linen, etc., for one person

Cover charge—Payment required for service in addition to menu prices; does not include tip or gratuity

Crab meat—Cooked flesh of hard crab removed from shell; large pieces are called crab lump, small pieces, crab flakes

Cranshaw melon—Oval shaped melon with mottled yellow and green skin and deep orange meat

Crayfish—Small freshwater shellfish akin to shrimp in flavor

Cream of tartar—White powder, product of grape fermentation, used as a component in baking powder or as an aid in preparing meringue from egg whites

Cream sauce—Sauce of fat, flour and milk enriched with cream

Crème anglaise (Fr.)—Term for English custard cream, a cooked mixture of milk, egg yolks, sugar and flavoring; known in US as custard sauce

Crème vichyssoise (Fr.)—Cold cream soup of pureed onions, leeks and potatoes

Crêpe—Thin delicate pancake, often rolled and stuffed, served as appetizer, entrée or dessert

Croquette—Mixture of chopped cooked meat, poultry or seafood bound in a thick sauce, shaped, breaded and fried

Crouton—Bread, cut into dice or slices, either toasted, fried or browned in oven, served as a garnish usually with soups; also meat, jelly or vegetables cut into small shapes

Crown of pineapple—Top leaves of pineapple

Crown roast of lamb—Whole rib sections of lamb, tied or otherwise joined to form a crown with trimmed rib bones at the top, roasted with or without stuffing

Cuisine—Term for a type of cooking such as haute cuisine meaning elegant classical cookery; also specialized cookery of a certain restaurant or region; also the kitchen itself

Cumin—Acrid, pungent seed of Middle Eastern plant, usually ground; used in curries, chili preparations, etc.

Curdle—To coagulate or change into curds; used to describe a mixture that has lost its smoothness, such as curdled cream of tomato soup

Custard—Mixture of beaten eggs, milk, and usually flavoring; made with sugar as dessert; sugar omitted when custards are made for soup

Cutlet—Thin slice of meat, usually breaded, for sautéing; also a croquette of meat, poultry or seafood made in a flat shape rather than round or conical

Cutting board—*See* Carving board

Deep fry—Too cook in fat deep enough for food to float

Deglaze or déglacer (Fr.)—To dilute concentrated juices or drippings in a pan in which food has been roasted or sautéd, by adding wine, stock or cream and scraping pan bottom and sides

Demiglaze or demiglace (Fr.)—*Espagnole* or brown sauce reduced with brown stock to half its original volume

Diable (Fr.)—Deviled or prepared with pungent spices, condiments, etc.

Dice—To cut into square pieces

Dill—Fresh or dried herb of thin delicate green leaves used in sauces, soups and marinades

Dot—To add small pieces such as butter or other fat by scattering it on top of foods

Dough—Mixture of flour, liquids and other ingredients stiff enough to knead

Drawn—Poultry with inner organs removed

Drawn butter—Same as clarified butter (*see above*)

Dredge—To thoroughly coat food with flour, bread crumbs or other ingredients

Dressed—Poultry cleaned, drawn, ready for cooking

Dressing—Stuffing for meat or poultry; also cold salad sauces such as French dressing

Drippings—Fats and other liquids which flow to pan bottom and become concentrated

Drumstick—Leg of poultry

Dry—When term is applied to wines or spirits, indicates a low sugar content or absence of sugar

Du jour (Fr.)—Literally "of the day"; referring to a menu item often not specifically named such as *"potage du jour"* or soup of the day

Duchesse potatoes—Potatoes which have been mashed, mixed with egg and formed into individual shapes with pastry bag and tube

Dust—To lightly coat food or a utensil by spraying it with a substance such as flour or cornmeal

Duxelles (Fr.)—Chopped mushrooms, seasonings and bread crumbs for stuffing vegetables

Eel—Long snake-like fish of which there are over 20 families, found in fresh and saltwaters, many without scales; skin color varies from gray to brown; flesh firm but mellow in flavor

Egg wash—Beaten eggs sometimes mixed with milk, water or oil, used to coat foods as a step in breading, or to coat pies, biscuits, rolls, etc., before baking

Eight-cut ribs of beef—Largest cut of beef rib roast containing eight ribs

Emincé (Fr.)—Finely sliced food

Emulsion—Mixture of an oily or fatty ingredient held in suspension with a liquid, such as mayonnaise

En (Fr.)—Word meaning "in" or "on" such as *en casserole* (served or baked in a casserole) or *en bordure* (shaped in a border around other ingredients)

Endive, French—Small tightly folded elongated head of white leaves with faintly bitter taste, used for salads

Entree—Intermediate course between soup and main dish on party menu; or alternately a dish (not a roast) served as a main course usually on a luncheon menu

Entremets (Fr.)—Desserts

Escalopes (Fr.)—Thin slices of meat flattened and sautéd; same as Italian scallopine

Escarole—Broad-leafed salad green with yellow center and faintly bitter flavor

Espagnole (Fr.)—Brown sauce

Estouffade (Fr.)—Brown stock

Faggot—*See* Bouquet garni

Farce (Fr.)—Stuffing; also called forcemeat

Fatback—Upper portion of side of pork after shoulder, loin, ham and belly are removed; also known as back fat

Feather bones—Small bones joining vertebrae in ribs of beef

Fennel seeds—Aromatic seeds resembling anise or licorice in flavor, used in marinades, bouquet garni or some spaghetti sauces

Fifth—A fifth of a gallon or four-fifths of a quart; common unit of bottled wine or spirits

Filet (Fr.) or fillet (Eng.)—A strip or long piece of tender meat or fish without bone or skin; to cut meat or fish into a fillet

Filet mignon—A slice of beef fillet, also called tenderloin, thick enough to be broiled or sautéd

Fines herbes—A combination of chopped fresh herbs frequently including parsley, chives, chervil and tarragon, used in omelets, salad dressings, etc.

Fire—In kitchen parlance, the source of heat in a range or broiler; food is "taken off" or "put on" the fire even though the heat source may be a gas flame, electricity, heated ceramic materials, coals, etc.

Fish boiler—Long narrow pot with lid for cooking large whole fish

Flambé—To set spirits ablaze around food in a pan or chafing dish

Flip—To turn over food in a pan by moving the pan in a quick motion without the use of a spatula

Flounder—Flatfish of which there are more than 300 species; one side of fish with eyes is pigmented, usually dark brown, while other side is white; much fish appearing on menus as sole is taken from flounder

Fluke—Species of summer flounder common on middle Atlantic coast

Flute—To cut parallel narrow strips off outside of food such as lemons or cucumbers; also name of narrow long loaf of French bread

Fold—To gently incorporate an ingredient such as beaten egg whites or whipped cream into a heavy mixture in order to lighten the mixture

Fonds blanc (Fr.)—White stock (*see* Stock)

Fonds blanc de volaille (Fr.)—Chicken stock

Fonds de cuisine (Fr.)—Literally "foundations of the kitchen" or basic stocks; less frequently used to identify some basic sauces such as *velouté* or hollandaise

Fonds de poissons (Fr.)—Fish stock

Food cost—The cost of all foods actually used in cooking (not foods purchased), calculated on a daily or monthly basis

Food cost percentage—The percentage which results when the receipts of a restaurant for a specific period are divided into the food cost for that period

Food mill—Device for pureeing food by forcing it by means of rotating blades through a strainer

Forequarter—Front end of half an animal such as beef, veal or lamb

Fowl—Old hen usually in egg production over a year, used for chicken broth and dishes requiring boiled chicken; also any edible bird, wild or domestic

French knife—Most widely used cook's knife with triangular blade

Fricassee—Chicken with bone, sautéd or boiled, cooked in a gravy of chicken stock

Fritter—A light fried cake made from a batter, named for its principal ingredient, such as corn fritter or clam fritter

Froid (Fr.)—Cold

Fry—To cook in deep or shallow fat; latter is called sautéing

Fumet (Fr.)—Stock with an intensified flavor made by boiling down or reducing normal stock; used to enhance sauce flavors

Garde manger (Fr.)—Member of kitchen staff in charge of leftover foods, preparing cold dishes, salad dressings, etc; also section in which he works

Garnish or garniture (Fr.)—Preparation placed alongside food on a dish in order to decorate it, enhance or complement its flavor; to add a garnish to a dish

Gaufrette potatoes—Waffle-shaped deep-fried potatoes

Gel—To form into, or produce, a gelatin

Genoa salami—Hard dry sausage of cured beef and pork, sliced thin, served as an appetizer; may be imported or domestic

Gherkins—Pickles with firm flesh made of very young cucumbers

Giblets—Heart, gizzard and liver of chicken or other poultry

Gizzard—Muscular stomach of chicken or other poultry

Glaçage (Fr.)—Procedure of glazing

Glaze—To brown under the broiler a white sauce poured over cooked fish, eggs, chicken, etc.; to brown, under the broiler or in a pan, food that has been sprinkled with sugar; to coat food with a glossy, clear substance such as a gelatin preparation, pureed fruit, jam, etc.

Goulash—Stew of Hungarian origin heavily flavored with paprika and onions

Grain—Arrangement or direction in which meat fibers run; cooked meat is carved, when possible, against the grain to produce tender slices

Gratinée (Fr.)—To brown a food sprinkled with cheese or bread crumbs; or a food covered with a sauce that turns brown under a broiler flame or in intense oven heat

Gravy—Liquid preparation which derives its flavor from the natural juices of a food with which it is cooked; as opposed to a sauce, usually cooked apart from the food with which it is later combined

Greaves—Solid residue of fat after it has been melted

Grenadine—Sweet red syrup made from meat of pomegranate

Grid—Bars forming a shelf beneath or over a broiler flame; can be moved toward or away from source of heat

Griddle—Cooking equipment of thick flat metal sheet above source of heat

Griddle stone—Special stone for cleaning residue on griddle after cooking; used normally after a meal period

Grill—To broil; also hinged wire rack in which food is placed and turned when broiled

Gristle—Tough cartilage of meat or poultry

Gruyère—Swiss cheese with small holes, somewhat softer and richer than the better known Swiss Emmentaler; also made in France

Gumbo—Vegetable okra or a soup containing okra

Haddock—Member of cod family but smaller in size, ranging from 1 to 4 lb each; skin gray on top side, lighter gray below; flesh usually more tender than cod

Halibut—Largest flatfish, some of which reach 30 to 40 lb; most commercial sizes range from 10 to 20 lb; on pigmented side color ranges from brown to nearly black; opposite side of fish is white; flesh very tender and flaky

Ham—Thigh of pig; may be fresh or smoked

Ham slicer—Long knife with flexible blade and straight tip end, used in carving ham

Haute cuisine—Classical cuisine developed by noted chefs of France often featuring rich or decorated foods; as opposed to *"cuisine de famille"* or family cooking and *"cuisine régionale"* or cookery featuring the regional specialties of France

Heavy-duty—Descriptive term for various types of restaurant equipment designed and built to withstand continuous hard usage in commercial kitchens as opposed to lighter household equipment

Heel of knife—Rear of blade of French knife

Hindquarter—Posterior end of half an animal such as beef, veal or lamb

Hollandaise sauce—Rich sauce of egg yolks and butter

Hone—To sharpen a knife on a whetstone or the stone itself

Honeydew—Large melon with creamy white skin and noticeable aroma when ripe; juicy pale green flesh

Hors d'oeuvres—Appetizers, may be hot or cold, served at dining table as first course or eaten with fingers at buffet featuring drinks

Hotel pans—Rectangular pans with a depth of 2 1/4 in.; length varies from 13 to 18 in. and width from 10 to 12 in.; used for baking as well as storage; sometimes called utility pans

Hydrogenated fat—Fat processed so that it reaches varying degrees of firmness and is not likely to become rancid during normal storage periods; remains solid at room temperature with high smoking point; noted for good plasticity (*see* Smoking point)

Ice (dessert)—Frozen mixture of sugar or sugar syrup, fruit puree or flavoring and water

Ice chest—Refrigerator for storing fresh fish packed in ice

Iceberg lettuce—Lettuce with tight compact leaves, medium green outside, lighter green at center

Icing—Sweet preparation for covering and filling cakes; also called frosting

Inset pans—Round or square pans which fit in a fixed position in steam table or refrigerated counter

Irish lamb stew—Lamb stew with white gravy and potatoes

Italian marrow—Zucchini

Jambon (Fr.)—Ham

Jardinière (Fr.)—Assortment of fresh vegetables in dice or fancy shapes used to garnish a main coarse

Joint—Term used in England or by English chefs for a large cut of meat such as a roast

Journeyman—Worker in the kitchen (or other trade) who has completed his apprenticeship

Julienne—Food cut into thin matchstick size pieces

Jus (Fr.)—Juice; used mainly to describe the natural juice and drippings of a roast diluted with stock to form a thin gravy; used in the phrase "*au jus*" meaning with natural gravy

Kebab—Skewered small chunks of meat (*see* Brochette)

Keel bone—Center bone separating halves of chicken breast

Kingfish—Member of whiting family; skin gray on top with oblique crossbands running down and forward; flesh firm and light

Kippered herring—Smoked herring usually from the British Isles, served as breakfast item

Kirsch—Colorless white brandy made from cherries; frequently used in desserts as flavoring

Knead—To work dough by hand or machine into a smooth mass

Knife steel—Steel rod with handle used for restoring edge to knife

Ladle—Long-handled utensil with dipping bowl at end; used not only for dipping but for measuring; sizes range from two tablespoons to one quart

Lake trout—Freshwater fish sometimes called salmon trout because of its orange colored flesh resembling salmon; skin gray with pinkish spots; flesh fatty and very tender

Langouste—Lobster-like shellfish without claws, also called spiny lobster; sold frozen in most of US except southern coastal states; much of it is imported from South Africa, Australia and South America

Lard—Soft fat of pork which is rendered and used for shortening

Larding pork—Fat from top of pork next to skin, used for barding (*see above*) and for larding or threading, by means of a special needle, long pieces of fat into lean cuts of meat; also called fatback (*see* Bard; Fatback)

Leavening—Substance such as baking powder or yeast which creates bubbles of gas in batters and doughs causing them to rise

Leek—Seasoning vegetable resembling a large spring onion with wide leaves, always cooked, and used as a seasoning vegetable in soups, stews, etc.

Legumes—Dried fruit or seeds of pod vegetables such as dried beans or dried lentils

Liaison (Fr.)—Process of thickening liquids such as sauces and soups, applies mostly to the use of egg yolks for thickening purposes; also method of adding rich body to a liquid as when butter is slowly melted in soups off the fire after cooking has been completed

Liquor—Natural juice of a food such as oyster liquor in shells or oysters or mushroom liquor that collects in pan when mushrooms are sautéd

Lyonnaise (Fr.)—Cooked in the style of food prepared in a region of France (Lyons) famed for excellent onions; prominent examples are omelet *lyonnaise* and potatoes *lyonnaise* both cooked with sautéd onions

Mace—Spice made from dried skin of nutmeg; somewhat less pungent than nutmeg; used in sauces and baked products

Macédoine (Fr.)—Mixture of fruit or vegetables cut into dice

Madeira—Wine from island of Madeira with a rich flavor resembling sherry; used in Madeira sauce

Maitre d'hotel—Head of dining room, in charge of all dining room staff; must understand food preparation, menu terms, seasonal foods, food specialties, etc.

Maitre d'hotel butter—Mixture of butter, lemon juice and parsley brushed on broiled foods after cooking

Malt vinegar—Vinegar with deep brown color made from fermented barley

Marbled—Term describing beef, especially steaks and roasts, with visible flecks of fat mingled with lean, indicating top quality

Marinade—Liquid in which food is marinated, usually containing seasoning vegetables, spices, vinegar, wine, water, etc.; French dressing and similar preparations are sometimes used as marinades

Marinate—To steep a food in a marinade long enough to modify its flavor

Marjoram—Aromatic herb of the mint family but not resembling mint in flavor, usually dried, used in poultry stuffings, sauce dishes, etc.

Marmite (Fr.)—Cooking or serving vessel of metal or earthenware, with straight sides, resembling round pot with short or stub handles; individual earthenware *marmites* used for onion soup and a rich clear beef soup called *petite marmite*

Marron (Fr.)—Chestnut

Marrow—Soft, rich substance taken from cavities of bones especially shin bones of beef

Marsala—Sweet Italian wine used in sauces and desserts

Mask—To coat a cooked food with a sauce before it is served; cold foods are frequently masked with a mayonnaise mixture which gells when refrigerated or a white sauce, called *chaud froid*, which also gells after chilling

Menu—Printed list of foods and their prices for a particular meal

Meringue—Mixture of egg whites and sugar beaten to a stiff foam

Meunière (Fr.)—Usually listed on menus as sauté *meunière* or *a la meunière*, describing a food, frequently fish, dipped in flour and sautéd in butter

Milanaise (Fr.)—Food cooked in a style developed in Milan, Italy, such as minestrone *milanaise*; also raw foods dipped in flour, eggs and bread crumbs mixed with cheese and sautéd

Mince—To chop fine

Minestrone (Ital.)—Term for hearty soup

Mirepoix (Fr.)—Mixture of chopped seasoning vegetables usually including onions, celery and carrots

Mis en place (Fr.)—Preparatory work before food is ready to be put on the fire, including gathering materials, cutting vegetables; also the assembling of all foods and seasonings necessary for quickly preparing dishes made to order during the meal period

Mix—To combine different ingredients; may be done by stirring, tossing, beating, whipping, etc.

Mongole soup—Thick soup of pureed peas and tomatoes

Monosodium glutamate—Granular white seasoning made from vegetable proteins, used for enhancing natural flavors of soups, sauces, stews, etc.; has no pronounced flavor of its own

Mornay sauce—White sauce flavored with cheese and thickened with egg yolks

Mortadella (Ital.)—Large fresh sausage made with pork and prominent pieces of pork fat; sliced thin and frequently served as appetizer

Mousse—Frozen dessert with fruit or other flavors, whipped cream and sugar; also a cold dish of pureed chicken or pureed seafood, etc., with egg whites, unsweetened whipped cream and gelatin

Mulligatawny—Thick soup of Indian origin with curry

Mussel—Bivalve with thin dark shells, oblong in form, frequently cooked in the shell with wine, cream and seasonings

Mutton—Old sheep nearly two years of age; little is sold in the US where lamb (sheep under one year of age) is the preferred meat

Nesselrode—Mixture of diced fruits in a rum sauce used in pies, ice cream, etc.

Newburgh sauce—Sauce of cream, sherry and egg yolks frequently combined with lobster and other shellfish

Noisette potatoes—Potato balls, somewhat smaller than parisienne potatoes; usually fried

Nutmeg—Pungent spice in whole or ground form used in sauces, chopped meat dishes, cakes, pies, etc.

Oeuf (Fr.)—Egg

Oil—Fat used for cooking, salads and salad dressings; stays liquid at room temperature; cottonseed, corn, soybean, peanut and olive oils are prominent types

Oilstone—Flat stone lubricated with oil, used for sharpening knives; also known as whetstone

Okra—Long vegetable with fuzzy pod, usually green in color; snaps easily when fresh; used in gumbo soup; may be fresh, frozen or canned

Oregano—Herb with pronounced aroma, related to marjoram; may be fresh or dried; used widely in Italian cookery for soups, stews, pasta sauces, etc.

Oyster—Well-known seafood; term also used to identify two small oval-shaped pieces of meat on back of turkey, chicken, duck, etc.

Paella (Span.)—Dish of Spanish origin with rice, seafood, chicken, seasoning vegetables, served in a wide shallow pan in which it is cooked, or cooked separately in a large pot and served in individual paella pan

Palette knife—Flexible spatula used for icing cakes

Panbroil—To cook in an ungreased shallow frying pan

Papillote (Fr.)—Style of food preparation in which meat, chicken or fish is cooked in closed paper container in shape of a heart; also paper frill attached to end of cooked lamb chops, chicken legs, etc., just before serving

Paprika—Ground dried sweet pepper; best known types are from Hungary or Spain

Parboil—To partially boil food in order to clean its surface, to make it firm or to prepare it for later cooking

Parfait—Dessert of ice cream or mousse served in a tall narrow glass often with flavoring syrups or fruit

Paring knife—Small knife with 3- to 4-in. blade used mainly for peeling, trimming or cutting vegetables into fancy shapes

Parisienne potato cutter—Utensil with cup-shaped ends for cutting balls of potatoes or other vegetables, melons, etc; smaller size is used for cutting potatoes *noisette*

Parisienne potatoes—Small balls of potatoes usually fried, cut with a parisienne potato cutter or fruit baller

Parmesan cheese—Hard light yellow grating cheese from Parma, Italy, or same type made in other countries

Parmigiana—Parma style, particularly cooked veal, chicken or eggplant covered with tomato sauce, mozzarella cheese, Parmesan cheese and browned under broiler or in oven

Pass—To transfer food partially prepared by one cook to another, to complete cooking; also to dredge or roll food in a substance which covers it

Pasta (Ital.)—Literally "dough"; term used for macaroni products including spaghetti, noodles and lasagne

Pastry bag—Bag of cloth or other material shaped in a cone used for extruding potatoes, butters, icings, etc., for decorating purposes

Pastry tube—Small cone-shaped piece of metal with specially cut ends to make fancy designs; tube is inserted in small opening of pastry bag

Patty shell—Cylinder-shaped pastry case with top made from very flaky dough called puff paste

Pâte (Fr.)—Dough or batter (pronounced pat)

Pâté (Fr.)—Pastry shell or case (pronounced pa-tay)

Pâté de foie gras (Fr.)—Goose liver cooked and often seasoned with truffles; available in cans or crocks; originally made in a rich pastry case

Paysanne (Fr.)—Literally peasant; term for hearty vegetable soup; also a style of cutting vegetables in a small flat shape

Peach melba—Dessert of peach half (cooked or canned), ice cream and sweetened raspberry puree called Melba sauce

Pelvic bone—Flat bone in thigh of animals such as lamb or pork; bone is removed to facilitate carving

Pepper pot soup—Thick vegetable soup containing tripe and sometimes dumplings

Peppercorns—Whole black or white pepper

Persian melon—Large melon with skin resembling cantaloupe, with thick sweet meat

Petite marmite (Fr.)—Rich beef broth with small pieces of beef, chicken and vegetables, served in an earthen casserole with grated cheese and sliced bread croutons

Pheasant—Game bird resembling chicken in appearance with somewhat pungent but subtle flavor

Pilaf, pilaff or pilaw—Rice with flavoring vegetables, frequently containing ingredients like chicken livers, mushrooms or seafood

Pimientos—Sweet red peppers; when canned, seeds and skin are removed

Piquant—Food characterized by pleasantly pungent or sharp flavor

Planked steak—Broiled steak served on a wooden plank, surrounded with small mounds of vegetables within a potato bordure

Plum tomatoes—Small oval-shaped meaty red tomatoes, often canned

Poach—To cook gently in a liquid

Pocket—Cavity made in meat such as breast of veal, large pork chop, etc., for inserting a filling

Poire Hélène (Fr.)—Vanilla ice cream, poached fresh pear or canned pear, covered with chocolate sauce

Pomme (Fr.)—Apple

Pomme de terre (Fr.)—Potato (literally "apple of earth")

Pompano—Flatfish from southern waters with very delicate flavor and texture

Portion—Quantity of food for one person

Portion control—System of regulating food by weight or size so that all portions sold are of a specific unvarying size

Pot roast—Dish of beef which is first browned, and then cooked with a liquid until tender

Potage (Fr.)—Soup usually of a thick type

Potato ricer—Device with plunger for mashing potatoes

Potatoes in jacket—Potatoes boiled in skin

Poularde (Fr.)—Roasting chicken from 3 1/2 to 5 lb

Poulet (Fr.)—Chicken weighing from 1 1/2 to 3 lb; in US a broiler, spring chicken or fryer-broiler

Poulette (Fr.)—Rich white sauce of chicken broth, cream and mushrooms

Poultry seasoning—Combination of dried spices and herbs used for poultry stuffing

Poussin (Fr.)—Very young chicken less than 1 1/2 lb; in US squab chicken (not to be confused with squab)

Prawn—Term now loosely used to describe large shrimp

Profiteroles—Small hollow balls of pastry made from the batter used for making eclairs (*choux* paste); larger ones are filled with custard or ice cream as dessert

Prosciutto (Ital.)—Ham of Italian origin, salted, spiced, air dried and pressed into a flat shape; sliced very thin; served as an appetizer and as a component in veal dishes

Provolone—Hard cheese of Italian origin, rich, smoky and somewhat sharp in flavor

Puff paste—Rich dough made flaky by repeated folding and rolling

Puree—Food cooked to a pulp and forced through a sieve

Quahog or quahaug—Round hard-shell clam of Atlantic coast

Quartz lamp—Heating lamp positioned to keep cooked food hot which has been dished on plates or platters and is waiting to be served

Quenelle (Fr.)—Light small dumpling made of pureed seafood, poultry, etc., cream and egg whites

Quiche Lorraine—Appetizer made of custard, cheese and seasonings baked in a pie shell, served warm

Quick breads—Muffins, biscuits and other baked items leavened with baking powder rather than yeast and which require no rising preliminary to baking

Rack—Rib section of lamb, veal or pork; also hinged wire device called broiler rack for holding and turning broiled meats; also a wire shelf placed in roasting pans to allow fat and drippings to flow off

Raft—Floating layer of ground meat, vegetables, etc., which forms in consommé during cooking

Ragoût (Fr.)—Stew

Range—Stove, usually heavy-duty, including oven and sometimes top shelf or broiler, with either closed or open top flames

Ravioli—Small pillow-shaped stuffed pieces of dough, boiled and served with a sauce

Red snapper—Fish with rose-red scales, 3 to 10 lb in size

Reduce—To cook a liquid so that its volume diminishes, and flavors become blended and concentrated

Relief cook—Cook who replaces another cook on the latter's day or days off; also called roundsman

Rémoulade sauce—Mixture of mayonnaise, chopped sour gherkins and other seasonings

Render—To melt solid fat and strain it

Ris de veau (Fr.)—Calf's sweetbread

Risotto (Ital.)—Rice dish with meat, vegetables, seafood, cheese or other accompaniments

Rissoler (Fr.)—To brown

Roast—To cook meat or poultry by dry, indirect heat as in an oven

Roast beef slicer—Long knife with flexible blade of which the end is rounded, used for carving large roasts

Roasting pans—Rectangular or square pans of heavy-gauge metal, reinforced by bottom steel straps, ranging in size from 12 × 18 in. to 24 × 24 in.; pans are designed to contain heavy loads without buckling

Robert sauce—Piquant brown sauce with chopped pickles, vinegar, white wine and mustard; also a bottled sauce of the same type served cold at the table

Rock Cornish game hen—Young chickens from 1 to 2 lb each, with plump breast meat; despite name, chickens may be of no special strain, and lack gamey flavor

Roll—To dredge or coat a food with another substance; also, in omelet making, to move the contents of the pan so that they roll into an oblong shape

Romaine—Type of lettuce with green long leaves, yellow or light green in center of head

Root vegetables—Vegetables such as potatoes or carrots, of which the root is the edible part

Roquefort cheese—Blue-veined cheese from France made from sheep's milk

Rosemary—Very pungent herb used in marinades, stews, etc.; frequently included with lamb dishes

Rôtisseur (Fr.)—Roast cook

Roulade—Rolled thin piece of meat usually stuffed and roasted or braised

Roundsman—Relief cook

Roux—Mixture of melted fat and flour used for thickening purposes

Royale—Baked custard mixture, cut into small pieces, used as a garnish for thin soups

Russian dressing—Mixture of mayonnaise, chili sauce, catsup and other seasonings

Rutabaga—Yellow turnip with smooth skin and more pungent flavor than white turnip; frequently served mashed

Sabayon—Rich sweet dessert or sauce of egg yolks, sugar and wine

Saffron—Dried stigmas of flowers of saffron plant; adds rich yellow color and pronounced flavor to rice, fish stews, etc.

Sage—Dried, somewhat bitter, whitish green herb used in poultry stuffings, sausages and other pork dishes

Salamander—Broiler, usually mounted above a range, smaller in size than independent floor units

Salmon—Long-bodied fish with silvery skin, pinkish orange flesh

Salpicon (Fr.)—Food cut into small dice, bound with a sauce, used for stuffing small patty shells, vegetables, etc.

Salt pork—Fat from belly of pig, with streaks of lean meat like bacon, salted but not smoked

Sauce—Liquid preparation usually cooked apart from dish with which it is subsequently combined; enhances flavors, adds piquance, etc.; may be hot or cold (*see also* Gravy)

Saucepan—Small size saucepot; may have loop handles on opposite sides or one long handle and one loop handle

Saucepot—Round deep vessel, ranging in size from 8 to 60 qt, with loop handles and cover, and with larger diameter than depth; used for cooking sauces, foods in sauce, stews, braised dishes, etc.

Saucer champagne glass—Stemmed glass with wide bowl used not only for drinking champagne but for serving seafood cocktail, fruit cocktail, etc.

Saucier (Fr.)—Sauce cook

Sausage—Chopped meat, frequently pork, with seasonings stuffed into a long casing; may be fresh or smoked; served hot or sliced cold

Sausage meat—Chopped seasoned meat used for stuffing, shaped into flat cakes or otherwise cooked

Sauté—To cook quickly in a small amount of fat

Sauté pan—Round pan with flaring sides and long handle used mostly for sautéing meats, fish, etc., which are served without a sauce

Sauteuse (Fr.)—Sauté pan

Sautoir (Fr.)—Large round pan with straight low sides and long handle; used for sautéing food in quantity before cooking it with a sauce

Scald—To bring milk up to the boiling point but avoid boiling; also to cleanse in very hot water or steam

Scallop—Seafood from a bivalve having ribbed shells; only the muscle which opens and closes the shells is used; also to bake in a shallow casserole or dish

Scallopine (Ital.)—Small flat pieces of meat, usually veal, sautéed and served with a sauce

Scum—Extraneous matter which rises to the top of liquids being cooked and which is removed by skimming

Sea trout—*See* Weakfish

Season—To add salt, spices and other flavoring elements to food; also to treat a new or used pan by heating it with fat and salt so that its interior surface does not cause food to stick

Second joint—Dark meat of poultry between breast and drumstick

Segment—To remove pieces of peeled citrus fruit between inner membranes

Set—To allow large pieces of meat or poultry to stand for a brief period before carving so that free-flowing juices subside, facilitating carving

Seven-cut ribs—Large standing beef rib roast containing seven ribs (*see* Eight-cut ribs of beef)

Shad—Freshwater fish; skin blue on top, often with spots below, silvery belly; very bony; roe considered great delicacy

Shallot—Small flavoring vegetable of onion family, less pungent than garlic and more aromatic than onion, used mostly in small quantities for seasoning purposes

Shank—Upper part of foreleg of beef; also cut from foreleg of lamb or hind leg of veal

Shell of beef—Short loin of beef without fillet or tenderloin

Sherbet—Frozen dessert similar to ice (*see above*) usually made with egg whites

Sherbet glass—Stemmed, usually thick, glass for serving sherbet; also frequently used for seafood cocktails, fruit cocktail and desserts

Sherry—Amber-colored aperitif and dessert wine, used in preparing many sauces and dishes, such as lobster Newburgh, sautéd veal, etc.

Shift—Hours during which a cook or other restaurant employee is regularly on duty

Shin—Lower part of foreleg of beef

Shir—To cook eggs in an individual round shallow baking dish with flared sides

Shish kebab—Chunks of meat, frequently lamb, cooked on a skewer

Short ribs—Chunks of beef, from 4 to 6 oz each, cut from ends of beef ribs, usually braised

Shortening—Solid fat such as butter, hydrogenated fat or lard used for making baked products rich or "short"; may also be used for certain frying purposes

Shuck—To remove meat of bivalves such as oysters or clams; also outer coating of vegetables such as corn, chestnuts, etc.

Silver onions—Small white onions left whole for cooking; also called picklers

Simmer—To cook slowly below boiling point

Skewer—Long narrow pointed pin of metal or bamboo used for piercing meat to hold it together for broiling

Skim—To remove extraneous matter rising to top of liquids such as soups, stews, etc; also to remove top of liquids that separate such as cream from milk, fat from stews, etc.

Skimmer—Perforated, very shallow scoop attached to long handle; also similar utensil made of continuous wire

Slab bacon—Whole unsliced bacon with rind

Smelt—Slender freshwater fish with silvery skin, usually served 3 to a portion

Smoking point—Temperature at which fat being heated releases visible fumes and begins to decompose

Smother—To cook in a covered pan or to cook sliced food such as onions in a mass so that end product resembles food cooked under a cover

Snow peas—Extremely small peas in nearly flat pods; pods and contents are edible; also known as sugar peas

Sole—True sole are seldom found in American waters; fish which appear on menus as sole, unless imported from Europe, are usually flounder; type called lemon sole is large size with meaty fillets, also called winter flounder; smaller gray-brown fish called gray sole

Soufflé—Very light baked preparation made of a sauce foundation, egg yolks, flavoring ingredient and beaten egg whites

Sous chef (Fr.)—Second in command in a kitchen working under chef; may be sauce cook; often called second cook

Spanish onions—Mild very large onions, globe shaped, sweet in flavor

Spareribs—Ribs from belly side of pork with small amount of flavorful flesh

Spatula—Utensil with square or rectangular flexible blade used for turning foods or for spreading substances such as icing; handle and blade may be on same plane or handle may be offset for easier turning

Spit—Long rod pierced at one end on which meat or poultry is fastened for rotating above fire or alongside source of heat

Squab—Young pigeon usually domesticated or raised in confinement, weighing from 14 to 18 oz when dressed

Steak—Slice of various foods at least 1/2 in. thick; although term is frequently used for meats such as beef or lamb, it may also apply to other menu items such as salmon steak, eggplant steak, etc.

Steam—To cook in the vapors of boiling water in an enclosed pan or in closed compartment of heavy-duty equipment

Steam-jacketed kettle—Large kettle, of floor or counter type, surrounded by, and sealed from, outer chamber containing steam; heat is regulated by valve controlling amount of steam which enters outer jacket; steam may be direct or generated by gas or electricity

Steam cooker—Cooking equipment with compartments in which food to be cooked is placed in solid or perforated pans; compartments are sealed and steam is turned on for specific periods, using either high- or low-pressure steam

Steel—*See* Knife steel

Stew—Small pieces of meat, poultry, etc., cooked in liquid which combines with the juices of the food being cooked to form a gravy; also seafood dishes such as oyster stew, clam stew, etc., cooked quickly in milk, cream and seasonings

Stick cinnamon—Quill-like dried bark of cinnamon plant, used whole in cooking fruits, pickled vegetables, etc.

Stir—To mix by moving spoon or beater in a rotating motion

Stock—Extraction resulting from simmering solid food such as meat, poultry, bones, vegetables, etc., in water; used as a base for soups, sauces, etc.

Stockpot—Large pot for cooking stock, with straight sides and loop handles often fitted with spigot and strainer, heated over top flame of range; larger floor models are heated in the same manner as steam-jacketed kettles

Strain—To put a liquid preparation through a sieve or filter in order to separate solids from liquids or in order to make a puree

Striped bass—Fish with design of dark parallel bars on sides; most commercial sizes range from 1 1/2 to 10 lb

Stuffing—Seasoned bread, rice or other food used as an accompaniment to poultry or meat; in restaurants usually prepared apart from poultry rather than stuffed in cavity; also mixtures prepared for filling pockets of veal, pork, etc.

Suprême (Fr.)—Breast of chicken removed from carcass, usually sautéd and served with a sauce; also same type of preparation for pheasant, guinea hen or other game birds

Supreme glass—Footed glass container with ice and inset collar for serving grapefruit, seafood cocktail, etc.

Sweat—Term describing sautéd food that gives off its own juices, forming a noticeable pool of liquid in pan

Sweetbread—Thymus gland of an animal

Swordfish—Large saltwater fish with upper jaw and snout formed into swordlike appendage; firm but tender flesh usually cut into steaks; commercial sizes range from 120 to 250 lb per fish

Synthetic stock—Stock, in dehydrated or paste form, made of vegetable proteins and other substances, resembling natural stocks made from beef, chicken, etc.

Tabasco sauce—Trade name of hot pepper sauce

Table d'hôte (Fr.)—Type of menu in which the price includes all the courses offered for the complete meal as opposed to a menu in which each item is priced individually

Tang—Extension of knife blade to which handle is attached

Tarragon—Fresh or dried herb of long slender leaf with semi-pungent aroma used in flavoring vinegar, in fines herbes (*see above*) in sauces and stews

Tart—Dessert of a pastry shell, with or without a cream filling, usually topped with fruit; also any food which is sharp in taste

Tartar sauce—Cold sauce of mayonnaise with finely chopped pickles, capers and olives

Tartar steak—Steak of raw chopped beef with egg yolk and seasonings

Terrine—Earthenware dish which serves as a form for baking pâtés of poultry, game and other foods served cold

Thyme—Very small gray-green leaves of low growing herb used in chowders and other soups, stuffings and sauces

Tilt kettle—Kettle in a fixed position on counter or floor, which can be released for emptying into another container

Tilting braising or tilting frying pan—Large rectangular pan in fixed position with wide range of controlled temperatures used for sautéing, braising, stewing, etc; pouring lip and tilting device facilitate emptying contents

Timbale—Small cylindrical mold of metal, earthenware or china used for baking chopped meat, poultry, eggs, etc., in a custard mixture; also a small pastry case in same shape

Tom turkey—Male turkey, usually larger than hen of same age, preferred for roasting

Tomalley—Green liver of lobster noted for delicate flavor

Tomato paste—Tomato puree reduced to a solid content of 20 to 25%

Tomato puree—Tomato meat cooked, strained and reduced to consistency of heavy sauce

Toss—To lightly mix ingredients such as salad materials, keeping them intact

Tournedos—Small steaks cut from beef fillet weighing 3 to 4 oz each

Tripe—Lining of stomach of cattle

Truffle—Edible fungi which grows underground, considered one of world's greatest delicacies; most truffles from France are black; white truffles are found in Italy

Trunnion kettle—Tilt kettle of counter type; pivots so that it can be emptied easily after cooking

Truss—To tie poultry so that it remains compact in shape during cooking

Try out—Popular term for sautéing solid pieces of fatty meat until fat melts from lean

Turbid—Condition of stock or soup containing particles of extraneous matter requiring clarification

Tureen—Deep vessel for serving soup; may contain individual or multiple portions

Turn—To transfer ingredients from one container to another; also to trim vegetables into small fancy shapes

Veal—Young of cow, less than 12 weeks old (*see also* Calf)

Vegetable peeler—Mechanical peeler; consists of revolving drum the inside of which is covered with a special abrasive; used mainly for potatoes but can also peel turnips, beets, etc.; hand peeler is utensil with floating blade

Vegetable plate—Main dish of assorted vegetables sometimes served with poached egg

Velouté (Fr.)—White sauce made from fat, flour and white stock, chicken stock or fish stock

Venison—Flesh of deer

Vert-pré (Fr.)—Garnish of julienne potatoes and watercress served with broiled or sautéd meats or poultry

Vichyssoise—*See Crème vichyssoise*

Vinaigrette (Fr.)—French dressing with chopped capers, chopped eggs and herbs; also oil and vinegar dressing for salads mixed at table

Vol-au-vent (Fr.)—Pastry case, either round or rectangular made of flaky dough (*see* Puff paste) filled with chicken, seafood, etc., in a sauce

Volume—Number of customers in dining room for specific meal, day or other period; volume cooking refers to mass feeding operations

Waldorf salad—Salad of diced apple, diced celery and mayonnaise

Walnut meat—Halves or broken pieces of walnuts removed from shell

Water ice—*See* Ice

Watercress—Salad green of small flat leaves on stem with pleasant, sharp flavor

Waxy potatoes—New potatoes with thin skin and yellowish white moist flesh

Weakfish—Popular fish of middle Atlantic coast, with pale, blue-gray skin on top and white belly; also called sea trout; popular sizes run from 1 1/2 to 6 lb

Welsh rabbit—Dish of melted cheddar cheese, ale or beer, mustard and other seasonings, served in casserole on toast

Whetstone—*See* Oilstone

Whip—To beat at high speed by hand or mechanical means in order to incorporate as much air as possible

White peppercorn—Dried berry of pepper plant, fully ripened; after drying, outer shell is removed, leaving white interior; less pungent than black pepper; used whole or ground

White sauces—Sauces made with light colored liquids such as milk, white stock, etc.

White stock—Stock made of unbrowned veal bones or combination of beef and veal bones and vegetables

Whitewash—Slang term for mixture of flour and cold water used for thickening purposes

Whiting—Small fish with elongated body, grayish green skin; also called silver hake; small whiting, 2 or 3 to the portion, called "pencil" whiting

Wiener schnitzel (Germ.)—Breaded veal cutlet frequently served with tomato sauce, lemon and anchovy

Wing tip—End of wing of poultry usually cut off and used for broth or stock

Wire whip—Hand utensil or beater of mixing machine made of looped wire usually in shape of bulb, designed to provide fast aeration of batters, egg whites, etc.

Yam—Sweet potato of moist, deep orange flesh

Yellow turnip—*See* Rutabaga

Yorkshire pudding—Accompaniment for roast beef, made of eggs, milk and flour, baked in drippings of roast beef

Zabaglione (Ital.)—*See* Sabayon

Zampino (Ital.)—Boiled Italian salami sometimes used as appetizer

Zeste (Fr.)—Peel of citrus fruits such as orange or lemon which contains aromatic oil

1

Introduction

If, as a student of commercial cooking, you walk into a large hotel kitchen or restaurant kitchen, you may be temporarily confused, if not baffled, by the kitchen organization. You will see cooks busy at various stations. But when you try to match each cook's duties with the sections of a cookbook, you will be understandably frustrated. It's easy, for instance, to spot the pastry cook making pies in the dessert section or to guess that the cook working near the stockpots is making soup. But as you continue to observe cooks behind the ranges, you will fail to find a cook whose sole duty it is to prepare meats or to find another cook specializing in poultry or to find a third cook whose exclusive duty it is to prepare seafood.

If you happen to be interested in the preparation of chicken dishes, and if you observe long enough, you eventually will see that one cook makes the chicken a la king, another undertakes the job of making the fried chicken, a third cook is assigned to broiling chicken, while still a fourth cook prepares the roast chicken. In substance, what you will have seen is that each of the cooks assigned to the critically important main courses of the menu specializes in a broad basic method of cooking adaptable to a wide variety of preparations. For instance, the broil cook (sometimes called the grill cook) not only uses his broilers for obvious jobs like broiling steaks, chops, split lobsters or shish kebabs, but at other times may use his broilers for making large quantities of toast for a banquet, or for browning grated cheese on potatoes au gratin, or for crisping the skin of carved roast duckling.

In time you will learn that even cooks' titles are not always the clues to their complete roster of duties. For example, the sauce cook (*saucier*) makes not only conventional sauces like hollandaise sauce, tomato sauce, etc., but more importantly is responsible for all those main courses cooked with moist heat like stews, pot roasts, boiled beef, poached fish, etc. A fry cook naturally will be found at his battery of fry kettles and sauté pans during the busy lunch or dinner periods. But in the morning the fry cook may also have the assignment of breakfast cook, preparing anything from oatmeal to country sausage to kippered herring. In other words, at certain times during the work day the specialized cook, for pratical reasons, assumes duties apart from his main specialty. In most restaurants there is a roundsman or relief cook whose duty it is to fill the job of each cook on the latter's day off, and who must be capable of performing any of the specialized jobs of cooks working at the ranges. Despite the fact that one cook will often take on the job of another cook's specialty, the best possible way for beginners to learn quantity cooking is to study one specialty at a time, explore it and master its elements before proceeding to another specialty.

This book, unlike a standard recipe book, concentrates on occupational skills rather than mere divisions of food. It aims to train beginner cooks to learn the specialized jobs in the kitchen, and to teach, through recipes, the skills involved in those specialties. Students thus learning basic skills and combinations of skills from one specialty to the next will not only catch the drift of what seems like the complicated organization of a kitchen but will be learning their trade in the tradition of European cooks and chefs who, for generations, have spent their apprentice and journeymen's years in just this manner.

If a cook's skill, like that of a watch repairman, were one that was performed at the worker's own bench, it would be easy to point out that patience, orderliness and the ability to master countless details were obvious signposts to success. But a cook in a busy restaurant (unless he is the sole cook in a small eating unit) should never look upon his specialized job in a kitchen as a sealed compartment in which he works alone, not affecting, or being affected by, other cooks. A dish as simple as corned beef hash browned is not a one-man job in a commercial kitchen. The raw corned beef is received by a butcher who soaks it overnight before cooking. A sauce cook simmers the meat the day it appears on the menu as corned beef and cabbage or New England boiled dinner. The leftover corned beef is trimmed and cut into dice by the *garde manger* (the cook responsible for preparing leftovers, hors d'oeuvres, etc.). A vegetable cook boils the potatoes for mixing with the hash. Again the sauce cook becomes involved, and prepares the mixture of diced corned beef, hashed potatoes, cream and seasonings, blending them until the hash is ready to sauté or brown. Finally, just before and during the meal period, the fry cook sautés the corned beef hash browned in single portions for the dining room. In this particular job five members of the kitchen staff take part in the preparation of a dish which, in a home kitchen, would be the work of one person.

This division of labor makes for the utmost speed and efficiency. But if any one of the five steps in preparing corned beef hash browned is not completed in time or is poorly done, the end product or final dish may be a partial, or perhaps complete, failure. Student cooks should never make the mistake of thinking that, robot-like, they are performing a single mechanical duty as factory workers sometimes do on an assembly line. Far from being robots, cooks must constantly probe, use fine judgment and make fresh decisions in their daily work. For example, the sauce cook simmering corned beef briskets in water must be alert to the fact that one brisket of corned beef may become tender 20 to 30 min before another brisket in the same pot, even though both briskets were of the same weight and grade. The *garde manger* must recognize that if his heavy French knife is not razor sharp, the corned beef cannot be cut into the uniformly small dice necessary for good eye appeal. The fry cook must be aware that if one of his sauté pans is covered with a film of built-up fat and other food from previous uses, the hash will stick to the pan and will not be formed into an attractive oval shape. Countless decisions of this type always remain in the cook's hands. The one person whose overall duty it is to see that each cook performs his individual assignment, and who coordinates the whole job, is the chef. But neither a student cook nor an experienced cook has a chef watching over his shoulder every minute of the working day and, therefore, each of the cook's daily jobs is a continuous test of his ability to appraise, judge and make rapid decisions. Like the nine men on a baseball team, each must act alone and act together.

Because the interdependence and teamwork of cooks is the lifeblood of a successful kitchen, student cooks at the very beginning must understand that the one overriding personal trait on which a cook's career stands or falls is his ability to get along with others. They must remind themselves that their ability to cooperate is not a characteristic with which we are born like the color of our hair or eyes. It must be learned and often relearned. The roast cook may be the best *rôtisseur* in the world, but if he cannot get along with the sauce cook on his right and the broil cook on his left, he chronically will join the ranks of the unemployed. Aspiring cooks will find that all the manual skills they acquire will be worthless without the ability to reason with others, be flexible in discussions and constantly adaptable to new circumstances.

At the beginning of each chapter on specialized cooking, the duties of the cook are described. These include not only the main routines of his job but the extra or overlapping duties which may vary considerably from one restaurant kitchen to another. Also listed and described are the equipment and working conditions of the job. These introductions should give a balanced view of the job and prepare the student for the recipes that follow.

Normally a recipe, like a job sheet in an industrial plant, is a list of ingredients for a dish and a brief outline of what to do with these ingredients. Normally it does not consider food cost control, food eye appeal, safety, sanitation, personnel relations and all the other factors which affect the professional cook every minute of his working day. To highlight these factors from job to job, recipes in *Quantity Cooking* will be longer than usual in order to underscore for the beginner those elements in his day-to-day working habits which he must master if he is to be a professional rather than an amateur cook.

A recipe is not a simple chemical formula like H_2O for water, a formula which is unvarying and unchallenged. Recipes vary widely for a number of reasons. Student cooks are often confused by different recipes for the same dish, and unless they are able to adequately understand the different approaches to recipes, whether they be in this or another book, they will find themselves lost in a fog of words rather than carefully guided for a specific job.

To illustrate how one must approach recipes and learn to use them, consider a simple dish like onion soup. There are only two principal ingredients in it, stock and onions, so that differences in ratios from one recipe to the next can be easily perceived. Here, from four established authorities in the field of commercial cooking, are four versions of onion soup. Recipes are adjusted so that each contains 12 qt stock.

Book and Author	Stock	Onions
Large Quantity Recipes American Dietetic Association	12 qt	48 oz
Food Preparation for Hotels, Restaurants and Cafeterias Robert G. Haines	12 qt	66 oz
Food For Fifty Fowler, West and Shugart	12 qt	128 oz
Quantity Cookery Treat and Richards	12 qt	160 oz

What are you, as a learner, to believe when four published recipes for onion soup not only give you four different ratios, but at one end of the scale tell you to use more than three times as many onions as at the opposite end of the scale? To get the answer, you must ask another question. For what type of restaurant is the onion soup intended? An onion soup served in a hospital or nursing home, for instance, might be close to a clear broth with only a small amount of onions included as a vegetable garnish. An onion soup in a metropolitan restaurant with a continental tradition, where quality rather than other considerations was the guide to kitchen standards, might be flavored with Madeira wine and thick with onions like a rich potage. The soup in the latter restaurant might be garnished with bread croutons and freshly grated imported Parmesan cheese, or it might be baked in an earthenware marmite pot with a crust of bread and cheese covering the top.

Chefs not only differ in the ratios of food in a recipe but often disagree on just what ingredients go into a particular dish. For example, the common but important sauce called white sauce or cream sauce in this country is called sauce *béchamel* in France. Since French cuisine is noted for the excellence of its sauces, a student might look up four French authorities and he would find these results:

Book and Author	Ingredients in Sauce *Béchamel*
A Guide to Modern Cookery A. Escoffier	Butter, flour, milk, veal and onions
Classic French Cuisine Joseph Donon	Butter, flour, milk, onions, parsley and cream
Cooking à la Ritz Louis Diat	Butter, flour, milk and onions
Larousse Gastronomique (Encyclopedia of Food, Wine and Cookery) Prosper Montagne	Butter, flour and milk

Here, the confusion can be resolved quickly for the student by asking *when* the recipes were written. *A Guide to Modern Cookery*, by the most eminent of all French food writers, was first printed in 1907 and represents the type of cuisine fashionable in elegant European hotels in the 19th century. Both Mr. Donon and Mr. Diat were French chefs working in New York City during the first half of this century. The last and simplest recipe is correctly described in the *Larousse Gastronomique* as the modern version replacing the older dishes known for their elaborate overdressed garnishes and rich complicated seasonings.

The recipes in this book, although planned for beginner cooks, are projected for quality kitchens rather than institutional kitchens where food and labor costs and convenience factors are necessary guides. This does not mean that the ingredients in this book's recipes and its methods of cooking are chosen just because they sound elegant or their costs are high. Rather, they are written with the aim of maximum training for excellence in kitchen skills. There are many commercial kitchens where cooks are almost completely unskilled and where it is customary to make onion soup from precut dehydrated onions and dehydrated artificial stock rather than a fine, fresh beef or chicken stock. At the opposite extreme, if one were determined to make the most expensive fresh onion soup conceivable, one could include dry French champagne along with the stock as the liquids for the soup, a practice actually followed in some Parisian kitchens. Neither extreme will be found in *Quantity Cooking.*

Although many recipes, as previously stated, are just a list of ingredients and what to do with them, student cooks must be prepared to recognize other implications in recipes which accompany every kitchen job. If, for instance, a recipe for rice calls for brushed French truffles selling at six dollars an ounce, you will automatically ask: Can a rice dish with an ingredient of this cost be allowed on the menu? If a recipe tells you to garnish a planked steak with small mounds of vegetables, you will naturally begin to think of bright green asparagus, tiny red beets, small silver onions and other vegetables that would provide colorful contrast to enhance eye appeal. If a recipe tells you that a soup may be stored up to a week in the refrigerator, you will probably wonder about the safekeeping of the soup—will it be as safe, from the public health standpoint, on the seventh day as it was on the first day? Experienced cooks naturally consider these things in their day-to-day jobs. Student cooks must make a special effort, when they read and work with recipes, to weigh these other considerations that are always involved with the recipe.

RECIPES AND TRADITIONAL SPECIALTIES

Many eating places are noted for specific dishes which they feature constantly and which are "drawing cards" on their menus. Normally a creamed chicken hash is a combination of diced cooked chicken and a cream sauce. One club restaurant in New York City for years has been famed for its creamed chicken hash made from diced breast of boiled fowl, sherry, heavy cream, a very small amount of cream sauce and a small amount of hollandaise sauce folded in at the last moment. It is a rich velvety dish always made to order, and the club's patrons who order it would rebel if they were offered any other version. A new cook joining the kitchen staff would have to learn the recipe for this particular chicken hash down to the last dash of cayenne pepper. This does not mean that when your schooling is completed, and you enter the trade, the owner, manager or chef under whom you work will ask you to obliterate all or any of the recipes you have mastered. Sometimes, in fact, a restaurant owner or manager will welcome innovative recipes and will encourage cooks to be creative as long as the new recipes are improvements rather than just change for change's sake.

RECIPES AND FOOD COST

It goes without saying that any restaurant, whether it be a large industrial cafeteria or an expensive hotel, expects its cooks to work in an economical manner with as little waste as possible. Students or apprentice cooks, working with new or familiar recipes, must keep a sharp lookout for possible waste. Newer cooks lacking the experience of veteran cooks in trimming and carving foods must make a special effort to be cost conscious of recipes. Recipes in this book will regularly cite possible sources of waste of which the student must always be conscious. When the recipe indicates that a sauce is to be strained through a china cap (a conical utensil commonly used for straining or pureeing foods), the sauce must be completely strained with no appreciable sauce remaining on the inside or outside of the china cap, on the spoon used for straining or in the pot in which the sauce was cooked. Often economy is a matter of simply following a recipe literally and precisely. If, for example, the recipe tells you to roast ribs of beef at 325°F and the meat is inadvertently put in ovens at 425°F, the shrinkage of the cooked meat will increase from its normal 15% to 25%, a prodigious difference for this expensive cut of meat.

RECIPES AND SANITATION

Personal cleanliness and cleanliness of uniforms, equipment and work stations are part of the orientation and ongoing training of every student cook. But food sanitation includes wider areas such as bacterial hazards, temperature control, refrigeration, use of leftovers and other procedures directly related to recipes. Factors which affect sanitation are cited and stressed in the recipes of this book. For example, a student preparing a crab meat croquette mixture on Monday to be used on Tuesday may take the hot mixture off the fire and, in a busy moment, set it aside on a shelf or work table for later refrigeration. Bacteria in food multiply at temperatures from 40° to 140°F. The crab meat, the milk, the eggs and other ingredients in the croquette mixture are well-known mediums for bacterial development. Let the crab meat stand in a hot kitchen for several hours, and the possibilities for food contamination are very great indeed. The recipe instructions, therefore, are not to be regarded as just a series of how-to steps, but as information that may directly affect the health of patrons in any public eating place.

RECIPES AND EYE APPEAL

It has often been said we eat not only with our mouths but with our eyes as well. Experienced cooks can sometimes look at a recipe and visualize what the completed dish will look like on the plate or platter. Time and again the attractiveness of a food will depend on the details of the recipe meticulously carried out. If lamb chops, for instance, are broiled under a strong broiler flame, following recipe directions, they will emerge crisply browned and attractive. If they are broiled slowly under a weak flame, they may emerge with the grayish cast of boiled meat. If they are brushed lightly with softened butter and lemon juice, they will have an appealing natural sheen. If this small step is ignored, the visual effect will be downgraded. If French fried potatoes are hand cut rather than put through a machine, and the recipe directs the cook to cut them 3/8 in. thick, any variation from this dimension can only result in a less tempting product.

RECIPES AND EQUIPMENT

Whenever utensils are called for in a recipe it is important: (a) to use the exact utensil the recipe indicates—don't attempt to use a curved butcher's knife for dicing carrots if the recipe indicates a heavy French knife; (b) to remember that a single utensil may have many uses—a kitchen spoon, for instance, may be used for stirring, beating, straining, folding, etc., but in a particular job should be used only as the recipe directs; (c) to be sure that hand equipment is in working order for the job in the recipe—a dull knife is not only harder to handle than a sharp knife, it is actually more dangerous; a carving board that is not perfectly flat will be a handicap in following a recipe that calls for dicing, slicing, chopping, etc. Frequently recipes must be adjusted to certain heavy-duty equipment. If, for instance, you are bringing liquid to a boil in a conventional pot on a closed top range, it may take an hour before the liquid reaches the boiling point. If, however, you are using one of the newer steam-jacketed kettles, boiling may occur in 1/4 the time. If the recipe calls for roasting meat in a conventional oven, the approximate time will be indicated in the recipe. If one of the newer high-speed convection ovens is used, the roasting time will be noticeably reduced. The student or apprentice cook working in a new kitchen for the first time, following recipes he has learned elsewhere, must be certain that he understands the use of any of the equipment that is unfamiliar to him.

RECIPES AND THE CLOCK

Chefs and cooks are constantly mindful that their work lives and dies by the clock on the kitchen wall. If one is preparing a soup at home, and the soup is not ready at the usual mealtime, members of the family may grumble. But if a cook in a hotel is preparing a special soup for a party of 200 people, and the soup is not ready when guests sit down at the banquet tables, the grumbling swells to an unremitting roar. The ability to follow the cooking times in a recipe means more than merely glancing at the clock. It means not only knowing specific cooking times for specific foods on the fire, but total preparation times.

If the large assortment of vegetables for a mulligatawny soup takes a half hour to dice, and the soup must be ready by 11 A.M. for a noon meal, the job of dicing would not seem too formidable for a cook starting work at 8 A.M. But the soup cook may have other assignments at 8 o'clock. He may have to take the place of a cook unexpectedly absent, and this contingency may seriously delay him. A student or apprentice cook undertaking the job for the first time may actually take an hour or an hour and a half for the same work the experienced cook completes in a half hour. In many kitchens a job like cutting the vegetables for a mulligatawny soup is performed the day before, during slack times. If a recipe calls for cooked chestnuts in a poultry stuffing, the chestnuts must be sorted beforehand to eliminate defective chestnuts. The chestnuts must be subsequently slit, baked until the shells open, again sorted, boiled until tender, cooled and broken into pieces for the stuffing. Obviously this job must be carried out long in advance of the moment when the stuffing is ready for the fire. For such reasons students must be particularly time-conscious of the recipes they are learning during their apprenticeship. Even when students are concentrating intensely on a new recipe, they must be conscious of routine steps that involve wasted motion and wasted time. Often simple distractions like a conversation with another cook, while seemingly harmless, can become a costly liability when time is at a premium in carrying out a recipe. Recipes, therefore, are much more than reading matter in a textbook to be learned in a classroom. In a down-to-earth sense, they are a form of strategy to be worked out beforehand between the chef or instructor on the one hand and the apprentice or student on the other. Careful estimates must be made for the time required for the principal steps in each recipe, and an estimate of the total time it will take before the food is removed from the fire and ready to serve. Cooks must consider other jobs with different recipes that must be performed beforehand or simultaneously with the main job. Having made the estimates, the wise student will allot his time as prudently as he would allot his money if he were spending it on a new expensive project. He will carefully note how much the actual time varied from the estimated time in carrying out a new recipe. Working with the same recipe repeatedly will show him the progressive speed which is the real score of one's experience.

RECIPES AND LEFTOVERS

There are kitchens (such as feeding units of the armed services and many school cafeterias) which each day, starting from scratch, prepare all fresh food using no leftovers. Most commercial restaurants, however, as a realistic business practice regularly use leftovers. It is the policy to have a minimum of leftovers, and all leftovers must be judiciously chosen to avoid foods which have deteriorated in quality or show signs of incipient spoilage. There are some recipes like croquettes calling for previously cooked food which may or may not include certain leftovers. In other cases a leftover soup like a gumbo soup might be strained and included in the stock of puree of lentil soup with excellent results. In still other instances a leftover food like tomato sauce, properly stored, suffers no distinctively noticeable flavor loss if it is used the second or the third day after it is prepared. Some dishes like goulashes and curries are considered improved on the second or third day because of greater blending and mellowing of flavors. For these and other reasons apprentice cooks starting work in restaurants for the first time should expect to adjust many of the recipes they have learned to accommodate the normal and necessary use of leftovers.

CONVERTING RECIPES

In some restaurants all food is weighed. In others it is measured in quart containers and other measuring units. In the majority of eating places a combination of both forms is followed. A cook requisitioning butter from the storeroom will always ask for it in pounds. When he orders canned tomato puree, he will order cans of a certain size, but use measuring quarts or measuring cups for his recipes. Weighing is a more precise method of using food in large quantities, but there are many practical objections to it. For instance, in a busy restaurant featuring an a la carte menu where most of the dishes are made to order, it would be extremely impractical and cause serious delays in the service if each spoonful of hollandaise sauce on the cauliflower or each portion of cauliflower or fresh asparagus had to be put on a scale to be measured in ounces or fractions of ounces. This book features a combination of weighing and measuring. For example, a recipe for braised beef indicates the weight of the beef just as it is customarily bought while such ingredients as the sliced vegetables—onions, leeks and carrots—are indicated in quarts or cups of the vegetables, trimmed and ready for cooking. Food calculations would be routinely easy if a recipe for 50 portions were always made for 50. But more often than not a recipe for 50 must be made for 75 or for 12 or for some other quantity different from the original recipe. For this important reason, as well as the necessity of using leftovers in many daily jobs (described above), every cook and every student must be able to perform simple mathematical calculations as part of his daily work. This is particularly important in a cookery class where obviously every student or every team of students could not, as a practical matter, prepare food in large quantities for each assignment.

2

Using The French Knife

Professional cooks use a number of well-known utensils, many of which are simply heavier or larger versions of those used in homes. Skills in handling them are easily learned. In a matter of minutes, a student can understand how to use a vegetable peeler, a spatula, a parisienne potato cutter or a skimmer. But one cutting tool, the French knife, takes months or sometimes years of practice before one uses it skillfully, speedily and with complete control. The French knife is to the cook what the chisel is to the sculptor, a hand instrument without which he could hardly function. Although cooks use a variety of knives from small paring knives to long roast beef slicers, the French knife is employed for so many jobs that it is as much a symbol of the cooking craft as is the tall chef's hat. It is variously known as the French knife, the chef's knife or the cook's knife.

Students should understand that certain utensils are always supplied by the kitchen in which you work. These include mixing or serving spoons, skimmers, ladles, wire whips, china caps (strainers), etc. Certain other utensils including knives are bought by the cook as his personal possessions, are kept under lock and key at his station, and are taken by him when he leaves a job and starts new employment. As a beginner, you are not expected to own a full complement of knives and other utensils. In time, as your experience grows, you will want to acquire those tools which you find best suited for your own working habits. If you are on the staff of a large commercial kitchen, you will note that for certain jobs cutting machines are used instead of knives. If diced potatoes, for instance, are needed for a banquet of 800 people, a machine would be used to cut the potatoes automatically. But if potatoes are to be cut in a special shape and thickness for 80 portions of minestrone soup, the potatoes very likely would be cut by hand using a French knife. As a beginner, the best size French knife for learning purposes is one with an 8-in. blade.

It is large enough not only for most cutting jobs but also for many jobs of meat carving. It is not so large that it is cumbersome to handle. Besides an 8-in. French knife, you will probably want to acquire the following utensils as the beginning of your permanent collection:

12-in. roast beef slicer
6 1/2-in. utility knife
4-in. paring knife
14-in. knife steel
Sharpening stone
9-in. fork, heavy duty, 2 pronged
8-in. spatula
4× 2 1/2-in. offset spatula
Parisienne potato cutter

CHOOSING A FRENCH KNIFE

In considering the purchase of a French knife, the first fact probably brought to your attention is that there are two kinds of steel blades. The older type is made of carbon steel, and is considered the best by many cooks because of its ability to hold a keen cutting edge for a long time before it needs sharpening. The second, and newer type, is made of stainless steel. From a practical standpoint, a carbon steel knife must be wiped after each use, or it will rust. Sometimes, if it is being used to cut an acid fruit such as grapefruit or an acid vegetable such as tomatoes, rust spots will show up while it is in use. Until a few years ago, most cooks agreed that the carbon steel blade was easier to sharpen and held its sharp edge longer than a blade made of stainless steel. Recent versions of stainless steel knives, particularly those from Solingen, Germany, seem to equal the best of the carbon steel knives in retaining a sharp working edge.

Note in Fig. 2.1 that while the French knife is usually described as having a triangular blade, the cutting edge is turned to a gentle curve toward the tip, a basic design that makes it easy to cut foods when the knife is used in the common down–forward motion described in a subsequent section. When selecting a French knife, you will want to examine it for its balance, that is, the distribution of weight from the handle to the tip. When the balance is good, it is easy to maneuver the knife quickly and efficiently. If you are selecting from a number of knives, look at the top of the blade. The knife with the thickest top is probably the best for heavy-duty use. Ex-

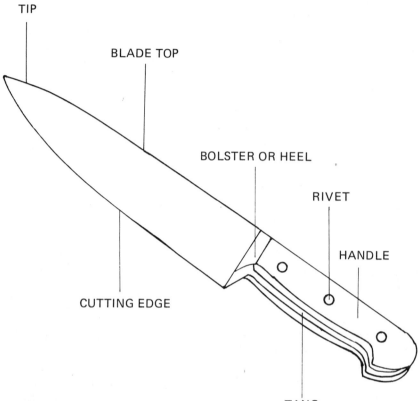

TIP

BLADE TOP

BOLSTER OR HEEL

RIVET

HANDLE

CUTTING EDGE

TANG

FIG. 2.1. THE FRENCH KNIFE

amine the bolster which abuts the handle; it, too, should be heavy to provide weight and force at the rear of the knife where most use occurs. Make sure the tang is thick, runs the whole length of the handle, and is visible on top and bottom. Handles may be of wood or wood impregnated with plastic; the latter can withstand the use of frequent washings in hot water. Choose a handle which feels comfortable to you. Be sure there is enough room so that your knuckles do not hit the cutting board when chopping or dicing. Make sure the rivets are absolutely flush with the handle. Finally, if you are considering a particular brand, consult other cooks who may have owned or used the knife in question.

KNIFE SAFETY

Listing a number of safety rules does not guarantee that you will be immune from accidents. Using almost any tool or machine in the kitchen is a serious activity fraught with many possible dangers of which the student must be aware. There are certain work habits one should consciously cultivate in using any kind of knife from a small paring knife to a large roast beef slicer.

(1) In the same way that an athlete is reminded to keep his eye on the ball, a cook must not only keep his eye on the knife but on the food being cut. If you must look up from the cutting board for any reason whatever, stop cutting.

(2) Be sure your knife is as sharp as possible. A dull knife will cause you to push or tug in an awkward way that may cause loss of control.

(3) Under no circumstances place a knife in a sink with water where it can not be seen. Wash and dry the knife as you hold it.

(4) Make certain that the handle of the knife is dry and free of grease. Wipe it as often as necessary.

(5) Do not attempt to catch a falling knife; step aside.

(6) When a knife is not in use, keep it in its rack, case or drawer.

(7) When a knife is in use, and you have stopped cutting momentarily, place the knife with its cutting edge to the side, never with its sharp edge facing up.

(8) In handing a knife to another person, place it so that it can be grasped by the handle, not the blade.

(9) Learn the traditional ways of holding, pivoting, chopping and slicing as described below. Correct form is not only designed for speed and efficiency but for safety's sake as well.

(10) Do not attempt to cut food in a work area cluttered with pans, trays and other equipment. Nothing but the food about to be cut should be on the cutting board. If there are large reserve quantities of food to be cut, keep them adjacent to the cutting board until needed.

(11) After batches of food are cut to the proper size, do not allow them to accumulate in haphazard piles on the cutting board. Remove them to containers so that the cutting board is free for working on the next batch.

(12) When walking with a knife, hold the blade down, top of the blade forward.

(13) Whenever a cutting board becomes wet, slippery or greasy, wipe it dry so that food will not slide about as you are cutting.

(14) When working under pressure in order to complete a job within a specified time, do not use the knife with such excessive speed that you may lose control of it.

The top of Fig. 2.2 shows the correct grip on the French knife. Note that the thumb is on the left side of the blade, while the first finger is on the right side. Remaining fingers are under the handle, directly behind the bolster. Holding the knife in this position provides maximum force for the rear of the blade where most cutting occurs. It also enables you to hold the blade securely, move it and pivot it with complete control. The grip on the knife must be secure but relaxed. If the knife is held too tightly, the hand can quickly become tired, and cutting is difficult. If the handle is grasped too

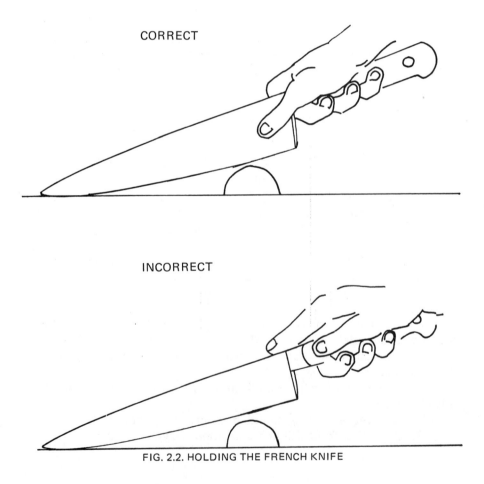

CORRECT

INCORRECT

FIG. 2.2. HOLDING THE FRENCH KNIFE

tightly for prolonged periods, one can develop cramps in the hand muscles. Beginners are advised not to adopt too circumscribed a stance in front of the cutting board. Attempts to use a strictly delineated position for the shoulders, elbows and forearm often result in unnecessary tension. The bottom (incorrect) knife grip shows a position commonly adopted by beginners perhaps because it is seen in homes and elsewhere. It is an attempt to steady the knife movement. Actually, when the finger is placed on top of the blade, the knife will often wobble, and slicing will be haphazard. Some cooks use the finger on top the blade, as shown, when marking portions of a cake or when scoring a ham. If it is used for such purposes, the blade must be moved very slowly. It is not recommended for general use with the French knife.

The French knife is commonly used for carving such foods as pot roast, boiled beef, smoked tongue and other boneless cuts of meat. Learners have a tendency to move the knife rapidly back and forth in short, restricted saw-like motions. As a result, slices are often irregular, and meat tends to break. The longer sweeping motion shown on the bottom of Fig. 2.3, with the knife drawn well to the rear, and moved well forward, not only results in fewer movements but in more accurate, controlled slicing. The same long, rather than short, movement should be used for slicing any food in this manner whether it be a loaf of bread or a tomato. The student is again reminded to hold the knife firmly but not grip it too tightly. The cutting edge of the knife does the work, not the force with which you grip the handle.

The style of cutting depicted in Fig. 2.4 is the most frequently used by cooks behind the range. The knife is placed at an angle to the cutting board and moved forward and down. When the first slice is completed, the knife, with its tip remaining on the board, is returned to a position above the food, and the forward–down motion is repeated. Initially the tip or middle of the blade cuts into the food. When the slice is completed, the heel of the knife is on the cutting board, while the tip of the knife is raised slightly. The entire motion is somewhat like a partial arc of a pendulum. The distance the knife traverses on the cutting board depends upon the size of the food being cut. If a carrot, for instance, were being sliced, the knife tip would move only slightly forward as shown in the illustration. If a large head of cabbage were being cut, the motion would be considerably extended.

For most cutting jobs, both hands are used in the position shown in Fig. 2.5. Strips of celery are being cut into dice. The right hand holds the knife handle for a down–forward slice as shown in Fig. 2.4.

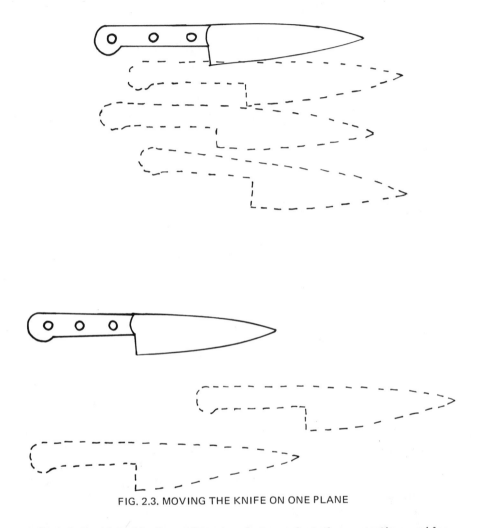

FIG. 2.3. MOVING THE KNIFE ON ONE PLANE

The left hand holds the celery in place, and at the same time guides the knife for each downward thrust. Note that the middle finger of the left hand is placed directly against the blade. All fingers of the left hand except the thumb are bent inward at the ends as though one were scratching a surface. The tip of the knife rests on the board. The blade, moving down and forward, cuts the pieces of celery extended beyond the blade. After each slice is completed, the left hand moves slightly to the rear, the knife pivots to the new position, and again, in one slice, cuts the exposed ends of celery into dice. Also note that the left hand holds the celery strips in a uniform row for dicing. The same position of the left hand is used

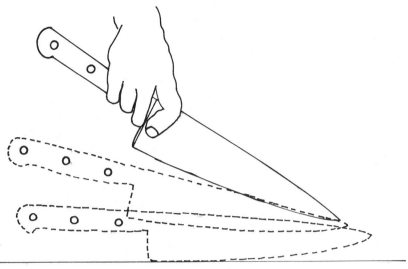

FIG. 2.4. SLICING DOWN AND FORWARD

not only for holding food cut into strips, such as celery or leeks, but also for whole pieces of food, such as onions, carrots, turnips, etc. The lower part of Fig. 2.5 shows the wrong and extremely dangerous use of the left hand. Instead of guiding the knife blade, the fingers are exposed to it, if the knife should slip. The hand held in this manner forces the cook to aim visually for the correct slicing position each time the blade is used, slows the job, and results in food cut into irregular sizes.

For numerous jobs in which food is finely chopped, the tip of the blade is kept on the cutting board while the knife is swiveled in an arc. When chopping parsley, for example, the stalks of parsley in a bunch are first chopped coarsely to reduce the size of the mass and to make the leaves more compact, after which they are chopped as shown in Fig. 2.6. Note that the handle of the knife is held in its regular manner. The tip of the knife is placed on the board with the left hand fingers extended, resting on top of the blade near the tip. Some cooks rest four fingers, others, three. The purpose of positioning the left hand in this manner is to hold the tip down while guiding it as it swivels around the board. With the knife held in this manner, the cook moves the blade very rapidly up and down, and reduces the food to the desired size. Certain foods, like garlic, are sometimes chopped so fine they are almost pureed. Students are again reminded to keep eyes constantly on the job before them. When chopping in this manner, foods will usually cling to the sides of the blade. Chop-

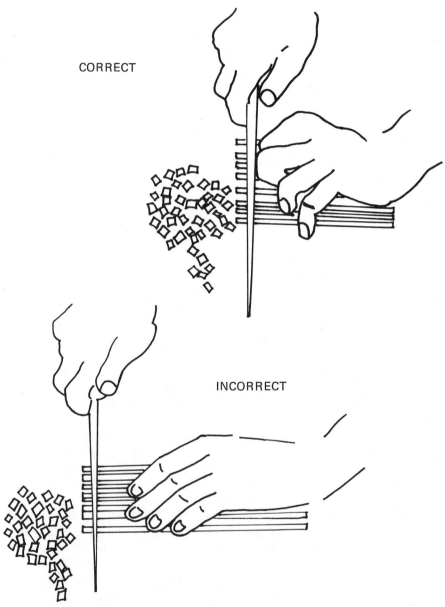

CORRECT

INCORRECT

FIG. 2.5. GUIDING THE KNIFE WITH THE LEFT HAND

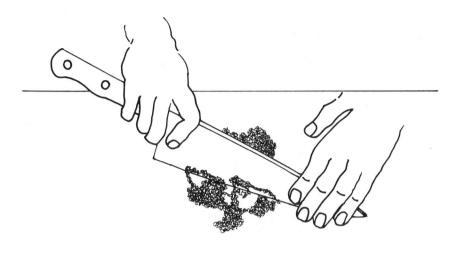

FIG. 2.6. CHOPPING AND SWIVELING

ping should be stopped periodically, and the blade should be wiped to return the food to the cutting board whenever necessary.

Two knives are sometimes employed when large quantities of food must be chopped quickly (Fig. 2.7). Unlike the swivel action shown in Fig. 2.6, both knives are moved rapidly in a down–up motion, on and off the board. Note the changed position of the hand. The thumb of both hands is placed on top of the handle providing maximum force in hitting the cutting board. Although the entire length of the blade may be used, most of the cutting takes place on the middle of the blades. Both knives are moved in tandem or alternately, to provide uniform chopping. From time to time, the food scattered over the cutting board must be scraped from the ends of the board toward the center. As chopping progresses, the pieces of food will scatter less, and tend to cling in one mass. Occasionally it may be necessary to wipe the blades of food particles adhering to them.

Although it differs from the French knife shown in previous illustrations, all students learning the art of roasting should become familiar with the roast beef slicer, sometimes called the meat slicer. The knife shown in Fig. 2.8 has a long flexible blade and rounded tip. Sizes of the knife range from 12- to 18-in. blades. It is used for large cuts of meat such as roast ribs of beef or for carving very thin slices of cold Smithfield ham. It cannot be used, as the French knife is, for severing the joints of poultry. It is convenient not only for slicing meat but for supporting the slice as it is carried to the serving plate or platter. Usually the thumb of the right hand is

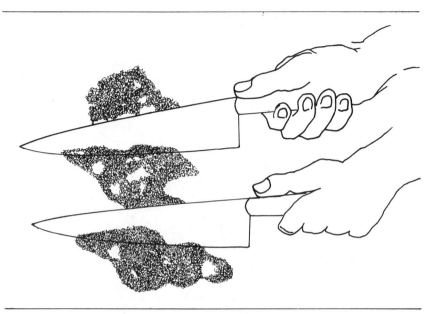

FIG. 2.7. CHOPPING WITH TWO KNIVES

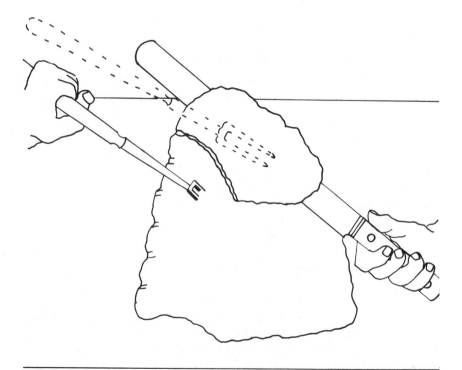

FIG. 2.8. USING THE ROAST BEEF SLICER

placed on top of the knife handle, a convenient way of holding and steadying the knife while carving in a horizontal position as shown. Note that the fork in the left hand is inserted between the rib bones to hold the roast firmly while it is being carved. After the slice is carved, the fork (shown by dotted lines) is placed on top of the slice to aid in moving it to the serving plate. Some roast cooks do not insert the fork into the rib section, but place it on top of the roast and hold it there, in order to steady the meat as each portion is being sliced.

The knife steel, sometimes called the butcher's steel, is a tapered rod with handle and guard, used for restoring the edge of the blade just before the knife is used (Fig. 2.9). It does not actually sharpen the knife edge—an oilstone is needed for that job—but eliminates the burr or microscopic ragged edge that forms on a knife blade. In buying a knife steel, select one that is at least 12 in. long, preferably 14 in. Make sure that the guard between the steel and the handle is large enough to prevent the knife from accidentally hitting the left hand. Whenever the steel is used, make sure that the handle is clean and dry, not greasy. Hold the knife with the normal grip described previously. Note that the left hand is well away from the steel guard. Place the knife heel at the top of the steel. The knife should be held at an angle of about 30 degrees. Too sharp an angle will make the steel ineffective. Bring the knife across the steel, as shown by positions on the dotted lines, so that the entire length of the blade edge sweeps across the steel. Repeat the same motion on the other side of the steel to hone the edge of the opposite side of the blade. Alternating in this manner, run the knife over the steel about 8 or 10 times. For safety's sake hold both knife and steel in the line of your vision while honing the knife.

In those kitchens which use the services of a specialist knife sharpener, cooks do not find it necessary to sharpen knives on a stone, sometimes called the oilstone or whetstone. This utensil may also be characterized by the material from which it is made, such as a carborundum stone or silicon carbide stone. Unlike the steel in Fig. 2.9, which merely restores an edge, the stone is used to regrind the blade to its original edge. The knife, as shown in Fig. 2.10, is drawn across the stone in such a way that the entire length of the blade is covered in one sweep. The bevel may be restored either by:

(a) Drawing the knife with the blade facing you (as illustrated), or

(b) Drawing the knife with the blade pointed away from you. Both techniques are used by cooks, and both are effective. What sharpens the edge is the friction of the stone and steel at a specific angle which should be from 15 to 20 degrees, no higher. In the

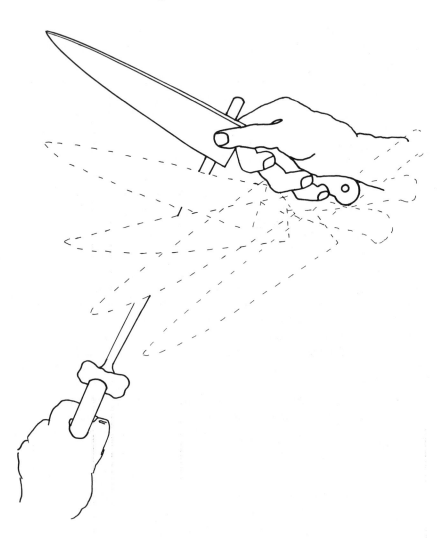

FIG. 2.9. USING THE KNIFE STEEL

recommended technique as shown, the fingers of the left hand are placed on top of the knife blade with its tip at the end of the stone near you. With slight but steady pressure on the tip, move the blade in one sweep so that the knife traverses the stone until it reaches the heel. The blade is then flipped over, and the knife drawn from the far end, starting at the heel and ending at the tip of the knife. If a knife has been neglected, and is extremely dull, one may have to pass

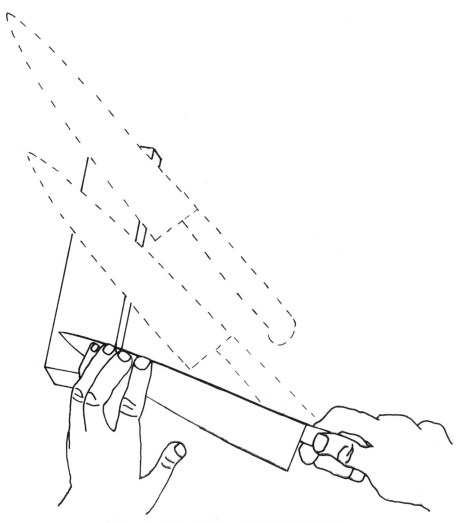

FIG. 2.10. SHARPENING A KNIFE ON A STONE

the knife over the stone from 50 to 100 times. For knives in normal condition, 8 or 10 sweeps should produce a sharp bevel. It is impossible to see the feather edge of a sharp knife, but you can feel it by passing your thumb very lightly over the blade edge. Ask your instructor or supervisor to check the sharpness with you. After using the stone, pass the knife over the steel a few times to make the edge ready for cutting.

CUTTING VEGETABLES

Learning to cut vegetables is often one of the first assignments of an apprentice cook. It is a common job, and no matter how far a cook progresses in his field, it takes a large part of his daily time and attention. Frequently, a newly hired cook joining a kitchen crew will be observed by the chef as the cook cuts vegetables. His accuracy and speed in this basic skill are often a clue to the cook's overall ability behind the range. Although one of the main goals in learning to cut vegetables is speed, the beginner is advised to start slowly and pay major attention to accuracy and uniformity in cutting.

Cutting Onions

Cut a thin slice from the neck with a paring knife, and remove skin from neck to root end, folding the skin back rather than cutting it. If any of the outer layers of onion are wilted or discolored, remove them; they may be used for stock. Trim the root end, but *do not cut deeply into it.* It is the section to which the onion layers are attached, and holds the onion intact on the cutting board as it is being cut.

Onion Rings

Place the peeled whole onion on the cutting board, root end to your left. Holding onion with left hand, cut vertical slices perpendicular to front of board. Cut slices 1/4 in. thick or larger if desired. Cut slowly; the whole round onion on the flat board will wobble if not held securely. Cut as close to the root end as possible while still holding onion in left hand. Turn flat side of onion down on cutting board, and cut horizontally for remaining few slices. Root end may be used for stock. Separate onion slices into rings.

Onion, Diced

(1) Cut peeled onion in half from neck to root end.

(2) Place flat side of onion on cutting board, root end to your left.

(3) Cut vertical lengthwise slices, parallel to front of cutting board, about 1/2 in. from root end to stem end of onion. Thickness of slices will vary with thickness of dice required. For small dice, cut slices 1/4 in. thick; for medium dice, 1/2 in.; for large dice, 3/4 in.

(4) Holding the knife blade horizontally, cut lateral slices toward root end of onion, choosing thickness desired for specific dice size. Do not cut into root end. Onion must stay intact on board.

(5) Cut vertical slices, perpendicular to front of cutting board,

beginning at stem end, choosing thickness desired. Continue cutting until root end of onion is awkward to handle.

(6) Place large flat end of onion on board, and cut criss-cross slices to size of dice required.

(7) Cut remaining half of onion in same manner.

Onion, Finely Chopped

(1) Follow preceding method of dicing onions. Cut slices no larger than 1/8 in. thick, or

(2) Cut onions into large dice, and chop as shown in Fig. 2.6.

Onion, Chopped Extremely Fine

Continue chopping as in preceding step (2) until onion particles are no larger than 1/16 in.

Onion, Julienne

(1) Cut peeled onion in half through root end.

(2) Place flat side of onion on board, root end to your left.

(3) Beginning at stem end of onion (your right side), cut vertical slices across onion, perpendicular to front of cutting board, 1/8 in. thick.

(4) Toss slices with finger tips to separate slices into strips. If onions are to be cooked, whole slices may be placed in cooking vessel; slices will separate into julienne strips as onions are stirred with spoon.

Onion, Sliced

(1) Cut a thin lengthwise slice off one side of peeled whole onion so that onion can rest flat on cutting board.

(2) Place onion on its flat side, root end to your left.

(3) Beginning at right side of onion, cut vertical, parallel slices, perpendicular to front of board. Cut slices to desired thickness.

Cutting Celery

For most cutting jobs, the larger outer stalks of celery are used, while the small inner stalks clinging tightly together are either turned over to the pantry to be served as iced celery hearts or are passed to the *garde manger* to be used in salads. Stalks should be separated from the bunch as close to the root end as possible. Celery must be washed well. Pay particular attention to the insides of the stalks which often need vigorous washing to remove clinging soil. Use a vegetable scrub brush if necessary. Cut off all leaves of celery, and turn them over to the soup cook for possible use in stocks. For most cutting jobs, celery should be peeled, using a vegetable peeler with floating blade; run the peeler over the outside of the stalks to remove stringy outer portion. If celery stalks are unusually thick, they may be cut laterally so that each stalk is sliced to 1/2 or 1/3 its normal thickness. Check with your instructor or supervisor. If stalks are too thick, place stalk on cutting board, outer side up, parallel to front of board. Holding stalk firmly with left hand on top of stalk, very carefully slice from right to left.

Celery, Diced

(1) Cut celery lengthwise into strips. For small dice, strips should be 1/4 in. wide; medium dice, 1/2 in.; large dice, 3/4 in.

(2) Place enough celery strips in a bundle so that you can conveniently hold them with your left hand while cutting.

(3) With knife tip on board, cut across strips to make dice of desired size.

Celery, Chopped

(1) Cut celery into large dice as described above.

(2) Chop, with knife tip on board (as described previously), until celery is reduced to proper size.

Celery, Julienne

(1) Cut celery stalks laterally as described above into slices no thicker than 1/8 in.

(2) Cut slices crosswise into 1 1/2-in. pieces.

(3) Cut pieces lengthwise into strips no larger than 1/8 in.

Cutting Leeks

Determine whether whole leeks, including green and white parts, are to be used for the job you are doing. Usually the white and the firm part of the green are required; for some soups only the white part of the leek is used; top green ends of leeks may be used for stock. For all jobs, cut off loose root ends, but solid part of root should be left intact. Leeks need special washing to remove soil which remains between layers. After cutting leeks lengthwise, as directed below, hold them under cold running water, separating layers to remove sand. After washing, examine leeks under good light to make sure they are completely clean.

Leeks, Diced

(1) Cut leeks lengthwise toward root end, slicing to within one inch of end, making halves, quarters, sixths or eighths, depending upon size of leeks and size of dice required. Small dice should be 1/4 in., medium dice, 1/2 in., and large dice, 3/4 in.

(2) Hold leeks under cold running water, separating layers, until completely cleaned.

(3) Place leeks on cutting board, root end to your left.

(4) Cut crosswise into size of dice required.

(5) When root end of leeks is reached, cut it first lengthwise and then crosswise to make dice of specified size.

Leeks, Chopped

(1) Cut leeks into 1/2-in. dice as described above.

(2) Chop, with tip of knife on board.

Leeks, Julienne

(1) Cut leeks lengthwise and wash as described above.

(2) Cut crosswise into 1 1/2-in. pieces.

(3) Cut 1 1/2-in. pieces lengthwise into 1/8-in. strips.

Cutting Carrots

For almost all cooking purposes except making stock, carrots are peeled before they are cut into various shapes. The stem end is cut off. Peelings and stem ends should not be indiscriminately thrown into the stockpot. When used in excess, their pronounced flavor can be undesirable. Turn any trimmings over to the soup cook to dispose of as he sees fit.

Carrots, Sliced

(1) Cut a thin lengthwise slice off each peeled carrot. The slice should be just thick enough to permit the carrot to rest flat on the cutting board without wobbling.

(2) Cut carrots crosswise into 1/4 or 1/2 in. thick slices. Carrots may be sliced diagonally if desired.

Carrots, Diced

(1) Cut a thin lengthwise slice off each peeled carrot to rest flat on cutting board.

(2) Cut into lengthwise slices to the desired thickness of the dice. Small dice should be 1/4 in., medium dice 1/2 in., and large dice 3/4 in. (Only large storage carrots with tops off would be used for 3/4-in. dice.)

(3) Cut slices into lengthwise strips the desired thickness of the dice.

(4) Place strips in a bundle large enough to comfortably hold in your left hand. Strips should be placed parallel to the front of the cutting board. Cut strips crosswise into dice of desired size.

Note: In some kitchens, cooks are instructed to cut a thin lengthwise slice off four sides of the carrot so that dice will show no rounded side.

Carrots, Julienne

(1) Follow steps (1) and (2) above, but cut lengthwise slices no larger than 1/8 in. thick.

(2) Cut slices crosswise into 1 1/2-in. pieces.

(3) Cut pieces lengthwise into strips no larger than 1/8 in.

Chopped Garlic or Shallots

Both of these flavoring vegetables with aromatic properties like the onion are almost always chopped extremely fine except in a few instances when they are lightly crushed and left whole for bouquet garni or similar uses. Garlic comes in clusters called a bulb or head which is separated into sections called cloves (not to be confused with the dried spice also known as a clove). To separate garlic cloves, place the whole bulb on the cutting board at an angle; holding it with your left hand, press or strike it with the palm of your right hand until the cloves come apart.

Shallots, like onions, are individual bulbs or twin bulbs. To detach garlic or shallots from their skin, place one or several on a cutting board; hold the flat side of a French knife against them, and strike the knife sharply with the right fist. The outer skin will become loose. Remove the skin, and discard it. Place the partly crushed garlic or shallots on the cutting board, and chop with the knife tip on the board.

FRENCH CUTTING TERMS

The following four French culinary terms appear frequently on English menus. They are simply variations on styles of cutting previously described.

Allumette: Strips of potatoes cut in a size between julienne and French fried, about 1/4 in. thick.

Bâtonnets: Vegetables cut into strips 1/4 in. thick and 1 to 1 1/2 in. long; used as a garnish for clear soups and sauce dishes.

Brunoise: Vegetables cut into tiny dice no more than 1/16 in. thick; used as a garnish for clear soups.

Paysanne: Small slices of vegetables, 1/8 or 1/16 in. thick, with a diameter not exceeding 1/2 in. in any direction; used as a garnish for both clear and thick soups.

3

Stocks

When you cook solid food in water, and the food does not absorb the water as it would, for instance, in making oatmeal, you make stock. Thus if you put turnips in a pot of water and boil them until the turnips become tender, the water acquires some of the turnips' flavor and becomes, in a sense, turnip stock. You're not likely to find turnip stock listed in any book of recipes. But the simple illustration describes what a stock is: namely, the liquid that results when the soluble flavoring constituents of food are extracted after cooking in water. When chefs refer to stocks they usually mean the basic stocks made of meat, bones, poultry or seafood and seasoning vegetables. One stock, court bouillon, is made only from vegetables. In classical French cooking stocks were called *fonds de cuisine* or foundations of the kitchen. They are extremely important, but when Escoffier said, "Stock is everything in cooking . . . without it, nothing can be done," he obviously was exaggerating. You don't need stock to make caviar canapés, broiled lamb chops, fillet of sole sauté *meunière*, hollandaise sauce, grilled mushrooms or dozens of other important dishes. But you do need stocks to make soups, many sauces, gravies and braised dishes—almost all those menu items which are the responsibility of the soup cook and the sauce cook.

Usually the soup cook is in charge of making the principal stocks in a kitchen and keeping their quality uniform. The stockpots, usually steam-jacketed kettles, are located at, or near, the soup cook's station. In some very large kitchens, stockpots are kept in a separate area or separate room. If there is no soup cook on the staff, soups will be prepared by the sauce cook, and the latter will be responsible for producing stocks in the kitchen.

There are five principal stocks:

(1) White stock (*fonds blanc*) made from beef and beef bones, veal and veal bones, chicken carcasses, vegetables and water.

(2) Brown stock (*estouffade*) used in most dishes with brown sauces or brown gravies and in certain soups.

(3) Chicken stock or chicken broth (*fonds de volaille*) used in many soups or poultry dishes.

(4) Fish stock (*fonds de poissons*) used in the preparation of individual pieces of fish poached and served with a sauce.

(5) Vegetable stock for fish (*court bouillon*) used in the preparation of large whole fish such as boiled whole salmon and certain shellfish.

Stocks may be made in large quantities in steam-jacketed kettles on the floor or in smaller kettles or pots on top of the range. A stock-pot, as distinguished from a regular pot, is one fitted with a faucet and strainer for drawing stock from the bottom of the kettle free from the fat on the top.

There are some minor stocks made for special dishes such as lamb stock used in Scotch lamb broth, clam stock better known as clam broth used in making clam chowder, etc. These special stocks are described in the recipes in which they appear.

It would simplify things if every time you started a stockpot, you would simply follow a recipe for stock with a given amount of solid ingredients and water, and then repeat the same process each time stock was needed. But stocks as a matter of actual restaurant practice and as a matter of economy are frequently made with leftover raw bones and raw meat trimmings, and these leftovers vary considerably from day to day. Even in those kitchens which purchase portion-controlled meats (rather than use meats trimmed and cut by a butcher on the premises) and where the amount of leftover meat trimmings and bones is at a minimum, chefs are faced with the problem of utilizing leftovers including meat, raw bones, carcasses, vegetable trimmings, etc. The stock maker must, therefore, use careful judgment in determining what may or may not be used in the stockpot. The following guides are planned for kitchens where stock is produced regularly.

14 GUIDES FOR MAKING STOCKS

(1) Kettles for stock must be kept scrupulously clean. They must be well scrubbed with detergent and a stiff brush after each use. Special attention should be paid to the strainer and faucet. If there is a hinged lid on the kettle, be sure that it is very carefully cleaned. Any residue of scum, grease or soap left on the lid may spoil the next batch of stock.

(2) Any meat, bones or carcasses which have remained in the refrigerator for several days and feel sticky to the touch or which have an unnatural odor should be washed, blanched, washed a second time and carefully examined for signs of spoilage before they are added to the stockpot. Fresh meat and bones should be examined for bone splinters, coagulated blood or foreign matter, and wiped clean with a damp cloth. Vegetables should be sound. They need not be young, but they should not be so old that they are decomposing or show signs of mold or rot. Besides the specified vegetables in the stock recipes, trimmings of vegetables within limits may be added. The stockpot should not become a catchall for any leftovers in the kitchen. For instance, strong-tasting vegetables such as broccoli or cabbage must be excluded. The quantity of vegetables must be controlled. If there happens to be an unusually large quantity of carrot trimmings from peeled carrots, and they are indiscriminately added to the stock, they may impart a sweet overpowering carrot flavor to the stock which radically alters its mild flavor. A good rule of thumb is never to allow the vegetable trimmings to exceed more than one third of those normally used. Herbs and other spices are omitted in some stocks or are used conservatively since the basic stock is only the first step in the preparation of a soup or stew each of which requires its own specific herbs and spices.

(3) When members of the kitchen staff other than the sauce cook or soup cook have accumulated vegetable trimmings, the best procedure is for them to turn such trimmings over to the soup cook rather than indiscriminately add them to the stockpot. The soup cook can then decide whether they should be added.

(4) A moderate flame or heat should be used when water is first added to the stockpot. It should be brought to a boil slowly before the first skimming. A small amount of cold water is sometimes added to stop the boiling and cause the scum to rise to the top for skimming. The stock should be simmered and skimmed when necessary to eliminate as much scum as possible.

(5) Since the flavoring ingredients extracted depend upon long slow cooking, frequent attention must be paid to the temperature of the stockpot whether the source of heat is steam, gas or electricity. Gas pressure sometimes changes during the day, and this may cause the stock to boil rather than simmer. The metal in certain kettles becomes "saturated with heat" after several hours, and the heat buildup or retention may make it necessary to adjust the temperature. Thus a stock which is barely simmering at 10 A.M. may be found to be boiling vigorously at noon even though the heat application was unchanged.

(6) The contents of a stockpot, particularly during the first hour

of simmering should be stirred once or twice. The weight of certain foods such as heavy shin bones may cause them to stick to the sides or bottom of the kettle. Use a long paddle and move the contents gently. Excessive or continued stirring may cause the stock to become turbid.

(7) Fat may accumulate on top of the stock during the long period of simmering and should be removed. Fat is important in imparting the flavor of certain meats, but excessive fat beyond a thin film on top serves no purpose. Add it to the container of used fat which is generally saved and sold by most restaurants.

(8) As the stock reduces during cooking, a rim of scum may form on the side of the kettle. Wipe it off to keep the deposit from concentrating and sticking to the kettle.

(9) The length of time the stockpot should be kept simmering depends upon the type of stock made, the kitchen needs and the day-to-day kitchen procedures. For instance, stock which is completed by noontime may be drawn during the afternoon for certain dishes. In other cases the stock may be completed, and may not be needed until the following day. It was once the accepted practice in some hotel kitchens to keep the stockpot simmering day and night for three or four days. Stock that was drawn off would be replenished with water and other ingredients including fresh bones. This method of stock making is rarely followed nowadays. The old-fashioned stockpot which would run continuously for several days required less labor but the quality of the stock was subject to continual variance, and its flavor was often too intense or stale tasting. The best practice is to make the stock, particularly the white stock, during the course of a single day, drawing off the stock when it reaches its peak of flavor and refrigerating it until needed.

(10) It was once considered a blight on a soup cook's ability if he used a so-called artificial or synthetic stock. Some of the dehydrated stocks available in the past conveyed sham, unnatural-tasting flavors. But the dehydrated stocks available today in concentrated form, when used judiciously, can sometimes make a good thing better. Stocks in granular form are largely vegetable proteins, and, when employed in small amounts to enhance stocks or sauces made from stocks, they have a definite value in the kitchen. When manufactured stocks are used to completely supplant natural stocks, their factory-made flavors are usually apparent.

(11) The large amount of liquid drawn from stockpots and the frequency with which stock is drawn often cause spillage in the work area, and accidents are possible. Whenever spills occur, be sure the floor is mopped and dried immediately. Do not leave the open

faucet of a stockpot untended. Be prepared to shut off the faucet; use a heavy dry towel to avoid burns.

(12) In setting up a quality standard or goal for a good stock, one should attempt to achieve the quality of a good broth. It should have a pleasant meat, poultry, seafood or vegetable flavor with a minimum of salt. It should leave a distinct, mild, pleasant aftertaste.

(13) Special stocks are sometimes made from previously cooked carcasses. Thus, if there were a large party with roast pheasant, the backs, necks and carcasses of the cooked birds might be used to make a pheasant soup the following day. In such cases the amount of bones needed for a stock with a pronounced flavor would be about double the quantity needed if uncooked bones were used. Such stocks are best if made the same day the birds were roasted rather than after the carcasses and trimmings have been kept overnight in the refrigerator.

(14) Because of the extended time required for stock making, it is necessary to coordinate the work of several cooks assigned to different shifts. A stock begun during the morning may not be completed until the late evening. Make sure that you understand your duties during the time you are tending the stockpot, and that the jobs of drawing off, cooling and refrigerating stock, removing bones, etc., are properly coordinated with other cooks who may be on duty before or after your workday.

Note: In the recipes below the words *kettle* and *pot* are used interchangeably. It is the practice in trade terminology to refer to either a stock*pot* or a steam-jacketed *kettle*. Both are the same type of equipment.

White Stock (Fonds Blanc)   Approx 10 Gal

This is the most common, most widely used of all stocks. It may be made fresh each day or made two or three times a week depending on menu requirements, dining room count, special parties, size of staff, etc. At one time a white stock was made with all veal bones. The modern tendency is to combine beef and veal bones and sometimes to include chicken carcasses in order to create a stock with good body while keeping the flavor sufficiently neutral for use in a wide variety of dishes. Normally a 30-gal stockpot is used to make 10 gal of stock. This allows room for both solid and liquid ingredients as well as headspace between the stock and the lid of the kettle. As the stock simmers, it reduces so that the finished stock may contain about one third less liquid than the original volume of water added to the kettle, depending upon the number of hours the stock was simmered. This reduction is a variable quantity. It depends not only on the total time the stock was cooked, but also on the width of the kettle, the temperature of the stock and the use of a lid that helps trap and return vapors to the kettle. If bones are large, cut them into 3-in. pieces using a saw rather than cleaver. Note that only bones are included in the recipe below rather than bones with meat. In restaurants where whole shin of beef is bought for stock making, the meat is removed from the bones and boiled separately. Note also that no salt is indicated in the recipe. As meat stocks are reduced, the natural salt in them becomes concentrated. Salt is best added in the finished dishes in which the stock is incorporated. In some restaurants where consommé is regularly prepared, the "raft" or ground cooked meat from the strained consommé is sometimes added to the stockpot for flavor.

Before starting work: If you are using a steam-jacketed kettle, make sure you are completely familiar with its operating features including steam supply, whether direct or self-generating, steam inlet valve and its control for specific temperatures, outlet valve, pressure gauge, and the operation and control of the faucet. The kettle should be absolutely clean; inspect it carefully on bottom, side and lid. The bones will be blanched before they are simmered. But if they feel sticky or slimy or if they have an off-odor (not a normal meat odor), check with your instructor or supervisor. Be sure you have an adequate supply of dry towels when drawing off stock for transfer to other containers. If you are using a saw for the first time, be sure you are adequately instructed in its use.

(1) Assemble the following ingredients:
> 60 lb shin, shank or shoulder bones of beef cut into 3-in. pieces
> 20 lb veal bones cut into 3-in. pieces
> 6 lb fowl carcasses (optional)
> 4 lb onions, coarsely chopped
> 2 lb carrots, coarsely chopped
> 3 lb celery, coarsely chopped
> 1/2 lb white turnips, coarsely chopped
> 1/2 lb parsnips, coarsely chopped
> Bouquet garni of 4 doz whole black peppercorns, 12 whole cloves, 8 bay leaves, 1 large bunch parsley, 2 teaspoons leaf thyme
> 15 gal water

(2) Examine stockpot very carefully to make sure it is clean.
(3) Place beef bones, veal bones and fowl carcasses in pot.

(4) Add 15 gal water or additional water if necessary to cover bones. (Amount of water needed will depend upon dimensions of pot.)

(5) Bring water to a rapid boil.

(6) Skim surface of water. Turn off heat.

(7) Drain stockpot, discarding water.

(8) Run cold water over bones, covering them. Move bones gently so that any scum on bones is washed away. Drain water used for washing bones.

(9) Fill pot with 15 gal water.

(10) Slowly bring to a boil.

(11) Carefully remove all scum with skimmer. If scum reappears quickly after skimming, add a small amount of cold water to pot to stop the boiling. Again bring to a boil, and repeat skimming.

(12) Reduce heat so that liquid barely simmers. Simmer for 2 hours.

(13) Add vegetables and bouquet garni; simmer 4 to 5 hours longer.

Note: If vegetable trimmings have been turned over to you by other cooks, check with your instructor or supervisor before adding them to stockpot. In some cases, trimmings should be saved for the next white stock job; keep them well-covered in the refrigerator.

(14) Remove scum from time to time as it appears. Skim fat occasionally.

(15) Strain stock using a china cap lined with cheesecloth. It may be necessary to use several pots for holding finished stock.

(16) If steam-jacketed kettle is the type into which cold water may flow in the jacket for cooling purposes, follow this procedure:

(a) Turn off heat and drain *jacket* of pot (not the pot itself).

(b) Remove solid ingredients from kettle. Use a large wire skimmer.

(c) Run cold water through jacket of kettle, and stir stock gently from time to time until it is cool.

(d) If kettle is fitted with automatic stirrer, use it at low speed while cooling stock.

(e) Draw off stock straining it through china cap lined with cheesecloth; be prepared to turn off faucet if liquid rises too high in china cap.

(f) Place cool stock in refrigerator in covered containers.

(17) If above procedure is not possible with equipment in your

kitchen, strain through china cap lined with cheesecloth. It may be necessary to use several pots to hold stock. Chill as follows:

(a) Place pot of drained stock in deep sink so that brim of pot is above brim of sink. Rest pot on several bricks or other flat heavy objects such as iron popover pans so that water can flow beneath pot. Tie the pot handles to the faucet or other object so that it will not tip when surrounded with water.

(b) Run cold water into sink so that it surrounds the pot. Water should be regulated so that it can run continuously and be drawn into overflow outlet until stock is cool.

(c) Stir stock gently from time to time to hasten cooling.

(d) Place stock in refrigerator until needed.

Brown Stock (Estouffade)   Approx 10 Gal

This is the stock used as a base for brown sauces, stews, braised dishes and some soups. White stock becomes brown stock if the bones and vegetables used in its preparation are browned before they are simmered in water. The flavor of the browned ingredients gives a special quality to the stock, just as a browned onion conveys a flavor very distinct from a boiled onion. Any white or light sauce can be made to look brown by the simple addition of brown coloring, using either the commercially prepared products or caramel coloring made in your kitchen. Sauces that are completely dependent upon prepared coloring substances, however, lack the genuine flavor of naturally browned ingredients. The color of brown stock is a light clear brown. If a deeper more opaque color is required, it is best to add coloring to the finished stew or braised dish rather than to the basic brown stock. While white stock may be made daily, or two or three times a week, brown stock is prepared less frequently. With proper refrigeration there should be no spoilage if brown stock is stored for a week, although it should be carefully checked to be sure it is sound. When is brown really brown? Actually there are countless shades of brown, and students should seek the guidance of the instructor or supervisor in determining when the optimum shade of brown is reached whenever browning is indicated. Bones and vegetables may be browned so lightly that they hardly affect the color of the stock at all. At the opposite extreme they may be browned so deeply they become charred and convey a burnt taste to the stock. Your own experience will be your eventual guide to the brown color spectrum.

Before starting work: Bones for the stock should be assembled, checked for quality and sawed. The job of browning bones, simmering, straining and cooling brown stock may extend beyond the normal work day. If you are a student working on a team with others, plan the job so that it is adequately covered from start to finish by someone on the team. If you are an apprentice cook in a commercial restaurant, consult with the chef or supervisor so that any unfinished details are covered during your absence.

(1) Assemble the following ingredients:

    60 lb shin, shank or shoulder bones of beef, 3-in. pieces

    20 lb veal knuckle bones or other veal bones, 3-in. pieces

    3 lb lean smoked ham trimmings (optional)

    3 lb carrots, coarsely chopped

    4 lb onions, coarsely chopped

    2 lb celery, coarsely chopped

    2 lb white turnips, coarsely chopped

    1 lb parsnips, coarsely chopped

    Bouquet garni of 4 doz whole black peppercorns, 12 whole cloves, 6 bay leaves, 1 bunch parsley, 2 teaspoons leaf thyme

    15 gal water

(2) Preheat oven to 450° F.

(3) If bones show any trace of stickiness, blanch them following steps (4) to (8) in the preceding recipe. If bones are freshly removed from meat, place bones, ham and all other ingredients except bouquet garni in two shallow roasting pans. (Do not pile all ingredients into a single pan. They will tend to steam in the oven rather than brown.)

(4) Place bones in oven. After 15 min, stir ingredients in pan to permit even browning. After 30 min, check with instructor or supervisor to see if browning is sufficient. Keep ingredients in oven until browning is complete.

(5) Remove pans from oven using 2 dry heavy towels, and transfer ingredients of pans into steam-jacketed kettle or stockpot. Pan may be held above kettle and ingredients carefully moved into kettle. Take special care when lifting and holding pan to avoid burns.

(6) Pour 1 qt water into each roasting pan, and place pans over top flames of oven. Bring to a boil. Scrape pan bottoms to loosen drippings.

(7) Pour pan drippings into stockpot.

(8) Add balance of water (14 1/2 gal) to stockpot. Add bouquet garni.

(9) Slowly bring to a boil.

(10) Carefully remove all scum. Reduce heat so that liquid barely simmers.

(11) Remove scum from time to time as it appears. Skim fat if there is any noticeable layer. Simmer 6 to 8 hours or until stock flavor is developed. Stir gently several times with long paddle to make sure no ingredients are sticking to pot. Avoid excessive stirring.

(12) Turn off heat. Let stock rest about an hour.

(13) Strain stock, using a china cap lined with cheesecloth.

(14) Cool stock, following directions discussed previously.

(15) Refrigerate stock until needed.

Chicken Stock or Chicken Broth   **Approx 10 Gal**
(Fonds Blanc de Volaille)

Whenever fowl (the term for old chickens that have been in egg production) are boiled, chicken broth is produced. For many years some American restaurants have used turkeys instead of fowl for boiling purposes. But in those restaurants where chicken rather than turkey is still used for such dishes as chicken a la king, club sandwiches, chicken salad, etc., the broth is regularly produced and is available without the necessity of setting up any special chicken stockpot. There are many eating places, however, such as hospitals, which regularly serve fresh chicken broth in large quantities and which use chicken trimmings such as necks, backs, gizzards, etc., to produce chicken stock or broth.

There are two types of chicken broth. The older one is made by simmering fowl in lightly salted water with no flavoring vegetables. It is purposely a strong broth with a pronounced "straight" flavor. The second type, as in the recipe below, uses flavoring vegetables but omits herbs because of their pungent flavor. Raw chicken parts which have been handled by several persons on a purveyor's assembly line need very careful washing and blanching before the stock is cooked. It has been the experience of many chefs that chicken stock tends to spoil more readily than beef or veal stock. Be sure the stock is chilled as quickly as possible after cooking. Be sure the temperature of the refrigerator in which the stock is stored is no higher than 38°F. Check the refrigerator thermometer regularly. Avoid storing stock in a walk-in refrigerator where there is heavy kitchen traffic and where the temperature may rise drastically during busy periods.

After chicken parts are cooked, they may contain a considerable amount of edible meat. They should be returned to the butcher or *garde manger* after cooking. Chicken carcasses, that is, the bones of leftover cooked chicken, may be used as part of the recipe. Because their flavor has already been partly extracted you should allow 2 lb of carcasses for each pound of fresh chicken parts substituted.

Before starting work: Examine chicken parts for any off-odor or signs of spoilage. If you are in doubt about the condition of any chicken parts, consult your instructor or supervisor. Be sure the chopping board or block on which the parts are cut is dry and clean. If whole fowl or whole turkeys are being boiled, the two jobs may be combined. If there is leftover chicken broth and it is sound, it might be reheated and combined with the new batch. Again, check with your instructor or supervisor.

(1) Assemble the following ingredients:

    60 lb chicken parts (necks, backs, gizzards, feet, etc.)
    12 gal water
    3 lb peeled onions, whole
    3 lb celery, whole stalks
    2 lb carrots, whole
    3 lb leeks, cut lengthwise in half and washed well
    Salt, pepper

(2) Examine chicken carefully. Be sure there are no signs of spoilage.

(3) Chop necks and backs crosswise in halves or thirds. Either a heavy French knife or cleaver may be used. Do not use your regular cutting board for this purpose: If the board is made of wood, it can be damaged. Use either a wooden block or a board reserved for chopping with a cleaver.

(4) Place chicken parts in batches in a large colander, and wash under cold running water. Drain well.

(5) Place chicken parts in stock pot. Cover with cold water.

(6) Bring water to a boil. Remove scum. Drain chicken parts.

(7) Wash again with cold water and drain. Stir chicken while washing so that all parts are cleaned.

(8) Cover chicken with the 12 gal water or enough to cover chicken completely.

(9) Bring to a boil. Remove scum carefully.

(10) Reduce heat and simmer chicken parts 1 hour.

(11) Skim fat from time to time as it accumulates.

(12) Add vegetables. Continue to simmer 1 hour longer or until chicken flavor is well developed.

    Note: When fowl are used for chicken stock, the stock is cooked until the fowl are tender. This may take 2 to 3 hours depending on size of fowl. Chicken parts, however, may become tender in an hour's time. A stock made from chicken parts is done not when the chicken is tender but when the stock flavor is completely extracted.

(13) Drain stock through a triple thickness of cheesecloth (muslin) in a china cap. Add salt and pepper to taste.

(14) Cool stock as rapidly as possible. Use 2 pots for cooling if practical.

(15) Refrigerate stock until needed.

Note: If stock is to be used in dishes such as chicken a la king, creamed chicken hash, etc., it need not be further clarified. If it is to be served as chicken broth, it may be clarified with egg whites as in making consommé. This is an optional procedure. Many patrons who order chicken broth with rice or chicken broth with noodles do not expect chicken broth to have the clarity of a fine consommé.

White Fish Stock (Fonds De Poissons Blanc)   Approx 10 Qt

Like chicken stock, fish stock differs from meat stocks in its comparatively brief cooking time. It takes a mere 30 min of simmering to extract the flavors from fish bones. It is an easy stock to make, and it is surprising that so few restaurants take advantage of this simple-to-prepare *fonds*, and fail to use it in fish dishes. Even restaurants which are not fish specialty houses can use a white fish stock in soups like fish chowder or to supplement and enhance the clam broth used in clam chowder. It is invaluable in almost all fish dishes served in a sauce. Whenever such dishes as broiled split striped bass or broiled split red snapper are featured on a menu, it is a simple matter for the butcher or *garde manger* to simply save the heads, backbones and other trimmings of the fish and turn them over to the soup cook or sauce cook for fish stock. Fish stock may be frozen if it is not needed within a day or two, and may be thawed when needed. Normally about 1 lb of fish bones and trimmings is used for each quart of stock. The best bones and trimmings are those from white-fleshed fish. Bones from mackerel, salmon or other fish with rather strong individual flavors are less desirable although they can be used in moderation. In some French restaurants white fish stock is always made with half white wine and half water since so many fish dishes with sauce include white wine. In American restaurants, however, where fish stock is widely used in preparing fish chowder, the inclusion of wine would be against tradition. It is more practical to make the stock with all water, as in the recipe below, and then add wine whenever the recipe indicates it. Fish bones and trimmings should, if possible, be used the same day they are available. They should not be stored several days, as meat bones are, since they deteriorate rapidly.

Before staring work: Since fish bones are merely washed and not blanched as meat bones are, it is important to be sure the fish bones, heads, trimmings, etc., are sound with no sign of spoilage or incipient spoilage. Fish bones should have the characteristic clean smell of fresh seafood. Be sure the special cutting board on which the bones, heads, etc., are chopped is well washed before and after it is used. Make certain that the cheesecloth (muslin) used for straining the stock is well rinsed before it is used and well washed after it is used. If fish stock is not to be used within a day or two after it is made, make arrangements for freezing it for future use.

(1) Assemble the following ingredients:

    10 lb bones, heads and trimmings of white flesh fish, coarsely chopped
    1/4 lb butter
    2 lb onions, sliced thin
    1 lb celery, sliced thin
    4 oz parsley stems and/or roots
    4 oz lemon juice
    2 doz whole black peppercorns
    1 tablespoon salt
    12 qt water

(2) Melt butter in heavy saucepot or brazier over low to moderate flame.

(3) Place fish bones and trimmings in pot.

(4) Add onions, celery, parsley, lemon juice and whole black peppercorns.

(5) Cover pot with tight lid, and let ingredients simmer 6 to 8 min.

(6) Add water and salt. Stir gently.

(7) Slowly bring to a boil. Keep pot covered, but check frequently until water reaches the boiling point.

(8) Skim well.

(9) Reduce heat, but keep at a gentle boil 30 min.

(10) Remove pot from fire. Let ingredients remain in pot an additional 30 min.

(11) Strain, using a triple thickness of cheesecloth over china cap.

(12) If stock is not to be used at once, cool it, following directions presented previously.

(13) Refrigerate stock if it is to be used within a day or two.

(14) If stock is to be held beyond a day or two, freeze it. Check

with your instructor or supervisor for appropriate containers
for freezing.

Court Bouillon   Approx 10 Qt

The French words *court bouillon* mean short or quick bouillon or
quick stock. Like the previous recipe for fish stock, it takes only
3/4 to 1 hour of cooking time. Its main use is as a vegetable stock
for cooking large fish such as whole boiled salmon or whole boiled
striped bass. It is also sometimes used for cooking shellfish such as
shrimp. There are recipes for court bouillon which include white
or red wine. The recipe below, following modern practice in most
places, omits wine which may be added later to any specific dish in
which the court bouillon is used. The main purpose of using court
bouillon instead of water is to impart the aromatic flavors of vegetables and spices to the dish being prepared.

Unlike fish stock, which is made whenever enough fish bones are
on hand to make a stock, court bouillon usually is prepared at a
special time in anticipation of specific dishes. Thus, if whole cold
boiled salmon is to be served on Friday, the court bouillon might
be prepared on Wednesday and cooled. On Thursday it would be
used to boil the salmon. The salmon would then be allowed to cool
in its court bouillon overnight to absorb the optimum flavoring components of the stock in which it was cooked, and would be served
the following day. Court bouillon is also sometimes used for cooking
other dishes such as calf's brains. This is a stock which is boiled
rather than simmered.

Before starting work: Find out what dish or dishes are being prepared for which court bouillon is needed. Increase or decrease the
recipe, if necessary, to suit the needs. Since court bouillon contains
no fat or bones with fat, such as marrow bones, it may be cooked
in a stockpot with a faucet or any conventional pot. In either case
choose a deep pot with a narrow diameter, rather than a large saucepot with a wide diameter in which the reduction may be excessive.

(1) Assemble the following ingredients:
    11 qt water
    1/4 cup salt
    1 pt cider vinegar
    8 oz carrots, coarsely chopped
    12 oz onions, coarsely chopped
    8 oz celery, including leaves, coarsely chopped
    Bouquet garni of 3 large bay leaves, 2 teaspoons leaf thyme,

2 teaspoons coarsely ground black pepper, 1 bunch parsley and 1 bunch dill

(2) Combine water, salt, vinegar, carrots, onions and celery in stockpot or conventional pot.

(3) Add bouquet garni.

(4) Place over a slow to moderate flame. Bring to a boil.

(5) Remove scum.

(6) Flame may be reduced slightly but court bouillon should be kept boiling rather than simmering until flavors are pronounced—from 45 min to 1 hour.

(7) Strain court bouillon through a triple thickness of cheesecloth in a china cap.

(8) Chill, unless it is to be used at once.

(9) Refrigerate until needed.

Soup Cook (*Potager*)

In small or moderate size restaurants, soups and soup garnishes are made by the sauce cook. In larger establishments, the job is handled by one person devoting his full workday to this specialty. Usually he also maintains the stockpots from day to day, since he is the principal user of stocks. Stocks, however, are needed by other cooks in making sauces, stews, braised dishes, etc., and the soup cook has the responsibility of keeping abreast of their requirements. This means that when he reads the chef's menus in advance, he must be able to anticipate stocks that will be needed for the next three or four days. He usually works near the sauce cook and at times may assist him. The soup cook, in very large kitchens, may have his own assistant (*commis*) to aid in cutting vegetables, lifting pots, straining soups, etc. Sometimes the soup cook may receive garnishes prepared by other cooks, such as *profiteroles* (small pastry shells) made by the pastry cook or cheese croutons made by the broiler cook. The soup cook is expected to have the ability to taste food with a cultivated palate and to use seasonings with finesse. Since soup is frequently the beginning of the meal, dining room reactions to the first course make the work of the soup cook extremely important.

JOB SUMMARY

The soup cook (1) prepares and serves soups, including heavy and clear soups, hot and cold soups; (2) makes fresh soups daily for table d'hôte menu as well as a la carte soups on permanent menu requiring preparation on weekly or semiweekly basis; (3) prepares soup garnishes such as bread croutons; (4) prepares special soups for banquets; (5) cooks stock and maintains stockpot used for soups, stews, braised dishes, etc.; (6) receives, reserves and uses broths and stocks made by other cooks such as chicken broth, ham stock, etc.; (7) places soups in steam table; (8) may serve soups during meal period; (9) cools soups and stocks, and reserves them for future use; (10) consults with *sous chef* or chef on future menus and use of leftovers.

MANUAL PROCEDURES

Soups

The soup cook (1) cuts vegetables by hand or machine in a variety of shapes and sizes as seasoning vegetables or main ingredients in soups; (2) soaks dried vegetables in pots or bowls; (3) sautés seasoning vegetables in soup pot; (4) adds flour or roux to soup pot; (5) adds stock or combinations of stocks, milk or other liquids; (6) stirs soup with paddle or spoon, simmers and removes soup for tasting; also skims soups with wire skimmer, perforated skimmer or spoon; (7) controls heat under soup kettles by adjusting flames, by moving kettles near or away from flames, by adjusting steam valves on steam-jacketed kettles; (8) prepares, by boiling, starch ingredients such as macaroni products, barley and rice; (9) cuts cooked meats, poultry or seafood and adds them to some preparations; (10) seasons soups during and after cooking using spices, bottled seasonings, etc.; (11) strains cream soups and purees soups with china cap, puree machine, etc.; (12) draws off prepared soups from large kettles and pours them into smaller *bain marie* pots or steam table insets; (13) chops parsley, chives and other herbs for addition to finished soups; (14) cools soups for future use by placing pots with soup in sinks with running water.

Stocks

He (1) soaks in water or blanches bones of beef, veal, poultry or game which are added to stockpot along with water; (2) cuts and adds vegetables to stockpot; (3) receives vegetable trimmings from other cooks, selects those which are useful, and adds them to stock-pot; (4) adjusts heat of stockpot to keep stock simmering; (5) skims stock with wire skimmer, perforated skimmer or spoon; (6) simmers stock until full flavor is developed; (7) draws off stock and strains it; (8) cools stock in sinks with running water or in kettles with cooling jackets; (9) stores stock in refrigerator; (10) makes special stocks, such as court bouillon, for fish soups, lamb broth, oxtail broth, etc.

EQUIPMENT AND UTENSILS

In his work he uses (1) steam-jacketed kettles, usually of 20- to 80-gal capacity; (2) trunions or tilt kettles; (3) large kettles of heavy metal for cooking on range tops; (4) small, medium and large kettles with lids for storage of soups, stocks and garnishes in refrigerator; (5) *bain marie* pots or steam table insets; (6) ladles of assorted sizes; (7) French knives, small, medium and large; (8) paring knife, knife steel, cleaver, and parer with swivel blade; (9) spoons and paddles of wood or metal; (10) china caps; (11) puree machine; (12) electric blender; (13) cloths for straining; (14) wire whips; (15) cutting board; (16) wire and perforated skimmers.

WORKING CONDITIONS AND HAZARDS

The soup cook (1) works in hot, humid environment; (2) works near and over boiling or simmering soups on range top as well as in vicinity of stockpots; (3) must stand and walk on slippery area near stockpots and floor drains; (4) is exposed to risk of cuts from long, intense use of French knife; (5) is exposed to burns from hot kettles; (6) frequently lifts heavy pots either alone or with designated helper.

PLACE IN JOB ORGANIZATION

The apprentice cook or vegetable cook may advance to soup cook in rare instances. The usual line of advancement is from fry cook, broil cook or roast cook to soup cook. Because of his close cooperation with the sauce cook, the soup cook is often promoted to that position.

SOUP CLASSIFICATIONS

Menu writers, whether they be chefs or others, often use cooking terms and menu terms so loosely that classifying them is often like beating the wind. The word bouillon, for instance, is *generally* used to mean a thin clear beef soup with pronounced beef flavor. Yet on menus you will sometimes find a tomato bouillon or a mushroom bouillon listed. On French menus you will sometimes see "Essence of Celery" listed when what is meant is simply a celery consommé. The following soup classifications are the most widely accepted uses of the terms.

Thin Soups

(1) *Broths*—thin soups made from cooking meat, poultry or seafood in water, such as chicken broth or clam broth. They are always strained but usually not clarified with egg whites. Scotch mutton broth—an old and defiant exception to the rule—is a thick soup with meat, vegetables and barley.

(2) *Consommés*—thin soups made from stock, chopped beef and clarified with egg whites. They are always strained after clarification and may be served with many garnishes, such as rice, small pieces of custard, vegetables, etc. Some consommés without a garnish may be given the flavor of a particular vegetable—such as consommé Madrilene with a pronounced tomato flavor. Sometimes consommés are served cold and jellied.

(3) *Bouillons*—consommés with extra rich beef flavor. The old term *consommé double* or consommé with double strength is synonymous with bouillon.

Thick Soups

(1) *Unstrained Vegetable Soups*—soups which when finished contain a large amount of solid ingredients, usually from 1/4 to 1/2 of their volume. Typical soups in this class are gumbo soups with vegetables, rice and chicken, or clam chowders with vegetables and clams.

(2) *Puree Soups*—soups whose thickness usually derives from mashed or strained dried vegetables such as green split pea soup, lentil soup, black bean soup, etc.

(3) *Cream Soups*—soups which are purees with fresh vegetables as the principal ingredients. They are normally thickened with flour or roux and contain milk or cream. An exception is *crème vichyssoise*, a soup of potatoes, leeks and onions made with no added starch. The old-fashioned soup term *velouté* was a cream soup made with chicken or meat stock thickened with egg yolks and cream; it is seldom found in American kitchens today. (The word *velouté* is used nowadays for a type of sauce.)

(4) *Bisques*—cream of shellfish soups such as bisque of shrimp or bisque of oyster. At one time bisques were thickened with some ingredient other than wheat flour, such as pureed cooked rice, in order to keep the soup's delicate flavors intact.

(5) *Thick Fish Soups*—soups which are closer to stews than soups. They may be listed in either the soup or fish sections of menus. Examples are the French *bouillabaisse* or the Italian *cioppino*. Both soups contain large amounts of fish and shellfish, with more solid than liquid components.

12 GUIDES FOR MAKING AND SERVING SOUPS

When restaurant supervisors or consultants check on the quality of food in a particular kitchen, one of the first items sampled is the soup. Frequently, though not always, the quality of the soup is an index to the caliber of many other dishes. There are kitchens where the soup cook is not permitted to take the soup off the fire for serving unless the soup is first checked by the chef for flavor, thickness, clarity, color, etc. Among the things which the chef stresses, and which you as a student should pay particular attention to, are the following:

(1) Any soup, whether it be thick or thin, should convey a pronounced but pleasant flavor of its principal ingredient. Thus a beef bouillon should have a rich mellow beef flavor. A cream of celery soup should have a lively bright flavor of fresh celery. If the raw celery used in making the soup is limp and weak in flavor, the flavor of the finished soup may have to be enhanced with the use of celery seed, celery salt, MSG seasoning, a small amount of lemon juice, etc.

(2) There should be a balance of the soup's principal flavor and its minor flavoring ingredients. Thus a Manhattan clam chowder should have a sturdy clam flavor, but the minor flavoring ingredients such as onions, celery, tomatoes, potatoes, etc., should be combined in such ratios and cooked until their separate flavors are homogeneously blended. If the flavor of either the onions or the tomatoes is overpowering, the soup would score low in flavor. When you taste the liquid of the chowder without any of its solid ingredients, it should convey the flavors of all the solid ingredients melded into what is recognized as a characteristic "chowder" flavor.

(3) Finished soups should be as tempting to the eye as to the mouth. Colors of vegetables should be natural looking, and as close as possible to their raw appearance rather than looking overcooked. Purees and cream soups should show no sign of lumps or soup "skin." There should be no conspicuous layer of fat on the finished soup. A very thin sheen of tiny fat globules may be allowed on certain thin soups such as *petite marmite* for their flavor value, but such soups should never coat a spoon with fat or leave an impression of greasiness. Uniform cutting of vegetables is extremely important not only for uniform cooking but for eye appeal. If there is a soup garnish, that is, something added to the soup just before it is served, and the garnish is a julienne of vegetables, each vegetable should be of no greater thickness than a match stick and of uniform length. If the garnish is bread croutons, the croutons should be uniformly small, golden brown in color, and crisp looking.

(4) Soups should be served neatly. If the soup is to be served in silver tureens, the tureens should be brightly burnished. If there is a drop of soup on the rim of the soup plate or soup dripping down the side of a tureen or on a tureen plate, these should be wiped clean by the soup cook or the cook serving the soup.

(5) Soups on the fire should only be brought to the boil for a brief period to remove the scum on the surface; during the rest of the cooking period, they should be simmered, not boiled. As soup simmers, the flavors are blended and the liquid is reduced. This reduction must take place slowly not only to develop flavors but to keep the liquid component from reducing too quickly or too drastically. A soup planned to yield 3 gal may yield 4 if it is not sufficiently reduced. Conversely, it may yield less than 3 gal if it is boiled or kept on the fire too long. A tall pot with a narrow diameter will keep soups from over-reducing; a shallower pot with a wider diameter, exposing a larger surface area of the liquid to the air, will allow the liquid to evaporate more quickly. Check with your instructor, chef or supervisor in choosing the pot that best serves the job on which you are working.

(6) In many soup recipes, seasoning vegetables are sautéd before the stock is added. This is done to reduce the sharp raw flavor of such ingredients as onions and leeks and to impart the sautéd flavor of the vegetables to the soup. A boiled onion has one flavor, a sautéd onion a perceptibly different flavor, a deeply browned onion still another flavor. Be sure the sautéing is always over a low flame, and stir the vegetables frequently to avoid the undesirable flavor and unpleasant appearance of scorched, browned or partially browned vegetables—a common soup fault.

(7) The ideal soup is one which derives its blended flavor from its natural raw components. Since natural stocks used for soups are not always uniform in flavor (although ideally they should be so) and since the flavors of vegetables vary from season to season, the soup cook may have to make flavor adjustments, using artificial stock, MSG seasoning, bottled seasonings, etc. The goal in soup making is to keep these flavor additives to a minimum, and to use them very sparingly at first, making small additions at a time only as needed. As artificial stocks vary considerably from one brand to the next, the soup cook should use a new brand conservatively at first until its usefulness is understood.

(8) No soup ever reaches its peak of flavor development if poor ingredients are used in its making. The soup cook is not a food buyer, but if any of the raw ingredients with which the soup cook works are

of poor or doubtful quality, are old or shows signs of incipient spoilage, it is important to call these facts to the attention of the supervisor for possible correction.

(9) Thick cream soups or puree soups which are exposed to air for
long periods of time in the steam table acquire a thick skin on top
which is sometimes stirred into the soup and is unappetizing in appearance. To avoid this, small pieces of unmelted butter may be distributed over the top of the soup. As the butter melts, it forms a
protective film on top. Just before the soup is served, the butter is
stirred into the soup. Thereafter, the soup should be stirred occasionally, even though it is unserved, to prevent the skin from forming.

(10) Soups may need attention if they remain in the steam table
for long periods of time. Often a layer of fat will form on the surface. If it is considerable, it should be skimmed and removed. If it is
a small amount of fat, it may be stirred into the soups (for cream
soups or purees). Sometimes starchy soups need thinning as the
starch expands during the meal period. These soups are thinned with
milk, cream or stock, depending on the type of soup.

(11) Hot soups should be hot. This means that the completed soup
should be in the steam table in ample time for the soup to reach $170°$
to $180°$F. Be sure to check the water level and temperature in the
steam table; it should not be boiling fiercely nor should it be lukewarm; adjust the steam valve, gas flame or other source of heat.
Keeping serving dishes stacked in a plate warmer is not necessarily
the cook's responsibility, but the soup cook should be conscious of
this step and should check the plate warmer occasionally. Cold soups
should be cold, from $38°$ to $42°$F. If cold soups have been removed
from the refrigerator during the meal period for faster service, they
should be placed in serving pots surrounded by cracked ice.

(12) When thick vegetable soups like pepper pot soup or minestrone soup are served, the soup ladle should be used to stir the ingredients so that each portion contains the proper amount of liquid
and solid ingredients. The best way to do this is not to use a stirring
motion with a spoon, but to tap the bottom of the soup pot once or
twice with the soup ladle and then immediately ladle the soup while
it is in motion.

Consommé   100 Portions, Approx 8 Oz Each

In restaurants where the menu and cuisine reflect continental traditions in cooking, consommé usually appears on the menu in some
form. On banquet menus it is universally popular because it is light,
zestful and appetite-whetting before the fish and main courses that

follow. The garnish used with consommé may vary from day to day, but the consommé itself, except in very large restaurants, is prepared only once or twice a week. Its components are stock, ground beef and finely chopped vegetables clarified with egg whites. Those restaurants which feature hollandaise sauce every day usually have a large accumulation of raw egg whites which are turned over from the sauce cook to the soup cook for use in consommés. The soup should always be a clear, amber-to-brown color. The word consommé is derived from the French *consommer* meaning to complete or to finish. As a soup, consommé represents the soup cook's skill in its most consummate form. Its beef flavor should be mellow but with pronounced body, using the word body in the sense of flavor intensity. As the soup is simmered, the natural salts in the stock and beef become concentrated, and therefore salt should be added as a seasoning at the end rather than the beginning of the cooking process. In old recipe books carcasses of fowl were added to consommé, but the modern white stock recipe usually includes fowls' carcasses. They are, therefore, omitted in the recipe below. When a consommé is brought to the table, you should be able to very clearly see the bottom of the soup cup or tureen. The process of clarification consists of four main steps:

(1) Ground beef and finely chopped vegetables are mixed with slightly beaten egg whites and stock.

(2) As the whites coagulate when they are heated, the solid ingredients in the pot adhere to the whites, forming a thick layer or raft that rises to the top of the soup.

(3) The simmering stock slowly bubbles through and around the raft without breaking it up but extracting the flavors of the raft and clarifying the soup.

(4) When the soup is strained, the cook, using extreme care, slowly ladles the soup through a linen or muslin strainer, leaving the raft undisturbed.

Before starting work: Make sure the stock to be used for the consommé is well chilled. Remove any fat from its surface. If the stock has gelled in the refrigerator, it may be placed in the steam table briefly—only until it is no longer gelled. Best results are obtained when the consommé is started with cold stock. Be sure the pot to be used for the consommé is immaculately clean. A slight film of soap from a previous washing or foreign matter may cause the consommé to be turbid. If in doubt about the cleanliness of the pot, scald it and dry it well. The vegetables below may be chopped by hand or machine; the more finely chopped they are, the more quickly their flavors will be released.

(1) Assemble the following ingredients:
    8 gal cold stock
    20 lb ground shin of beef
    3 1/2 lb onions, finely chopped
    2 lb celery, finely chopped
    1 lb leeks, white and green parts, finely chopped
    2 lb carrots, finely chopped
    24 egg whites
    Bouquet garni of 1 bunch parsley, 2 teaspoons leaf thyme, 24
        whole black peppercorns, 6 whole cloves, 12 whole allspice
        and 4 bay leaves
    Salt, pepper, MSG seasoning (variable)
    Caramel coloring (variable)
    Red coloring (variable)

(2) Pour the egg whites into the pot in which the soup is to be
    cooked. Tilt the pot so that the egg whites are in a corner of
    the pot.

(3) Beat whites with a wire whip only until they are foamy on
    top. They should not be beaten stiff.

(4) Add the beef and mix well. Add the onions, celery, leeks and
    carrots, mixing well.

(5) Pour the stock into the pot and mix well.

(6) Tie the bouquet garni in muslin and fasten it to pot handle.
    Place in pot.

(7) Heat over a moderate flame. Stir several times before the soup
    comes to a boil.

(8) Allow the soup to boil about 5 min before removing the scum
    the first time. Use a perforated skimmer for removing scum.

(9) After removing scum, add 2 cups cold water to retard boiling.
    When it again comes to a full boil, remove scum. This pro-
    cess should be repeated at least twice for thorough skimming.

(10) Wipe the edge of the soup pot to remove any scum deposit
     that may have adhered to it.

(11) Place pot over low flame or move it on top of a closed range
     so that the soup simmers very slowly. It should not boil for
     the balance of the cooking period.

(12) When the raft has cohered into a solid mass, move a portion of
     the raft with a spoon so that the bubbling liquid can move
     through and around the raft.

(13) Continue simmering the soup 3 to 4 hours or until flavor of
     consommé is fully developed. Remove any scum from time to
     time when it appears. Do not disturb the raft during this
     period.

(14) Remove soup from fire. Let it set at least 15 min before straining.

(15) Although some stocks and broths are strained by drawing the soup from the bottom of the pot through a strainer and spigot, consommé should be strained by ladling it from the top of the pot. The bottom of the pot may contain sediment separated from the raft on top. Move the raft gently to one side and ladle the soup from the pot, pouring it through a double thickness of linen (discarded table tops or napkins, well rinsed, may be used) or a triple thickness of muslin into a clean pot. Soup may be strained a second time in this manner if it is not perfectly clear. Add the unstrained raft to the stockpot if stock is being made.

(16) Add salt, if necessary; add pepper to taste; and MSG if necessary to point up flavors.

(17) Add caramel coloring if necessary; this should be added in driblets at a time, stirring well after each addition. A few drops of red coloring may be added to enhance eye appeal (use very conservatively).

(18) Place as much consommé as is needed for the next meal in a steam table pot and reheat for serving.

(19) Serve with any of the garnishes for clear soups (pp. 56-57).

Storing consommé.—Since consommé is normally prepared in large amounts and may be stored up to an entire week in the refrigerator, spoilage is possible. It is extremely important to take the following steps for rapidly cooling the soup before it is placed in the refrigerator.

(1) After the soup has been strained and is to be chilled, place the pot of soup in a deep sink surrounded with cold running water.

(2) To permit the water to circulate beneath the pot as well as around the sides, place a heavy object under the kettle to raise it off the sink bottom. Several bricks or two heavy popover pans or a similar device may be used.

(3) Stir the soup occasionally, about every 15 min, to hasten cooling.

(4) When the soup has cooled to approximately room temperature, place it in the refrigerator.

(5) If any fat accumulates and solidifies on top, permit it to remain; it acts as a seal.

(6) Take off for each day's use only as much as you reasonably anticipate will be used.

Consommé Madrilene.—Prepare consommé above using either

white stock or chicken broth. When assembling ingredients, add 2 No. 10 cans tomatoes and 8 lb fresh tomatoes coarsely chopped. Cook and strain as above. Red coloring may be added after consommé is finished; consult your instructor or supervisor.

Jellied Consommé Madrilene.—Prepare consommé Madrilene. Soak 1 lb plain gelatin in cold water. Add to consommé 15 min before cooking is completed. Stir well to make sure gelatin is completely dissolved. Strain soup in usual way. Add red coloring if desired. Chill until gelled.

Consommé Garnishes

In those restaurants where consommé is listed on the menu every day, there is usually a daily variation which, in most cases, is simply a different garnish added to the basic soup. Thus, consommé with the garnish *brunoise* below would be listed as consommé *brunoise*, or consommé with tapioca or consommé julienne, etc. The garnishes are planned for approximately 50 portions of consommé, 8 oz each.

Brunoise.—Cut the following vegetables into dice no larger than 1/16 in.: 2 lb carrots, 1 1/2 lb white turnips, 1 lb leeks (white part only), 1 lb onions, 1 1/2 lb celery. The preceding vegetables are prepared by boiling in salted water until tender, after which they are drained, covered with just enough consommé to keep vegetables moist and kept warm in a steam table inset. Add to consommé just before serving.

Barley, Rice or Tapioca.—Boil until tender 1 1/2 lb each of either pearl barley, long grain rice or pearl tapioca. Drain. Add to consommé just before serving.

Chiffonade.—Cut 2 lb lettuce and 2 lb sorrel into julienne strips or shreds. Blanch in salted water until just tender. Drain. Combine with 1/2 cup very finely chopped chervil leaves (no stems). Add to consommé just before serving.

Julienne.—Follow the same preparation as for *brunoise*, except that vegetables are cut julienne no larger than 1/8 in. thick and 1 1/2 in. long.

Pasta Garnishes.—Boil 1 1/2 lb of any of the various forms of pasta in salted water, drain well, and keep warm in steam table in just enough consommé to cover pasta. Add to consommé just before serving.

Royale.—Beat 8 eggs and 8 egg yolks until well-blended. Slowly stir in 1 qt hot consommé. Add salt and pepper to taste. Strain through a fine china cap. Pour into buttered shallow casseroles to a depth of 1 in. Place casseroles in pan surrounded with hot water. Bake at 375° F until firm to the touch—about 20 min. Let cool, and unmold. Cut into small diamond-shaped pieces, and add to consommé just before serving.

Profiteroles.—Very small balls of *choux* paste (the dough used in making cream puffs and eclairs) are forced through a pastry bag and baked. They are usually prepared by someone in the pastry department, and may be used on both consommés and cream soups.

Vegetable Soup   **50 Portions, Approx 8 Oz Each**

What Americans call vegetable soup would be called *potage paysanne* or peasant soup in France. It is reminiscent of hearty zestful soups like the Italian minestrone *milanaise;* though the soup is extremely popular, it is almost impossible to find two recipes alike. It is a catchall soup, not in the sense that you can indiscriminately dump any and all vegetables into the pot, but that you can vary the recipe during the vegetable seasons to utilize fresh vegetables available for a limited time. Fresh asparagus might be one of the ingredients in the soup during the spring and early summer, fresh corn in midsummer and Hubbard squash in the fall. In this recipe and many of the following recipes for soups of this type a small amount of flour is included in the ingredients. This is an optional step that not all chefs follow. The flour does two things: (1) it helps absorb the butter used in sautéing the seasoning vegetables, and (2) it changes the consistency of the stock from a thin clear liquid to one with a more substantial mouth-feel. The liquid of some canned vegetables or the cooking liquid of some fresh vegetables may be used as part of the stock. If this is done, avoid vegetable liquid with poor eye appeal such as the juice of canned or cooked spinach.

White stock is indicated here, but beef broth from boiled fresh beef or chicken broth or a combination of them may be used.

Before starting work: Review use of the French knife and cutting of vegetables (Chap. 2). Are your knives sharp? Is your cutting board clean and cleared of all vegetable trimmings? Are you familiar with lighting and adjusting flames on the ranges where you will be working? If, after consulting your instructor, supervisor or chef, the substitution of vegetables is being considered, do not substitute any of the principal seasoning vegetables: onions, leeks, garlic and celery. If canned vegetables are substituted for fresh, add them when the cooking is almost completed, merely long enough for the vegetables to heat through. Prolonged heating may make some canned vegetables mushy. If raw fresh vegetables, like asparagus, cauliflower or squash are to be used, cut them as close in size as possible to the medium size dice of the other vegetables. Add them toward the end of the cooking period so that they become tender as the soup is completed.

(1) Assemble the following ingredients:

2 gal, 1 qt white stock
1/2 lb butter
1 1/2 lb onions, medium dice
3/4 lb leeks, white part and solid part of green, medium dice
1 tablespoon garlic, chopped extremely fine
1/2 lb celery, medium dice
3/4 lb sweet green peppers, medium dice
3/4 lb sweet red peppers, medium dice
1/4 lb flour
1 lb carrots, medium dice
1/2 lb rutabaga turnips, medium dice
Bouquet garni of 2 large bay leaves, 1 teaspoon leaf thyme, 24 whole black peppercorns, 6 whole cloves, 6 whole allspice
1 No. 10 can tomatoes, chopped fine, juice reserved
3 lb potatoes, medium dice
3/4 lb cabbage, medium dice
2 teaspoons Worcestershire sauce
1 cup parsley, chopped extremely fine
Salt, pepper, MSG seasoning (variable)

Note: If stock is cold, it should be heated over a moderate flame to the boiling point.

(2) Choose a 4- or 5-gal soup pot. Examine inside the pot to make sure it is clean, and rinse or scald the pot if necessary.

(3) Melt butter in pot over low flame. Do not permit it to sputter or brown.

(4) Add onions, leeks, garlic, celery, green peppers and red peppers. Stir well to coat all vegetables with butter. Raise flame slightly or move pot toward center of closed top range.

(5) Sauté slowly, stirring very frequently, until vegetables have lost their crispness and are limp. However, they should not turn deep yellow or brown. Stir corner of pot, turning vegetables up so that you can examine them to prevent browning; move pot under hood light, if necessary, to examine vegetables.

(6) Stir in flour, blending well, until no dry flour is visible.

(7) Slowly and carefully pour stock into pot. Hold head back when pouring stock; avoid spilling stock on range. Mix well.

(8) Add carrots, turnips and tomatoes together with their juice. When adding these ingredients, hold them close to the surface of the stock to avoid splattering.

(9) Place bouquet garni in piece of muslin. Tie it shut and fasten it with cord to pot handle; place in pot.

(10) Stir in 1 tablespoon salt.

(11) Bring soup to a boil over a moderate flame.

(12) When soup is at a rapid boil, skim surface well.

(13) Reduce flame so that soup merely simmers.

(14) Stir soup using paddle. Move paddle in corner and over pot bottom to make sure no ingredients are sticking to pot.

(15) Simmer soup for approximately 1 hour; skim soup during this period whenever necessary.

(16) Add potatoes and cabbage. Cook until potatoes and cabbage are tender but not mushy.

(17) Skim fat from soup, using a soup ladle or large kitchen spoon. Add fat to used fat receptacle.

(18) Taste solid ingredients; if some are not tender, continue cooking soup. Taste soup liquid; add more salt to taste and stir well when making additions to correct seasoning. Add pepper to taste, usually up to 1 teaspoon. Add MSG seasoning if necessary to intensify soup's flavor; add Worcestershire sauce. If soup liquid still seems weak in flavor, a small amount of prepared soup stock base may be added—check with instructor or supervisor.

(19) Pour soup into steam table (*bain marie*) pots; use an extra large ladle for dividing soup among steam table pots, stirring soup well before each addition to distribute liquid and solid ingredients evenly.

(20) Place soup in steam table for serving.

(21) Just before soup is to be served, check again and remove any noticeable layer of fat.

(22) Add parsley to soup just before mealtime.

Manhattan Clam Chowder 50 Portions, Approx 8 Oz Each

Although the word chowder is derived from the French *chaudière* meaning a three-legged pot that once was suspended over an open fireplace, chowder in this country is almost exclusively a thick vegetable soup made with clams. Clam chowder had its origin in colonial America: starving New Englanders discovered the clam by observing wild pigs rooting in the shore sands, and later produced the first clam chowder. Occasionally one will see on menus such terms as corn chowder or vegetable chowder, but these are the exceptions. Clam chowder is made with clam broth, clams and vegetables, always including potatoes. Manhattan clam chowder includes tomatoes and no milk; New England clam chowder contains milk and no tomatoes. Although the flavor of dried herbs in soups should be subtly conveyed, Manhattan clam chowder is usually cooked with a pronounced flavor of the herb thyme. Usually, when making Manhattan clam chowder, thyme is not placed in a muslin bag (like the typical bouquet garni which is later removed from the soup) but is added directly to the soup. Pieces of thyme floating on top of the soup are not considered to detract from the soup's eye appeal. The clam stock should never be weak or lifeless in flavor. This means using enough clams to produce a strong clam broth or else reducing the broth until the flavor is sufficiently concentrated. In many restaurants fish stock or white stock is combined with clam broth, although the use of white stock made from meat bones is not followed in those restaurants where the chowder is literally meatless. Likewise, the salt pork in the recipe below will not be used in kitchens that observe meatless Fridays or fast days.

Hard-shell clams called quahogs are the ones most commonly used for clam chowder except in New England where soft-shell clams or steamers are used. Clams and their shells are often sandy, and need thorough washing under cold water and scrubbing with a stiff vegetable brush before they are cooked. Clam broth is produced by covering clams with cold water and bringing the water to a boil, or by steaming the clams until the shells open. The liquid that remains in the pot, a combination of the cooking water and the released juice of the clams, is clam broth. Even though clams are well-scrubbed beforehand (sometimes clams are put on a diet of water and cornmeal to help their bodies expel the sand), clam broth is usually not completely free from sand, and must be well-strained through linen or muslin. Hard clams, even in their raw state, are somewhat chewy. If they are overcooked, they can become almost inedible. For this reason the clams which have been cooked in a separate pot until open should not be added to the soup during cooking but after the completed soup is in the steam table, ready to serve. Hard clams must be alive when they are purchased, that is, the shells must be tightly shut. The shells open during cooking. Do not use any clams (a) that are not tightly shut before cooking or (b) that are not opened after cooking. Although the salt pork in the recipe below conveys its rich, characteristic flavor to the soup, butter or margarine may be used as alternatives for sautéing the vegetables.

(1) Assemble the following ingredients:

8 dozen scrubbed, large hard-shell chowder clams (quahogs)
1 lb salt pork, chopped extremely fine
2 tablespoons garlic, chopped extremely fine
2 1/2 lb onions, medium dice
1 1/2 lb celery, medium dice
1 1/4 lb sweet green peppers, medium dice
1 tablespoon leaf thyme
1/4 lb flour
3 qt fish stock or white stock
1 No. 10 can tomatoes, chopped fine (juice reserved)
5 lb potatoes, medium dice
1/2 cup tomato catsup (optional)
1/2 cup chili sauce (optional)
2 teaspoons Worcestershire sauce
Salt, pepper, MSG seasoning (variable)
1 cup parsley, chopped extremely fine

(2) Place clams in a pot with a tight fitting lid. Add 1 gal cold water and bring to a boil. Boil until shells are wide open; avert head when lifting lid of pot to examine clams.

(3) Remove clams in their shells from pot with a wire skimmer; set aside in refrigerator.

(4) Strain clam broth through a triple thickness of linen or muslin placed in a china cap. Avoid pouring sediment in bottom of pot into strained broth; discard sediment.

(5) Place salt pork in clean soup kettle (do not use the pot in which the clams were steamed open).

(6) Place pot over a moderate flame until fat melts; if butter is substituted for salt pork, melt it in the pot over a low flame.

(7) Add garlic, onions, celery, green peppers and thyme. Sauté, stirring frequently, only until vegetables are limp and begin to turn yellow. Do not brown vegetables.

(8) Add flour, stirring well until no dry flour is visible.

(9) Add clam broth, fish stock or white stock, and tomatoes together with their juice. Pour all ingredients carefully to avoid splattering.

(10) Bring soup to a boil, stirring frequently.

(11) Skim soup well.

(12) Lower flame so that soup simmers slowly; skim when necessary. Simmer 1 to 1 1/2 hours or until flavors are well blended.

(13) While soup is simmering, remove clams from their shells, and discard shells. Examine clams, and, if they are sandy, wash them under cold running water and drain well.

(14) Cut away "blade" or tough edge of clams. Chop "blades" very fine with heavy French knife or put through meat grinder using fine blade.

(15) Cut balance of clams into small dice; store clams in refrigerator until needed.

(16) About 20 min before soup is completed, add potatoes, and simmer until potatoes are tender.

(17) Remove soup from flame, and skim off surface fat.

(18) Add catsup, chili sauce and Worcestershire sauce, stirring well for thorough blending.

(19) Add salt and pepper to taste, allowing for natural saltiness of clam broth; add MSG seasoning if necessary to point up flavors.

(20) Pour soup, using an extra large ladle, into steam table pots. Stir soup to make sure solids and liquids are distributed evenly.

(21) Place soup in steam table.

(22) Add diced and chopped clams and parsley just before mealtime.

New England Clam Chowder   **50 Portions, Approx 8 Oz Each**

New England clam chowder differs from Manhattan in that it contains milk and no tomatoes. On restaurant menus the New England type is sometimes called Boston Clam Chowder. Frequently the clams used in New England clam chowder are soft-shell clams rather than hard-shell or quahogs. Hard clams are tightly shut. The shells of soft clams are usually open. The neck of the clam protrudes from the shell. Because the shells are normally open in their natural habitat, soft clams tend to be sandy, and the soup cook should follow 3 important steps in removing the sand:

(a) The raw clams in the shell must be well-scrubbed under cold running water before they are steamed open.

(b) The cooked, shucked clams must be washed carefully before they are added to the soup.

(c) The clam broth must be strained through a double or triple thickness of cheesecloth or linen before it is added to the soup pot.

New England clam chowder is one of the American recipes that traditionalists insist should be made in one and only one way. Other Americans challenge the tradition, and add such vegetables as green peppers, celery, leeks or parsley to the chowder. The recipe below hews to the traditional method of preparing the soup. Students may be familiar with home recipes in which the raw clams are removed from the shell and cooked in water to produce the broth. The practice differs in commercial kitchens where clam broth is made by steaming the clams open as in the previous recipe.

Before starting work: Examine the raw clams, and discard any with broken shells. Soft-shell clams that show no sign of motion when touched may be dead; discard them. They are a possible cause of food contamination. Examine the cheesecloth or linen to be used for straining the clam broth. It should have no odor. If necessary, wash and rinse it well before using. Examine the salt pork to be used in the recipe. If it feels salty, wash it well or blanch it before chopping. Be sure to keep diced potatoes in cold water until needed.

(1) Assemble the following ingredients:

8 lb soft-shell clams
6 qt cold water
1 lb salt pork, finely chopped
3 lbs onions, small dice
1/2 lb flour
6 lb potatoes, small dice
2 qt milk
1 qt light cream
Salt, pepper
1/2 lb butter

(2) Place clams carefully in wide colander.

(3) Place colander in sink.

(4) Run cold water over clams, washing well, scrubbing if necessary to remove dirt or sand.

(5) Place clams in soup pot. Pour the 6 qt cold water into the pot. Place tight fitting lid on pot.

(6) Place pot over moderate flame, and bring water to a boil.

(7) Reduce flame and simmer until shells are wide open.

(8) Remove pot from fire. Remove lid, slowly raising side of lid opposite you to permit steam to escape. Let clams remain in pot about 15 min to cool slightly.

(9) Remove clams from pot with large skimmer. Place clams in large shallow pan to cool. Cool 5 to 10 min.

(10) Remove clams from shells. Discard shells.

(11) Place clams in wide colander and wash well under cold running water. Examine clams to make sure they are free of sand.

(12) Remove sheath, the filmlike covering, from necks of clams.

(13) Cut neck from body of clams.

(14) Chop necks finely in chopping machine with upright blades, or chop by hand using heavy French knife.

(15) Cut body of clams into small dice, about 1/4 in.

(16) Chill clam meat in refrigerator until needed.

(17) Strain clam broth using a double or triple thickness of cheese-cloth (muslin) or linen. Avoid pouring sediment in bottom of pot.
(18) Place salt pork in pot over moderate flame. Stir frequently, while it is sautéing, to prevent browning.
(19) As soon as salt pork melts or is rendered, tilt pot to spread fat over entire bottom. Add onions.
(20) Sauté onions until light yellow, stirring frequently. Onions should not brown.
(21) Stir in flour, blending well.
    Note: In many recipes flour is not included. A small amount of it, however, gives body to the soup.
(22) Slowly stir in clam broth, using a large wire whip, blending well. Shake whip to dislodge pieces of onion in whip.
(23) Bring to a boil. Skim well.
(24) Add potatoes. Bring to a boil. Skim well.
(25) Reduce flame. Simmer until potatoes are tender and flavors are well blended, about 20–30 min.
(26) In a separate pot combine milk and cream. Heat over a low flame, but do not boil.
(27) Remove soup from fire. Slowly stir in milk and cream.
(28) Taste soup before seasoning. Both salt pork and clam broth are salty. Add salt and pepper sparingly to taste.
(29) Place soup in steam table until mealtime. Dot surface of soup with butter. Cover pot with tight lid until mealtime.
(30) Add clams just before serving.

Navy Bean Soup   **50 Portions, Approx 8 Oz Each**

Ever since 1903, when the US Senate passed a resolution request-ing that bean soup be served every day in the Senate restaurant, this thick soup has been a favorite in restaurants, mass feeding establish-ments and homes all over the country. If you have ever opened a household size can of concentrated bean soup which requires the addition of a can of water, you probably noted that the contents of the can were almost a complete mass of solid ingredients. The soup did not flow from the can, and it was probably necessary to spoon the beans into the soup pot. This unusually large ratio of solid ingre-dients (beans) to liquid is the main characteristic which patrons expect when they order navy bean soup. The beans in the finished soup should be largely intact with a minimum of broken beans and loose skins. Beans will be broken if they are of poor quality, if the soup is cooked at a rapid boil rather than simmered, or if it is over-cooked or carelessly stirred during cooking. Therefore, keep the soup at a simmering temperature, checking it frequently to avoid boiling, stirring it with a large paddle. Since the quality of navy beans varies, and one brand may require more or less time on the fire, the cook should use careful judgment in deciding when cooking is completed. There are five sizes of dried white beans, and navy beans are next to the smallest in size. The recipe below calls for half white stock and half ham stock. If ham stock is not available, all white stock may be used and the flavor of smoked meat may be conveyed by any of the following steps:

(a) Add the bones from two smoked hams; blanch the bones before adding them to the soup.

(b) Cook smoked meat such as smoked calas, smoked pork butts or smoked spareribs along with the soup.

(c) Add the rind of untrimmed slab bacon to the soup.

If ham stock is used and has been stored in the refrigerator for days, check it to make sure it is unspoiled. Make sure all fat has been removed from it. Since ham stock is frequently salty, add salt sparingly to taste when the soup is seasoned. The celery and tomatoes in the recipe below are optional ingredients. If they are omitted, increase the stock by 2 qt.

Before starting work: After soaking and cooking, the 3 lb of dried beans in the recipe below will weigh approximately 9 lb. Because the weight of this ingredient may cause it to settle to the bottom of the pot, the danger of scorching is present. Be sure the soup pot you use is of heavy metal. If a steam-jacketed kettle is used, keep it within a low temperature range. Be sure the beans, which require overnight soaking, are kept in the refrigerator rather than at room temperature which, during hot spells, may cause souring.

(1) Assemble the following ingredients:

    3 lb navy beans
    1/2 lb butter
    1 lb onions, small dice
    2 tablespoons garlic, chopped extremely fine
    1 lb celery, small dice
    1/4 lb flour
    1 1/2 gal white stock
    1 1/2 gal ham stock
    1 qt canned tomatoes
    Salt, pepper

(2) Wash beans in china cap under cold running water.

(3) Cover beans with cold water to a height 2 in. above beans. Remove any defective beans or foreign particles that float to the top. Soak beans overnight in refrigerator.

(4) Place beans in heavy pot together with the water in which

they were soaked. Add 1 tablespoon salt. Stir well. Slowly bring to a boil. Skim foam from top.

(5) Reduce flame and simmer slowly about 1 hour until beans are half cooked. Check water level of beans frequently. Beans must be completely covered with water during this step.

(6) In another heavy pot, melt butter over low flame.

(7) Add onions, garlic and celery. Stir well. Keep flame low.

(8) Sauté, stirring frequently, until vegetables are semitender and onions are beginning to turn yellow.

(9) Stir in flour, blending well. No dry flour should be visible.

(10) Add beans together with their liquid. Add white stock and ham stock. Stir gently.

(11) Slowly bring to a boil. Skim foam. Lower flame at once so that soup barely simmers.

(12) Drain tomatoes, reserving juice. Chop tomatoes fine. Add tomatoes and their juice to the soup.

(13) Simmer soup slowly, stirring occasionally with large paddle until beans are tender and flavors are well blended.

(14) Season to taste with salt and pepper.

(15) Remove ham bones if used, lifting them out carefully with 1 or 2 wire skimmers and transferring them to a container nearby.

(16) Place soup in steam table. Stir pot well before serving each portion.

Minestrone Milanaise   **50 Portions, Approx 8 Oz Each**

The Italian word *minestra* means soup. *Minestrone* means a thick, hearty soup of which there are countless versions. In the United States the best known of the minestrones is the Milan style soup called minestrone *milanaise*. It is replete not only with fresh vegetables but with several starches including potatoes or rice and a macaroni product as well as dried beans both mashed and whole. Often there are more solid than liquid ingredients in the finished soup. In most of the previous soups flavoring vegetables were sautéd in butter. Many Italian chefs prefer chopped salt pork in place of butter. Sometimes the chopped pork is melted with a little oil in the soup pot. The flavor of dried beans is emphasized by mashing half the beans and leaving the balance whole.

Instead of the usual dice into which most vegetables are cut for thick soups, the vegetables for minestrone are often cut into flat disc-shaped pieces, a style of cutting known in France as *paysanne* (see Chap. 2). When making minestrone, chefs like to take advantage of vegetables which are in season. For this reason, any recipe for minestrone may vary throughout the year by substituting vegetables which are seasonally available, such as fresh asparagus, fresh corn, fresh tomatoes, etc. In place of white beans, red kidney beans or cranberry beans may be used. Grated cheese is always passed as an accompaniment to the soup. Since the salt pork used to sauté the vegetables and the cheese are both salty, salt should be used in moderation as a seasoning. Like navy bean soup, minestrone must be stirred especially well before each serving in order that each portion contains a proper ratio of solid and liquid ingredients.

Before starting work: Soak the beans in cold water the night before the soup is to be cooked. Check with your instructor or supervisor the day before to make sure all vegetables are on hand or will be available. If necessary, discuss substitutions beforehand. Make sure you have a large heavy French knife for chopping the salt pork. Chopping salt pork with garlic and herbs such as basil and parsley will keep the pork from cohering into a solid mass, but it cannot be done effectively with a light or medium weight knife. The tubetinni in the recipe below are small tubular forms of pasta. If they are unavailable, thin spaghetti broken into 1-in. pieces may be used instead.

(1) Assemble the following ingredients:
   2 lb white pea beans
   1/2 lb salt pork
   1/4 cup fresh basil leaves or 2 tablespooons dried basil
   1 tablespoon dried oregano
   2 tablespoons garlic, finely chopped
   1 cup parsley sprigs (no stems) packed firmly into measuring cup
   1/4 cup olive oil
   1 1/2 lb onions, cut paysanne
   1 lb celery, cut paysanne
   1/2 lb flour
   1 qt canned tomatoes, chopped (juice reserved)
   8 qt white stock
   1 1/2 lb carrots, cut *paysanne*
   1/2 lb white turnips, cut *paysanne*
   2 1/2 lb potatoes, cut *paysanne*
   1/2 lb cabbage, cut *paysanne*
   1 lb spinach
   1/2 lb tubettini or thin spaghetti (1-in. pieces)
   Salt, pepper
(2) Wash beans well. Remove any foreign particles. Cover with cold water to a height of about 2 in. above beans. Soak overnight in refrigerator.
(3) In the morning, cook the beans apart from the soup. Add 1

teaspoon salt to beans. Add cold water (some of it will have
been absorbed by the beans during soaking) so that water is
about 2 in. above beans. Simmer over low flame, stirring
occasionally, until beans are tender about 1 1/2 to 2 hours.
Add water, if necessary, to keep beans covered during
cooking.

(4) Cut salt pork into 1/2-in. slices. Place salt pork and garlic in
a mound on cutting board. Add basil, oregano and parsley.
Chop in a hacking motion (do not rest tip of knife on cutting board) until salt pork and other ingredients are extremely fine.

(5) Pour olive oil into soup pot, and swirl oil so that it completely
coats bottom of pot.

(6) Add chopped salt pork mixture and heat over a moderate
flame.

(7) As soon as pork shows signs of melting, stir it with a spoon
to spread the mixture as much as possible. Avoid browning
garlic; reduce flame if necessary. Dried herbs like basil or
oregano will turn dark during sautéing, but this is normal
and is expected in a minestrone.

(8) Add onions and celery. Sauté until onions turn yellow, not
brown.

(9) Stir in flour, blending well.

(10) Add stock slowly. Stir well.

(11) Add tomatoes and tomato juice.

(12) Add carrots and turnips. Add 1 tablespoon salt.

(13) Bring soup to a boil. Skim foam. Simmer soup 1/2 hour.

(14) Add potatoes and cabbage.

(15) Remove tough ends of spinach. Wash spinach well. If spinach
is "unwashed" type, wash it in clear cold water 6 times.
Chop coarsely. No piece of spinach should be larger than
1/2 in. square. Add spinach to soup.

(16) Drain cooked beans, reserving juice. Mash half the beans by
forcing them through a china cap or food mill. Add whole
beans, mashed beans and bean liquid to soup.

(17) Simmer about 1/2 hour longer or until all vegetables are tender. Skim soup from time to time to remove foam.

(18) In a separate pot cook the tubettini until tender. Drain well.
Add to soup.

(19) Season soup to taste with salt and pepper. Skim fat.

Note: In most soups the fat is thoroughly skimmed from the
top before serving. A certain amount of fat in minestrone
(melted salt pork) is expected and, therefore, the skimming is
not as complete as it is with most other hearty soups.

Chicken Gumbo Soup   50 Portions, Approx 8 Oz Each

Sometimes a regional soup will be cooked in a noticeably different way when it appears in restaurants outside the region in which it was created. Gumbo soup, whose home is in the southern states—particularly Louisiana—is actually more of a stew than a soup when eaten in New Orleans. Restaurants there feature gumbos which are a rich medley of crab meat, oysters, lobster, chicken, ham, rice, seasoning vegetables and herbs ranging from fresh coriander leaves to dried sassafras. One of these southern gumbos is a hearty meal served in soup form. In commercial restaurants outside the southern region, however, gumbo soup is of a much different character—usually a chicken soup with rice and vegetables.

The one ingredient found in every restaurant version of gumbo soup no matter where it is served is the vegetable okra, a green pod with mucilaginous or sticky characteristics. The stock for chicken gumbo soup is, of course, chicken broth. But a pale or watery broth should be avoided. Chefs sometimes color the broth with caramel coloring. In other cases they brown the fowl briefly in the oven before it is put in a pot to make chicken broth. Anyone who has ever opened a can of okra has probably noticed that the liquid in the can is quite thick. The same thickening action occurs when fresh okra is cooked in a gumbo soup. An additional thickening agent is often used—gumbo filé powder, a mixture of dried sassafras and thyme. Gumbo filé powder is never added while the soup is cooking, since boiling or even simmering will often cause the filé powder to form thin, rope-like strands. It should be added to the soup only when the soup is in the steam table ready to serve.

Before starting work: Note that in the recipe below the rice is cooked separately from the soup and is only added after the soup is completely cooked. This step is taken to avoid overcooked or mushy rice. If cold rice is left over from another meal, it can be used in the soup provided there are no off-flavors. Check it carefully if this change is being made. Wash the previously cooked rice if necessary before adding it to the soup. Determine beforehand if the okra is fresh, frozen or canned. If it is canned, it should be drained and washed before it is added to the soup. Frozen okra usually requires less cooking time than the fresh. The boiled chicken below should preferably be from the fowl used to make the chicken broth.

(1) Assemble the following ingredients:

2 gal chicken broth
1/2 lb butter
2 lb onions, small dice
1 lb celery, small dice

3/4 lb sweet green peppers, small dice

3/4 lb sweet red peppers, small dice

Bouquet garni of 1/2 bunch parsley, 4 large bay leaves, 1 teaspoon leaf thyme, 48 whole black peppercorns, 12 whole allspice, 8 whole cloves

2 qt canned tomatoes

3 lb fresh okra

1/2 lb rice

1 1/2 lb boiled chicken cut into 1/4-in. dice (edible portion without skin or bone)

Salt, pepper, Tabasco sauce

4 teaspoons filé powder

(2) Cook rice separately from soup. Avoid overcooking. Set rice aside.

(3) Melt butter over low flame, using heavy soup pot.

(4) Add onions, celery, green and red peppers.

(5) Sauté vegetables, stirring frequently, only until onions are light yellow, not brown.

(6) Add chicken broth and bouquet garni. Bring to a boil. Skim foam from soup.

(7) Drain tomatoes in colander, reserving juice.

(8) Chop tomatoes fine. As tomatoes are being chopped, juice will accumulate on cutting board; move it toward center of board to avoid spillage.

(9) Add tomatoes and reserved tomato juice to soup pot.

(10) Wash okra. Remove stem ends of okra, and cut crosswise into 1/2-in. slices. Add okra to pot.

(11) Simmer soup 30 to 40 min or until okra is very tender.

(12) Add rice and chicken to pot. Stir well to break up rice if necessary. Simmer slowly 10 min. Remove bouquet garni.

(13) Add 1/4 teaspoon Tabasco sauce and salt and pepper to taste.

(14) Skim excess fat from soup. Pour a small amount of soup into a soup dish to observe color. Add a small amount of caramel coloring, red coloring, or both if necessary.

(15) Place soup in steam table.

(16) About 15 min later or just before serving, stir in filé powder.

Onion Soup   50 Portions, Approx 8 Oz Each

In this country, onion soup is often listed on menus as French onion soup presumably because France is its country of origin. Its main ingredients are onions and broth or stock. There are many European variations of onion soup: in France one finds it made with tomatoes or mushrooms, or with milk, cream or wine. American restaurants, however, feature two main types. The first is an onion soup ladled into a dish and garnished at the table with bread croutons and grated cheese. The second is an onion soup served in individual earthenware tureens with bread and cheese formed into a crust during baking or placed under the broiler for the cheese to brown. Instructions for both types are given below. Since onion soup includes only two principal ingredients, one would think there would be few variables in the finished product. But onions, from their raw to their finished state, change their face many times, and the stock you select may be anything from stock drawn from the general stock pot (*fonds blanc*) to a rich brown consommé good enough to be served in its own right. Raw onions differ significantly in flavor. There are freshly harvested onions with a pronounced, volatile flavor and other onions kept in storage for weeks with a much less vivid flavor. There are yellow globe onions, flat white onions, red onions, Bermuda onions and Spanish onions. Each contributes its individual flavor to the soup. Large Spanish onions are the favorite of soup cooks for their easy handling and mellow flavor. Onions may be sautéd until they are merely limp, until they are wilted, or still further sautéd until they are light yellow, deep yellow or brown. The deep yellow stage is the one that most chefs prefer. In the best restaurants chefs also prefer either a consommé or a rich chicken broth (made from fowl browned in the oven before being boiled) rather than a white stock drawn from the regular stockpot. In some restaurants onion soup is thickened with a very small amount of flour, a practice that many chefs avoid, particularly if the liquid component in the soup is a fine chicken broth or consommé whose delicate flavor would be impaired with flour. Finally, in many eating places it is traditional to season onion soup with a generous amount of freshly ground pepper to give the soup a pungent, bracing quality many patrons expect.

Before starting work: Check raw onions to be sure there are none with a soft or soggy "neck," indicating possible spoilage. Is your cutting board and work area cleared so that sliced onions can be gathered in batches and set aside in a container to keep your station uncluttered? Is your knife honed so that you can cut the onions in uniformly thin slices? If it is your job to peel onions (in most restaurants the vegetable cook peels the onions, while the soup cook cuts them for soup), they may be held under water briefly to keep eyes from watering.

(1) Assemble the following ingredients:
   3 gal consommé or chicken broth
   8 lb peeled onions
   2 tablespoons garlic, chopped extremely fine

3/4 lb butter

Salt, freshly ground pepper (variable)

2 tablespoons Worcestershire sauce

1/2 teaspoon Tabasco sauce

(2) Cut onions in half through stem end.

(3) Place onion flat on cutting board, root end to left.

(4) Slice onion thinly; slices should not exceed 1/8 in. in thickness. When onion is almost completely cut and is awkward to handle, place it down on the side on which it was sliced, and continue to cut slices to end. As onions collect into large batches, set them aside.

(5) Place butter in soup pot over moderate flame.

(6) As soon as butter is melted, toss pot to coat bottom and several in. of side of pot with butter. Do not permit butter to foam or brown.

(7) Add onions and garlic. Stir well with spoon or paddle.

(8) Stir pot frequently, and check color of onions frequently. Sauté onions until they are yellow. Move pot to lower flame or change flame to prevent browning of onions.

(9) If consommé or chicken broth has noticeable layer of fat, remove it. Pour consommé or chicken broth into pot with onions. Stir well.

(10) Bring to a boil. Skim well.

(11) Lower flame, and simmer moderately, approx 1/2 hour or until flavors are well blended.

(12) Taste soup before adding seasonings. If consommé or chicken broth was previously salted, add salt sparingly to taste.

(13) Add 1 tablespoon freshly ground whole pepper; either black or white may be used.

(14) Add Worcestershire sauce and Tabasco sauce.

Cheese Croutons for Onion Soup.—Cut 150 slices of narrow French bread, diameter no larger than 1 1/2 in. Bread of this type is called a *flute.* Place slices on greased shallow baking sheets in a single layer. Sprinkle with grated Parmesan cheese. Sprinkle lightly with paprika. Sprinkle lightly with melted butter. Bake in preheated oven at 375° F for 15 to 20 min or until light brown. Croutons are placed on soup by waiter in dining room. Parmesan cheese, freshly grated if possible, is also passed by waiter to customer at dining table.

Baked Onion Soup Au Gratin (50 Portions).—Prepare onion soup recipe above multiplying ingredients 1 1/2 times. The larger quantity is necessary to accommodate size of most individual marmites (ceramic tureens) in which the soup is baked and served. Preheat oven to 450°F. Prepare 200 cheese croutons instead of 150. Ladle soup into marmites. Float 4 cheese croutons on top of each portion of soup. Sprinkle generously with additional Parmesan cheese. Sprinkle lightly with melted butter and paprika. Place marmites in heavy duty baking pans filled with approx 2 in. of hot water. Place soup in oven. Bake 20 to 30 min or until cheese crust on top is browned. Remove baking pans very carefully, using a triple thickness of dry towel or very heavy pot holders to avoid burns. Remove tureens from hot water, handling each very carefully with a dry towel. Serve at once while very hot. Additional Parmesan cheese may be passed at table.

Note: Baked onion soup au gratin in sometimes listed on a la carte menus. To prevent extended delays at the table, the hot onion soup is poured into an individual marmite as above. The soup is then topped with cheese croutons, grated cheese, melted butter and paprika. The soup is not literally baked. For the sake of speed, it is placed under a broiler flame until the cheese browns. It is not as attractive as the soup which is baked in the oven.

Chicken Mulligatawny Soup   50 Portions, Approx 8 Oz Each

The dominant flavor of most soups comes from its principal ingredient—like the peas in puree of split pea soup, the tomatoes in cream of tomato soup, etc. One might anticipate that the principal flavor in chicken mulligatawny soup would be chicken. Actually, instead of chicken, a spice (curry powder) dominates the blend of flavors. Curry is not one spice but a mixture of anywhere from 12 to 20 spices. It contains cumin, fenugreek and other spices associated with Indian cookery. The word mulligatawny is derived from two Indian words *milagu tannir* meaning pepper water. But the mulligatawny soup served in the Western world usually is not fiery hot with pepper. The soup's stock is chicken broth which contains diced chicken. Students may note two ingredients not normally found in thick soups with vegetables. They are eggplant and apple. As the soup is cooked, both the eggplant and the apple tend to rise to the top of the soup rather than settle, as other ingredients do, on the bottom. Later, when the finished soup remains in the steam table, the eggplant and apple absorb liquid and mix more easily with the other components. In any case, the soup must be well stirred before each portion is ladled out, in order to ensure a proper distribution of all ingredients. When adding curry powder to this soup or any other dish containing curry, it is best to first dissolve the curry in water or blend it with butter to prevent lump formation.

Before starting work: Review dicing vegetables (Chap. 2). When you assemble your ingredients for the soup, remember that both apples and eggplant tend to discolor when exposed to the air. Discoloration can be prevented in two ways: (1) by immersing these ingredients in a liquid with an acid such as water and lemon juice; or (2) by cutting them at the last moment, just before they are added to the soup pot. Arrange your work schedule so that if there is any last minute job of cutting, it can be performed expeditiously.

(1) Assemble the following ingredients:

    2 gal, 1 qt hot chicken broth
    1 1/2 lb onions, small dice
    2 tablespoons garlic, chopped extremely fine
    1 lb leek, white and solid part of green, small dice
    1 lb celery, small dice
    1 1/2 lb sweet green peppers, small dice
    1 lb butter or vegetable fat
    1/4 cup curry powder
    1/2 lb flour
    1 lb peeled eggplant, small dice
    1 lb apples, peeled, cored, small dice
    1 1/4 lb boiled chicken, skinless and boneless, small dice
    1 lb rice
    1/2 cup parsley, chopped extremely fine
    1 pt hot milk
    1 pt hot light cream
    Salt, pepper, MSG seasoning

(2) Melt butter in soup pot over low flame.

(3) Add onions, garlic, leeks, celery and green peppers. Stir well.

(4) Sauté, stirring frequently, until vegetables are tender but not browned.

(5) Stir in curry powder. The curry must be well blended with the butter and vegetables. No dry curry powder should be visible. Examine ingredients in pot under good light to make sure blending is complete.

(6) Stir in flour, blending well. No dry flour should be visible.

(7) Slowly stir in hot chicken broth. Use a long wire whip for stirring. Shake whip to release any vegetables caught in center of whip. (A paddle may be used for stirring but the blending may be incomplete.)

(8) Bring soup to a boil. Skim well.

(9) Reduce flame. Simmer 1/2 hour, skimming when necessary.

(10) While soup is simmering, cook rice in a separate pot, and set aside.

(11) Add eggplant and apples to soup. Continue to simmer 1/2 hour, stirring frequently with paddle.

(12) Add chicken and rice to pot. Stir well. Simmer 15 min longer. Add parsley.

(13) Remove pot from fire.

(14) Stir in milk and cream.

(15) Add salt, pepper and MSG to taste.

(16) Store soup in steam table until serving time.

Green Split Pea Soup   **50 Portions, Approx 8 Oz Each**

Soups like split pea, black bean and lentil are, in a sense, self-thickening. They are made from dried starchy vegetables which become soft during cooking and turn into a puree. The puree is not perfectly smooth, and the soup must be strained later. It may seem odd, therefore, to find flour as an additional thickening agent in recipes for these soups. The flour, however, serves an important purpose. When such soups are completed and are placed in the steam table for serving, the heavy puree tends to separate from the thin stock. To keep the puree in suspension, a small amount of flour is added to the soup after the seasoning vegetables are sautéd. While puree soups are expected to be thick, they should never be so thick that a spoon drawn across the soup leaves a furrow. As a soup of this type stands in the steam table, it tends to thicken. The soup cook should check the soup for its consistency, and thin it with stock when necessary. A good practical way to test the thickness of a puree soup is to pour a small amount on a plate. When the plate is tilted slightly, the soup should flow more rapidly than a medium sauce; it should not flow like water.

Most soups of this type are flavored with a smoky meat (not a meat which is merely cured like corned beef). This can be achieved by using half ham stock and half white stock. All ham stock produces a somewhat overpowering flavor. If ham stock is not available, ham bones from cooked smoked hams or bacon rind may be added to the soup pot. Other smoked meats like smoked spare ribs, smoked shoulders of pork, etc., are sometimes added to the soup to be cooked with it. Trimmings from such meats are sometimes added to the soup as meat croutons.

Formerly all dried legumes intended for soup were soaked overnight before cooking. The newer "quick-cooking" dried vegetables eliminate this step. In some restaurants a small amount of light cream (about a cup per gal of soup) is added to the finished soup. The cream should never be added in such quantities that the soup approximates a cream soup such as cream of mushroom. Popular garnishes with split pea soup are sliced frankfurters, bread croutons, diced ham, etc. (Instructions for soup garnishes are given subsequently.)

Before starting work: The day before, find out whether the peas are the quick-cooking variety. If soaking is necessary, the peas should be soaked the night before in cold water and kept in the refrigerator, not at room temperature, which may cause souring. Determine beforehand whether ham stock, ham bones, bacon rind, etc., are available. A heavy soup of the puree type, because of its weight, tends to stick to the bottom of the pot during cooking and may become scorched. The unpleasant flavor of the scorched layer is soon imparted to the entire batch of soup. To avoid scorching, be prepared to stir the soup frequently during cooking; stir well, scraping the pot bottom and corners of the pot; use a slow to moderate flame for cooking; a closed top range is better than an open flame for soups of this type.

(1) Assemble the following ingredients:

    4 lb quick-cooking green split peas

    2 gal hot white stock

    2 gal hot ham stock

    1 lb salt pork

    2 tablespoons garlic, chopped extremely fine

    3 lb onions, coarsley chopped

    1 lb leeks, white and solid green part, coarsely chopped

    1 lb celery, coarsely chopped

    1/2 lb flour

    Bouquet garni of 1/2 bunch parsley, 1 teaspoon leaf thyme, 24 whole black peppercorns, 2 teaspoons leaf sage, 4 large bay leaves

    1 tablespoon sugar

    2 teaspoons Worcestershire sauce

    1/4 teaspoon Tabasco sauce

    Salt, pepper, MSG seasoning (variable)

(2) Place peas in a small pot or bowl. Cover with cold water and stir well; remove any foreign particles that have floated to the top. Drain peas in a china cap.

(3) Chop salt pork coarsely. Add garlic to salt pork and chop until pork is finely minced.

(4) Place pork in soup pot over moderate flame; stir frequently until fat melts.

(5) Add onions, leeks and celery. Sauté until vegetables are tender, not browned.

(6) Add flour; stir until no dry flour is visible.

(7) Pour both kinds of stock carefully into pot, adding only about a quart at first. Stir well to dissolve roux (fat and flour mixture) before adding balance of stock.

(8) Add peas to pot, holding them as close as possible to surface of stock to prevent splattering.

(9) Tie bouquet garni in a piece of muslin, fasten it to handle of pot and place in pot.

(10) If ham stock is very salty, add no salt to soup. If salt is added, use from 1 teaspoon to 1 tablespoon—avoid oversalting.

(11) Bring soup to a boil over a low to moderate flame, stirring frequently until soup comes to a boil.

(12) Skim soup well.

(13) Reduce flame or move pot so that soup merely simmers. Stir soup frequently, making sure no thick layer forms on bottom of pot.

(14) Simmer soup from 1 to 1 1/2 hours or until peas are very tender; when pressed through fingers they should disintegrate; most of them should have turned into a puree.

(15) Let soup cool 15 to 20 min.

(16) Strain soup through china cap, forcing as much of the solid ingredients through the china cap as possible.
Note: If a heavy-duty blender is used for pureeing the soup, the yield will be somewhat larger; after using the blender, the soup should still be put through a china cap to eliminate any unblended particles.

(17) Season soup to taste with salt and pepper, and use MSG seasoning if necessary to point up flavors. Add sugar, Worcestershire sauce and Tabasco sauce.

(18) Thin soup with stock if it seems too heavy.

(19) Pour soup carefully into steam table (*bain marie*) pots, and place in steam table for meal service. Thin soup during meal service if necessary.

Yellow Split Pea Soup.—Substitute yellow split peas for green split peas.

Lentil Soup.—Substitute lentils for green split peas. This is sometimes cooked as cream of lentil soup. Add 1 pt hot light cream and 1 pt hot heavy cream to finished soup in steam table.

Black Bean Soup.—Substitute black beans for green split peas, and increase cooking time from 1/2 to 1 hour or until black beans are very soft. It is usually flavored with dry sherry wine after soup is strained and put in steam table. Individual portions are sometimes garnished with chopped hard egg and a slice of lemon.

Mongole Soup.—Prepare with equal quantities of green split pea soup or cream of green peas and cream of tomato soup. It may be garnished with green peas and a julienne of cooked onions, carrots and celery, added to finished soup in steam table.

Scotch Lamb Broth   **50 Portions, Approx 8 Oz Each**

Scotch lamb broth is not a broth in the dictionary sense of a thin, simple soup but actually a thick vegetable soup with barley and pieces of lamb. Its origin was in the British Isles where lamb or mutton was frequently boiled. In this country, boiled lamb or boiled mutton rarely appears on restaurant menus. Some commercial kitchens, however, often have leftover lamb bones from such dishes as boneless lamb stew, roast boned shoulder of lamb, curry of lamb, etc., and these bones are used to make a special lamb stock which should be prepared the day before the soup itself is cooked. If such bones are not available, lamb shanks may be purchased and boiled both for their stock and their meat which is added to the soup as in the recipe below. In either case the accumulated bones or lamb purchased for the soup should be blanched before making the stock. The vegetables for Scotch lamb broth are cut *brunoise* style or in very small cubes no larger than 1/8 in. thick, preferably 1/16 in. thick. Cutting vegetables uniformly in this small size may seem tedious at first, but with experience, speed and ease will develop. The student is reminded of the importance of uniform cutting for eye appeal. Barley may be cooked in the soup or separately as in the recipe below. The latter procedure eliminates the thick, cloudy liquid which results when barley is boiled.

Before starting work: Check 2 days beforehand to see if there are accumulated lamb bones which may be used for stock. Check to see if there is sufficient meat on the bones to supply the lamb croutons which are expected in this soup. Check with the butcher or your supervisor on these points. Review cutting vegetables *brunoise* (Chap. 2). The recipe below is in two parts, one for making the stock, the second for the soup itself.

(1) Assemble the following ingredients for lamb stock:

   12 lb lamb shanks (or bones that yield meat equivalent of lamb shanks)

   4 gal water

4 large whole peeled onions

2 large carrots

2 teaspoons salt

(2) Blanch lamb, that is, cover it with cold water, bring it to a boil, throw off water, wash with cold water and drain.

(3) Place blanched lamb in pot with the 4 gal water, onions, carrots and salt.

(4) Bring to a boil. Skim well.

(5) Reduce flame and simmer approx 2 hours. Be sure stock is kept below boiling point at all times.

(6) Strain stock through fine china cap, and chill until needed.

(7) Remove meat from lamb bones in large pieces. Place in a bowl. Add enough lamb stock to cover meat, and chill until needed.

(8) Assemble the following ingredients for soup:

12 qt lamb stock.

Note: The 16 qt water used for stock above will have been reduced to approximately 12 - 14 qt after cooking.

1 lb butter

1 1/2 lb onions, cut *brunoise*

3/4 lb leeks, cut *brunoise*

1 lb celery, cut *brunoise*

1 lb carrots, cut *brunoise*

1 lb white turnips, cut *brunoise*

1 tablespoon garlic, chopped extremely fine

1/2 lb flour

Bouquet garni of 1/2 bunch parsley, 2 bay leaves, 2 teaspoons rosemary, 1 teaspon thyme, 24 whole black peppercorns

3/4 lb pearled barley

1/2 cup parsley, chopped extremely fine

Salt, pepper, MSG seasoning

(9) Remove fat from surface of lamb stock.

(10) Heat lamb stock over moderate flame.

(11) In another soup pot melt butter over low flame.

(12) Add onions, leeks, celery, carrots, turnips and garlic. Stir well.

(13) Sauté, stirring frequently, until onions turn light yellow. Do not let vegetables brown.

(14) Stir in flour, blending well. No dry flour should be visible.

(15) Slowly stir in hot lamb stock. Stock should be added in 3 or 4 batches, stirring well after each addition. A large wire whip may be used for stirring. Tap whip over edge of soup pot to release any vegetables caught in center of whip. Add bouquet garni.

(16) Bring soup to a boil. Skim well.

(17) Reduce flame and simmer soup approx 1 1/2 hours.
(18) In a separate pot bring 3 qt water to a boil. Add 1 1/2 teaspoons salt. Slowly add barley, stirring well. Simmer barley 1 1/2 to 2 hours or until very tender.
(19) Drain lamb meat. Add stock to soup pot, covering meat.
(20) Cut lamb into cubes approximately 1/8 in. thick.
(21) Drain barley in fine china cap. Wash barley under cold running water.
(22) Add barley to soup.
(23) Skim excess fat from soup.
(24) Stir lamb croutons into soup. Add salt, pepper and MSG to taste.
(25) Add parsley to soup.
(26) Place soup in steam table. Stir soup pot well before serving each portion to distribute ingredients uniformly.

Cream of Tomato Soup   **50 Portions, Approx 8 Oz Each**

In most restaurants, including those with the highest standards of food quality, this extremely popular cream soup is usually made with canned tomatoes and canned tomato puree rather than fresh tomatoes. The reason canned products are used is that the quality of fresh tomatoes is so poor throughout the year, except for the brief period when fresh tomatoes are harvested, that best results are obtained from the canned products. Cream of tomato soup is notoriously subject to curdling. It curdles because the high acid content of the tomatoes causes the protein in the milk or cream to coagulate in the same way that a tablespoon of vinegar added to a cup of milk will cause the milk to curdle instantly. For this reason most recipes for cream of tomato soup include baking soda as an ingredient for neutralizing somewhat the acidity of the tomatoes. Baking soda, however, has a sharp flavor and pronounced aftertaste if used carelessly. It should be used only in minimal amounts. Besides the use of baking soda, the following guides help in avoiding curdling:

(1) Do not add milk or cream to the soup during the cooking process when the soup is on the fire or immediately after the soup is removed from the fire. It will still be hot enough to curdle milk and cream.
(2) After the soup has been cooked and is strained, set it aside for further cooling to about 140° F.
(3) Heat the milk and cream until they are warm, about 140° F.
(4) Place the soup in the steam table; be sure the water in the steam table is at a simmering, not boiling, temperature.

(5) Slowly stir the hot milk and cream into the soup.

(6) Keep smaller than normal batches of soup in the steam table for serving. When one batch has been served, replace it with another batch combined as above.

For a richer, creamier soup than the recipe below, decrease the amount of milk and substitute an equal amount of light cream. Many cream soups and puree soups are made richer by adding butter *after* the soup is in the steam table. The butter melting in the hot soup, giving richness, smoothness and body to the soup, is known by the French culinary term *liaison*.

(1) Assemble the following ingredients:

> 6 qt white stock
> 1 No. 10 can tomatoes, chopped fine (juice reserved)
> 1 No. 10 can tomato puree
> 1 1/2 lb butter
> 1 1/2 lb onions, chopped fine
> 2 tablespoons garlic, chopped extremely fine
> 1 1/4 lb carrots, chopped fine
> 1 lb celery, chopped fine
> 3/4 lb flour
> Bouquet garni of 1/2 bunch parsley, 1 tablespoon basil, 1 teaspoon oregano, 36 whole white peppercorns, 6 whole cloves and 6 whole allspice
> 2 ham bones
> 2 teaspoons baking soda
> 2 qt, 1 pt milk
> 1 pt light cream
> Salt, white pepper, sugar (variable)

(2) Melt butter in soup pot over low flame. Tilt pot as butter melts so that entire bottom and a few inches of sides of pot are coated with butter.

(3) Before butter sputters or browns, add onions, garlic, carrots and celery.

(4) Raise flame slightly or move pot for increased heat. Sauté vegetables, stirring frequently, until onions are deep yellow but not browned.

(5) Stir in flour, blending well. There should be no dry flour visible.

(6) Slowly add tomatoes together with their juice, tomato puree and stock, lowering each of these ingredients carefully into pot to prevent splattering. Stir well.

(7) Place bouquet garni in a piece of muslin, tie it closed and fasten it with cord to handle of pot; place in pot.

(8) Stir well with a large wire whip to blend puree with other ingredients. Shake whip above kettle to release any ingredients caught inside whip.

(9) Add ham bones.

(10) Raise flame so that it is moderate, or move pot on closed top range for added heat. Stir frequently.

(11) When soup comes to a boil, skim well.

(12) Lower flame or move pot so that soup simmers very slowly. Again, stir frequently with large paddle, scraping bottom and corners of pot to prevent scorching.

(13) Simmer soup 1 to 1 1/2 hours or until flavors are well blended and vegetables are very tender.

(14) Mix 2 tablespoons salt, 1 teaspoon ground white pepper, 2 tablespoons sugar and soda, blending well. Add to pot, stirring well. Add more salt, pepper or sugar to taste if necessary.

(15) Remove bouquet garni from soup; remove ham bones with a wire skimmer.

(16) Strain soup through china cap. Let soup stand at room temperature 20 to 30 min.

(17) Pour soup into steam table (*bain marie*) pots. Be sure water in steam table is simmering, not boiling.

(18) Combine milk and cream and heat in steam table pot. Do not boil it over a top flame. Remove any skin that may form on milk mixture.

(19) About 10 min before meal period, slowly stir milk and cream into tomato mixture, and correct seasoning if necessary.

(20) Be sure tomato soup does not rest on bottom of steam table. Place a heavy object under steam table pot if necessary to keep pot off bottom. If soups are stored in steam table insets, this step will not be necessary.

(21) Serve soup with bread croutons or *profiteroles.*

Note: For richer soup use 2 qt milk and 1 qt light cream. For more intense tomato flavor, substitute 1 cup tomato paste for 1 cup tomato puree.

Cream of Chicken Soup   50 Portions, Approx 8 Oz Each

Cream of chicken soup is not only served under its own name but is also frequently used as a foundation for other cream soups, such as cream of celery or cream of asparagus. To prepare the latter soups, the named vegetable is added to the soup pot and is pureed when the soup is finished. Cream of chicken soup should, if possible, be made from chicken broth rather than white stock. To intensify the chicken flavor, whole fowl or carcasses of fowl as well as chicken feet, wing tips, gizzards and other chicken parts are frequently added to the pot during the cooking and later removed before the soup is strained. All cream soups should be velvety smooth in appearance and to the palate, but the modern tendency is not to make them indiscriminately rich with an overabundance of heavy cream, egg yolks, etc. The soup should never be pasty looking or leave a furrow when you draw a spoon through it. Like many dishes containing flour, cream of chicken soup tends to thicken as it stands. It should be thinned with chicken broth, milk, cream or a combination of these ingredients before and during the meal period when necessary. Cream soups, like cream sauces, tend to form a skin on top if they are unstirred for long periods. To prevent skin formation before the meal, dot the surface with bits of butter, and cover the pot with a tight lid. As the butter melts, it will form a coating on the surface which later is stirred into the soup before the first portion is served.

Before starting work: The day before, check with the instructor or supervisor to find out how much chicken broth is available. If it is insufficient for the recipe, white stock may be used for balance of the stock component. Also determine beforehand if there are carcasses of fowl and/or chicken parts which may be added to the soup pot. If whole fowl are to be used, they normally require 2 to 2 1/2 hours in the pot before they are tender. Plan to allow this longer cooking time if necessary.

(1) Assemble the following ingredients:

3 gal chicken broth

1 pt plus 1 cup white roux (p 202)

5 lb chicken parts, such as boiled fowl carcasses, raw feet, wing tips, etc.

1 1/2 lb onions, 1/2-in. slices

1/2 lb leeks, white part only, 1/2-in. slices

Note: Leeks should be cut in halves or quarters lengthwise and well washed before slicing.

1/2 lb celery, 1/2-in. slices

1 qt milk

3 cups light cream

1 cup heavy cream

3/4 lb boneless and skinless boiled chicken, 1/4-in. dice (the cooked chicken parts will furnish some of this item)

Salt, white pepper, MSG seasoning

Note: The vegetables above are not sautéd as they are in many soups. Sautéing is not necessary for the soup's flavor in this case, and the white vegetables, when strained, maintain the natural color of the soup.

(2) Blanch the chicken carcasses and chicken parts, that is, put

them in cold water, bring the water to a boil, throw off the water, and wash the contents of the pot under cold running water. If chicken feet are included, they should be scraped to remove the scales before blanching.

(3) Warm the roux, if it is cold, over a low flame until it is no longer solid.

(4) Bring chicken broth to a boil. Be sure to use a pot large enough to hold the broth as well as fowl carcasses, etc.

(5) Skim the chicken broth.

(6) Keeping the broth at a rapid boil, slowly add the roux, stirring well with a long wire whip.

(7) Add chicken parts. Lower them slowly and carefully into the pot, holding them as close as possible to the surface of the liquid, rather than dropping them from above, to prevent spattering.

(8) Add onions, leeks and celery.

(9) Bring to a boil. Remove scum from surface.

(10) Reduce heat so that soup simmers. Stir frequently with a paddle, scraping bottom and corner of pot to prevent thick layer from forming.

(11) Simmer until flavors are well developed, about 1 1/2 hours.

(12) Remove soup from fire.

(13) Remove chicken parts, using a wire skimmer.

(14) Put soup with its vegetables through a food mill or puree machine.

(15) Pour milk and both kinds of cream into a pot, and scald them, that is, bring them up to the boiling point but do not boil.

(16) Slowly stir milk-cream mixture into soup, stirring well with wire whip.

(17) Add diced fowl. Stir well.

(18) Season to taste with salt, pepper and MSG.

(19) Thin soup if necessary with additional milk and cream.

(20) Place soup in steam table for service.

Cream of Chicken Soup A La Reine.—Put 1 lb cooked fowl through a meat grinder using fine blade. Add this ground chicken to the soup just before it is put through the food mill or puree machine. Additional thinning may be necessary.

Cream of Mushroom Soup   **50 Portions, Approx 8 Oz Each**

The previous recipe referred to cream of chicken soup as a base for other cream soups. (Other cream soups do not contain pieces of diced chicken.) In a large restaurant where a different cream soup might appear on the menu each day, the soup cook would make his basic cream of chicken soup once or twice a week. He would omit the milk and cream, and store the cream soup base in the refrigerator until needed, at which time he would make the necessary modification for the cream soup for that particular day. The student should understand, however, that there are many restaurants where this traditional method of making cream soups is not followed, and where all cream soups are made with a simple white stock or even synthetic stock in order to save costs.

The principal flavoring ingredient in cream of mushroom soup consists of chopped sautéd mushrooms. If the mushrooms are not fresh or of top quality, they should be soaked in cold water beforehand to partially restore their freshness. Mushrooms are of top quality when the caps are tight fitting around the stems, the stems are short and firm and the caps are firm, dry and heavy for their size without any spongy feeling when you handle them. Mushrooms for soup are chopped medium fine. They may be chopped with a French knife if necessary. The job is more quickly and efficiently done in a chopping machine with vertical blades. When mushrooms are sautéd, they normally give off juices which collect in the pan, forming a pool of liquid. In certain dishes, this mushroom liquor is reduced in a pan without a lid until it is evaporated. When cooking cream of mushroom soup, however, the mushrooms are sautéd with a lid to conserve the juice, an important component of the soup's liquids.

Before starting work: Check to see if there is leftover cream of chicken soup which may be incorporated into the cream of mushroom soup. If there is none, follow the steps as indicated in the recipe. However, if cream of chicken soup is available, make sure it is sound, and adjust mushroom soup recipe accordingly. Before using the chopping machine with vertical blades to chop the mushrooms, be sure you are familiar with handling it, and observe all safety precautions.

(1) Assemble the following ingredients:

3 lb fresh mushrooms, chopped medium fine
1/2 lb butter
2 tablespoons lemon juice
3 gal chicken broth
1 pt plus 1 cup white roux (p 202)
5 lb chicken parts such as boiled fowl carcasses, raw feet, wing tips, etc.
1 1/2 lb onions, 1/2-in. slices
1/2 lb leeks, white part only, 1/2-in. slices

1/2 lb celery, 1/2-in. slices
1 qt milk
3 cups light cream
1 cup heavy cream
Salt, white pepper, MSG seasoning, cayenne pepper, ground
    mace

(Follow steps (2) to (11) in preceding recipe for cream of chicken soup.)

(2) While soup is simmering, melt butter in saucepan large enough to hold mushrooms.
(3) Add mushrooms and lemon juice. Sprinkle with salt and pepper. Stir well.
(4) Sauté, stirring occasionally, keeping pan covered until mushrooms have lost their raw flavor and raw color. Do not attempt to brown. Set aside.
(5) Remove soup from fire.
(6) Remove chicken carcasses and chicken parts, using a large wire skimmer.
(7) Force soup through a food mill or puree machine.
    Note: Half the mushrooms may be forced through food mill if desired.
(8) Add mushrooms and their liquor to strained soup.
(9) Scald milk and both kinds of cream.
(10) Stir milk-cream mixture into soup.
(11) Season with salt, pepper and MSG to taste.
(12) Stir in cayenne pepper and mace to taste. Both seasonings should be used sparingly.
(13) Thin soup, if necessary, with milk and cream.
(14) Place soup in steam table until serving time.

Cream of Asparagus Soup.—Instead of sautéd chopped mushrooms, add 1 No. 10 can asparagus. Use appropriate grade of asparagus for soup. Simmer and strain as above. For fresh cream of asparagus soup add 5 lb fresh asparagus trimmings (end pieces, peelings, etc.). Diced cooked asparagus may be added to strained soup as croutons.

Cream of Broccoli Soup.—Instead of chopped sautéd mushrooms, add 5 lb chopped fresh or frozen thawed broccoli to soup pot before simmering. Strain as above.

Cream of Celery Soup.—Instead of chopped sautéd mushrooms, add 5 lb chopped fresh celery to soup pot before simmering. Strain as above. Use celery salt as one of the seasonings. Diced cooked celery may be added to finished soup as croutons.

Cream of Cauliflower Soup.—Instead of chopped sautéd mush-rooms, add 5 lb fresh cauliflower (trimmed weight) to soup pot before simmering. Strain as above.

Cream of Spinach Soup.—Instead of chopped sautéd mushrooms, add 5 lb chopped, washed, fresh spinach or frozen thawed spinach to soup before simmering. Strain as above.

Cold Crème Vichyssoise   **50 Portions, Approx 8 Oz Each**

Vichyssoise is a cold puree soup made of potatoes, leeks and onions. Sometimes the French name for a dish is better known than its English equivalent. *Crème vichyssoise*, however, is the French name for a soup created in the United States by chef Louis Diat of the Ritz Carlton hotel in New York City, and as a matter of fact is not well known in France. Most cream soups like cream of tomato or cream of celery are thickened by flour and sieved ingredients such as tomato puree. No flour is used in making vichyssoise. Its thickness is derived from potatoes, one of its principal ingredients. It is one of the few soups in which changes in the soup's ingredients, while not calamitous, will usually upset the soup's delicate flavor. Even a mild vegetable like celery, when added to the recipe, seems to adulterate the soup's subtle balance of flavors. If the soup is made in the morning, a 6- to 8-hour chilling period should be allowed before the soup is served. Like other cold soups it should be served between 38° and 42°F. The bouillon cups or soup bowls in which it is served should be prechilled. It is always garnished with chopped chives sprinkled on top; the chives are best if fresh rather than dried or freeze-dried. In many restaurants where vichyssoise appears on the menu throughout the year, the soup is prepared in sufficient quantities to last for a 3- or 4-day period. Where this is the practice, under no circumstances should the soup be held beyond a 4-day storage period in the refrigerator, since the soup contains milk and cream, and these tend to hasten spoilage. The soup should be checked before each meal period by the *garde manger* or cook responsible for storing and serving the soup. As vichyssoise stands in the refrigerator, the starch in the potatoes swells, thus causing the soup to be thicker than when it was first made. To thin it to its original consistency, milk or milk and cream should be added in small quantities at a time until it is properly thinned.

Before starting work: Examine peeled potatoes to make sure there are no eyes, black spots or other blemishes. Make certain peeled potatoes are in cold water to prevent discoloration. The interval between the time the potatoes are peeled and the time they are used in the soup should be as brief as possible. Check with the vegetable cook on this matter. When preparing leeks, cut them lengthwise in half or quarters if leeks are very thick. Spread leaves apart slightly and hold under cold running water to wash off sand. If, after cutting leeks, there are still evidences of sand, wash leeks again. When slicing potatoes, the cutting board will become wet and slippery. Dry it as often as necessary to keep potatoes firmly on board when slicing, in order to avoid accidents with the knife.

(1) Assemble the following ingredients:

7 lb (peeled weight) peeled potatoes, 1/2-in. slices
2 lb leeks, white part only, 1/2-in. slices
1 1/2 lb onions, 1/2-in. slices
1 tablespoon garlic, chopped extremely fine
1/2 lb butter
2 1/2 gal chicken broth
1 qt milk
1 qt light cream
Salt, white pepper
1 cup fresh chives, very finely chopped

(2) Melt butter in soup pot over a low to moderate flame. Do not permit butter to foam or brown.

(3) Tilt pot so that butter coats a few inches of side of pot.

(4) Add leeks, onions and garlic. Stir well.

(5) Place a lid on pot, but be prepared to check pot frequently.

(6) Sauté, stirring frequently, until vegetables are limp and beginning to turn soft. Under no circumstances should they be permitted to color to the brown stage.

(7) Add chicken broth and potatoes, lowering both ingredients carefully into pot.

(8) Bring to a boil. Let boil 1 or 2 min.

(9) Using a skimmer remove foam from top. Do not skim fat from surface. It should remain with soup to be later blended into the puree.

(10) Simmer 1/2 to 3/4 hour or until potatoes are very soft.

(11) Combine milk and cream in another pot or saucepan. Heat up to the boiling point but do not boil.

(12) Add milk and cream to soup.

(13) Remove soup from fire. Force soup through food mill, puree machine or china cap. Soup may also be pureed in heavy duty blender in small batches. Soup should be strained after blending to make sure no unblended particles remain.

(14) Season to taste with salt and pepper.

(15) Cool soup following directions on p 55.

(16) Chill in refrigerator, keeping soup covered with tight fitting lid.

(17) Before each meal period, check soup for thickness. Thin with milk or milk and cream, adding small quantities at a time, stirring well until soup is of proper consistency. Check with instructor or supervisor.

(18) Sprinkle chopped chives on top of each portion of soup just before serving.

Bisque of Lobster Soup   **50 Portions, Approx 8 Oz Each**

The word bisque generally means a cream of shellfish soup such as bisque of lobster, bisque of shrimp, etc. Originally bisques were thickened with some ingredient other than wheat flour, such as rice flour or cooked rice. The reason for this step was to preserve the delicate seafood flavor, keeping it as natural as possible. Nowadays, regular white flour or rice flour is used. What makes the bisque a successful soup is not its thickening agent, but the amount of fresh lobster used and the way the lobster is prepared. On menus you will sometimes find such terms as vegetable bisque or tomato bisque, soups that turn out to be nothing more than ordinary cream soups with perhaps some added cream for richness. Although the ingredients in a bisque may be costly and the preparation somewhat more complex than other cream soups, the procedure is something with which every student of quantity cooking should be familiar in order to understand the various ways in which stocks are created and their flavors developed. When making clam chowder, the soup's stock (clam broth) was produced in 10 or 15 min, as soon as the clam shells were widely opened. When you boil lobsters for 10 or 15 min, however, and taste the water in which they were cooked, the liquid or lobster stock is almost flavorless. If you continue to cook the lobsters for an hour or longer, you ruin the lobster meat by overcooking. To solve this dilemma, the cook, preparing bisque of lobster, follows a special procedure:

(a) Raw lobsters are cut into chunks and sautéd briefly until the shells change color and the lobster meat is cooked with its flavor and texture intact.

(b) The lobsters are removed from the pot. The lobster meat is removed from the shells, and the meat is set aside.

(c) The empty lobster shells (which contain a concentrated lobster flavor) are chopped and returned to the soup pot and are slowly simmered in a thickened court bouillon (vegetable stock), along with flavoring vegetables.

(d) The soup or bisque is strained.

(e) Part of the lobster meat, not all, is returned to the soup as lobster croutons. The balance of the lobster meat is used for other dishes.

(f) Hot cream is added along with seasonings to finish the soup.

Before starting work: Prepare the court bouillon the day before if possible. Be sure to use a heavy French knife for cutting the lobsters—a medium or light weight knife is impractical. Check lobsters to make sure they are all alive. They should show movement when lifted.

(1) Assemble the following ingredients:
   8 live lobsters, 1 1/4 lb each
   2 1/2 gal hot court bouillon (Chap. 3)
   1 lb butter
   2 1/2 lb onions, medium dice
   1 lb celery, medium dice
   1 lb carrots, medium dice
   1 cup (8 oz) brandy
   1/2 lb rice flour or white wheat flour
   Bouquet garni of 1/2 bunch parsley, 4 bay leaves, 1 teaspoon leaf thyme, 24 whole black peppercorns, 6 whole cloves, 6 whole allspice
   1 pt (16 oz) dry white wine
   1 qt canned tomatoes, drained, chopped fine, juice reserved
   1/2 cup tomato paste
   1 pt hot light cream
   Salt, pepper, cayenne pepper, MSG seasoning

(2) Wash lobsters under cold running water, removing any seaweed clinging to them.

(3) Place lobster on cutting board with the head forward.

(4) Insert tip of heavy French knife at the spot where the head joins the body. This kills the lobster, although movement will still be noticeable.

(5) Cut the lobster tail in half lengthwise.

(6) Turn the lobster, head facing you, and cut the head in two lengthwise. The lobster is now split in two parts.

(7) Using the heel of the knife, with a chopping motion, cut off lobster claws close to body.

(8) Again using heel of the knife, crack the lobster claws open in the large and small sections of each claw.

(9) Remove sac behind head of lobster. Discard sac.

(10) Remove tomalley (green substance) and roe, if any, from lobster. Set tomalley and roe aside.

(11) Cut all lobsters in manner described in preceding steps.

(12) Melt butter in a soup pot over a low flame.

(13) Add onions, carrots, celery and lobsters. Move the pot to a high flame. Stir well. Cover pot.

(14) Sauté, stirring frequently, and shaking pan to toss all ingredients until lobster shells are red, and lobster meat has lost its raw color and has just become firm.

(15) Add brandy. When brandy is warm, set ablaze. As soon as flames subside, remove pot from fire.

Note: Some cooks prefer to blaze the lobster in a shallow *sautoir* rather than a deep pot. By simply moving the *sautoir* around an open flame, the vapors are set ablaze. When a deep pot is used, a long taper or straw should be used for blazing (flambéing). Hold head back to avoid rising flames.

(16) With slotted spoon or skimmer, lift lobster pieces from pot. Vegetables should remain in pot.

(17) Stir flour into pot, mixing until no dry flour is visible.

(18) Slowly stir in hot court bouillon, mixing well with wire whip. Shake whip from time to time to dislodge any pieces of vegetable caught in whip.

(19) Add white wine and bouquet garni. Add tomatoes together with their juice and tomato paste, stirring very well to blend tomato paste with liquid in pot.

(20) Return pot to a moderate flame, and bring to a boil, stirring frequently.

(21) Skim well. Reduce flame so that liquid simmers.

(22) As soon as lobster is cool enough to handle, remove all lobster meat from shells including tail meat and claw meat. Use an oyster fork or paring knife with pointed edge. Keep claw meat apart from tail meat.

(23) Chop lobster shells, using a heavy French knife or cleaver.

(24) Return shells to soup pot. Add 1 tablespoon salt.

(25) Continue to simmer soup 1 hour, skimming when necessary. Stir frequently with large paddle especially in corner of pot.

(26) Strain soup through a fine china cap. Press ingredients well to extract all soup.

(27) Force tomalley and roe through a china cap with holes large enough to permit sieving. Stir into soup.

(28) Cut claw meat into small croutons no more than 1/16 in. thick.

(29) Add claw meat and cream to soup. Add salt, pepper, cayenne pepper and MSG to taste.

(30) Place soup in steam table until serving time.

Note: Balance of lobster should be chilled, kept well covered, and used for dishes such as lobster Newburgh, curry of lobster, etc.

Garnishes for Cream Soups and Puree Soups

Although the French word *croûton* literally means end of a long loaf, and the most common croutons for thick soups are those made of bread, there are other soup croutons and garnishes with which the student should be familiar.

Bread Croutons.—White bread, preferably without crust is cut into 1/4- or 1/8-in. dice and baked in a moderate oven 10 to 15 min or until lightly browned. The croutons should be stirred during baking to brown evenly, and must be watched carefully or they may burn. They may be sprinkled with melted butter before browning, or may be fried in clarified butter, rather than baked, until brown. Allow about 2 tablespoons per portion or about 1 qt and 1 pt for 50 portions.

Vegetable Croutons.—These are widely used for cream vegetable soups. They are made of the principal flavoring ingredient, such as diced cooked celery for cream of celery soup, diced cooked asparagus for cream of asparagus soup, etc. Because of the texture of many vegetables, such as cauliflower, the croutons are often chopped rather than diced.

Bacon or Ham Croutons.—Frequently these are served with puree soups made of dried vegetables such as green split peas, yellow split peas, etc. Dice should be 1/8 in. thick. The croutons may be added at one time to finished soup in steam table or added to individual portions just before soup is served. Allow about 2 tablespoons per portion or about 1 qt and 1 pt for 50 portions.

Frankfurters.—Sliced cooked frankfurters are frequently served with puree soups made of dried vegetables such as lentil, black bean, etc. The croutons may be added all at once to finished soup in steam table, or added to individual portions just before soup is served. Allow about 1/2 oz per portion or about 1 1/2 lb for 50 portions.

Whipped Cream.—Unsweetened whipped cream may be used plain or flavored with curry, horseradish, paprika, etc. It should be kept on cracked ice during meal, and added to soup just before serving in dabs of about 2 tablespoons per portion or about 1 qt and 1 pt for 50 portions.

Chopped Fresh Herbs.—Very finely chopped herbs such as parsley, dill, chervil, tarragon or chives may be sprinkled on cream soups just before serving. Allow about 1 teaspoon per portion or about 1 cup for 50 portions. (Also served with consommés)

5

Fry Cook (*Friturier*)

In many restaurants the fry cook's duties go considerably beyond the job of frying. Sometimes the fry cook is also the breakfast cook since many breakfast items like eggs, bacon, sausage, etc., involve frying. There are kitchens where the fry cook works closely with, or may supervise, the vegetable cook. In still other places certain sautéd dishes like calf's liver or minute steak may be assigned to the sauce cook. From the student's viewpoint, however, it is important to understand the two main categories of frying:

(a) Deep fat frying: cooking with deep fat in a large kettle or pot with straight sides. The kettle must be large enough for the food to float. Food is lowered into the hot fat in a frying basket and withdrawn by the same means.

(b) Sautéing or cooking with shallow fat in a frying pan or *sauteuse* (a pan with a long handle and flared sides to permit steam to escape and to allow easy turning of the food). There must be just enough fat to cook the food on one side at a time and to keep the food from sticking to the pan.

Note: There is a third type of frying in which no *initial* fat is used in the pan, and which is employed in cooking such foods as bacon or sausage which give off their own fat during cooking and do not require added fat but are still a form of frying. In household cookery, the procedure is called panbroiling.

The fry cook's job of sautéing, popularly called panfrying, should not be confused with the job of sautéing chopped vegetables for soups, sauces, stews, etc. This type of sautéing does not produce fried foods in the usual sense of the term. The French word *sauter* means to jump. When a soup cook sautés seasoning vegetables for a soup he frequently tosses the vegetables by moving the pot quickly back and forth, causing the vegetables to jump so that he need not stir them with a spoon or paddle. A fry cook never attempts to flip such foods as breaded veal cutlets or fillets of fish by simply moving the pan, but carefully lifts each piece of food with a spatula and turns it when necessary.

For the sake of gaining proficiency in frying skills, this chapter is devoted to deep and shallow fat frying. Another chapter covers the work of the breakfast cook and the preparation of such foods as eggs, bacon, ham, etc.

Students should understand that much of the food handled by the fry cook is made ready for him by others on the kitchen staff. If fried oysters are featured on the menu, the job of breading the oysters may be handled by the *garde manger* or his assistant, while the fry cook does the actual frying as each order is received in the kitchen. When French fried potatoes are on the menu, the vegetable cook may peel and cut the potatoes while, again, the actual frying and finishing are handled by the fry cook. In this chapter, however, the recipe steps in the jobs are described from beginning to end so that the student may acquire an overall view of some of the typical jobs of frying. Ideally each portion of fried food, if it is to be hot and crisp, should be made to order at the last moment just before it is served. This ideal situation is not possible in large institutional kitchens and cafeterias where multiple orders must be prepared in advance for fast quantity service. In fine restaurants, however, fried foods are still prepared individually to order.

JOB SUMMARY

The fry cook (1) consults with the chef or *sous chef* in estimating daily needs, advance menus and banquet menus; (2) fries in deep or shallow fat, meats, poultry, seafood, eggs, vegetables, fruits and fritters; (3) receives breaded foods from *garde manger* in single orders or batches; stores breaded foods in nearby reach-in refrigerator; orders and receives solid, semisolid or liquid fat in quantity containers, and butter or margerine in pound quantities; (4) receives peeled raw potatoes, cut raw potatoes, cooked potatoes and other vegetables from vegetable cook; (5) fries individual portions of food to order as well as multiple portions for cafeteria service or banquets; (6) fries some foods partially, such as fried chicken, and finishes the chicken by baking; (7) may use oven for certain foods listed as fried on the menu such as bacon, sausage, etc.; (8) orders and receives sauces for fried foods such as tomato sauce, tartar sauce, etc.; (9) may prepare egg dishes which are not fried such as poached eggs;

(10) renders fat from beef suet if available in quantity; (11) may assist roast cook or vegetable cook at certain times.

MANUAL PROCEDURES

In his work, he (1) fills deep frying kettles to proper level with liquid, semisolid or solid fat; (2) heats kettles of fat until fat reaches specific frying temperature; (3) sets thermostats for appropriate frying temperature; (4) may heat iron kettles of deep fat over top flames of range or other source of heat; (5) may use frying thermometer to check accuracy of thermostatic control; (6) lowers food in wire baskets into wells of deep fryers; (7) drains fried food, suspending it above fat; removes and empties baskets of fried food; (9) seasons fried foods after frying; (10) checks doneness of certain fried foods by piercing with fork and checking color; (11) drains fried foods on absorbent paper; (12) mixes batters of flour, milk, eggs, etc., for fritters and for coating foods before frying; (13) heats shallow frying pans, adds fat, and sautés foods turning them to brown on both sides; (14) dredges some foods in flour or (in absence of *garde manger*) coats them with flour, eggs and bread crumbs before frying; (15) heats frying pans with fat for egg dishes; (16) adds whole eggs for frying or beaten eggs for scrambling or omelets; (17) fills and turns omelets into appropriate shape; (18) boils water in saucepan for poached eggs, and adds eggs for poaching; (19) cooks bacon or sausage in shallow baking pans in oven; (20) garnishes fried foods with parsley, lemon wedges, etc.; (21) adds vegetable accompaniments to fried foods on serving plates or platters; (22) strains and filters used deep fat; (23) cleans frying equipment with detergent, brushes, etc., if kitchen helper is not assigned to this task.

EQUIPMENT AND UTENSILS

Important equipment includes (1) deep fry kettles using gas or electricity as source of heat; (2) iron kettles with straight sides designed for deep fat frying; (3) frying baskets; (4) French fry potato cutters; (5) parisienne potato cutters; (6) frying pans, assorted sizes; (7) baking pans; (8) utility pans; (9) bowls, forks, ladles, spoons, French knives, and spatulas; (10) deep fat thermometer; (11) dispensers for salt, pepper, etc.; (12) fat filters or mechanical filtering equipment.

WORKING CONDITIONS AND HAZARDS

The fry cook (1) works with deep kettles of fat heated to temperatures ranging between 300° and 400°F; (2) works at extremely hot ranges when sautéing; (3) is exposed to sputtering fat and fat spillage; (4) must be constantly alert to possibility of fires caused by fat spillage; (5) is exposed to fumes from frying foods; (6) must move quickly to check foods during frying and must be prepared to remove them quickly from kettle or sauté pans; (7) must be able to work quickly on varied orders.

PLACE IN JOB ORGANIZATION

The breakfast cook, vegetable cook or cook apprentice may be promoted to fry cook. The fry cook may be promoted to roast cook, broiler cook or roundsman.

FAT ABSORPTION

Americans in both restaurants and homes eat fried foods avidly and frequently. From the quality standpoint good fried foods are an appetizing brown, crisp and tender on the outside, and moist and flavorful inside. But the many terms which have come into slang usage over the years, such as "grease pot" or "grease joint," referring to restaurants, reflect only too realistically the common reaction to cooks who are unskilled in frying. The technical term for greasiness in fried foods is fat absorption. All fried foods absorb some fat. Excessive fat absorption occurs if:

(a) The fat temperature is too low; the general range of temperatures for frying is between 300° and 400°F.

(b) The frying pan is overloaded with food causing the fat temperature to sharply drop and to become slow in recovering its initial temperature.

(c) There is insufficient fat in the pan for the quantity of food, causing the food to remain in the pan too long before it is browned.

(d) Uneven pieces of food, including some which are much thicker than others, are placed in the same frying pan with smaller pieces and are all left in the pan until completely cooked.

(e) The fat has been excessively used, and has not been strained or replenished.

(f) The food for any reason is kept in the fat too long.

FRYING FATS

In Chap. 6, the student learns that the broiler cook's mastery of his job depends upon his control of a piece of equipment—the restaurant heavy-duty broiler. The fry cook's success depends not only on the correct use of his equipment but just as importantly on his cooking medium—fat. Gaining an expert hand in the art of frying depends, among other things, upon the kind of fat he uses and the skilled way he uses it. There are some fats whose appearance, aroma and flavor change almost constantly when used for frying. Butter, for instance, is solid when cold. It turns soft at room temperature, and liquifies when heated. As cooking continues, its color deepens from light yellow to light brown. It begins to foam, and gives off a nutty aroma. Eventually it burns black. The trained fry cook must constantly anticipate each of these phases every time he uses butter. Even the newer so-called stabilized fats used for deep frying are continually affected by foods cooked in them. A full kettle of fat used for deep frying is soon less than a full kettle as the fat is absorbed by foods cooked in it, and must be replenished from time to time. Crumbs from breaded foods fall into the fat, settle into a sludge at the bottom of the kettle, and must be strained out. Oils with a pale yellow color used for deep frying gradually turn dark upon repeated use. When large amounts of food with a pronounced flavor, like onions or certain fish, are fried in deep fat, flavor transference occurs, and the use of the fat may become limited. The student aspiring to be a fry cook must become aware of all these constantly altering factors, and must be able to deal with them in a practical way.

Before any frying job is attempted, the student should know the characteristics of the principal fats used in frying.

Butter: Because butter is churned from milk or cream it contains a large amount of water. The water content is useful when butter is used as a spread for sandwiches; but in frying, it causes the butter to foam or sputter at relatively low temperatures. When exposed to intense heat, butter turns black and acquires a burnt flavor. Since its flavor is desirable in many dishes such as sautéd fish or fried eggs, it is frequently clarified so that it can withstand more heat than in its original form. To clarify butter, it is simply left in a warm place or placed over a low flame until melted. The foam on top is then skimmed off, and the clear or clarified butter is poured off, avoiding the solid matter in the bottom of the container. Frequently a combination of clarified butter and oil is used for sautéing, a step which reduces the likelihood of the butter burning. Butter is never used for deep fat frying because, even when clarified, it smokes or decomposes at normal deep frying temperatures. The French term *beurre noir* which literally means black butter is actually butter heated until it is brown; its use is illustrated in fillet of sole *beurre noir* (p 109).

Margarine: This butter substitute is usually made from vegetable oils with added skim milk, processed in such a way that it can be used in the same way as butter for cooking. Some brands of margarine tend to brown or burn even more readily than butter when exposed to high heat in a frying pan.

Lard: The rendered (melted) fat of hogs is known as lard. Like butter it turns solid when refrigerated, and has an individual, recognizable flavor which is imparted to food fried in it. It is seldom used for deep fat frying these days, although it was once popular for this purpose. Its flavor may be acceptable in cooking sautéd pork chops, sautéd ham steaks, etc.

Rendered beef fat: In some restaurants beef fat is rendered on the premises from the fat trimmings of beef. (Lamb fat is never included because of its strong flavor. Veal fat may be included with the beef fat, but the amount available is usually insignificant.) The best quality beef fat is from the kidney area. In those restaurants which do not use pre-portioned meats and where the usual wholesale cuts of beef are trimmed on the premises into roasts, steaks, stewing meat, etc., there is normally a regular accumulation of raw beef fat. The fat may be melted down or rendered by the fry cook so that, after straining, it is available for deep frying. It has its own characteristic flavor, but may be used successfully in frying French fried potatoes, chicken or meat croquettes, etc. It must be kept under refrigeration except when in use, and tends to break down or become unusable more readily than hydrogenated fats. Beef fat is rendered by cutting it into pieces preferably no larger than 4 in. thick and by placing the pieces of fat in a very heavy deep pan (often a square pan for fitting in the oven), adding 1 pt of water to every 10 lb of beef fat. It is cooked either on top of the range or in the oven until the fat melts and most of the water has evaporated. It should be stirred occasionally. The solid pieces of fat remaining, called greaves, are removed, and the fat is strained through a triple thickness of cheesecloth (muslin). There are many restaurants today which prefer to sell their raw fat to a fat processor rather than render it.

Chicken fat: Accumulated chicken fat may be rendered in the same way as beef fat. It has a distinct flavor which some chefs find useful in making panfried chicken, sauces with a chicken base, etc. Other chefs prefer butter or fats which are relatively flavorless.

Cooking oils: These include olive oil and the well-known vegetable oils such as corn oil, cottonseed oil, soybean oil, etc. Most olive oil is imported from Europe. It has its own individual flavor, although the highest quality olive oils have the mildest, least assertive flavors. Olive oil is still used in a few restaurants for sautéing, despite the fact that it tends to smoke at low frying temperatures. Most of it finds its way into salad dressings rather than in cooked dishes. The American vegetable oils like corn, cottonseed, soybean, etc., are excellent both for sautéing and deep frying. Their smoking point is high, and they have the ability to withstand repeated use without breaking down. They are easy to handle, are stored easily, and may be used for both cooking and for salad dressings.

Hydrogenated vegetable fats: These are both solid and semisolid and are the most widely used fats for commercial deep frying or sautéing. The process of hydrogenation changes the oils from a liquid to a solid state when the fats are kept at room temperature. They are comparatively tasteless and odorless, and are preferred for their capacity to be used repeatedly without quickly breaking down or turning rancid.

FAT SMOKING POINTS

When any of the above fats are heated for frying, their temperatures rise to a range of 300° to 400°F. One of the most important facts for the fry cook to know is the smoking point of the fat being used. This is simply the temperature reached when the fat gives off a blue vapor and sharp fumes. Fats at the smoking point not only break down chemically but give an unpleasant flavor and odor to foods fried in them and cause the foods to be less digestible. When crumbs from breaded foods, flour and other substances used for coating foods fall into fat, they begin to lower its smoking point. Foods with a large amount of moisture such as potatoes tend, in time, to break down fats. Fats in continuous use at a given temperature will eventually smoke at a lower point than when fresh fat is used. If the amount of clean fat which is normally absorbed by deep-fried foods is regularly and quickly replaced by fresh fat, the smoking point of the fat will be close to normal. Fats which have reached the smoking point a number of times tend to become rancid more readily than fats which are kept below the smoking point. Finally, fat in a deep kettle with a comparatively narrow diameter will smoke less readily than fat in a kettle with a wider diameter and more shallow depth.

The smoking points of fats varies with different brands, and is affected by age, storage conditions, etc. Butter may begin smoking at 300°F, and therefore should only be used for sautéing at relatively low temperatures, usually between 250° and 300°F. If butter is clarified, its smoking point will rise to between 325° and 350°F; it is used for sautéing meats, poultry or seafood. Olive oil smokes at approximately 350°F, adequate for sautéing but not practical for most deep fat frying which takes place at about 370°F. Hydrogenated vegetable fats as well as vegetable oils such as corn, cottonseed and soybean all have smoking points above 400°F, frequently up to 450°F. Some of the newer fats especially formulated for deep fat frying reach smoking points between 475° and 500°F, a range which makes them best of all for sustained deep fat frying.

Generally speaking, foods for deep frying are best cooked in fats with a high smoking point. Foods for sautéing are generally fried at lower temperatures, and therefore fats with a lower smoking point may be used. Once you know the distinctive qualities of a fat, including its smoking point, you will be able to use it to best advantage. For instance, you may choose butter for fried or shirred eggs, clarified butter for sautéing brook trout, a mixture of clarified butter and oil for sautéing calf's liver, pure olive oil for sautéing veal scallopine, semisolid vegetable oil for French frying potatoes, etc. But whatever fats are used, you should follow certain proven guidelines in frying. They are divided below into two sections.

DEEP FAT FRYING

Before kettles are used for deep frying they must be regularly checked for cleanliness. If the fry cook himself does not wash the kettles at the end of the shift or the end of the day, he must still make sure they are absolutely clean. Manufacturers' instructions usually describe in detail the procedure for cleaning their equipment. The kettle may be gas-fired or electric. In general, deep fryers heated with gas burners are cleaned in position by filling the empty kettles with water and a cleaning agent, boiling the solution, flushing with clean water and drying. Electric fry kettles are disassembled and washed in a pot sink like other cooking equipment. Since the heating elements in a deep electric fryer are in the kettle itself (rather than beneath the kettle as in the case of gas equipment), the elements after use become discolored and must be cleaned by soaking the elements overnight in a fry kettle cleaning solution.

18 GUIDES TO DEEP FAT FRYING

(1) Be sure the fat is preheated to the recommended temperature before any food is deep fried. Automatic fry kettles usually have a light indicator which tells you when the fat is correctly preheated.

(2) If you are using deep fat in a kettle which is not automatically controlled for temperature, clip a frying thermometer to the side of the kettle to make sure the temperature is correct.

(3) If an automatic frying kettle does not seem to be functioning properly (that is, if it seems to be browning food too quickly or too slowly), check its temperature with a frying thermometer or report the matter to your instructor or supervisor. The thermostat may need adjustment or replacement.

(4) When food at room temperature or cold food is lowered into hot fat, the temperature of the fat drops instantly. A certain margin of lowered temperature is expected, but in a properly functioning kettle the initial temperature will soon be recovered. It will not, however, return to its correct temperature if the frying basket is overloaded with food. In most cases do not add food in quantities which cannot float in a single layer when the food rises to the top of the fat. The exception to this rule is the type of deep frying equipment fitted with two frying baskets which permit food to be fried in two layers.

(5) Always lower food slowly into deep fat. Always be prepared to withdraw the food if the fat shows signs of bubbling too high or bubbling over the side of the kettle.

(6) When, after frying, a basket of food is raised from the fat, suspend it above the fat momentarily until excess fat drips back into the kettle.

(7) Do not sprinkle fried food with salt while the basket is suspended over the fat, as salt hastens the decomposition of the fat. Season the food away from the fat.

(8) All foods should be as dry as possible before frying. The crumbs on breaded foods which have been kept in the refrigerator too long may become moist. If necessary, dip them lightly in dry crumbs before frying. Potatoes for French frying should be as dry as possible since moisture causes fat to break down.

(9) In large kitchens with a battery of 3 or 4 fry kettles, use each one, whenever possible, for a specific purpose, i. e., one for French fried potatoes, a second for seafood, the third for meats, poultry, etc.

(10) If, before a meal period, semisolid fat is poured into a deep fry kettle, the heat may be turned on at once for preheating. If

solid fat is used, pack it down thoroughly before turning on the heat to prevent an air pocket forming around the heating coils.

(11) Keep temperatures low, about 200°F, while melting fat during preheating, or in slack periods when kettles are not in active use. If there is a battery of kettles, turn off the heat completely in those that are not being used during slack periods.

(12) Whenever particles of food such as ends of potatoes, pieces of batter, etc., are found floating on the fat, remove them with a wire skimmer or perforated spoon to prevent their burning and discoloring the fat.

(13) When kettles are in constant use, be alert to the level of the fat at all times. Replace fat when necessary to keep it at the correct level for frying.

(14) Remember, when adding fat to bring it up to the correct level during a meal period, that you are lowering the temperature of the fat remaining in the kettle. Wait until the temperature is again normal before proceeding to add food for deep frying.

(15) At the end of the shift or end of the day, drain the fat and strain it through a fat filter, a fine mesh screen or a triple thickness of cheesecloth (muslin). Check the condition and color of the fat with your instructor or supervisor before reusing it.

(16) Always replace the entire contents of a fry kettle when:
    (a) It is deeply discolored, much darker than its original color;
    (b) It is broken down as indicated by brown bubbling at the rim of the kettle (not to be confused with the bubbling of moist foods such as potatoes);
    (c) It has acquired an off-flavor or strong aroma.

(17) Taste the fat at least once a day. In a very busy kitchen, taste it twice a day to make sure its naturally bland flavor has not been impaired. Do not taste hot fat.

(18) Do not exceed the load ratio of the specific equipment with which you are working. Load ratio simply means the weight of the fat in relation to the weight of the food in it. For example, if the load ratio recommended by the manufacturer of the frying equipment is 8 to 1, and if the fryer holds 24 lb of fat when properly filled, and you are frying French fried potatoes, there should never be more than 3 lb of potatoes in the frying basket at any one time.

SAUTÉING

When a student is apprenticed to a fry cook, one of the first things he notices is that the fry cook uses his black iron frying pans over and over without washing them, merely wiping them dry after each use. The extremely high heat of the fat in the pan, sometimes almost twice that of boiling water, destroys bacteria that would normally flourish in an unwashed saucepan. Even when the frying pans are made of another metal such as aluminum or when the pans are lined with stainless steel, the washing may be deferred until the end of the meal. Routine washing of a black iron pan would actually cause the food to stick, while wiping the pan dry leaves a very thin film of fat on the surface, permitting the food to brown or become done, and slide easily from the pan. A new black iron pan must be "seasoned" before it is put into use. This is the fry cook's responsibility. Seasoning means simply that the inside surface of the pan must be prepared in such a way that foods such as eggs, corned beef hash, etc., may be cooked and easily removed from the pan with their shape intact. The steps below should be followed in seasoning a pan.

(a) It is washed with a detergent, rubbed with steel wool, rinsed and wiped dry.

(b) It is then vigorously rubbed with salt.

(c) The salt is removed and the pan is filled with cooking oil.

(d) The pan is heated over a low flame for 30 min.

(e) The oil is discarded, and the pan is wiped dry. After long repeated use, the built-up film of fat on the pan will be mixed with residues that may cause food to stick. When this occurs, the salt–oil treatment or seasoning must be repeated until the pan is again usable.

18 GUIDES TO SAUTÉING

(1) At the beginning of the shift, check frying pans to make sure they are clean and ready for frying. Wipe them dry, or use the salt-oil treatment described above.

(2) Make sure the frying pans are sufficient in number and of the correct size for the menu items to be fried that day.

(3) Keep frying pans within easy reach; make certain that your supply of towels is sufficient and available nearby.

(4) If clarified butter is to be used for sautéing, check to see that there is an adequate supply for the entire meal period. If another liquid fat such as oil is to be used, it should be available in a pitcher for easy pouring or in a container with a small ladle for easy dipping.

(5) Many foods to be sautéed are first dipped in flour. The flour should be sifted and seasoned with salt and pepper if this is indicated

for the food being sautéd. Keep the flour within easy reach, in a shallow pan big enough to accommodate multiple portions.

(6) In some kitchens, it is the practice to dip certain foods for sautéing, such as fish, in milk before dipping in flour. Keep a small quantity of milk available in a shallow pan or bowl, and replace it when necessary rather than let it stand at room temperature for an extended meal period.

(7) When dipping food in flour prior to sautéing, shake or pat off excess flour to minimize burnt particles in the pan.

(8) The amount of fat used in the pan will vary with the thickness of the food being sautéd. If you are sautéing thin fillets of flounder, fat poured to a depth of 1/8 in. will be sufficient. If you are sautéing whole small sea bass, about 3 in. thick, from 1/4 to 1/2 in. of fat will be required in the pan.

(9) Be sure the fat for any sautéing job is sufficiently hot before the food is added to the pan. It should be heated to the 350° to 400°F range. Since a fat thermometer cannot be used in a shallow frying pan, you must judge the temperature by other means. The fat will be hot enough when:

(a) Its surface is shimmering; small wavelike motions are visible;
(b) The first wisp of smoke appears (too much smoke means the fat is too hot and is breaking down);
(c) The fat begins to sputter somewhat as the first portion of food is lowered into the pan; the sputtering should not be excessive.

(10) Be prepared to lower the flame under the pan or move the pan if excessive heat causes the food to brown too rapidly or unevenly.

(11) Use a long, heavy-duty offset spatula for turning the food. Examine each piece before turning to make sure the browning is completed. Check the browning on the second side before removing the food from the pan.

(12) When thick pieces of food such as breaded pork chops are being sautéd first before they are placed in the oven, sauté them only to a light brown color, since the oven will continue to brown the chops as their cooking is completed.

(13) Use the proper flame for the job on hand. A wide flame is needed for a wide frying pan containing multiple portions of food; a much smaller flame is needed for a single omelet.

(14) Be prepared at all times to raise or lower the flame if browning is proceeding too slowly or too rapidly.

(15) When wiping a black iron pan after each use, examine it to make sure there is no residue of food sticking to the pan.

(16) If the same pans are being used repeatedly, they will retain built-up heat and will require less time for preheating than if the pans are cold. Allow for this difference when placing foods in the pans for sautéing.

(17) Certain foods which are coated with flour before sautéing, such as calf's liver, fillet of sole sauté *meunière*, etc., require a moderate flame for proper sautéing. Meats which are not coated with flour such as minute steaks, lamb steaks, etc., should be exposed to a strong flame which sears them properly and browns them deeply.

(18) Never crowd the sauté pan. Food in the pan must fit comfortably so that one side is always in complete contact with the pan bottom. As portions of food are sautéd, they shrink somewhat and there will be additional room in the pan. Food may be added in the space thus provided, but the pan should still never be crowded.

Fillet of Sole Sauté Meunière   **50 Portions, Approx 3 Oz Each**

Even though the foreign names of dishes are avoided on many American menus, some French cooking terms are traditionally used for certain dishes. One of the most common is *sauté meunière*, and it appears with anything from sautéd calf's brains to sautéd kingfish. It is used to identify food dipped in flour, sautéd with clarified butter or oil, transferred to a serving dish, sprinkled with chopped parsley and lemon juice and then covered with butter browned in the same pan in which the food was sautéd. The French word *meunier* means miller. According to culinary legend, Napoleon was supposed to have eaten a magnificent dish of sole in an inn called *La Belle Meunière* where the miller's wife did the cooking. Word origins aside, it is a common procedure which nevertheless requires the cook's most careful attention. (The student is again reminded that sautéd dishes of this type are often prepared by the sauce cook rather than the fry cook.)

The fillets may be taken from gray sole weighing 2 lb apiece or from lemon sole weighing 6 lb apiece. The fillets may be 1/4 in. thick or 3/4 in. thick. Each requires a different cooking time which the student can only learn by experience rather than from a strict time schedule. There are two common mistakes in preparing fish sauté *meunière*, and the student should be alerted to them. First, if the fat in the pan is not sufficiently hot, the fish steams rather than browns. Second, if there is too much fat in the pan, the fish is neither sautéd nor deep fried, but simmered in fat and usually becomes grease-laden. Portions of fillet of sole sauté *meunière* should not be prepared in advance but always made to order. Note that, while the ingredients for 50 portions are indicated in the recipe below and are available before mealtime, the individual orders of fish should only be cooked when orders are received from the dining room.

Before starting work: Review 18 guides to sautéing. If the range space assigned to you for sautéing is crowded with pots or pans, arrange to move them so that you will have room for several sauté pans to be used at one time.

(1) Assemble the following ingredients:

12 lb fillet of gray sole
1 lb flour
2 tablespoons salt
2 teaspoons celery salt
1 teaspoon white pepper
1 teaspoon paprika
Oil or hydrogenated fat (variable)
3 lb butter, soft but not melted
50 lemon slices
2 large bunches washed parsley (variable)
4 lemons, cut in half for juice

(2) Remove stems of 1 bunch parsley. Give stems to soup cook who may add them to stockpot. Place parsley on clean cutting board. With 1 or 2 French knives, chop parsley following directions in Chap. 2. Place chopped parsley in a cloth napkin or small clean kitchen towel. Bring ends of towel tightly around parsley so that towel can be twisted. Squeeze parsley over sink until it is very dry. Place parsley in container and keep nearby.

(3) In a utility pan or shallow bowl combine flour, salt, celery salt, white pepper and paprika. Stir to blend ingredients well. Keep nearby.

(4) If fillets have just been washed and are still wet, dry them with clean toweling. Keep fillets in nearby reach-in refrigerator until needed.

Note: The practice in some restaurants is to pass individual portions of the raw fish from the *garde manger* to the fry cook, or pass small batches at a time so that raw fish is never held for long periods at room temperature.

(5) Select a frying pan in which the number of fillets about to be sautéd can be placed comfortably without crowding.

(6) Roll the fillets in the flour mixture, i. e., coat the fillets with

flour by rapidly moving the pan back and forth. Pat the fillets by hand to be sure flour coating is intact. Shake fillets above flour to remove excess flour.

(7) Heat oil or melt fat to a depth of 1/4 in. in frying pan. Fat must not smoke but should be sufficiently hot to "seize" the fish. The word "seize" in kitchen parlance means the coating on the fish begins to brown in a matter of seconds.

(8) Holding each fillet by the end, lower it quickly but carefully into the pan. Do not drop it from a height causing the fat to splash. If any fat splashes onto range top, wipe it immediately unless it flames. If it flames, stand back, and wait until flames subside. If flames do not burn out in a few seconds, smother them with a piece of coarse burlap kept nearby or by dousing with salt. If flames persist, follow instructor's or supervisor's directions.

(9) Check browning of bottoms of fillets. Browning of edges may be noted first. Lift fillets partially with long offset spatula to check bottom browning.

(10) When fillets are medium brown, turn them, using spatula. If turning is awkward, a second spatula or kitchen fork in left hand may be used to steady fish as it is being turned. Turn fish quickly but not in such a manner that fat splashes.

(11) When second side is browned, transfer fillets from pan to warm serving plates or platters.

(12) Sprinkle fillets with chopped parsley.

(13) Sprinkle fish sparingly with a few drops lemon juice on each fillet.

(14) Quickly wipe pan in which fish was sautéd. Add butter to pan allowing about 2 tablespoons for each portion of fish.

(15) Place pan over high heat, and melt butter to medium brown (called hazlenut brown). Watch pan constantly; do not let butter turn black.

(16) Immediately pour hot butter from pan over fillets.

(17) Garnish each portion with 2 or 3 parsley sprigs depending upon size. Keep sprigs bunched together for each portion.

(18) For each portion dip a lemon slice in chopped parsley so that half the lemon slice is covered with parsley.

(19) Place a lemon slice on each portion of fish. Fish should be served at once. If platters are used, place platter covers in position. Follow whatever routine is used in the kitchen to notify waiter that order is ready and should be picked up for serving.

Fillet of Sole Beurre Noir.—Omit sprinkling parsley over fish. Melt butter until it is dark brown but not black. Add 1 teaspoon parsley and 1 teaspoon drained capers in vinegar. Pour over fish just before serving.

Fillet of Sole Amandine.—Prepare fillet of sole sauté *meuniére.* When butter is melted in pan, add 1 tablespoon almonds cut julienne. Almonds may be toasted beforehand in moderate oven until lightly browned.

Batter-fried Fillet of Fish   **50 Portions, Approx 3 Oz Each**

When a food to be fried is very delicate in flavor, such as certain fish like sole, pompano, etc., it is sometimes covered with a thin batter instead of the common coating of flour, eggs and breadcrumbs. The principal ingredients in such a batter are flour, milk and eggs. The batter should be thick enough to coat the food but not form a heavy layer on it. As in the previous recipe, orders are prepared individually as they are received in the kitchen, and the dining room staff should be alerted to pick up such orders as soon as they are ready. For optimum quality, foods of this type must be freshly fried and piping hot when served. While fish fillets are kept refrigerated until cooked, batters are held at room temperature for best frying results. One may prepare a batter, following a specific recipe, only to find that the batter is too thick or too thin. Variable factors such as the kind of flour, moisture content of the flour, size of eggs, mixing procedures, etc., may cause a batter to vary in consistency from time to time. Normally a fry cook tests his batter just before the meal period by dipping a small piece of food into the batter and frying it. If the coating is too thin and does not adhere properly or is too thick and cakey, it may be adjusted with additional flour or thinned with additional milk. Best results are obtained from batters of this type if they are made in advance and allowed to stand for about an hour before they are used. Batters are more tender if not used immediately. During this period, the batter "relaxes," i.e., any toughening factors in the flour are avoided.

Before starting work: Since this job requires deep fat, allow enough time to filter the fat if necessary and to preheat the deep kettles to the proper temperature. Allow the one hour standing period for the batter. Set up your station so that the fish, the flour (for coating the fish before dipping in batter), the batter and the kettles are as close as possible for efficient operation.

(1) Assemble the following ingredients:
12 lb fillet of fish such as lemon sole, flounder, fluke, etc.
Bread flour for dredging
Salt, celery salt, pepper
8 eggs
1/2 cup cooking oil
1 qt milk
2 lb pastry flour
4 teaspoons baking powder
Fat for deep frying
2 bunches parsley, washed, patted dry, stem bottoms removed
3 qt tartar sauce (p 280) or remoulade sauce (p 280)

(2) Open eggs, 2 at a time, into a small dish. Check to make sure no pieces of shell remain with eggs and that eggs are sound.

(3) Turn eggs into mixing bowl, 2 at a time.

(4) Beat eggs by hand, using a wire whip until eggs are foamy.

(5) Slowly add oil and milk to eggs while continuing to beat.

(6) Sift 2 lb pastry flour, baking powder and 1 tablespoon salt into bowl containing egg mixture.

(7) Stir batter with wire whip until blended. If there are some small lumps of dry ingredients, they may remain; they will disappear as the batter stands or will disappear when the fish is fried.

(8) Let the batter stand at room temperature one hour.

(9) Preheat fat to 370° F.

(10) Place about 1 lb bread flour into a utility pan for dredging the fish.

(11) As individual orders of fish are received, sprinkle the portions to be fried with salt, celery salt and pepper on one side.

(12) Roll the fish in the pan containing the bread flour. Fish may be rolled by placing the fish in the flour, turning it on both sides to coat it completely, and then shaking off excess flour. It may also be rolled by placing the fillets in the flour and moving the pan back and forth so that the fish is coated on both sides in one step. Excess flour should be shaken off.

(13) Dip fish in batter, holding each piece by the end. Keep the bowl of batter as close to the frying kettle as possible to prevent spillage. After fish is coated with batter, hold it briefly above batter to allow excess batter to drip off.

(14) Lower, don't drop, fish into the fat. Hold it as close to the surface of the fat as possible before releasing it. Fish may be held by hand or fork when lowering it into the fat.

(15) Fry the fish, turning once, until it is medium brown. Fish may be lifted out of the fat with the frying basket or with a per-

forated skimmer or slotted spoon. Take special care in lifting and transferring the fish not to break the coating.

(16) Place fish on warm uncovered plates or platters.

(17) Garnish with parsley sprigs.

(18) Serve with tartar sauce or remoulade sauce, allowing about 1/4 cup per portion.

Note: Batter-fried fish may be served with or without lemon wedges.

Corn Fritters   **50 Fritters**

One of the fry cook's most important basic skills is making batters. The principal ingredients of a batter are flour, milk or water and eggs. Thin batters such as the one in the previous recipe are used to coat foods like fish, shrimp, apples, etc. Batters of a different type are employed in making small fried cakes containing chopped ingredients or small pieces of food, such as clam fritters, corn fritters, etc. On French menus, fritters are called *beignets.* One of the most popular of these is known as *beignets soufflés*, and is made from a batter that is cooked before it is fried. The batter is rich in eggs and is made light with vigorous, prolonged beating. Many fritter recipes depend on baking powder for leavening action or lightness. The recipe below follows the method of the *beignets soufflés*, and is important to learn because fritters of this type hold their shape well after frying and are more suitable for mass production than fritters made with baking powder. Corn fritters are a widely used garnish with fried chicken. They may be made with cooked kernels removed from corn on the cob or with canned whole kernel corn or crushed corn. Corn fritters are sometimes served as a luncheon course with bacon and hot maple syrup (allowing about 3 fritters per portion). The ideal way to make fritters is to fry them as they are ordered which is sometimes impractical in large kitchens. Although the recipe below is planned for 50 fritters, the best procedure is to make the batter beforehand and then, during the meal period, fry the fritters in small batches as needed.

Before starting work: Check with instructor or supervisor to determine kind of corn to be used. If fresh corn off the cob is planned, allow enough time to cook the corn and cool it so that the kernels can be removed in time to make the batter. Allow 6 to 8 large ears of corn to make the quantity needed for the recipe.

(1) Assemble the following ingredients:

2 lb whole corn kernels, either freshly cooked corn off the cob or drained canned whole corn kernels

Note: If canned whole corn is used, drain corn, reserving

liquid from can. Add enough water to make 1 pt liquid and use in place of 1 pt water below.

1 pt milk
1 pt water
1/4 lb butter
2 teaspoons salt
1/2 teaspoon ground nutmeg
1 lb flour
16 eggs
Deep fat for frying

(2) Pour water and milk into a heavy deep saucepan.

(3) Place pan over a low flame and scald the milk, that is, heat the milk up to the boiling point but do not allow it to boil.

(4) Add butter, salt and nutmeg. Stir until butter dissolves.

(5) Add flour all at once. Stir with a mixing spoon until all ingredients form into a solid mass, and batter leaves sides of pan cleanly. This requires considerable vigorous stirring. Stirring should not stop until all ingredients are thoroughly blended.

(6) Remove pan from fire. Turn mixture into bowl of mixing machine. Choose appropriate size bowl for amount of batter. Use heavy flat beater, not wire beater.

(7) Set machine at slow speed. Start beating, and gradually increase speed to medium.

(8) Add unbeaten eggs, about 2 at a time, beating well after each addition, until all eggs are incorporated into the mass.

(9) Add corn. Continue mixing until corn is blended into batter.

(10) Chill batter from 1/2 to 1 hour before frying.

(11) When ready to fry fritters, heat deep fat to 370° F. Empty frying basket should be in fat, not suspended above it.

(12) Drop batter by large spoonfuls into fat. Spoonfuls should be equivalent of No. 24 ice cream scoop. Spoon or scoop should be dipped into hot fat before dipping into batter for easy release of batter into deep fat. Do not crowd kettle with fritters. Fry them in small batches at a time.

(13) Fry, turning once, until medium brown on both sides. Fritters may be tested for doneness by piercing with a skewer or single prong of kitchen fork. The skewer should show no sign of wet batter when withdrawn.

(14) Using frying basket remove fritters from fat and drain at once on absorbent paper toweling. If fritters must be held before they are served, place them in a shallow tray in a warm dry

spot such as the shelf above the ranges rather than in an enclosed food warming unit where the fritters may become soggy.

Potatoes Lyonnaise   **50 Portions, Approx 4 Oz Each**

Potatoes *lyonnaise* are prepared by sautéing boiled sliced potatoes as well as onions. Sautéd potatoes without onions are normally listed on menus as home fried potatoes. When onions are added, the French term invariably is used. If only one or two portions of potatoes *lyonnaise* are being prepared for an a la carte order, the fry cook browns them in a long oval shape in the corner of the pan, and turns them out onto a plate or platter, brown side up. But when large quantities of potatoes *lyonnaise* are prepared, they are sautéd in extra large frying pans, browned on the bottom and then flipped over and browned on the other side. The job of flipping a large quantity of food while keeping its shape intact is something a student cannot learn by written directions. It must be mastered by first observing experienced cooks and then by flipping small portions at a time. Gradually the portions are increased until the cook learns how to confidently handle larger and larger quantities. In some modern kitchens, volume sautéing is done in a tilting frying pan, a rectangular unit with a large cooking surface and a wide range of temperatures. When this equipment is used, the potatoes and onions are not flipped but merely stirred from time to time for uniform browning.

Normally potatoes are boiled by the vegetable cook who passes them to the fry cook for browning. It is important to alert the vegetable cook to the fact that potatoes should not be overcooked, or the slices will disintegrate in the frying pan. To keep slices intact, whole cooked potatoes are first cooled for several hours before they are sliced. Sometimes potatoes are cooked unpeeled, cooled and then sliced in order to keep the potatoes from breaking apart when they are sautéd. Finally, in some large volume feeding operations, potatoes *lyonnaise* or home fried potatoes are ovenized, that is, cooked in baking pans in a very hot oven. The procedure requires less attention on the part of the fry cook, but the potatoes sometimes develop a "steamy" leftover flavor, and their color is not the deep brown of potatoes sautéd in a pan.

Before starting work: Review slicing onions. Examine large frying pans to make sure there are no built-up deposits from previous uses which might cause food to stick. If pans need cleaning and seasoning, follow the procedure on p 104.

(1) Assemble the following ingredients:

16 lb medium size potatoes in the jacket, boiled until just tender, drained and cooled several hours

3 lb onions, cut julienne

1 lb hydrogenated vegetable fat or oil

1/4 lb clarified butter

Salt, pepper

Paprika (optional)

(2) Peel potatoes. Remove any eyes or discolored portions. For this kind of peeling cooks usually use a table knife or paring knife.

(3) Cut potatoes lengthwise into halves or quarters in order to make slices approx 1 in. square in size. Because of their shape, potatoes will not be literally square, but they should be as close to this size as possible.

(4) Spread potatoes in shallow baking pans or utility pans. Potatoes should be no more than 2 in. deep to permit exposure to air so that potatoes are as dry as possible before sautéing. Keep them in pans for an hour or longer if possible.

(5) Heat butter over a moderate flame in a frying pan large enough to accommodate onions. Add onions. Sprinkle lightly with salt.

(6) Sauté onions, stirring frequently, only until onions are limp. Avoid cooking to the yellow or brown stage. Set aside.

(7) Melt shortening or pour oil to a depth of 1/4 in. in 2 extra large frying pans. When shortening or oil are hot (wave-like motion may be observed) lower potatoes carefully into pans. Spread potatoes in pans so that they are uniformly distributed to edge of pans. Sprinkle generously with salt and pepper. Sprinkle lightly with paprika if desired. (Paprika is a flavoring component and also adds to browning.) Spread onions over potatoes.

(8) After several minutes, stir a small portion of potatoes from bottom with spatula. If they are browning slowly, stir all the potatoes gently. (Stirring will distribute seasonings and onions).

(9) Keep potatoes on moderate to high heat until potatoes are uniformly browned on bottom. A spatula may be used to check color of potatoes around edge of pan without disturbing bottom.

(10) Flip potatoes so that bottom crust is on top.

(11) Continue to sauté potatoes, without stirring, until a medium-brown crust is formed on bottom.

(12) Before turning potatoes out of pans, move potatoes in pans

to make sure they are not sticking to bottom or sides. Loosen potatoes on side of pans, if necessary, with spatula. Turn potatoes onto steam table pans, keeping top and bottom crusts intact if possible.

(13) Before serving, check portions with instructor or supervisor.

Fried Oysters   **50 Portions, 6 Oysters Each**

The procedure for breading foods prior to frying, called *à l'anglaise* in French kitchens, has many variations. Normally it is a coating of flour, beaten eggs and bread crumbs, each applied successively to the food to be fried. Some chefs skip the flour, and dip the food only into eggs and bread crumbs in order to keep the coating as light as possible. Some recipes call for white bread crumbs made from somewhat stale, but not hard, white bread from which the crusts have been removed. White crumbs made in this manner help preserve the delicate flavors of such seafoods as scallops and oysters. Other formulas call for cracker crumbs or a mixture of bread crumbs and cornmeal. Each combination is designed to give a preferred texture to the particular food being fried.

Oysters have a large moisture content, a factor which causes breaded oysters to become "sweated" or soggy especially if they are held for prolonged periods before they are fried. To deal with this problem, some chefs apply a double breading to the oysters, that is, dip them in eggs and bread crumbs and then repeat the process a second time, a practice which makes for a thick coating. Still others bread the oysters with a single coating and then liberally sprinkle them with additional crumbs while the oysters are held in the refrigerator prior to frying. Excess crumbs are shaken off before frying. No matter which of these optional methods of breading is used, it is best not to bread oysters too far in advance of the cooking. If a period of about a half hour is allowed after breading and before frying, the oysters will not ooze excess moisture.

Before starting work: If oysters are freshly opened on the premises, and are in their own liquor, allow the oysters to drain about 1/2 to 1 hour before breading. Allow enough time to examine the oysters carefully to remove any pieces of shell or foreign matter. (Normally oysters are breaded by the *garde manger* and are passed to the fry cook for frying.) If you are handling the complete job, check with your instructor or supervisor on the type of crumbs to be used.

(1) Assemble the following ingredients:

   300 large size shucked oysters (selects), drained
   2 lb flour
   2 tablespoons salt

1 tablespoon celery salt
2 teaspoons ground black pepper
16 eggs
1/4 cup cooking oil
1 pt milk
2 lb (approx 2 qt) white bread crumbs
1 cup cornmeal
Fat for deep frying
Salt
50 lemon wedges
3 qt tartar sauce

(2) Combine flour, salt, celery salt and pepper in a utility pan, mixing well.
(3) Beat eggs, oil and milk in a shallow bowl, using a wire whip; no whites of eggs should be visible after beating.
(4) Combine bread crumbs and cornmeal in a utility pan, mixing well.
(5) If oysters are draining in colander, gently stir oysters to drain as thoroughly as possible. Oysters are soft and tender, and careless handling may break them.
(6) Spread oysters between clean paper or cloth toweling and gently pat dry.
(7) Examine oysters a second time to make sure there are no pieces of shell or foreign matter.
(8) Place oysters in batches in flour mixture. Do not crowd pan, or oysters may become matted. Roll oysters in flour by moving pan back and forth.
(9) Lift oysters from flour and drop into bowl with egg mixture.
(10) Move bowl back and forth or rotate bowl to cover oysters with egg mixture.
(11) Lift oysters from egg mixture, holding momentarily to let excess egg wash flow into bowl, and drop into bread crumbs.
(12) Roll in bread crumbs by moving pan back and forth to coat oysters completely. Pat crumbs lightly onto oysters to make coating firm.
(13) Carefully lift breaded oysters to shallow pan or tray which has been sprinkled lightly with bread crumbs. Do not pile oysters more than 2 deep in pan or tray.
(14) Chill oysters in refrigerator about a half hour before frying.
(15) Preheat deep fat to 370° F.
(16) Place oysters in frying basket (no more than a single layer at a time).
(17) Lower oysters slowly into deep fat; be prepared to withdraw basket if bubbling rises too high.

(18) Fry until medium brown, usually about 2 min.

(19) Drain oysters briefly in basket over fat. Remove basket from fat, and sprinkle oysters lightly with salt.

(20) Carefully turn oysters onto serving plates or platters.

(21) Garnish each portion with a wedge of lemon. Serve tartar sauce in sauce boat or paper soufflé cup, allowing about 1/4 cup per portion.

Breaded Fried Chicken   48 Portions

In kitchens where there is a *garde manger*, the latter breads the chicken and passes it to the fry cook. The entire procedure is outlined below. Foods for frying usually are of uniform size to ensure that some pieces are not kept in the frying pan so long that they absorb excess fat. Chicken cut up for frying, however, is a food that cannot be of uniform thickness. The wing, leg, second joint and breast are all of different dimensions. To ensure uniform browning without undue fat absorption, all pieces of chicken are fried only until their color is light brown; they are still raw in the center. The chicken is then removed from the frying pan and baked in a slow oven until all pieces are tender and done. Chicken prepared in this manner may be fried either in shallow or deep fat. Because of the considerable amount of bread crumbs that fall into the pan, many chefs prefer to fry the chicken in shallow fat, and then discard the fat after it is used. Special care must be taken to ensure that the crumb coating adheres firmly to the chicken, as the coating may fall off if the chicken is carelessly handled in the frying pan or carelessly transferred to the baking pan.

In kitchens which have an abundance of chicken fat, the fat is sometimes rendered and strained. It is then combined in equal proportions with hydrogenated fat or oil and used for frying. Another fat combination, somewhat more expensive, is half oil and half clarified butter. The chicken fat emphasizes the chicken flavor. Clarified butter gives a somewhat more delicate flavor to the final product. In the majority of restaurants, hydrogenated fat or vegetable oils are used for their neutral flavor and economy.

Before starting work: If bread crumbs were previously used for breading, strain them through a china cap or wire strainer. Make sure they have no off-odor or stale flavor. Arrange your work station so that it is possible to work from left to right with the containers of flour, eggs and bread crumbs arranged in that order.

(1) Assemble the following ingredients:

12 chickens, 2 3/4 to 3 lb each, cut for frying. (Chicken thus prepared is first drawn, washed and dried; the neck is

removed and the chicken is separated into breast pieces, legs and second joints, allowing 1 piece of white meat and 1 piece of dark meat per portion.)

2 lb flour (variable)
2 tablespoons salt
1 1/2 teaspoons white pepper
16 eggs
1/4 cup cooking oil
1 pt milk
2 lb bread crumbs (variable)
Fat for frying, either hydrogenated fat or oil

(2) Preheat oven to 325° F.
(3) Pour flour into a utility pan or steam table size pan. Add salt and pepper. Stir well.
(4) In a large bowl beat eggs with wire whip until whites are no longer visible. Add cooking oil and milk. Stir until well blended.
(5) Place bread crumbs in utility pan or larger size pan.
(6) Place chicken in a large pan at left hand side of pan with flour.
(7) Place 2 utility pans at end of line for receiving breaded chicken.
(8) Roll chicken in flour. Place enough chicken in pan so that the pan can be moved back and forth, coating the chicken completely. If necessary to coat some pieces of chicken by hand, use right hand.
(9) With right hand lift chicken from flour, shake to remove excess flour, and lower into egg wash, adding only enough pieces to coat chicken without crowding bowl.
(10) Move or rotate bowl so that chicken is completely covered by egg wash. Be sure each piece is completely coated—there should be no "bald" spots which permit excessive fat absorption.
(11) With left hand, lift chicken from eggs, holding pieces briefly above bowl to let excess fat drip off.
   Note: The reason for using one hand only for dipping in egg wash and the other hand for coating chicken with bread crumbs is to keep the hands from becoming matted while applying coating.
(12) Lower chicken into bread crumbs.
(13) With right hand roll chicken in bread crumbs by moving pan quickly back and forth. Use right hand to move pan, and to

pat bread crumb coating so that it adheres firmly to chicken. Place breaded chicken in reserved pans.

(14) Heat fat to a depth of 1/2 in. in very large frying pans. Use a moderate flame.

(15) When fat is hot, lower pieces of chicken into pan. Sauté chicken on both sides until chicken is light brown. Use a pair of tongs or spatula to turn chicken. Avoid breaking bread crumb coating.

(16) Place browned chicken on lightly greased baking sheets in a single layer. Do not use deep roasting pans which prevent chicken from browning in oven.

(17) Continue to sauté chicken in this manner until all of it is ready to bake. Wipe pans clean and add fresh fat when necessary.

(18) Place chicken in oven. Bake 30 to 40 min or until chicken is medium brown, and chicken feels tender when second joint and drumstick are pierced with skewer or kitchen fork. It is not necessary to turn chicken on baking sheets, although pans may be moved for uniform browning.

(19) If chicken is to be held for service, store it in a warming unit set at 160° F. It may also be stored in a steam table pan with cover.

Chicken Velouté Sauce or Cream Sauce.—Either may be served with fried chicken. Pour sauce on serving plate or platter before adding chicken so that crisp coating is not covered. Either sauce may also be served in a sauce boat. Prepare 3 qt sauce for 50 portions.

Bread Crumb Coating.—This may be omitted, dipping chicken merely in seasoned flour before sautéing it.

Chicken a la Maryland.—Prepare fried chicken as above. Serve it with one or two slices of crisp bacon, a corn fritter and cream sauce.

Breaded Veal Cutlet, Tomato Sauce   12 Portions, Approx 4 Oz Each

Breaded veal cutlet is normally made one portion at a time, or if it is featured on a table d'hôte menu, a half dozen portions at a time may be made for rapid service. It is seldom prepared in large quantities because the flat thin cutlets rapidly lose their crispness upon standing in the steam table. Unlike breaded chicken in the previous recipe, which is cooked in both the frying pan and the oven where the pieces of chicken become uniformly browned, veal cutlets are cooked only in the pan. Although they are flat, the cutlets are not always in complete contact with the pan bottom. Some of the cutlets will become brown before others. It may be necessary to move the pan from time to time for uniform browning. Each cutlet must be turned at the right moment to brown both sides evenly. If multiple orders are being prepared (the recipe below calls for 2 batches of 6 orders each), the pan must be quickly wiped and dried, and then reheated with fresh fat before sautéing can be continued. If the temperature of the fat in the pan is too low, the cutlets will be grease soaked. If it is too high, the breading may be burned while the meat is undone. Fat from the pan sputters almost constantly on the range which must be wiped dry to avoid dangerous flaming. It is, therefore, a frying job which requires constant alertness on the part of the cook.

Before starting work: Check quantity of leftover tomato sauce, if any. Check sauce for soundness. It should have no off-odor or off-flavor, and should show no sign of bubbling or fermentation when stirred. Notify instructor or supervisor if additional sauce is needed. Review procedure for breading chicken in previous recipe.

(1) Assemble the following ingredients:

> 12 veal cutlets, 4 oz each, 1/2 in. thick when cut, pounded with meat mallet to 1/4 in. thickness
> 1/2 lb flour
> 1 teaspoon salt
> 1/2 teaspoon black pepper
> 3 eggs
> 2 tablespoons cooking oil
> 1/2 cup milk
> 1/2 lb bread crumbs
> Fat for sautéing, either hydrogentated fat or oil
> 3 cups tomato sauce (p 220)

(2) Heat sauce in steam table or over moderate flame. Keep in steam table until needed.

(3) Pour flour into utility pan or steam table size pan. Add salt and pepper. Stir well to blend seasonings.

(4) In shallow bowl beat eggs, 2 tablespoons oil and milk until well blended.

(5) Pour bread crumbs into utility pan or steam table size pan. If bread crumbs were previously used for a breading job, strain them.

(6) On work table, beginning at left hand side, arrange from left to right the veal in a pan, flour, egg wash and bread crumbs.

Place an empty pan or container at end of line to receive the breaded cutlets.

(7) Place cutlets in flour. Roll veal in flour by quickly moving pan back and forth with right hand.

(8) With right hand, lift veal from flour, shaking cutlets to remove excess flour.

(9) Lower cutlets one by one into egg wash.

(10) Coat cutlets with eggs by moving bowl back and forth or rotating it, tossing veal in liquid. Be sure each piece is completely coated; any uncoated spots will keep bread crumbs from adhering.

(11) With left hand, lift cutlets from eggs, holding cutlets briefly above bowl to allow excess egg wash to drip off.

(12) Still using left hand, lower cutlets into bread crumbs.

(13) Roll cutlets in bread crumbs, moving pan quickly back and forth with right hand so that crumbs swirl over cutlets. Pat bread crumbs into meat so that coating is firm.

(14) Place cutlets in reserved pan. Cutlets may be refrigerated a half hour if not needed at once. If refrigerated for a longer period, check bread crumb coating to make sure it is not moist. Pat additional crumbs into cutlets if necessary.

(15) Choose a long-handled frying pan large enough to hold 6 cutlets at one time. Wipe it clean if necessary.

(16) Melt fat or heat oil to a depth of 1/4 in. in pan.

(17) When fat is hot, with visible wave-like motions (but not smoking), lower cutlets carefully, one at a time, into pan.

(18) Sauté until cutlets are medium brown. Check bottoms of cutlets from time to time for browning. Move pan if necessary to brown uniformly.

(19) When each cutlet is brown on bottom, turn it carefully but quickly with spatula. A finger of the left hand may be used to "steady" the cutlet as it is being lifted to turn so that it will not splash in pan. Hold head back to avoid sputtering fat.

(20) Sauté cutlets until brown on second side.

(21) Drain cutlets on absorbent paper. If not served at once, keep in steam table pan or in pan placed on oven shelf.

(22) Drain fat from pan. Wipe pan clean. Repeat steps 16 to 21 with remainder of cutlets.

   Note: Experienced cooks might use 2 pans at a time for a job of this size.

(23) To serve each cutlet pour 1/4 cup tomato sauce on plate or platter. Place veal cutlet on top of sauce. Do not pour sauce over cutlet.

Veal Cutlet a la Holstein.—Prepare cutlets as above. Garnish each cutlet with a lemon slice half covered with chopped hard egg and remainder with chopped parsley. On top of the egg place an anchovy filet wrapped around a pitted green olive.

French Fried Potatoes   **50 Portions, Approx 3 Oz Each**

Many of the recipes in this chapter have dealt with foods that are coated before being fried. Potatoes, however, are one of the few foods which are uncoated before frying. Of all types of fried potatoes, French fried are not only the most popular, but are an example of a fried food which is usually superior in the restaurant version as against the same food cooked in homes, assuming the restaurant is a quality eating place. Homemakers usually fry French fried potatoes by cooking them in a one-step operation in the fry kettle. Fry cooks in commercial eating places, however, generally use a two-step procedure called blanch–finish or blanch and brown, which produces potatoes with a crisp but tender brown crust and a light moist interior. The two-step operation, described in the recipe below, permits the fry cook to prepare potatoes during off-meal periods, to complete the frying in a final step which takes less than 2 min, and guarantees that the potatoes are piping hot when the waiter picks them up in the kitchen for serving.

Many restaurants now buy frozen French fried potatoes which are precut and are ready to be fried. In top quality kitchens, however, the fry cook must know this job from the raw to the finished state. If raw potatoes have been stored in a cool area, 40° to 60°F, they should be held at room temperature, approx 70°F, for one day before they are prepared. The best potatoes for French frying are the so-called baking potatoes. Their size is uniform. They have a smooth skin with shallow eyes and a mealy texture which makes them light and tender. Potatoes are usually peeled by machine, using an abrasion method. Eyes and dark spots or other defects are removed by hand. The round edges of the potatoes should be cut off so that the potatoes are flat on the ends. Potato trimmings may be used for home fried, hashed brown or other potato dishes. The ideal length of the potatoes is from 3 to 3 1/2 in. Since potatoes cut by hand cannot be exactly uniform in size, a French fry cutter should be used. If raw potatoes are to be held for more than 15 min after they are cut, they should be steeped in cold water to prevent discoloration.

Before starting work: Review 18 guides to deep fat frying. The job of paring and trimming potatoes is usually assigned to the vegetable cook who may or may not trim and cut the potatoes for French frying. Check with your instructor or supervisor on your exact duties. Since the recipe below is for the two-stage preparation, allow enough time for the potatoes to cool so that they are ready to be finished during the meal period.

(1) Assemble the following ingredients:
20 lb peeled potatoes (weight after peeling)
Fat for deep frying
Salt

(2) Using a paring knife, remove any eyes, dark spots, green sections or any other defects from potatoes. If job is inter-rupted or potatoes must be held during the following steps, steep potatoes temporarily in cold water.

(3) Cut off a slice from each end of the potatoes so that ends will be flat. Cut off any irregular protuberance of potatoes which would prevent them from being uniformly cut.

(4) Force potatoes through French fry cutter using die with 3/8-in. thickness.

(5) Place potatoes in 1 or 2 bowls or pots and wash with slowly running cold water to remove surface starch.

(6) When wash water is clear, drain potatoes in colander.

(7) Preheat deep fat to 350°F. Use several kettles if possible to complete blanching as quickly as possible.

(8) Dry potatoes as much as possible, using clean towels, dis-carded table tops, table cloths or some other material. (Wet potatoes lowered into fat will cause excess bubbling and also cause fat to deteriorate rapidly.)

(9) Fill baskets with no more than the maximum load ratio suggested by the equipment manufacturer.

(10) Lower potatoes very slowly into fat. Be prepared to withdraw the basket if bubbles rise too quickly and fat shows signs of overflowing. Return potatoes very slowly to fat as bubbling subsides.

(11) Fry potatoes until they are barely tender but not brown. Test potatoes by piercing them with a kitchen fork. The amount of time required for blanching usually varies from 5 to 7 min.

(12) Let potatoes drain above fat for a minute or two. Do not salt potatoes. They will be salted later. Turn potatoes into shallow pans or baking sheets. They should not be piled high, or steam will form and potatoes may break and become soggy. Spread potatoes to a depth of 2 to 3 in., no higher.

(13) Let blanched potatoes reach approx room temperature, allowing about an hour.

(14) Preheat deep fat to 375° F for finishing potatoes.
(15) As potatoes are ordered, fry them until medium brown. Remove basket from fat, drain for a moment and sprinkle potatoes with salt. When the basket is shaken to distribute the salt, the potatoes will have a sound which is compared to the rustle of peanuts and indicates crispness.
(16) Turn potatoes from basket onto warm serving plates or platter. A cold dish will spoil crispness of potatoes. Platters may be lined with paper doilies or cloth napkins. Potatoes, however, should not be covered for service. Use whatever routine is in effect in your kitchen to have waiters pick up potatoes at once. Keeping them for any length of time on a warm shelf or under warming lamps will cause quality to deteriorate.

Long Branch Potatoes or Allumette Potatoes.—Cut potatoes 1/4 in. thick instead of 3/8 in. thick.

Parisienne Potatoes.—Cut potatoes into balls with parisienne potato cutter, using large end of utensil. In some restaurants, parisienne potatoes are sautéd rather than deep fried.

Noisette Potatoes.—Using a parisienne potato cutter, cut potatoes into balls using small end of utensil. In some restaurants, *noisette* potatoes are sautéd rather than deep fried.

Gaufrette Potatoes.—Using whole potatoes, cut slices from end of potatoes using a *gaufrette* (waffle-shaped) cutter. Allow potatoes to blanch as briefly as possible until barely tender. Total cooking time is usually about 5 min.

Julienne Potatoes or Shoe String Potatoes.—Cut whole potatoes into slices no thicker than 1/8 in. Cut slices into strips about 1/8 in. thick, forming julienne strips. Potatoes may be cut in mechanical vegetable cutter. Reduce blanching time until potatoes are barely tender.

Calf's Liver and Bacon, Maitre d'Hotel Butter   **12 Portions**

Although the recipe below specifies quantities for 12 portions, calf's liver, when sautéd, is almost always made to order for optimum quality which means the liver must be hot and tender, with a crisp coating and juicy inside. The maitre d'hotel butter is made ready beforehand, while the bacon is partially cooked and finished at the last moment. Like other very tender meats, calf's liver is often ruined by overcooking. Two or three minutes of sautéing on each side are sufficient to cook thin slices of calf's liver to a proper stage of doneness. Just before cooking, the liver is dipped in seasoned flour to form a light, crisp coating. If the liver is dredged in flour and is allowed to stand for prolonged periods, or if the fat in which it is sautéd is not sufficiently hot, the flour coating will be gummy and greasy. As in testing broiled foods, the doneness of liver may be checked by simple hand pressure or by touching it with the tines of a fork. It is resilient when rare, and becomes firm when well-done. When the meat has been sautéd on one side, the top side will show droplets of pink juice when the meat is medium rare. Calf's liver should be sliced just before it is to be sautéd. If sliced and left standing, there will be an excessive loss of juice and flavor. The *garde manger* should be ready to supply the liver quickly when the fry cook calls for it.

Before starting work: If there is any leftover partially cooked bacon from breakfast or any leftover maitre d'hotel butter, check them for quality and, if possible, use them in the recipe below. Arrange to have 2 or 3 different size frying pans on hand, wiped dry, ready for sautéing. Plan to arrange the sliced liver, pan with seasoned flour, and fat or oil for frying within a compact area for fast efficient movement.

(1) Assemble the following ingredients:

    24 slices calf's liver, about 2 oz each and about 3/8 in. thick

    24 slices bacon

    1/2 lb butter

    1 tablespoon lemon juice

    2 tablespoons very finely chopped parsley

    1/2 lb flour

    1 teaspoon salt

    1/2 teaspoon black pepper

    Hydrogenated fat or cooking oil

    1 bunch watercress, 1 in. cut off stem bottoms, washed and dried

(2) Preheat oven to 375° F.

(3) Separate bacon slices. Avoid tearing slices. If bacon is very cold and slices are not easily separated, let bacon stand at room temperature until it softens somewhat, and is less brittle. Place slices in a shallow baking pan with fat side of each slice overlapping the lean portion of the next slice.

(4) Place bacon in oven, and bake until it loses its raw appearance

and shows signs of curling, about 10 to 12 min. Lift bacon from pan with spatula or fork, and place bacon over back of plate for draining. Place in steam table or warming unit until needed. Very carefully pour off accumulated bacon fat, holding pan with 1 or 2 heavy towels. Check with instructor or supervisor on disposition of bacon fat; it may be used for cooking.

(5) Let butter stand at room temperature until it is soft enough to spread easily. Stir in lemon juice and parsley until well blended. Set aside until needed. Do not allow butter to melt. Return to refrigerator briefly if necessary.

(6) Pour flour, salt and pepper into utility pan, and stir until well blended.

(7) Heat fat to a depth of 1/4 in. in frying pan. Fat must be hot but not smoking. A wavelike motion is visible when it is hot.

(8) Roll calf's liver in flour, coating thoroughly. Shake off excess flour. Allow 2 slices liver per portion.

(9) Lower—do not drop—liver into pan. Sauté about 2 min on each side or until medium brown. Look for droplets of juice just before turning.

(10) While liver is sautéing, place bacon under broiler flame or in deep fat at 370° F until bacon is crisp. Allow 2 slices per portion. It may also be finished on a griddle or in a frying pan. Bacon is sometimes finished by the broiler cook rather than by the fry cook if it is impractical for the latter to use the broiler.

(11) Place 2 slices liver per portion on warm plate or serving platter. Dab with maitre d'hotel butter, using a pastry brush or spoon.

(12) Arrange 2 slices bacon on each portion calf's liver. Garnish with several sprigs of watercress placed alongside liver.

Beef Liver.—This may be prepared in same manner as calf's liver.

Turkey and Mushroom Croquettes   50 Portions, 2 Croquettes Each

Croquettes are made from a cooked or leftover food, such as turkey or chicken, bound with a sauce thick enough to allow the mixture to be shaped, breaded and deep fried. The French word *croquer*, from which croquette is derived, means to crunch. Often croquettes are fried too far in advance and become soggy in a steam table, before being served. Sometimes the sauce accompanying the croquettes is poured over them rather than on the plate beneath the croquettes, thus destroying the crunchiness which is the first indication of quality. In some restaurants turkey for croquettes is chopped until it is finely minced or else put through a meat grinder. In better kitchens the turkey meat is cut by hand into very small dice no larger than 1/4 in. thick. Some of the dice may break up during cooking, but sufficient will remain so that distinct pieces of turkey are evident in the finished product. The recipe below calls for both soft bread crumbs and dried bread crumbs. The former are made from white bread, 2 or 3 days old, trimmed of all crust; the latter are made from 4- or 5-day-old bread including the crust.

Before starting work: The job of making croquettes is one in which the steps are normally shared by a number of cooks. Check in advance with your supervisor or instructor to find out if you are to perform the whole job or part of it. If you are assigned to cut the turkey, this phase of the job should be started early on the day before the croquettes are to be served. This will allow the croquette mixture to be made and chilled overnight for proper handling and shaping. Be sure the fat for frying the croquettes is either fresh or has been well filtered and is not discolored.

(1) Assemble the following ingredients:

    7 lb (weight after trimming) cooked turkey, preferably boiled, trimmed of all skin, fat, gristle or hard ends, 1/4-in. dice

    2 lb fresh mushrooms, 1/4-in. dice

    1 lb onions, chopped very fine

    1 1/2 lb butter

    12 oz flour

    1 qt hot milk

    1 qt hot chicken broth

    6 egg yolks, beaten slightly

    1/2 lb soft bread crumbs (variable)

    Salt, pepper

    2 lb flour (variable)

    12 eggs

    1 pt milk

    3 lb dried bread crumbs (variable)

    Fat for deep frying

    3 qt 1 pt sauce *suprême* (p 212)

(2) Melt butter in heavy saucepan over low flame.

(3) Add onions, and sauté only until onions are light yellow.

(4) Add mushrooms and sauté, stirring frequently, until all mushroom liquor has disappeared from pan.

(5) Remove pan from fire. Stir in 12 oz flour slowly, blending until no dry flour is visible.

(6) Return pan to moderate flame.

(7) Slowly stir in hot milk, mixing well as milk is added.

(8) Slowly stir in hot chicken broth, mixing well as broth is added.

(9) Bring mixture to a boil.

(10) Add turkey, blending well.

(11) Slowly stir in 6 egg yolks.

(12) Simmer 5 min, stirring frequently, until mixture again bubbles.

(13) Stir in 1 cup soft bread crumbs. (Check with supervisor or instructor on thickness of mixture.) Add more crumbs if necessary. Mixture must be very thick.

(14) Preheat oven to 375° F.

(15) Season croquette mixture with salt and pepper. Turn mixture into a greased shallow baking pan. Use 2 pans if necessary.

(16) Bake in oven 1/2 hour. Stir mixture every 10 min to make sure it is not sticking.

Note: Baking the croquette mixture eliminates the taste of raw flour and helps bind the mixture.

(17) Remove from oven. Chill, covered, overnight in refrigerator.

(18) Divide mixture into croquettes, using a No. 20 scoop for each croquette.

(19) Roll each croquette between palms of hands. If mixture seems too moist to handle, add a small amount of soft bread crumbs; use sparingly. Roll each ball on clean surface, using palm of hand to shape ball into cylinder. Tap each end of cylinder gently to flatten it. Arrange croquettes in shallow pan.

(20) Beat 12 eggs and milk in large shallow bowl.

(21) Set up 2 lb flour, beaten eggs and dried bread crumbs for breading; see procedure for breading chicken (p 118).

(22) Roll croquettes successively in flour, eggs and bread crumbs.

(23) After croquettes are breaded, tap ends or roll lightly again with palm of hand if necessary to reshape them.

(24) Place croquettes on pans lightly sprinkled with bread crumbs. Store in refrigerator until needed. Make sure sauce *suprême* is hot and in steam table ready for service.

(25) Heat deep fat to 360° F.

(26) Fry croquettes to order. Keep in fat until well-browned, about 3 min. Do not fill frying basket with more than a single layer of croquettes at one time.

(27) For each order, pour a 2-oz ladle of sauce *suprême* onto plate or platter.

(28) Place 2 croquettes on top of sauce.

Corned Beef Hash Browned   **50 Portions, Approx 8 Oz Each**

Like croquettes in the previous recipe, corned beef hash is a dish whose principal ingredient, corned beef, should be finely diced rather than chopped in a haphazard way. Corned beef hash is a mixture of cooked meat and potatoes. The potatoes bind the meat so that it coheres into a mass as it is being sautéd. If it is too dry, the hash will lose its shape and disintegrate in the pan. If it is too moist, it will stick to the pan and will not brown properly. To make the mixture cohesive, some of the potatoes may be mashed, and a small amount of cream added for moisture and flavor. If, after all the ingredients have been combined, the mixture seems too moist, it may be spread out in shallow pans so that exposure to the air will dry it. This means that the hash mixture should be ready for frying several hours before the meal period. If, at meal time, the hash still seems too moist, a small amount of white bread crumbs may be added, but this addition should be minimal to avoid flavor alteration. In the recipe below, the hash is browned one portion at a time in individual frying pans.

Before starting work: Make sure all pans are properly seasoned, that is, their surface is such that they do not cause food to stick.

(1) Assemble the following ingredients:
    10 lb boiled corned beef
    14 lb (cooked weight) peeled, freshly boiled potatoes
    Cooking oil
    2 1/2 lb onions, chopped very fine
    2 tablespoons garlic, chopped extremely fine
    1 pt light cream (variable)
    2 tablespoons Worcestershire sauce
    Salt, pepper
(2) Cut corned beef into 1/4-in. dice.
(3) Chop 2/3 of the potatoes fine.
(4) Put balance of potatoes through a potato ricer.
(5) Heat 1/2 cup oil in sauté pan over low flame.
(6) Add onions and garlic, and sauté until onions are tender but not brown. Stir frequently to prevent browning.
(7) In large shallow mixing bowl place corned beef, potatoes and onions.
(8) Combine cream and Worcestershire sauce, and pour over hash.
(9) Sprinkle with salt and pepper.

(10) Mix hash thoroughly. Add more cream if hash is not cohesive. Add salt and pepper if necessary.

(11) Sauté a small portion of hash to determine if it is too moist or too dry. Make corrections above if necessary.

Note: Before sautéing hash at mealtime, measure several portions on portion control scale as guide.

(12) When ready to brown hash, pour oil into frying pan, allowing about 2 tablespoons oil per pan. Swirl oil in pan, and pour back excess oil so that bottom and sides of pan are covered only with a light film of fat.

(13) Add corned beef hash to pan, and sauté over a moderate flame. Allow hash to brown lightly on bottom, and heat through.

(14) Move hash with spatula to corner of pan opposite handle so that it forms an oblong shape and rests on side of pan.

(15) Place pan over high heat until hash is deeply browned on bottom. Before serving, move hash slightly to make sure it is not sticking.

(16) To serve, place edge of pan on rim of serving plate. Tip pan quickly so that browned side of hash is up.

(17) If hash seems greasy, press it briefly with a clean towel, keeping shape of hash intact.

Poached Egg with Hash.—Poached egg is sometimes served with hash. Place egg on top center of hash.

Roast Beef Hash Browned.—Use cooked fresh beef instead of corned beef.

Chicken or Turkey Hash Browned.—Use cooked chicken or turkey instead of corned beef.

6

Broiler Cook (*Grillardin*)

When a sauce cook performs a routine job like making 50 portions of lamb stew, he sets about his work deliberately, simmering the stew in a single kettle until the meat slowly becomes tender, and the gravy's flavor is fully developed. He paces his work schedule so that the stew is finished comfortably before the lunch or dinner period. But a broiler cook who is required to turn out 50 a la carte orders of steaks, chops and seafood within the lunch or dinner period literally faces 50 distinct jobs, no 2 of which may be exactly alike. He must work quickly, weigh decisions with a glance, and be aware that if he is not constantly alert, the rare steak in a matter of minutes may become well-done, the chicken, dry, and the fish, tough. Some of the foods he handles are tender in their raw state, like fish, or can be made tender in a brief time like chops and steaks. These are among the most expensive items on the menu. The broiler cook, therefore, has special responsibilities to both management and customers, requiring unfaltering skill and attention.

There are charts which tell the student broiler cook how many minutes to cook typical menu items such as a 1-in. thick filet mignon, a 1/4-in. fillet of sole or a 2-in. English lamb chop. But if the student watches an experienced broiler cook in action, he sees that the veteran cook does not, and cannot, consult a chart for broiling time while watching the clock on the wall during a hectic meal period. As a matter of fact, the student will learn that if he compares the charts for one type of broiler with the charts for another type, they may differ radically. A 2-in. rare sirloin steak according to one set of directions will take 20 min total cooking time. A chart for another type of broiler shows 10 min total cooking time for the same job. The actual time taken for broiling the steak in a specific kitchen may differ from both charts. All these differences would suggest that, while first-hand job experience is the most important factor in learning the many-sided art of the broiler cook, experience itself in turn is governed by the particular broiler equipment with which the cook works. The two main types of broilers are described below.

JOB SUMMARY

The broiler cook (1) broils meats, poultry, seafood, game, vegetables and fruit; (2) may use broiler equipment, or make it available to other cooks, for completing au gratin dishes or other dishes where rapid top browning is required, (3) may use broiler for miscellaneous jobs such as making toast for broiled dishes or in large quantities for banquets, making croutons for onion soup, browning the skin of roast duckling, etc.; (4) orders foods cut into portions, ready for broiler, from butcher or *garde manger*; (5) may cut raw meat into individual portions and trim it for broiling when butcher or *garde manger* is off duty; (6) may broil in advance food in large quantities for banquets, for cafeteria service or for dining room service where a large number of orders of broiled foods are received within a short time during busy periods; (7) normally prepares broiled foods individually to order; (8) adds sauces prepared by sauce cook to certain broiled foods; (9) may make butter sauces for broiled foods; (10) garnishes broiled foods with watercress, toast, etc.; (11) places broiled foods on warm plates or platters, and may include, with the dish, vegetable components prepared by other cooks; (12) may assist fry cook or roast cook when necessary.

MANUAL PROCEDURES

Among his responsibilities he (1) checks broilers and broiler drip pans for cleanliness, and brushes or scrapes equipment, if necessary, to remove residues; (2) may add water to drip pans and replace it when necessary; (3) preheats broilers by lighting gas or turning electric switch; if charcoal fires are used, lights fires, spreads charcoal for even bed of fire, adjusts fires by adding fuel or dousing it with water to restrain flare-ups; (5) dips food in oil or clarified butter before broiling; (6) dips certain foods in bread crumbs or flour before broiling; (7) places food between wire broiler racks and tightens or loosens racks; (8) places racks on broiler grids, and turns racks to broil both sides of food; (9) places individual pieces of food directly on broiler grids, and turns food with fork, tongs or spatula to brown on both sides; (10) may season food before or after broiling by sprinkling with salt, pepper, paprika, etc.; (11) arranges small pieces of food on skewers for broiling; (12) turns skewers for browning food on both sides; (13) adjusts heat application of broiler by raising or lowering food from source of heat; (14) tests food for doneness by pressing with fingers or fork; (15) finishes cooking large pieces of food by removing them from broiler grid and placing them in oven above or below broiler; (16) sometimes pours drippings over broiled foods; brushes finished foods with butter sauces.

EQUIPMENT AND UTENSILS

He uses (1) heavy-duty broilers, sometimes with oven sections above or below broilers; (2) smaller broilers, called salamanders, positioned above range or other working surface; (3) broilers with heat source beneath food using either charcoal, chunks of ceramic material or other radiant elements; (4) broilers with heat source above food using gas or electricity; (5) hinged wire broiler racks; (6) utility pans for holding flour, bread crumbs, oil, etc.; (7) compartment pans with seasonings; (8) brushes for oil and butter sauces, brushes for dousing charcoal with water, knives, cleaver, meat mallet, tongs, forks, skimmers, spoons, spatulas of assorted sizes; (9) extra heavy towels for use with hot equipment; (10) burlap towels for wiping broiler grid; (11) scrapers and wire hair brushes or heavy-duty pot scrub brushes for cleaning broiler grids.

WORKING CONDITIONS AND HAZARDS

The broiler cook (1) works under pressure of producing varied orders in limited time; (2) must be constantly alert to sputtering flames, flare-ups, etc.; (3) must avoid sputtering fat as food broils or is being turned; (4) if ventilation is not adequate, may be exposed to heavy fumes and smoke; (5) space between broilers and serving areas is often, although not always, cramped.

PLACE IN JOB ORGANIZATION

The fry cook, breakfast cook or vegetable cook may be promoted to broiler cook. The broiler cook may be promoted to roast cook, roundsman or sauce cook.

TYPES OF BROILER EQUIPMENT

There are two main types of broilers, known as underfired or over-head, the former with the heat source beneath the food and the latter with the heat source above the food. There are also broilers with a radiant surface and source of heat on the side such as the revolving rotisserie type broiler with food fastened to a spit. These are found mostly in food shops where cooking takes place in view of the customers.

Underfired Equipment

Fifty years ago charcoal grills or coal-fired grills were common in restaurants. Some eating places still feature charcoal broilers in special areas of the dining room where showmanship is an important factor. Commercial charcoal broilers are operated on the same principle as outdoor home-style charcoal stoves. A bed of charcoal is lit and maintained with a draught of air beneath the fire. The fire is ready when the charcoal turns ashen gray. Charcoal must be added from time to time to maintain uniform heat and a bed of coals sufficiently deep for quantity broiling. To diminish the intensity of the heat, food is raised above the fire. To increase the heat, food is lowered toward the fire. Since flare-ups occur when melting fat drops into the fire, steaks and chops must be closely trimmed of most of their visible fat. Thick steaks of 4 to 6 portions each are difficult to broil since often they become excessively charred while remaining raw in the center. Certain delicate foods like sweetbreads or fillets of fish are not easily cooked in this manner. In many restaurants, instead of the charcoal fire, char broilers are used. These produce a charcoal broiled flavor, but instead of charcoal, chunks of long-lasting ceramic material are heated by gas or electricity. Meat juices and fat, falling into the bed of heat, convey the smoky flavor characteristic of wood or charcoal outdoor broilers. Thick steaks or steaks cooked to the medium or well-done stage are difficult to produce.

Overhead Broilers

In large volume kitchens, broilers with the heat source above the food are the most popular type used. The heavy-duty broiler which stands on the floor is often equipped with an oven section above or below the broiler. Some heavy-duty broilers are double-deck equipment, permitting the broiler cook to turn out a large quantity of food within a limited space. (Bending is necessary to check the food in the bottom section.) The salamander is a smaller broiler above a range or spreader area, and is useful in restaurants with limited broiler needs as well as in busy restaurants during slack periods.

12 GUIDES TO BROILING

(1) The performance of all types of broilers varies. Even the same models from the same manufacturer will sometimes produce different results. Some broilers are relatively slow, others fast. Some, like the infrared broilers, preheat in a minute or less, while others may take from 5 to 30 min to preheat. Some deliver heat with relative uniformity while others broil in a spotty pattern. If one were to pull forward the grid of a broiler, place slices of bread on it for toasting, and were then to place the grid under a preheated broiler flame, the chances are very good that some slices would become brown faster than others, and that some slices might even become charred while others were lightly browned. This common phenomena of unequal heat distribution is one of the first things the student must learn about any broiler with which he is working. Only when the pattern of heat distribution is accurately known will the broiler cook be able to control broiling by raising or lowering the grid or by shifting food from one section of the grid to another when necessary to avoid "hot" or "cold" spots. This is particularly important if the entire grid surface is covered with a large quantity of food being broiled at one time. Before starting any job of broiling, the student should determine the normal position of the grid for the specific food being cooked.

(2) Food just removed from the refrigerator will take a longer broiling period than food which has been standing at room temperature. For example, if broiled lamb chops are featured on a table d'hôte menu on a particular day, and are to be made to order, the broiler cook will receive a quantity of raw chops from the butcher and will keep the chops uncooked at his station rather than order them one by one from the butcher. (In some kitchens, the broiler cook works alongside a reach-in refrigerator where he can take the precut chops as needed.) The colder chops will take a slightly longer cooking period than those at room temperature. The broiler cook must also remember that thin chops at room temperature may become done in the center before the outside is sufficiently browned. Only chops, therefore, of medium or double thickness should be held at room temperature before broiling. Thin chops or thin steaks, 3/4 of an in. or less in thickness, should always be at refrigerator temperature for best broiling results.

(3) One of the broiler cook's most important skills is the ability to

recognize degrees of doneness. Time and again amateur cooks broil meat to a crisp brownness, and then cut the meat only to find that it is raw in the center. Theoretically, one could insert a specially designed thermometer with a thin stem into each piece of broiled food, but this procedure is not practical in a busy restaurant. All sensory evaluations are subjective and vary from one person to another. But, in spite of individual variations, certain senses are not only useful but absolutely indispensable in learning the art of broiling including determining when foods are done.

The sense of *taste* is of little practical use to the broiler cook. A soup cook or sauce cook can, and should, taste soups and sauces, but a broiler cook cannot cut a slice off the broiled chicken or the thick steak before it is taken to the dining room.

The sense of *smell* may tell us in a limited way that broiling is progressing. The aroma of lobsters under the fire or the aroma of thick hamburgers browning on a char broiler reveal that the process of broiling is taking place but do not tell us how far the broiling has progressed except in certain instances where food is excessively charred and, perhaps, ruined. Another reason why the sense of smell is of limited value is the fact that cooks working for prolonged periods at broilers giving off a large amount of fumes are exposed to so many food odors, often of great intensity, that they temporarily suffer from "nose fatigue" and, at times, may be indifferent to odors that they would recognize more easily in a different setting.

The sense of *sight* tells us when broiled food is browned, and the degree of brownness is extremely important. For instance, if a cook is broiling sea trout 3/4 in. thick, the fish will usually be done when it is a deep golden brown. This is one case where the fish is not turned during broiling, since the heat is able to completely penetrate fish of that thickness from one side. The cook notes that as the broiling proceeds, the fish shrinks somewhat and that eventually the reduced size is a clue to the fact that the trout is done. Other foods like thick steaks, thick chops, etc., may become well-browned on both sides and remain undone in the center. Such foods are transferred from the broiler to the oven to complete the cooking. Not all foods brown at the same rate. Shell steaks, for instance, which are well-marbled, that is, contain a large quantity of small fat pieces mixed with the lean, will brown easily without added fat. The cook recognizing the degree of marbling will expect a certain browning result to follow. The sense of sight also reveals the altered shape of certain foods as they become done. A lamb chop, for instance, not only shrinks during broiling, but as the cooking continues, the chop tends to round out on both sides, assuming a somewhat bulging shape; the outside muscles contract noticeably because the exterior temperature of the chop is higher than the interior. As the meat changes shape, the cook notices small droplets of juice that appear on the surface, indicating that the meat has reached the medium-rare stage. The juice that flows from broiled chicken tells another story. Chicken is always broiled to the well-done stage. It is one of the few broiled foods pierced with a fork to determine its doneness. When the juice flowing from the chicken is clear rather than pink, the broiled chicken is done. If no juice is seen to flow, it is overdone.

To the broiler cook, the most valuable of all senses for judging doneness is the sense of *touch*. Chops or steaks at the very rare stage will be resilient, almost "bouncy", when they are pressed. As they become more well-done, the meat becomes more firm. At one time all broiler cooks were taught to quickly touch and test meats by pressing them with the first and second fingers. The practice is still widely followed. Many cooks prefer to test the meat by pressing it with the back of a fork. One must be careful in testing meats in this manner not to be misled by a loose muscle which will yield under pressure no matter how well-done the meat may be. Using the tactile sense in this manner is something the student cannot learn from a table or chart. Only careful observation working alongside, and with an experienced broiler cook will develop mastery of this important skill.

(4) It was mentioned above that certain thick foods are browned on the broiler, and then are transferred to the oven to complete the cooking. If the oven is above the broiler, and receives its heat from the broiler flame, the oven temperature will usually be in the high heat range, and foods may become overcooked if not frequently checked for doneness. The broiler cook should, therefore, be as familiar with the oven and the way it performs as he is with the broiler itself. In a busy kitchen where the broiler cook receives a large variety of orders, he must not only be in the habit of keeping his eyes on the visible food on the broiler, but also must remember and check the unseen foods placed in the oven for finishing.

(5) Almost all meats, poultry and seafood are brushed with oil or dipped in oil before broiling. Oil hastens browning and helps to prevent dryness and shriveling. It also helps to prevent food from sticking to the grid and possibly tearing when it is turned or removed from the broiler. Any vegetable oil used for cooking purposes may be used. If foods are dipped in flour before broiling, the flour coating should be applied first and the food should then be dipped in oil or brushed with oil. At one time it was the practice to add salt, pepper

and paprika to oil used for broiled foods. Salt, however, retards browning of meat, and should be added after broiling. Most broiler cooks nowadays use unseasoned oil, and add seasonings when necessary.

(6) Skill in using hand tools is extremely important for the broiler cook. The important utensils are a two-tined heavy fork, a pair of tongs, spatulas, including a heavy offset spatula as well as a thin spatula (palette knife), and hinged wire grills called broiler racks. When a fork is used for turning food extreme care must be taken not to jab steaks or chops in such a way that the juice of the meat is lost. The fork should be inserted into the fat side of the steak or chop rather than through the lean section of the meat. Using tongs eliminates the danger of unnecessary piercing, although some cooks find tongs awkward in handling large pieces of food. If meat is not held firmly by the tong ends, it may easily be dropped. A wide offset spatula is best for turning delicate foods such as fish which may break if the spatula is not large enough. A thin pliable spatula is helpful in loosening foods which may stick to a wire grill or pan sometimes used in broiling. Hinged wire grills are used for broiling and turning large quantities of the same item. A single lamb chop might be placed directly on the rack. Six or eight lamb chops would be placed within a wire grill. The grill should be cleaned as often as necessary during use, and oiled when necessary to prevent sticking. Special care must be taken in loading, turning and unloading the wire grill to avoid touching the metal, a common cause of burns. Whenever foods are placed on the broiler grid or foods need turning, the grid should be pulled forward away from the broiler flame. Before starting work, the broiler cook should always make sure the safety latch of the grid is properly fastened. The temptation, during a busy period, to reach under the broiler flame with fork or spatula should be avoided.

(7) Foods which tend to curl or lose their shape when broiled like split lamb kidneys should be fastened with skewers to keep them intact and as flat as possible for uniform exposure to the heat. Chickens, squabs, lobsters, etc., whether broiled singly or in quantity should be placed within a wire grill for broiling. Steaks and chops are slashed on the fat side to prevent curling.

(8) Years ago it was customary for the broiler cook to "quadriller" or sear food with the checkered marks of a broiler grid or wire broiler. The custom is still followed in some restaurants, and the student should be familiar with it. The grid or rack is made extremely hot by positioning it close to the flame. It is brushed with oil, and

food is placed on it so that the parallel rods sear the meat in one direction. A few minutes later, the cook turns the steak or chop so that perpendicular lines form an attractive crossbar pattern. The job is always difficult with delicate foods such as fish. In most eating places broiler cooks do not mark food with the "quadrillé." Instead, the normal parallel lines of the grid are seen on the food. It is desirable, however, to broil the food so that the seared lines appear in a diagonal pattern if possible.

(9) Skewered foods like shish kebab need special attention. Small pieces of food placed on a skewer for broiling are known by the term brochette such as a brochette of sweetbread, brochette of scallops, etc. If the skewered foods are delicate like a brochette of oysters, it is best to broil them in a shallow pan so that they may be turned and remain intact. If such foods are being broiled in quantity, they are placed in a hinged wire broiler rack, and the rack is used for turning them at one time. Such items are brushed generously with oil or clarified butter to prevent drying. When turning individual brochettes, it is important that all the pieces on the skewer are turned simultaneously. Sometimes a skewer is turned, and the food does not revolve with it. If this occurs, the cook should use a fork or spatula to make sure all the pieces on the skewer are turned and browned at the same time. Oriental chefs sometimes use two parallel skewers instead of one to ensure complete turning in one step. The broiler cook should remember that when metal skewers are used, the metal conducts heat quickly, and that overcooking should be avoided.

(10) The terms rare, medium and well-done, when applied to broiled steaks, chops, hamburgers, etc., are not scientific terms indicating exact interior temperatures of food. Experienced broiler cooks know that what some people call rare, others may term medium. In different localities, the terms are variously used, and subject to personal bias. Many household cookbooks and meat thermometers for roasting indicate rare beef as having an internal temperature of 140°F, medium, 160°F, and well done, 170° to 180°F. In most restaurants specializing in steaks and chops, a lower range is followed: 110° to 120°F is usually considered rare, 130° to 140°F, medium, and 160° to 170°F, well-done. Rare meat is recognized by its interior color. It is red in the center, tapering off to brownish gray at the edges. There are some meat items where only a small area of the center is bright red, depending on the cut, thickness of the meat, etc. In other instances, such as very thick steaks, the redness extends beyond the center. Aged beef will not show the same

amount of red color as fresh beef when both are cooked to the same internal temperature. The juice that flows from rare meat may be darker than the flesh. Apart from color, meat that is rare does not lose as much juice as well-done meat, and is, therefore, larger, heavier and more succulent. Meat to be cooked rare is, if possible, placed close to the source of heat for deep browning, medium, farther away, and well done at a still greater distance. Again, charts showing the number of inches from the heat source vary greatly depending upon the kind and efficiency of broiler equipment in use. Effective guidelines can only be learned through on-the-job experience and may have to be relearned when cooks change jobs and use equipment which is new to them.

(11) When broiled foods, especially cuts of meat, are removed from the fire, the meat's interior temperature continues to rise somewhat. This occurs because heat is still being conducted from the outer to the inner meat fibers. The broiler cook must make allowance for this phenomena. If, for example, a broiled 3- or 4-in. steak has been cooked rare as ordered, the interior of the meat may have a temperature of only $100°$ to $110°$F, considered by some on the raw side. But there is a normal interval between the time the steak is removed from the fire, placed on the platter, garnished, etc., and the time the steak is picked up by the waiter, taken to the dining room, carved and served. During this interval the center of the steak becomes somewhat less rare while still keeping its bright red color.

(12) Cooks and waiters are constantly being reminded that hot foods must be hot, that is, hot when they arrive at the table. Heat is not just a matter of temperature but an extremely important factor in palatability, especially when broiled foods are considered. The sizzling hot steak, chicken or lobster simply tastes better than the same food served lukewarm. Broiled foods kept warm in a covered steam table pan or under plate covers too long become steamy and lose their broiled succulence. All plates or platters should be prewarmed in a plate warmer or other unit. If silver platters are not sufficiently warm, the cook may place them briefly under a broiler flame to prevent the loss of heat by transference. In spite of the wide use of heating lamps for foods ready to be picked up, the job of getting food rapidly to the table is the dual responsibility of both the broiler cook and the waiter. If food is not picked up within a reasonable time, the broiler cook should notify the chef, second cook, captain or other person responsible. In many restaurants there is a routine set up between the kitchen and the dining room staff to expedite the service of all foods, particularly broiled items.

Maitre d'Hotel Butter   Approx 1 Pt

Almost all broiled foods and many sautéd foods are brushed or dabbed with butter after cooking. The butter is semisoft so that it clings to the food, gently melting. Usually a compound butter is prepared, that is, one mixed with other flavoring ingredients which may be chopped or pureed. The best known of the compound butters is the one called maitre d'hotel, a mixture of butter, chopped parsley and lemon juice. It is normally available at the broiler cook's station for both lunch and dinner.

(1) Assemble the following ingredients:
    1 lb sweet butter
    Note: If salted butter is used, the salt below should be omitted.
    2 tablespoons lemon juice
    1/4 cup parsley, chopped extremely fine
    Salt, white pepper

(2) Let butter stand in a bowl at room temperature only until it is soft enough to spread easily. If it is a very hot day or if the temperature of the kitchen is very hot, the butter may melt. Place the container of butter in another one with water and ice if necessary to prevent melting.

(3) Add lemon juice slowly, stirring with a spoon or small paddle until lemon juice and butter are blended.

(4) Stir in parsley, blending well.

(5) Season lightly with salt and pepper.
    Note: Cold butter, broken into pieces, may be placed in a small mixing machine and blended with other ingredients. At meal time, however, the butter should be soft.

(6) Spread maitre d'hotel butter on broiled meats, poultry and seafood just before they are served. The amount of butter will depend upon the portion of food which has been broiled. There should be enough butter to moisten and flavor the dish; there should not be so much butter that a large pool of it forms on the plate. Sometimes the meat juices of broiled steaks and lamb chops will collect on the plate. The meat juices and the butter mingle, forming a gravy, and are poured over the meat just before it is served by the waiter.

Anchovy Butter.—Chop very fine 3 oz anchovy fillets in oil, well drained. Rub through fine china cap. Blend with 1 lb softened butter and 2 tablespoons lemon juice. Season lightly with freshly ground pepper. Use with broiled seafoods.

Bercy Butter.—Chop 1/4 cup shallots extremely fine. Cook shallots in 2 cups dry white wine until wine is reduced to 1/2 cup. Blend with 1 lb softened butter and 2 tablespoons parsley, chopped extremely fine. Add salt and pepper to taste. Use with broiled steaks or chops.

Chive Butter.—Substitute 1/4 cup chives, chopped extremely fine, for parsley in recipe for maitre d'hotel butter. Use with broiled meats or seafood.

Marchand De Vin Butter.—Prepare like *Bercy* butter substituting dry red wine for dry white wine. Use with broiled steaks or chops.

Lamb Chop, Mixed Grill   10 Portions

A mixed grill is the ideal job for a student learning the varied routines of the broiler cook. The dish is a variety of 4 meats and 2 vegetables. All of the components are cooked in a broiler; the oven is used for partial cooking of the bacon and tomatoes. The composition of a mixed grill varies in different restaurants. The items below are lamb chop, lamb kidney, sausage, bacon, tomato and mushrooms. In some restaurants a slice of liver is used in place of the lamb kidney. Others may add a slice of shell steak, substitute ham for bacon, etc. A mixed grill, to be of top quality, should be delivered to the dining table within a few minutes after the food is removed from the fire. Since the different items take different cooking times, the broiler cook's main objective is to complete the cooking of the assorted foods at one time if possible. Bacon, for example, is blanched or partially cooked beforehand and made crisp at the last moment. If some of the items are ready, while others need further cooking, they should be kept hot in an uncovered steam table pan. Lamb, unless ordered otherwise by the customer, is usually cooked to a medium or slightly rare stage rather than well-done. The grilled tomato should be cooked only until barely done; overcooking may cause the tomato skin to split. In the steps below it will be noted that the mushrooms are briefly sautéd before they are broiled. This procedure keeps the mushrooms from becoming excessively dry, which would occur if they were placed directly under the broiler flame. Lemon juice sprinkled on the mushrooms aids in keeping them from discoloring and improves their flavor. Lamb kidneys

should be broiled as close to the flame as possible, and cooked briefly. Overcooking toughens them and mars their flavor.

Before starting work: Shallow au gratin pans, which are commonly
used for broiling, will be needed for the mushrooms, tomatoes and
sausages. Arrange to have the pans or similar equipment on hand
before starting the job. If two broilers are available, plan to broil the
kidneys on a grid close to the broiler flame. The other items may be
broiled 8 to 10 in. from the source of heat or even farther if a strong
infrared broiler is used.

(1) Assemble the following ingredients:

    10 rib lamb chops, 1 in. thick

    10 slices bacon

    10 lamb kidneys, trimmed of fat and membrane, split for
    broiling

    10 small link sausages

    5 large firm tomatoes, stem ends removed, cut in half hori-
    zontally

    10 extra large or 20 medium size mushrooms, stems cut off

    1/2 lemon

    Cooking oil

    Salt, pepper, paprika

    Maitre d'hotel butter

    Note: Quantity of maitre d'hotel butter is not specified
    since it is kept as a standard item at the broiler cook's
    station; it is used for this and other jobs of broiling.

    1 bunch watercress, bottoms of stems cut off, washed, patted
    dry

(2) Preheat broilers. Preheat oven to 400° F.

(3) Fasten kidneys on skewers. Pierce each kidney on one side,
run skewer through bottom of kidney and come out other
side. Several kidneys may be fastened on one skewer.

(4) Separate bacon slices if necessary. Place slices, slightly overlapping, in au gratin pan. Bake about 8 to 10 min, turning
once, or until bacon is partially cooked but not crisp. Remove
from oven. Drain excess fat. Set bacon aside.

(5) Heat 2 tablespoons oil in a sauté pan large enough to contain
mushrooms. Add mushrooms. Sprinkle with salt and pepper.
Sprinkle with juice of half lemon. Sauté only until mushrooms
lose raw appearance. Remove mushrooms to lightly greased
au gratin pan. Set aside.

(6) Arrange lamb chops in wire broiler rack. Fasten rack. Brush
chops with oil. Set aside.

(7) Arrange tomatoes, cut side up, in greased au gratin pan. Brush

tops of tomatoes with oil. Sprinkle with salt, pepper and paprika. Set aside.

(8) Pierce sausage links with fork. Place links in ungreased au gratin pan. Set aside.

(9) Place lamb chops, tomatoes and sausages under broiler.

(10) Broil chops until brown on one side. Sprinkle browned side with salt and pepper. Turn to brown second side.

(11) As soon as tops of tomatoes are brown, remove tomatoes to oven to complete cooking, 5 to 8 min.

(12) Turn sausages to brown on second side.

(13) Brush kidneys with oil and place on hot broiler close to flame. When one side is brown, move broiler grid away from flame, sprinkle browned side with salt and pepper and turn to brown second side. Again position kidneys close to flame. Total broiling time should be 5 to 6 min. Kidneys should be rare.

   Note: Insert tine of fork into loop of skewer to turn kidneys. Do not attempt to turn skewers by hand unless a very heavy, folded dry towel is used.

(14) Place mushrooms under broiler. Broil 3 to 4 min, turning mushrooms once.

(15) Shortly before broiling is completed place bacon slices under broiler to brown. Turn once.

(16) Open wire grill carefully with fork and dry towel. Remove chops. On each platter or serving plate, place a lamb chop. Use fork and dry towel to remove kidneys from skewers. Place a kidney and link sausage alongside chop. Place half tomato on platter or plate. On top of tomato place 1 or 2 mushrooms.

(17) Dab all items on the plate generously with maitre d'hotel butter.

(18) Place a slice of bacon across each chop.

(19) Garnish each portion with sprigs of watercress.

Broiled Double Shell Steaks,   **3 Steaks, 2 Portions Each**
Smothered Onions

In some apprentice training programs, it is the practice not to permit beginner students to perform such jobs as broiling thick shell steaks. Such steaks are normally expensive, and an error like overcooking is irretrievable. Actually the job is neither very difficult nor cumbersome. The two critical steps are testing the steak's doneness when it is turned and determining when it is ready to be removed from the fire. Both steps should be checked by the supervisor or instructor. Sometimes the quality of the finished steak depends more on the quality of the raw meat than on the cooking, assuming the cooking is correct.

Shell steaks are taken from the short loin of beef, considered the finest of all beef cuts for broiling. Filet mignon, an extremely tender steak, as well as the chateaubriand (double filet mignon) below, is part of the short loin. Thin shell steaks of one portion are best sautéd. The butcher or *garde manger* who passes the steak to the broiler cook usually flattens it slightly with the side of the cleaver, and slashes the fat side of the steak at intervals of about one inch to prevent curling. Steaks of approximately two inches in thickness, as those in this recipe, are usually placed directly on the broiler grid rather than on a wire rack. Some extra large shell steaks are cut as thick as five inches. These are browned on the broiler, finished in the oven, and then sliced either in the kitchen or at the table. One of the popular garnishes with steaks is smothered onions. In a busy restaurant, they might be prepared by another cook such as the sauce cook or fry cook. Often the broiler cook assumes the job since the onions are made to order at the same time the steak is being broiled. The dish is another example of how a specialist cook takes on a job apart from his regular duties.

Before starting work: Review guides to broiling, No. 3. If steaks are not slashed on the fat side, cut fat edge diagonally at 1-in. intervals. Do not cut so deeply that lean meat is exposed. Be sure that clean warm platters are on hand for serving steaks. Determine beforehand to what degree of doneness the steaks are to be broiled.

(1) Assemble the following ingredients:
   3 boneless shell steaks, 20 oz each, slashed for broiling
   Cooking oil
   Salt, pepper
   2 lb Spanish onions, peeled
   2 teaspoons garlic, chopped extremely fine
   2 tablespoons clarified butter
   1 1/2 cups dry red wine
   1 tablespoon *glace de viande* (p 217)
   Maitre d'hotel butter
(2) Preheat broiler.
(3) Cut onions in half through stem end.
(4) Cut onions crosswise into thinnest possible slices.
(5) Heat butter and 1 tablespoon oil in sauté pan large enough to accommodate onions.

(6) Add onions and garlic. Sauté, stirring frequently, until onions turn slightly yellow, not brown, and become limp.

(7) Sprinkle onions with salt and pepper.

(8) Add wine. Cook until wine is reduced to approx 1/2 cup. Tip pan to check amount of wine left in pan.

(9) Add *glace de viande*. Stir to coat onions thoroughly. Simmer 2 to 3 min longer.

(10) Correct seasoning of onions if necessary. Keep onions warm until served.

(11) Raise grid of broiler as close to flame as possible. Keep it in that position about 3 min.

(12) Brush steaks with oil. Do not season.

(13) Lower broiler grid to normal position for broiling. Pull grid forward. Place steaks on grid, pressing steaks with back of fork so that grid marks will appear diagonally on steaks. Return grid to normal position for broiling.

(14) After a few minutes, move steaks to a 90-degree angle so that grid marks form a crossbar pattern on bottom of steaks.

(15) Continue to broil steaks until brown on top. Check with supervisor or instructor on doneness of meat. When meat is ready to turn, sprinkle the top or browned side with salt and pepper. Turn steaks to brown other side.

(16) When second side has become brown, test for doneness. Check with supervisor or instructor.

(17) If further broiling is indicated, return grid to normal position. Just before steaks are removed from broiler, season second side with salt and pepper.

(18) Place steaks on preheated platters, with crossbar pattern on top. Brush steaks generously with maitre d'hotel butter.

(19) Place onions on platter alongside steaks. If platter covers are available, place them in position.

Chateaubriand Steak.—Chateaubriand is a double or triple portion of filet mignon in one piece cut from the center of the filet. It may be anywhere from 3 to 6 in. thick before broiling. It is usually flattened somewhat with the side of a cleaver, brushed with oil or clarified butter, and broiled to the rare stage. If the broiler is very fast, the steak is browned quickly under the flame and transferred to the oven to finish cooking. It is sliced diagonally at the table.

Filet Mignon.—A single filet mignon usually weighs about 6 oz. It should either be broiled very close to a strong broiler flame and cooked to the rare stage, or else sautéd in a small amount of hot oil.

Broiled Split Mackerel
10 Portions

Mackerel for broiling should weigh 1 1/2 to 1 3/4 lb each. Each fish provides 2 portions. It is cut in half lengthwise, and the backbone is removed, leaving a few small bones in the belly side of the fish. Mackerel of this size are thin, and it is only necessary to broil them on one side. The broiler heat penetrates the fish, cooking it completely. Turning the fish for further broiling, after one side is brown, would only make it dry and possibly toughen the flesh. This is an example of a fish which is best handled in a shallow baking sheet or au gratin pan rather than on a wire grill or on the broiler rack.

Mackerel, as prepared below, are dipped in fine bread crumbs on the side exposed to the flame. The bread crumbs not only protect the fish from excessive drying but form a crisp coating which enhances the mackerel's natural flavor. The skin of mackerel is thin and tends to stick to the pan; therefore, be sure the pan is well greased. For removing the fish from the pan, use a large thin spatula (palette knife). Some au gratin pans are made of copper lined with tin. When the tin is exposed to extreme dry heat, as under a broiler or in a very hot oven, the tin may melt and small pellets may form in the pan. Be on the lookout for this phenomena. Aluminum pans do not present this problem.

Before starting work: Plan your work so that all ten portions of fish are breaded beforehand and placed on a heavy-duty baking sheet that will not warp under the broiler. If all ten portions are to be served at one time, they can easily be broiled by using the baking sheet as a broiler pan. If individual orders are received, simply transfer the fish needed to a small au gratin pan for broiling.

(1) Assemble the following ingredients:

    5 fresh mackerel, 1 1/2 or 1 3/4 lb each, cleaned and split for broiling

    Cooking oil

    Salt, celery salt, pepper, paprika

    Sifted bread crumbs

    Maitre d'hotel butter

    1 large lemon

    1 bunch parsley, washed, patted dry, bottoms of stems removed

(2) Preheat broiler.

(3) Brush a heavy-duty baking sheet generously with oil.

(4) Brush mackerel with oil on flesh side.

(5) Sprinkle flesh side with salt, celery salt and pepper.

(6) Dip flesh side in bread crumbs. Pat crumbs to make firm coating. Keep fish, flesh side up, on work table.

(7) Sprinkle crumb coating lightly with paprika. Drizzle lightly with oil.

(8) Place fish on baking sheet, skin side down. Do not crowd fish in pan.

(9) If fish are not to be broiled at once, place pan in refrigerator until needed.

(10) Place pan in normal position for broiling. Broil until crumb coating is medium brown. Move pan, if necessary, for uniform broiling. Fish is done when it flakes easily. Test doneness by inserting fork and moving gently without noticeably disturbing crumb coating.

(11) Cut a thin slice off ends of lemon. Cut lemon lengthwise into 10 wedges.

(12) Using a large spatula, remove mackerel from pan to warm serving plates or platters. Transfer fish gently to avoid breaking.

(13) Just before serving, dab each portion with maitre d'hotel butter.

(14) Garnish each portion with parsley. Place a lemon wedge alongside parsley.

Broiled Deviled Mackerel.—Follow steps (1), (2), (3), and (5) above. [Omit step (4).] Prepare a mixture of 1/2 lb butter at room temperature, 1 tablespoon prepared mustard, 1 teaspoon dry mustard, 1 tablespoon lemon juice and 2 teaspoons Worcestershire sauce; blend to a smooth paste. Spread butter mixture on flesh side of fish, coating uniformly. Follow steps (6) to (14) above.

Broiled Salmon Steak, Anchovy Butter   10 Steaks, 3/4 In. Thick

A salmon steak is a 3/4 in. thick slice of fresh salmon cut across the whole fish. Slices are taken from a 10 to 12 lb salmon. If larger salmon are used, portions will be larger unless the thickness of the slice is reduced. Like most fish, salmon is soft in its raw state. When exposed to the broiler heat, the outside of the fish becomes firm. Actually, salmon, when cooked, is more firm than some filleted fish such as broiled mackerel. Unlike mackerel, which is cooked on one side only, salmon should be turned to give both sides of the steak the characteristic brown coating people expect when eating this fish. Instead of a bread crumb coating used with mackerel, salmon is dipped in flour and then dipped in, or brushed with, oil. Salmon steak may be broiled either on a wire broiler rack or in a shallow pan. To determine doneness, it may be touched for its resiliency, but it should not be carelessly pressed with a fork or fingers, or it will break. A better method of judging salmon is to pierce it very gently with one tine of a fork or with a small pointed knife; if the flesh begins to flake, it is done. Also, if the long belly bone (not the center bone) is visible and comes away easily, the fish is done.

Before starting work: Discuss with your supervisor the proper position of the broiler rack for salmon steaks. If you are using broiler racks, examine them carefully to make sure they are clean with no residue of meat drippings from a previous use. After the rack is used, remember to clean it very carefully before its next use to remove any pieces of fish or fish skin which may adhere to the rack.

(1) Assemble the following ingredients:

    10 salmon steaks, 3/4 in. thick

    Salt, celery salt, pepper, paprika

    Flour

    Cooking oil

    Anchovy butter (half recipe, p 141)

    1 large lemon

    1 bunch parsley, washed, patted dry, bottoms of stems removed

(2) Preheat broiler.

(3) Sprinkle salmon steaks on both sides with salt, celery salt and pepper.

(4) Dip fish in a pan of flour. Remove excess flour by shaking fish and patting steaks lightly.

(5) Dip in oil or brush with oil, coating both sides completely. If fish is dipped in oil, hold it briefly over pan of oil to allow excess to drain off. Sprinkle salmon lightly with paprika.

(6) If a wire rack is used, fish may be placed on top the closed rack or inside the rack with the two parts locked in place. Be sure the rack is well oiled before placing fish on it. If a shallow baking pan is used, it too should be well oiled.

(7) Place fish in normal position for broiling.

(8) When flour coating is lightly browned, turn the salmon carefully. If a spatula is used for turning the fish, be sure it is large enough to hold the fish and keep it intact.

(9) Broil until second side is lightly browned.

(10) Test salmon for doneness as directed above. If fish is inside a wire rack, open the rack carefully. If necessary, gently loosen any steaks which may stick to the wires. Avoid breaking fish.

(11) Place fish on warm serving plates or platters.

(12) Dab each portion generously with anchovy butter.

(13) Cut a slice off each end of lemon. Cut lemon into 10 wedges.

(14) Garnish each portion of fish with parsley sprigs and a wedge of lemon.

Broiled Codfish Steaks.—Substitute codfish for salmon. Because of its extreme flakiness, codfish should be broiled on top, rather than within, a wire broiler rack. It may also be broiled on a shallow au gratin pan or similar pan.

Broiled Halibut Steaks.—Substitute halibut for salmon. Broil as directed for codfish steaks.

Shish Kebab   10 Portions

Shish kebab (a Turkish phrase meaning broiled meat on a skewer) is a dish of broiled marinated lamb chunks cooked on a metal or bamboo rod. Usually the skewer includes pieces of vegetables such as sweet peppers, mushrooms, etc. The greater the amount of vegetables on the skewer, the smaller the amount of meat, and vice versa. Vegetable components vary from place to place according to individual recipes, and may include such items as pineapple, olives, whole bay leaves, etc. Normally the butcher or *garde manger* marinates the lamb in a mixture of oil, lemon juice and seasonings, and later fastens the ingredients on skewers. Just before cooking, the broiler cook receives the skewers and puts them on the fire.

In order to better understand the complete job in this recipe, the student is directed to marinate the meat and arrange it on the skewer. Before the skewers are arranged, there is a preparatory broiling job: removing the skins of sweet peppers by exposing them to a strong broiler flame, a procedure all cooks should master. Leg of lamb is usually used for shish kebab. Since this is a lean cut, the oil marinade is important not only for flavoring the meat but for keeping it from drying excessively. During the broiling, the meat is basted with the marinade. Since the pieces of meat are relatively small, the skewer should be placed very close to the broiler flame for rapid browning. All skewered foods like brochette of scallops or brochette of chicken livers (the French word *brochette* means skewer) may be placed directly on the grid of the broiler provided it is clean and well oiled to prevent sticking. A more convenient way to handle skewered foods, if a large quantity is being prepared at one time, is to place them in a wire broiler rack or in a shallow baking pan. Most skewers (except those of bamboo) are made of flat or round metal pins with a hook at one end for turning. Others are twisted ribbon fashion in order to hold the meat more securely when it is turned.

Before starting work: Review guides to broiling, No. 9.

(1) Assemble the following ingredients:

4 lb boneless leg of lamb, fat well trimmed, cut into 40 cubes approx 1 1/4 in. thick

Cooking oil (may be vegetable oil, olive oil or a combination of both)

1 lb onions, thinly sliced

2 large cloves of garlic, mashed lightly

Salt

1/2 teaspoon freshly ground black pepper

1/2 cup lemon juice

1 large bay leaf, finely chopped

3 large sweet green peppers

20 large mushrooms, stems removed

Maitre d'hotel butter (p 141)

(2) Place the lamb, 1 cup oil, onions, garlic, 1 teaspoon salt, black pepper, lemon juice and chopped bay leaf in a bowl.

(3) Mix ingredients well.

(4) Cover bowl and marinate in the refrigerator at least 4 hours or overnight. Stir the contents of the bowl several times while it is being marinated.

(5) Preheat broiler.

(6) Wash peppers and cut in half lengthwise.

(7) Cut away curved stem ends of peppers and turn them over to the soup cook for possible use in stock pot.

(8) Tap peppers to remove seeds.

(9) Cut each pepper in half again lengthwise. Cut away inner membranes.

(10) Place peppers, skin side up, on baking sheet or shallow pan.

(11) Place pan on broiler, close to flame, and broil until peppers are charred. They should be almost completely black.

(12) Remove peppers from pan and steep in cold water about 5 minutes. Drain.

(13) Rub skins off peppers, using fingers or dry clean towel. (Although skins of peppers are burnt, peppers will show only a few dark traces from broiler heat.)

(14) Cut peppers into approx 40 1-in. squares or as close to that size as possible.

(15) Heat 2 tablespoons oil in sauté pan large enough to accommodate mushrooms. Sauté mushrooms only until they lose their raw color. Stir during sautéing. Set aside and cool.

(16) Remove pieces of lamb from marinade. Lamb should be free of onion or garlic, but pieces of bay leaf may adhere to lamb. Strain marinade and set aside for basting shish kebabs.

(17) Fasten a mushroom, cap side out, on end of a skewer near the loop.

(18) Fasten 4 pieces of lamb and 4 squares of green pepper alternately on each skewer. Do not crowd skewer. Fasten a mushroom, cap side out, on the end of the skewer.
(19) Sprinkle shish kebabs lightly with salt.
(20) Broil close to flame until medium brown. Turn skewers once during broiling. Baste at least once during broiling, brushing with strained marinade.
(21) Place skewers on warm serving platters or plates.
(22) Brush with maitre d'hotel butter.

Broiled Deviled Half Chicken   **10 Portions**

Plain broiled chicken is prepared by placing the chicken in wire broiler racks, and positioning the grid as far from the flame as possible, since chicken must be cooked very slowly. If the chicken shows signs of charring, it is removed from the broiler and finished in the oven. Broiled deviled chicken, like broiled deviled mackerel, is prepared with a mustard mixture and bread crumbs, with the significant difference that mackerel is broiled in about five minutes, while chicken takes approximately a half hour. If you coated the chicken beforehand with bread crumbs, the crumb coating would be charred long before the chicken was done. The procedure, therefore, in this case is to start broiling the plain chicken until it is about half done. The broiling is then interrupted. The chicken is cooled somewhat, coated with mustard butter and bread crumbs, and returned only briefly to the broiler to brown the bread crumbs. Again the chicken is removed from the broiler and transferred to the oven where the cooking is completed. Unlike the flesh of broiled red meat which should not be pierced with a fork, broiled chicken (like roast chicken) is tested for doneness by inserting a fork into the breast section and the leg or second joint. The liquid that flows should be clear rather than pink, since chicken is always cooked to the well-done stage but should not be overdone.

Before starting work: Make sure there are clean wire broiler racks to hold the chickens during the initial broiling. Clean the racks, if necessary, using a stiff brush and heavy coarse towel. The normal position for broiling chicken is much lower than that for broiling steaks or chops. Ask your instructor or supervisor to indicate the correct position.

(1) Assemble the following ingredients:
    5 spring chickens, 2 1/4 lb each, singed if necessary, cleaned and split for broiling

Cooking oil
Salt, pepper, paprika
1/2 lb butter, softened until it can be spread easily
2 tablespoons Dijon mustard
2 teaspoons dry English mustard
2 teaspoons Worcestershire sauce
1/8 teaspoon cayenne pepper
Sifted bread crumbs
1 bunch watercress, bottoms of stems removed, washed, patted dry

(2) Preheat broiler.
(3) Brush chickens on both sides lightly with oil. Be sure wing tips are fastened under breast.
(4) Place chickens in wire broiler racks.
(5) Broil, skin side up, until lightly browned. Check color of skin frequently. There should be no charring.
(6) Sprinkle browned side with salt and pepper.
(7) Reverse broiler racks and broil underside of chickens. Broil until medium brown.
(8) Remove chickens from broiler racks. Use a fork and heavy dry towel to unload racks. Let chickens cool slightly for handling.
(9) Mix butter, both kinds of mustard, Worcestershire sauce and cayenne pepper to a smooth paste.
(10) Rid the cavity of the chickens of any bones that can be easily removed, including the keel bone, cartilage and rib bones.
(11) Sprinkle chickens on underside with salt and pepper.
(12) Preheat oven to 375° F.
(13) Using a sandwich spreader or knife, spread both sides of chickens with butter mixture.
(14) Place bread crumbs in utility pan. Roll chickens in bread crumbs, moving pan back and forth to coat surface of chickens completely.
(15) Sprinkle chickens lightly with paprika. Drizzle lightly with oil.
(16) Place chickens, skin side up, on a greased baking sheet or shallow pans. Do not use pans with deep sides.
(17) Return chickens to broiler. Broil only until crumbs are light golden brown. Avoid charring. Do not turn chickens.
(18) Place chickens in oven and bake 15 to 20 min or until juice is clear when chickens are pierced with fork.
(19) Cut chickens in half just before serving. Serve a half chicken per portion. Garnish each portion with watercress.

Broiled Calf's Sweetbreads With Ham   **10 Portions**

Broiling changes the flavor of meats and softens their fibers. Some meat items, however, like brains or sweetbreads are soft, almost limp, in their raw state and must be made firm and compact before they can be properly handled in the broiler. Calf's sweetbreads are the thymus glands of the calf. They are sold in pairs; each pair is two portions. (There are also beef and lamb sweetbreads, but calf's sweetbreads are considered superior to the others.) In order to make them ready for broiling, they are first soaked in cold water to remove excess blood and to whiten them. After the soaking, they are drained and blanched in simmering water for a few minutes until they become firm. Their shape, however, remains irregular. To make them uniform for broiling and to keep them from shrinking excessively, they are placed under a weight for at least an hour, after which they are broiled. In this recipe sweetbreads are served on toast with ham. When the broiler cook needs toast for a job like this, he usually uses the broiler rather than the automatic toaster. All three components of the dish require different times under the broiler. Toast takes the least time; ham may require 2 to 4 min, while the sweetbreads take 5 to 10 min depending on the type of broiler used. It is the broiler cook's responsibility to see that all three components are finished at approximately the same time.

Before starting work: The day before, check to see if the sweetbreads are frozen. Allow enough time for thawing if necessary. If there is any leftover maitre d'hotel butter in the refrigerator, check to see that its flavor is still fresh. Make a fresh batch if necessary; melt the older butter, strain it, and use it for another cooking purpose if possible.

(1) Assemble the following ingredients:
  5 pairs calf's sweetbreads
  10 slices smoked cooked ham, 1/4 in. thick, 2 oz each
  10 slices white bread
  Salt, pepper
  Flour
  Cooking oil
  Maitre d'hotel butter (p 141)
  1 bunch watercress, bottoms of stems cut off, washed, patted dry

(2) Place sweetbreads in a container with ice-cold water. Add ice cubes to water if necessary to chill it. Let sweetbreads remain in water 3 to 4 hours or overnight. Change water once during soaking.

(3) Drain sweetbreads and place in a saucepan with ample cold water to cover. Add 1 teaspoon salt.

(4) Over a low flame, slowly bring water to a boil. Stir sweetbreads gently with a wooden spoon. Skim water. Let sweetbreads simmer 3 min, no longer.

(5) Lift sweetbreads out of water with a skimmer. Do not dump them. Place them in another container with cold water to cover.

(6) When sweetbreads are cool enough to handle, drain them. Cut each pair in half. Remove tubes and connecting tissue.

(7) Place sweetbreads, in a single layer, in a shallow pan lined with a clean cloth towel. Place another cloth on top of the sweetbreads. On the cloth place a board or another pan. Put a weight, such as a No. 10 can of food, on the board. Keep sweetbreads in the refrigerator, weighted down, 1 to 2 hours.

(8) Preheat broiler.

(9) Remove sweetbreads from weight. Roll in flour. Pat off excess flour.

(10) Brush sweetbreads with oil, coating completely. Season with salt and pepper.

(11) Place sweetbreads in broiler rack.

(12) Broil 5 to 7 min on each side or until medium brown.

   Note: If broiler flame is strong and browning takes place quickly, remove sweetbreads from broiler rack as soon as they are browned. Place them on a greased au gratin pan, and transfer to a 375°F oven to finish cooking. To test for doneness, pierce end of sweetbread gently with fork. If pieces seem about to separate, sweetbread is ready.

(13) About 3 to 4 min before sweetbreads are done, place ham on wire racks (not inside racks) and broil about 2 min on each side. (Since ham is cooked, it need only be heated through.)

(14) Just before sweetbreads are to be served, place bread under broiler, and toast on both sides. Watch bread as it toasts; it may scorch quickly under a broiler flame.

   Note: Toast is usually trimmed of crust. It may be left in a square shape or may be cut in any of the following ways.

   (a) Cut in half diagonally, and place lengthwise on plate so that halves no longer form a square shape.

   (b) Cut into a round shape with a large cookie cutter.

   (c) Trim into a heart-shaped piece.

(15) Place toast on warm serving plate or platter. Place ham on toast, and sweetbread on ham.

(16) Brush generously with maitre d'hotel butter. Garnish with sprigs of watercress.

Broiled Ham Steak, Apple Rings   10 Steaks, 6 Oz Each

Sometimes foods which were previously cooked by some method other than broiling are put under the broiler to be reheated and made ready for serving. Examples are the two main components of this recipe, cooked ham and apple rings. The ham is the ready-to-eat type. The apple rings are first sautéd until tender, and later are glazed (browned with sugar under the broiler) just before they are served. Other instances of this use of the broiler are Canadian bacon, deviled ribs of beef, canned fruits such as pineapple slices, and crepes. Since the ham steak is a slice of meat usually from 1/2 to 3/4 in. thick, it will take more time under the broiler than the softer apple rings. The student should keep this time differential in mind when planning the job. Ham steaks are slices taken from the center of the ham. The larger the ham, the wider and thinner the slice. Ham steaks should be broiled close to the flame and as quickly as possible to give the meat its broiled or grilled flavor. The apples, on the other hand, should be glazed farther from the flame to keep the sugar, which burns quickly, from charring.

Before starting work: A whole slice of ham may provide 3 or 4 portions depending upon the size of the ham. Portions are normally cut by the butcher or *garde manger* and passed to the broiler cook. If slices are not cut into portions, weigh them and estimate how many portions can be cut from each slice. Slash the fat edge of the ham at 1-in. intervals to prevent curling.

(1) Assemble the following ingredients:

    10 ham steaks, 6 oz each, cut from center of ready-to-eat ham
    5 large Delicious apples
    1/2 lemon
    Flour
    Cooking oil
    Maitre d'hotel butter
    Sugar
    Cinnamon

    Note: Students may observe that 5 of the above items are not listed in specific quantities. These are standard items normally available at the broiler cook's station or other nearby stations. They are used for this and similar jobs. At the end of the shift or the end of the day, the containers or bulk items are returned to their normal place.

(2) Preheat broiler.

(3) Fill a bowl with cold water. The bowl should be large enough to hold the apples when sliced. Squeeze juice of 1/2 lemon into water to prevent discoloration of apples.

(4) Peel and core apples. Check cavities of apples with finger to make sure no sharp pieces of the core remain. Place apples in water.

(5) Cut each apple crosswise into four apple rings. While working with apples, keep them in water as much as possible.

(6) When all apples are sliced, drain them. Pat dry with paper toweling.

(7) Place apple rings in utility pan with flour. Move pan back and forth quickly to coat with flour.

(8) Heat oil to a depth of 1/4 in. in large frying pan. Oil is sufficiently hot when small wave-like motions are noticed. Oil should not be heated until it smokes.

(9) Place apple slices in pan to sauté. (Gently lower them into oil to prevent splattering.)

(10) When apples are browned on bottom, turn and brown second sides.

(11) Remove apples from sauté pan and place in a single layer on a greased baking sheet. Set aside.

(12) Move empty broiler grid as close to flame as possible. Keep it in that position 3 to 5 min.

(13) Brush ham steaks with oil. (Do not season with salt and pepper.)

(14) Lower broiler grid to normal position for broiling ham steaks. Place steaks on grid so that grid bars will form diagonal lines on meat. Press steaks briefly with back of fork or with spatula to form grid marks.

(15) Broil ham steaks until fat is light brown.

(16) Turn and broil second side. (Check with instructor or supervisor on doneness.)

(17) Sprinkle apple slices generously with sugar. Sprinkle lightly with cinnamon. (If there is a cinnamon-sugar mixture in the kitchen, use it instead of the separate ingredients.) If can of cinnamon is used, hold it high above apples so that spray will be evenly distributed.

(18) Place apples under broiler in normal position for apples. Broil apples only until sugar melts. Move pan if necessary to glaze evenly. Watch apples carefully to avoid charring.

(19) Place ham steaks on warm serving plates or platters. Brush generously with maitre d'hotel butter. Garnish each portion with 2 apple rings.

7

Roast Cook (Rôtisseur)

In previous chapters we learned how important it was for both the fry cook and broiler cook to react quickly at their respective stations, to make rapid-fire decisions and to constantly focus on the performance of the equipment they used for their jobs. By contrast, the roast cook has the time to study and weigh each job assignment beforehand and to work deliberately. His most important decisions are made in an unhurried atmosphere between meal periods when there are few if any customers in the dining room, and when the large cuts of meat or poultry are slowly browning for the meal ahead. On the other hand, although his work is less hectic, any error in his judgment can be enormously costly. The cook who keeps a steak on the broiler too long ruins one portion. The roast cook who keeps a 7-cut beef rib roast on the fire too long ruins at least 25 portions.

Jobs of roasting that may seem routine often call for the most skillful judgment. The roast cook, for instance, may place three legs of lamb in the oven at one time. One might assume that the three legs would be finished at the same time. Actually, it may be necessary to take each one off the fire at a different time. The weight of each leg, its quality, shape, age, position in the roasting pan and other factors all may make what seems like a cut-and-dried job one that, in fact, calls for highly developed judgment. Students learning the art of roasting usually recall that a roast cooked at home was always planned so that it would be ready when the family, as a group, sat down to dinner. In restaurants, however, the lunch or dinner period may extend over a three-hour period or longer, with guests coming and going at different times. Obviously, menu items such as roast ribs of beef or roast turkey cannot be made to order for consumption at a specific time (except in the case of banquets), but must be cooked in advance, kept warm for several hours without the meat noticeably losing its savor, and carved into portions when individual orders arrive in the kitchen.

The term roasting means to cook by dry heat using an indirect flame. (At one time it meant to cook on a revolving spit over an open fire, a process that is rarely found in commercial restaurants nowadays.) Baking is exactly the same cooking process. Though the terms are interchangeable, menu tradition arbitrarily fixes their usage. Thus, we say roast duckling and baked Virginia ham, roast pork and baked potato.

One aspiring to the roast cook's job must learn not only the cooking of meat and poultry but also the art of carving. Carving usually takes place in the kitchen. There are some restaurants, however, where certain roasts like ribs of beef are kept on a special roast beef wagon in the dining room, and are carved there by a buffet attendant or sometimes by the headwaiter or dining room captain. Carving is extremely important not only because a well-carved portion of roast has great eye appeal but because the actual yield in portions usually is greater when carving is efficient than when it is irregular or haphazard. For slicing large roasts, the carver uses a long, thin flexible slicing knife with a rounded end, called a roast beef slicer. The shape of the knife permits it to easily slide along bones and remove slices cleanly. For carving smaller roasts, like chicken or duckling, a heavy French knife is used to cut the meat into chunks rather than slices. A small French knife or sometimes a boning knife is used for detaching shoulder pieces, removing wishbones, etc. The roast cook's knives must always be razor sharp and must be frequently honed on the knife steel (see Chap. 2).

Normally all of the raw meat and poultry which the roast cook receives from the butcher or *garde manger* is oven-ready, that is, trimmed and tied to keep the meat in as symmetrical and compact a shape as possible. Since large roasts need long hours of preparation, it is important that all meat or poultry items for roasting be ready in advance and issued in time for the meal ahead. This means a close working relationship between the roast cook and the butcher or *garde manger*. Brillat-Savarin, the eminent food philosopher and amateur cook who lived in the last century, once said that roast cooks are born, not made. It was a thought that professional cooks now regard as extremely foolish. The student must understand that although roasting is a job that calls for sensitive, mature judgment, there is no mystique or instinctive talent which will make him a fine *rôtisseur*. Only careful attention to the work habits of an experienced roast cook and to the proven down-to-earth guidelines in roasting will lead to practical success in this esteemed branch of cookery.

JOB SUMMARY

The roast cook (1) roasts meats, poultry and game for regular dining room and banquets, in absence of banquet chef; (2) in absence of other cooks may bake potatoes, stuffed vegetables, etc.; (3) may use ovens for finishing certain large cuts of broiled foods; (4) makes stuffings for poultry; (5) prepares gravies from drippings in roast pans; (6) prepares garnishes for roasts; (7) carves meat and poultry to order; (8) serves vegetable accompaniments to roast menu items; (9) returns leftover portions of roasts to *garde manger;* (10) may assist broiler cook or vegetable cook during certain times; (11) consults with chef or *sous chef* and butcher or *garde manger* on amounts of meat for roasting.

MANUAL PROCEDURES

In his work the roast cook (1) may rinse and dry poultry for roasting if this job is not performed by butcher or *garde manger;* (2) preheats ovens and regulates heat by adjusting thermostat during roasting; (3) brushes meat or poultry with oil or other fat before roasting; (4) sprinkles seasonings on foods to be roasted either before or after roasting; (5) selects appropriate pans for roasting based on size of roasts and places meat in pans or on racks in pans; (6) may add stock to pan for drippings; (7) cuts seasoning vegetables (*mirepoix*) for roasts and adds them to pans before or during roasting; (8) bastes roasts with drippings; (9) turns roasts in oven for uniform browning; (10) tests roasts for doneness by sight, touch and the use of meat thermometers; (11) removes roasts from oven; (12) cuts twine from finished roasts; (13) places roasts in covered steam table pans for holding during meal period; (14) skims fat from drippings; (15) pours stock into roast pans with drippings; (16) heats drippings over top flames; (17) thickens gravies by mixing cornstarch solution or adding roux and simmers gravies until flavor is developed; (18) just before carving, trims meat with small French knife; (19) cuts and removes bones in certain roasts preparatory to carving; (20) carves meat and poultry with thin flexible meat slicer or French knife, producing slices of uniform thickness and portions of uniform weight; (21) pours gravy over roasts; (22) garnishes roasts; (23) places vegetable accompaniments on serving plates or platters.

EQUIPMENT AND UTENSILS

The roast cook uses (1) gas or electric ranges; (2) carving board; (3) steam table; (4) roasting pans of assorted dimensions suitable for size, shape and number of roasts; (5) saucepans; (6) china caps; (7) steam table pans; (8) forks, spoons, long-bladed flexible carving knives, French knives of assorted sizes; (9) meat thermometers; (10) oven pan racks; (11) dispensers or compartment trays for oil, salt, pepper, etc.

WORKING CONDITIONS AND HAZARDS

He (1) works near and over hot ranges; (2) is exposed to high oven heat as well as surface heat of range tops; (3) must carry and move roasting pans with heavy loads of meat or poultry; (4) must turn and lift heavy roasts during cooking; (5) works quickly while basting or testing doneness of roasts, exposed to interior oven temperatures; (6) is subject to burns and cuts while trimming and carving roasts; (7) is exposed to heat of steam table throughout meal period.

PLACE IN JOB ORGANIZATION

The fry cook, broiler cook or breakfast cook may become roast cook. The roast cook may in turn be promoted to sauce cook or second cook.

21 GUIDES TO ROASTING

(1) Only tender or semitender cuts of raw meat lend themselves to roasting. As far as beef is concerned, this means those cuts which are least exercised such as the ribs, loin, etc. Almost the entire carcass of smaller animals like lamb or pork may be roasted, although, from a practical standpoint, the back and the hindquarter are best for roasting and carving. Among poultry items, young rather than old birds are roasted. The tougher cuts of animals must be

cooked by moist heat such as braising or boiling. In actual practice, the roast cook does not decide which cuts of meat are purchased for roasting. This is the responsibility of the manager, buyer or chef. But, having been given the proper meats or poultry for roasting, the cook must be constantly aware that any item held in the oven beyond certain norms of doneness will result in roasts that are not only dry but, in some cases, unnecessarily tough. Roast pork, for instance, must always be cooked to the well-done stage. Cooking beyond this point, however, only produces meat that is both chewy and unpalatable.

(2) The exemplary finished roast is one which is well browned. It may be deeply browned as in the case of roast beef or light-to-medium brown as in the case of chicken. It should never be pale, with an uncertain finish, leaving the customer in doubt as to whether the meat was roasted, braised or boiled. The carved portions may be blood rare, if it is roast beef, or they may show only white droplets of juice, if it is pork, but in no case should the roast be cooked to the dry, overdone stage with a stringy appearance. If the cook removes a roast from the oven and it is underdone, it may be returned to the fire for further cooking. An overdone roast cannot be salvaged.

(3) Whenever meat or poultry is roasted, there are cooking losses. Such losses are represented by melted fat, meat juices, drippings and evaporation. Restaurant owners expect the roast cook to keep these losses at the lowest possible rate while turning out roasts of high palatability. Generally speaking, roasts cooked at low oven temperatures suffer less loss than roasts cooked at high temperatures. A low oven temperature is considered in the 250° to 350° F range. At low oven temperatures, roasts are often more tender, retain greater natural flavor and are more easily carved. Studies have shown that beef roasted at 225° F to the rare stage suffered a loss of only 7% in weight shrinkage. When similar cuts were roasted at 325° F, the loss in weight rose to 15%. At 425° F, losses reached 25%. From the restaurant owner's standpoint, a $100 purchase of meat roasted at 425° F has a value of only $75 when it is taken from the oven. The objection to low temperature roasting is that, in many cases, it does not produce meat with the brown, appetizing crust and characteristic crust flavor which are universally popular. To minimize cooking losses and still achieve a brown exterior, cooks sometimes use both temperatures—that is, they sear the meat briefly and then reduce the heat drastically for the long period until the meat reaches the desired stage of doneness. There are a few outstanding exceptions to low temperature roasting. Wild game birds, such as mallard ducks, are

cooked in an extremely hot oven of 500° F for a mere 20 min; the meat is expected to be served very rare.

(4) Rare, medium and well-done, applied to roasts, are terms that are always subject to personal bias. In household cookbooks rare meat is usually described as that which has an internal temperature of 140° F. Medium doneness is listed as 160° F, and well-done, 170° to 180° F. Restaurant chefs, however, consider rare meat as 110° to 120° F, medium, 130° to 140° F, and well-done, 160° to 170° F. Rare red meat shows the bright color of retained meat juices. Medium doneness means less redness and somewhat reduced juiciness. Well-done roasts may show no red color whatever and still less juice, although the meat should not be dry.

All roast cooks in previous times judged when meat was finished by its external appearance (shrinkage, brownness, change of shape, etc.) and its firmness when pressed or thumped by hand. No matter how experienced and how skillful the roast cook, the only accurate indication of the doneness of meat is a thermometer reading of its internal temperature. Veteran roast cooks often resist using the thermometer as though its use were a reflection on their skill. Student cooks should not be swayed by this outmoded viewpoint. Whether a particular roast should be cooked rare, medium or well-done is a decision normally made by the chef, and the roast cook should follow his directions. In certain restaurants, roast squabs are cooked slightly rare, while in other eating places they are always well-done. It is the practice in most army mess halls to serve all roast beef well-done. Those restaurants in which roast ribs of beef is a featured speciality always offer patrons a choice of rare, medium or well-done. As an apprentice roast cook, you should carefully determine what the traditional practices are in the kitchen in which you are working.

(5) Roasts with a high percentage of internal fat like roast ribs of beef will shrink more than lean roasts such as roast round of beef. Roasts which are lean in their raw state, such as certain game birds, are often covered with a layer of fat to prevent excessive shrinkage. The process is called barding. In addition to reducing loss of juices, it protects the tender outside layer of meat from drying and becoming tough. The untrimmed outside layer of fat in some roasts may exceed one inch. If the fat were left on, the roasting time would be increased unnecessarily. In such cases the butcher will trim the fat down to 1/2 or 1/4 in. The exterior fat of ribs of beef is very thick on one end and tapers off at the other. To balance the fat distribution, butchers trim one end and add the fat thus removed to the other end for more uniform roasting. The melting outside fat,

because of the high temperature it reaches, may speed up the cooking time in certain roasts.

(6) Shrinkage of meat and the rate at which it shrinks often depend upon the shape of the roast being cooked. Roasts which are chunky will require more time in the oven than those which are thin, rangy and long. In the latter case, the heat penetration will obviously be faster than in the thicker cuts. Thus a roast strip loin of beef weighing 18 to 20 lb and about 4 in. thick will take less time in the oven than a roast top round of the same weight but double the thickness. Because thickness and shape are such important factors in roasting, the timetables which indicate how long meat should remain in the oven can sometimes be misleading. This fact again points up the importance of using a thermometer as an accurate guide in roasting.

(7) Boned roasts such as ribs of beef or leg of lamb take a longer period of time per pound in the oven because the boned version, after being tied, is more compact and chunkier. Also, bones are a better conductor of heat than flesh. In homes the boned version makes for easier carving. Boneless roasts are not common in restaurants except in mass feeding establishments where meat is cut on a slicing machine. Some cuts of meat, like fillets of beef, are naturally boneless, and the roasting time is always governed by the weight and the shape of the meat.

(8) Large meat thermometers for indicating the internal temperature of roasts such as ribs of beef are always placed in the thickest part of the meat. Thermometers of this type are left in the roast until the desired temperature is reached, and are then removed. If there is only one thermometer available for several roasts, it should be inserted in the smallest roast first and, when removed, placed in the next larger size, etc. A more accurate procedure is to insert a thermometer in each roast, since one may become done before another because of its position in the oven and other factors. There are also smaller testing thermometers which can be inserted in small roasts like fillet of beef, loin of pork, etc., and which give an instant reading of the meat's internal temperature. These thermometers can be inserted and withdrawn not only for testing the temperature of meat roasts but also for indicating the temperatures of other foods like casseroles, pureed dishes, etc., which must be held sometimes for long periods at minimum temperatures below which spoilage is possible.

(9) All meats and poultry should be roasted in uncovered pans, since covered pans, while possibly helping to make meat more tender, tend to give it a steamed or braised flavor, and retard browning. Pans should be of the proper dimensions to accommodate the particular roasts for which they are being used. Several squabs, for

instance, may be roasted in an au gratin pan with sides only an inch high. The sides of the pans chosen should be high enough to keep juices from splattering but not so high as to prevent the lateral flow of heat from browning the meat properly. A pan for a 24 lb roast turkey should have higher sides than a pan for a 12 lb ham with its almost flat shape. Never overcrowd a roasting pan, and never overcrowd an oven. One of the conditions of successful roasting is the circulation of dry air around the food. Both overcrowded pans and overcrowded ovens result in excess moisture around the roast, preventing the normal browning within the time needed for cooking the roast.

(10) Seasonings such as salt and pepper, sprinkled on the roast before cooking, penetrate the flesh only a fraction of an inch. Excessive salting will cause undue loss of meat juice and meat flavor. For these reasons, do not season meat highly before it is roasted. At banquets, where guests seem to use salt and pepper less avidly than they do in the regular dining rooms, it is sometimes the practice for the roast cook or whatever cook carves the meat to very lightly salt the slices of meat on the serving plates before they are taken to the dining room.

(11) Some roasts, particularly poultry, are cooked with a *mirepoix*, the French term for a mixture of flavoring vegetables, usually carrots, onions and celery. The addition of a *mirepoix* serves two purposes: It adds a slight flavor to the roast itself and conveys a distinct flavor to the pan gravy or *jus*. When very large cuts of meat like ribs of beef are roasted, the *mirepoix* has little if any effect on the meat's flavor. Small birds like Rock Cornish game hens or squabs are sometimes mixed with the vegetables the night before and kept in covered containers so that the volatile flavors of the vegetables blend with the flesh before roasting. Sometimes the *mirepoix* is sautéd before it is added to the roast; more often the raw vegetables are added to the roasting pan. When roasting large cuts of meat, the *mirepoix* should not be added to the pan until the cooking is 1/2 or 3/4 completed; if added too soon, the vegetables may become charred and give the gravy a burnt flavor.

(12) During roasting, a layer of melted fat usually collects on the pan bottom. If the meat rests in this fat, it becomes grease-soaked and that part of the meat in contact with the fat may actually fry. To prevent this, certain roasts, such as duck, are placed on a metal rack rather than on the pan bottom. Other roasts, such as ribs of beef or saddles of lamb, when placed fat side up in the pan, form a natural rack of their own which keeps the fleshy side of the meat from contact with the pan bottom.

(13) To ensure uniform browning, it may be necessary to turn

certain roasts in the pan or to turn the pan itself. There are roasts such as those previously cited which form their own natural rack in the pan and which usually do not require turning. Other roasts such as chicken may have to be turned several times to ensure even browning on top, bottom and sides. If the roast is large and bulky, such as a 24-lb turkey, it is sometimes more convenient to turn the pan if there is an uneven heat pattern in the oven causing irregular browning.

(14) Recipe instructions will sometimes tell you to baste the meat periodically. Basting is simply pouring the juices which collect in the pan over the roast. Basting enhances the natural flavor of a roast and keeps the skin of poultry moist and pliable. (Some customers may prefer the skin crisp, but for carving purposes somewhat moist skin is better.) Sometimes, when there is insufficient natural juice in the pan, cooks add stock for basting purposes. Care should be taken not to add so much stock that the meat become steamy and loses the distinctive flavor of roast meat. The natural layer of fat on top of such roasts as ribs of beef or loin of pork melts during roasting and helps the basting process. Normally a roast cook uses a long kitchen spoon for basting. If the spoon is inconvenient, a basting syringe may be used instead.

(15) It is extremely important to be familiar with the performance characteristics of the particular oven equipment with which you are working. A high speed convection oven requires less cooking time than a conventional oven. It is important to know the preheating time of an oven, the proper use of oven controls such as thermostats, timer, etc., the capacity of the oven for efficient roasting, the uniformity or unevenness of heat application and other factors which affect its operating efficiency. Since the performance of any oven varies with its model, age and use, a roast cook must remain attentive while roasts are in the oven in order to control the job from start to finish.

(16) The French term *au jus* literally means with juice, and it is often combined with English terms, such as roast ribs of beef *au jus* or roast leg of lamb *au jus*. When the term is used on a menu, the customer expects to receive the roast with unthickened natural pan gravy. Such pan gravies whether accompanying beef, veal, lamb or pork are known as *jus de rôtis*. In the best restaurants gravies of this type always convey the pronounced but mellow flavor of the specific roast being served. Thus the *jus* served with lamb should have the definite flavor of lamb, and not pork or beef. There are some kitchens where a *jus* pot is kept simmering on the back of the

range. A variety of browned bones from different roasts are placed in the pot as they are made available and are simmered with water and vegetables. It is a catch-all kind of small stockpot, and, while the *jus* is always ready and is a labor saver, it is not recommended for serving with fine roasts. Pan gravies are not thickened with flour or cornstarch, but are sometimes made richer and given body by swirling a small amount of butter with the gravy after it is removed from the fire and placed in the steam table.

(17) After a finished roast is removed from the oven and while it is setting in the steam table, you may observe that the reading on the meat thermometer continues to rise for approx 20 min or longer in some cases. This phenomenon merely shows that the heat is still being conducted from the hotter outer portions of the meat toward its center. If you were to carve the meat while its temperature was still rising, you would notice an unusual amount of free-flowing juices, and carving would be somewhat difficult. If, however, the meat is permitted to set during this post-roasting period, the juices are reabsorbed into the meat, and carving is facilitated. Do not, therefore, carve any roast the minute it is removed from the oven, except in an emergency. The best practice is to allow the meat to set in a steam table pan uncovered until the setting is complete, and then to keep the roast covered except when it is being carved.

(18) Many roast poultry dishes are accompanied with a stuffing or dressing such as oyster stuffing, chestnut stuffing, etc. In homes the stuffing is packed into the cavity of the bird's carcass. In restaurants, as a general practice, it is baked in a pan apart from the bird for the following reasons:

    (a) The cavity of some birds like turkeys is not large enough to accommodate the number of portions of stuffing required.

    (b) Stuffing in the bird increases the total cooking time needed for the heat to penetrate. This increased cooking time may cause the turkey to be overdone and dry.

    (c) Stuffing can be handled and divided into portions more efficiently when it is baked in a shallow pan. Any loss of flavor can be compensated by using poultry stock, such as chicken broth, in place of water.

(19) A roast of prime meat may be cooked to just the right internal temperature, may be impressively browned and may be properly set after being removed from the fire, but the job is not completed. It still requires the roast cook's observant care for the next 2 to 3 hours during the meal period when the roast is being carved. The roast must be kept warm for serving, but must not be further cooked.

One cannot always rely on the heat of steam tables, especially when working with older equipment. They may be too hot or not hot enough, and this means the roast cook must keep the meat covered or uncovered for varying periods. Sometimes, if there is too much bottom heat in a steam table pan, it may be necessary to place a tray between the pan and the roast. Sometimes, it may be necessary to remove the roast from the steam table to the dry heat of a shelf above the oven. If roast duck or goose is not kept properly hot in the steam table, the cook may place the carved portions, skin side up, under a broiler flame for a very brief reheating period. At other times, he may bring the gravy up to the boiling point and pour it over the roast just before it is taken to the dining room. Some electrically heated holding units which are designed to keep food at a specific serving temperature for long periods of time are not always accurately controlled. The roast cook, therefore, must be continually mindful of the temperature and condition of the meat he has roasted, and must be prepared to take whatever steps are necessary to keep the meat at optimum serving temperature. Cooks sometimes lightly touch food with the knuckles to judge its serving temperature.

(20) Meat, whenever possible, should be carved against the grain. The grain of meat means the arrangement or direction in which the meat fibers run. Very often the grain is apparent to the eye. Cutting against the grain results in slices that are more tender than those cut with the grain. In several of the dishes in this chapter, such as roast leg of lamb and baked ham, most of the slices are cut against the grain. A small section of each of these roasts, however, must be cut with the grain for practical reasons. Since both of these meats are normally very tender, the departure from the rule is not serious.

(21) The roast cook must be constantly aware of the operating efficiency of the ovens with which he is working. Oven thermostats, for instance, may be set for the correct temperature, but if the thermostats are not properly calibrated or are malfunctioning for any other reason, the job of roasting may be seriously impaired. No oven temperature for a specific job should vary more than 25° plus or minus. Sometimes the heat input of gas or electric equipment may not be normal because of conditions outside of the kitchen in which you are working, and this can cause ovens as well as other cooking equipment to malfunction. If a roast seems to be browning too quickly or too slowly, if oven controls such as timers, pilot lights, switches, etc., are not working properly, or if oven doors, shelves, etc., need repair, you should report such matters at once to your supervisor or instructor.

Roast Chicken   48 Portions

There are at least three different methods of roasting chickens, and, as a student, you should be acquainted with them. The first procedure is to place the chicken breast side down for almost the entire roasting period, and then, toward the end of the cooking, turn it breast side up for brief browning. A second set of directions advises that the chicken be cooked breast side up without any turning whatever. Finally, the third method, and in fact the one used in most restaurants and outlined in the recipe below, requires the chicken to be roasted on its side for half the cooking time, and then reversed for the balance of the roasting. Students on apprentice training programs may find roast cooks following these and other methods. It is important, however, for them to remind themselves that the dual objectives in this job are (a) to make the chicken brown for the sake of palatability and appearance, and (b) to cook the chicken in such a way that the flesh becomes tender while remaining moist rather than dry.

If you roast chicken breast side down throughout most of the cooking period to prevent excessive drying of the white meat, the very opposite result may occur; most of the juices of the bird flow to the bottom of the pan rather than over the flesh of the chicken; the skin of the white meat may tear when the bird is turned; the white meat may be dry and grease-soaked. If you roast it breast side up, without turning, the chicken may be tender and juicy throughout, while the bottom and parts of the side lack brown color. But if you roast it on its two sides, both bottom and top will turn a medium golden brown without excessive cooking, and the bird will, to a considerable extent, be self-basted as juices flow from one side to the other. Students should be aware that, if chickens have been frozen with subsequent loss of juices during thawing, or if chickens are of poor quality, no technique whatever will produce a juicy, flavorful well-browned bird.

When it comes to basting, the student may again be puzzled by the diversity of directions. One cookbook writer says basting should occur every 5 min, a second, every 10 min, a third, every 15 min, while a fourth advises no basting whatever. Basting is pouring pan juices over the bird while it is roasting. Its purpose is to moisten the chicken with its own juices and fat for the sake of flavoring (just as one can give a butter flavor to chicken by basting it with melted butter) and to make the browned skin pliable rather than so brittle that it tears into uneven pieces when the chicken is carved. Basting a chicken every 5 min would, on the face of it, be highly impractical for a roast cook in a large restaurant where several hundred portions were being roasted. The cook would hardly finish basting the last pan, when he would again start to baste the first pan. Also, the heat loss while the oven door was being kept open would make browning difficult. Most cooks find that basting approximately every 20 min results in well-flavored birds with tender brown skin. Finally, the technique of roasting chickens often depends on the age, efficiency and performance characteristics of the particular ovens with which you are working. Some ovens have strong bottom heat, others strong top heat while the new convection ovens with forced air produce heat delivery from the sides or walls of the oven. It is extremely important, therefore, that you choose roasting pans which are shallow rather than deep so that the flow of heat reaches the surface of the chicken as uniformly as possible, no matter what type of equipment is being used.

Before starting work: Do not roast chickens too far in advance. Plan your work schedule so that the chickens will be ready when the dining room opens for business. Time must be allowed for making gravy after chickens are removed from the pan, during which interval the flesh of the chickens will set.

(1) Assemble the following ingredients:
12 roasting chickens, 3 1/2 lb each, tied for roasting
3/4 lb butter
Salt, pepper
2 lb onions, coarsely chopped
1 lb celery, coarsely chopped
1/2 lb carrots, coarsely chopped
3 qt chicken broth
1 cup dry white wine
1 cup brown roux (p 202)
Caramel coloring

(2) Preheat oven to 350° F.

(3) Place 1/2 lb butter in small saucepan. Heat over low flame only until butter melts. Do not allow butter to foam.

(4) Select roasting pan large enough to hold the 12 chickens. Place chickens in pan. Brush chickens with melted butter. Sprinkle chickens with salt and pepper. Arrange chickens on their side in pan.

(5) Heat balance of butter in large frying pan. Sauté onions, celery and carrots until onions are light yellow, not brown.

(6) Scatter vegetables in pan. Add 1 pt chicken broth to pan. Place pan in oven. (Check with instructor on whether top or bottom shelf is to be used. Pan should be placed on shelf

which is best for uniform browning.) Baste chickens approximately every 20 min during roasting.

(7) Roast chickens until top side is medium brown. Turn pan, if necessary, for uniform browning. Some chickens may become brown before others. Turn chickens.

(8) Continue to roast chickens until second side is brown. Add more chicken broth to pan if necessary for basting. If chickens are fresh and top quality, their own juices will increase basting liquid.

(9) Test chickens for doneness. Lift each chicken up so that liquid flows from cavity into pan. Pierce second joint and breast of several chickens; clear, not pink, juice should flow. Drumstick should feel soft when pressed. It may be necessary to remove some of the chickens from pan before others.

(10) Place chickens in steam table pan. Do not remove twine until chickens are carved. Keep cover over pan.

(11) Place roasting pan on top range. Tip pan so that liquid flows to one side. Skim off chicken fat. Do not skim clear liquid in pan.

Note: In some kitchens, the chicken fat is kept in the pan and mixed with flour or flour and water to make gravy. In other restaurants, the chicken fat is always removed because of its slightly strong flavor. Some of the fat in the pan will have been the butter used to brush the chicken before it was roasted.

(12) Add wine to pan. Scrape pan bottom and sides to loosen all drippings. Carefully pour liquid from pan and *mirepoix* (seasoning vegetables) into saucepot. Add balance of chicken broth.

(13) Bring gravy to a boil. Slowly stir in roux until gravy is thickened. Reduce flame and simmer 20 min.

(14) Strain gravy through fine china cap into steam table pot. Skim fat if necessary. Add caramel color if necessary, to make gravy medium brown. Add salt and pepper to taste. If gravy flavor seems weak, it may be strengthened by a small addition of dehydrated chicken bouillon. Use only if necessary.

(15) Carve chicken as follows:

(a) Cut twine and remove it.

(b) Make a V-cut in back of chicken and remove neck section. Neck section may be added to brown stockpot. Insert small pointed knife in front of breast and remove wishbone.

(c) With chicken, breast side up, on cutting board, slice down body separating leg and second joint from body. Hand may be used to complete separation. Cut between second joint and leg, separating them.

(d) Cut down back of chicken, splitting chicken.

(e) Place chicken, breast side down, on cutting board. Remove keel bone and cartilage by hand. Split breast lengthwise. Cut each breast crosswise into 2 chunks. One piece on each side will have shoulder attached.

(16) To serve chicken, place a piece each of dark and white meat on warm serving plate or platter. Each piece should be skin side up.

Note: If a stuffing is served, place stuffing on plate first. Place chicken pieces on stuffing.

(17) Pour hot gravy over chicken just before waiter picks up order.

Roast Half Spring Chicken.—Use 2 or 2 1/4 lb chickens instead of 3 1/2 lb chickens. Allow 1/2 chicken per portion. Roast at 400°F. for approximately 1 hour. The hot oven is necessary for browning.

Roast Pheasant.—Bard the pheasant, that is, cover the breast with a thin piece of larding pork which prevents drying of flesh. Roast in a hot oven, 400° F, 30 to 40 min or until just done.

Roast Duck, Apple Stuffing   48 Portions

Most of the ducks grown commercially in the United States are very fatty birds. The amount of fat which melts during roasting is so great that a 5- to 6-lb duck yields only as much edible meat as a 3 1/2-lb chicken. It is desirable, therefore, to roast ducks on racks so that the fat drains off while the meat browns in the dry oven heat rather than simmers in a large pool of fat in the pan. It may be necessary to pour off the accumulated fat 2 or 3 times during roasting. Cooks often pierce the skin of a duck with a fork in several places to facilitate melting and draining the fat. After ducks have been roasted, and while being kept warm on the steam table, the skin often loses its crispness. It may be restored by briefly placing the cut portions of the duck, skin side up, under a broiler flame. Tart accompaniments such as applesauce or apple stuffing are popular with the rich meat of duck. The bones are relatively large. In carving the birds, you should use a large heavy French knife with which you can chop the carcass almost in the same way a cleaver is used. When making the gravy, it may seem unthrifty to discard the duck fat and then thicken the gravy with a roux made of butter. But duck fat, like chicken fat, has a strong, individual flavor which patrons may or may not like, depending on area tastes and other factors. Note that while most forms of poultry are brushed with oil or other fat before roasting, this step is omitted in preparing ducks because of their abundance of natural fat. Since ducks are placed on racks, they are roasted breast side up for uniform browning.

Before starting work: Ask supervisor or instructor if duck fat is to be saved for cooking purposes or otherwise disposed of. Sometimes the fat is used for sautéing certain foods such as chicken livers, chicken, etc. Assemble racks of the correct size for the roasting pans that are to be used.

(1) Assemble the following ingredients:

12 ducks, 5 1/2 to 6 lb, cleaned, drawn and trussed
Salt, pepper
2 lb onions, coarsely chopped
1 lb celery, coarsely chopped
1/2 lb carrots, coarsely chopped
1/4 cup cooking oil
2 cups dry white wine
3 qt chicken broth
1 cup brown roux (p 202)
Caramel coloring
Apple stuffing (p 183)

(2) Prepare apple stuffing while ducks are roasting.

(3) Preheat oven to 325° F.

(4) Sprinkle ducks with salt and pepper.

(5) Place ducks, breast side up, on racks in roasting pans. Do not crowd pans. (Basting is unnecessary when ducks are on racks.)

(6) Roast for 1 hour. Drain fat from pans. The best procedure is to remove the ducks by inserting a fork and holding the ducks up so that fat drips into pans. Remove both ducks and racks from pans. Place ducks temporarily on baking sheets. With 2 heavy dry towels, tip roasting pans toward receptacle on floor for collecting fat. Replace racks and ducks in pans, in original position, and continue roasting 1 hour longer.

(7) Sauté onions, celery and carrots (*mirepoix*) in oil in large frying pan until onions are limp, not brown.

(8) Again remove ducks from pans and discard fat. Let drippings remain in pans. Do not return racks to pans. Return ducks to pans. Add sautéed vegetables to pans. If ducks have not browned evenly, place them on their side or breast if necessary.

(9) Continue to roast until ducks are tender and show no pink juice when pierced. Drumstick should feel tender when quickly pressed, and should move easily from second joint.

(10) Remove ducks from roasting pans. Place in steam table pans.

(11) If there is additional fat in pans, pour it off. Place pans over top flame on range.

(12) Add wine to pans and scrape pan bottoms and sides to loosen drippings.

(13) Add chicken broth to pans and bring to a boil. Pour gravy into a saucepot.

(14) Bring to a boil. Slowly stir in roux. Stir until roux is completely dissolved and gravy thickens.

(15) Reduce flame and simmer slowly 20 min.

(16) Strain gravy through fine china cap into steam table pot. Press vegetables in china cap to extract all gravy.

(17) Add caramel coloring if necessary to make gravy medium brown. Skim fat from gravy if necessary. Season with salt and pepper. If gravy flavor seems weak, it may be strengthened by adding dehydrated chicken bouillon. Use sparingly. Place gravy in steam table.

(18) To carve ducks:

    (a) Cut twine and remove it.

    (b) Make a V-cut in back of duck and remove neck section. Neck sections may be added to brown stockpot. Insert small pointed knife in front of breast and remove wish bone.

    (c) With duck breast side up on cutting board, slice down body separating leg and second joint from body. Section may be separated by hand. Cut between second joint and leg, separating them.

    (d) Cut down back of duck, splitting back. Use a heavy French knife.

    (e) Place duck breast side down on cutting board. Remove keel bone and cartilage by hand. Split breast lengthwise. Cut each breast crosswise into 2 chunks. One piece of each side will have shoulder attached.

(19) When orders are placed for ducks, check to see if skin is soft and more browning would be desirable. If so, arrange pieces of duck on shallow pan, skin side up, and place under broiler flame until skin is deep brown and crisp. Watch broiler constantly to avoid charring skin. This last browning step should take place only before ducks are ready to be served.

(20) Place a portion of stuffing on warm serving plate or platter.

(21) On top stuffing place 1 piece of breast meat and a second joint or leg.

(22) Pour gravy over duck just before serving.

Note: Sometimes when duck is carved in dining room in view of guests, the breast of the duck may be cut alongside breastbone and detached in one piece from the bone. It may be then cut in long strips called, in French, *aiguillettes.*

Roast Turkey, Bread Stuffing   **50 Portions**
Giblet Gravy   **Approx 4 Oz Each**

Roasting a large turkey need not be unduly complicated. A problem for many roast cooks is the fact that most turkeys are frozen. There are fresh turkeys during the fall holiday season and at other times in certain areas. Frozen turkeys must be thawed before they are cooked. In thawing, they lose their natural juices, the very thing the roast cook wants to save, not only because juices mean flavor but because they affect the tenderness and texture of the turkey meat. This built-in handicap makes it doubly important, therefore, for the roast cook to avoid the cardinal fault in turkey roasting— overcooking. To prevent excessive loss of juices, the roast cook should observe the following steps:

(a) After a frozen turkey has been thawed, cook it as soon as possible to avoid further losses.

(b) Spread a fat-soaked cheesecloth over the turkey during roasting; it will reduce losses of juice and still permit the skin of the turkey to brown with a delicate sheen.

(c) If roasted turkey is sliced in advance for a banquet, cook it only to an internal temperature of 165°F instead of the usual 180°; subsequent reheating will bring it to the desired stage of doneness.

(d) Use a slow to moderate oven, 325° to 350°F.

The old practice of barding a turkey—that is, tying a sheet of salt pork over the breast to keep the white meat moist—is not widely followed these days. The salt pork on large turkeys melts long before the turkey is finished. Aluminum foil may be wrapped around the bird to create, in effect, a secondary oven, but many cooks prefer not to use it in order to control brownness and doneness more effectively.

When turkeys are roasted for large parties in which guests are served at one time, the turkey and stuffing are prepared as follows:

(a) Individual portions of stuffing are placed in utility pans or steam table pans; each portion of stuffing is covered with a portion of dark and white turkey meat; this is done considerably in advance of serving time.

(b) Pans containing the portions thus arranged are covered with aluminum foil and refrigerated.

(c) Before the turkey is reheated, a small amount of chicken or turkey broth is poured into the pans, just enough to prevent sticking and to create a moist atmosphere in the pans.

(d) Turkey and stuffing in the covered pans are baked in the oven until they reach serving temperature, about 180° F.

(e) Portions are transferred to serving plates and covered with hot gravy.

All forms of poultry, particularly turkey, are candidates for food contamination. The wet surface and interior of turkeys, as they are being thawed, are well-known areas for bacterial growth. Washing the turkeys before they are trussed is the job of the butcher or *garde manger* who passes the cleaned, drawn and trussed birds to the roast cook. If there is any doubt about the condition of turkeys when you receive them, if you can feel any sticky or slimy spots, or detect any off-odor, call this fact to the attention of your supervisor or instructor. After cooking, the turkey, stuffing and gravy should not be held below 140° F while in the steam table or during the meal period. Check temperatures, if possible, with a small food-testing thermometer.

Before starting work: In large mass-feeding establishments turkeys are often roasted a day in advance in order to be ready for a noon meal. Discuss the work schedule with your instructor or supervisor so that all the main steps of the job can be carried out in ample time.

(1) Assemble the following ingredients:
   2 18-lb young tom turkeys, cleaned, drawn and trussed
   Cooking oil
   Salt, pepper
   2 lb onions, coarsely chopped
   1 lb celery, coarsely chopped
   1/2 lb carrots, coarsely chopped
   1 pt dry white wine
   1 pt turkey or chicken broth
   1 gal turkey or chicken broth
   1 1/2 cups brown roux
   Bouquet garni of 8 sprigs parsley, 12 peppercorns and 1 large
      bay leaf
   Turkey giblets: necks, wing tips, gizzards and hearts
   Moist bread stuffing (p 181)

Note: Arrange your work so that while the turkey is roasting, the stuffing can be made.

(2) Preheat oven to 350° F.

(3) Brush turkeys with oil.

(4) Sprinkle turkeys with salt and pepper on all sides.

(5) Cut two pieces of cheesecloth, each large enough so that a double thickness of the cloth will fit completely around each turkey.

(6) Dip cheesecloths in oil. Wrap each turkey with cheesecloth, covering it completely.

(7) Place turkeys on sides on wire racks in roasting pans. If oven is large, both turkeys may fit into one pan.

(8) Pour 1 pt broth into pan. Place pan in oven.

Note: While turkeys are roasting, the weight may cause them to stick to the racks. If no racks are used, the turkeys may stick to the pan bottom. Move turkeys slightly, while basting them, to make sure they are not sticking. Baste turkeys about every 20 min.

(9) Pour 1 gal broth into saucepot. Add turkey necks, wing tips, gizzards and hearts. Add bouquet garni to pot, fastening it to handle.

(10) Bring broth to a boil. Reduce flame. Simmer slowly until gizzards and necks are very tender, about 1 1/2 hours.

(11) After turkeys have roasted on one side for an hour, turn them on the other side and roast an additional hour. Lift cheesecloth slightly from time to time to make sure it is not sticking. If cheesecloth seems to be too dry and turns very dark, brush it with oil.

(12) After 2 hours roasting, remove turkeys and racks from pans, and add chopped vegetables to pan. Remove cheesecloths. Return turkeys to pan, breast side up, without racks.

(13) Continue to roast turkeys, breast side up, until they are done. Doneness may be checked as follows.

    (a) Meat thermometer placed in thickest part of thigh registers 180° F. (Roast only to 160° F if turkeys are to be sliced, chilled and reheated for later serving.)

    (b) Leg and thigh joint may be easily moved.

    (c) Drumstick feels soft when pressed.

    (d) When a fork is inserted in breast or thigh, clear, not pink, juice flows.

(14) Lift turkeys so that any juice from cavities flows into pan. To hold turkeys, use two kitchen forks, one in cavity of bird and one in front between breast and neck. Avoid tearing skin.

(15) Remove turkeys from roasting pan to steam table pans.
(16) Prepare giblet gravy as follows:
   (a) Using skimmer, lift wing tips, necks, gizzards and hearts from broth. Set aside.
   (b) Remove meat from neck. Cut away meat from gizzards, discarding tough inner skin. Add wing tips to stockpot.
   (c) Put neck meat, gizzards and hearts through meat grinder, using fine blade. (This step is usually handled by *garde manger* or his assistant.) Set aside.
   (d) Place roasting pan with drippings and chopped vegetables on top of range. Tip pan and skim off as much fat as possible.
   (e) Add wine to pan. Scrape pan bottom and sides to loosen drippings. Pour drippings and contents of pan into saucepot with broth.
   (f) Bring to a boil. Reduce flame. Simmer 20 min.
   (g) Strain gravy through fine china cap into another saucepot.
   (h) Place gravy over moderate flame, and bring to a boil.
   (i) Stir in roux. Stir until roux is dissolved and gravy is thickened. Simmer 10 min. Add ground giblets.
   (j) Skim fat if necessary. Add salt and pepper to taste. Add caramel coloring if necessary to make gravy medium brown. Place giblet gravy in steam table.
(17) To carve turkey, follow this procedure:
   (a) Place turkey on side on cutting board.
   (b) Using a small trimming knife or boning knife, make a circular cut around shoulder. Remove shoulder. Shoulder may be served whole or the meat may be removed and added to sliced white meat.
   (c) Cut between second joint and body of turkey to separate light from dark meat. Pull second joint and drumstick away from body.
   (d) Separate drumstick from second joint either by hand or with a small knife.
   (e) Turn second joint, skin side down, on cutting board. Remove thigh bone. Use a small trimming knife or remove by hand. Cut meat of second joint in 1/2 in. thick slices. Keep warm in steam table.
   (f) Remove meat from drumstick by hand or cut into 1/2 in. thick slices, and place alongside meat of second joint. Check with instructor or supervisor on amount of turkey to cut for orders on hand.

(g) Turn turkey on other side and remove shoulder, thigh and drumstick in same manner, slicing dark meat.

(h) With turkey on its side, make a vertical cut the length of the turkey breast, so that turkey breast is divided into two sections. This facilitates slicing so that entire breast need not be sliced. Slices are smaller as a result of this step, but portions are more easily managed. If whole breast slices are desired, eliminate this step.

(i) Turn turkey breast side up. Cut breast meat in slices no larger than 1/4 in. thick. Slices may be 1/8 in. thick. Check with instructor or supervisor on thickness and amount of breast meat to cut.

(j) On bottom of turkey are two solid pices of meat called "oysters." Remove them and add them to dark meat.

(18) Place a portion of dressing on warm serving plate or platter.

(19) On top of dressing, place slices of dark meat, then slices of white meat. Check with instructor or supervisor on size of portions. Use portion control scale for first several portions.

(20) Pour hot giblet gravy over turkey. Serve with cranberry sauce, cranberry relish or any other designated garnish.

Roast Squab   **6 Portions**

An old guideline in cookery says, "The smaller the roast, the hotter the oven." In spite of the general advantages of low temperature roasting, poultry of very small sizes like squabs, squab chickens or small Rock Cornish game hens, weighing about a pound or less each, are roasted in a hot oven 400°F. If the oven heat is less than 400°F, the birds will cook, but will remain pale and steamy looking. They will lack the succulent brown skin and rich flavor which make them such distinguished menu items. To accelerate the browning, small birds of this size are often sautéd before they are roasted. They are then kept in the sauté pans, provided these pans are shallow, or are tr · isferred to au gratin pans for roasting. Pans of this type permit quick heat penetration on most of the surface of the birds.

Squab is another name for pigeon, although the squabs purchased by restaurants are specially bred birds that have not been allowed to fly. They have a slightly gamey but not strong flavor and are frequently served with a tart accompaniment such as red currant jelly or blackberry jelly. If they are stuffed or boned and stuffed, the stuffing is usually cooked by the roast cook who gives it to the butcher or *garde manger* for stuffing before the squabs are trussed.

Before starting work: Review ways of cutting toast (p 155). Examine squabs carefully to make sure they were properly singed, that is, exposed to a gas flame to burn off hairs or feathers.

(1) Assemble the following ingredients:

6 squabs weighing 14 to 16 oz each, cleaned, drawn and trussed
3 tablespoons clarified butter
Salt, pepper
4 oz onions, coarsely chopped
2 oz celery, coarsely chopped
2 oz carrots, coarsely chopped
1/2 cup dry white wine
1 pt hot chicken broth
1/4 cup brown roux
Caramel coloring
6 slices white bread, crusts removed
1/2 bunch watercress, washed, patted dry, bottoms of stems cut off
3/4 cup red currant jelly

(2) Preheat oven to 400° F.

(3) Sauté onions, celery and carrots in 1 tablespoon butter, stirring frequently, until onions are deep yellow but not brown.

(4) Choose another sauté pan large enough to accommodate 6 squabs. Heat balance of butter in this pan over moderate flame.

(5) Add squabs to pan. Sauté squabs until skin loses raw color, turning birds as necessary.

(6) Add sautéd vegetables (*mirepoix*) to pan with squabs. Add 1/2 cup chicken broth to pan. Place squabs on side in pan.

(7) Place squabs in oven. Roast 30 to 40 min or longer until squabs are browned, turning squabs once to brown on both sides. Baste squabs several times during roasting.

Note: Metal handle of sauté pan becomes very hot. Do not impulsively grab it. When necessary to turn or remove pan, be sure to have a double or triple thickness of dry towel in hand.

(8) Test squabs for doneness by piercing breast with fork. Juice should be clear, not pink, when squabs are done. (In some European restaurants, squabs are sometimes served rare; this is not usually the practice in the United States.)

(9) Remove squabs from pan. Gently scrape off any vegetables remaining on squabs. Keep squabs warm in covered steam table pan until served.

(10) Add white wine to pan. Place pan over moderate flame. Sim-

mer until wine is reduced to a few tablespoons liquid. Scrape pan to loosen drippings.

(11) Add balance of chicken broth to pan and bring to a boil.

(12) Reduce flame. Simmer 5 min.

(13) Add brown roux. Stir well until roux is dissolved, and gravy is thickened. Simmer 5 min. Add caramel coloring if necessary to make gravy medium brown.

(14) Strain gravy through fine china cap. Skim gravy of fat.

(15) Toast bread under broiler. Cut into any of the shapes described on p 155.

(16) Remove twine from squabs. Place squabs on toast, on warm plates or platter.

(17) Pour gravy over squabs.

(18) Garnish squabs with watercress.

(19) Place currant jelly in a sauceboat to be passed at the table.

Moist Bread Stuffing   **50 Portions, Approx 3 Oz Each**

On menus you will find the words stuffing and dressing used interchangeably. Both mean an accompaniment to roasted poultry. (Dressing is also used for the cold sauce served with salads, such as French dressing.) As previously explained, the stuffing for poultry prepared in restaurants is usually not literally stuffed into the bird but baked separately. Bread stuffings are made from stale bread which is soaked and seasoned. The most common faults of moist bread dressing are sogginess and overseasoning. Sogginess is caused by soaking bread which is insufficiently staled, by using bread which is heavy in its fresh state or by adding too much liquid to the bread. Often stale bread is simply tossed into a large container, covered with cold water for a period, and then squeezed to eliminate excess water. If the bread is squeezed tightly, it becomes too compact. The addition of beaten eggs in the recipe below makes for a lighter stuffing. When seasoning stuffing, it is best to use spices sparingly. Students sometimes taste stuffing before it is baked, which is not always an accurate guide. The flavors of certain herbs such as thyme or marjoram are released by heat, so that after the stuffing is baked the flavoring elements become much more pronounced. Dried herbs which are too old or have been exposed to the air too long lose flavor. Thus a package of dried sage which is freshly opened will have a vivid aroma. If the sage remains unused on the shelf for a long period, its aroma and flavor will diminish. In many restaurants bread stuffing for poultry is prepared by the *garde manger* rather than the roast cook.

Before starting work: Stale bread may be found either in the *garde manger's* section or in the pantry. Ideally, the bread should be about 4 days old and should be staled in the refrigerator. Students should read menus in advance, just as experienced cooks do, and should set bread aside for a job such as this. Examine bread carefully to make sure there is no sign of mold. Do not use muffins, biscuits or other quickbreads which cause stuffing to be heavy.

(1) Assemble the following ingredients:

    4 lb stale white bread

    1 to 1 1/2 qt cold chicken broth

    Note: If chicken broth is gelled, it should be placed over a low flame only until it becomes liquid; it should not be hot.

    1 lb melted butter

    2 lb onions, small dice

    1 lb celery, including leaves (leaves chopped fine, balance of celery, small dice)

    2 oz parsley, chopped extremely fine

    1 tablespoon leaf sage

    1 teaspoon leaf thyme

    1 teaspoon ground marjoram

    5 eggs, well beaten

    1 1/2 tablespoons salt

    1 teaspoon ground black pepper

(2) Cut bread into 1/2-in. cubes and place in large wide mixing bowl. (In some restaurants it is the practice to use bread without crust. If crust is trimmed, bread should be added so that the trimmed weight is 4 lb.)

(3) Melt 1/4 lb butter in wide shallow saucepan. Do not permit butter to brown.

(4) Add onions and celery to saucepan. Sauté, stirring frequently until vegetables are tender. Use a low to moderate flame. Keep saucepan covered as much as possible during sautéing. If onions are tender and celery remains too crisp, a small amount of water may be added to saucepan to complete cooking without browning vegetables.

(5) In another small saucepan, melt balance of butter.

(6) Very slowly pour chicken broth and balance of melted butter over bread while tossing lightly. The purpose of pouring the broth slowly is to use just enough to make the bread moist rather than soggy.

(7) Scatter sautéed vegetables over bread. Sprinkle with parsley,

sage, thyme and marjoram. Sprinkle with salt and pepper. Toss bread to blend seasonings.

(8) While tossing bread, slowly add beaten eggs.

(9) Turn dressing into greased baking pans. If steam table inset pans are available (the pans from which the stuffing will be served), they may be used for baking the stuffing. Cover pans with aluminum foil or greased heavy paper.

(10) Preheat oven to 350° F.

(11) Bake stuffing 1 hour.

(12) Serve stuffing with spoon or scoop, allowing 3 oz per portion. Use a portion control scale to estimate size of portions for first several orders.

Oyster Stuffing.—Add 2 qt shucked small-to-medium size oysters. Simmer oysters in their own liquor only until edges of oysters curl. Drain oysters, reserving liquor. Cool liquor and substitute it for an equivalent amount of chicken broth. Combine oysters with other ingredients when mixing stuffing.

Chestnut Stuffing.—Add 1 qt coarsely chopped, shelled, roasted chestnuts or 1 qt canned chestnuts in water, drained and coarsely chopped. Combine with other ingredients when mixing stuffing.

Sausage Stuffing.—Add 2 lb bulk fresh sausage meat, sautéd until brown, and broken up so that pieces of meat can be well distributed with other ingredients. Add to bowl when mixing stuffing.

Apple Stuffing.—Add 2 qt pared, cored, diced cooking apples, rolled in flour and sautéd until tender. Add to bowl when mixing stuffing.

English Bread Stuffing   **50 Portions, Approx 3 Oz Each**

English stuffing is dry and crumbly rather than moist as in the preceding recipe. It is lighter than the moist stuffing since the only liquid added to it is melted butter. It should be made from white unsliced sandwich bread. The bread should be four days old for best results. The crusts of the bread are sliced off, and the bread is made into crumbs in a chopping machine with vertical blades. Some types of white sandwich bread have additives in them which retard staling. If this is the case, the crumbs should be made the day before the stuffing is to be baked to allow for additional staling. English stuffing may be served as an accompaniment with any form of roast poultry but is most popular with chicken or pheasant.

Before starting work: Review Chap. 2 on chopping vegetables with the French knife. The vegetables are chopped fine by hand rather than diced as in the previous recipe. Make sure you are familiar with the operation of the chopping machine with vertical blades, used for making white bread crumbs.

(1) Assemble the following ingredients:

5 lb (trimmed weight) stale white sandwich bread without crust

1 1/2 lb butter

2 lb onions, chopped fine

1 lb celery (no leaves), chopped fine

3 oz parsley, chopped extremely fine

1 tablespoon ground poultry seasoning

1 tablespoon salt

1/2 teaspoon white pepper

(2) Cut bread into 1-in. chunks.

(3) Chop bread into fine crumbs by placing it in chopping machine with vertical blades. Do not overload machine. Chop bread in batches.

(4) Place chopped crumbs in wide mixing bowl.

(5) Melt 1/4 lb butter in saucepan large enough to accommodate onions and celery. Add onions and celery. Sauté, stirring frequently, until tender. Vegetables should not brown. If onions are tender and celery remains firm, a small amount of water may be added to saucepan; cover saucepan with lid and continue cooking until celery is tender.

(6) Sprinkle sautéd vegetables over breadcrumbs. Sprinkle parsley, poultry seasoning, salt and pepper over breadcrumbs.

(7) Melt remaining butter in saucepan.

(8) Toss breadcrumbs to blend ingredients, slowly adding balance of melted butter while continuing to toss mixture.

(9) Preheat oven to 325° F.

(10) Turn stuffing into heavily greased baking pans. Cover pans with aluminum foil or greased heavy paper. Greased side of paper should be on top crumbs.

(11) Bake stuffing 30 to 40 min or until completely heated through. Crumbs should not be browned. Stuffing should be stirred once during baking to prevent browning on bottom.

(12) Place stuffing in steam table pans or in deep pots and keep in steam table for serving. If stuffing seems to become too dry during meal period, it may be moistened with a small amount of stock; use as little as possible.

Note: Any of the variations with moist bread stuffing (p 183) can be used with English bread stuffing.

Baked Glazed Ham, Madeira Sauce   50 Portions, Approx 5 Oz Each

There are two kinds of ham, smoked and fresh. When the unmodified word ham appears on a menu, such as ham sandwich or baked ham, it means the smoked type. A fresh ham cooked in the oven is listed as *roast* fresh ham. Baked ham is usually coated with sugar or some other sweet substance during the baking process, and the brown coating forms an attractive glaze. At one time most of the hams served in restaurants were raw, requiring soaking and subsequent simmering in water before they were baked. Nowadays ready-to-eat hams are widely used. These are hams with the bone in, not the canned boneless type. They are processed in such a way that the baking and glazing does not cause them to become noticeably dry. A baked glazed ham is one of the few jobs in which the roast cook does not prepare the usual *jus* or gravy made from the drippings. Because the meat was previously cooked, the drippings in the baking pan are minimal. In this case the roast cook prepares a sauce made apart from the meat. Thus, on a menu, you may read "Baked Ham with Raisin Sauce" or "Baked Ham, Madeira Sauce," etc. As far as the technique of carving is concerned, ham is similar to leg of lamb (p 189).

Before starting work: Determine the day before whether the hams you are using are the ready-to-eat type or whether they need to be simmered in water. In the latter case, they should be simmered the day before and cooled before baking. The hams you receive from the butcher or *garde manger* should have the hip bone removed, the skin taken off and the fat in excess of 1/4 in. trimmed off. Test the thickness of the fat by inserting a small pointed knife. As soon as the tip of the knife touches the lean part, you will feel resistance. If there is excess fat, trim it away by slicing laterally.

(1) Assemble the following ingredients:
   2 smoked, ready-to-eat hams, 14 to 16 lb each
   Whole cloves
   1 lb light brown sugar
   1 cup corn syrup
   1 cup orange juice or pineapple juice
   3 qt sauce *espagnole* (p 213)
   1 pt ham stock
   3/4 cup Madeira wine
(2) Preheat oven to 325° F.
(3) Make sure fat on ham is smooth and gently beveled at the shank and butt ends. Trim fat if necessary.
(4) Place hams in roasting pan, fat side up. Pan should be large enough so that hams are not crowded. Insert meat thermo-

meters so that point of thermometers is in center of thickest part of hams. Thermometers should not touch bones.

(5) Bake hams without turning approximately 2 hours or until thermometers show readings of 130°F. Remove hams from oven.

(6) Remove hams from pan. Remove thermometers from hams.

(7) Pour corn syrup, orange juice and brown sugar into saucepan Stir well. Heat over low flame, stirring frequently, until sugar dissolves.

(8) With small sharp French knife, using tip only, score the ham— that is, cut very shallow diagonal slices in fat, no more than 1/8 in. deep and about 3/4 in. apart so that diamond-shaped sections are formed on fat. Insert a clove into each diamond section. Return hams to roasting pan.

(9) Spoon half the brown sugar mixture over the hams.

(10) Return hams to oven and bake 20 to 30 min or until glaze begins to form. Spoon balance of sugar mixture over ham and bake until top is brown. Baste with sugar mixture about every 10 min.

(11) Heat sauce *espagnole* and ham stock until it comes to a boil. (If no ham stock is available, add several ham bones to sauce.) Reduce flame, and simmer 30 min. Add Maderia wine. Remove from fire and place sauce in steam table.

(12) Remove hams from baking pans to steam table pans. Hams should set at least 1/2 hour before carving. Remember when transferring hot hams from one place to another that hams are fatty and glaze is very hot. Insert a heavy fork into bottom of ham with one hand and hold protruding shank bone with other hand covered with heavy towel. Carry carefully to keep intact.

(13) To carve ham, follow this procedure:

(a) Place ham on cutting board, butt end down, shank end up. (Some cooks place the ham in a tureen or box into which butt end fits. This keeps the ham in one position during carving.)

Note: You may use either a French knife, a roast beef slicer or a kitchen slicer in carving hams. Some roast cooks use a French knife to start carving the ham when the slices are small. As slices become wider, they change to the roast beef slicer.

(b) Pull out thin bone on top, alongside main bone.

(c) Cut a V-shaped piece, about an inch thick from top of ham.

This piece is given to the *garde manger* for chopped ham, ham omelets, etc. Subsequent slices will be small at first and then become larger as ham is sliced.

(d) Begin cutting slices about 3/8 in. thick, with knife perpendicular to bone. Cut as evenly as possible. Run knife along bone to free slices from ham.

(e) When middle of ham is reached, fewer slices will be needed per portion.

(f) As carving progresses, slices should be cut from lean side of ham. Cut perpendicular to carving board. Mix lean and fatty slices when placing portions on plate.

Note: During carving, hands and knife handle become greasy. Wipe frequently. Use knife steel frequently. Keep knife steel handle free of grease.

(14) Place sliced ham on warm serving plates or platter. Pour Madeira sauce over ham. (Whole cloves may fall off ham as it is carved. Do not attempt to restore them on serving plate. They are used for flavor rather than eye appeal.

Roast Leg of Lamb, Mint Sauce   50 Portions, Approx 5 Oz Each

No dish illustrates the differences in eating habits between France and the United States as distinctly as leg of lamb. In France it is customarily eaten rare. In this country waiters do not ask patrons whether they want their roast lamb rare, medium or well done. It is served medium to well done in most restaurants. However, when the lamb is of fine quality—that is, the lamb is young with no hint of a "woolly" taste—the best restaurants tend to serve the lamb slightly pink with a hint of rareness. Your instructor or supervisor will advise you on this matter.

Among meats, leg of lamb is one of the smaller roasts. This means that some of the initial slices from the narrow end of the leg are conspicuously small. To make the first portions more attractive, larger slices from the lean side of the leg are combined with the smaller pieces. Sometimes a roast cook will carve a leg of lamb until he reaches the middle where slices are large, and then begin carving a second leg of lamb so that slices of different size can be combined. Other cooks carve the meat on the bias to increase size of slices. Mint sauce, one of the popular accompaniments for lamb, is not the typical gravy but a sauce cooked apart from the meat. Both mint sauce and pan gravy are served with lamb. The pan gravy or *jus* made from

the drippings of the meat is poured over the sliced meat on the serving plate, while the mint sauce is served in a sauce boat, in the same
way that mint jelly would be served on the side at the table.

Before starting work: Mint sauce is sometimes made in large
batches and stored in the refrigerator to be used for a number of
meals. Check to see if there is any leftover mint sauce which should
be used before the fresh batch.

(1) Assemble the following ingredients:

    5 legs of lamb, 6 to 7 lb each, with pelvic bone, backbone and
        tail bone removed, tied for roasting
    Salt, pepper
    Cooking oil
    2 lb onions, coarsely chopped
    1 lb celery, coarsely chopped
    1 lb carrots, coarsely chopped
    3 qt brown stock
    1 qt cider vinegar or malt vinegar
    2 qt and 1 pt water
    2 cups very finely chopped fresh mint leaves
    1 cup sugar
    1 tablespoon salt

(2) Preheat oven to 350°F.

(3) Brush lamb with oil. Sprinkle with salt and pepper.

(4) Place legs of lamb fat side up in roasting pans.

(5) Fasten meat thermometers in lamb in thickest part of leg. If
only one or two thermometers are used, insert them in smallest
legs. When first legs are done, insert thermometers in larger
legs.

(6) Roast lamb 1 hour.

(7) While lamb is roasting, pour vinegar, water and 1 cup chopped
mint leaves into saucepan. Bring to a boil. Reduce flame and
simmer until liquids are reduced to 2 qt. Strain through a
china cap lined with cheesecloth. To the strained liquid add
balance of mint, sugar and 1 tablespoon salt. Stir well. Bring
to a boil. Remove from flame. Mint sauce may be served hot
or cold. If served hot, keep in steam table container. If served
cold, chill in refrigerator.

    Note: The purpose of simmering the first batch of mint
    leaves with the water is to give the sauce a pronounced mint
    flavor. The second cup of leaves which are only brought up
    to a boil conveys a fresh aroma of mint.

(8) After lamb is roasted 1 hour, scatter chopped vegetables in
roasting pans. Add 1 qt stock or enough so that there is about

1/2 in. of liquid in each pan. Lift legs of lamb so that they rest on vegetables.

(9) Baste lamb with liquid in pans about every 20 min. Continue to roast lamb, fat side up, until thermometer registers 160° F, if this is the stage of doneness to which lamb is roasted in the kitchen where you are working. To roast lamb to the well-done stage, keep it on the fire until a temperature of 170° to 180° F is reached. Total cooking time is usually 1 1/2 to 2 hours.

(10) Remove pans from oven, using a double or triple thickness of heavy dry towel in each hand.

(11) Transfer legs of lamb to steam table pans. Do not remove twine used to tie the lamb until just before the meat is carved.

(12) Pour balance of stock into roasting pans. Bring to a boil over a top flame. Scrape pans to loosen drippings. Simmer slowly 20 to 25 min.

(13) Pour pan gravy (*jus*) through china cap, lined with cheesecloth into steam table pot.

(14) Skim fat carefully from gravy. Season with salt and pepper. If gravy seems pale in color, a small amount of caramel coloring may be added. To test color of gravy, pour a small amount onto a white dinner plate. Keep gravy hot in steam table.

(15) To carve leg of lamb, follow this procedure:

(a) Place leg in a vertical position. The shank or narrow end of the leg is up. The thick meaty portion or bottom of the leg is rested in a soup tureen or other suitable receptacle so that the leg can be held securely while it is being carved. The shank end of the leg is held with the left hand rather than a meat fork.

(b) Cut a small wedge at the top of the leg about 2 in. from end of shank. The wedge thus removed may be used in hashes or similar dishes.

(c) Cut 1/4-in. slices perpendicular to leg bone. For larger slices, cut on the bias. Use either a French knife, a kitchen slicer or roast beef slicer. As you approach the middle of the leg, use the kitchen slicer or roast beef slicer for neat uniform slices. After cutting in this manner, run knife along leg bone to free slices for serving.

(d) From the lean side of the leg (opposite fatty side) cut slices perpendicular to carving board. Mix these slices with slices from fatty side when arranging portions on plates. These slices are carved with, rather than against, the grain and should be used sparingly.

(16) Place slices on warm serving plates or platter. Check with supervisor or instructor on size of portions.

(17) Pour hot gravy over lamb just before orders are taken from kitchen. Allow 1 1/2 oz gravy per portion.

(18) Serve mint sauce separately in a sauceboat. Stir mint sauce well before each serving; mint will settle to bottom of container. Use a No. 2 ladle or 2 oz mint sauce per portion.

Roast Loin of Pork   **50 Portions, 2 Chops Each**

In roasting pork, the cook has no choice in determining whether the meat is to be rare, medium or well-done. It must always be well-done because of the possible presence of trichinae. On the outside chance that trichinae might be present, the meat is always cooked to a sufficiently high temperature (170° F) to eliminate the danger of trichinosis. Even without this danger, pork cooked to the well-done stage seems to have greater palatability than pork roasted to medium doneness. The gravy is usually slightly thickened rather than left thin like the *jus* served with beef and lamb. To enrich the pork flavor of the gravy, the chine bone or backbone which is removed for easier carving is added to the saucepot. When carving a loin of pork, the roast cook usually uses a heavy French knife rather than a thin pliable blade, since the job of carving in this case is merely a matter of cutting uniform slices between the rib bones. Fresh pork is popularly regarded as a fat meat, and for this reason it is often served with tart garnishes such as applesauce, spiced apples, etc. Actually modern breeding methods have produced pork which is much less fatty than it once was. The lean parts of some pork cuts may have no more fat than the lean of corresponding cuts of beef.

Before starting work: Review the use of the French knife (Chap. 2). The day before, find out if there are 3 qts of sauce *espagnole* in the refrigerator. If not, prepare sauce in time for use as gravy. The recipe calls for meat thermometers. If thermometers are not used in the kitchen where you are working, review testing doneness of meat (pp 137, 163, 164).

(1) Assemble the following ingredients:
   5 center cut pork loins, about 6 lb each
   Salt, pepper
   2 lb onions, coarsely chopped
   1 lb celery, coarsely chopped
   1 lb carrots, coarsely chopped
   2 bay leaves
   1 teaspoon leaf thyme

2 qt white stock

1 cup dry white wine

2 qt sauce *espagnole* (p 213)

(2) Preheat oven to 350°F.

(3) Sprinkle pork loins with salt and pepper. Place meat thermometers in center of thickest part of loins.

(4) Place pork loins, fat side up, on racks in roasting pan.

(5) Roast 1 1/2 hours. Remove meat from racks.

(6) Remove racks from pan. Very carefully, using heavy dry towels, pour off accumulated fat in pan. Let drippings remain.

(7) Add onions, celery, carrots, bay leaves and thyme to pan, spreading vegetables evenly.

(8) Return pork loins to pan, fat side up. Pour 1 qt stock and wine into pan.

(9) Continue to roast. Baste meat about every 20 min. Roast pork until thermometers register 170°F. Total cooking time is usually about 3 hours, depending upon thickness of loins.

(10) Remove meat from pan. If chine bones have been sawed through and are still attached to meat, remove them from loins. Use a boning knife or small trimming knife, detaching bones cleanly. To avoid burns, use a fork to hold meat; fat and bones are very hot.

(11) Place pork loins in covered steam table pan until mealtime.

(12) Scrape pan bottom and sides to loosen drippings.

(13) Very carefully pour liquid and vegetables from roasting pan into saucepot. Add balance of stock, sauce *espagnole* and chine bones. Chine bones may be chopped with a cleaver if necessary to fit them into pot.

(14) Bring gravy to a boil. Reduce flame and simmer until gravy is reduced to approx 3 qt liquid.

(15) Strain gravy through fine china cap into steam table pot.

(16) Skim fat carefully from gravy.

(17) Check gravy for color. Add caramel coloring if necessary to make it medium brown.

(18) Season gravy with salt and peper.

Note: Gravy may also be seasoned with Worcestershire sauce and MSG seasoning. Add them in small amounts to taste. Some cooks add a very small amount of sugar, 1 or 2 teaspoons, to enhance this type of gravy.

(19) Place gravy in steam table. If any noticeable amount of fat collects on gravy during meal period, skim fat off.

(20) To carve pork:

(a) Place loin on cutting board.

(b) Hold meat steady with fork in left hand. Fork should be inserted near but not adjacent to section of meat being carved.

(c) Cut between ribs to bottom of loin. Watch thickness of slices carefully to cut uniform portions. Check portions with instructor or supervisor.

(21) For each portion allow 2 slices pork, each containing a rib. Place pork on warm serving plate or platter.

(22) Pour about 2 oz (No. 2 ladle) gravy over each portion.

Roast Ribs of Beef   50 Portions, 8 to 9 Oz Each

Many restaurants have established eminent reputations on a single dish—roast ribs of beef. There are other roasts which are more tender such as roast fillet of beef, or roasts which are more expensive such as roast loin of veal. For generations, however, in both England and the United States, no example of the roast cook's art has enjoyed wider popularity than roast ribs of beef. There are three modern methods of preparing the roast. It may be:

(a) Roasted at a very low temperature of 250°F from start to finish;

(b) Roasted in a slow to moderate oven of 325° to 350°F throughout the roasting period; or

(c) Briefly roasted in a hot oven of 450°F about a half hour until browning starts, and then finished in a very low oven of 250°F.

All of the above methods avoid undue cooking losses. The last mentioned (c), followed in the recipe below, ensures good browning while the subsequent low oven heat minimizes shrinkage. The half hour initial period in the hot oven is not to be confused with the old-fashioned searing technique when an oven of 500°F or hotter was often used for a period of one hour or longer on the mistaken assumption that the extremely hot oven "sealed" in the meat juices. The ribs you receive from the butcher or *garde manger* will be oven-ready, trimmed and tied. The blade bone will have been removed. The chine bone or back bone will have been sawed loose. It may still be attached to the meat so that after cooking is completed, the bone may be easily cut away and used to make a richer flavored gravy or *jus*.

There is no *mirepoix* (flavoring vegetables) in the recipe below. The *mirepoix* used in most roasts is intended to add the flavoring of the seasoning vegetables to the *jus*. Many chefs in restaurants specializing in roast ribs of beef want the *jus* to have a straight, pronounced beef flavor unmodified by vegetables. In almost all restaurants, roast ribs of beef are cooked to the rare stage. The outer (top and bottom) slices are medium to well-done. But the largest part of the roast is kept rare for the larger number of patrons who prefer it this way. At the beginning of the meal period, when the first orders from the dining room arrive in the kitchen, customers may ask for rare roast beef. In this case the roast cook cuts off an outside chunk, including one or two ribs, and sets it aside for later customers who may want their meat well-done. If an unusually large number of patrons ask for well-done beef, the roast cook either pours hot *jus* several times over each portion, which quickly converts the meat from rare to medium or well-done, or else places individual slices very briefly under a broiler flame.

Before starting work: Ask your supervisor or instructor what time the meat is to be put in the oven in order to have the finished roast ready for the meal ahead. See whether both rib roasts can fit comfortably into one roasting pan. Use two pans or two ovens if necessary.

(1) Assemble the following ingredients:

2 7-cut ribs of beef, each weighing 20 to 22 lb, ready for the oven

Salt, pepper

4 1/2 qt brown stock (p 38)

(2) Place meat in oven. Remove top oven shelf if necessary.

(3) Preheat oven to 450° F.

(4) Select a heavy-duty roasting pan. Make sure that it is clean; there should be no residue from a previous job. If it is not large enough for the two roasts to fit comfortably, use two pans. Have two meat thermometers ready. Be sure stem of each thermometer is clean.

(5) Sprinkle meat on all sides with salt and pepper.

(6) Place ribs, fat side up, in pan. The ribs will form a natural rack in the pan, keeping the roast out of the melting fat.

Note: Roast ribs of beef are one of the heavier roasts to handle, requiring strength and balance in placing them in the pan and removing them. Do not hesitate to ask for assistance if needed.

(7) Insert meat thermometers so that stems rest in the center of the thickest part of the meat. Placement of the stem can be estimated beforehand by holding the stem outside the meat, noting its possible depth when inserted. The thermometer should not touch fat or bone.

(8) Roast the ribs approx 1/2 hour or until browning commences. The meat should not be deeply browned at this point, but the first streaks of browning should be apparent.

(9) Reduce oven heat to 250°F. If oven is an old type, and thermostat is not quick-acting, the oven door may be left open for several minutes to reduce heat quickly. (An oven thermometer may be used to check the heat.)

Note: During roasting, melting fat in the pan may begin smoking. If this occurs, the roasts may be removed from the pan briefly, and the fat poured off. Drippings or brown crusty residue should not be removed from pan.

(10) Continue to roast at 250°F until each thermometer registers 110°F, at which time meat should be removed from oven. Total cooking time is usually 4 to 4 1/2 hours. Interior temperature will continue to rise after meat has been setting, to approx 120°F. This temperature, indicating rare doneness, represents the thickest part of the roast; portions of the meat close to the ends will have a higher internal temperature.

(11) Remove roast ribs from pan, using a heavy-duty kitchen fork and dry folded heavy towel. Insert the fork in the fat side of the meat. Lift the meat, using the fork in one hand and holding a protruding rib in the other hand covered with a towel. Two forks, one in each hand, may be used if this is more convenient. Place the meat, small end up, on steam table. Keep steam table cover over ribs. Meat should set at least 30 min before carving.

(12) While meat is setting, prepare the gravy or *jus*. Pour off fat from the pan, but permit drippings to remain. To pour off fat, use a fork wedged under handle of pan to steady it; use a heavy towel in second hand; very carefully tip pan so that fat flows from one corner into a container. Add stock to pan. Scrape pan bottom with spoon to loosen drippings. Place pan over a top flame. Simmer gravy 20 to 35 min.

(13) To prepare meat for carving, remove ribs from steam table to cutting board. Cut off twine. Remove loose fat. Cut off chine or large bone from bottom. Cut off small feather bones. Place chine bone and feather bones in pan with *jus*. Return roast to steam table pan. Roast should be placed with small end up. If necessary, put a small dish under roast so that the top of the roast is level for carving; the roast may naturally lean to one side if not supported in this manner.

(14) Taste stock for flavor. If flavor seems week, a tablespoon or two of *glace de viande* or beef extract may be added and simmered until dissolved. Skim off any noticeable amount of fat. Add salt and pepper to taste.

(15) Strain *jus* through a china cap lined with cheesecloth into a steam table pot. Place in steam table. (In some restaurants several tablespoons butter are swirled into finished *jus*; other chefs prefer the *jus* as clear as possible with no added fat.) While roast stands in steam table pan, and when it is being carved, some of its natural juices may collect in the pan. Remove them and pour into pot with *jus*.

Note: Roast ribs of beef should always be carved to order. Instructor should be consulted on thickness of slices. First slices at small end of roast must be thicker than wider slices at bottom. If working area permits, roast should be carved while meat is in steam table pan. Otherwise it may have to be removed to an adjacent cutting board. Use the knife steel frequently while carving. Wipe knife handle frequently to keep it dry.

(16) Carve meat in the following manner:

(a) Place roast so that rib bones are on your left.

(b) With left hand insert fork between two of the ribs below the meat you will be slicing. If ribs are resting firmly in steam table pan or on cutting board, it may not be necessary to insert fork into roast. Instead, place bottom side of fork, tines up, on top slice you are carving.

(c) Holding roast beef slicer horizontally, cut meat in clean, long steady strokes. The first stroke should be toward your body. Do not use small mincing strokes. Keep your eye on the knife, making sure that each slice is uniformly thick. Some carvers cut only toward the body, sliding the knife forward without cutting on the up-stroke. It makes for uniform carving, but it is time-consuming. Slice the meat until the knife reaches the bone end of the meat.

(d) To free the slice, cut upward when bone is reached, or remove the knife from beneath the slice, and cut alongside the rib with the tip of the knife. Transfer the slice to a warm serving plate or platter.

Note: Some roast cooks, using a small trimming knife, cut alongside the rib bones for a few inches before slicing meat so that, when the meat is sliced, portions will automatically come free from the bone.

(17) Pour hot *jus* over meat just before waiter picks up order. Use a No. 2 ladle for each portion.

(18) When sufficient slices have been removed, and a rib bone has no more meat alongside it, cut off the bone. (In some restaurants, these bones are served in the dining room along with the

roast beef when requested by customers. In other places, the bones together with the meat between the bones are served as a menu item—broiled deviled roast rib bones. The bones are spread with mustard, rolled in bread crumbs and broiled until browned. Finally, in some kitchens, the bones are heated with brown stock for a *jus* to be served at a subsequent meal as the gravy for hot roast beef sandwiches.)

8

Sauce Cook (*Saucier*)

If the sauce cook only made sauces, his job would be relatively simple. But his daily work includes the huge array of dishes which are loosely characterized as moist heat preparation. These are braised dishes, boiled meats, poultry and seafood, stews and sautéd dishes with sauces. In some kitchens the sauce cook makes sautéd dishes such as calf's liver or breaded veal cutlets, jobs which are described in Chap. 5 as the work of the fry cook. There are certain specialty restaurants such as the so-called steak houses which do not require a sauce cook. In the great majority of restaurants, however, whose menus are not limited to a few prominent specialties, the sauce cook has the pivotal job. It is impossible to imagine a cook attaining the rank of sauce cook who has not mastered all the other specialties in the kitchen. His training takes longer than that of any other cook, his wages are higher, he ranks next to the chef in authority, and often fills the job of *sous chef* or assistant chef and may be responsible for carrying out the chef's orders. In the United States he is sometimes known as the second cook. The number of his daily preparations is so far-ranging that it may seem to the student that the sauce cook bears a manifestly disproportionate share of the work behind the ranges. To an extent this is true in some kitchens, but the sauce cook's higher salary and the possibility of his promotion to chef are compensating factors.

In large restaurants there are usually one or two sauce cook assistants who share the work, or there may be a fish cook who prepares seafood dishes with or without sauce. The sauce cook must have the ability to handle a multitude of different jobs in preparation, keeping a vigilant eye on each. It is not uncommon in busy restaurants for the sauce cook to have 8 to 12 pots on top of the ranges simmering at the same time. Normally most of his specialties are prepared before the lunch or dinner periods, then stored in the steam table for serving at mealtime. But in those eating places where there is a large a la carte offering of such dishes as lobster Newburgh, curry of chicken or Welsh rabbit, he must be able to produce these dishes quickly while serving the regular lunch or dinner items. He and the chef normally confer before, during and after the meal period. Both often jointly decide when a dish has reached its optimum point in preparation and is ready to be removed from the fire. The sauce cook's knowledge of herbs and spices must be extensive, and he must be able to use these seasonings with a sensitive hand. Because of the wide range of his duties, this chapter will be divided into the following categories, each with a set of guidelines: Sauces, Sauce Dishes, Boiled Dishes, Braised Dishes and Stews.

JOB SUMMARY

The sauce cook (1) prepares and serves sauces and dishes with sauce; (2) cooks and serves stews, braised dishes and boiled meats, poultry or seafood; (3) prepares sauces on a daily basis for specific menu items as well as sauces to be stored for a week's use such as sauce *espagnole*, tomato sauce, etc.; (4) in the absence of a soup cook, may make soups and stocks; (5) supplies sauces to other cooks when dishes they are preparing need sauce accompaniments; (6) prepares garnishes for stews and braised dishes; (7) serves vegetable accompaniments to menu items for which he is responsible; (8) requisitions groceries from storeroom for himself and other cooks; (9) confers with chef before and during meal period; (10) may prepare and serve food for banquets.

MANUAL PROCEDURES

Sauces

The *saucier* (1) cooks meat, poultry and seafood in water for stocks; (2) chops vegetables for stocks; (3) simmers, skims and strains stocks; (4) sautés vegetables for use in brown stocks; (5) browns bones and meat by sautéing in pan or roasting in oven for use in brown stocks; (6) combines vegetables, meat, bones and stock for sauce preparation; (7) heats milk, cream, white stocks or combinations of these for sauces; (8) makes roux, using fat and flour, and cooks to varying shades of color depending on sauce being prepared; (9) combines roux and liquids to make sauces; (10) simmers, skims and strains sauces; (11) seasons sauces with bouquet garni and other spices and herbs; (12) colors sauces when necessary; (13) cools and stores some sauces in refrigerator for subsequent use; (14) during meal period keeps sauces hot in steam table; (15) skims and thins hot sauces in steam table when necessary; (16) checks quality of stored sauces in refrigerator and reheats sauces for daily use; (17) makes compound sauces from basic sauces by adding cooked vegetables, wine, seasonings, etc.; (18) chops vegetables for unstrained sauces such as pasta sauces and cooks them with tomato products; (19) simmers unstrained sauces to proper consistency; (20) clarifies butter and combines butter with egg yolks for sauces made by emulsification.

Sauce Dishes

He (1) sautés raw meats, poultry or seafood for combining with sauces; (2) boils raw meats, poultry or seafood to be combined with sauces; (3) dices or otherwise cuts cooked meats, poultry or seafood to be used in sauces; (4) chops and sautés seasoning vegetables; (5) reduces wine for flavor intensification; (6) blazes spirits; (7) cooks vegetable garnishes; (8) combines cooked meats, poultry or seafood with sauces and simmers combination until flavors are blended; (9) seasons sauce dishes with spices, wine and other flavor components; (10) garnishes sauce dishes with vegetables and/or starch components.

Boiled Dishes

In preparing boiled dishes, he (1) blanches meat or poultry, if necessary, before boiling; (2) simmers meat or poultry in water, using pots over top flame or steam-jacketed kettle; (3) may use seasoning vegetables in whole pieces for simmering; (4) checks stock frequently to maintain simmering temperature; (5) skims stock when necessary; (6) tests each piece of meat or poultry individually for tenderness; (7) removes meat from stock when tender; (8) strains stock; (9) combines stock with roux for sauces; (10) strains sauces; (11) may add flavoring ingredients to sauces; (12) poaches or simmers seafood in fish boilers using water or court bouillon; (13) poaches or simmers seafood in shallow baking pans using water or court bouillon; (14) carves meat or poultry into slices or pieces prior to serving; (15) garnishes boiled meats with cooked vegetables; (16) pours sauce over boiled meat or poultry or serves sauce separately.

Braised Dishes

The sauce cook (1) browns large pieces of meat by sautéing or roasting; (2) deglazes pan in which food was browned; (3) may dip meat in flour prior to sautéing; (3) marinates meats in vinegar, water and spices or other marinades prior to browning; (4) chops and sautés or otherwise browns seasoning vegetables; (5) simmers browned meat and seasoning vegetables in marinade and stock; (6) thickens gravy with flour or roux; (7) tests meat for tenderness by inserting fork; (8) skims, strains and seasons gravies; (9) colors gravies if necessary; (10) carves meat; (11) covers meat on serving plates with gravy and adds garnish vegetables and/or starch.

Stews

In addition, he (1) blanches small pieces of meat, if necessary, prior to browning; (2) sautés meat in fat; (3) chops and sautés seasoning vegetables with meat; (4) adds herbs and spices to sautéd meats; (5) may brown meat in shallow pans in hot oven prior to adding to stew pot; (6) adds flour to sautéd meat for gravies; (7) adds stock to sautéd meats; (8) simmers stews until gravy flavor is developed and meat is tender; (9) cuts vegetables for garnishing stews; (10) may add garnish vegetables to stew pot or may cook them separately; (11) skims gravies; (12) corrects gravy seasoning; (13) colors gravy if necessary; (14) skims fat from gravy, if necessary, while stews are in steam table.

EQUIPMENT AND UTENSILS

In his work he uses (1) stock pots; (2) steam-jacketed kettles; (3) tilt kettles; (4) tilting-braising pans; (5) saucepots with loop handles; (6) stewing pots or *braisières*, round and rectangular; (7) saucepans with long handles; (8) sauté pans or *sautoirs*; (9) fish boiler; (10) oval and round gratin pans; (11) steam table or hotel pans; (12) wire whips of assorted sizes and gauges; (13) skimmers; (14) assorted spatulas; (15) stirring paddles; (16) china caps; (17) cutting board; (18) French knives, slicing knives, paring knife.

WORKING CONDITIONS AND HAZARDS

The sauce cook (1) works with equipment containing hot liquids in humid atmosphere; (2) moves and carries heavy pots, sometimes with assistance of another cook or kitchen helper; (3) must constantly be alert for spillage of hot foods on hands or body; (4) must work rapidly when skimming foods; (5) must exercise special care when pouring hot foods from one container to another; (6) is exposed to heat of steam table during meal period.

PLACE IN JOB ORGANIZATION

The sauce cook may be promoted from soup cook, roundsman or roast cook. He may advance to chef or executive chef.

SAUCES

In learning the sauce cook's job, it is important for the student to understand the difference between a sauce and a gravy. A sauce is a liquid preparation, usually thickened, cooked apart from the food with which it is later served. Thus, a *béchamel* or cream sauce is cooked in one pot and later combined with sautéd mushrooms which have been cooked separately. The resultant dish is creamed mushrooms. A gravy, on the other hand, is a liquid preparation which derives its flavor from the raw solid food with which it is cooked in the same pot. When chunks of lamb, for example, are cooked together with stock in the same pot, the stock takes on the distinctive flavor of lamb. The resultant stew contains lamb gravy. We do not refer to it as lamb sauce. The purpose of any sauce is to enhance the flavor of the food with which it is served. It may emphasize the natural flavor of the food as when a *velouté* or sauce made with chicken broth is combined with chunks of chicken and sweet peppers to make chicken a la king. It may add a totally different flavor as when hollandaise sauce, made from egg yolks and butter, is poured over cooked asparagus. There are many categories of sauces with hundreds of variations. The basic sauces, however, sometimes called the mother sauces in French cooking terminology, are the following:

(1) *Béchamel* or cream sauce, in which the principal ingredients are fat, flour and milk or cream

(2) *Velouté*, a sauce made of fat, flour and white stock

(3) *Espagnole* or brown sauce, in which the principal ingredients are fat, flour and brown stock made of meat and bones

(4) Tomato sauce made of fat, flour, tomato products and white stock

(5) Hollandaise sauce made of egg yolks and butter.

In addition to these basic sauces and their variations, there are thick unstrained tomato sauces, such as those served with spaghetti, sweet dessert sauces, seafood cocktail sauces, barbecue sauces and cold sauces such as tartar sauce. Many of these miscellaneous sauces are not made by the sauce cook. But the five basic sauces, in many of the best restaurants, are available at all times and are used on a daily basis.

Students may note that four out of the five basic sauces contain fat and flour. A mixture of melted fat and flour is called roux, and it is the common thickening agent in many sauces. When melted fat and flour are combined and cooked very briefly—only until the taste of raw flour disappears—the mixture is called a white roux. When the cooking is allowed to continue, the mixture takes on a deeper yellow color and is called a blond roux. If the mixture is still further cooked until it takes on a light tan color, it is known as a brown roux and is the base for brown sauces. To make 1 pt roux, mix until smooth 11 oz melted butter or other fat and 7 oz flour.

The ability to judge a fine sauce from a mediocre one is something that students can learn only with practical accumulated experience. One of the best standards, however, for judging a hot sauce is this: The sauce should have a mellow delicious flavor if tasted alone; and it should flatter the food with which it is served. Even a sauce with a sharp piquant flavor like curry sauce, when used with a bland food like shrimp, should not be so overpowering or aggressive in flavor that the natural taste of the shrimp is lost.

23 GUIDES TO SAUCE COOKERY AND SAUCE DISHES

(1) Excellent sauces can only be made with excellent ingredients. Simple basic components like butter, milk, cream or eggs should be carefully checked for freshness, flavor and odor before each job. All stocks for sauce should be of pronounced strength. If stocks are weak, they should be cooked or reduced until their flavor is intensified or should be supplemented with flavor-strengthening seasonings.

(2) The quantity of sauce to be prepared each day should be carefully estimated on the basis of the menu and the probable lunch or dinner load to keep leftover sauces to a minimum. Some sauces may be used the next day; others may have to be discarded. This is particularly important in the case of those sauces that are made fresh each day, such as hollandaise sauce or those containing milk or cream.

(3) For all sauces that need simmering, use heavy saucepans over

low flames. A saucepan of thin metal can easily result in a scorched sauce, particularly one containing milk or cream.

(4) For stirring the ingredients of a sauce when they are first combined, use a fine wire whip, rather than a coarse whip, to prevent lump formation.

(5) For stirring a small quantity of sauce after it is simmering on the fire, use small spoons or paddles. For stirring large quantities use a long stainless steel paddle. Stirring means not only moving the liquid in the pot but scraping the bottom of the pot and the corners where excessive thickening usually occurs.

(6) Plan your work so that saucepots are on the fire in ample time to allow long slow simmering. Extended cooking is necessary for two reasons:

(a) To develop a mellow, finished flavor
(b) To reduce the liquids so that the sauce in time acquires sufficient body to coat food and adhere to it without conveying a thick starchy mouth-feel.

(7) The well defined flavor of a sauce depends more on the ingredients used and the way the sauce was cooked than on the last-minute seasonings that may be added to it. While a sauce is in the process of cooking, avoid excessive seasonings. Many stocks contain natural salts and flavoring components which intensify as the sauce reduces.

(8) Sauces (except those of the emulsion type like hollandaise) are usually placed in the steam table at least one hour prior to the meal period. During that time skin formation may occur on top of the sauce. To prevent it:

(a) Dot the sauce with small pieces of butter, or
(b) Place a piece of greased paper on the surface of the sauce; cut the paper to fit the diameter of the pot and remove it at mealtime
(c) During the meal period, occasionally stir sauces that are not served for long intervals.

(9) Sauce flavor additives such as the wide variety of instant bouillons, gravy flavors, etc., now available may be used to improve sauces. They should be used in moderation or their synthetic flavors will become very apparent.

(10) When flour, the common thickening agent for sauces, is combined with melted fat to make roux, the mixture should always be heated over a low flame. High heat diminishes its ability to thicken liquids.

(11) Because we usually see the sauce before we see the food it coats, special attention must be paid to eye appeal. The light sauces such as *béchamel* and *velouté* should show the gloss which comes

from long slow cooking. Brown sauce should be richly brown. Tomato sauce should be bright red. When colorings are added to sauces, they should be used in small quantities progressively to obtain a rich hue without making the sauce look artificial. It is not always possible to obtain expected color tone with natural means.

(12) A variety of fats can be used to make sauces including butter, margarine, chicken fat, rendered pork fat, hydrogenated vegetable fat, etc. French tradition holds that butter provides the best flavor and that sweet butter is superior to salted butter.

(13) Some special sauces such as Newburgh sauce (see lobster Newburgh, p 236) are thickened with egg yolks rather than flour. The egg yolks are usually mixed with a small amount of cream, and the mixture is called a *liaison*. It is never added directly to the liquid in the saucepan. Some of the hot liquid in the pan is first combined with the egg yolk mixture, and the resultant mixture is slowly added to the pan to complete the cooking. Excessive or prolonged heat must be avoided or the *liaison* may curdle.

(14) A common fault of sauces is lump formation. If flour, for instance, is tossed directly into a hot liquid, the outer starch particles are cooked almost instantly while the inner particles remain raw. Lumps are thus formed. To prevent lump formation, a thickening agent such as flour, cornstarch or arrowroot should be dispersed with another ingredient before it is added to the sauce. To avoid lump formation mix the starch:

(a) With melted fat such as in making a roux
(b) With enough cold liquid such as water or milk to make a paste, or
(c) With sugar if the sauce is a sweet dessert sauce.

(15) If, in spite of all precautions, lump formation occurs in a sauce, the sauce should be beaten with a wire whip. If lumps still remain, the sauce should be strained through a fine china cap, through cheesecloth or both.

(16) The basic stocks used in soups such as white stock, brown stock and chicken stock are also used in sauce making. In some restaurants these stocks are prepared by the soup cook who makes them available to the sauce cook. Since a sauce is expected to have a more concentrated flavor than a soup, the sauce cook should check the flavor of stocks before using them. In some cases, it may be necessary to reduce the stocks before adding them to the sauces. In other cases, the sauce may have to be cooked longer than usual for additional strength. It is the sauce cook's responsibility, therefore, to frequently set his own guidelines for cooking times rather than to follow the specific time set in a recipe.

(17) The drippings which form the base for some sauce dishes may be a very small quantity in the pan. When a liquid is added to the pan, such as Marsala wine in veal scallopine Marsala, the drippings are usually dissolved. If they do not dissolve quickly, scrape the pan bottom and sides so that the pan is completely deglazed.

(18) When a food is dipped in flour and sautéd before it is simmered in a sauce, be sure there is only enough flour to lightly coat it. Excess flour only falls into the pan, turns dark and discolors the sauce.

(19) The ideal sauce dish results when the solid food and the sauce accompanying it are slowly simmered until the flavors are well blended. Certain sauce dishes, however, are made to order during the meal period when extended simmering is not possible. In such cases the sauce must be rapidly boiled. Use heavy saucepans for such dishes to avoid scorching; stir the ingredients or shake the pan frequently until flavors are blended.

(20) When sauce dishes are prepared for a table d'hôte menu, they should be kept in the steam table at a serving temperature from 140° to 160° F. If the steam table heat is too intense, the solid food may disintegrate, and flavors become unpleasant. Check the temperature of the water in the steam table to make sure it is not too high.

(21) When a rich sauce like hollandaise is poured over another food cooked in water such as poached fish or poached eggs, be sure the fish or eggs are not surrounded with a rim of water before the sauce is added. If there is excess water on the plate or casserole, wipe it with a clean towel.

(22) When serving sauce dishes, the sauce cook must always be mindful of eye appeal. Drops of sauce on the rim of a plate or casserole should always be wiped off before the waiter receives the dish. If toast triangles, rice mounds or other garnishes are served with sauce dishes, they should always be neatly placed or arranged on the dish.

(23) Sometimes sauces which have been completely cooked will be too thick or too thin even though a recipe was followed precisely. Different brands of flour and even the same brand at different times will produce sauces which do not have the same consistency. Sometimes the acid content of a liquid in a sauce will affect the thickness of a sauce one way or the other. If brown or white sauces are too thick, they may be thinned with stock or milk. If they are too thin, they may be thickened with cornstarch. Cornstarch is dissolved in cold water or other liquid, using 1 part cornstarch to 2 parts cold liquid. The sauce is brought to a boil, and the cornstarch solution is slowly added while stirring constantly. The sauce must then be cooked

further until all starch taste disappears. Use cornstarch very sparingly, as it has almost twice the thickening property of flour.

Sauce Béchamel (White or Cream Sauce)   1 Gal

In many restaurants staffed by Americans who do not use the French language in their daily work, French terms for sauces such as sauce *béchamel* are still frequently used. The name *béchamel* is traced to a financier who was steward of the royal household of Louis XIV. As previously pointed out, the modern version of this sauce consists of melted fat, flour and milk or milk and cream. Students familiar with the common white sauce made in homes know that the sauce becomes thick in a matter of minutes. Mere thickness, however, does not mean a sauce is ready to serve. The French practice in making this sauce is to allow long slow simmering. What starts out as a simple thick sauce with a starchy aftertaste in time becomes a smooth creamy elixir with no hint of the taste of flour. The best flour to use is pastry or all-purpose, rather than bread flour, because bread flour has less thickening ability. For best results, fresh whole milk should be used rather than powdered milk, and a small amount of cream should be added for both rich flavor and body. Any cook who has ever spilled milk over a flame on a hot stove knows that the milk instantly scorches. Sauces made with milk cooked over a high flame will, in the same way, tend to quickly burn on the bottom of the saucepot. It is particularly important, therefore, to use a pot of heavy metal when making sauce *béchamel* and to stir the sauce frequently and thoroughly.

In busy restaurants the sauce is made fresh each day. Any sauce *béchamel* left over from a previous day should be checked carefully for flavor and odor if it is to be added to a fresh batch. The sauce cook often supplies this sauce to other cooks. The fry cook may need it for croquettes. The vegetable cook may need it for a creamed vegetable. For this reason the sauce cook should consult with the chef or other cooks in estimating his daily needs. The sauce may be thin, medium or thick depending on the particular use. For most purposes the medium sauce is used. A thin sauce *béchamel* might be needed for a casserole, a thick sauce for croquettes. Proportions for all three versions are indicated in the recipe below.

Before starting work: Check milk and cream for freshness. Choose heavy pots both for scalding the milk and cream as well as for making the sauce. Examine interior of pots under good light to make sure they are absolutely clean. Choose a wire whip and mixing paddle of the appropriate size for the pot you are using. If you are making more or less sauce than indicated in the recipe, check your calculations carefully and submit them to the chef or instructor for approval.

Note: Some cooks make only the thick sauce, and then later add liquid, if and when necessary, to make it medium or thin.

(1) Assemble the following ingredients:

Ingredient	Thin Sauce	Medium Sauce	Thick Sauce
Butter or margarine:	8 oz	1 lb	2 lb
Pastry flour:	4 oz	8 oz	1 lb
Milk:	1 gal plus 1 pt	1 gal plus 1 pt	1 gal plus 1 pt
Light cream:	1 pt	1 pt	1 pt
Salt:	1 tablespoon	1 tablespoon	1 tablespoon
White pepper:	1/2 teaspoon	1/2 teaspoon	1/2 teaspoon

(2) Pour milk and cream into saucepot.

(3) Heat over low to moderate flame until mixture is scalded, that is, until it comes almost up to the boiling point but does not boil. Bubbles will appear around edge of saucepot. Milk mixture may also be heated in steam table.

(4) While milk is heating, melt butter in heavy saucepot, at least 1 1/2 gal capacity. Use a low flame.

(5) When butter is melted, remove saucepot from heat.

(6) Add flour slowly, stirring with fine wire whip until well blended. No dry flour should be visible. Check corner of pot to make sure blending is complete.

(7) Return to low flame, and simmer approximately 5 min. At this point a white roux will have been made. The color is not literally white because of the butter.

(8) Slowly stir in hot milk, adding milk in batches of about a quart each. Beat well after each batch is added, and cook until sauce becomes thick after each addition.

(9) When all milk has been added, continue to cook over low flame. Stir sauce from time to time with paddle, scraping bottom and corner of pot to make sure that no thick layer forms on bottom. If a layer does form, stir vigorously with wire whip.

(10) Simmer for approximately 1/2 hour over very low flame, stirring about every 5 min, until sauce is smooth and glossy. There should be no "floury" taste.

(11) Remove sauce from fire. Stir in salt and white pepper, mixing well.

(12) Force sauce through fine china cap into *bain marie* (steam table) pot or two pots if part of the sauce is to be retained for a later meal. Place sauce for next meal in steam table.

(13) Dot sauce with butter allowing 1/4 lb butter to 1 gal of sauce. Butter will melt slowly and will prevent skin formation.

(14) At serving time stir in butter on surface of sauce. Correct seasoning if necessary.

(15) If sauce thickens noticeably as it stands in steam table, stir in hot milk in very small batches until sauce is restored to original consistency. If any lumps or thick layers appear, strain the sauce again through a fine china cap.

Onion Flavor.—Before adding flour, sauté 1 cup onions or shallots, chopped extremely fine, in butter until onion is wilted but not colored. Onion will be removed when sauce is strained but flavor will remain.

Grated Nutmeg Flavor.—This variation is preferred by some chefs. Add 1/2 teaspoon freshly grated nutmeg along with salt and pepper.

Cheese Sauce.—Add 1 lb freshly grated Parmesan cheese or 1 1/2 lb shredded sharp Cheddar cheese (preferably white rather than yellow) to sauce when sauce is finished cooking and is in steam table. Parmesan cheese will blend instantly. Cheddar cheese will melt in a few minutes.

Egg Sauce.—Add 16 hard-boiled eggs, finely chopped, to finished sauce.

White Mushroom Sauce.—Cut 3 lb fresh mushrooms in slices 1/8 in. thick. Sauté mushrooms in 6 oz butter until tender and until all mushroom liquid has evaporated from pan. Combine mushrooms and sauce *béchamel*. Simmer 5 min.

Horseradish Sauce.—Add 1 pt prepared horseradish, well drained. Mix well. Dissolve 2 tablespoons dry mustard in 1/2 cup milk, mixing well. Add to sauce. Mix well.

Butter for Finishing.—Just before a sauce is ready for serving, cooks sometimes add a few pats of butter and stir it until it melts, resulting in a delicate rich flavor.

Sauce Mornay   1 Gal

Each of the variations in the preceding recipe for sauce *béchamel* contains one added principal ingredient. Sauce *Mornay* contains two added components—egg yolks and grated cheese. They must be very carefully combined if the sauce is to be successful. Sauce *Mornay* is one of the most widely used variations in the white sauce category. It is incorporated with poultry, seafood, eggs, vegetables and pasta in dozens of different recipes. Usually in such combinations the dish is sprinkled with additional cheese and browned under the broiler or in the oven. When adding eggs to a hot sauce, the cook should observe the following steps to make a successful blend:

(1) The egg yolks are diluted with cream

(2) A small amount of hot sauce is added to the egg yolk mixture, raising its temperature slightly

(3) The resultant mixture is slowly stirred into the hot sauce and briefly cooked while being stirred constantly.

The three steps make what is known as a *liaison*. After sauce *Mornay* has been completely cooked and seasoned, it should not be kept directly in contact with the water in the steam table for any prolonged period. It may "break" or appear to be curdled. Rather it should be kept in a steam table pot inside a larger one in contact with the water. When orders are received for a *Mornay* dish, the sauce is combined with the food it accompanies, sprinkled with additional cheese and placed under a broiler or in a very hot oven for last-minute browning or glazing. To ensure that the glazing will be attractive, a small amount of unsweetened whipped cream is sometimes folded into the sauce just before it is browned.

Before starting work: Review guides to sauce cookery (pp 202–206). Check both milk and cream for freshness. *Mornay* dishes are usually served in shallow individual casseroles. Make sure these are clean and available. Sauce *Mornay* is usually made right before the meal period. Schedule your work so that you can complete the sauce without any last-minute rush.

(1) Assemble the following ingredients:

    1 gal milk
    1 lb butter
    8 oz flour
    1 tablespoon salt
    1/2 teaspoon white pepper
    16 egg yolks
    1 cup light cream
    8 oz grated Parmesan cheese

(2) Pour milk into saucepot.

(3) Heat over low to moderate flame until mixture comes almost up to the boiling point but does not boil.

(4) In another saucepot melt butter.

(5) When butter is melted, remove saucepot from heat.

(6) Add flour slowly, stirring with wire whip until well blended. No dry flour should be visible. Check corner of pot to make sure blending is complete.

(7) Return to low flame and simmer approximately 5 min, stirring occasionally.

(8) Slowly stir in hot milk, adding milk in batches of about a quart. Mix well after each batch is added, and cook until sauce is thick after each addition.

(9) When all milk has been added, continue to cook over low flame. Stir sauce from time to time with mixing spoon or paddle, scraping bottom to make sure no thick layer of sauce is forming.

(10) Simmer for approximately 1/2 hour or until sauce is smooth and glossy with no "floury" taste.

(11) Stir in salt and pepper. Correct seasoning if desired. Keep sauce on fire.

(12) Beat egg yolks with wire whip. Slowly stir in cream and beat until well blended.

(13) Slowly stir about 1 cup hot sauce into egg yolk mixture. Blend well.

(14) Slowly pour egg yolk mixture in a small stream into hot sauce, beating constantly as mixture is added.

(15) Continue to cook over low to moderate flame, stirring constantly, until sauce almost comes up to boiling point.

(16) Remove saucepot from fire. Stir in grated cheese. Add more salt and pepper if desired.

(17) If sauce is not used at once, dot sauce with 1/4 lb butter broken into small pieces. Butter will gradually melt and prevent skin formation. Stir melted butter into sauce just before it is to be used.

Sauce Velouté   1 Gal

The French word *velouté* means velvety. It is an apt description for a sauce known for its mellow smoothness. It is made like sauce *béchamel* except that instead of milk, chicken broth or veal stock is the main liquid ingredient. Needless to say the strength of the chicken broth or stock is all important. If the broth or stock is weak, the sauce should be cooked longer than the normal time indicated below in order to concentrate its flavor. If there is time to strengthen the stock before it is added to the sauce, this may be done by adding chicken parts such as necks, wing tips or backs, and cooking them with the stock until its flavor is pronounced. In a restaurant where fresh mushrooms are frequently used, the peelings or trimmings of mushrooms including stems may be added to give the sauce a richer flavor; later the sauce is strained to remove the mushroom pieces. Chicken broth or stock has less opacity than milk, and for this reason sauce *velouté* may seem to be less thick than a sauce made with milk. To judge the thickness of a sauce, cooks frequently pour a small amount on a plate and tip the plate, noting how rapidly the sauce flows. Unlike sauce *béchamel*, which can be used as a thin, medium or thick sauce, sauce *velouté* is always prepared for medium thickness.

Before starting work: Carefully check the chicken broth or veal stock to make sure it has not soured. Stir it well; there should be no sign of fermentation. Check the broth or stock for flavor strength. Follow directions above for increasing strength if necessary. If chicken bouillon powder is used, add it in minimal amounts. It may be later added to the finished sauce if necessary.

(1) Assemble the following ingredients:
     1 lb butter or margarine
     10 oz pastry flour
     1 1/2 gal chicken broth or white stock or a combination of the two
     1 tablespoon salt
     1/2 teaspoon white pepper
     1/8 teaspoon cayenne pepper
     1 lb mushroom stems or trimmings (optional)
(2) Pour chicken broth or white stock into saucepot.
(3) Heat over low to moderate flame until it comes to a full rolling boil.
(4) Reduce flame so that broth or stock simmers, just below the boiling point.
(5) Melt butter in heavy saucepot of 2 gal capacity. Use very low flame.
(6) Stir in flour with wire whip until well blended. No dry flour or pockets of flour should be visible. Check corner of pot to make sure blending is complete.
(7) Continue to keep flame very low, stirring frequently, until roux deepens in color but does not begin to turn a light brown. When roux attains a deep golden color, it is known as a blond roux rather than the white roux in sauce *béchamel*.

(8) Slowly stir in hot broth or stock. Add liquid in batches of about a quart each. Beat well after each batch is added, and cook until sauce is thick after each addition.
(9) Add mushrooms if available. Bring sauce up to a boil.
(10) Reduce flame so that sauce simmers. Stir from time to time with mixing spoon or paddle, scraping bottom and corner of pot. If thick layer forms on bottom, stir it vigorously with a wire whip.
(11) Simmer for approximately 1 hour or until sauce is smooth and glossy, and flavor is well-developed.
(12) Stir in salt, white pepper and cayenne pepper. A few drops of yellow (egg shade) coloring may be added if desired to improve appearance of sauce. Check with chef or instructor before adding coloring. It is best to pour the coloring onto a spoon in very small amounts, and then add it to the sauce rather than to pour it directly from the bottle into the saucepot.
(13) Force sauce through fine china cap into *bain marie* (steam table) pot.
(14) Dot sauce with butter, allowing 1/4 lb butter to 1 gal of sauce, to prevent skin formation.
(15) At serving time, stir in butter on surface of sauce. Correct seasoning if necessary.
(16) While sauce remains in steam table, stir periodically to prevent skin formation. If skin does form, it is best to lift it out and discard it, rather than stir it into balance of sauce.

Fish Velouté.—Use fish stock (p. 42) instead of chicken broth or white stock. Add 2 tablespoons lemon juice to finished sauce in steam table.

Sauce Suprême.—Use 5 qt chicken broth or white stock instead of 1 1/2 gal. After sauce has been strained, scald 1 pt light cream and 1 pt heavy cream, and slowly stir into strained sauce. Simmer, do not boil, 15 min longer.

Sauce Poulette.—Sauté, in 4 oz melted butter, 4 oz shallots, chopped extremely fine, and 1 lb mushrooms, chopped fine. Sauté until mushrooms are tender and all mushroom liquid has evaporated from pan. Chop 2 oz parsley extremely fine. Stir shallots, mushrooms and parsley into sauce *suprême* above. Simmer slowly 10 min. Correct seasoning if necessary.

Sauce Allemande.—Beat 16 egg yolks and 1 cup light cream to make a *liaison*. When sauce *velouté* is finished, slowly add 1 cup of it to egg yolk mixture, mixing well. Slowly pour egg yolk mixture into hot sauce over moderate flame. Cook, stirring constantly, until sauce comes up to the boiling point but does not boil. Remove from fire at once. Correct seasoning if necessary.

Sauce Espagnole (Basic Brown Sauce)   5 Gal

The French word for basic brown sauce, *espagnole*, meaning Spanish, should not be mistakenly identified with Spanish cooking. The sauce may have been inspired by Spanish chefs who came to France centuries ago, but this is uncertain. At one time the sauce required several days preparation. It was cooked, skimmed and reduced in a protracted way that is no longer followed. The old-fashioned sauce *espagnole* conveyed an intense flavor that has given way to the lighter tasting sauce which most modern chefs have adopted. It is made brown by starting out with a brown roux, that is, by cooking butter and flour until the flour acquires a tan color. The sauce includes browned vegetables and brown stock, and is simmered until the flavors are well developed. Unlike sauce *béchamel* which is made fresh every day, brown sauce is normally made once a week. It does not contain milk, and therefore its keeping qualities are better.

There is a stronger flavored brown sauce named *demiglace* (frequently called demiglaze). It is simply the basic brown sauce combined with an equal amount of brown stock and cooked a second time until it is reduced to the original quantity of brown sauce. Some chefs use the heavier flavored *demiglace* in all instances where brown sauce appears on the menu; others prefer the lighter version or the basic sauce which is the recipe below. The argument for using a milder flavored brown sauce is that it is frequently combined with chicken, veal and pork dishes whose natural flavors are distinctively delicate, and that an excessively concentrated brown sauce makes the sauce, rather than the food it accompanies, the dominant flavor.

Students will find during their apprenticeship that, as a matter of actual practice, there are many impromptu combinations of brown sauces and brown gravies from day to day. For instance, the leftover gravy of a beef pot roast will often be combined with sauce *espagnole*. Sauce *espagnole* may be combined with the gravy of a goulash or used to supplement the gravy of a brown beef stew if there is insufficient natural gravy. If carried too far, this shuffling of brown gravies and brown sauce, while saving labor and perhaps food costs, can only lower standards. It is a common practice, however, of which the student should be aware. Note that in the recipe below the ratio of flour to butter is double what it was for sauce *béchamel*. This is because the browned flour has less thickening property than flour which has not taken on color.

Before starting work: Review preparation of brown stock (Chap. 3). Brown stock should be ready a day in advance of the sauce preparation. Check brown stock in the refrigerator to make sure there is sufficient for the quantity of sauce you are preparing. Check it for flavor and color. If it has been stored for a considerable length of time, make sure it has no off-odor or shows no signs of incipient spoilage. Since the recipe below calls for 5 gal of sauce, you should use a 12 gal pot to allow for flavoring vegetables, reduction of sauce, etc.

(1) Assemble the following ingredients:

    10 gal brown stock

    3 lb butter or melted strained beef fat or pork fat

    Note: If melted beef or pork fat is used in whole or in part, it should be carefully checked to be sure it has no charred flavor, brown specks, etc.

    5 lb onions, coarsely chopped

    2 lb carrots, coarsely chopped

    2 lb celery, coarsely chopped

    3 lb pastry flour

    8 large cloves of garlic, mashed

    1 cup chopped parsley stems

    6 large bay leaves

    2 teaspoons leaf thyme

    1 qt tomato puree

    Salt, pepper

    Caramel coloring (optional)

(2) Heat brown stock until it comes to a boil.

(3) Melt butter or other fat in saucepot over low flame. Do not let it bubble or brown.

(4) Add onions, carrots and celery. Stir well.

(5) Increase flame to moderate. Sauté vegetables until onions and celery are browned. "Browned" means a deep golden color (which may be streaky in some vegetables) but not charred. There should be no black edges or black pieces of vegetables showing excessive carbonization.

(6) Reduce flame again and stir in flour, using a wire whip. Shake the whip to dislodge vegetable pieces. Scrape bottom and

corner of pot with paddle to make sure there is no unblended flour.

(7) Continue to sauté over a low flame until fat and flour mixture turns brown. "Brown" in this case means a deep tan color sometimes compared to the color of a light cigar. Move pot near or under light, if necessary, to check color. Stir frequently to avoid burning flour. Time required for browning usually takes from 12 to 20 min. If flour becomes too brown, it will result in a charred flavor. There should be no black specks. Keep flame low or flour will lose thickening property. The browned fat-flour mixture is called a brown roux.

(8) Remove pot from flame, or turn flame off.

(9) Stir hot brown stock into brown roux in batches. Add about 2 qt at a time, stirring constantly with a wire whip. Stir well after each addition. Continue to add balance of stock in this manner.

(10) Make a bouquet garni of garlic, parsley, bay leaves and thyme. Add to pot.

(11) Slowly bring sauce to a boil, stirring occasionally.

(12) When sauce comes to a full, rolling boil, skim well.

(13) Reduce flame and continue to simmer—don't boil—until sauce is reduced to about half its original volume. Do not use a lid on pot. Stir from time to time with large paddle, scraping bottom and corner of pot. Cooking time should be from 2 to 3 hours depending upon flame, diameter of pot, etc. The finished sauce, after addition of all ingredients and reduction is to be approximately 5 gal.

(14) Add tomato puree. Stir well. Continue to simmer about 1/2 hour longer. (For a less thick sauce, canned chopped tomatoes together with their juice may be used in place of tomato puree.)

(15) Add salt and pepper to taste, stirring well before tasting. The amount of salt varies depending upon the natural salts in stock. Undersalting is preferable to oversalting.

(16) Let sauce cool slightly, approximately 30 to 45 min.

(17) Strain through fine china cap and cheesecloth.

(18) Add caramel coloring if necessary. Correct seasoning if necessary. If stock flavor was weak, it may be necessary to add a sauce, or gravy, strengthener such as powdered bouillon. Use only if necessary and in minimal amounts.

(19) Set aside, and place in steam table the amount of sauce needed for the meal at hand. Balance of sauce should be

precooled in sink and then stored, covered, in the refrigerator for future use.

Demiglace (1 Gal).—Simmer 1 gal sauce *espagnole* and 1 gal brown stock until the 2 gal of liquid are reduced to 1.

Mushroom Sauce Madeira (1 Gal).—Slice and sauté 3 lb mushrooms, caps and stems, and 1/2 cup shallots, chopped extremely fine, in 1 cup melted butter. Use low flame. Avoid browning shallots. Sauté until all mushroom liquid has evaporated from pan. Add 1 gal brown sauce and simmer 30 min. Add 1 cup (8 oz) dry Madeira wine or dry sherry. Correct seasoning if necessary.

Sauce Robert (1 Gal).—Prepare 1 cup onions chopped fine, 1/4 cup shallots, chopped very fine, 2 tablespoons garlic, chopped extremely fine, 1 cup sour pickles, chopped extremely fine, and 1/4 cup parsley, chopped extremely fine. Sauté onions, shallots and garlic in 1/2 cup melted butter only until onions and shallots are wilted and light yellow in color. Add 1 pt dry white wine and 1 cup vinegar. Simmer until liquids are reduced to 1/2 cup. Stir in 1/4 cup French mustard until well blended. Add 1 gal brown sauce. Simmer slowly, stirring frequently, 20 to 30 min. Add pickles and parsley. Correct seasoning if necessary.

Sauce Bordelaise (1 Gal).—Combine in saucepot 1 cup shallots, chopped extremely fine, with 2 qt dry red wine. Simmer slowly until wine has been reduced to 2 cups liquid. Add 1 gal sauce *espagnole*. Simmer slowly until total contents of pot are 3 1/2 qt. Cut 2 lb beef marrow into small dice, and poach in salted water 2 min. Drain and add to sauce. Add 1/4 cup parsley, chopped extremely fine.

Sauce Diable (1 Gal).—Combine 1 cup shallots, chopped extremely fine, 2 tablespoons freshly ground black peppercorns, 1 pt dry white wine and 1 pt white wine vinegar. Simmer slowly until mixture has been reduced to 2 cups. Add 1 gal sauce *espagnole* and 2 tablespoons Worcestershire sauce. Simmer until sauce has been reduced to 1 gal. Add 1/2 cup parsley, chopped extremely fine.

Caramel Coloring.—Pour 2 lb granulated sugar and 1 1/3 cups cold water into heavy saucepan. Stir until sugar dissolves. Heat over moderate flame until liquid turns very dark brown, almost black. Slowly stir in 1 cup cold water. Hold head back; mixture will bubble vigorously. Again bring to a boil. Simmer, stirring frequently, until liquid is syrup-like, thicker than water. Cool. Strain, and keep in a bottle for adding brown color to sauces, gravies, etc. Many restaurants use commercial preparations such as Kitchen Bouquet, Gravy Aid, etc., in place of caramel coloring prepared on premises.

Glace De Viande.—*Glace de viande* or meat glaze is an extract made from brown stock, cooked until it has an almost paste-like consistency. Like caramel coloring, it is prepared by the sauce cook, but may be used by other cooks for special needs. It is normally stored in the refrigerator for weeks or even months, and corresponds to commercial products which are sold as concentrated bouillon and are available in jars under the original French name of *glace de viande.* It is used to improve the flavor of brown sauces or dishes with brown gravy. It is one of the ingredients in *béarnaise* sauce, and may be used to coat certain cold dishes giving them a rich brown color. Its preparation consists mainly of reducing strained brown stock over a period of several days. Heavy saucepans must be used in order to reduce the stock very gradually. As the quantity becomes noticeably reduced, smaller saucepans are used. Whenever the stock is transferred to a smaller container, it should be strained through muslin. Cooking should continue at least until the meat glaze is reduced to 1/16 its original volume. Thus, if 4 gal brown stock are used, the *glace de viande*, when finished, should be no more than 1 qt. Some chefs prefer an even more concentrated reduction. *Glace de viande* is considered ready when it is thick enough to heavily coat a spoon. It should be stored in the refrigerator in wide-mouth jars kept tightly closed. It becomes thicker when cold.

Hollandaise Sauce   1 Qt

Hollandaise is a light creamy sauce of egg yolks and butter served with vegetables such as asparagus and broccoli, with eggs Benedict and other dishes. It is sometimes incorporated into other sauces. There is a culinary tradition about hollandaise sauce which intimidates newcomers into believing that the job of making the sauce is so intricately difficult that it should never be attempted by students of elementary cooking. It is an expensive sauce; the main ingredients are egg yolks and butter. But lobster is expensive, too, and boiling a lobster is one of the simplest jobs in the kitchen. What discourages student cooks is the fact that the sauce may "break" if improperly made. The smooth emulsion may disintegrate leaving the egg yolks and butter separated so that the sauce looks curdled. If this crisis should occur, the sauce can be remade in a brief time using the broken ingredients beaten a second time into a few additional egg yolks. Unlike the white or brown sauces, hollandaise is not cooked over a flame or simmered for long periods. Butter is melted and drawn or clarified. A mixture of beaten egg yolks and a small amount of water is cooked over hot water only until the yolks lighten in color and show the first signs of thickening. The melted butter is then very slowly beaten into the egg yolks until the ingredients are emulsified into a sauce. Egg yolks are the emulsifying agent. In procedure it is similar to making mayonnaise which is a cold emulsion of egg yolks, oil and vinegar. During the meal period hollandaise sauce is not kept in a steam table like other sauces, or it will break; it is kept in a warm, not hot, place. This *should* concern students as well as experienced cooks, because at warm temperatures, around 100° to 120°F, bacterial growth and food contamination can occur in sauces. To avoid this danger, hollandaise sauce should:

(a) Be made as close to mealtime as possible

(b) Be made for only one meal at a time.

There will be leftover egg whites after the sauce is prepared. Consult the chef or instructor who will direct you to give the egg whites either to the soup cook who may use them for clarifying soup or to the pastry department for use in desserts.

Before starting work: Make sure that all containers and utensils including wire whip, spoon, bowl, etc., are immaculately clean. Run utensils through scalding water of mechanical dishwasher if possible. The whip should be one of fine wire called piano wire. The ingredients to be assembled below call for 12 egg yolks. To separate yolks from whites, the eggshells are cracked in the center. Do not hit them so sharply that the shells shatter into many small pieces. Pour the yolks back and forth between the empty shells permitting the whites to fall into a container. Have another container nearby for the yolks. Avoid getting any yolk into the whites. (If a meringue is being made from the whites, the mixture of yolks and whites may make it impossible to beat the whites successfully.)

(1) Assemble the following ingredients:

2 lb butter, preferably sweet rather than salted

12 egg yolks

1/2 cup cold water

2 tablespoons lemon juice

Salt, white pepper, cayenne pepper

(2) Melt butter in small pot in steam table or over very low flame

(3) As soon as butter is melted, carefully remove foam from top using a small sauce ladle or spoon.

(4) Carefully pour off butter into another small container, saving the clear butter and discarding the solid matter on the bottom.

(5) Pour egg yolks and water into small narrow saucepot or steam table pot. The pot must be large enough to accommodate the wire whip so that the mixture can be beaten thoroughly as it cooks.

(6) Beat egg yolks and water until well blended before heating.

(7) Heat egg yolks and water over barely simmering water in steam table, beating constantly with wire whip. If water is boiling vigorously, the yolks will be cooked too quickly and the emulsification will not take place. (The conventional double boiler may be used in the place of the steam table. Again the water in the bottom of the double boiler should be barely simmering, not boiling.) Continue to beat until the yolks lose their deep yellow color and turn creamy yellow in appearance. The yolks will begin to change from their fluid state and suddenly begin to thicken. At this point they should be removed from the heat and beaten about a minute longer. The heat of the container will continue to thicken them. Avoid excessive thickening by beating vigorously. Scrape bottom and corner of pot.

(8) Very slowly, starting with driblets, pour melted butter into egg yolks while continuing to beat with wire whip, hitting bottom of container with whip and stirring corner of pot from time to time.

(9) As sauce becomes an emulsion, continue to add butter in a very slow stream, until all butter has been added.

(10) Slowly stir in lemon juice.

(11) Add salt to taste. (If salted butter has been used, add salt sparingly.) Add white pepper and cayenne pepper very sparingly to taste.

(12) Check with chef or instructor to find best place to keep sauce warm until mealtime. Sometimes it is kept near, but never in, a steam table. Sometimes it is kept near or on an oven shelf if there is not too much bottom heat.

(13) If, for some reason, sauce should break, beat 2 egg yolks and 1 1/2 tablespoons water as in step (7) above. Then very slowly add the broken sauce into the fresh egg yolks until

the emulsification is completed. If sauce seems too thick, it may be thinned with a very small amount of cold water. Check with chef or instructor before adding water.

Thick Hollandaise.—Use 16 egg yolks instead of 12.

Béarnaise Sauce.—Prepare hollandaise sauce omitting lemon juice. Heat 1 cup tarragon vinegar, 1 tablespoon shallots, chopped extremely fine, 1 tablespoon *glace de viande* until liquid is reduced to 1/4 cup. Slowly add to cooked hollandaise sauce, blending well. Stir in 1 tablespoon parsley, chopped extremely fine, and 1 tablespoon fresh tarragon chopped extremely fine.

Mousseline Sauce.—Fold 1/2 cup unsweetened whipped cream into hollandaise sauce.

Maltaise Sauce.—Heat 1 cup orange juice until it is reduced to 1/4 cup liquid. Cool slightly. Stir into hollandaise sauce. Stir in 2 tablespoons grated orange rind.

Choron Sauce.—Cook 2 cups tomato sauce until it is reduced to 1/2 cup. Cool slightly. Stir into hollandaise sauce.

Tomato Sauce (Puree Type) 1 Gal

The recipe which follows is the strained tomato sauce served in small quantities with such dishes as breaded veal cutlets, breaded pork chops, fried fish, etc., and is not to be confused with the thick unstrained tomato sauce (p 224) served with pasta. In almost all restaurants in the United States the sauce is made with canned tomato products rather than fresh tomatoes. The reason for this is simply that the fresh tomato season is brief, and since tomato sauce is served all year long, the canned tomato products are more consistent in quality. If fresh tomatoes are available, however, they may be combined with the canned products for a more lively flavor. Tomato sauce to a great extent is self-thickening, that is, the tomato products are reduced until they reach a sauce consistency. Only a small amount of flour is added as a binding agent. Tomato sauce, as it simmers, must be carefully and frequently stirred to prevent scorching. Like brown sauce it is cooked once a week in many restaurants; its keeping quality is relatively good. The flavor of a fine tomato sauce should convey the tartness of fresh tomatoes, but should never be so sharp or acidy that it becomes unpleasant. Because of its natural tartness, the seasoning is usually balanced with a small amount of sugar. Note that pork fatback rather than butter is used for sautéing the vegetables. Pork fat gives the sauce a mellow meaty flavor.

Before starting work: Check to see if there is any leftover tomato sauce, tomato puree or tomatoes in the refrigerator which might be used in the recipe. If, after assembling the ingredients for the recipe below, there are some leftover canned tomato products, be sure to remove them from the cans, transfer them to clean storage containers, and cover well before placing in the refrigerator.

(1) Assemble the following ingredients:

    6 oz fatback pork or bacon, without rind, in one piece
    1 tablespoon garlic, chopped fine
    1 lb onions, coarsely chopped
    1/2 lb celery, coarsely chopped
    1/4 lb carrots, coarsely chopped
    4 oz flour
    3 qt hot white stock
    2 qt tomato puree
    2 qt canned tomatoes with juice
    3 large bay leaves
    1 tablespoon basil
    1/2 teaspoon leaf thyme
    24 whole black peppercorns
    Salt, black pepper
    Sugar
    2 ham bones (optional)

(2) Cut the fatback pork or bacon into small dice.

(3) Sprinkle the garlic on the fatback pork and chop vigorously with a heavy French knife until the pork mixture becomes smooth and paste-like. It may also be put through the meat grinder using fine blade.

(4) Place the chopped pork mixture in a heavy saucepot over a low flame.

(5) Heat, stirring frequently, until the pork fat is rendered (melts). Avoid burning pork or browning garlic.

(6) Add onions, celery and carrots. Stir well.

(7) Still using a low flame, sauté vegetables until tender but not brown.

(8) Stir in flour, blending well. Use a long spoon or paddle for blending. If pockets of dry flour are visible, stir with wire whip. Shake whip to dislodge vegetables.

(9) Slowly stir in hot stock in batches, about a pint at a time,

blending well after each addition. Heat may be increased slightly. Slowly bring to a boil, stirring occasionally.

(10) Drain tomatoes in colander, reserving juice. Press tomatoes by hand to release juice.

(11) Chop tomatoes coarsely, and add together with their juice to saucepot. Stir well.

(12) Add tomato puree, blending well.

(13) Make a bouquet garni of the bay leaves, basil, thyme and peppercorns. Add to pot.

(14) Add ham bones if desired. (The flavor of smoked ham is considered desirable by many chefs but is not obligatory.)

(15) Bring sauce to a boil, stirring frequently with a paddle.

(16) Reduce flame to keep sauce simmering. Cook for 1 1/2 to 2 hours or until sauce is reduced to about 5 qt. (After straining, sauce should yield approximately 1 gal.)

(17) Season sauce with salt and pepper. Add sugar to taste.

(18) Remove bouquet garni. Strain sauce through a fine china cap.

(19) Remove as much sauce as is needed for the meal ahead. Chill balance of sauce and store, covered, in refrigerator until needed.

Spanish Tomato Sauce   **1 Gal**

What is known in the United States as a Spanish omelet is not found in Spain under that name. But in this country the Spanish omelet has always been a very popular menu item. The same sauce used for this omelet is sometimes listed as creole sauce and is served with such dishes as mackerel creole or shrimp creole. Its principal ingredients are chopped tomatoes and fresh vegetables cut julienne. For eye appeal the julienne should be cut as uniformly as possible. Use a sharp French knife, and use the knife steel frequently. When the sauce has finished cooking, it should be tested for thickness. The sauce should barely flow when a small amount is poured on a plate, and the plate is tipped. If the sauce flows too freely, the sauce should be cooked further or thickened by adding more tomato paste.

Before starting work: Review cutting julienne (see Chap. 2). The recipe below calls for fresh green and red peppers to be skinned or peeled. To skin peppers, cut them in half lengthwise. Remove stems, tap peppers to remove seeds and cut away thick inner membrane. Place peppers skin side up on shallow pans. Place under a preheated broiler flame. Broil until peppers turn very dark brown, almost black. If the peppers are arched on the pan, they may be pressed with a long spoon to flatten as they soften under the broiler heat. If the broiler is high speed, the skin may turn dark very quickly. Watch the peppers carefully, and move the pan if necessary to broil evenly. Remove peppers from pan and wash with cold water. Using a clean towel, rub off pepper skins.

(1) Assemble the following ingredients:

    1 No. 10 can tomatoes
    1 pt tomato paste
    1/2 cup cooking oil, preferably olive oil
    1 lb onions, julienne
    1 lb celery, julienne
    1/2 lb sweet green peppers, skinned and cut julienne
    1/2 lb sweet red peppers, skinned and cut julienne
    1 tablespoon garlic, chopped extremely fine
    1 teaspoon basil
    1 teaspoon leaf thyme
    Salt, black pepper, cayenne pepper
    Sugar

(2) Place tomatoes in a colander over a bowl or pot. Press tomatoes to release juice. Reserve juice.

(3) On cutting board chop tomatoes fine. Set aside.

(4) Heat oil in sauce pot over low flame.

(5) Add onions, celery, sweet peppers, and garlic. Stir well.

(6) Rub basil and leaf thyme between thumb and forefinger, and add herbs to pot.

(7) Sauté slowly, stirring frequently, until vegetables are tender but not brown.

(8) Add tomatoes and their juice.

(9) Add tomato paste, stirring well to blend thoroughly.

(10) Add 1 tablespoon salt, 1/2 teaspoon ground black pepper, 1/8 teaspoon cayenne pepper and 2 teaspoons sugar.

(11) Simmer over low flame, stirring frequently until vegetables are tender and sauce is reduced to 1 gal. If sauce seems too thick, it may be thinned with tomato juice. If sauce seems too thin (the consistency of the sauce may vary with the amount of water in the tomatoes), it may be thickened with additional tomato paste. Use tomato paste very sparingly as it may alter taste of sauce. Check consistency of sauce by pouring a small amount on a plate. It should flow very slowly when the plate is tipped.

(12) Correct seasoning if necessary with salt, pepper and sugar.

(13) Pour sauce for meal ahead into a steam table pot.

(14) Unused sauce may be placed in pot, chilled, covered, and stored in refrigerator up to a week's time.

Tomato Sauce (Pasta Type)   1 Gal

Tomato sauce of the pasta type, that is, one served with macaroni products, is a basic sauce from which variations like meat sauce and mushroom sauce may be made. It is a sauce which is equally as important as the food it covers. Like the Spanish tomato sauce for omelets, it should be thick enough so that it barely flows on the plate. As in other sauces, seasoning vegetables are sautéd as the first step. Because most of these sauces are of Italian origin, olive oil or other cooking oil rather than butter is used for sautéing. Herbs like basil, oregano and bay leaf are always used, but the sauce cook should use them with a light hand. The tomatoes are either chopped on a cutting board or forced through a colander. In either case, the solid pieces of tomatoes should be small in size. In making the Spanish tomato sauce, the vegetables were cut julienne so that distinct pieces of vegetables could be seen in the finished sauce. By contrast, the seasoning vegetables in this sauce are chopped extremely fine. In some Italian restaurants this type of tomato sauce is sometimes flavored, after the cooking has been completed, with a small amount of freshly grated Parmesan cheese and a small amount of sweet heavy cream. Both ingredients are added to tone down the acid flavor of the tomatoes. A cook may use the same recipe in making this sauce on two different occasions and produce sauces of different flavor and thickness. This is because different brands of tomatoes, tomato puree and tomato paste may have been used. Tomato products are known to vary noticeably from one brand to another. The cook cannot change the flavor of the canned tomato products used; but if a sauce is too thick, it may be thinned by the addition of tomato juice; if it is too thin, it may be thickened by the addition of tomato paste.

Before starting work: For straining tomatoes, choose a colander with small openings and a bowl or pot of the proper size on which the colander may rest. If there are any leftover tomato products in the refrigerator which are to be used, check them carefully to make sure they are sound, with no off-flavor, off-odor or signs of mold. Wash hands well if they are used for forcing tomatoes through colander.

(1) Assemble the following ingredients:

    1 No. 10 can Italian plum tomatoes

    1 qt and 1 pt tomato puree

    1 pt tomato paste

    1/2 cup olive oil or other cooking oil

    1 lb onions, chopped very fine

2 tablespoons garlic, chopped extremely fine
2 teaspoons basil
1 teaspoon oregano
4 large bay leaves
Salt, pepper, sugar
1/4 cup freshly grated Parmesan cheese (optional)
1/2 cup heavy sweet cream (optional)

(2) Place a colander over a bowl or saucepot.
(3) Add tomatoes. With heavy spoon or by hand force tomatoes through colander so that tomato meat is broken into small pieces. If there are any pieces of tomato which cannot be forced through colander, remove them to cutting board, and chop into small pieces. Reserve tomatoes and their juice.
(4) In a heavy saucepot heat oil over a low flame.
(5) Add onion and garlic. Shake pot or stir ingredients so that onions are distributed evenly over bottom of pot.
(6) Rub basil and oregano between thumb and forefinger and add to pot. Add bay leaves.
(7) Sauté until onions are light yellow. Do not brown. (The herbs will turn dark; this is their normal appearance.)
(8) Add tomatoes, tomato puree and tomato paste. Do not drop them from the top of the pot, but lower the containers with the tomato products as close to the bottom of the pot as possible to prevent splattering. Mix well with wire whip. Some vegetables may get caught inside whip. Tap whip over pot to release vegetables.
(9) Slowly bring sauce to a boil. Stir again with wire whip. Make sure tomato paste is blended with other ingredients.
(10) Add 1 tablespoon salt, 1/2 teaspoon ground black pepper and 2 teaspoons sugar. Mix well.
(11) Reduce flame so that sauce merely simmers. Stir occasionally with paddle.
(12) Simmer approximately 1 hour or until flavors are well blended.
(13) Correct seasoning, if necessary, with salt, pepper and sugar.
(14) Pour sauce into steam table pot. Remove bay leaves.
(15) Just before mealtime, add Parmesan cheese and cream if these ingredients are desired. Cream should be heated up to the boiling point before adding to sauce.

Mushroom Sauce.—Chop 2 lb mushrooms fine. Use caps and stems. Chopping machine with upright blades may be used. After onions and garlic are sautéd, add mushrooms and sauté until all mushroom liquid has evaporated from pot.

Meat Sauce.—After onions and garlic are sautéd, add 3 lb chopped beef or 2 lb chopped beef, 1/2 lb chopped veal and 1/2 lb chopped pork. Stir meat frequently with fork, while sautéing, to break meat into smallest possible pieces. A wire whip may be used for breaking up meat; shake whip to release pieces caught in wires.

Marinara Sauce.—Reduce onions to 1/2 lb. Add 1/2 lb carrots chopped extremely fine to seasoning vegetables. Add 2 oz fillet of anchovies, chopped fine, after adding tomato products. Stir well so that anchovies are blended with other ingredients. Reduce salt because of saltiness of anchovies.

Shrimp Creole   50 Portions, 3 Oz Shrimp Each

Shrimp creole is an example of how the sauce cook prepares a dish by simply combining a standard sauce which is part of his normal routine with a cooked food—boiled, peeled and deveined shrimp. The sauce in this case is Spanish sauce which, it was pointed out, is another name for creole sauce. When the sauce and the shrimp are merely warmed together, however, the sauce seems to lack the delicate but definite taste of shrimp. In other words, the shrimp and the sauce flavors remain unblended, even though they are combined in the same pot. To emphasize the blending, the sauce cook first sautés the cooked shrimp briefly in butter, and then combines them with the sauce. This may seem like an unimportant detail, but butter is an ingredient which quickly picks up the flavors of other foods. In this case it transmits the shrimp flavor to the sauce, and the blending is complete. Normally the sauce cook does not boil the shrimp. This is the job of the *garde manger*, and it is done a day in advance, permitting ample time for boiling the shrimp, removing shells and veins and cooling them in their own cooking liquid.

Before starting work: See if there is any leftover Spanish sauce in the refrigerator. Check it for quality, and consult instructor or supervisor to decide if the leftover sauce should be incorporated in the recipe. If a dish like Spanish omelet is planned for the menu within a few days, additional Spanish sauce beyond the quantity needed in the recipe may be prepared at the same time. Examine shrimp carefully to make sure they are free of all pieces of shell.

(1) Assemble the following ingredients:
10 lb (cooked weight) shrimp, boiled, peeled and deveined (equal to 20 lb raw shrimp in the shell)
3/4 lb butter
2 tablespoons chili powder

2 gal Spanish tomato sauce (p 222)
Salt, pepper, sugar

(2) If Spanish sauce is cold, heat it over moderate flame to serving temperature, 160° F.

(3) In large saucepot melt butter over low flame.

(4) As soon as butter melts, add shrimp. Do not let butter brown. Move pot quickly back and forth tossing shrimp so that they are covered with butter.

(5) Sauté shrimp only until they are heated through, 3 to 5 min.

(6) Sprinkle chili powder over shrimp, and stir with mixing spoon, so that shrimp are uniformly coated with chili powder.

(7) Add Spanish sauce to pot with shrimp. Stir well. Simmer about 5 min.

(8) Taste sauce. Correct seasoning if necessary with salt, pepper and sugar.

(9) Turn shrimp into steam table pots. Keep hot in steam table.

Note: Shrimp creole is normally served with rice. An attractive way to serve the dish is to make a rice mound in an individual casserole. This may be done by dipping a teacup in hot water, so that the inside of the cup is moist, filling the cup 3/4 full with rice and pressing the rice firmly into the cup. The cup is then inverted over one side of the casserole, and shaken until the rice is unmolded. The shrimp are spooned alongside the rice.

Curry of Chicken and Mushrooms   50 Portions, 3 Oz Chicken Each

Curry is a term describing dishes cooked in an Indian style. But the curries served in the Western world are usually far different from those prepared in India where the word curry vaguely means any of countless dishes cooked with freshly ground dried spices. In most American restaurants a curry is a dish made with a sauce containing curry powder—a prepared blend of ground spices with the emphatic taste of cumin, coriander, ginger and turmeric among others. The usual curry powder may contain anywhere from 15 to 20 spices. When it is added to such dishes as curry of shrimp or curry of chicken, it should always be first mixed with melted butter or water to prevent lumping. Like all spices, curry powder should be heated when it is put into the pan to release its aromas. Generally the proportion of curry powder to sauce is from 1 to 2 teaspoons per pint of sauce, although this may vary greatly depending upon whether the sauce is to be mild or strong tasting. In Indian restaurants many curried sauce dishes use tomatoes as the sauce base. American and European chefs usually choose sauce *velouté* as the base for a curry.

Thus, for curry of chicken, the *velouté* would be made from a strong chicken broth; for seafood curry the *velouté* would be made from a fish stock. Rice is almost always an accompaniment with curry, and, if the curry is served in a casserole, the rice is placed in a mound alongside it. Chutney, a condiment made of raisins, apples, mangoes, etc., is frequently served with curried dishes. Sometimes sauce cooks will chop a small amount of chutney and add it to the completed curry sauce for a slightly sweet flavor accent.

Before starting work: If sauce *velouté* is freshly made, it need not be reheated for the curry. If it is cold, it should be reheated either in the steam table or over a low flame so that it will be hot when it is added to the curry. In most restaurants the fowl is diced by the *garde manger* who passes it to the sauce cook. Also the mushrooms are washed and sliced by the *garde manger* rather than the sauce cook. Check the procedures with your instructor or supervisor so there will be no confusion in carrying out your job.

(1) Assemble the following ingredients:

    6 5-lb boiled fowl, trimmed of skin and bone, cut into 3/4-in. dice

    2 gal sauce *velouté*

    1 lb butter

    1 lb onions, chopped fine

    1/4 lb shallots, chopped extremely fine

    1 tablespoon garlic, chopped extremely fine

    4 large bay leaves

    1/2 cup curry powder

    5 lb fresh mushrooms, 1/4-in. slices, caps and stems

    Salt, pepper

    1 pt heavy sweet cream

    2 oz fresh lemon juice

(2) Melt butter in heavy saucepot over low flame.

(3) Add onions, shallots, garlic and bay leaves. Stir well.

(4) Sauté slowly, stirring frequently, until onions are limp but not brown. Use a long paddle for stirring.

(5) Stir in curry powder, blending well with butter in pan. There should be no pockets of dry curry powder. Continue to sauté over low flame 5 min.

(6) Add mushrooms. Sauté, stirring occasionally, until mushroom liquid in pan is evaporated. Tip pan to check mushroom liquid.

(7) Add fowl. Mix well with large spoon or paddle so that all pieces of fowl are covered with curry mixture. Avoid breaking fowl into shreds.

Note: If fryers or roasters rather than fowl are used, special care must be taken to avoid breaking pieces of chicken. Two saucepots instead of one may be used to avoid excessive mixing.

(8) Add sauce *velouté*. Stir well. Slowly heat until sauce bubbles. Use a low to moderate flame. Scrape bottom and corner of saucepot to avoid scorching.

(9) Let sauce simmer 20 min or until flavors are well blended.

(10) Stir in cream carefully. Stir in lemon juice.

(11) If sauce seems too thick, it may be thinned with additional stock, milk or cream.

(12) Add salt and pepper to taste. Although curry powder is considered "hot" because of its spices, it sometimes lacks sufficient pepper.

(13) Turn curry of chicken and mushrooms into steam table pots, and place in steam table until serving time. If part of the curry is to be served at a later meal, it should be chilled as quickly as possible and kept in the refrigerator until needed.

(14) During mealtime, stir curry occasionally from bottom of steam table pot. Thin with milk, cream or stock if necessary.

(15) If chutney is served, spoon it into a sauce boat. Rice should be placed in a mound alongside the chicken. In some restaurants the rice may be placed in the bottom of a casserole and the curry spooned on top the rice.

Apple Flavor.—Curry dishes are sometimes enhanced by the addition of a small amount of applesauce or shredded apple.

Coconut Flavor.—Add shredded fresh or dried coconut when cooking the sauce *velouté*. Strain it before combining with other ingredients.

Veal Scallopine Marsala   **4 Portions, 3 Oz Each**

Veal scallopine Marsala—thin slices of sautéd veal in a wine sauce—is almost always made to order. If it is cooked in large quantities and held in the steam table, it loses its "bloom" or fresh-from-the-pan flavor which is all important in this dish. Veal scallopine should never be overcooked. Long cooking may toughen the meat and cause undue shrinkage. Note that even when the veal is properly cooked, the 4 oz of raw meat per portion shrink to approximately 3 oz after sautéing. The sauce cook must be prepared to efficiently handle individual orders from the waiters, keeping his pan, sliced meat, wine and seasonings within easy reach. Veal scallopine is usually dipped in flour before it is sautéd, although some cooks do not follow this practice. After dipping it in flour, it is important to shake off all excess flour, or the surface of the meat will be pasty and starchy. Care must be taken not to crowd the pan so that the meat can be quickly sautéd to a light streaky brown. If the pan is too full, juices will collect and the veal will tend to steam rather than brown. Normally a black iron frying pan is not used for making a dish with a sauce. Veal scallopine, however, is an exception to the rule. When a black iron pan is used in this manner, it must be very clean with no built-up residue of fat or drippings. Otherwise, an aluminum, copper or stainless steel pan should be used, and washed clean before being reused. The wine for this dish is Italian Marsala. The recipe indicates dry (not sweet) Marsala, but even the driest of this type of wine has some sweetness to it, and therefore should be used sparingly. The meat will be cut into thin slices and pounded for tenderizing by the butcher or *garde manger* who passes it to the sauce cook.

Before starting work: Arrange to keep a pan of seasoned flour on hand for coating the meat. Also arrange, if possible, to keep the meat in a nearby reach-in refrigerator from which portions may be taken as needed. Keep a section of the range clear of other pans so that if it is necessary to prepare several orders simultaneously there will be room for them on the fire.

(1) Assemble the following ingredients:

8 thin slices leg of veal, each slice about 2 oz, pounded thin
Seasoned flour

Note: Seasoned flour is flour mixed with salt and pepper; the usual proportions are 1 cup flour, 1 teaspoon salt and 1/4 teaspoon white pepper. Check with the instructor or chef on the amount of seasoned flour to prepare for the estimated portions in the meal ahead. If seasoned flour is not used, the meat is simply sprinkled with salt and pepper and then dipped in flour.

1/4 cup clarified butter, or 2 tablespoons clarified butter and 2 tablespoons cooking oil
1/2 cup brown stock
1/2 cup dry Marsala wine
2 tablespoons unmelted butter

(2) Pass veal through flour, that is, dip it in the flour to coat it thoroughly; then, holding it above the flour, shake the slices or pat them to eliminate excess flour.

(3) Pour clarified butter into pan large enough to comfortably hold the 8 slices of veal in a single layer. Heat over high flame.

(4) When butter is hot, lower veal slice by slice into pan.

(5) Sauté veal until slices are light streaky brown; check brownness by lifting slices with a fork.

(6) Turn veal and brown other side.

(7) Remove veal from pan. Keep in a warm place. If a silver platter is used, the veal may be placed on the platter and kept warm on a range shelf. Do not wipe pan clean.

(8) Add stock and Marsala to pan. Quickly bring to a boil. Scrape pan bottom and side to loosen drippings.

(9) Boil until liquids are reduced to about half the original quantity. There should be about 1/2 cup gravy, 2 tablespoons per portion. The meat should not be swimming in gravy when served.

(10) Remove pan from fire. Add unmelted butter. Stir or swirl ingredients in pan until butter melts.

(11) Pour hot gravy over veal on platter or serving plates just before order is picked up to be served.

Chicken Fricassee   50 Portions

The word fricassee is another one of those loosely used menu terms which means different things in different restaurants. In some places it consists of chunks of boneless boiled chicken combined with a chicken sauce *velouté*; it may or may not be garnished with mushrooms and small white onions. In other kitchens the whole boiled chicken is left on the bone; the skin is removed, and the chicken is cut into portions just before serving; a chicken sauce *velouté* is poured over the chicken on the serving plate or platter. In the classic French kitchen, however, and in the recipe below, small broiler-size chickens with skin and bone are sautéd; a *velouté* sauce is simmered in the same pan in which the chickens were cooked; the sauce is poured over the chicken on serving plate or platter and the dish is garnished with mushrooms and glazed white onions. When chicken fricassee is prepared in this manner, the sauce develops a pronounced natural flavor that is missing when the chicken is merely boiled. If individual servings of chicken fricassee are prepared to order, the sauce is sometimes enriched with cream and egg yolks. Since the sauce must be served at once (the sauce may break upon standing), the latter sauce is not recommended as a procedure where large quantities must be prepared in advance. The chickens which the sauce cook receives from the butcher will have been split, each portion containing the breast in one piece and the leg and second joint in another piece. Usually the breast will become done before the dark meat. The sauce cook, therefore, should cook the breasts in one pan and legs with their second joint in another to allow for different cooking times. During sautéing it is very important to use a low to moderate flame so that while the chicken slowly browns, it does not become overcooked.

Before starting work: Saucepans, pan lids, and pots will be needed for sautéing both chicken and mushrooms, for boiling the onions and later glazing them, and for storing both the cooked chicken and the fricassee sauce. Make sure all these utensils are available before starting work. Make sure there is enough burner space on the ranges to accommodate the pots and pans needed for the job. Raw chickens should always be washed by the butcher before cooking. If they are still wet when you receive them, dry them with clean towels to avoid excessive sputtering on the fire.

(1) Assemble the following ingredients:

25 2-lb chickens (broiler size), cut for fricassee
3 cups (variable) clarified butter
1 lb shallots or onions, chopped extremely fine
2 tablespoons garlic, chopped extremely fine
1 qt dry white wine
100 large size mushrooms, stems cut close to cap
100 small white onions
2 tablespoons sugar
3 qt chicken sauce *velouté*
1 qt light sweet cream
1 cup chopped parsley

(2) Pour clarified butter to a depth of 1/8 in. in two or four large *sautoirs*, or in tilting-braising pans, and heat over a low to moderate flame.

(3) Place chickens, skin side down, breasts in one pan, second joint and leg in another. Sauté slowly until chicken is a medium brown. Moisture in chicken will cause sputtering; use a long fork to turn chicken, and hold head back when examining chicken for brownness.

(4) Turn chicken to brown on second side. Cover pan tightly. Continue to sauté until chicken is tender. Test for doneness by inserting a fork into chicken. When chicken is done, the juice should be clear, not pink. Legs and second joints may need longer cooking than breasts.

(5) While chickens are sautéing, sauté mushrooms in another pan. Use clarified butter for sautéing. Sprinkle mushrooms with salt and pepper. Sauté until no mushroom liquid remains in

pan. Transfer mushrooms to steam table pot and keep warm until serving time.

(6) Boil onions in salted water until just barely tender, 10 to 15 minutes, depending on size of onions.

(7) Drain onions and let cool slightly.

(8) Sauté onions, using just enough clarified butter to coat pan bottom. Add sugar to pan and continue to sauté until onions are glazed and lightly browned. Transfer onions to steam table pot, and keep warm until serving time.

(9) When chickens are tender, remove from *sautoirs*. Do not wash *sautoirs*. Stack chickens in shallow pans, and keep warm in steam table or on range shelf.

(10) Add shallots and garlic to *sautoirs* in which chickens were cooked. Sauté, stirring frequently, until shallots are yellow not brown.

(11) Add wine to pans. Scrape pans to deglaze drippings. Cook until wine is reduced to 1/4 its original quantity.

(12) Add sauce *velouté* to pan and simmer 20 min, stirring frequently.

(13) Add cream to sauce. Bring to a boil. Reduce flame and simmer 5 min.

(14) Skim excess fat from sauce.

(15) Strain sauce through fine china cap. Turn sauce into steam table pot, and keep warm until serving time.

(16) For each portion of chicken, place a breast and second joint with leg on serving plate or platter.

(17) Garnish each portion with 2 mushrooms and 2 glazed onions.

(18) Pour sauce over chicken and garnish on serving plates or platter.

(19) Sprinkle with chopped parsley.

Chicken a la King   **50 Portions, 3 Oz Chicken Each**

The job of making chicken a la king is an outstanding example of how the sauce cook and other cooks must plan and coordinate their individual assignments to produce a simple dish. Chicken a la king is a combination of diced cooked chicken in a sauce containing green peppers, pimientos and mushrooms. Normally the chef is in charge of coordinating the details of such a job, but since the sauce cook often works as the chef's assistant it sometimes becomes part of his normal routine to plan all the preliminary work. Chicken a la king is sometimes served in a patty shell, a light form of pastry. If this is the case, patty shells must be ordered from the pastry chef at least two days in advance. The chicken must be boiled the day before, and this means the *garde manger* or butcher must have the chickens (usually fowl) cleaned and drawn, and turned over to the sauce cook or soup cook in ample time for cooking. After the chickens are cooked, the sauce cook or soup cook returns it to the *garde manger*. The soup cook stores the cold broth in the refrigerator. Sometime later the *garde manger* removes bone and skin from the chicken and cuts it into dice. He dices peppers and pimientos and slices mushrooms. If the peppers are to be skinned, the *garde manger* may turn them over to the broiler cook who sears them under a very hot flame before they are diced. On the day the dish is cooked, the sauce cook orders the necessary chicken broth from the soup cook and makes a sauce *velouté*. If rice is to be served with the chicken a la king, the vegetable cook prepares this item. If toast is to be served with it, the broiler cook supplies it as needed, or in some kitchens the toast may be made by the pantryman. In all, five members of the kitchen staff may be involved in the preparation of chicken a la king. Like any good sauce dish, chicken a la king should blend all the components of the recipe, so that if you tasted the sauce alone, you would at the same time recognize the distinct flavors of chicken, green peppers, pimientos and mushrooms.

Note: The job of boiling chicken may be handled by either the soup cook or the sauce cook. Since boiling meat and fowl is one of the sauce cook's basic skills, recipe directions below call for the sauce cook to boil the fowl as well as perform the remaining steps in the job.

Before starting work: Steps (1) to (11) below should be carried out the day before chicken a la king is prepared. Make sure all other preliminary steps mentioned above which involve other cooks are completed before the balance of the job is started.

(1) Assemble the following ingredients:
    6 fowl, 5 lb each, cleaned and drawn
    2 gal sauce *velouté*
    Cooking oil
    3 lb green peppers, cut into 3/4-in. dice
    2 cans pimientos, 16 oz each, cut into 3/4-in. dice
    3 lb mushrooms, 1/4-in. slices
    Salt, pepper
    1 pt heavy sweet cream
    3/4 cup (6 oz) dry sherry
(2) Place fowl in pots or in steam-jacketed kettle. Add cold water to cover fowl.

(3) Bring to a boil.

(4) Drain water from fowl. Run cold water over fowl to wash off any scum.

(5) Again cover fowl with cold water. Add 1 tablespoon salt per 2 gal of water.

(6) Bring to a boil. Let water boil for a minute or two until scum forms. Remove it with skimmer.

(7) Reduce flame so that water merely simmers. It must be below the boiling point with bubbles occasionally breaking on top or side. Keep pot covered during simmering. Skim when necessary.

(8) Continue to simmer until fowl is tender.

Note: The cooking time varies with the quality and age of the fowl. Fowl are hens that have been in egg production and usually are at least a year old. Average cooking time for fowl is 2 to 2 1/2 hours. Young chickens of the same size will become tender, if cooked in water, in about an hour.

(9) Test fowl for tenderness. Insert fork in back of fowl alongside shoulder. Hold each fowl upright above pot to drain. Quickly pinch drumstick. When fowl is tender, the flesh yields easily when pressed. Test each fowl, one by one, in this manner. Remove fowl from broth when each one is tender. Some may require longer cooking times than others.

(10) Return fowl to *garde manger* who will remove skin and bone, when fowl is cool enough to handle, and will cut fowl into cubes 3/4 to 1 in. thick.

(11) Remove fat from chicken broth. Strain broth and use it or other chicken broth to make sauce *velouté.*

(12) Sauté green peppers in oil over a moderate flame, using only enough oil to coat pan bottom, until green peppers are tender. Toss peppers in pan occasionally, or stir with spoon for uniform cooking.

(13) In another pan sauté mushrooms in oil, using as little oil as possible to coat pan bottom. Sauté mushrooms until tender. If any mushroom liquid remains in pan, it may be added to sauce *velouté.*

(14) In large saucepot combine sauce *velouté* and heavy cream, blending well. Bring to a boil. Reduce flame so that sauce simmers.

(15) Add chicken, green peppers, pimientos and mushrooms. Stir gently.

(16) Simmer slowly until flavors are well blended, 20 to 30 min after simmering begins. Use a low flame and stir ingredients

with large paddle or spoon, scraping pan bottom and corner
of pot from time to time.

(17) Slowly stir in sherry, blending well.

(18) Simmer 5 min longer. Season to taste with salt and pepper.

(19) Turn chicken a la king into steam table pots, and hold in
steam table until serving time.

(20) Serve with rice, noodles, toast or patty shell as designated by
menu.

(21) Before serving, spoon a portion onto plate or into individual
casserole, and check size with instructor or chef.

Lobster Newburgh   **4 Portions**

Although lobster Newburgh is an expensive menu item, it is not a
job of such complex difficulty that it cannot be learned by students
of elementary cooking. It is usually made for individual a la carte
orders rather than in large quantities. The principal ingredients are
sliced boiled lobster meat, butter, sherry wine, cream and egg yolks.
In most restaurants the sauce cook usually adds a small amount of
sauce *béchamel* to each order, although egg yolks are the main thickening agent. There are kitchens where Newburgh dishes of this type
are made with all sauce *béchamel* colored with a large amount of
paprika. It is not a practice followed in fine seafood restaurants. The
sauce cook receives the boiled lobster meat removed from the shell
by the *garde manger*. It may be sliced when he receives it or may be
in chunks. In any case great care must be taken by the sauce cook
not to overcook the lobster meat. It has been cooked once. When it
is cooked a second time it should be:

(a)   Sautéd over a low flame

(b)   Simmered only a few minutes with cream until flavors are
blended

(c)   Thickened quickly with egg yolks and served at once.

Any sauce thickened with egg yolks rather than flour will curdle if
cooked too long. The sherry in this dish is briefly flambéed, that is,
set ablaze for a few moments before the cream is added. Flambéing
reduces the sherry so that its flavor is more concentrated and trans-
forms the raw flavor of the wine to a cooked one. (Usually spirits
with a large alcohol content like brandy or rum are flambéed. Sherry,
however, is a wine with about twice the alcoholic content of red and
white table wines and will blaze when heated.) The process of flambéing should not be regarded by the student as one with great
mystique and hidden complexities. Sherry wine like spirits contains

alcohol. As the alcohol is heated, it gives off vapors. These vapors above the wine can be set ablaze by applying a match or moving the pan near or over a stove top burner or a chafing dish burner. The flames will evenually disappear when the alcohol is completely evaporated. They will also disappear as soon as the cream is poured into the pan.

Before starting work: Choose a copper or cast aluminum saucepan large enough to hold four orders of lobster Newburgh; it should be a somewhat shallow pan with enough depth to stir or move the ingredients without spillage. Make sure cream is available but do not remove it from refrigerator until it is needed. Plan to make fresh toast just before the dish is ready to be picked up by the waiter. (Sometimes the sauce cook toasts the bread. In a busy restaurant the waiter might bring the toast from the pantry to the sauce cook, or the broiler cook might toast the bread under the broiler and pass it to the sauce cook.)

(1) Assemble the following ingredients:
Meat from 4 boiled 1 1/2-lb lobsters, cut into 3/4-in. slices
4 tablespoons (1/4 cup) clarified butter
Salt, celery salt, white pepper, paprika
Cayenne pepper
1/2 cup dry sherry wine
2 cups light sweet cream
1/4 cup sauce *béchamel*
4 egg yolks
6 slices toast, cut in half diagonally

(2) Pour butter into saucepan. Move pan to coat bottom and sides of pan with butter.

(3) Heat over low to medium flame.

(4) Add lobster. Sauté about 3 min, tossing pan or stirring with spoon until all lobster is coated with butter and heated through.

(5) Season lobster with salt, celery salt, white pepper and paprika. Again toss ingredients in pan.

(6) Add sherry wine. When wine is hot, move pan toward open flame. Move pan forward and backward, tossing ingredients gently, until wine is set ablaze. Avoiding spilling wine.

(7) Keep pan over flame until flames subside and almost disappear. Add 1 1/2 cups cream.

(8) Simmer 3 to 4 min.

(9) Add sauce *béchamel*, stirring well.

(10) Using a kitchen fork or small wire whip mix balance of cream

with egg yolks in small mixing bowl or deep dish, blending well.

(11) Remove a small amount of cream from the pan (about 1/4 cup) and combine it with the egg yolk mixture, blending well.

(12) Slowly stir egg yolk mixture into pan.

(13) Bring to a boil and stir constantly with mixing spoon for 1 min—no longer; do not stop stirring or mixture may curdle.

(14) Remove pan from fire. Add a dash of cayenne pepper, and correct seasoning with salt and white pepper if needed.

(15) Place a half slice of toast on the bottom of each of 4 individual shallow casseroles.

(16) Divide lobster among the 4 casseroles.

(17) On each portion place two half slices of toast on opposite sides of lobster. Sprinkle lobster very lightly with paprika.

Poached Salmon Steaks, Hollandaise Sauce   50 Portions

Salmon steaks are slices cut across the fish, usually from 1/2 to 3/4 in. thick. Although cold boiled whole salmon are frequently presented on buffet tables during the summer when fresh salmon are in season, hot salmon steaks, either broiled or poached, are also a very popular menu item. The term poaching, when applied to fish, simply means simmering or cooking in liquid below the boiling point. Rapid boiling causes the fish to break apart, whereas poaching keeps it intact. Salmon may be poached in water. Better results, however, are obtained if it is poached in the vegetable stock known as court bouillon. It is best to prepare the court bouillon a day in advance so that the stock is cold when the salmon steaks are placed in it. The stock is then slowly brought up to a simmering temperature of 160° to 180° F and maintained at that temperature until the fish is done. For quantity cooking shallow baking pans rather than saucepans are generally used so that the fish rests in a single layer in the pan, and can be conveniently removed in portions as ordered. After the salmon steaks are cooked, they may be placed in the steam table for serving. Reserve pans of prepared fish may be kept warm on the range shelf or in warming cabinets with a temperature of 140° to 150° F.

Before starting work: Plan to make the court bouillon a day in advance. Plan to prepare the hollandaise sauce as close to the meal period as practical. The salmon may be poached in batches rather than all at one time. Thus, if a lunch or dinner period is spread over a 2- or 3-hour period, one pan of fish at a time may be poached fresh, since cooking time is only from 10 to 15 min after simmering begins.

Use several clean cloth towels for draining fish when individual portions are removed from cooking liquid; do not use these towels for any other purpose.

(1) Assemble the following ingredients:

50 salmon steaks, 8 to 10 oz each

1 gal hollandaise sauce

6 qt court bouillon (p 44)

Butter

Cooking oil

2 large bunches parsley, well-washed, most of stems removed

(2) Spread butter on bottom and sides of 6 or 7 shallow baking pans or steam table pans 12 by 20 in. (The number of pans needed will depend on diameter of salmon steaks. Thick steaks cut from small salmon will take less room than wide steaks cut from large fish.)

(3) Arrange salmon in a single layer in pan. Do not crowd fish.

(4) Pour cold court bouillon over fish using enough liquid so that court bouillon is level with top of fish.

(5) Cut pieces of heavy brown paper to fit pans.

(6) Cut a hole about 1 in. in diameter in center of each sheet of paper.

(7) Grease paper sheets with oil on one side.

(8) Place paper, greased side down, on fish

(9) Place pans on range top over slow to moderate flame.

(10) Bring almost up to boiling point, but do not boil. From time to time check pans to make sure liquid is not boiling. Lift paper carefully, avoiding burns.

(11) After 10 min simmering, check fish for doneness. Salmon is done when small round bone in center can be lifted easily from fish. A small pointed knife should be used to test fish in this manner.

(12) Keep pans in warm place. Liquid in pans should be about 140° to 150°F. Pans may be kept in food warmer set at 140° to 150°F.

(13) To serve salmon steaks, lift each portion carefully from pan with long wide spatula or slotted spatula. Place the fish (while on spatula) on clean towel to drain.

(14) Transfer fish to warm dinner plate or platter. Platter is sometimes lined with clean white napkin.

(15) With small pointed knife lift out small center bone of fish. Lift off skin of fish in one piece.

(16) Garnish salmon with several parsley sprigs.

(17) If salmon is on dinner plate, spoon hollandaise sauce over fish,

allowing about 1/3 cup sauce per portion. If salmon is on platter from which it will be transferred to plate at table, spoon hollandaise sauce into sauce boat.

Poached Fillets of Sole with Mushrooms   50 Portions
(Filets de Soles a la Bonne Femme)

The preparation of this dish differs in two important respects from the previous one of poached salmon steaks with hollandaise sauce. First, fillet of sole is a thin fish, and to keep the pieces intact as well as present a substantial appearance, the fillets are folded in halves or thirds lengthwise. Secondly, the sauce is not simply poured over the fish but is placed under the broiler to brown. There are four main steps:

(1) The fillets are cooked in shallow pans with wine, court bouillon, shallots and mushrooms.

(2) After cooking, the fillets, mushrooms and shallots are lifted from their cooking liquid and removed to other pans or shallow serving casseroles.

(3) A *velouté* sauce is made of the liquid in which the fillets were cooked.

(4) The sauce is poured over the fish and is browned under the broiler.

When the mushrooms and shallots are sprinkled over the fillets, and later when the cooked fillets are transferred from one pan to another. it is important to divide these ingredients carefully so that portions are uniform and intact. Fillets are easily broken after cooking if not handled with meticulous care. The final browning under the broiler (*glaçage*) must be watched constantly or the entire batch of fish may be charred. To make sure the sauce turns attractively brown, unsweetened whipped cream is folded into the sauce just before the sauce is placed under the broiler, taking advantage of the special property of cream for browning purposes. The cold whipped cream naturally melts when it is folded into the hot *velouté*, but it is dispersed sufficiently so that browning takes place in a matter of seconds. In some kitchens hollandaise sauce is also folded into the *velouté* for a *glaçage*; it makes the sauce richer, but is not absolutely necessary. The fillets which the sauce cook receives from the *garde manger* or butcher will have been cut into long strips along their natural seam.

Before starting work: If, after receiving the fillets, there is a delay in poaching them, do not allow them to stand at room temperature; store them temporarily in the refrigerator. Make sure the court bouillon is prepared a day in advance so that it is cold when poured over the fish. Check to make sure there are enough available pans for poaching. Usually 12×20-in. utility pans are preferred for poaching fish. Final browning may be done at one time for banquets, or may be done in individual orders throughout the meal period.

(1) Assemble the following ingredients:

   12 lb fillet of sole

   4 lb mushrooms, stems and caps cut separately into 1/4-in. slices

   1 lb shallots, chopped extremely fine

   Butter

   Salt, white pepper

   3 qt court bouillon (p 44, variable)

   1 qt dry white wine

   1 1/2 lb butter

   1 lb flour

   1 pt heavy sweet cream, whipped (unsweetened)

(2) Preheat oven to 400° F.

(3) Butter 6 to 8 shallow baking pans or utility pans for cooking the fillets

(4) Fold each pieces of fillet in half or in thirds so that it is at least double its normal thickness. Folding will depend upon the thickness and length of individual fillets. Check with instructor or chef before proceeding with this step.

(5) Place fillets in pans in uniform rows. Do not crowd fillets in pans.

(6) Sprinkle fillets with salt and pepper.

(7) Arrange the shallots and mushrooms on fillets so that they are distributed uniformly.

(8) Slowly pour wine into pans. Pour court bouillon into pans using only as much as necessary to barely reach top of fillets.

(9) Cut brown paper to fit pans. Cut a 1-in. circle in the center of each piece of paper. Butter the paper on one side only. Place the paper, buttered side down, on the fillets.

(10) Place pans over top flames and bring court bouillon up to a boil.

(11) Very carefully, holding a dry towel in each hand, lift pans from top flame to oven shelves.

(12) Bake 10 min.

(13) Remove pans from oven, again using a dry towel in each hand, lifting pans very carefully to avoid spillage.

(14) Remove brown paper carefully. Discard paper.

(15) With a flexible spatula lift fillets from pans onto clean shallow

baking pans or serving casseroles. Be sure, when transferring fish from one container to another, that each portion is covered with a uniform amount of mushrooms and shallots. Place fish in steam table, oven shelves or other place to keep warm.

(16) Pour off court bouillon from pans into single pot and set aside. Keep hot.

(17) Melt butter in heavy saucepot over low flame.

(18) Stir in flour, blending well.

(19) Heat roux in heavy saucepan over moderate flame until roux is deep yellow.

(20) Slowly pour hot court bouillon into roux in batches, about a pint at a time, while stirring constantly with wire whip.

(21) When all court bouillon has been added, bring sauce to a boil. Reduce flame and simmer slowly 1/2 hour, stirring frequently.

(22) Remove sauce from fire. Correct seasoning of sauce.

(23) Let sauce cool about 10 min.

(24) Fold whipped cream into sauce, using a down-over-up stroke with mixing spoon, adding about 1/3 of cream at a time.

(25) Pour sauce over fish.

(26) If individual casseroles are used, place casseroles on large metal trays. If pans are used, place one pan at a time under broiler flame, watching pan constantly, and turning pan when necessary to brown uniformly. *Glaçage* is done when top of sauce is a light mottled brown.

Note: For a richer *glaçage* fold in 1 1/2 cups hollandaise sauce before folding in whipped cream.

STEWING

Stewing is the process of simmering small pieces of meat or poultry in a liquid until tender. The same cooking method includes dishes like goulash which are not listed as stews on the menu. There are seafood stews like oyster or clam stew which are cooked in a matter of minutes and which are closer to soups rather than the type of stew which in France is called a *ragoût*. In some stews the meat is first sautéd until brown before it is cooked in its gravy. In other stews the meat is sautéd only until it loses its raw color. The stew is covered with its cooking liquid which is generally stock or a combination of stock with tomato juice, wine or other flavoring components. The meats used for stewing are the tougher cuts of the animal, but the cooking time for different stews may vary from 1 1/2 hours for a lamb or veal stew to 3 hours for a beef stew.

17 GUIDES TO STEWING

(1) The meat for stews generally is boneless. If bones are included, however, it is important to examine meat and remove any bone splinters which are loose or which may be loosened as the stew simmers.

(2) If the meat seems wet before it is to be sautéd, wipe it dry with clean towels to aid in browning.

(3) In those restaurants where butchering is done on the premises, meat for stew may be collected over a period of days, and may include freshly cut meat as well as older meat and trimmings. Examine meat. If there is any evidence of stickiness, sliminess or off-odor, call this fact to the attention of the supervisor or instructor. In some cases the meat should be blanched before it is put in the stew pot.

(4) Meat for brown stews may be sautéd in three ways:

    (a) It may be sautéd in a large frying pan and then transferred to the stew pot. The advantage of this method is that the fat for sautéing which sometimes becomes charred is largely eliminated. Some fat clings to the meat, but the fat on the pan bottom does not become part of the stew. Its disadvantage is that the meat juices that flow onto the pan are lost.

    (b) It may be sautéd in the same pot in which it is to be simmered. This is the most common method. In this case, however, the browning must be more moderate than in method (a).

    (c) It may be browned in shallow pans in a hot oven. The meat must be spread out in thin layers in order to brown as much as possible. The method results in a deeper brown color because of the dry oven heat. The pans are deglazed in order to save the drippings for the stew pot. Its disadvantage is that the high oven heat sometimes causes excessive shrinkage.

(5) When sautéing meat for stews, stir it frequently to bring as much meat as possible in contact with the pan bottom or sides of the pot.

(6) Use brown stock for brown stews and white stock for light stews such as Irish lamb stew. Be sure the stock is not excessively concentrated in flavor; it will acquire additional flavor from the meat. If stock flavor is too intense, it may be necessary to dilute it with water.

(7) The liquid in the stew which eventually becomes the gravy should be brought to a boil initially to remove the scum; thereafter it should always be kept at a simmering temperature to make the meat tender.

(8) Check the stew pot frequently to make sure the gravy is not boiling. Boiling will leave the meat chewy and ragged in texture no matter how long it is kept on the fire. Even though the fire beneath the pot or the heat input of the steam-jacketed kettle may be constant, the heat that gradually builds up in the metal of the pot or kettle may cause the temperature of the gravy to reach the boiling point.

(9) Stews may be thickened in four ways by:
  (a) Dredging the meat in flour before it is sautéd
  (b) Sprinkling flour over the meat after it is sautéd but before the cooking liquid is added to the stew pot
  (c) Adding a flour-water or flour-stock paste to the liquid in the pot
  (d) Adding a roux to the gravy while it is simmering.

Procedure (b) is preferred by most chefs, particularly in making brown stews. It permits the flour to brown slightly and eliminates any raw flavor. The fat that has already gone into the pot to sauté the meat is joined with the flour, making a roux while the meat is still browning. If procedure (d) is followed, the additional fat of the roux adds excessive richness to the stew. This, plus the fat of the meat that melts during cooking forms an excessive layer of fat on top which must eventually be skimmed off.

(10) Remove excess fat from the stew both while it is cooking and after it stands in the steam table. The pot may be tilted slightly to remove the fat from one side of the pot.

(11) Some pieces of meat in a stew are usually done before others. Check at least a half dozen pieces of meat before removing the stew from the fire.

(12) The ideal stew is one in which the flavor of the gravy is fully developed at the same time the meat is done. If, because of prolonged cooking, the gravy flavor becomes too concentrated, it may be diluted with a mild stock or water. If the flavor seems too weak, it may be strengthened with gravy flavoring aids, powdered bouillon, etc., always used in minimal amounts.

(13) Vegetables are important components of many stews. Besides the flavoring vegetables (such as chopped onions and garlic), large pieces of carrot, whole silver onions, potatoes, etc., are often added. Be sure these added vegetables are carefully cut as in the case of carrots and potatoes, and that they are as uniform in size and as symmetrical as possible.

(14) Vegetable components for a stew are sometimes cooked apart from the stew in order to enhance the eye appeal of the dish. In such

instances, be sure to avoid overcooking the vegetables in order to preserve as much of their natural color as possible.

(15) Stews may be served on a dinner plate, in a soup dish or in an individual casserole. Be sure to check with the instructor or supervisor on:

    (a) The dish in which the stew is to be served

    (b) The number of pieces of meat and amount of gravy to be allotted to each portion. This is particularly important if the meat is cut into pieces of irregular size.

(16) When stew meat is cooked in quantity in one tall pot, the weight of the meat will cause pieces on the bottom to stick or become crushed. Use a large paddle to frequently and carefully stir the bottom of the pot.

(17) When assembling the ingredients for a stew, the sauce cook will get the meat from the butcher or *garde manger*, and may get vegetables like carrots and potatoes from the vegetable cook. If the vegetables are to be shaped in a special way—such as carrots cut into olive-shaped pieces or potatoes cut parisienne (small balls)—these instructions should be given to the vegetable cook in ample time to allow proper preparation. In some kitchens, vegetables cut into fancy shapes for stew are the job of the sauce cook rather than the vegetable cook.

Old-fashioned Beef Stew   **50 Portions, 4 Oz Beef**

The slang phrase "slum combo" for stew both shows contempt for the way stews are often prepared and reinforces the common notion that a stew is a haphazard mixture of meat and vegetables thrown into one pot. Actually the best stews follow strict procedures and require the sauce cook's unerring judgment. When the phrase "old-fashioned" appears before a stew, it means that the stew is made in a brown rather than a light gravy. The phrase also sometimes means that both meat and vegetables are cooked in the same pot. Modern chefs prefer to cook some of the vegetable components apart from the stew and add them just before it is served for the sake of a more impressive appearance. When a recipe states that the meat should be browned, it does not mean it should have the brownness of a well-done steak cooked over charcoal, but neither should the meat have the grayish color that results when meat is piled high in a pot, and its own juice causes it to acquire a steamy-looking dull color. Theoretically, the stock in every stew should be made from the same meat as the stew itself. Thus beef stew should be made with beef stock, lamb stew with lamb stock, etc. While this is conceivably possible, modern chefs prefer a mild stock with no flavor so strongly assertive that the finished gravy becomes unpleasantly concentrated. Thus, in a beef stew, if you use a mild stock made with beef and veal bones or with all veal bones rather than a strong beef bouillon made from boiled beef, the resultant gravy will have a mellow flavor reflecting the meat in the stew itself whose natural flavor becomes fully developed by long slow simmering. Different cuts of meat require different cooking times. Chuck will sometimes require a longer cooking period than top round. Even in the chuck itself there are muscles which take longer cooking than others. This means that the sauce cook must make multiple tests for tenderness when the stew is finishing.

Before starting work: Make sure the weight of the meat is what the recipe specifies. If an increased or decreased number of portions is to be prepared, check the calculations carefully. If the beef is freshly cut and oozing an unusual amount of juice, wipe it dry with clean towels. If rendered beef fat is to be used for sautéing, be certain that it has no strong or acrid flavor caused by excessive heat.

(1) Assemble the following ingredients:
   20 lb boneless beef chuck, 1-in. cubes
   Vegetable fat, cooking oil or rendered beef fat
   Salt, pepper
   2 lb onions, chopped fine
   1 tablespoon garlic, chopped extremely fine
   3/4 lb flour
   6 qt hot brown stock
   3 cups juice from canned tomatoes
   Bouquet garni of 4 stalks celery, 12 sprigs parsley, 1 teaspoon
      leaf thyme and 4 bay leaves
   8 lb potatoes, 1-in. cubes
   8 lb carrots, olive-shaped pieces, 1 in. long
   4 lb fresh or frozen peas, boiled
   100 small silver onions

(2) In large saucepot, brazier or tilting-braising pan, heat 1/8 in. fat over high flame.

(3) Add meat. Sprinkle with salt and pepper. Sauté, stirring frequently until brown.

   Note: If necessary, use two saucepots or braziers so that meat is not piled too high. Alternatively, meat may be placed in shallow baking pans in a hot oven of 475° F and browned; stir occasionally to prevent charring; deglaze baking pans after meat is browned.

(4) Reduce heat to low. Add chopped onions and garlic. Stir very well. Allow meat to sauté about 5 min longer. Stir frequently to prevent onions from browning.

(5) Add flour. Flour may be placed in wire strainer and shaken over meat to distribute it uniformly. Stir well. Continue to cook over low flame 5 to 8 min longer or until flour begins to brown.

(6) Add hot brown stock slowly, stirring well, scraping bottom and sides of pot.

(7) Bring gravy to a boil. Remove scum. Reduce flame so that gravy merely simmers.

(8) Add tomato juice and bouquet garni. Simmer very slowly about 2 1/2 hours or until meat is tender. Check surface of stew frequently to make sure it is not boiling.

(9) While meat is simmering, boil silver onions until almost tender, about 15 to 20 min; drain onions; melt 3 tablespoons butter in a *sautoir;* add onions and 2 tablespoons sugar. Sauté until onions are light brown; remove onions to steam table pot; place in steam table in time so that when stew is served, onions will be hot.

(10) About 20 min before cooking of stew is completed, add potatoes and carrots to pot; when cold vegetables are added, it may be necessary to increase heat to keep gravy simmering. Stir well. Cover pot with lid.

(11) Continue to simmer until meat and vegetables are tender. Test meat by inserting kitchen fork. Test at least a half dozen pieces of meat.

(12) Remove pot from fire. Skim fat from gravy. Remove bouquet garni. Correct seasoning with salt and pepper and gravy strengthener if necessary.

(13) Add caramel coloring if necessary; use sparingly, a small amount at a time, stirring well.

(14) Turn stew into steam table pots.

(15) Heat peas or keep peas in steam table pot.

(16) Serve stew in individual casseroles if available. Check with instructor or supervisor on size of portions.

(17) Sprinkle peas on top each portion of stew. Add 2 glazed onions on top each portion.

Beef Stew Bourguignonne.—Cut 2 lb salt pork into 1/4-in. cubes; blanch if very salty; sauté in fat until light brown before adding beef; remove from pot and set aside. Follow recipe above substituting 1 gal dry red wine and 2 qt stock in place of all stock. Omit potatoes in recipe. Add salt pork to stew after it is completely cooked.

Beef Goulash   **50 Portions, 4 Oz Beef Each**

Dishes like stews and braised meats, which in homes are always cooked in pots over a top flame, are sometimes cooked in the oven in restaurants. During the initial browning of the meat, a top flame may be used, but after the stock is added, the balance of the cooking takes place in the oven using a regular stew pot with metal loop handles. The advantage of the oven is that the heat reaches the pot or brazier from all sides rather than merely the bottom where scorching is possible. Goulash is a form of stew which is usually cooked until it is extremely tender; the meat should almost break apart. The long slow oven heat makes this possible. Students must remember that when they check and stir the contents of a pot in the oven that the pot lid and handles are extremely hot and must be handled with a heavy folded dry towel or heavy potholders to avoid burns. Goulash is flavored with paprika, the ground dried pod of sweet red peppers. In many dishes cooks tend to use paprika more for coloring than for flavoring. Paprika, however, is a spice with a definite flavor, and it must be used in sufficient quantity so that its flavor is apparent. Paprika burns rather easily; use a very low flame when stirring it into the pot. Dried caraway seeds, another spice used in goulash, should be pounded in a mortar to release the flavor of the seeds. Unlike old-fashioned beef stew, goulash is cooked only with finely chopped flavoring vegetables rather than chunks of potatoes, carrots, etc. It is usually served with noodles as an accompaniment.

Before starting work: In the recipe below note that the amount of flavoring vegetables is larger than in the usual stew. Review Chap. 2 on chopping vegetables. Be sure that you have sufficient dry towels or potholders for handling the stew pot in the oven.

(1) Assemble the following ingredients:

> 20 lb top or bottom round of beef, cut into 3/4-in. cubes
> 1 lb lard or vegetable fat
> Salt, pepper
> 3 lb onions, chopped fine
> 2 tablespoons garlic, chopped extremely fine
> 2 lb sweet red peppers, chopped fine
> 2 1/2 oz sweet Hungarian or sweet Spanish paprika
> 3/4 lb flour
> 6 qt hot brown stock
> 3 cups juice from canned tomatoes

      3 tablespoons caraway seeds, pounded in mortar

      4 bay leaves

      24 whole peppercorns

(2) Melt lard or vegetable fat in large saucepot or brazier. Use a moderate flame.

(3) Add meat. Sprinkle with salt and pepper. Sauté, stirring frequently, until meat is brown.

(4) Remove meat from pot, using a wire skimmer. Drain off fat. Do not wash pot. Let drippings remain.

(5) Return meat to pot.

(6) Add onions, garlic and sweet peppers. (There will be enough fat remaining in pot and on meat to continue sautéing.) Stir well.

(7) Turn flame low and continue to sauté until vegetables are tender but not brown.

(8) Add paprika and flour, stirring very well so that no dry pockets of paprika or flour form in pan.

(9) Continue to sauté, using very low flame, until flour loses raw flavor, about 10 to 15 min.

(10) Add brown stock slowly, stirring well while adding stock, scraping bottom and sides of pot.

(11) Add tomato juice.

(12) Bring gravy to a boil. Remove scum. Reduce flame so that gravy merely simmers.

(13) Make a bouquet garni of the caraway seeds, bay leaves and whole peppercorns. Add to pot.

(14) Place pot in slow oven of 325°F. Place lid on pot. Remove top oven shelf if necessary.

(15) Continue to cook until meat is very tender about 2 to 2 1/2 hours. Check pot occasionally. Use dry towels or potholders. Bring oven shelf forward so that goulash can be stirred. If gravy is bubbling, reduce oven heat so that gravy merely simmers.

(16) Remove pot from oven.

(17) Skim fat from surface of gravy. Remove bouquet garni. Correct seasoning.

(18) Turn goulash into steam table pots.

Irish Lamb Stew   **50 Portions, 4 Oz Lamb Each**

Like Indian curry, Irish lamb stew is generally not made in US restaurants as it would be in homes in its country of origin. In Ireland an Irish stew is a combination of lamb, potatoes and onions placed in alternate layers in a pot with a small amount of liquid, and cooked until the meat is tender and most of the liquid has evaporated. This native homemaker's version, while delicious, has practical problems for commercial service where the stew must be cooked and held during a two-or three-hour meal period. In a restaurant there must be sufficient gravy so that the meat does not dry out and can be easily served. The ideal stock would seem to be lamb stock. But a stock made from lamb bones alone has a pronounced, sometimes sharp flavor. Best results are attained with a combination of lamb and white stock. Usually the stew is made with boned shoulder of lamb. If the lamb is boned on the premises, the butcher will have lamb bones which can be used for stock, and the stock should be made the day before the stew is cooked. Generally carrots, silver onions, turnips or other garnish vegetables are not served with an Irish stew. In some restaurants the gravy is slightly thickened with flour, but better results are achieved if a small quantity of mashed potatoes is mixed with the stock, just enough to give the gravy a creamy rather than a soup-like consistency.

Before starting work: Review guides to stewing. If both the mealy Idaho potatoes and the moist, waxy potatoes are available, choose the latter since they hold their shape better during cooking. Since Irish lamb stew, like beef goulash, is cooked in the oven, review the procedure for goulash, noting the safety procedures for handling pots in the oven.

(1) Assemble the following ingredients:
   20 lb boned shoulder of lamb, 1-in. cubes
   2 gal stock, half lamb and half white stock
   12 lb peeled potatoes
   2 lb onions, finely chopped
   2 lb leeks, white part only, finely chopped
   2 tablespoons garlic, chopped extremely fine
   6 pieces of celery
   1 bunch parsley
   2 teaspoons dried basil
   4 bay leaves
   Salt, white pepper
   1 cup parsley, chopped extremely fine

(2) Set aside 4 lb potatoes. While stew is cooking, boil the potatoes in salted water until tender. Mash through potato ricer. Set aside.

(3) Cut balance of potatoes lengthwise in half. (If potatoes are very large, cut lengthwise in quarters.) Cut potatoes into 1/2-in. slices. Set aside in cold water.

(4) Blanch the meat, that is, cover it with cold water and bring to a boil. Discard water, and wash lamb.

(5) Combine chopped onions, leeks and garlic.

(6) Tie celery, whole bunch of parsley, basil and bay leaves into a bouquet garni.

(7) Fill pot half full with alternate layers of meat, sliced potatoes and onion mixture.

(8) Add bouquet garni to pot.

(9) Add balance of meat, sliced potatoes and onions in alternate layers.

(10) Pour stock into pot.

(11) Add 1 tablespoon salt and 1 teaspoon pepper.

(12) Bring stew to a boil over top flame. Remove scum.

(13) Place pot in oven preheated to 300° F. Cover pot with lid.

(14) Simmer slowly, turning down oven heat if necessary, for 1 1/2 hours or until meat is tender. Paddle may be inserted into pot to make sure stew is not sticking to bottom.

(15) Remove pot from oven. Skim fat from stew. To aid in skimming, pot may be tilted at a slight angle so that fat flows to one side of pot.

(16) Remove bouquet garni from stew.

(17) Stir in mashed potatoes, blending well.

(18) Correct seasoning of stew if necessary.

(19) Place stew in steam table pots for serving. Keep hot in steam table.

(20) Sprinkle each portion of stew with chopped parsley just before serving.

Chicken Cacciatora   48 Portions

Chicken cacciatora is a stew of sautéd chicken and tomatoes. It is prepared in either of two ways. In the first method, pieces of chicken are sautéd in a pan until done, fresh tomatoes and mushrooms are sautéd in another pan until tender, and the contents of the two pans are combined and briefly simmered. This method is practical in restaurants where a la carte orders are prepared one by one. For quantity cooking, however, the dish is prepared in advance, and the two principal ingredients become a true gravy. This is the method followed in the recipe below. The butcher or *garde manger* cuts the chicken into pieces and passes it to the sauce cook. Each chicken is cut into two breast pieces, two legs and two second joints. The breasts are later divided, making eight pieces per chicken. The chicken is not browned in extremely hot fat but sautéd in clarified butter and oil until it turns a deep yellow to brown color; it is not expected to have the deep brown color of fried chicken. Since pieces of chicken are irregular in shape, they should be sautéd slowly or edges will become dry and tough while other parts remain under-done; slow heat also prevents the chicken from shriveling excessive-ly. It is not necessary to dip the chicken in flour even though some chefs sometimes follow this procedure; excess flour may fall into the pan and frequently cause the drippings to acquire a charred flavor. While sautéing chicken, it is necessary to watch the pan with special care; no matter how heavy the pan or how uniform the heat, some parts of the chicken will become brown before others, and must be turned as soon as they are colored. To speed the job chicken may be sautéd in two pans. After deglazing, the drippings may be combined in one pan for subsequent cooking.

Before starting work: Be sure chicken is dry before sautéing it. Wipe with clean towels if necessary. Count breast pieces, legs and second joints to make sure there is the quantity specified in the recipe. Have on hand a long-handled fork or long tongs to avoid burns while sautéing chicken.

(1) Assemble the following ingredients:

12 3-lb chickens, cut for stewing
1 lb butter, clarified
Cooking oil
Salt, pepper
3 lb onions, chopped fine
2 tablespoons garlic, chopped extremely fine
1 teaspoon dried basil
1 teaspoon oregano
4 lb mushrooms, caps and stems cut in 1/4-in. slices
3 cups dry white wine
4 qt canned tomatoes with juice
2 qt tomato puree
1 pt tomato paste
1 cup parsley, chopped extremely fine

(2) For sautéing chicken use equal quantities of clarified butter and oil. Pour enough to fill large *sautoirs* to a depth of 1/4 in. Heat over a low to moderate flame.

(3) Add chicken to pans in a single layer. Place chicken skin side down.

(4) Sauté until chicken is a light streaky brown. Check color of chicken frequently, and turn as necessary; avoid sputtering fat.

(5) Turn chicken to cook on second side until lightly browned. Sprinkle with salt and pepper.

(6) Drain tomatoes, reserving juice. Chop tomato meat coarsely.

(7) Turn chopped tomatoes and their juice, tomato puree and tomato paste into a brazier or two braziers large enough to hold chicken. Stir well to blend tomato paste with other ingredients. Heat over low flame.

(8) Remove pieces of chicken, after they are browned, to brazier with tomatoes.

(9) Add onions and garlic to pan or pans in which chicken pieces were sautéd. There will usually be sufficient fat in pan for sautéing. Use additional fat only if necessary.

(10) Sauté onion and garlic until yellow and limp. Add basil and oregano. Sauté about 2 min longer.

(11) Add mushrooms to onion mixture. Sauté until mushrooms are tender and all mushroom liquid has disappeared from pan.

(12) Add wine to pan. Scrape pan bottom and sides to loosen drippings.

(13) Simmer until the 3 cups of wine are reduced to about 1 cup.

(14) Add mushroom mixture to chicken. Hold pan carefully tilted above brazier, and carefully use spoon to move all contents of pan into brazier. Add 1 tablespoon salt and 1 teaspoon pepper, stirring well.

(15) Bring to a boil over a moderate flame. Skim carefully.

(16) Reduce flame so that tomato mixture simmers very slowly.

(17) Simmer 30 to 40 min or until chicken is tender. Skim fat from surface. There may be considerable fat depending upon the quality of the chickens. Correct seasoning if necessary.

(18) Turn chicken into deep steam table pans or pots.

(19) To serve chicken cut each breast piece crosswise in half. Allow a piece of white and a piece of dark meat for each portion. Spoon tomato mixture over chicken. Sprinkle with chopped parsley.

Note: Chicken cacciatora is usually served with rice. If individual serving casseroles are used, place rice in a mound alongside chicken.

BRAISING

The culinary term braising is one of those words with multiple meanings which often leave the student confused. For instance, cooks may add sautéd chopped meat to a spaghetti sauce and say they are braising the meat when they are doing nothing of the sort. What occurs is that the meat, as it sautés, gives off liquid so that if you look into the pan, you will see a temporary pool of meat juice. This liquid is one of the main elements found in all braising no matter how the term is defined. The student should simply remember that in most of the best restaurants today the term braising describes pieces of meat (much larger than the pieces of meat used in stews) which are first browned and then cooked with liquid until tender. A braised dish frequently is made of pieces of meat weighing from 3 to 5 lb. In some cases the meat may weigh up to 15 lb, as in the case of braised fresh ham. Sometimes the term applies to smaller pieces of meat, as in the case of braised pork chops. In household practice, braised meat is cooked with a small amount of liquid, sometimes just enough to give a moist atmosphere to the pot. Restaurant sauce cooks, on the other hand, generally use a much larger amount of liquid for the gravy that is normally served with each portion.

12 GUIDES TO BRAISING

(1) Meat for braising may be browned in three ways:
    (a) Rolled in flour and sautéd in fat
    (b) Sautéd in fat without a flour coating
    (c) Browned in a hot oven without a flour coating.
Method (c), used with large cuts of meat, gives the deepest color to the meat; and the drippings in the pan, when deglazed, result in a gravy with a rich brown color.

(2) If the meat is insufficiently browned, the color may wash away when the meat is later cooked with a gravy, and the braised dish will look somewhat like boiled meat. Be patient during the browning process. A large piece of meat may take 20 to 30 min before it is evenly browned. Turn the meat as often as necessary to brown uniformly.

(3) Meat for braising is sometimes marinated for several days such as beef a la mode. The marinade in which it is soaked will tend to retard browning. Wipe the meat well before browning it.

(4) Braised dishes may be cooked in braziers (large pots with more width than depth), in steam-jacketed kettles or in tilting-braising pans. In smaller kitchens, the brazier, because of its shape, permits the cook to check the meat carefully for tenderness as it is being cooked. In large institutional restaurants the steam-jacketed kettle or tilting-braising pan is preferred for its convenience in handling large quantities.

(5) Although some of the larger cuts of meat may take 3 to 4 hours braising, other cuts may be done in 1 1/2 to 2 hours. Check the meat for tenderness by piercing it with a two-pronged fork. When the meat is done, the fork can be inserted and withdrawn without undue tugging. Check with your instructor or supervisor on the doneness before removing any meat from the pot. If the fork seems to quickly slide in and out of the meat, the braised dish is probably overdone and will be difficult to carve.

(6) Keep cooking temperatures about 30° below boiling for all braised dishes. If you permit the gravy of a braised dish to boil rapidly, the meat invariably will be chewy rather than tender no matter how long it is cooked.

(7) In restaurants braised dishes are generally cooked with just enough gravy to barely come to the top of the meat. Use a tight-fitting lid on the pot and a low flame to prevent excessive reduction of gravy.

(8) Meat in a brazier which has been browned and is combined with its liquid may be cooked on a top flame or in the oven. The former permits the cook to check the meat more conveniently than when the oven is used. The slow oven heat, however, is sometimes more uniform than a top flame. It is extremely important, therefore, for the student to familiarize himself with the particular equipment with which he is working.

(9) Although braised meats are always cooked for a long period on a slow flame, they should not be overcooked. There is a point beyond which there is excessive shrinkage.

(10) Sometimes the gravy in a braised dish will not develop its full flavor sufficiently even though the meat is tender. If this is the case, the gravy may be strengthened with *glace de viande*, bouillon powder or some other gravy strengthener. If there is time, after the meat is removed from the pot, the gravy may be reduced to intensify its flavor.

(11) Skim the fat off the gravy during cooking as often as necessary. Some of the fat that rises to the top in the brazier will be the fat that was used to sauté the meat. Some of the fat is rendered from the meat itself. The student should remember that it is impossible to taste the gravy objectively when there is a thick layer of fat on top. When the braised dish is served, there should be no fat visible on top of the gravy.

(12) After the braised dish has finished cooking, let it set at least a half hour in a warm place apart from the gravy or in the gravy itself. If the meat rests in the gravy, it will absorb some of the juices lost during cooking. Carving will be easier after the setting interval.

Braised Beef (Pot Roast)   **50 Portions, 3 Oz Beef Each**

Braised beef is a large piece of tough or semitender meat which is first browned then cooked with liquid until tender. How much and what kind of liquid are variables that depend on the version being prepared. In France braised beef is usually marinated in, and cooked with, red wine. German sauerbraten is another braised beef dish in which the meat is marinated in a mixture of vinegar, wine, water and seasonings for several days before it is cooked. In US restaurants the meat is cooked with stock and is sometimes listed on menus as Yankee pot roast. The amount of liquid may very greatly. There are cooks who completely submerge the meat in liquid while it is being cooked, making considerably more gravy than they actually need, and then reserve the surplus gravy as brown sauce for other dishes. The disadvantage of this practice is that the meat covered in gravy sometimes acquires a steamy boiled flavor not characteristic of a pot roast. Other cuts of meat such as short ribs, stuffed breast of veal, or boned shoulder of lamb all follow the general pattern of the recipe below.

Before starting work: Check available stock for braising the meat. The traditional stock is brown stock (see Chap. 3). However, a white stock or even chicken broth may, in an emergency, be used to supplement the brown stock. Taste the stock to make sure it is sound. Place stock on a low flame so that it is hot when added to the brazier. Review 12 guides to braising at the beginning of this unit.

(1) Assemble the following ingredients:

  20 lb top or bottom round of beef in 5- to 6-lb pieces, tied as for roasting
  Salt, pepper
  12 oz vegetable fat or rendered beef fat
  1 lb onions, coarsely chopped
  1 tablespoon garlic, chopped fine
  1 lb carrots, coarsely chopped
  1/2 lb celery, coarsely chopped
  6 oz flour
  1 gal hot brown stock
  12 sprigs parsley
  4 bay leaves
  1 teaspoon leaf thyme
  24 whole black peppercorns
  12 whole allspice
  1 qt canned tomatoes with juice

(2) Preheat oven to 475° F.

(3) Place meat in shallow pans. Sprinkle with salt and pepper. Do not add fat to pans.

(4) Roast meat until it is deep brown, about 30 min. Turn meat once or more to make browning uniform.

(5) While meat is roasting, melt fat in brazier or heavy stew pot.

(6) Over moderate flame add onions, garlic, carrots and celery. Sauté until browned but not scorched. Stir frequently.

(7) Stir in flour, blending well. Place pot over low flame, stirring frequently until flour turns light brown.

(8) Slowly stir in 3 1/2 qt hot stock in 3 or 4 batches, beating with wire whip until gravy is thickened. Keep flame low.

(9) Remove browned meat from oven and transfer meat to brazier. Do not wash pans in which meat was browned.

(10) Add balance of stock to pans used for browning meat.

(11) Scrape bottoms and sides of pans to loosen drippings. If necessary, heat pan over top flame to dissolve all drippings.

(12) Pour drippings into brazier with meat.

(13) Drain tomatoes, reserving juice. Chop tomatoes coarsely.

(14) Add tomatoes and their juice to the pot.

(15) Make a bouquet garni of the parsley, bay leaves, thyme, peppercorns and allspice. Add to pot.

(16) Simmer meat slowly, covered with tight lid, until tender, for 2 1/2 to 3 hours. Check pot occasionally to make sure gravy is barely simmering. Lift or move meat from time to time to make sure it is not sticking to bottom of pot.

(17) Test each piece of meat for tenderness by inserting fork. Hold meat in a fixed position. You should be able to insert and withdraw the fork without special effort.

(18) Remove meat from pot and place in steam table.

(19) Strain gravy through a fine china cap into steam table pot.

(20) Correct seasoning of gravy if necessary. If roast meat flavor is very pronounced, a pinch of sugar is sometimes added for flavor correction.

(21) Add caramel coloring to gravy if necessary. Keep gravy in steam table.

(22) Keep meat in steam table pans. It should set for about 1/2 hour before serving.

(23) Slice meat across the grain with very sharp knife, using knife steel frequently. Check thickness of slices with instructor or supervisor.

(24) Pour gravy over meat on serving plates or platter.

Beef a la Mode   **50 Portions, 3 Oz Beef Each**

Beef a la mode is a variation on the previous recipe, braised beef. The main difference in its preparation is that the meat is marinated, or steeped in a flavoring liquid, for a day before it is cooked. The marinade is a mixture of wine, stock, seasoning vegetables and spices. The flavors of the marinade penetrate the meat and give it a distinctively tart flavor of wine and spices. The recipe below calls for marinating the meat one day. If a more pronounced flavor is desired, the marinating period should be extended to two or even three days. In Europe where the quality of beef generally is inferior to American beef, the meat frequently is larded, that is, strips of salt pork are inserted into the meat for added richness. Sometimes, during the summer months, beef a la mode is served cold with a jellied gravy. To help the gravy gel, calves' feet are added to the liquid ingredients. Their gelatinous quality enhances the flavor of the gravy and causes it to gel when chilled. Note that there is no bouquet garni in the recipe below. In its place mixed pickling spices are added directly to the marinade. Mixed pickling spices are a prepared mixture of whole spices used for marinades in preparing beef a la mode, sauerbraten, etc., and they are removed when the gravy is strained.

Before starting work: Meat which is marinating, if not completely covered by the marinade, may need turning several times before cooking. Arrange with another cook, if necessary, to turn the meat when you are off duty. For marinating meats, choose pots, bowls or other containers of stainless steel or containers lined with enamel to keep flavors intact. Sometimes deep refrigerator storage pans or deep steam table pans may be used for this purpose.

(1) Assemble the following ingredients:
   20 lb top or bottom round of beef in 5 to 6 lb pieces, tied as
      for roasting
   Salt, pepper
   2 qt brown stock
   2 qt dry red wine
   1 lb onions, coarsely chopped
   1/2 lb carrots, coarsely chopped
   1 lb celery, coarsely chopped
   2 tablespoons mixed pickling spices
   6 large cloves of garlic, cut in half
   12 sprigs parsley
   1 qt canned tomatoes with juice
   12 oz vegetable fat or rendered beef fat
   6 oz flour

(2) Place beef in one or several containers with stock, red wine, onions, carrots, celery, pickling spices, garlic, parsley and 2 tablespoons salt. Stir to dissolve salt.

(3) Place beef and its marinade in refrigerator, cover, and marinate 24 hours. Turn meat, if necessary, to marinate on all sides.

(4) Preheat oven to 475° F.

(5) Remove meat from marinade. Wipe meat dry with clean cloth or paper towels.

(6) Place meat in shallow baking pans. Sprinkle with salt and pepper.

(7) Roast 25 to 30 min or until well browned. Turn meat to brown uniformly.

(8) Melt fat in large brazier. Use 2 braziers if necessary.

(9) Stir in flour, blending well.

(10) Heat over low flame, stirring frequently, until roux is light brown. Avoid excessive heat.

(11) Remove 1 pt liquid from marinade. Set aside.

(12) Heat balance of marinade until it comes to a boil.

(13) Slowly stir marinade, in batches of about 1 qt each, into brazier, stirring well with wire whip after each addition. Wait until each batch of marinade begins to thicken before adding more.

(14) Remove meat from oven when browned, and place in brazier.

(15) Drain tomatoes, reserving juice. Chop tomatoes coarsely and add with their juice to the brazier.

(16) Pour reserved pint of marinade into pans in which meat was browned. Scrape pan bottoms and sides to loosen drippings. Place pans over top flame if necessary to deglaze drippings. Add to brazier.

(17) Simmer meat slowly over low flame until meat is tender, from 2 1/2 to 3 hours. Be sure flame is low at all times. Mix gravy and scrape pan bottom with heavy paddle from time to time. Lift or move meat to make sure it is not sticking.

(18) Test each piece of meat for tenderness by inserting and withdrawing fork. Check tenderness with instructor or supervisor.

(19) Remove meat from brazier, and place in steam table pan.

(20) Strain gravy through fine china cap lined with muslin. Squeeze muslin, if necessary, to strain all gravy.

(21) Skim gravy if necessary. Correct seasoning. Keep hot in steam table pot.

(22) Slice meat with very sharp knife. Cut loop strings only when necessary to carve meat.

(23) Pour gravy over sliced meat on serving plates or platter.

Note: Beef a la mode, in some restaurants, is garnished with tiny carrots, glazed onions and green peas.

Braised Pork Chops, Sauce Robert   50 Portions, 2 Chops Each

Sometimes even tender meat, such as loin pork chops, is braised for the sake of the flavor that develops rather than for tenderness itself. Unlike braised beef which takes 2 1/2 to 3 hours cooking, braised pork chops will become tender in about an hour. Sauce *Robert* is a tart brown sauce, one of the variations of sauce *espagnole* or basic brown sauce. In some restaurants pork chops prepared in this style are merely sautéd until done, and then the sauce *Robert* is poured over the chops just before they are taken to the dining room. When, however, the chops are braised, as in the recipe below, the flavors of both the meat and the sauce are joined so that each is enriched as the result of mutual blending. Pork chops cooked in this manner are ideally suited for busy restaurants where most of the cooking takes place before the meal period. Braised pork chops which are leftover may be safely refrigerated for up to a week's time, or may be frozen in their sauce and kept for service at another time. The sauce cook must heed one important precaution: because the meat is tender, it is important not to overcook it to the point where it disintegrates, and to handle it carefully after cooking so that the chops stay intact in the steam table and on the serving plate. Since sauce *Robert* is enriched with pungent spices, the dish is usually served with a mild accompaniment such as buttered noodles, rice or mashed potatoes.

Before starting work: If possible, sauce *Robert* should be prepared the day before the chops are cooked to permit deliberate careful attention to the job. Examine pork chops to make sure there are no bone splinters. If the kitchen is equipped with a large tilting-braising pan, arrange to have it available at the time it is needed. Otherwise saucepans should be used.

(1) Assemble the following ingredients:

100 loin pork chops, 3 to 4 oz each, trimmed weight

Salt, pepper

Lard or vegetable fat

Note: Excess fat which butcher trims from pork loin may be coarsely chopped and heated slowly in a heavy pan until the fat is melted or rendered. Such fat is then strained and may be used in place of prepared lard or vegetable fat.

1 gal sauce *Robert* (p 216)

2 qt white stock

(3) Melt fat to a depth of 1/8 in. in tilting-braising pan or sauce pans. Sprinkle chops with salt and pepper.

(4) Sauté the chops over a low to moderate flame until they are medium brown. Check their color frequently, and turn when necessary to brown uniformly on both sides. Avoid sputtering fat; hold head back when turning chops.

(5) After chops have been sautéd, remove them from the pan and set aside temporarily in shallow pans.

(6) Pour off fat from braising pan or *sautoirs*. Do not, however, wipe pans clean. Let drippings remain.

(7) Add stock to pans.

(8) Heat over low flame. Scrape pans to loosen drippings.

(9) Pour sauce *Robert* into pans. Stir well with wire whip.

(10) Bring sauce to a boil. Skim well. Reduce flame so that sauce merely simmers.

(11) Return pork chops to pans. If any meat juice has accumulated while pork chops were set aside, add it to the sauce pans.

(12) Simmer chops, covered, until very tender, about 1 hour. Check occasionally to make sure no chops are sticking to pan bottom.

(13) Remove chops to steam table pans, lifting carefully one by one. Do not dump them.

(14) Skim fat carefully from sauce.

(15) Taste sauce. If it is too concentrated in flavor, it may be thinned with additional stock. If it is somewhat weak, reduce it by further cooking until it is of desired strength.

(16) Pour sauce over chops in steam table pans. Keep hot until meal time.

(17) Serve two chops per portion. Lift chops carefully from steam table pan to serving plates or platters to keep chops intact.

(18) Pour gravy over chops on serving plates or platter.

Note: If during the meal period, additional fat accumulates on surface of gravy, skim it carefully.

Braised Stuffed Shoulder of Lamb	**50 Portions, 3 Oz Lamb, 1 Oz Stuffing Each**

While leg of lamb is generally roasted and is therefore the job of the roast cook, shoulder of lamb may be either roasted or braised as in the recipe below. In the latter case it becomes the sauce cook's assignment. To facilitate carving, the shoulder is boned. The bones which are removed should be sawed into pieces about 3 in. long.

Usually, when the shoulder is boned, it is also stuffed. The stuffing may be made by either the *garde manger* or the sauce cook. Its preparation is described below to familiarize the student with a typical stuffing for a braised meat. The same stuffing might be used in other meat dishes such as stuffed breast of veal. Note that in the bouquet garni in the recipe below, there is more garlic than usual and that rosemary, a rather pungent herb, popular in lamb dishes, is included. Young spring lamb has a mild flavor, and the seasonings in the gravy may be more pronounced than in a beef dish. When braised shoulder of lamb is carved, the sauce cook uses a sharp French knife rather than a roast beef slicer. The meat is cut by simply placing it on the carving board, inserting a fork to hold the meat steady, and slicing downward as one would slice a loaf of bread. Some of the slices, however, may not stay intact because of the boning. If this occurs, the slices should be re-formed on the serving plate or platter before adding the gravy. The cord used for tying the meat should be left on and only removed as each loop is reached when carving. Be careful, when cutting the cord, not to slice into the meat; use the tip of the knife.

Before starting work: Since the job below contains two phases—stuffing the raw meat and then braising it—allow at least three hours time for the total preparation. If this is not practical, the shoulders should be boned and stuffed the day before they are cooked. Check the quality of the bread crumbs. If the white crumbs have already been made, and some have been used for breading fried foods, be sure they are sifted carefully. If fresh crumbs must be made, cut chunks of unsliced white bread from which the crusts have been removed, and make crumbs in a chopping machine with vertical blades.

(1) Assemble the following ingredients:

> 16 lb (boned weight) boned shoulder of lamb
> Lamb bones from shoulders, cut into 3-in. pieces
> Salt, pepper
> 1 qt and 1 pt white bread crumbs
> 1/2 lb onions, chopped fine
> 4 oz butter
> 2 lb sausage meat
> 1 1/2 lb spinach, boiled, drained, chopped fine
> 1/2 cup parsley, chopped extremely fine
> 4 eggs, beaten slightly
> 2 lb onions, sliced
> 1/2 lb carrots, sliced
> 3/4 lb butter

6 oz flour
8 cloves of garlic, mashed lightly
2 teaspoons rosemary
1 teaspoon leaf thyme
4 bay leaves
1 gal hot brown stock
1 qt canned tomatoes with juice

(2) Prepare the stuffing in the following steps:

    (a) Sauté the 1/2 lb onions, chopped fine in 4 oz butter until onions are light yellow.

    (b) Add sausage meat and continue to sauté until meat is browned. Break meat up as it is sautéing, using a fork.

    (c) Remove sausage from fire.

    (d) Add bread crumbs, spinach, parsley, eggs, 1 teaspoon salt and 1/4 teaspoon pepper. Mix well. Correct seasoning if desired.

(3) Sprinkle the inside of each lamb shoulder with salt and pepper.

(4) Fill the pocket of each lamb shoulder with the stuffing.

(5) Roll up lamb shoulders and tie securely to make meat compact. Loops of twine should be uniformly spaced around meat.

(6) Preheat oven to 450° F.

(7) Place shoulders in shallow baking pans. Sprinkle with salt and pepper.

(8) Roast shoulders, turning once, until brown, about 30 min.

(9) While meat is roasting, melt 3/4 lb butter in brazier.

(10) Add sliced onions and carrots, and sauté until brown.

(11) Stir in flour, blending very well. No dry flour should be visible. Continue to sauté until roux is light brown. Use a low flame to prevent scorching.

(12) Slowly stir in 3 1/2 qt brown stock in batches of about a qt, blending well before and after each addition comes to a boil. Use a wire whip.

(13) Bring gravy to a boil. Add lamb bones. Reduce flame so that gravy simmers.

(14) Make a bouquet garni of the garlic, rosemary, thyme and bay leaves. Add to gravy.

(15) Transfer meat from roasting pan to brazier.

(16) Add balance of stock to roasting pans. Scrape pan bottoms to loosen drippings. Add drippings to brazier.

(17) Drain tomatoes, reserving juice.

(18) Chop tomatoes coarsely, and add tomatoes together with their juice to brazier.

(19) Simmer lamb until tender, about 1 1/2 to 2 hours. Test

meat for tenderness by inserting and withdrawing fork. Hold each shoulder firmly, while testing with fork, so that meat does not bob about in gravy as it is being tested. If necessary, lift shoulders from brazier to cutting board to test for tenderness.

(20) Remove meat to steam table.

(21) Skim fat from gravy.

(22) Remove bouquet garni from gravy, and strain gravy through fine china cap.

(23) Correct gravy seasoning. Add caramel coloring if necessary. Keep gravy hot in steam table.

(24) Cut meat into 1/4-in. slices, taking care to keep slices intact. Pour gravy over meat on serving plates or platter.

Braised Short Ribs of Beef   **50 Portions, 2 Pieces Each**

In those restaurant kitchens where the butcher trims meat for roast ribs of beef and where roast ribs are regularly featured, there are always short ribs on hand. These are the strips or ends of the ribs which are cut off when the roasts are trimmed to the oven-ready stage. Braised short ribs are, in a sense, miniature pot roasts. Each portion usually consists of 2 chunks of meat and bone, weighing 4 to 6 oz each. (In some restaurants a single strip weighing about 10 to 12 oz is served.) The cooking procedure is similar to that followed in making braised beef, that is, the meat is first browned in the oven, and then transferred to a brazier to complete the cooking. Each piece of meat contains layers of lean and fat and some of the rib bones. It is important to cook the meat until tender but not overcook it to the point where the individual pieces are no longer intact. For handling the meat, it is best to use a large kitchen spoon or skimmer rather than a fork. Because of the rich flavor of short ribs, they are usually cooked in a piquant gravy with tomatoes and dry wine, tart accents that create a pleasant balance of flavors. Like stews, short ribs are sometimes garnished on the serving plates or casseroles with carrots, glazed silver onions and green peas.

Before starting work: Examine short ribs to make sure there is no off-odor, stickiness or other signs of deterioration indicating meat has been held too long in the refrigerator. If in doubt, check with instructor or supervisor. Count the number of pieces of meat. There should be 100 for 50 portions. As short ribs cook, they give off considerable fat. Keep a container handy for collecting the skimmed fat and, when it is filled, add it to the large can or receptacle for used kitchen fat.

(1) Assemble the following ingredients:
   40 lb short ribs of beef, cut into cubes approx 2 to 2 1/2 in.
   Salt, pepper
   3 lb onions, sliced
   1 lb carrots, sliced
   1 lb celery, sliced
   12 garlic cloves, lightly mashed
   4 bay leaves
   12 sprigs parsley
   36 whole black peppercorns
   12 whole allspice
   4 whole cloves
   1 teaspoon leaf thyme
   1 fifth dry red wine
   2 qt canned tomatoes with juice
   1 gal brown stock
   1 pt brown roux
   1 cup finely chopped parsley
(2) Preheat oven to 450° F.
(3) Place short ribs in shallow baking pans. Sprinkle with salt and pepper. Add onions, carrots and celery to pans. (Do not use deep pans; they will not permit browning of ribs.)
(4) Bake approximately 30 min or until short ribs are well browned.
(5) Make a bouquet garni of the garlic, bay leaves, parsley, peppercorns, allspice, cloves and thyme.
(6) Remove meat and vegetables from baking pans. Transfer to braziers.
(7) Add wine to baking pans. Place pans over top flames. Scrape pan bottoms to deglaze drippings. Simmer until wine is reduced to about half its original quantity. Pour wine into braziers.
(8) Drain tomatoes, reserving juice. Chop tomatoes coarsely.
(9) Add tomatoes with their juice and stock to braziers.
(10) Add bouquet garni.
(11) Bring stock to a boil. Skim well.
(12) Reduce flame slightly while keeping stock at a boil.
(13) Slowly stir brown roux in small batches into gravy, mixing well after each addition.
(14) Reduce flame so that gravy barely simmers.
(15) Cook, skimming fat occasionally, until meat is very tender, about 1 1/2 to 2 hours.
(16) When meat has finished cooking, tip brazier slightly so that fat flows to one side. Skim fat carefully.

(17) With two kitchen spoons or skimmer, lift meat from braziers to steam table pans, keeping pieces of meat intact.
(18) Strain gravy through fine china cap. Correct seasoning if necessary. Keep gravy hot in steam table.
(19) For each portion place two pieces of meat in individual casserole. Pour gravy over meat. Sprinkle with chopped parsley.

14 GUIDES TO BOILING MEAT AND POULTRY

Time and again the term boiling is applied to foods that are not literally boiled at 212°F but are simmered at temperatures ranging from 160° to 180°F. As a student you must remember that although the menu lists boiled corned beef as an item, you should actually cook the corned beef about 30° below the boiling point. As stated elsewhere in this book, a temperature of 212°F applied to meat cooked by moist heat, leaves the meat dry and coarse, with muscle fibers that fall apart as the meat is carved. Simmering, on the other hand, not only produces meat that is more tender and flavorful but meat with less shrinkage, and is therefore an important factor in food cost control. French chefs often use the word "poaching" for cooking food in liquid at a simmering temperature. The word poaching is particularly applicable to fish or seafood cooked in liquid.

(1) Students are sometimes confused about whether a liquid is simmering or boiling. When a liquid simmers, the bubbles come to the surface slowly and only occasionally. For moments there may be no bubbling visible. It is a good idea for students to own a pocket testing thermometer (sold in laboratory supply houses) which can be inserted into liquids as well as into certain solid foods to take an exact temperature reading. A thermometer ranging from 0° to 220°F is practical for testing most foods cooked behind the range.

(2) All foods kept at a simmering temperature must be watched frequently. The built-up heat of a utensil, variations in gas pressure, steam pressure and other factors may cause a liquid to eventually boil even though the heat input is thought to be steady. Make whatever adjustments are necessary to maintain a simmering temperature.

(3) Meats and poultry listed on the menu as boiled are frequently blanched as the initial step in their cooking. The meat or poultry is placed in cold water and heated until it comes to a boil; it is then removed from the water and washed. Blanching is sometimes necessary to remove surface impurities, possible off-odors, etc. Blanching also helps in producing a more clear, clean-tasting broth.

(4) Meats which have been cured in a salt solution like corned beef are usually soaked overnight in water before they are boiled in order to remove excess salt. If soaking is required, wash the meat first, steep it in cold water and keep refrigerated until the meat is drained before cooking.

(5) If there is not time to soak cured meats, they may be cooked by changing the water two or three times during the cooking period.

(6) Certain cured meats like country smoked hams from some southern states may require two days soaking before cooking. It is important to check the menu several days in advance to determine if this is necessary.

(7) Be sure the container you use for soaking and the pot you use for simmering are large enough to hold the meat comfortably with ample water to spare. If necessary use a steam-jacketed kettle rather than a pot.

(8) Although beef broth or chicken broth are, in a sense, by-products of simmering beef or chicken, it is sometimes advisable to add bones and vegetables to the pot in order to strengthen the flavor of the broth.

(9) Whenever meat or poultry is simmered it is important to coordinate the jobs of sauce cook and soup cook. Chicken broth and beef broth are *"fonds"* or foundation stocks for which there are many uses. When smoked hams or other smoked meats are simmered, the stock may be useful in split pea soup or bean soup. The sauce cook, therefore, should regularly consult with the soup cook on preparations of this type.

(10) The cooking time of poultry and pieces of meat, even though they are of the same approximate weight, varies. Thus if one is simmering six 5-lb fowl, each of the six may conceivably be removed from the pot at a different time. Do not assume a piece of meat is tender unless it is individually checked.

(11) It is sometimes difficult to check meat or poultry for tenderness while it is floating in the pot. Hold the piece to be checked against the side of the pot or remove it, if necessary, to a pan or work surface and then insert the fork to test tenderness. Fowl may be lifted above the pot and tested for tenderness by pinching the drumstick.

(12) In transferring hot boiled meats from one container to another, liquid may be easily spilled and cause an accident. If hot liquid is spilled on the floor or work surface, it should be wiped as soon as possible.

(13) Boiled meat like roast meat should, after cooking, be allowed to set for at least a half hour before it is carved. During this setting period, the meat should be in a deep steam table pan covered or near-

ly covered with its own cooking liquid. Excess fat should be trimmed off the meat just before the meal period.

(14) Boiled meats like fresh beef brisket or corned brisket, even though properly simmered, may disintegrate if not properly carved. Carve against the grain, and use an extremely sharp knife, honed frequently during the meal period.

Boiled Fresh Beef Brisket   **50 Portions, 4 Oz Each**
Horseradish Sauce

Note that the name of the dish is fresh beef brisket. There is also corned beef brisket which has been cured in a brine. Fresh beef may be blanched or put directly into the pot with water. Corned brisket is usually soaked overnight. The approximate cooking time for fresh brisket is 3 to 4 hours; corned brisket takes 4 to 6 hours. Because of the prolonged cooking time in both cases, students who may report for duty at a time which doesn't coincide with this long period should make arrangements for another cook on duty—sometimes the breakfast cook or vegetable cook—to start the job. When cooks repeat the old phrase, "The pot smiles," they are simply reiterating the importance of keeping the cooking liquid at a simmering, not boiling, temperature. The liquid used in cooking fresh beef becomes beef bouillon. The liquid used for cooking corned beef is sometimes used for cooking cabbage, or is discarded. If beef bouillon is to be served the same day, the sauce cook should coordinate his work with the soup cook. Frequently to give the bouillon a richer flavor, beef bones or veal bones and vegetables are added to the water in which the meat is simmered. If beef bouillon is not to be served as a soup the same day, the sauce cook should turn the bouillon over to the soup cook when the job is completed. He may use some of the bouillon, however, for making horseradish sauce. (Horseradish sauce is made by combining a sauce *suprême* or a sauce *béchamel* with prepared horseradish.)

Before starting work: Review the preparation of sauce *suprême* (p 212) and horseradish sauce. Check with the soup cook the day before to see if beef bouillon is to be served at the same meal. Plan your work accordingly. Keep plenty of dry towels available for wiping spillage and wiping utensils when handling the meat. If a strong bouillon is needed for the menu, use all stock for simmering the meat. For a less strong bouillon use half stock and half water or all water.

(1) Assemble the following ingredients:
    25 lb fresh beef brisket

6 lb beef shin bones, 3-in. pieces
6 lb veal bones, 3-in. pieces
4 gal white stock, or 2 gal stock and 2 gal water, or 4 gal water
4 lb whole peeled onions
1 lb whole carrots
1 lb whole white turnips
1/2 lb whole parsnips
8 large leeks, split lengthwise, well-washed
8 stalks celery
1 bunch parsley
1 teaspoon leaf thyme
1/2 teaspoon whole cloves
4 bay leaves
2 teaspoons whole black peppercorns
Salt, pepper
1/2 gal sauce *suprême*
12 oz prepared horseradish
1 tablespoon dry mustard

(2) Place brisket, beef bones and veal bones in a large pot with cold water to cover.

(3) Bring to a boil over high heat. Boil 5 min, no longer.
   Note: This brief period of boiling affects only surface of meat. Interior of meat remains raw.

(4) Pour off water by draining contents of pot.

(5) Run cold water over meat and bones to wash away all scum.

(6) If necessary, wash pot.

(7) Return meat and bones to pot.

(8) Add stock or stock and/or water. Bring to a boil. Remove scum.

(9) Add onions, carrots, turnips, parsnips, leeks, celery and parsley.

(10) Again bring to a boil. Remove scum. Reduce flame so that liquid simmers.

(11) Make a bouquet garni of the leaf thyme, whole cloves, bay leaves and whole black peppercorns. Add to pot. Add 1 tablespoon salt.

(12) Simmer meat until tender, about 3 to 4 hours. Skim surface fat from time to time.

(13) Test tenderness of meat by inserting meat fork in each piece of meat in three or four places.

(14) Turn off flame. Let meat remain in its cooking liquid 1/2 hour before removing from pot.

(15) Transfer meat to deep steam table pans. Pour cooking liquid over meat in steam tables to a depth of about 1 in. to keep meat moist.

(16) Strain beef bouillon through china cap lined with muslin. Correct seasoning with salt and pepper if desired. Turn bouillon over to soup cook.

(17) Place horseradish in double thickness of clean muslin, and squeeze by hand to eliminate juice.

(18) Add horseradish to sauce *suprême*, stirring well.

(19) Dissolve mustard in 1/4 cup cold stock or cold water. Add to sauce. Stir well. Keep sauce hot in steam table pot.

(20) Carve brisket against grain in thin slightly diagonal slices. As carving continues (meat is carved to order), it will be necessary to turn brisket to carve against grain. Use a very sharp knife, honed frequently. Check portions with instructor or supervisor.

(21) Place meat on serving plates or platter. Moisten slices with a small amount, about 1 or 2 tablespoons, of reserved bouillon in steam table pan. Horseradish sauce may be poured over meat or may be served separately in sauce boat.

Corned Beef Brisket.—Soak brisket in cold water overnight. Discard water. Cover with fresh water and simmer for 4 to 6 hours or until tender. Omit bones, seasoning vegetables, bouquet garni and other seasonings as well as horseradish sauce.

New England Boiled Dinner.—Cook corned beef brisket as above and serve with a vegetable garnish of cabbage wedges cooked in corned beef stock, and whole peeled carrots and potatoes cooked in water. In some versions of this dish there are slices of both boiled fresh brisket and boiled corned brisket. Other versions include a slice of boiled salt pork, and sometimes include boiled parsnips, onions or turnips as vegetable accompaniments.

Boiled Smithfield Ham, Cider Sauce   50 Portions, 3 Oz Ham Each

Students should not confuse this job with the popular menu item called baked Virginia ham which is merely any kind of cooked smoked ham or canned ham baked with sugar and spices. Smithfield hams come from hogs raised on a special diet; the meat is cured in a heavy salt brine, smoked and hung to age for up to two years. A similar type of ham, called country ham, is produced in other parts of the South, and is cooked in the manner described below. They have a salty, concentrated flavor which distinguishes them from other hams such as the regular tenderized ham or "ready-to-eat" ham. They are another example of the importance of reading menus several days in advance of preparation. Because of their heavy salt content, hams of this type are soaked at least one full day and sometimes two days. How long they should be soaked is something each chef must decide. If a particular brand of Smithfield ham or country ham is used regularly, experience will be the best guide. If a brand is unknown to the chef, the chef may consult the purveyor and ask his advice on the optimum soaking time. Because of their long aging, the surface of the ham becomes very hard and should be scrubbed with a stuff brush before soaking and cooking. Their keeping quality is good, and after cooking they may be held for two to three weeks without deterioriation. Frequently the cooked cold ham is served on buffet tables and is carved into very thin slices. If the ham is simmered in a conventional pot, the water level should be checked occasionally; water should be added if necessary to keep the ham covered at all times. Sometimes cider or vinegar is added to the cooking water, about a pint for each ham.

Before starting work: At least three days in advance, check with instructor or supervisor on soaking time required. Review the steps in carving ham (see Chap. 7).

(1) Assemble the following ingredients:

2 12-lb Smithfield hams, soaked 1 to 2 days

2 qt cider

3 qt sauce *espagnole* (p 213)

(2) Scrub hams under cold running water with clean, stiff vegetable brush.

(3) Place hams in a large pot or in a steam-jacketed kettle.

(4) Cover with cold water. Water should be at least 2 in. above hams. Add 1 qt cider.

(5) Bring to a boil. This may take 1/2 to 1 hour if a conventional pot is used rather than a steam-jacketed kettle.

(6) Reduce flame so that liquid simmers. Simmer approximately 4 hours or until small bone at shank end of ham becomes loose and is protruding. Do not test meat for tenderness with fork, it may not be accurate and may cause loss of meat juice.

(7) Remove hams from stock. Save 1 cup of stock without fat. If pot is equipped with spigot, the stock without fat may be drained off.

(8) Allow hams to cool slightly. Peel or cut skin off ham. Cut off any fat in excess of 1/4 in. Tip of knife may be inserted to gauge depth of fat. The fat feels soft; the solid meat is firm.

(9) Place hams in steam table pans. A small amount of stock or water, about 1/2 in. in depth, may be added to keep hams moist.

(10) In saucepot combine sauce *espagnole*, remaining 1 qt cider and 1 cup ham stock.
(11) Bring to a boil. Skim well. Reduce flame and simmer until sauce is reduced to 3 qt. Use a wide saucepan if necessary to hasten reduction. Better results will occur if sauce is slowly reduced. Correct seasoning if necessary.
(12) Carve ham, following directions on page 186, but carve Smithfield ham in thinner slices. Consult instructor or supervisor on size of portions.
(13) If ham is served with cabbage, place cabbage on serving plate, place overlapping slices of ham on cabbage, and pour sauce over ham allowing approximately 2 oz sauce per portion.

9

Cold Meat Man (*Garde Manger*)

The French term *garde manger* means two things. First, it is that section of the kitchen where fresh as well as leftover meat, poultry and seafood are stored. It includes walk-in and reach-in refrigerators and ice chests for seafood. Secondly, *garde manger* means a member of the kitchen staff in charge of this department. As such he may have two sets of duties:

(a) He may perform the work of butcher—storing, boning, trimming, trussing and slicing raw meat, poultry or seafood.

(b) He may prepare foods from leftovers or cooked foods to be served cold, including cold platters, canapés, seafood cocktails, and salads of meat, poultry or seafood. He may prepare salad dressings. He may prepare raw or cooked meats, poultry or seafood by slicing, dicing, chopping them, etc., for cooks behind the range.

It is the latter role (b) with which this chapter is concerned. There are many modern restaurants where the job of butcher has virtually been eliminated through the use of preportioned cuts of meat, drawn poultry, trimmed oven-ready roasts, etc. But the *garde manger* assigned to the preparation of hors d'oeuvres, salads, leftovers, etc., is an indispensable link in the kitchen organization. Actually the phrase "cold meat man" does not accurately describe his total job. There are times when he is behind the range boiling such foods as lobster, shrimp or hard eggs. Much of his daily work is spent in trimming and cutting leftovers for hashes, croquettes, etc., which he subsequently passes to the sauce cook, fry cook, and others. Handling leftovers is a phase of his work that keeps him in daily contact with the chef in planning dishes for future menus, ordering daily supplies, etc. When cooks need meat, poultry or seafood before and during the meal, the *garde manger* supplies them; they may be raw foods in portions, whole pieces like meats for roasting or boiling, or breaded foods. Although sandwiches are discussed in a separate chapter, there are kitchens where the *garde manger*'s duties include sandwich making or supervision of sandwich making. Even cold soups which are pre-pared by the soup cook are turned over to the *garde manger* for storing, thinning, garnishing, etc. Because of these many duties the *garde manger* usually has one or two assistants to work with him. Since the foods the *garde manger* handles are often the largest components of the kitchen food cost, he must have considerable experience in estimating portions, portion control, calculating batches of raw food to be passed for a given dish, etc. When food cost percentage shows any significant rise, and the rise is not due to corresponding increases in the cost of raw food, the chef or manager normally turns to the *garde manger* to help check the possibilities of excessive waste in leftovers or pilfering.

JOB SUMMARY

The *garde manger* (1) receives, stores and distributes fresh meat, poultry, seafood, tomatoes and mushrooms for preparation behind range or for use in *garde manger* section; (2) takes daily or more frequent inventories of raw and leftover foods in refrigerators in his section, and transmits data to chef for planning future menus and for daily ordering; (3) consults chef or *sous chef* in planning use of specific leftovers; (4) requisitions grocery supplies from storeroom for preparation of cold dishes; (5) prepares cold hors d'oeuvres for cocktail parties, bar service, and dining table service; (6) arranges platters of cold whole cooked meats, poultry or seafood for buffet table; (7) prepares large salads for buffet table, individual salads of meat, poultry or seafood and salad dressings for dining room; (8) shapes cooked mixture for croquettes; (9) breads raw and cooked foods for frying; (10) may prepare sandwiches or supervise sandwich preparation; (11) may supervise pantry preparation; (12) stores, serves and garnishes cold cream soups or cold jellied soups.

MANUAL SKILLS

He (1) trims with knife whole cooked meats including roasts, boiled or braised meats or boiled whole fish, arranges on platters and garnishes such whole foods for buffet service; (2) with French knife or roast meat slicer cuts cooked meats and poultry into slices for cold cuts; (3) uses slicing machine for cutting cold cuts; (4) dices or chops cold cooked meats, poultry and seafood for salads;

(5) shapes and garnishes cold salads on large platters for buffet service; (6) slices hard eggs, tomatoes, pickles, radishes and other foods for cold garnishes; (7) mixes meats, poultry, seafood and other foods with salad dressings for main course salads; (8) slices cabbage by hand or cutting machine for cole slaw; (9) mixes by machine oil, vinegar, eggs and seasonings for mayonnaise and other salad dressings; (10) adds spices and chopped foods to basic dressings for variations such as tartar sauce; (11) toasts and butters bread, and spreads or arranges foods on bread for canapés; (12) cuts canapés into various shapes and garnishes canapés; (13) prepares cold purees by mixing, and uses pastry bag and tube for stuffing eggs, celery, etc., with purees; (14) peels, slices or dices cooked potatoes and mixes them with dressings and seasonings for potato salad; (15) boils seafood such as shrimp and lobster; (16) removes seafood from shells; (17) cleans and dices seafood; (18) mixes wine, vinegar and seasonings for marinades; (19) cuts stale bread into cubes and prepares bread crumbs in chopping machine; (20) dips raw or cooked foods in flour, eggs and bread crumbs for frying; (21) grinds raw or cooked meat, poultry or seafood in grinding machine and shapes ground mixtures into patties; (22) with French knife cuts cooked meat, poultry or seafood into dice or slices for croquettes, hash, creamed dishes, etc.

EQUIPMENT AND UTENSILS

In his work he uses (1) cutting or chopping machine; (2) grinding machine; (3) meat slicing machine; (4) mixing machine with cutting attachments; (5) mixing bowls; (6) cutting block, cutting tables and cutting boards; (7) French knives, roast meat slicer, paring knives; (8) wire whips, mixing spoons, spatulas; (9) pastry bags and tubes; (10) china caps; (11) cleaver and meat saw; (12) ladles, scoops, dippers.

WORKING CONDITIONS AND HAZARDS

The *garde manger* (1) moves from normal kitchen temperature of *garde manger* section to hot stoves or to walk-in refrigerators; (2) walks on wet or slippery tile floors of refrigerators; (3) assembles and disassembles cutting machines, slicing machines and grinding machines; (4) frequently works in limited space; (5) must be alert to orders from waiters as well as requests for food from cooks, pantrymen, etc.

PLACE IN JOB ORGANIZATION

The assistant to the *garde manger* or butcher may be promoted to *garde manger*. A well-qualified *garde manger* may be promoted to second cook or *saucier*.

30 GUIDES FOR THE GARDE MANGER

(1) All fresh foods whether cooked or raw have a limited life and become subject to spoilage. The *garde manger* is literally the guardian against spoilage, and daily or twice daily should check all foods in his section for signs of incipient spoilage, stickiness, off-odors, etc.

(2) Be sure refrigerator temperatures never rise above 40° F. If higher temperatures are noticed, report them at once to the chef or instructor. If refrigerator thermometers do not seem to be functioning properly, report this fact at once.

(3) Be sure all fans in refrigerators are working normally.

(4) Keep refrigerator doors open as briefly as possible.

(5) Store the same foods in the same place whenever possible so that they can be reached quickly or replaced quickly. It is sometimes advisable to place written markers on refrigerator shelf space reserved for specific foods.

(6) Place foods in packages, storage pans or other containers in such a way that air circulation is not impeded around the containers.

(7) Place drip pans beneath cuts of meat hanging from wall hooks.

(8) Any spillage on shelves or floors of refrigerators should be wiped immediately.

(9) Wash refrigerator shelves, walls and floors at least once a week.

(10) All storage pans containing sliced, diced or chopped meats or poultry should be lined with wax paper.

(11) Cover cooked foods in containers with tight-fitting lids, plastic wrap or other wrap to avoid moisture loss and to avoid transference of food odors and flavors.

(12) When working with cold leftover foods, do not keep them at room temperature for more than 20 to 30 min. If, for example, you are cutting cooked beef for hash, take a few pieces of beef at a time from the refrigerator, and return batches to the refrigerator as soon as the meat is cut.

(13) Beaten eggs used in breading should be made fresh daily or, if left from one day to the next, should be carefully checked and always discarded if there is any doubt as to their quality. Bread

crumbs for breading should be sifted after each use or during use to keep them from becoming matted with egg.

(14) When using a working table with wooden surface, a cutting board or block, be sure the working area is scrubbed frequently and scraped when necessary.

(15) All fresh fish should be packed in crushed ice, and the ice should be replenished or changed as often as necessary. The entire ice chest for fish should be emptied and washed at least twice weekly.

(16) Food in tins such as anchovies, if left over, should be transferred to containers of enamel or stainless steel.

(17) Food in glass jars or bottles, after being opened, should be kept tightly closed and kept in refrigeration.

(18) Slicing machines, cutting machines and food grinders are notorious hosts for bacteria. They should be washed well after each use and be scalded if possible. If this is the duty of the *garde manger*'s assistant or some other person in the kitchen, the *garde manger* should check both the cleaning procedures and the cleaned equipment.

(19) During the *garde manger*'s absence at off-peak periods or late at night, other cooks may go to the *garde manger*'s refrigerators for precut meat, breaded foods, etc. Access to his refrigerator should be limited to appointed personnel so that responsibility is established for the inventory and condition of the refrigerators.

(20) Since much of the *garde manger*'s work is concerned with uniformity in carving, slicing, dicing and trimming meat, the *garde manger* should be equipped with a complete set of heavy-duty knives, kept very sharp and well honed at all times, as well as a complete assortment of food cutters of assorted shapes and sizes. Such personal equipment should be under lock and key during the *garde manger*'s absence.

(21) The food under the *garde manger*'s supervision represents a large portion of the food cost. Portion control in his department, therefore, is of critical importance. To test the designated portion size of sliced meats, poultry, etc., use a portion control scale frequently. For such foods as chicken salad, potato salad, etc., use standard size dippers, scoops, etc., rather than kitchen spoons.

(22) Butter for canapés, sandwiches and spreads should be softened for spreading. Let butter stand at room temperature only until it can be worked to a smooth spreading consistency; do not let it melt. If it shows signs of melting, chill it briefly.

(23) When slicing meats for cold cuts, slice them to order if pos-

sible for the sake of both appearance and flavor. If quantities must be prepared in advance, slice them as close to serving time as possible and estimate quantities needed as conservatively as possible.

(24) Because salad dressings that are made on the premises contain no stabilizing additives, keep them under refrigeration at all times. If they are removed from the refrigerator during a meal period, they should be placed in a refrigerated well or should be surrounded with ice. The exception to this rule is French dressing made with olive oil which tends to become solid if kept more than 24 hours under refrigeration. In kitchens where olive oil French dressing is a standard item, it is often made fresh daily.

(25) While cooks are frequently reminded that hot foods should be hot and cold foods, cold, the *garde manger* must be constantly aware of this important directive. Salad bowls and plates for cold cuts should be chilled. Individual salads made in advance should be placed in the refrigerator until they are picked up by the waiters.

(26) Eye appeal in cold foods often depends upon color contrast. Do not, for instance, garnish a plate with red tomatoes, red beets and red radishes.

(27) The phrase, "Neat, not gaudy," is the modern *garde manger*'s constant guideline, whether he is making a canapé, a sandwich or a salad. Do not add garnishes that give foods an "overdressed" or artificial look.

(28) Just as an athlete keeps his eye on the ball, keep your eye on the meat or poultry being sliced or diced not only for uniform results but for safety's sake. You cannot assemble and garnish an attractive cold platter or salad while engaged in a conversation with another worker.

(29) Be meticulous about uniformity. If chicken is to be cut into 1/2-in. dice for salads or 1/4-in. dice for hash, cut the chicken as closely as possible to the designated size. If necessary, as a guide purely for training purposes, look at a ruler or use the ruler for the initial dice until your eye and hand become coordinated.

(30) The rim of the plate or the rim of the salad bowl should be wiped clean, if necessary, before the waiter picks up the food. Odd pieces of salad greens or other foods, drops of dressing, etc., should never appear on the rim.

Mayonnaise   1 Gal

There was a time when first class restaurants used only mayonnaise made on the premises. Today the great majority of eating places purchase prepared mayonnaise. Nevertheless, students learning the art of the *garde manger* should understand this job and be able to produce not only mayonnaise but also its important variations such as tartar sauce, Russian dressing, etc. Mayonnaise is to the *garde manger* what hollandaise sauce is to the sauce cook, that is, a rather difficult sauce thickened not by flour but by emulsification. Hollandaise is a hot sauce made of egg yolks, water and butter. Mayonnaise is a cold sauce made of egg yolks, vinegar and oil. Both sauces are susceptible to "breaking," which means that the emulsification is not stable, fat separation occurs, and the sauce looks curdled. Demulsification or breaking may take place if:

(a) The egg yolks are insufficiently beaten when the job is started;
(b) Too much vinegar is added at the beginning;
(c) Too much salt is used;
(d) The oil is added too rapidly; or
(e) The beating is insufficient or at irregular speeds throughout the job.

Commercial mayonnaises are made with domestic salad oils such as soybean oil, corn oil, etc., rather than with imported olive oil which has a more noticeable flavor than domestic oils. In some very distinguished American restaurants, the European practice of using olive oil is still followed. Finally, if in spite of precautions, demulsification occurs, the job may be started again with several beaten egg yolks to which the *garde manger* adds the broken mayonnaise in a very gradual stream while beating continuously.

Before starting work: Make sure the mixing bowl and wire whip are absolutely clean and dry. Scald them if necessary. Choose a mixing machine and bowl of the appropriate size for making 1 gal. Test eggs for freshness. Open several; be sure the yolks are firm and do not break when turned into a dish, and that the whites are not watery and "running." After separating egg yolks from whites, check with the chef or instructor who will tell you whether to give the whites to the soup cook or the pastry cook.

(1) Assemble the following ingredients:
  16 egg yolks
  2 1/2 tablespoons salt
  3 tablespoons sugar
  2 tablespoons dry mustard
  1 tablespoon prepared Dijon mustard
  1 teaspoon white pepper
  1 cup vinegar
  1/2 cup lemon juice
  3 qt and 1 pt salad oil (olive oil, corn oil, soybean oil, etc.)
(2) If machine is equipped with dispenser for oil, set it in place.

(3) Pour egg yolks, salt, sugar, both kinds of mustard and white pepper into bowl.
(4) Lift bowl to proper height. Selector should be on low speed.
(5) Turn mixer on. Gradually raise speed to medium. Blend well.
(6) Slowly pour in 1/4 cup vinegar. Blend well.
(7) Add oil in smallest possible stream. (Apprentices are sometimes told to add it in drops. Actually oil is not added drop by drop, but the advice is meant to insure emulsification by carefully controlling the amount of oil added.
   Note: Oil may be added in a special funnel used for making mayonnaise, or by puncturing oil can at top so that oil flows in a very small stream.
(8) When emulsification takes place (you will see the smooth mass of sauce forming in the bowl), oil may be added in a somewhat larger stream. When half the oil has been used and the mixture is smooth and thick, slowly mix in 1/2 cup vinegar in a small steady stream.
(9) Continue to add balance of oil until the total quantity is used.
(10) Slowly mix in balance of vinegar and lemon juice.
(11) Taste mayonnaise. Correct seasoning if desired.
(12) Remove mayonnaise and store in a clean glass jar or jars with tight-fitting lid. Keep refrigerated.

Tartar Sauce.—To each qt mayonnaise add 3/4 cup finely chopped sour pickles, 1/2 cup capers in vinegar, drained and chopped fine, 1/4 cup finely chopped green olives and 2 tablespoons chives, chopped extremely fine.

Russian Dressing.—To each qt mayonnaise add 1/2 cup chili sauce, 1/2 cup catsup, 1 cup hard egg chopped fine, and 1 tablespoon each chives, chervil and parsley, each chopped extremely fine.

Chantilly Dressing.—Into each qt mayonnaise fold in 1 pt heavy cream beaten until thick.

Green Sauce (Sauce Verte).—To each qt mayonnaise add the following ingredients, each chopped extremely fine (measurements are after chopping): 2 tablespoons cooked spinach, 1 tablespoon fresh tarragon, 1/4 cup watercress, 2 tablespoons chervil.

Remoulade Sauce.—To each qt mayonnaise add 1/2 cup finely chopped sour gherkins, 1 tablespoon Dijon mustard, 1/4 cup drained finely chopped capers, 1 tablespoon each chives, chervil and tarragon, chopped extremely fine.

French Dressing 5 Qt

As explained in the previous unit, mayonnaise is an emulsion of eggs, oil and vinegar. Because it keeps its shape and consistency after being mixed it is called a permanent emulsion. French dressing is a mixture of oil and vinegar, without eggs, and is known as a temporary emulsion. For this reason French dressing freshly prepared in a restaurant (as distinct from commercial dressings which contain stabilizers and may be permanent emulsions) must be shaken or stirred before it is served. In many restaurants French dressing is kept at the *garde manger's* section in a stoppered bottle and is shaken before each use.

Making French dressing is not so much a matter of culinary skill as it is assembling the combination of specific raw ingredients that will result in a particular blend of flavors. The choice of oil and vinegar is important. It was pointed out in the previous unit that most domestic salad oils like corn oil, soybean oil, cottonseed oil, etc., are characterized by their relatively neutral flavors. Peanut oil has a somewhat distinct flavor which is imparted when it is used in French dressing. Olive oil (the most expensive of the oils) is more distinctive and is the preferred oil for salads in restaurants which follow a continental tradition. The various vinegars used may include cider, tarragon, white wine, white (made from grain), red wine and malt vinegar. Different brands of vinegar vary in strength of flavor and acidity. Since the *garde manger* does not purchase the oil or vinegar used in his dressing, the chef or chef-steward who orders a particular product actually determines the outcome of the job no matter what procedure the *garde manger* follows. In the finest restaurants the *garde manger* uses a ratio of at least three parts of oil to one of vinegar; or, as tradition has it, he is a spendthrift with oil, a miser with vinegar. If French dressing is made with all olive oil, it will become thick in a day or two if stored in the refrigerator, and must be spooned rather than poured. French dressings made with other oils will remain pourable even though chilled. In some restaurants, as previously stated, olive oil French dressing is made fresh daily.

Before starting work: Choose a mixing bowl which is the appropriate size for 5 qt of French dressing. If it is too small, the dressing may splatter out of the bowl. If it is too large, the blending may be poor. Use standard graduated qt and cup measures. Do not guess at the quantities. Be sure the mixing bowl and wire whip are thoroughly clean. Check the salad oil to make sure there is no off-odor or sign of rancidity. Check available bottles with stoppers or jars with lids to make sure they are sufficient for storing the dressing after it is made. When pouring the dressing from the bowl into bottles or jars, stir well each time before pouring so that there is a proper ratio of oil to vinegar in each container.

(1) Assemble the following ingredients:

> 1 gal salad oil
> 1 qt vinegar
> 3 tablespoons salt
> 1/4 cup dry mustard
> 2 teaspoons white pepper
> 1 tablespoon sugar
> 2 teaspoons paprika (optional)

(2) Pour vinegar into mixing bowl.

(3) Add salt, mustard, white pepper, sugar and paprika.

(4) Beat with wire whip until well blended. Salt and sugar should be dissolved. Make sure there are no unblended lumps of dry mustard. If a machine is used, lift the whip out of the bowl before examining ingredients.

(5) Add the oil in a slow steady stream while beating well.

(6) Taste the dressing and correct seasoning if desired.

(7) Pour into clean dry bottles with stoppers, or jars with tight-fitting lids.

(8) Store in refrigerator.

> *Note:* If olive oil is used, store in cool, dry dark place rather than refrigerator. If a more tart dressing is desired, increase vinegar and decrease oil in equal amounts.

French Dressing with Egg.—Beat 8 whole eggs. Add slowly to French dressing while beating with wire whip.

Onion Flavor.—Chop 1 lb Spanish onion very fine. Place onion in triple thickness of cheesecloth. Gather ends of cheesecloth together, hold over bowl containing dressing, and squeeze to release onion juice. Mix well.

Garlic Flavor.—Gently smash with flat side of knife 16 medium to large size cloves of garlic. Remove skin from garlic. Add garlic to dressing. Let stand overnight. Strain dressing next day and discard garlic.

Lemon Dressing.—Use lemon juice or half lemon juice and half vinegar instead of vinegar. Additional sugar may be added to taste if dressing is to be used with fresh fruit salads.

Tomato Dressing.—Add 1 cup tomato puree and 1 cup catsup to recipe.

Sauce Vinaigrette.—Add 1 cup chopped drained capers, 1/4 cup each parsley, chives and chervil, chopped extremely fine, and 1 cup finely chopped hard egg.

Chiffonade Dressing.—Add 2 cups finely chopped hard egg, 1 cup each green pepper and pimiento, chopped fine, and 1/2 cup parsley, chopped extremely fine.

Antipasto   6 Portions

The Italian word antipasto means "before meal" (literally before the pasta), and the term is used in the same way as hors d'oevres in French or appetizer in English. In American restaurants featuring Italian food, however, antipasto is generally a plate of cold appetizers most of which are purchased rather than prepared on the premises. It may include some fresh items such as celery or radishes, but these involve trimming rather than cooking. Usually cruets of olive oil and red wine vinegar are offered to the customer at the table. Extreme neatness and a sense of color are important in assembling the plate. All ingredients should be ice cold when the antipasto is served. Thus if the *garde manger* is preparing 20 or 30 antipasti for a party, the best procedure is to assemble the individual plates, and then return them to the refrigerator until the moment the waiters are ready to serve them. Be circumspect in examining all foods in jars or cans (even though transferred out of the can.) which have been left over from a previous use. If anchovies are extremely salty, they should be washed, dried and brushed with fresh salad oil. If sardines show a hard or brown edge, do not use them.

Before starting work: At least two hours in advance prepare celery hearts and radish fans in recipe below. Celery hearts should be cut from the center of the celery bunch. Hearts are made by cutting the center of the bunch lengthwise into sixths or eighths, each of which should contain a wedge of the root end of the celery. The very small tender leaves of the heart stalks may be left on, but larger leaves should be removed. Refrigerate in a bowl with cracked ice. Prepare radish fans by cutting a thin slice off opposite ends of each radish, and then cutting very thin parallel slices down toward base of radish but not through stem end. Place radishes in a bowl with cracked ice, or cracked ice and water, and refrigerate until needed. Check all plates to make sure they are absolutely clean. Place them in the refrigerator to chill. Check list of ingredients needed in the recipe, and then check refrigerator stock to make sure all foods are on hand and are chilled. Meat to be sliced for antipasto should be sliced by machine, if available, rather than by hand, and should be sliced very thin.

(1) Assemble the following ingredients:

   3 hard-boiled eggs, shelled
   6 short asparagus tips, cooked or canned
   6 anchovy fillets in oil, drained
   3 slices mortadella sausage
   3 cups shredded lettuce (iceberg)
   6 very thin slices prosciutto ham
   6 boneless and skinless sardines
   6 pimiento strips, 1 1/2 in. long, 1/8 in. thick
   6 lettuce cups (Boston)
   6 artichoke hearts in oil, drained
   6 radish fans
   6 black olives
   6 celery hearts
   6 thin slices Genoa salami
   6 thin slices provolone cheese, 3 in. diameter

(2) Cut hard eggs in half lengthwise.

(3) Cut each asparagus tip if necessary so that it is about 1/2 in. shorter than the length of the egg. Place an asparagus tip on the center of each egg.

(4) Place an anchovy fillet diagonally across each asparagus tip.

(5) Cut each slice of mortadella sausage in half. (Mortadella sausage is usually quite wide in diameter.)

(6) Place a mound of shredded lettuce near the center of each plate.

(7) Place a sardine on top each portion of shredded lettuce. Place a pimiento strip lengthwise on each sardine.

(8) Place a lettuce cup alongside the sardines. On the lettuce cup place an artichoke heart, a radish fan and a black olive.

(9) Place a celery heart between the shredded lettuce and the lettuce cup.

(10) Place the hard egg with asparagus tip and anchovy near the center of the plate.

(11) On the rim of the plate arrange a slice of mortadella, a slice of prosciutto, a slice of Genoa salami and a slice of provolone.

(12) Return plates to refrigerator, if possible, to chill until serving time.

Assorted Canapés   48 Pieces, 8 Slices Bread

The French word canapé literally means couch or sofa, that is something on which to rest or raise food. In the restaurant trade a canapé is a piece of toasted or fried bread, cracker or other base on which an appetizer is placed. Usually canapés are served at cocktail parties or at receptions before dinner rather than as appetizers at the dining table. Hot hors d'oeuvres or appetizers are prepared by the sauce cook or some other cook designated by the chef. Canapés, like other cold hors d'oeuvres, are the job of the *garde manger*. There are an infinite number of food combinations used for canapés, including many spreads made of seafood, cheese, eggs, meat and poultry. One of the best known assortments is a tray of canapés made with four classical appetizers: caviar, smoked salmon, anchovies and sardines. The technique for preparing them is simple. Slices of white bread are toasted on one or both sides, then are buttered and spread with the four components. The bread is cut into quarters or sixths and arranged for serving on a large platter or platters. If canapés are made to order just before they are served, the bread may be toasted on both sides. If they are made in advance and held in the refrigerator until serving time, the following procedure is suggested:

(a) Toast the bread under the broiler on one side only.

(b) Butter the untoasted side. Plain butter or a compound butter (p 288) may be used.

(c) Cover the buttered side with the appetizer.

(d) Coat the smoked salmon, anchovies and sardines either with salad oil or with an aspic to give the canapés a sheen and to keep them from drying.

(e) Cut the canapés into bite-size pieces and arrange them on a platter. Canapés are sometimes decorated with butter, mayonnaise and other ingredients, using a pastry bag and tube for making decorative designs. The tendency in recent years is to present canapés which are not overdecorated. The number of canapés served at a cocktail party is always variable depending on the length of the cocktail period. One portion standard allows 6 small appetizers per person for a cocktail period from 1 1/2 to 2 hours. If canapés are supplemented with hot hors d'oeuvres, these would be included in the estimate of six per person. In any event, the *garde manger* should always be prepared to make additional canapés if called for.

Before starting work: Obtain trays, preferably silver, for arranging canapés. To keep canapés from sliding when they are passed or served, platters should be lined with white linen napkins or paper doilies; choose the correct size for the platters you will be using. Be sure there is shelf space in the refrigerators for the platters. Appetizers like canapés are only appetizing when they are neatly prepared and cleanly cut. Make sure that you have a sharp heavy French knife for cutting. A heavy knife, rather than a light one, enables you to cut the canapés without disturbing the arrangement of the toppings.

(1) Assemble the following ingredients:
   8 slices white sandwich bread, crust on
   1/4 lb butter (variable), worked until soft
   1/4 lb smoked salmon
   4 oz black or red caviar
   2 oz flat anchovy fillets in oil
   6 skinless and boneless sardines in oil
   1 canned pimiento
   1 hard boiled egg, chopped extremely fine
   1/2 cup jellied consommé Madrilene (p 56)
   1 lemon
   1 bunch parsley

(2) Heat the jellied consommé Madrilene until it melts. Return to refrigerator in a small bowl. Chill it until it becomes syrupy and is beginning to jell again.

   Note: In kitchens where cold dishes in aspic are prepared, there may be a special jelly available for coating cold foods.

(3) If salmon is in oil, drain it. If salmon is unsliced, cut it into very thin diagonal slices. Slices should be uniform in thickness. Use a very sharp knife, preferably a ham slicer or some other knife with a long thin blade. If there are any salmon bones, remove them. Set slices aside.

(4) Drain oil from anchovy fillets. Set aside on a plate. If fillets are excessively salty, they may be washed, patted dry, and brushed with salad oil.

(5) Drain sardines. Avoid breaking when lifting from can. With a small pointed knife carefully separate each sardine lengthwise into two pieces. Place sardines outer side up on plate.

(6) Place bread on a tray. Toast under broiler until medium brown on one side only.

(7) Arrange bread, toasted side down, and butter the untoasted side.

(8) On the buttered side of 2 slices of bread spread the caviar. Spread it evenly to the edge of the bread. Set aside.

(9) On the buttered side of 2 slices of bread, place the smoked salmon, covering the bread completely. Run the flat side of a knife over the salmon to smooth it. Set aside.

(10) On the buttered side of 2 slices of bread arrange the anchovies in parallel lines. Anchovies should be placed side by side so that no bread is visible. Use more than the 2 oz of anchovies if necessary. Run the flat side of a French knife over the anchovies to smooth them. Set aside.

(11) On the buttered side of 2 slices of bread arrange the sardines,

outer side up, in parallel lines. If the two slices of bread are not large enough to hold 12 pieces of sardine, toast and butter another slice. Cut pimientos into thin strips about 1/4 in. thick and 1 1/2 in. long. Place a strip lengthwise on top of each sardine. A toothpick or two may be used to transfer and place pimiento strips.

(12) When jellied consommé is syrupy and beginning to thicken, carefully brush or dab tops of the smoked salmon, the anchovy and the sardine canapés, covering them completely. If consommé is not sufficiently thick, it will flow off tops of canapés, the gel will not form, and the bread may become soggy. When applying the jellied consommé, the canapés may be placed on a wire rack so that any excess liquid runs off bread. Be especially careful when brushing the sardine canapés so that the pimiento strips remain in place; or brush the pimiento strips and the sardines separately and then place the strips on the sardines. Do not brush the caviar canapés.

Note: Instead of brushing canapés with jellied consommé or aspic, some *garde mangers* brush sardine, anchovy and smoked salmon canapés with olive oil just before serving to give them an attractive gloss.

(13) Place all canapés on a flat tray and return to refrigerator until jelly on top of canapés becomes firm, 1/2 to 1 hour.

(14) Remove canapés from refrigerator. Using a heavy sharp French knife, cut off crusts of bread.

(15) Cut smoked salmon canapés in half. Cut each half crosswise into thirds. Set aside.

(16) Cut each anchovy canapé into six finger-like strips. Sprinkle ends of each canapé with chopped egg. Set aside.

(17) Cut sardine canapés lengthwise so that each piece of sardine is a long canapé. Trim off excess bread beyond margin of sardine. Set aside.

(18) Cut each caviar canapé in half. Cut each half diagonally into thirds, making triangular shapes. (If red caviar is used, a few black capers may be placed in the center of each canapé. If black caviar is used, a little chopped egg may be sprinkled in center of each canapé. Use only enough chopped egg so that it looks like an attractive garnish and not something carelessly dropped on the canapés.)

(19) Line a large silver platter or two platters with white linen napkins or with white paper doilies.

(20) Arrange the canapés on the platter so that all four kinds are uniformly distributed.

(21) Cut a slice from each end of the lemon. Use a very sharp knife to cut neatly. Cut lemon in half. Cut each half lengthwise into 6 wedges. Cut each wedge crosswise into 4 pieces.

(22) Tear off very small sprigs of parsley with as little stem as possible.

(23) Place lemon wedges and parsley alternately between canapés. Use only enough parsley to provide a moderate amount of color contrast.

Cold Compound Butters   Approx 1 Cup

Just as the sauce cook or the broiler cook from time to time prepares hot butter sauces, so does the *garde manger* use cold compound butters for spreading on canapés. A cold compound butter is simply softened, not melted, butter mixed with another food of a pronounced flavor, usually pureed or chopped. The compound butter is spread on the canapé base, and then covered with smoked salmon, sardines or any other canapé item. Butters of this type provide a rich but not oily taste and subtly enhance the recognizable flavors of well-known canapé coverings. It is important to carefully calculate how much butter you will need for a job and then make the specific amount required, since leftover butter of this type cannot always be used for other daily dishes. Normally a single slice of bread for canapés will be spread with 2 teaspoons of butter. A pound of butter will be sufficient for 48 slices of bread. If there is leftover compound butter, check to see if it can be used by the sauce cook or the broiler cook. If not, it should be kept tightly wrapped in the refrigerator, or it may be frozen and held for future use.

Before starting work: Remove butter from refrigerator about 20 to 30 min before softening it. Break the butter into small pieces to hasten softening. Do not let butter melt. If it can be worked easily with a spoon or butter spreader, it is ready to be made into a compound butter. Use a clean mixing bowl of the appropriate size for the amount of butter you are preparing. A mixing bowl which is too large can cause waste. If the bowl is too small, thorough blending is difficult.

Anchovy Butter.—Mix 3/4 cup softened sweet butter, 1/4 cup anchovy paste and 1 teaspoon lemon juice. If mixture does not seem to be well blended, force it through a fine sieve and mix again. In place of anchovy paste, very finely chopped anchovy fillets may be pounded in mortar to a puree and then forced through sieve with butter.

Caviar Butter.—Mix until well blended 2/3 cup softened sweet butter and 1/3 cup black or red caviar. Do not rub through sieve unless caviar eggs (usually the red type) are very large.

Chive Butter.—Chop 2 tablespoons chives extremely fine. Blend well with 1 cup minus 2 tablespoons softened butter.

Chivry Butter (Green Butter).—Blanch for 3 min in boiling water 8 spinach leaves, 1 tablespoon parsley (leaves only, no stems), 1 teaspoon fresh tarragon (leaves only) and 1 teaspoon fresh chervil (leaves only). Drain well. Dip in cold water and dry in clean towel or napkin. Separately blanch for 3 min 2 tablespoons peeled chopped shallots. Combine spinach, herbs and shallots, and chop extremely fine or pound in a mortar until reduced to a fine paste. Rub through a fine sieve. Blend well with 1 cup minus 2 tablespoons softened butter.

Curry Butter.—Chop 1/4 cup onion or shallots extremely fine. Sauté in 2 tablespoons butter only until onions are slightly softened, not brown. Stir in 2 teaspoons curry powder and sauté about a minute longer. Cool onions. Mix onions with 3/4 cup softened butter, blending well.

Horseradish Butter.—Drain enough prepared horseradish so that there is 1/4 cup, drained measure. Blend well with 3/4 cup softened butter and 1 teaspoon lemon juice.

Lobster Butter.—With heavy French knife coarsely chop 1 lb cooked lobster shells including creamy part and roe if any. Place in a mortar with 1 cup slightly softened butter. Pound well. Force through a fine sieve. Be sure sieve (china cap) is fine to avoid pieces of shell. If in doubt, mixture can be melted in top part of double boiler, strained through a cheesecloth, then cooled until butter can be easily spread. An alternative procedure is to chop the shells and place them in a heavy-duty blender with the melted butter. Blend the mixture for 1 min, then strain through sieve lined with cheesecloth. Cool until butter is semisoft.

Mustard Butter.—Mix 1/4 cup Dijon mustard and 1 teaspoon dry mustard with 3/4 cup softened butter, blending very well.

Pimiento Butter.—Chop fine 1/3 cup pimientos, mix with 2/3 cup softened butter and force mixture through a fine sieve.

Smoked Salmon Butter.—Chop fine 1/3 cup smoked salmon. Mix with 2/3 cup softened sweet butter and 1 teaspoon lemon juice. Force mixture through a fine sieve.

Shrimp Cocktail   **50 Portions, 2 Oz Each**
                                                  1 Gal Cocktail Sauce

Shrimp cocktail is a dish of cold, peeled boiled shrimp, coated with cocktail sauce and served in a lettuce cup. In restaurants with an oyster bar, the oysterman normally prepares the cocktail sauce, and the *garde manger* cooks the shrimp. Cocktail sauce is composed almost entirely of prepared ingredients, that is, condiments out of cans, jars or bottles rather than anything cooked in the kitchen. There are some seafood cocktail recipes which call for chopped green pepper, chopped onion, etc., but these are the rare exceptions. Its principal ingredient is catsup. Although catsup itself contains many seasonings, cocktail sauce should be distinguished by sharp, tart accents that stand out in contrast to the relatively bland flavors of shrimp, crabmeat, etc. Shrimp may be cooked in salted water or in a stock-like liquid as in the recipe below. In either case, the two principal guidelines are:
  (a) Cook the shrimp at a simmering rather than boiling temperature.
  (b) Avoid overcooking which toughens the shrimp.
Raw shrimp in the shell are usually headless. Along the back of the shrimp there is a vein which may be black, pink or orange in color. It is always removed after shrimp have been cooked. To help in removing the vein, shrimp shells are sometimes cut down the back before cooking. But this additional step beforehand does not eliminate the vein and may actually increase the total time on the job.
Before starting work: Check condition of shrimp. If they are frozen on arrival, thaw them in the refrigerator if possible rather than at room temperature or by immersing in water. When they are unfrozen, they should be stored in the fish ice chest covered with cracked ice. Examine them before cooking. Top quality shrimp should be firm to the touch, not flabby; they should feel clean rather than sticky or slimy; they should have a characteristic "seashore" odor but no off-odor indicating deterioration. Check the number of raw shrimp per pound so that you can calculate the number of cooked shrimp per portion. The recipe below is for approximately 4 portions per pound of raw shrimp.
  (1) Assemble the following ingredients:
      12 1/2 lb shrimp (preferably 16 to 24 per lb)

2 gal plus 1 qt water
2 lb celery, large dice
2 lb onions, large dice
36 whole peppercorns
4 large bay leaves
Salt, pepper
2 1/2 qt catsup
1 qt chili sauce
1/2 cup vinegar
1/2 cup lemon juice
2 tablespoons Worcestershire sauce
1 cup prepared horseradish
1 teaspoon celery salt
1/2 teaspoon Tabasco sauce
1/8 teaspoon cayenne pepper
100 leaves Boston lettuce, trimmed, washed and dried

(2) Wash shrimp well in colander under cold running water.
(3) Pour 2 gal plus 1 qt water into saucepot.
(4) Add celery, onions, peppercorns, bay leaves and 3 tablespoons salt.
(5) Bring to a boil. Reduce flame and simmer 20 min.
(6) Add shrimp to pot.
(7) When water again reaches simmering point, cover pot and simmer (do not boil) 5 min.
(8) Remove pot from fire. Strain cooking liquid and reserve.
(9) Spread shrimp in shallow pans.
(10) When shrimp are cool enough to handle, remove shrimp shells by breaking and pulling underside of shells first, then lifting entire shells from back of shrimp. Be sure no pieces of shell remain on shrimp.
(11) With paring knife remove sand vein. In some types of shrimp it is possible to lift out entire vein by hand, starting at head end of shrimp. It may be necessary to wash some shrimp to remove residue of vein.
(12) Return shelled shrimp to strained cooking liquid.
(13) Store, covered, in refrigerator until needed.
(14) In large mixing bowl combine catsup, chili sauce, vinegar, lemon juice, Worcestershire sauce, horseradish, celery salt, Tabasco sauce and cayenne pepper.
(15) Stir well with wire whip. Add salt and pepper if desired.
(16) Pour cocktail sauce into glass jars or other containers with tight lids. Chill well, at least 2 hours before serving.

(17) For each order of shrimp cocktail, line cocktail glass or dish with 2 leaves of lettuce. Add 4 shrimp of 16-to-the-lb size or 6 shrimp of 24-to-the-lb size. Spoon cocktail sauce over shrimp allowing 3 oz cocktail sauce (No. 12 scoop or dipper) per portion.

Lobster Cocktail.—Substitute 2 oz (cooked weight) diced boiled lobster meat.

Crabmeat Cocktail.—Substitute 2 oz (cooked weight) freshly cooked crab lump. Examine crab lump very carefully to remove any pieces of shell.

Diced Celery.—This is sometimes added to shrimp cocktail. For each portion, use 1/4 cup celery cut into very small dice.

Cauliflower Greek Style (a la Grecque)   1 Gal

Cauliflower Greek style, like shrimp, is another example of a food which is boiled by the *garde manger* rather than by one of the regular cooks behind the range. Because it is served as an appetizer, its preparation is the *garde manger's* responsibility. It is a method of pickling a vegetable and is not to be confused with the household process of pickling vegetables in sterilized jars which are intended to be kept on the shelves for months. As prepared below, cauliflower Greek style might be stored in the *garde manger's* refrigerator for one to two weeks. There are four main steps in the job:

(1) Cauliflower is blanched and drained. Blanching is very brief or partial cooking and facilitates subsequent cooking in a marinade.

(2) A marinade is prepared. It consists of water, oil, vinegar and seasonings.

(3) The blanched cauliflower is then cooked in the marinade only until it is barely done; it should be semicrisp.

(4) The cauliflower is marinated at least one day before it is served.

For this dish the cauliflower should be firm, creamy white, with no "ricy" appearance, soft spots or other defects. Excessive blanching or overcooking in the marinade must be avoided, since any vegetable prepared Greek style, whether it be cauliflower, artichokes, mushrooms or silver onions, is expected to retain a certain characteristic firmness after it has been marinated. The amount of vinegar or lemon juice is variable; different brands of vinegar and fresh lemons vary from time to time in their flavor and acidity; the *garde manger* should be guided accordingly.

Before starting work: Examine cauliflower and if necessary remove any possible defects noted above. For blanching the cauliflower, choose a wide diameter saucepan rather than a narrow one so that the rapidly boiling water will blanch the cauliflower quickly. If a steamer is used, be sure you understand how it is operated to avoid overcooking.

(1) Assemble the following ingredients:
   6 lb cauliflower, as purchased, before trimming
   Salt, pepper
   1/2 lb onions, chopped fine
   1 qt water
   1 cup salad oil
   1 cup white wine vinegar or lemon juice or a combination of the two
   1 stalk celery cut into 1-in. pieces
   36 peppercorns
   2 large bay leaves
   12 fennel seeds
   24 coriander seeds
   1/2 teaspoon leaf thyme
   2 large cloves of garlic, lightly mashed, outer peel removed

(2) Cut off outer green leaves of cauliflower and heavy green stalks.

(3) Cut away as much of core as possible. Discard core. (Cauliflower leaves as well as core are not suitable for adding to stockpot.)

(4) Separate head of cauliflower into smallest possible flowerets.

(5) Boil flowerets in salted water 2 min or cook in steamer 1 min. Drain immediately. Set aside.
   Note: In some kitchens, steps (2) to (5) above may be performed by vegetable cook instead of *garde manger*.

(6) Make a bouquet garni of the celery, peppercorns, bay leaves, fennel seeds, coriander seeds, thyme and garlic.

(7) In saucepot heat 1/4 cup oil over moderate flame.

(8) Add onion and sauté, stirring frequently until onion is light yellow, not brown.

(9) Add balance of oil, water, vinegar and bouquet garni. Simmer slowly, do not boil, 10 min. Keep pot covered.

(10) Place cauliflower in a saucepan about 3 in. high, so that cauliflower is spread out as much as possible.

(11) Pour hot marinade over cauliflower. Add 1/2 teaspoon salt and 1/4 teaspoon pepper. Cover saucepan with tight lid. Simmer slowly until cauliflower is barely done. Remove from fire.

(12) Let cauliflower cool at room temperature about 1/2 hour.

Taste marinade. Add salt and pepper to taste. Add more vinegar if desired. Remove bouquet garni.

(13) Transfer cauliflower and marinade to enamel or stainless steel pan with tight lid. Spoon marinade over cauliflower. Cover with tight lid. Chill at least 24 hours, occasionally spooning marinade over cauliflower.

(14) After chilling, taste marinade again and correct seasoning if desired.

(15) Before serving, carefully mix marinade and cauliflower. Lift cauliflower from marinade with slotted spoon. Pour only enough marinade in hors d'oeuvres dish to moisten cauliflower.

Onions Greek Style.—Use peeled small silver onions instead of cauliflower.

Mushrooms Greek Style.—Substitute button mushrooms for cauliflower. Remove any long stems of mushrooms. Mushrooms may either be blanched in water or sautéd briefly in oil before cooking with marinade.

String Beans Greek Style.—Substitute fresh beans for cauliflower. Remove stem ends of beans. Cut beans julienne with string bean cutter or cut diagonally into 1-in. pieces before blanching.

Celery and Cucumber Salad, Mustard Dressing 2 Qt

Generally the *garde manger* is concerned with salads of meat, poultry or seafood. In those restaurants, however, where an hors d'oeuvres tray or cart is a regular feature of the luncheon or dinner menu, the *garde manger* may prepare appetizer salads such as celery and cucumber salad. Like other hors d'oeuvres of this type, celery and cucumber salad is eaten in small quantities, perhaps one or two serving spoonfuls per portion, as part of an assortment of hors d'oeuvres. Mustard dressing is made with fresh cream and lemon juice. The acid of the lemon gives the cream a thicker consistency than it would normally have. Fresh cream cannot be held for longer periods without spoiling. Sterilized cream, which does not spoil as readily as regular pasteurized cream, is now used in many eating places, but should still be checked before each use, especially in the warm months. Usually a salad of this type should not be kept for more than two days and on the second day should be checked for incipient spoilage. While stored in the refrigerator, it should be tightly covered to prevent assimilation of other food odors.

During the summer season when crisp Kirby cucumbers are available, the cucumbers are merely peeled and diced. At other times of the year, however, it is necessary to remove the watery, seedy section of large cucumbers as indicated below. The *garde manger* should plan on filling small bowls or dishes of the salad for hors d'oeuvres service and should be prepared to make replenishments when necessary.

Before starting work: For this dish the middle stalks of the celery bunch are best. Often the outer stalks are spongy and watery, while the heart of the celery is best reserved for olives and celery hearts as an appetizer. Check with the sauce cook or soup cook who may be able to use the outer stalks as a seasoning vegetable. Plan your work so that the celery and cucumber salad can marinate at least two hours before serving.

(1) Assemble the following ingredients:

   1 1/2 lb celery stalks
   1 lb cucumbers
   1/4 cup Dijon mustard
   2 oz lemon juice
   1 pt heavy cream
   Salt, white pepper, cayenne pepper

(2) Wash celery well, scrubbing inside of stalks with vegetable brush if necessary.

(3) Cut off celery leaves. Pass to soup cook.

(4) Dry celery with clean cloth or paper towels.

(5) Using vegetable peeler with floating blade, peel outside of celery stalks, eliminating stringy portion of celery.

(6) Cut celery lengthwise into 1/2-in. strips.

(7) Cut celery crosswise into 1/2-in. dice.

(8) Peel cucumbers.

(9) Cut cucumbers lengthwise in half.

(10) With small spoon scrape away seedy section of cucumbers.

(11) Cut cucumbers lengthwise into 1/2-in. strips.

(12) Cut cucumbers crosswise into 1/2-in. dice.

(13) In mixing bowl pour 1/2 cup cream, lemon juice and mustard.

(14) Beat with small wire whip until well blended. Do not attempt to whip cream.

(15) Gradually add remainder of cream mixing with wire whip.

(16) Add celery and cucumbers to cream mixture. Mix well.

(17) Season to taste with salt and pepper. Add a dash of cayenne pepper.

(18) Let mixture marinate at least two hours in refrigerator. Keep well covered at all times.

(19) Stir cucumbers, celery and mustard dressing several times while marinating. Stir well just before serving.

Stuffed Celery   100 Pieces, 1 1/4 In. Each

Celery is prepared as an appetizer by filling the hollow or concave side of the stalks with a soft cheese mixture and then cutting the stalks into bite-size pieces. For stuffing celery the *garde manger* uses a pastry bag and tube. The bag is a cone-shaped piece of canvas or other material with a small opening at one end into which a decorating tube is placed. The bag is filled with a cheese mixture, and, as the bag is pressed, the tube extrudes the contents in an attractive design. Tubes come in many shapes and sizes. One of the tubes most commonly used by the *garde manger* is the star tube, designated in the recipe below. The cheese mixture in the bag must be sufficiently plastic to easily pass through the tube, but not so soft that it fails to hold a distinct shape. The bag should never be more than three-fourths full. If a student has never handled the bag before, the bag may be filled and used for practice purposes by forcing the cheese mixture onto a clean platter or tray; the extruded mixture may then be returned to the bag and used to stuff the celery. All mixtures of this type used for stuffing should not be kept out of the refrigerator for more than 15 to 20 min at a time. In a recipe of this kind the yield or number of portions will depend upon the amount of filling in the celery and the uniform manner in which it is filled.

Before starting work: Examine the pastry bag and tube for cleanliness. Be certain there is no odor from a previous use. Normally a *garde manger* will have several pastry bags on hand so that if one needs washing, a clean dry bag is available. For cutting the celery into portions you will need a medium size French knife; it should be as sharp as possible for neat, clean cutting. Examine the work surface, whether it be a wooden table or cutting board, to make sure it is clean and dry as possible. Check to be sure there is sufficient refrigerator space available for storing the celery after it has been stuffed.

(1) Assemble the following ingredients:
   Enough celery stocks (estimated) for 100 1 1/4-in. pieces
   1 1/2 lb cream cheese
   1/2 lb blue cheese or Roquefort cheese
   1/2 cup heavy sweet cream (variable)
   2 teaspoons Worcestershire sauce
   1/4 cup chives, chopped extremely fine
   1/8 teaspoon cayenne pepper
   Paprika

(2) Detach celery stalks from bunch and wash well, paying particular attention to inside of stalks. Remove celery leaves and pass to soup cook or sauce cook.
   Note: Some stalks of celery may be 2 in. wide at bottom and

only 1/2 in. wide at top. Top ends may be cut away. Wide bottom ends may also be cut so that width of celery approximates 1 to 1 1/4 in.

(3) Using a vegetable peeler with floating blade, scrape outside of stalks eliminating coarse outer fibre of celery.

(4) Dry celery with clean cloth or paper towels.

(5) Using vegetable peeler or sharp paring knife, very carefully cut a thin slice down outside stalk center to that each stalks rests flat on the work surface and does not tilt from side to side.

(6) Arrange celery stalks thus prepared side by side on a clean tray.

(7) Place cream cheese and blue cheese in mixing bowl to blend. If there is a small mixing machine (household size), it may be used. Do not attempt to blend cheese in a large heavy-duty mixing machine. If no small mixing machine is available, soften and blend cheese by hand using a mixing spoon or paddle.

(8) To make cheese soft enough for the pastry bag, add cream in small amounts, blending well after each addition. Check with chef or instructor on the proper consistency of the mixture.

(9) Mix in Worcestershire sauce, chives and cayenne pepper, blending well.

(10) Fit star tube into pastry bag. Make sure the tube is fitted firmly into position.

(11) Fill bag no more than 3/4 full, pressing cheese mixture toward tube end of bag, but not out of tube.

(12) Fold over top end of bag, closing it. Hold top in right hand and press bag so that mixture reaches end of tube.

(13) Place tube over celery. Pressing bag with one hand and guiding with the other, fill celery, raising and lowering bag to make uniform swirls.

(14) When all celery stalks have been filled, sprinkle cheese mixture lightly with paprika.

(15) Carefully lift each stalk of celery from tray to cutting board.

(16) Cut celery crosswise into 1 1/4-in. pieces.

(17) Arrange pieces of celery on napkin-lined platter and place in refrigerator until served.

Note: Stuffed celery is sometimes combined with assorted canapés and other hors d'oeuvres on a platter.

Stuffed Deviled Eggs   50 Halves

Stuffed deviled eggs are served as either an appetizer or as a garnish with salads or cold cuts. To prepare them, cold hard-boiled eggs are cut in half lengthwise; the yolks are removed, made into a puree with spices (deviled) and are then returned to the hollow part of the whites with a pastry bag and tube. As in making stuffed celery, the *garde manger* must be unfailingly meticulous in each step of the job to avoid food contamination. Mayonnaise is one of the ingredients in making deviled eggs. Since both eggs and mayonnaise are easily subject to contamination, all equipment used on the job must be as clean as possible. The job should be carried out as speedily as possible, and, after the eggs are stuffed, they should be kept in the refrigerator until the moment they are called for. Twenty-five eggs are needed to make 50 halves, but it is best to boil several additional eggs; sometimes eggshells break during cooking; a few of the eggs may not be intact for stuffing. Hard eggs will sometimes show a dark unsightly rim around the yolk, due to overcooking or cooking at too high a temperature. The best method for cooking hard eggs without causing them to become toughened is to simmer them at a temperature of 180° to 190° F. After cooking, the eggs should be cooled as quickly as possible under cold running water.

Before starting work: Remove eggs from refrigerator about 1 hour before commencing work. In lifting raw eggs from one container to another, handle carefully to prevent cracking shells. Examine eggs; do not use any eggs with cracked shells; give such eggs to breakfast cook or fry cook. Check pastry bag for cleanliness; turn it inside out, and examine carefully. Hold pastry bag tube up to light to examine it. Wash hands well before and during job, since eggs require considerable handling. Review page 296 on handling pastry bag and tube.

(1) Assemble the following ingredients:

    28 eggs (any eggs not stuffed may be used for another purpose)

    1/2 cup butter, softened but not melting

    1/2 cup mayonnaise

    2 teaspoons Dijon mustard

    1 teaspoon dry mustard

    1 teaspoon Worcestershire sauce

    1/4 cup chives, chopped extremely fine

    2 tablespoons parsley, chopped extremely fine

    Salt, pepper, cayenne pepper

    1 bottle small capers in vinegar

(2) Choose a pot large enough to hold eggs comfortably. To avoid breakage, carefully lower eggs into pot.

(3) Fill pot with cold water.

(4) Slowly bring water to a boil. As soon as water boils, reduce heat so that water merely simmers.

(5) Cook eggs at simmering temperature 10 min.

(6) Place pot under cold running water. Let water run into pot 8 to 10 min.

(7) Pour off water from eggs.

(8) With lid on pot, shake pot so that shells partly crack.

(9) Again fill pot with cold water. Lift eggs one by one from pot and remove shells, occasionally holding eggs under water to facilitate removing shells.

(10) Examine each egg to make sure no pieces of shell adhere.

(11) With narrow sharp knife cut eggs in half lengthwise.

(12) Arrange eggs, hollow side up, on tray lined with clean towel. (Towel keeps eggs from slipping when filled.)

(13) Remove yolks with small spoon. Turn yolks into small china cap with fine-size holes or into wire sieve.

(14) Force yolks through china cap or sieve into bowl.

(15) To yolks in bowl add butter, mayonnaise, both kinds of mustard, Worcestershire sauce, chives and parsley. Blend well with mixing spoon. Season with salt and pepper. Add a dash of cayenne pepper. Blend well again.

(16) Turn egg yolk mixture into pastry bag with star tube.

(17) Force egg yolk mixture into cavity of white, forming three mounds with pastry bag. (Check with chef or instructor on amount of filling for each egg.)

(18) Place a caper at opposite ends of egg yolk mixture. A toothpick or two may be used for lifting and placing capers on eggs.

(19) Chill eggs in refrigerator until needed.

Curried Deviled Eggs.—Add 1 tablespoon curry powder to yolks when blending with other seasonings.

Anchovy Stuffed Eggs.—Add 2 tablespoons anchovy paste to yolks when blending with other seasonings.

Sliced Stuffed Olives.—Slice olives and dip in salad oil. These may be used in place of capers to decorate eggs.

Deviled Eggs with Ham.—Use 1/4 cup butter and 1/4 cup mayonnaise instead of 1/2 cup each. Add 1/2 cup pureed cooked Smithfield ham to egg yolk mixture.

Deviled Eggs with Liver.-Use 1/4 cup butter and 1/4 cup mayonnaise instead of 1/2 cup each. Add 1/2 cup pureed cooked chicken livers or prepared liver spread to egg yolk mixture.

Cole Slaw   50 Portions, 1/3 Cup Each

While potato salad is normally served with cold meats, cole slaw appears on the menu as an accompaniment to both cold and hot foods, particularly fried seafood dishes. At one time cole slaw, in many restaurants, was a simple combination of shredded cabbage and French dressing. Nowadays, it is usually prepared with mayonnaise and is marinated in its dressing overnight or longer. If you mix shredded cabbage and mayonnaise and taste it immediately, the flavors of the cabbage and the dressing are two distinct entities. But if the cabbage and mayonnaise are marinated several hours, the cabbage becomes limp and the juice of the cabbage mixes with the mayonnaise to form the blended flavor characteristic of cole slaw. Cabbage may be either the young green heads of spring cabbage or the more solid fall or winter strains of white cabbage. Because cabbage varies in flavor throughout the year, seasonings are variable and may be changed for each batch of cole slaw when it is prepared. For cole slaw, cabbage is cut into the thinnest possible shreds. This may be done by hand using a French knife (a rare procedure except when small quantities are needed), by hand on a cabbage cutting board with sliding box and diagonal knives or by machine using the vegetable slicing attachment of a food chopper. When cabbage is cut with a French knife, results are not as uniform as when using either of the other two methods. If cabbage is shredded by hand, the core should be left in so that the chunks of cabbage stay intact during cutting. If cabbage is shredded by machine, the core of the cabbage should be removed.

Before starting work: If a hand cabbage cutter is used, be sure that the blades are clean and free of rust and that the sliding box and sliding surface are clean and free of any noticeable odor. Adjust the blades, if necessary, to produce fine shreds. If a vegetable cutting machine is used, be sure you have been instructed in its operation and that the slice adjuster is set to the proper thickness for cole slaw. Do not fail to disassemble and flush the cutting mechanism after each use so that it will be clean for the next job.

(1) Assemble the following ingredients:

  10 lb cabbage, untrimmed weight
  1/2 lb carrots, peeled
  1/2 lb sweet green peppers (optional)
  1/2 lb sweet red peppers (optional)
  1 pt mayonnaise
  1/2 cup French dressing
  8 to 12 oz vinegar
  3 to 4 oz sugar

1/2 cup cream

Salt, pepper

(2) Cut away and discard all outside dark, spotted or wilted leaves from cabbage.

(3) Cut cabbage in half from top to bottom, slicing through core.

(4) Cut each half of cabbage through core into halves, thirds or quarters, depending upon size of cabbage, so that wedges can be easily handled.

(5) If cabbage is to be shredded in vegetable slicing machine, remove all core. (The core is usually discarded. If there is some other menu item in which cabbage is one of the ingredients, such as stuffed cabbage rolls, the cores may be reserved and turned over to the cook in charge of the job.) If cabbage is to be shredded by hand, leave cores on each wedge for holding wedges intact.

(6) Shred cabbage by machine or on cabbage slicer. Set aside in large mixing bowl.

(7) Cut sweet peppers in half through stem end. Remove and discard stems, seeds and inner membrane.

(8) Shred peppers and carrots. Add to cabbage in mixing bowl.

Note: Sweet peppers and carrots may be shredded by machine or on large holes of square metal grater.

(9) In a separate smaller bowl combine mayonnaise, French dressing, 8 oz vinegar, 3 oz sugar, cream, 1 teaspoon salt and 1/2 teaspoon pepper. Mix well with wire whip until all ingredients are thoroughly blended.

(10) Pour mayonnaise mixture over cabbage. Thoroughly toss all ingredients with large mixing spoon or two spoons.

(11) Turn mixture into stainless steel or enamel storage container and refrigerate at least 3 to 4 hours. Press down cabbage to facilitate marinating.

(12) Taste cole slaw. Correct seasoning, if desired, by adding small quantities as needed of vinegar, sugar, salt and pepper.

Red Cabbage.—Red and white cabbage may be combined. Use 7 lb white cabbage and 3 lb red cabbage.

Onion Flavor.—Chop 4 oz onion extremely fine, place onion in a triple thickness of cheesecloth, pull up ends of cheese cloth and squeeze over cole slaw. Blend well.

Celery Seed.—One tablespoon of celery seed may be added to cole slaw before marinating.

Potato Salad   **50 Portions, 4 Oz Each**

There are many restaurant owners who would no sooner eliminate potato salad from their menu than they would eliminate bread and butter. Now and then a *garde manger* will be called upon to make a salad rarity, such as crayfish and truffle salad or an elaborate aspic salad, but he prepares potato salad as a regular item throughout the year. Although the dish may be a routine one, it must be prepared each time with critical attention and judgment. Patrons will complain if the dressing is too thick or too thin, if the potatoes are broken, or if the salad is too sharp or too bland. In busy restaurants it is made two or three times a week. If it is held too long in the refrigerator, it will acquire a leftover flavor and aromas from other foods. Since it contains mayonnaise, it must be checked daily for flavor or possible signs of spoilage. This is particularly important for the *garde manger* working in those restaurants where potato salad may be kept on a buffet table without refrigeration.

One of the common faults of potato salad is the sogginess caused by overcooking the potatoes. Normally potatoes are boiled by the vegetable cook rather than the *garde manger.* The *garde manger* should remind the vegetable cook to remove the potatoes from the fire or from the steamer the instant they become tender. Raw potatoes for salad may be peeled, sliced and boiled, in which case the slightest overcooking will cause them to disintegrate. More often they are boiled in the jacket, after which they are peeled and sliced or diced. For consistent results the vegetable cook should select potatoes which are as uniform in size as possible. After boiling, they should be cooled several hours before they are peeled and sliced. If kept too long after cooking (overnight for example) and not mixed with salad dressing, their fresh flavor will dissipate.

The best potatoes for salad are the moist types which stay intact after boiling rather than the mealy types which are best for baking or French fried potatoes. If both types are available in your kitchen, choose the former for potato salad. Potatoes are starchy and when mixed with mayonnaise tend to thicken the dressing. It is important, therefore, before each meal period to check the potato salad and thin it, if necessary, with milk, water, vinegar or any combination of these which might be desirable.

Before starting work: Check to see if there is any leftover potato salad from a previous job. If it is no more than one day old, it may be combined with the new batch. If it is several days old and is of good quality, serve it first, and do not combine it with the new batch. Both raw and cooked potatoes which have been peeled tend to discolor when exposed to the air. To avoid oxidation, have all seasonings measured beforehand so that, as soon as the potatoes are peeled, the mixing can be completed.

(1) Assemble the following ingredients:

15 lb potatoes in the jacket, boiled until just tender
1 lb celery, small dice
6 hard-boiled eggs, chopped fine
4 oz scallions, white part only, chopped extremely fine
1/4 cup chives, chopped extremely fine
1/4 cup parsley, chopped extremely fine
1/2 cup vinegar (cider or white wine vinegar)
1 cup salad oil
3 cups mayonnaise (variable)
Salt, pepper

(2) Allow potatoes to cool 1 hour before slicing. Using a table knife, scrape skins off potatoes. Remove eyes or any discolored spots.

(3) Cut potatoes into 1/4-in. slices, about 3/4 in. in diameter or as close to that size as possible.

(4) In a mixing bowl combine scallions, chives, parsley, vinegar and oil. Mix well with wire whip.

(5) Add mayonnaise, 1 tablespoon salt and 1 teaspoon pepper.

(6) Spread about 1/3 of the potatoes, 1/3 of the celery and 1/3 of the eggs in a wide mixing bowl or roasting pan.

(7) Sprinkle 1/3 of the mayonnaise mixture over the potatoes.

(8) Continue making alternate layers of potatoes, celery, eggs and mayonnaise mixture until all ingredients are added.

(9) Toss salad lightly to blend all ingredients. Avoid, if possible, breaking potatoes.

(10) Correct seasoning, if necessary, with salt and pepper. Add more vinegar if desired.

(11) Chill well in refrigerator. Keep salad covered at all times in refrigerator.

Onion.—Extremely fine chopped or grated onion may be substituted for scallions.

Chopped Hard Eggs.—Eggs may be omitted from mixture, or may be sprinkled over salad just before serving.

Pimientos or Sweet Roasted Red Peppers.—Add 1 cup peppers or pimientos, cut into small dice, for flavor and color.

Chopped Sweet Green Peppers.—Add 1 cup chopped peppers to salad.

Mustard Flavor.—Add 1/4 cup prepared American or Dijon mustard to mayonnaise mixture.

Hot Potato Salad.—Omit mayonnaise. Increase vinegar to 1 cup. Add 1 cup French dressing and 2 cups hot stock to salad. Place in steam table about 1 hour before serving.

Lobster Salad	6 Portions, 4 Oz Lobster Meat Each

Lobster salad, often listed as fresh lobster salad on the menu, may be made from canned fresh lobster meat (that is, cooked by a processor and packed in cans that are not hermetically sealed but are refrigerated), from freshly boiled frozen lobster tails (*langouste*) or from boiled live lobsters taken from the North Atlantic. The latter are considered the best quality and are indicated in the recipe below. When the *garde manger* receives lobsters that are alive, they are normally packed in ice and seaweed. They should be examined upon arrival to make sure each lobster is alive, since a lobster which dies in transit and before cooking deteriorates very rapidly. When live lobsters are received, their claws are normally plugged so that they cannot snap. For safety's sake, however, when handling lobsters, always lift them from the back with head and claws forward. To make sure the lobster is alive, lift it; it should show rapid movement of the large and small claws. The tail, when straightened, should spring back to its former position. The lobster is cooked by plunging it into a pot of rapidly boiling water or by cooking it in a steamer. After the lobsters are boiled, they should be removed from the water as soon as possible, spread out in shallow pans, and then placed in the refrigerator to chill. If they are not used the same day they are cooked, they should be kept in the fish ice chest covered with cracked ice.

Since the *garde manger* prepares lobster for other dishes such as lobster Newburgh, he may boil more lobsters than indicated in the recipe below. In most restaurants fresh lobster salad is an expensive a la carte item and is not made in advance, but prepared to individual order. When this is the case, the lobster meat is removed from the cooked chilled lobster shell just before the salad is made. At one time it was the practice to put the diced lobster meat, celery and seasonings in a salad bowl, and simply spoon the mayonnaise (usually an excessive quantity) on top. The lobster was said to be "masked." Nowadays the lobster is coated with mayonnaise but not inundated by it, and in some restaurants the mayonnaise may be served separately at the table to be mixed either by the customer or the waiter.

Before starting work: Plan your work so that the lobsters can be boiled and chilled at least 3 hours before the salad is made. In choosing the pot for boiling the lobster, allow 1 1/2 to 2 qt water for each lobster. Make sure there is space on the range for the pot you will be using. If the lobsters are to be steamed, do not remove the live lobsters from the ice and seaweed until the steamer is available. Test to make sure each lobster is alive; if in doubt, consult your supervisor or instructor.

(1) Assemble the following ingredients:

> 6 1-lb chicken lobsters
> > *Note:* Larger lobsters will yield more meat per pound but the meat will be less tender.
>
> Salt, celery salt, pepper
> 2 tablespoons French dressing
> 2 tablespoons lemon juice
> 2 cups celery, small dice
> 2 cups mayonnaise
> 1 tablespoon horseradish
> 3 shelled hard-boiled eggs
> 2 medium size tomatoes
> 12 colossal ripe olives
> 2 tablespoons capers in vinegar, drained
> Boston lettuce leaves

(2) Bring 9 qt water to a rapid boil. Add 1/2 cup salt.

(3) Plunge lobsters, one by one, head first into water.

(4) Cover pot and let water again come to a boil.

(5) Reduce flame. Simmer 15 min.

(6) Remove pot from fire. Place a large colander in sink. Pour contents of pot into colander to drain. Hold head back to avoid burns. Pour carefully; try to keep lobsters intact. If poured carelessly, claws may become detached from body. In order to keep lobsters intact, they are sometimes lifted from pot with a skimmer.

(7) Place lobsters in shallow pans. Let them set at room temperature about 10 min.

(8) Chill in refrigerator at least 3 hours. If lobsters are not to be used the same day, store them in the fish ice chest, covered with cracked ice.

(9) Remove lobster meat from shells. Use a heavy French knife to cut lobster and to crack shells. Use a small pointed paring knife to remove meat from claws. In removing meat, follow this procedure:

(a) Place lobster on its back.

(b) Cut lobster in half lengthwise.

(c) Remove stomach, a gritty section in a sac in back of the head.

(d) With a small knife lift out and discard dark intestinal vein. Do not discard tomalley (green liver) or coral roe, if any. These are added to salad.

(e) Lift lobster meat from body in one piece, and set aside.

(f) With heavy French knife, using a sharp chopping motion, separate claws from body.

(g) Crack large and small sections of claws with French knife, using heel of blade.

(h) Dig lobster meat from claws, using small pointed knife. A lobster fork may also be used for this part of job. Avoid small pieces of shell.

(i) Cut lobster meat from back and claws into dice approx 1/2 in. thick or as close to that size as possible.

(j) Turn lobster meat into mixing bowl. Add tomalley to bowl. If there is any roe, break it into small pieces by hand and add to bowl.

(10) Sprinkle with salt, celery salt and pepper.

(11) Add French dressing and lemon juice. Toss lightly.

(12) Add celery, mayonnaise and horseradish. Mix well with spoon. Correct seasoning if necessary.

(13) Line 6 salad bowls with lettuce leaves.

(14) Spoon lobster salad into bowls, dividing mixture equally.

(15) Cut hard eggs lengthwise in quarters.

(16) Remove stem end of tomatoes. Cut each tomato into 6 wedges.

(17) Alternately place around edge of each salad two tomato segments and two pieces of hard egg.

(18) Place two olives on opposite sides of each salad.

(19) Sprinkle center of each salad with about a half dozen capers.

(20) Additional mayonnaise may be passed at table in a sauce boat. Allow about 1/4 cup mayonnaise per portion.

Cocktail Sauce.—Mayonnaise and cocktail sauce are sometimes combined in seafood salads. Allow 1/4 cup cocktail sauce per cup of mayonnaise.

Shrimp Salad.—Substitute 1 1/2 lb (cooked weight) boiled, peeled shrimp for lobster.

Crabmeat Salad.—Substitute 1 1/2 lb crab lump for lobster meat. Examine crab lump carefully to remove any pieces of shell.

Crabmeat and Avocado Salad.—Substitute 1 lb jumbo crab lump for lobster. Add diced meat of 3 medium size ripe avocados when mixing ingredients.

Tomato Stuffed With Chicken Salad   50 Portions

Uniformity in cutting, as the eye perceives it, is one of the most important clues to the *garde manger*'s experience and ability. Like cooks behind the range working with hot foods, the *garde manger* must be able to skillfully and rapidly use the French knife not only on foods that are displayed, such as cold buffet items, but also in the preparation of dishes where cutting might seem less important. For example, if the chicken used to stuff a tomato is cut into an assortment of irregular pieces, the quality of the salad will be disappointing.

If the chicken as well as the celery mixed with it is cut into pieces 1/4 in. thick, and if every morsel is that size or as close to it as possible, the texture of the salad will be recognizably first-rate. Tomatoes for stuffing must be very large, approximately 4 in. in diameter. The tomatoes are first peeled, a cap is cut from the top of the tomato, and a cylindrical piece of tomato meat is removed. The chicken salad is placed in this cavity, and the cap is returned to the top. The best chicken for salad is cold boiled fowl which will hold a distinct shape when cut. The proportions of chicken to celery will vary from one restaurant to another, but since chicken is the dominant flavor, the ratio of chicken to celery should be two or three to one. Since the *garde manger* is responsible for the use of leftover cooked foods, he may include pieces of roast or braised chicken provided they are moist and do not include hard ends or skin. Decisions of this type are always made in consultation with the chef or *sous chef.*

Before starting work: Examine tomatoes to be sure they are all firm and ripe. Bruised or overripe tomatoes should not be used. Boiling water will be needed for removing the tomato skins. Be sure to choose a large wide saucepot or *sautoir,* deep enough to hold at least a half dozen tomatoes at one time. Individual salads of this type, prepared before the meal period, are always placed in the refrigerator to chill until serving time. Be sure there is enough refrigerator shelf space to store the number of portions you are preparing. Plan your work so that the finished salads will be chilled at least one hour before serving.

    (1) Assemble the following ingredients:

        50 large fresh tomatoes about 4 in. in diameter

        10 lb boiled fowl, edible meat, without skin or bone

        3 lb celery

1 qt mayonnaise
1/3 cup lemon juice or vinegar
Salt, pepper
1 tablespoon Worcestershire sauce
1/4 teaspoon Tabasco sauce
25 hard-boiled eggs
100 extra large stuffed olives or ripe olives
8 heads Boston lettuce or 4 heads iceberg lettuce

(2) Bring 2 to 3 gal water to a rapid boil.
(3) Lower a wire frying basket filled with a single layer of tomatoes into water for about 15 to 20 sec. Do not allow tomatoes to remain in water longer than this, or they will become partially cooked and too soft to handle.
(4) Lift basket from water, and carefully place tomatoes on work surface.
(5) Continue to blanch balance of tomatoes in this manner.
(6) Using a sharp paring knife, peel off tomato skins, starting with top of tomatoes and peeling toward stem end.
(7) With small, sharp pointed knife cut out green stem of tomatoes; do not cut deeply as bottom of tomato must remain intact.
(8) Cut a horizontal slice about 1/4 in. thick from top of each tomato, opposite stem end. Carefully set tomato caps aside.
(9) Remove a cylindrical piece from inside each tomato for stuffing. Use a very sharp pointed knife with narrow blade, and cut in the following manner:
  (a) Holding the knife pointed toward work surface, cut a deep circle around tomato, leaving a "wall" of tomato about 1/4 in. thick. Cut toward bottom of tomato, but do not cut so deeply that bottom is pierced.
  (b) Loosen inner section or cylinder by inserting the knife horizontally through tomato near bottom. Move the knife back and forth until the cylinder of tomato is free.
  (c) Remove the inside of the tomato in one piece. Give the pieces thus removed to the sauce cook for possible use in soups or stock. In some restaurants the cylinder is placed alongside the stuffed tomato as a garnish.
(10) Carefully turn each tomato upside down to remove any excess moisture. Remove any seeds.
(11) Sprinkle inside of each tomato with salt. Set aside.
(12) Cut chicken into 1/4-in. dice.
(13) Separate celery into stalks. Wash well and dry with clean cloth or paper towels.

(14) Cut off celery leaves. Pass to sauce cook or soup cook.

(15) Using vegetable peeler with floating blade, peel outside of celery stalks to remove stringy matter.

(16) Cut celery into 1/4-in. dice.

(17) In large mixing bowl combine mayonnaise, lemon juice, Worcestershire sauce and Tabasco sauce. Mix very well with wire whip. Add chicken and celery, mixing well. Season with salt and pepper to taste.

(18) Very carefully pile chicken salad into each tomato. Use a large tablespoon or fruit spoon rather than a kitchen spoon. The salad should be mounded on top and should protrude from top of tomato. Smooth the mound with a spoon or wide-blade butter spreader.

(19) Separate lettuce into leaves for lining individual salad bowls. Wash lettuce and pat dry with clean cloth or paper towels.

(20) Place individual salad bowls on trays. Line bowls with lettuce leaves.

(21) Place a tomato in each bowl.

(22) Place a tomato cap on top of each salad.

(23) Cut hard eggs into quarters.

(24) Alongside each tomato alternately place two hard egg quarters and two olives.

(25) Chill salads in refrigerator until serving time.

Note: Another technique for stuffing tomatoes, particularly if tomatoes are medium size is as follows:

(a) Peel tomatoes as described above but do not remove inside.

(b) Cut tomatoes into four or six segments, slicing from top toward bottom but not cutting into bottom.

(c) Gently open segments fanwise leaving segments attached to bottom.

(d) Fill tomatoes in center with mound of salad, garnish as above, and chill.

Seafood Stuffings For Cold Tomatoes.—Diced cooked shrimp or lobster, crabmeat, boiled salmon or canned tunafish may be used in place of chicken.

Beef Salad (Hors d'Oeuvres) 1 Gal

People ordering salads in a restaurant usually consider two types on the menu. One is the main course salad such as lobster, shrimp or chicken—the sort of substantial salad which is very popular in hot weather. The second type is represented by tossed green salads and others which may precede, accompany or follow the main course. There is still a third very important class—the hors d'oeuvres salad— served as an appetizer before the soup and usually as one of the components of an hors d'oeuvres cart or tray. The French phrase *"hors d'oeuvres assortis"* on a menu indicates a choice of as many hors d'oeuvres as may be presented on the cart or tray. It may include many foods purchased ready-to-serve, such as olives, canned sardines in oil, sliced salamis of various kinds, artichoke hearts in oil, as well as sliced hard egg, sliced tomato, celery hearts, radishes, etc., all of which the *garde manger* arranges in appropriate dishes for serving. It will also include hors d'oeuvres salads which are made on the premises by the *garde manger*, and which often include leftover meats, poultry or seafood. For example, the day after boiled beef is served on a menu, the cold leftover beef might be converted into an hors d'oeuvres salad, such as the recipe below. This dish can be taken as a prototype from which many variations are possible by substituting the kind of meat. Note that the quantity of salad which the recipe yields is not expressed in portions but in measure, since it is practically impossible to indicate how much salad a customer may take in a selection of hors d'oeuvres. Beef salad, like others of this type, should be marinated at least one day before it is served.

Before starting work: Make sure there is no sign of off-odor or off-flavor in the beef. The best beef for this salad is boiled beef. If there is insufficient boiled beef, braised beef well-trimmed of any hard ends or hard surface may be included. Roast beef is not well adapted to this recipe. Check the refrigerator carefully for any leftovers that may be combined if necessary. Plan to use a very sharp French knife for slicing the meat to keep pieces of meat intact. Even though the meat may be tender, use the knife steel frequently. Be sure the beef is trimmed of all fat, gristle or hard ends before weighing it.

(1) Assemble the following ingredients:
    2 lb (trimmed weight) boiled beef
    6 medium size (approx 2 lb) firm ripe tomatoes
    2 lb medium size potatoes, boiled in jacket
    1 cup sour pickles
    1/2 cup scallions, white part only, chopped fine
    1 tablespoon chives, chopped extremely fine
    2 tablespoons parsley, chopped extremely fine
    1 tablespoon tarragon, chopped extremely fine
    1 cup French dressing (p 281)
    1 teaspoon Worcestershire sauce
    Salt, pepper

(2) Bring 1 gal water in a *sautoir* to a rapid boil. Lower tomatoes into water for 20 sec. Remove tomatoes and set aside.

(3) When tomatoes have cooled slightly, remove skins and stem ends with paring knife.

(4) Cut each tomato from top to bottom into 6 segments.

(5) Press out and discard tomato seeds.

(6) Cut tomatoes into julienne strips, 1 in. long and 1/8 in. thick.

(7) Peel potatoes and cut into slices 1/8 in. thick. Cut slices into julienne strips 1 in. long.

(8) Cut beef into slices 1/8 in. thick. Cut beef slices into julienne strips 1 in. long.

(9) Cut sour pickles into slices 1/8 in. thick. Cut into julienne strips 1 in. long.

(10) In mixing bowl combine scallions, chives, parsley, tarragon, French dressing and Worcestershire sauce. Mix well.

(11) Add beef, tomatoes, potatoes and pickles.

(12) Toss all ingredients lightly. Avoid, as much as possible, breaking potatoes, beef, etc., while tossing.

(13) Add salt and pepper to taste. Toss lightly.

(14) Place salad in container with tight lid, and marinate 1 day before serving.

Tongue Salad.—Substitute boiled corned or smoked tongue for boiled beef.

Corned Beef Salad.—Substitute boiled corned beef for boiled fresh beef.

Sweetbread Salad.—Substitute braised sweetbread for boiled beef.

10

Vegetable Cook (Légumier)

In many restaurants of moderate size the duties of the fry cook and the vegetable cook are handled by one person, once called the *entremetier*. But in larger kitchens the work is divided, and the vegetable cook may assist the fry cook or may devote his entire time to vegetable cookery. If one were to give a capsule description of a vegetable cook, one might say that for the most part he washes, trims, cuts and boils or steams vegetables. After the vegetables are boiled or steamed, he usually turns them over to another cook for seasoning or combining with a sauce and for serving during the meal period. For instance, if broccoli hollandaise is on the menu, the vegetable cook washes, trims and boils the broccoli. At that point his work ceases. The sauce cook prepares the hollandaise sauce, keeps the broccoli hot for service during the meal period, and when orders are received from the waiters, places portions of broccoli on serving plates and spoons hollandaise sauce over it.

Sometimes the vegetable cook merely cleans, trims and cuts raw vegetables, and then passes them to another person for cooking. When French fried potatoes are on the menu, the vegetable cook pares the potatoes in a machine, trims them if necessary, puts them through a French fry cutter, and then turns them over to the fry cook. If potatoes *rissolées* or oven browned potatoes are featured, the vegetable cook selects potatoes of the proper size, pares, washes, trims and may blanch them briefly. He passes them to the roast cook who browns them in the oven.

This division of labor may vary widely from place to place. But it is important to point out that the vegetable cook's station is not behind the range, but in a separate section usually near the pot washing area where large sinks, a potato peeling machine and other equipment are available. Sometimes the vegetable cook merely washes and trims raw whole vegetables which are then given to another cook. If braised spareribs and cabbage are being cooked, the vegetable cook washes, sometimes soaks, and trims the cabbage. Another cook cuts the cabbage into slices and wedges and combines it for braising with the spareribs. All cooks behind the range use raw onions for seasoning or other purposes in their special jobs. It is traditional for the vegetable cook to peel all onions, and then pass them to other cooks who chop, dice or slice them for specific jobs. The vegetable cook must know the approximate yield in portions of raw vegetables. Thus a bushel of string beans or so many pounds of string beans will normally be sufficient for a certain number of 3-oz portions when cooked. If there is a private party for 6 people or 60 people, and string beans are included in the menu, the vegetable cook should be able to calculate the amount of raw string beans he needs for trimming and boiling.

In his daily work he follows routines rather than recipes. Although he may perform the same jobs day in and day out, his work nevertheless demands the most careful judgment, or vegetables may be ruined. He may be working in a restaurant where frozen peas are cooked each day. A specific brand of frozen peas may normally become tender in 5 min cooking time. But frozen peas, like fresh peas, vary in quality even when packed under the same label. One batch may require only 4 1/2 min; another batch may need 5 1/2 min. The peas may vary in color, size, flavor and tenderness, despite the claims of the processors. Variations in the quality of all vegetables whether fresh or frozen mean variations in the cooking time. The vegetable cook must therefore be constantly alert to the quality features of vegetables and must be able to judge them by sight, touch, taste, etc. If there are noticeable blemishes or other defects in vegetables he has received, he reports such facts to the *sous chef* or his supervisor. He is responsible for the storage of both raw and cooked vegetables in the refrigerator and freezer.

Years ago vegetable cooks prepared their vegetables in large batches at a time before the meal period. Before lunch or dinner started, cooks behind the range would call for the vegetables needed on the menu. The vegetable cook would give them the boiled vegetables for the entire meal period. They would sauté the vegetables to make them hot, and store them in the steam table for a two- or three-hour period. The old practice resulted in vegetables that were soon limp and tasteless, often with poor color and with both their vitamin and mineral content badly dissipated.

The modern practice is to cook, on a continuing basis throughout the meal, small batches of vegetables at a time. This means that during the meal period, the vegetable cook must organize his work to quickly supply freshly boiled or steamed vegetables as needed. Not only are the flavor, texture, color and nutrients conserved by this procedure, but waste in overproduction is sharply reduced.

There are four types of vegetables which the vegetable cook handles: fresh, frozen, canned and dried. For the most part his skills and judgment are involved in the cooking of fresh or frozen vegetables. Canned vegetables are normally heated, and then turned over to a cook who seasons and serves them. Dried vegetables are sometimes washed, sorted if necessary, and soaked or blanched before cooking.

JOB SUMMARY

The vegetable cook (1) meets with *sous chef* or sauce cook and discusses daily as well as advance production schedules; (2) receives and stores fresh vegetables in refrigerator; (3) receives and stores root vegetables such as potatoes, onions, turnips, etc., on racks or bins; (4) receives and stores frozen vegetables in freezer; (5) stores certain standard canned vegetables such as tomatoes on shelves for emergency use; (6) stores opened canned vegetables in original tins or storage containers; (7) stores leftover cooked vegetables in covered containers; (8) reports any unusual condition of fresh vegetables on arrival (vegetables are routinely inspected by receiving clerk; vegetable cook provides secondary check after vegetables are unpacked); (9) sorts, washes and trims fresh vegetables for boiling; (10) prepares, by boiling or steaming, fresh, frozen or canned vegetables for daily use on table d'hôte and a la carte menus; (11) supplies peeled, washed and trimmed seasoning vegetables such as onions, leeks, carrots, celery, etc., to other cooks; (12) boils or steams certain vegetables in advance of meal time; (13) boils or steams vegetables in limited batches during meal period; (14) soaks and may boil dried vegetables such as navy beans, lentils, etc., to be subsequently prepared by other cooks; (15) may cook rice, macaroni products and cereals; (16) blanches vegetables such as squash or sweet potatoes for subsequent preparation by other cooks; (17) may assist cooks in preparation of certain vegetables such as stuffed baked potatoes, stuffed peppers, etc.; (18) may season vegetables with butter, salt, pepper, etc., or may leave seasoning to other cooks depending upon established procedures in certain kitchens; (19) may chop, dice or grind cooked vegetables for vegetable salad, vegetable fritters, etc.; (20) may completely cook, season and have ready for service an item such as mashed potatoes; (21) may assist fry cook during meal period; (22) may filter used fat for frying and clean deep fat frying equipment.

MANUAL PROCEDURES

The vegetable cook (1) washes vegetables under cold running water; (2) washes vegetables by steeping, soaking, etc.; (3) steeps certain vegetables like broccoli in heavily salted water to remove insects; (4) using paring knife, hand peeler or French knife trims vegetables, removing skin, root ends, blemishes, wilted leaves or rot; (5) pares root vegetables, mostly potatoes, by using potato peeling machine; (6) removes by knife or hand portions of vegetables such as tough base of asparagus stalks, artichoke stem and leaves, etc.; (7) hulls fresh vegetables in pods such as peas or lima beans; (8) may remove strings from certain vegetables such as beans or snow peas; (9) removes leaves and core end of vegetables such as cauliflower; (10) cuts or otherwise divides vegetables such as broccoli or cauliflower into sections before cooking; (11) shucks corn by removing husk; (12) peels onions leaving them whole; (13) turns peelings and trimmings of certain vegetables such as celery and carrots over to soup cook or sauce cook; (14) cuts certain vegetables by hand into slices, dice, hash, julienne, etc., before or after cooking; (15) boils vegetables in pots above top flame, in steam-jacketed kettles or tilt kettles; (16) may steam vegetables in covered pots without pressure; (17) steams vegetables in small high-pressure steamers (for limited batches) as well as in large compartment steamers; (18) uses mixing machine for mashed potatoes; (19) uses cutting machines for slicing, dicing, etc.; (20) uses cutting machine with vertical blades for chopped spinach, vegetable purees, etc.; (21) may season vegetables before and after cooking; (22) regulates heat of fire; (23) tests vegetables for doneness from time to time by testing with fork, by finger pressure or tasting; (24) sets pressure on steamer, operates steamer by closing door, and operating steam valve; (25) removes vegetables from steamer when done; (26) may bake vegetables in shallow pans in oven, and regulate oven temperatures.

EQUIPMENT AND UTENSILS

In his work, he uses (1) ranges; (2) refrigerators; (3) steam-jacketed kettles, tilt kettles, deep pots, and steamers; (4) steam tables; (5) potato peeling machine; (6) food cutter and food chopper; (7) deep sinks; (8) steam table (*bain marie*) pots and pans; (9) storage pots and pans; (10) cutting board; (11) colanders; (12) china caps; (13) hand vegetable parer and paring knife; (14) French knife; (15) forks; (16) mixing spoons, assorted sizes; (17) ladles; (18) wire and slotted skimmers.

WORKING CONDITIONS AND HAZARDS

The vegetable cook (1) works at large sinks in wet or damp surroundings; (2) bends over sinks for long periods; (3) lifts heavy containers of raw and cooked foods; (4) works with large pots filled with boiling water; (5) works with steamers under pressure; (6) is subject to scalds from hot water or steamer and burns from hot stoves or steamers; (7) must sometimes walk on slippery surfaces in kitchen or in walk-in refrigerators.

PLACE IN JOB ORGANIZATION

The vegetable preparer, pot washer or kitchen helper may become the vegetable cook. He in turn may be promoted to fry cook or breakfast cook.

30 GUIDES TO VEGETABLE COOKERY

(1) Refrigerate all vegetables upon arrival except root vegetables; examine all vegetables upon arrival, checking middle and bottoms of crates, baskets, etc.

(2) Keep root vegetables such as potatoes, onions, parsnips, etc., in a cool, dark, well-ventilated place, free of dampness, on racks or bins off floor.

(3) Remove vegetables to be washed and trimmed in batches rather than all at one time if large quantities are to be prepared; return all washed and trimmed vegetables to refrigerator unless they are cooked at once.

(4) Vegetables should be well-washed to remove harmful sprays, dirt, insects, etc., and should be examined after washing and re-washed if necessary.

(5) Make sure that any sink used for steeping vegetables in cold water is clean before each use.

(6) Wear heavy nonskid shoes on duty because of frequent spillage of water on floor.

(7) Mop water spillage whenever it occurs, either in the vegetable cleaning area or elsewhere.

(8) When steeping and washing vegetables in sink partially filled with water, lift vegetables out of water, then drain water to wash away sand, dirt, foreign objects, etc. Wipe sink bottom, refill sink and repeat process as many times as necessary to clean vegetables thoroughly.

(9) Drain all washed vegetables in colander or perforated rack before trimming or cutting; a second washing may be necessary after trimming or cutting.

(10) Before using any special equipment for paring, cutting or cooking vegetables, be sure you completely understand how to start it, handle it, adjust it, assemble it, disassemble it and clean it.

(11) Vegetables like cabbage, broccoli and others which may contain insects, worms, etc., not removable by simple washing should be placed in a container with cold water in which 1/4 cup salt and 1/4 cup vinegar, per gal of water, have been dissolved. Let vegetables steep in solution for approximately 1/2 hour.

(12) Consult with *sous chef* or sauce cook on disposition of vegetable trimmings such as celery leaves, onion ends, carrot peelings, etc.

(13) If vegetables such as potatoes or carrots are to be sliced, diced or otherwise cut, consult cook who is involved in final steps of preparation as to size of dice, thickness of slices, etc.

(14) Since the modern practice in vegetable cookery is to prepare small batches at a time and replenish them as often as necessary during the meal period, it is important to check each day with the *sous chef* on the size of the batches which vary from day to day, depending on anticipated number of luncheons, dinners, etc.

(15) In preparing vegetables for small batch cookery before and during the meal period, be sure that all preparation (washing, draining, trimming, etc.) is completed before the meal period begins.

(16) In areas where water is known to be hard and to contain large amounts of alkalis, take particular care to avoid overcooking and undue softening of vegetables. Water with a large alkaline content helps retention of green color, but can cause texture of vegetables to become unnaturally soft.

(17) Undercooking vegetables can sometimes be corrected; overcooking always means irretrievable losses in flavor and nutrients. The general guideline is to cook all green vegetables until just done, and to cook most root vegetables until completely tender but not mushy.

(18) Green vegetables cooked to the "just done" stage will have better color than if they are overcooked. Check vegetables by piercing with a fork, pressing between fingers or tasting before cooking is complete; make repeated frequent tests if necessary to avoid overcooking.

(19) Vegetables with red color such as beets or red cabbage retain color best when vinegar, lemon juice or some other acid is added to the water in which they are cooked or to the cooked vegetable when it is buttered and seasoned or combined with a sauce.

(20) The use of baking soda to retain green color in vegetables, once an almost universal practice, has been virtually eliminated in

commercial kitchens. A very small amount of baking soda may help retain green color and hasten cooking. But the possibility of adding too much is always likely, with destructive results to flavor, texture and nutrients.

(21) When vegetables are boiled in salted water, allow 1 tablespoon salt per gallon of water.

(22) Cooking vegetables under steam pressure speeds the tenderizing process. Since vegetables in sealed steamers cannot be checked for tenderness quickly and easily, it is extremely important to know the performance characteristics of the pressure equipment you are using and to take every precaution to avoid overcooking. Always check the first batch cooked, and make adjustments for subsequent batches. For best results use vegetables of uniform size. Large and small carrots, for instance, placed in the same steamer compartment will not yield uniform results. Certain leafy vegetables tend to cling together and may cook unevenly in steamers.

(23) Juice from canned vegetables or the cooking liquid from fresh or frozen vegetables can sometimes be used for stocks or for keeping vegetables hot in steam table pots or pans. Check with the *sous chef*, instructor or supervisor before discarding cooked vegetable liquids.

(24) Drain all vegetables as quickly as possible after cooking, keeping in mind the possible use of their cooking liquid. The heat of the cooking liquid as well as the retained heat in the vegetables may result in soggy texture. Therefore, cooked vegetables, after removal from the fire, are sometimes washed in cold water to arrest the cooking, particularly if the vegetables are not to be used at once. Otherwise, they may be spread in shallow pans to expose them to cold air as much as possible. When there is continuous small batch cookery, vegetables are simply quickly drained, seasoned and placed in the steam table for service.

(25) Because of differences in seasons, harvests and localities, fresh vegetables vary greatly in maturity, tenderness, texture and flavor; therefore, all cooking times—no matter what equipment is used—can vary greatly. The shape, size and efficiency of different pieces of cooking equipment are also variable factors that affect the outcome of different jobs. Be prepared to use individual judgment for each job of vegetable cookery no matter how often the same menu item is repeated or what the suggested cooking time may be.

(26) Most of the basic rules of fresh vegetable cookery apply to frozen vegetables except the preliminary washing and cleaning which are unnecessary; frozen vegetables are washed prior to freezing. Since they are also blanched prior to freezing, their cooking times are generally less than their fresh counterparts.

(27) Frozen vegetables such as peas, diced carrots, kernel corn, etc., which are loose and free flowing, will cook more uniformly than frozen vegetables in block form.

(28) All frozen vegetables should be stored in freezers at 0°F or less. If the thermometer in the freezer registers above 10°F, report this fact to your supervisor or instructor. Be sure to store frozen vegetables in such a manner that old stock is used before the new.

(29) If leftover vegetables are to be served, they should be reheated alone, and not mixed with a fresh batch whose color, flavor and texture may be different from the leftover batch.

(30) Whenever batches of hot vegetables are placed in the steam table for service, be sure the steam table water is simmering (approximately 180°F) and not boiling. There should be about 1/4 to 1/2 in. liquid in the steam table (*bain marie*) pot or pan containing the vegetables in order to prevent undue drying of the vegetables. The liquid may be vegetable stock, water or milk. All vegetables which are fragile such as asparagus, broccoli, etc., should be carefully placed in steam table pans rather than pots; they should be in a shallow layer; they should be carefully handled when transferring them from the steam table pan to the serving plate or platter.

FRESH VEGETABLE COOKERY

The important fresh vegetables the *légumier* handles in his daily routines are described below. Quality standards are indicated, since they determine the outcome of his cooking. If, for instance, fresh peas are on the menu, the fullness and color of the pods and the age and tenderness of the peas will all affect the cooking time. If the pods are partially empty, the yield or number of portions will be less than normal. Procedures for washing, trimming and boiling or steaming, which are the bulk of the work, are outlined. Finally, the most popular ways of serving each vegetable are listed.

The term *low-pressure steam* below indicates the traditional compartment type steamer with a pressure of 5 psi, equivalent to 225° F. *High-pressure steam* equipment performs at 15 psi, equivalent to 250°F. The student should again be reminded that all frozen vegetables require less cooking time than fresh vegetables because of previous blanching. If available, processors' directions for cooking frozen vegetables should be followed. After the first batch is cooked, however, the cook should check the quality of the vegetables and make adjustments in the cooking times if necessary.

The cooking times indicated for steam equipment apply to a load of 3 12×20×2 1/2-in. pans.

Artichoke, French or Globe   50 Portions

Quality Standards	Heavy for size; fresh-looking, dark green, tightly clinging leaves (loose spreading or discolored leaves indicate poor quality); compact globe
Amount	50 artichokes, approx 7–8 oz each
Preparation	Wash under cold running water. With heavy French knife, cut off 3/4 to 1 in. of top leaves at apex. Cut off stem 1/2 in. from base. Brush cut top leaves and stem with lemon juice to prevent discoloration; the sharp tips of remaining leaves are sometimes cut with scissors and brushed with lemon juice. Tie trimmed artichoke with string to keep it intact during cooking. Artichokes are done when leaves are loose enough to be easily detached, and artichoke bottom is soft when pierced with fork. Lift carefully with spoons or skimmer when transferring from pot to steam table pan. Turn upside down to drain. Remove string just before serving. Separate leaves partially and with small spoon carefully scrape and remove silky inner fibers called "choke."

Cooking Times	Boil	Low-pressure Steam	High-pressure Steam
	25–45 min	18–30 min	8–12 min

To Serve	Placed on white linen napkin; with hollandaise or drawn butter on side; stuffed, after removing choke, and served hot or cold; cold with French dressing; artichoke bottoms sometimes detached and served as vegetable garnish *Note*: Customer pulls off leaves at table and dips stalk end in sauce; the rest of the leaf is discarded. Artichoke bottom is eaten with fork.

Artichoke, Jerusalem   50 Portions

Note: The Jerusalem artichoke is an altogether different vegetable from the French or globe artichoke. It resembles the French artichoke only slightly in flavor and is a root vegetable.

Quality	Firm; heavy for size; knobby in shape but with
Standards	smooth skin; free from blemishes
Amount	14 lb as purchased
Preparation	Wash and scrub under cold running water. It may be peeled before cooking but is usually cooked in jacket. The Jerusalem artichoke may be sliced, diced or cut julienne before or after cooking.

Cooking Times

Boil	Low-pressure Steam	High-pressure Steam
20–35 min	18–24 min	10–15 min

To Serve   Sliced, diced or julienne; creamed; au gratin; sliced and sautéd in butter; pureed; fritters

Asparagus   50 Portions

Quality	Straight stalks; fresh green color (white asparagus
Standards	has virtually disappeared from American markets although it is still popular in certain parts of Europe); compact tips, not wilted, spreading or broken; stalks of uniform thickness; thicker rather than thinner stalks traditionally desirable for restaurant service; no more than an inch of white woody base; crisp and fragile rather than limp when stalks are bent
Amount	20 lb. as purchased (3 to 5 stalks per portion; yield variable depending upon amount of woody bottom removed)
Preparation	Wash under a moderate stream of cold running water, holding stems upright to wash sand away. With a floating blade vegetable peeler, peel length of stalks to eliminate scales and stringy outer fiber (in some sections of the US local asparagus freshly delivered from farms may not require peeling but may need extra washing or scrubbing with soft vegetable brush to remove sand). Break off by hand the tough woody bottoms of stalks; or, using a French knife, cut about 1/4 in. above white part. Both peelings of asparagus and tough bottoms may be turned over to soup cook for cream of asparagus soup. Tie into bunches of 8 to 10 stalks each, using butcher cord, and place upright in pot with water leaving tips exposed (thus permitting bottoms to cook while steaming tips). Tips may be cut off and cooked separately from stalks, since tips take

shorter cooking time, but avoid rapidly boiling water which may break tips. Tips thus cooked may be used as vegetable garnish. Stalks without tips, cut after cooking into 1-in. pieces, may be used for creamed asparagus, omelets, etc.

Cooking Times	Boil	Low-pressure Steam	High-pressure Steam
	8-15 min	6-9 min	1-2 min

To Serve — A la carte orders served on white napkin; with drawn butter, hollandaise sauce, *mousseline* sauce or *maltaise* sauce on side; with grated parmesan cheese; *beurre noir*; creamed; au gratin; *polonaise* (with chopped egg, chopped parsley and buttered bread crumbs)

Beans, Green Or Yellow (Snap Beans)   50 Portions

Quality Standards — May be round or flat; straight long pods; most varieties stringless; snap easily and quickly when bent; neither watery nor soft; bulging pods that ridge and feel thick usually tough; green beans, bright in color without yellowish or grayish steaks, free of dark rusty spots or other blemishes; yellow or wax beans, fresh looking, of uniform color without blemishes

Amount — 12 lb as purchased

Preparation — In the unlikely event that beans contain strings, it may be necessary to remove ends and strings. Otherwise only ends are removed by hand, pinching off as little as possible from tips at opposite ends of beans. Leave small beans whole or cut crosswise into 1-in. pieces, cut diagonally into 1-in. peices, or cut French style or julienne using hand string bean cutter or attachment to food cutting machine. Wash before cooking. Check doneness of beans frequently, when boiled, to avoid overcooking.

Cooking Times	Boil	Low-pressure Steam	High-pressure Steam
1-in. pieces	10-15 min	8-12 min	2-3 min
French	8-12 min	6-11 min	1-2 min
Whole	12-20 min	10-18 min	4-6 min

To Serve — Buttered with salt and pepper; creamed; au gratin; with toasted almonds julienne; mixed with lima beans; julienne with onions sauté (*lyonnaise*); cooked and seasoned with bacon fat and diced bacon

Beans, Lima   50 Portions

Quality Standards	Pods, fresh looking, dark green, firm, full but not bulging, free of blemishes or slime; beans, plump with tender skin, light green or greenish white, free of sprouts
Amount	25 lb as purchased
Preparation	Cut sliver from inner side of pods and twist pods to snap open. Remove beans by pushing with thumb. The cooking time may vary widely depending on size of beans. Shell as close to the meal period as practical, and keep refrigerated after shelling until cooked.

Cooking Times	Boil	Low-pressure Steam	High-pressure Steam
	15–25 min	10–16 min	1–4 min

To Serve	With butter, salt, pepper and dash of sugar; with whole kernel corn as succotash; creamed with light cream sauce or plain sweet cream; buttered with diced pimientos; au gratin; mixed with string beans

Beets   50 Portions

Quality Standards	Small to medium size more tender than larger beets; firm, globular in shape with smooth skin; larger beets with noticeable ridges usually woody; tops fresh-looking (although sometimes when beets are young, poor appearance of tops is not dependable guide to quality since beet tops deteriorate rapidly in shipping)
Amount	15 lb
Preparation	Cut off tops, leaving 1/2 to 1 in. of stems, but do not cut off root end. Wash, scrubbing with soft vegetable brush if necessary, but avoid breaking skin (if skin is broken before or during cooking, color will be lost). After cooking, if beets are young, steep in cold water 10 min and slip skins off. If beets are old, skins are removed with paring knife. Cut off stems and root ends. They may be

cut into slices, dice or julienne. Acids such as vinegar or lemon juice aid in brightening red color when beets are reheated.

Cooking Times

	Boil	Low-pressure Steam	High-pressure Steam
	30 min-1 hr	25–40 min	8–12 min

Note: Old beets without tops held in storage may require considerably longer cooking times.

To Serve Buttered and reheated with lemon juice or vinegar salt, pepper and sugar; as Harvard beets in a thickened sweet–sour sauce; with buttered beet greens

Broccoli   50 Portions

Quality Standards Compact heads with dark green or purplish green buds (yellow color or yellow flowers mingled with buds indicate old broccoli); stalks firm but tender when cut; leaves relatively sparse between buds

Amount 20 lb as purchased

Preparation Cut or tear off all outer leaves or leaves between buds, and cut off about an inch from bottom of stalks. Stalks may be peeled to hasten cooking. Cut stalks lengthwise about 1/2 in. from flowers to bottom of stalks to equalize cooking time of flowerets and stalks. Broccoli heads and stalks may be detached and cooked separately to avoid overcooking. Water should be simmering rather than boiling to avoid breaking heads apart. Test frequently for tenderness by piercing with fork. Cook until just done, and lift out of water with spoons or skimmer (do not dump from pot). Drain well. Broccoli is sometimes placed on towels to complete draining. Keep hot in steam table pans in single layer.

Cooking Times

	Boil	Low-pressure Steam	High-pressure Steam
	6–10 min	5–8 min	1 1/2–2 min

To Serve With drawn butter, salt and pepper; with hollandaise sauce, *mousseline* sauce, *maltaise* sauce or *Mornay* sauce au gratin; *polonaise* (buttered breadcrumbs, chopped egg and parsley)

| Brussel Sprouts | 50 Portions |

Quality Standards	Hard, compact; leaves fresh bright green rather than yellowish; uniform size; neither puffy nor elongated; no worm holes or smudge; should be examined carefully for signs of plant lice
Amount	12 lb as purchased
Preparation	If insects are suspected, soak in heavily salted water with vinegar for 1/2 hour. Wash well and remove outer spotted, yellowish or discolored leaves. Cut a thin slice from bottom of each steam and wash again. Cook only until barely done with slight crispness remaining. Cooking times may vary greatly because of variations in size.

Cooking Times

Boil	Low-pressure Steam	High-pressure Steam
8–10 min	6–8 min	1–2 1/2 min

| *To Serve* | Buttered with salt, pepper and dash of sugar; creamed; au gratin; with chestnuts |

| Cabbage, Green Or Red | 50 Portions |

Quality Standards	Heavy for size; early green cabbage not as firm as white fall or winter strains; leaves crisp looking and crisp to touch (a few outside leaves may lack crispness or be wilted, but balance of head should be solid); no discolored veins; no worm holes or yellow leaves
Amount	12 lb as purchased
Preparation	Remove wilted or discolored outer leaves and cut off thin slice from base. Wash under cold running water. If served in wedges, cut through core into appropriate size. If served sliced or shredded, cut in quarters or eighths, with most of core removed, but leave sufficient core to hold leaves together. It can be cut by machine, French knife or cole slaw cutter with blades adjusted to the appropriate size. Cabbage is sometimes cooked with meat such as spareribs, pork butt, etc., and the cooking time is governed by the meat recipe. When cabbage is cooked alone (such as wedges cooked in stock of corned beef), the cooking time is reduced so that

cabbage is still slightly crisp when removed from fire.

Cooking Times	Boil	Low-pressure Steam	High-pressure Steam
Shredded	5–8 min	4–6 min	1–2 min
Wedges	8–12 min	6–10 min	2–4 min

To Serve With butter, salt and pepper; with butter, cream, salt and pepper; braised with diced cooked bacon, salt pork, ham or garlic sausage; cooked in stock of corned beef, seasoned mildly with vinegar and sugar; red cabbage braised with stock, apples, onions, butter, vinegar, sugar, salt and pepper

Carrots   50 Portions

Quality Standards Bright but deep in color; no green shoulders; crisp, hard, symmetrical; free from rootlets; crisp green tops if any (both young and old carrots are marketed without tops); old carrots sometimes purchased for soup, stock, etc., rather than as a table vegetable

Amount 12–15 lb as purchased

Preparation Wash under cold running water and pare thinly using hand vegetable peeler with a floating blade. A machine vegetable peeler can be used but waste is considerable. If carrots are very young and fresh, they may be used without paring. Carrots may be left whole if very small, or may be cut into halves, quarters, crosswise slices, diagonal slices or dice.

Cooking Times	Boil	Low-pressure Steam	High-pressure Steam
Whole	12–30 min	10–20 min	3–6 min
Sliced	8–15 min	7–12 min	2–3 min
Diced	5–8 min	2–6 min	1–2 min

To Serve Buttered with salt, pepper and sugar; creamed; diced with peas; pureed with white turnips; glazed with butter and honey or syrup; Vichy style (suitable for only very young farm-fresh carrots), cooked with butter, salt, sugar and 1/4 in. water over very low heat in tighly covered pan until carrots are tender and all water has evaporated from pan

Cauliflower 50 Portions

Quality Standards	Outer leaves long, bright green and crisp; head white or creamy white, very compact and heavy for size; free from blemishes, loose spreading clusters or "riciness"; quality not affected by leaves which sometimes grow through curds; flowers in heads should not show growth
Amount	15 lb as purchased
Preparation	Cut away outer green leaves and any blemishes or bruise marks. If worms or insects are found or suspected, soak (heads down) in cold salted water with vinegar. Drain and wash well if soaked in this manner. Cut a cone-shaped piece out of the core, and break head into flowerets, or leave whole (whole cauliflower is sometimes planned for small parties or a la carte service). If left whole, remove part of the core, but do not cut so deeply that head will break apart during cooking.

Cooking Times	Boil	Low-pressure Steam	High-pressure Steam
Flowerets	8-12 min	2-4 min	1-2 min
Whole	20-30 min	12-18 min	10-12 min

To Serve	Buttered with salt and pepper; creamed; au gratin; with *Mornay* sauce au gratin; with hollandaise sauce; *polonaise* (with buttered bread crumbs, chopped hard egg and chopped parsley)

Celery 50 Portions

Quality Standards	Stalks or leaf stems crisp enough to snap easily; heavy for size; leaves fresh and green with some yellow near heart; inside of stalks smooth and firm rather than puffy; heart, full and well-developed rather than loose and limp
Amount	12 lb as purchased
Preparation	Cut or tear off leaves. Cut a slice from bottom end and remove stalks from bunch. Wash well, scrubbing outside and/or inside of stalks with vegetable brush if necessary. Scrape outside of stalks with vegetable peeler. Save the hearts, if requested as an appetizer; pass trimmings to soup cook or sauce

cook. Cut into slices or dice except for braised celery (see below).

Cooking Times	Boil	Low-pressure Steam	High-pressure Steam
	8–10 min	5 min	2–3 min

To Serve Creamed; with *Mornay* sauce au gratin; puree (with 1/3 mashed potatoes); braised (whole bunch cut into 3 to 5 pieces, cooked with seasoning vegetables and stock 30 to 40 min, pan juice reduced with *espagnole* sauce and poured over celery on serving plates)

Corn on the Cob 50 Portions

Quality Standards Bright shiny kernels either yellow or white, sometimes mixed in new varieties; no space between rows; kernels juicy when pressed; no stunted kernel growth; no kernels with flat or depressed tops or blemishes

Amount 50 ears

Preparation Remove outer husks and silk, using a soft vegetable brush or hand to remove silk. Examine carefully to make sure all silk is removed. Cut off tip or stem end if either protrudes noticeably. Shuck as close to cooking time as possible. Wash well under cold running water and keep refrigerated until just before cooking. After cooking if corn is kept in the steam table, keep 1/4 in. of milk in the pan.

Cooking Times	Boil	Low-pressure Steam	High-pressure Steam
	5–10 min	4–8 min	2–4 min

To Serve May be wrapped in white linen napkin; served with butter or clarified butter on side; sometimes lightly brushed with clarified butter just before serving; cut off cob, may be served buttered with salt and pepper, mixed with diced pimientos, with hot sweet cream or in cream sauce

Eggplant 50 Portions

Note: This vegetable may be stored by the *garde manger*, rather than the vegetable cook, and may be pared, sliced, breaded or otherwise prepared by him prior to cooking.

Quality Standards Heavy for size and firm to touch; skin, shiny dark purple over complete surface; may vary widely in size; rust spots or wrinkled skin signs of old stock or poor quality

Amount 12 lb as purchased

Preparation Cut off stem end and pare with French knife as close to cooking or breading time as possible. Soaking in salted water is not necessary. Cut into 3/8 in. horizontal slices for deep frying or sautéing; cut into finger-shaped 3/8 in. thick or 1/2 in. thick pieces for deep frying. For broiling, cut into horizontal slices 1/2 to 3/4 in. thick. For deep frying, prepare *a l'anglaise* (dip in flour, egg and bread crumbs in that order). For broiling, dip slices in flour first, brush well with oil and sprinkle lightly with salt and pepper. For sautéing, dip slices in milk first, then in flour; or in milk, flour and beaten egg in that order. Cook all styles to order if possible, with the exception of stuffed eggplant.

Cooking Times	Deep Fry	Broil	Sauté
	3–5 min	3–5 min	3–5 min

To Serve Sautéd; deep fried; broiled; baked with *duxelles* stuffing (see Glossary)

Greens   50 Portions

Note: The varieties of greens include spinach, beet tops, collards, dandelion, Swiss chard, kale, mustard and turnip greens.

Quality Standards Leaves crisp, large and tender, with fresh green color; leaves not wilted, yellowish or showing rot or sliminess; stems neither woody nor seedy; insect damage not apparent

Amount 24 to 30 lb as purchased

Preparation Cut off stem end and pare with French knife as well as coarse, large stems and all ends of small stems. Wash at least 4 times in clear cold water, lifting greens from the water each time and washing sand from bottom of sink. If after the fourth washing the greens are still sandy, wash 2 additional

times. Sometimes water adhering to leaves is sufficient for cooking.

Cooking Times

Boil	Low-pressure Steam	High-pressure Steam
5–20 min	8–12 min	3–5 min

To Serve With butter, salt and pepper; with olive oil, lemon
juice, salt and pepper; with diced bacon or diced
salt pork and vinegar or lemon juice; chopped and
creamed; with sautéd onions julienne (*lyonnaise*);
braised with chopped onions and garlic, bacon,
ham or salt pork and stock

Mushrooms   50 Portions

Note: Mushrooms are normally kept in the *garde
manger's* refrigerator and are washed, sliced, diced
or otherwise prepared by him in their raw state for
other cooks at the range. In some restaurants mushrooms may be handled by the vegetable cook.

*Quality
Standards* Vary in color from clean white (which are the best)
to creamy white to light brown; firm, plump,
heavy for size; short stems; caps enclose stems
(open caps indicate lack of freshness); are not fresh
if spotted or slimy; may be large caps 1 to 3 in. in
diameter or small "button" mushrooms

Amount 12 lb as purchased (served as vegetable side dish)

Preparation Soak in cold water briefly. Drain and repeat operation if necessary. Do not peel mushroom caps un-
less mushrooms are to be used for decorating
purposes. Cut off thin slice from stem if bottom is
dirty and discolored. The caps may be separated
from stems or left on stems, depending upon dish
for which they are intended. Mushrooms may be
sliced, diced, coarsely or finely chopped.

Cooking Times

Sauté	Broil
5–8 min	5–8 min

To Serve Sautéd in butter, seasoned with salt, pepper, lemon
juice and parsley; broiled served with maitre d'hotel
butter; creamed; au gratin; stuffed with *duxelles*
stuffing and baked; curried; with paprika sauce;
with Madeira sauce

Onions, Small White (Silver Onions)   50 Portions

Note: The most frequently used onion in the kitchen is the medium size domestic variety, usually globular, sometimes flat, in shape, with a yellow, red or white skin. These onions are used mostly as flavoring vegetables in soups, stews, etc., and the vegetable cook peels them and leaves them whole for other cooks to cut into various shapes and sizes. Large sweet Spanish onions are frequently used for the same purposes, but are also cut into rings and fried by the fry cook as French fried onions or made into smothered onions by the sauce cook. The small white onions above, however, are a separate vegetable item on the menu, prepared by the vegetable cook, usually by boiling, and are served whole.

Quality Standards Well-shaped, uniform in size, with skin dry enough to crackle; bulb hard with thin, bright neck; should not have damp or wet feeling at neck; no evidence of seed stems or sprouting

Amount 10 lb as purchased

Preparation Cut a slice from the stem end and root end, but do not cut so deeply that onion layers can break apart during cooking or serving. Peel thinly, making sure all white peel is removed. Remove first or second layers of onion if necessary to eliminate wilted or green spots, discoloration, etc.

Cooking Times

Boil	Low-pressure Steam	High-pressure Steam
18–25 min	10–15 min	4–6 min

To Serve Creamed; au gratin; with *Mornay* sauce au gratin; glazed (sautéd with butter, sugar, salt and pepper until sugar carmelizes slightly and browns onions); fines herbes (with butter, salt, pepper and very finely chopped parsley, chives, chervil and tarragon)

Peas   50 Portions

Quality Standards Pods large, smooth, with fresh green color, well-filled, snap easily when young (yellowish, swollen, dried-looking or specked pods indicate old stock);

Amount 25 lb as purchased

Preparation Shell as close to cooking time as possible. Press pods and twist to open. Empty peas into deep container. The shells are sometimes saved, chopped and used in the preparation of cream of pea soup or split pea soup. Wash the shelled peas before cooking. If peas vary considerably in size, the larger ones may be separated and cooked slightly longer than the smaller size.

Cooking Times

Boil	Low-pressure Steam	High-pressure Steam
6-9 min	3-6 min	1 min

To Serve With butter, salt, pepper and sugar; with diced carrots, buttered; creamed; creamed with diced carrots; French style with butter, shredded lettuce and small white onions; seasoned and served with chopped fresh mint leaves and butter; pureed with butter and cream

Potatoes, White   50 Portions

Note: In many restaurants, two kinds of potatoes are used: (1) the Idaho russet, a well-shaped long potato suitable for baking, French frying and mashing and (2) the cobblers, green mountains, red bliss or similar varieties suitable for boiling, home fries, au gratin, etc.

Quality
Standards Smooth skinned with no prominent eyes, if russets; clear, firm, unwrinkled skin with noticeable eyes, if other variety; free from cuts, prominent knobs or sprouts; when peeled, should be free of brown or gray spots, green spots called sunburn, black circle near skin or black interior known as black heart or hollow heart; uniform in size

Amount 20 lb variable, depending on mode of preparation

Preparation *Note:* In most commercial restaurants potatoes are pared by machine. The length of time potatoes are kept in machine will determine amount of raw weight loss. Different varieties and sizes of potatoes require different paring times. If in doubt, run machine for 1 1/2 to 2 min, and examine potatoes.

Continue paring only as long as necessary to remove skins without undue waste; consult *sous chef*, instructor or supervisor.

Boiled potatoes: If, after paring by machine, any skin, eyes, green, black or brown spots remain, trim potatoes by hand, using hand vegetable peeler or paring knife. Then store potatoes covered with cold water in refrigerator if storage time is brief, 30 min to 1 hour; if potatoes are to be held longer, use an antioxidant in water to prevent browning. For the best flavor and nutritional qualities, pare potatoes as close to cooking time as possible and keep in water, before boiling, as briefly as possible.

Potatoes can be boiled peeled or unpeeled. If unpeeled (potatoes in jacket), a 1/2-in. band of skin around the center of potatoes may be removed before cooking for easy handling at the dining table. A steam-jacketed kettle is more efficient than a conventional pot in that the recovery time in bringing water back to a boil, after potatoes are added, is shorter. Test medium size boiled potatoes for tenderness in 20 to 25 min; avoid overcooking. When potatoes are drained, do not carelessly dump them from one container to another, or they may break. If necessary lift them with a spoon from the cooking pot to the steam table container. Boiled potatoes in the steam table should have 1/4 in. of water in the bottom to prevent drying. If boiled potatoes seem watery but are not overcooked, they may be placed in dry pot over low flame and tossed gently for a brief period to dry. Peeled potatoes are sometimes parboiled for pan roast or potatoes *rissolées*.

Cooking Times	Boil	Low-pressure Steam	High-pressure Steam
Whole	30–40 min	20–30 min	8–16 min
Slices	8–12 min	4–8 min	1–3 min

To Serve — Boiled with or without jacket; with parsley butter; mashed; home fried; *lyonnaise* (slices sautéd with onions julienne); hashed brown; hashed creamed; au gratin; *duchesse* (mashed, baked with egg yolks, put through pastry bag and tube and browned); croquettes. Raw potatoes are prepared without boiling for baked potatoes, baked stuffed potatoes, French fries, julienne, *allumettes*, soufflé or parisienne (small balls French fried).

Potatoes, Sweet   50 Portions

Quality Standards
Thick and chunky; skins smooth, bright, clean-looking; free from blemishes, softness or other signs of decay; different varieties with skin colors ranging from almost white to yellow to deep brown; potatoes with deep orange-colored flesh, called "golden" sweets, most popular

Amount
20 lb variable, depending on mode of preparation

Preparation
Sweet potatoes may be pared by hand before boiling. If they are pared by machine, the waste can be high. Wash and scrub them if necessary before boiling in the jacket. Pare after boiling with table knife, removing any dark spots. They are sometimes baked instead of boiled for mashing and other uses.

Cooking Times

Boil	Low-pressure Steam	High-pressure Steam
25–35 min	20–30 min	6–8 min

To Serve
Mashed; mashed with pineapple; mashed and baked with brown sugar; candied; southern style (sliced with apples and syrup); croquettes; French fried (made with boiled sweet potatoes); fried in slices, quarters or halves; grilled. For baking, use raw sweet potatoes.

Squash   50 Portions

Note: There are many squash varieties, including summer, crooknecks, white scallops, long green or zucchini and Hubbard. Some varieties of summer squash are available all year long.

Quality Standards
Young, small to medium sizes more tender than large sizes which may be coarse and stringy; soft rind; firm to touch; crooknecks deep yellow in color; zucchini bright, deep green; acorn deep green and firm; Hubbard, or late squash, medium to large in size with hard, warted rind

Amount
25 lb as purchased

Preparation
Crooknecks and zucchini: Cut off ends and pare by hand. Zucchini skin is sometimes left on in which

case the vegetable must be well-scrubbed before cooking. If crooknecks are young, do not remove seeds; otherwise seeds must be scooped out. Cut into slices or large dice.

White scallops: If squash is very young, paring is unnecessary; prepare as crooknecks or zucchini.

Acorn: Cut in half and remove seeds and stringy area.

Hubbard: The rind may be left on, after being well-scrubbed, if the squash is to be served in single pieces. If it is to be mashed, the rind must be removed. Also remove the seeds and stringy area. The peel can also be removed after cooking. Hubbards are sometimes baked after steaming.

Cooking Times

	Boil	Low-pressure Steam	High-pressure Steam
Acorn	20–25 min	12–18 min	8–10 min
Crooknecks	10–15 min	5–8 min	2–3 min
White scallops	10–15 min	5–8 min	2–3 min
Zucchini	5–10 min	1–2 min	1/2–1 min
Hubbard	20–30 min	15–20 min	10–15 min

To Serve With butter, salt, pepper and sugar; with tomatoes, green peppers and onion baked with bread crumb topping; creamed; au gratin; Hubbard, mashed with butter and seasonings or baked in portion chunks with butter, cinnamon, sugar, salt and pepper

Tomatoes

Note: Tomatoes are normally kept in the *garde manger's* refrigerator, and are sliced, halved or otherwise prepared in their raw state by the *garde manger* for baking, broiling, stuffing, etc. On rare occasions the sauce cook or others will use raw tomatoes as a seasoning vegetable in sauces, stews, etc. The principal ways of cooking raw tomatoes are broiling, baking and stuffing.

Quality Standards Firm, heavy for size, plump; skin deep red, glossy, without yellow streaks; free from blemishes, scars, cracks, wrinkles or ridges; should not be angular or otherwise misshapen; when cut, are deep red, not excessively watery nor prominently seedy; interior meaty, moist and firm

Preparation   If not red, ripen at room temperature. To remove skin, lower into rapidly boiling water for 15 to 20 sec, dip in cold water, and peel off skins. The skin is removed only when tomatoes are used in sauces, stews, salads, etc. If tomatoes are large, leave skin on, cut out stem end with pointed small knife, and cut in half horizontally for broiling or baking. Before broiling or baking, dip cut side of tomatoes in oil or melted butter and season. They may be sprinkled on cut side with bread crumbs or grated cheese. If tomatoes are small to medium size, leave whole, cut slice off end opposite stem, remove stem, and season for broiling or baking. For stuffing, cut slice off top, remove seeds and liquid, and fill with *duxelles* or other stuffing topped with bread crumbs or grated cheese.

Cooking Times

Broil	Bake
8–12 min	15–25 min

To Serve   Broiled; baked; stuffed

Turnips, White and Yellow (Rutabagas)   50 Portions

Quality Standards   Generally marketed without tops (if tops are on turnips, they should be fresh and green); heavy for size; firm, smooth skin (wrinkled skin or scars around top indicate turnips are woody and strong in flavor)

Amount   18 lb

Preparation   Wash under cold running water. Pare by machine or pare thinly by hand. Leave turnips whole, if small, to be used for mashing. Cut into 1/4 or 1/2 in. thick slices or dice.

Cooking Times

	Boil	Low-pressure Steam	High-pressure Steam
1/4-in. slices or dice	8–12 min	6–10 min	2–4 min
1/2-in. slices or dice	18–24 min	15–20 min	4–6 min
Whole, small to medium size	20–30 min	12–15 min	10–12 min

Note: If rutabagas are very large and old, cooking time may have to be increased considerably until the tender stage is reached.

To Serve   With butter, salt, pepper and sugar; mashed; mashed (yellow) with potatoes; creamed; au gratin

Boiled Rice   Approx 1 Gal

Rice was once the hobgoblin of cooks. There were six grades, and despite a multiplicity of recipes, simple boiled rice was often sticky, gummy, hard to keep hot in the steam table and difficult to serve. The abundant amount of top-grade long grain rice as well as the type marketed by the trade name "converted" has made the job of cooking rice successfully a routine one. When rice is served as an accompaniment to a main dish, most chefs prefer the finished rice to be light and fluffy, with distinct grains. The easiest way to achieve this result is to allow a little more than twice as much water as rice by volume, and to simmer the rice (despite the fact that it is called boiled) until the water is absorbed and the rice is tender. During the simmering it is extremely important that the rice not be stirred. After cooking, it may be lightly fluffed with a kitchen fork.

Before starting work: Select a heavy saucepan, preferably aluminum rather than copper lined with tin. The tin lining as well as a lid lined with tin may melt as the rice becomes dry, and small pellets may drop into the rice. If there is any leftover rice from a previous meal, check to see that its flavor has not been impaired. Do not mix the leftover rice with the new batch as the latter is being cooked. Reheat, and serve the leftover rice before serving the new batch.

(1) Assemble the following ingredients:
   2 lb long grain rice or "converted" rice
   2 qt and 1 pt water
   1 1/2 oz salt
   2 large bay leaves (optional)
   1/4 lb butter
(2) Pour water into heavy saucepan.
(3) Add salt and bay leaves.
(4) Heat over a moderate flame. Bring water to a rapid boil.
(5) Add rice. Stir well.
(6) Allow water to come to a second boil.
(7) Stir once more. Reduce flame as low as possible to keep water barely simmering.
(8) Cover pan with tight-fitting lid. Cook, without stirring, until rice is tender, 15 to 20 min.
(9) Taste rice to test tenderness. Do not stir. Continue cooking if necessary.
   Note: Instead of cooking rice on a top flame, it may be

placed, after it has come to a boil, in a moderate oven of 350° F. Oven time is usually from 20 to 30 min.

(10) Remove rice from heat. Remove lid from pan. Let rice stand 5 min.

(11) Turn rice into a shallow bowl or into a large baking pan, spreading it out. Break butter into small pieces, and scatter it over the rice.

(12) With two-pronged kitchen fork, fluff rice to coat it with butter. Avoid excessive stirring or mixing. Remove bay leaves. Place rice in steam table pot for serving.

Rice Pilaf.—Melt 1/4 lb butter in recipe above in saucepan. Add 1/2 lb onions, chopped extremely fine. Sauté briefly until onions are light yellow. Add rice and bay leaves. Continue to sauté over low flame until rice grains are shiny and coated with butter. Add 2 qt and 1 pt white stock or chicken broth in place of water. Cook as above until tender.

Curried Rice.—Follow recipe for rice pilaf. When onions are sautéd, stir in 2 tablespoons curry powder, blending well so that no lumps of curry are visible. Dissolve 1 teaspoon turmeric in 2 tablespoons cold water; add to saucepan after rice has been added.

Saffron Rice.—Follow recipe for rice pilaf above. Add 6 large fresh tomatoes, peeled, seeded and chopped very fine, when sautéing onions. Add 2 teaspoons saffron after rice has been added. Cook as above.

11

Breakfast Cook

The breakfast menu is the one bill of fare that normally does not change from day to day. Several times during the year, perhaps, modifications may be made on the breakfast menu to include seasonal fruits such as berries, melons, etc. Otherwise the menu and the routines of the breakfast cook are more or less constant even though there are days of the week when the breakfast cook is busier than normal because of increased dining room volume. Frequently the breakfast cook is also the fry cook or may assist the fry cook before and during the midday meal. Almost all hot breakfast dishes, with the exception of hot cereals, are made to order. This means that the breakfast cook is often inundated with short orders that need immediate individual attention. While many of the menu items in a kitchen, such as soups, sauces, braised dishes, etc., are heavily influenced by European tradition, most breakfast dishes in this country are largely American with some English influence. Breakfast egg dishes like omelets and shirred eggs frequently appear on luncheon menus with fillings and garnishes. The ability to master egg cookery, therefore, becomes an asset for the breakfast cook who would advance to the job of fry cook and other higher positions. In some restaurants the breakfast cook is assisted by another worker such as a pantry worker or vegetable cook who may report for work an hour or so before the dining room is open for breakfast. The assistant may preheat equipment, bring water to a boil for coffee, start heating the steam table, receive morning supplies such as bread and rolls, etc. In very large restaurants or institutional feeding establishments, there may be a number of breakfast cooks depending on the dining room or coffee shop volume.

JOB SUMMARY

The breakfast cook (1) consults headwaiter or dining room captain on anticipated or special breakfast attendance; (2) orders and receives from storeroom standard breakfast items such as cereal, eggs, butter, etc.; (3) prepares hot cereals for storage in steam table during breakfast; (4) mixes batter for griddle cakes or waffles, and prepares griddle cakes or waffles to order; (5) mixes batter for French toast and prepares French toast to order; (6) prepares egg dishes such as scrambled, fried, poached, shirred, omelets, etc.; (7) may prepare scrambled eggs in quantity for large groups eating at one time; (8) blanches and finishes bacon; (9) grills and fries ham; (10) fries, grills or bakes sausage; (11) may prepare potatoes such as French fried, hashed brown, home fried, etc.; (12) toasts bread, English muffins or other muffins; (13) sautés corned beef hash, broils lamb chops and prepares other breakfast meat items.

MANUAL PROCEDURES

He (1) boils salted water in saucepans and stirs in cereals; (2) simmers and stirs cereals until done; (3) turns cereals into steam table pots and stores cereals for service; (4) spoons portions of cereal into appropriate dishes; (5) arranges bacon slices in baking pans, and blanches bacon until half cooked; (6) finishes bacon to crisp stage by placing and turning on griddle, in frying pan or under broiler; (7) cuts sausage into separate links, arranges sausages on baking pan, in frying pan, on griddle or under broiler and cooks until half done; (8) finishes sausages when individual orders are received; (9) places thin ham slices under broiler or on griddle and cooks until browned; (10) poaches eggs in water and vinegar; (11) beats eggs for omelets and pours eggs into frying pans; (12) fills, folds and garnishes omelets; (13) melts fat in frying pan or griddle, and fries eggs on one side or turns eggs by flipping or with spatula; (14) mixes eggs with fork or wire whip, pours eggs into frying pans with melted fat and stirs eggs with fork until scrambled; (15) garnishes egg dishes with bacon, ham, sausage, etc.; (16) makes batters from mixes by adding eggs, milk, etc., and reserves batters for griddle cakes; (17) mixes fresh batters by machine or by hand, combining flour, baking powder, salt, sugar, eggs and milk for griddle cakes and waffles; (18) pours batter from pitcher or from ladles onto griddle and onto waffle iron; (19) turns griddle cakes with spatula and stacks griddle cakes or waffles on serving dishes; (20) cuts boiled potatoes with knife and slices or chops potatoes; (21) sautés potatoes; (22) deep fries previously blanched potatoes; (23) sautés corned beef hash; (24) toasts bread or muffins in automatic toaster or under broiler.

EQUIPMENT AND UTENSILS

The breakfast cook uses (1) ranges; (2) broiler; (3) deep fat fryer; (4) mixing machine; (5) griddle; (6) steam table; (7) reach-in refrigerator; (8) waffle iron; (9) frying pans; (10) baking pans; (11) saucepans; (12) wire whips, spatulas, spoons, forks; (13) French knives; (14) measuring containers; (15) dispenser for salt, pepper, etc.

WORKING CONDITIONS AND HAZARDS

He (1) works under considerable pressure in front of ranges, griddle, steam table, broiler and deep fat fryer; (2) is subject to burns from sputtering fat.

PLACE IN JOB ORGANIZATION

The breakfast cook may be promoted from short order cook, counterman or pantry worker. He may eventually become fry cook or broiler cook.

USING THE GRIDDLE

The special piece of equipment which the breakfast cook must be able to use skillfully, and which other cooks may or may not use, is the griddle. It is widely found in coffee shops, breakfast shops and counter restaurants where much of the cooking takes place immediately adjacent to the serving area or in view of the customers. It is a heavy flat-top utensil with its source of heat, either gas or electric, beneath the top plate. For making griddle cakes, it is the only satisfactory piece of equipment. It may be used for certain egg dishes, ham, bacon, sausage, etc. Normally heavy-duty kitchen equipment such as ranges, steam tables, etc., are cleaned by a kitchen helper. Keeping the griddle clean, however, is important during as well as after its use, and is usually the responsibility of the breakfast cook.

16 GUIDES TO CLEANING AND USING THE GRIDDLE

(1) Any griddle which is new or has not been used for a long period, such as one in a seasonal resort kitchen, and which is covered with a grease coating to prevent rust, must be carefully cleaned with a grease-dissolving solution.

(2) Before a griddle can be used, it must be "seasoned"—that is, a film of fat must be applied in such a way that a nonstick surface covers the griddle. After a griddle has been in use for several meals or for an entire day and is thoroughly cleaned, it must be reseasoned.

(3) To season a griddle, follow these steps:

(a) Set the temperature at 400° F and preheat griddle.

(b) Pour unsalted shortening or oil onto griddle, using enough to coat entire surface.

(c) Spread shortening over entire surface with a heavy clean towel, a fat mop or brush.

(d) Allow shortening to remain until it smokes.

(e) Wipe griddle clean.

(f) Repeat steps (b) to (e) at least two times, wiping well after each application. Griddle is now seasoned.

(g) If some small spots on griddle later seem to cause food to stick, scrape them with a spatula, and reapply shortening as above.

(4) Griddle should be scraped after individual orders or batches of food have been cooked to remove food particles or residue. Scrape with edge of spatula. Remove food particles, and scrape fat toward rim of griddle to drain off. Wipe rim of griddle if all fat does not flow off.

(5) At the end of the shift or the end of the day, clean griddle for the next meal, following these steps:

(a) Set temperature of griddle at 150° F.

(b) Scrape off any remaining food or residue.

(c) Pour griddle-cleaner solution onto surface, using quantities suggested by manufacturer. Spread with cloth so that entire griddle is covered.

(d) Let solution stand 5 min.

(e) Scrape solution to rim of griddle to run off. Wipe griddle dry.

(f) Pour hot fresh water onto griddle to rinse and remove cleaning solution.

(g) Scrape water to rim of griddle. Wipe dry with clean cloth.

(h) Reseason griddle as described previously.

(6) Once a week or more often if necessary, rub surface of griddle

with griddle stone, following grain of metal. This removes any residue remaining after routine cleaning and leaves a fresh griddle top. It must be reseasoned as previously described before using again.

(7) Always preheat the griddle to the designated temperature considered best for the specific food to be cooked. Eggs, for instance, should be fried on the griddle at 300° F, bacon at 350° F, and griddle cakes at 390° F. Incorrect temperatures will give poor results.

(8) Make a note of any area of the griddle where the heat distribution may be irregular, that is, cause spotty cooking or uneven browning. Cook the food in such areas for a longer or shorter period than usual. Modern griddles with good performance characteristics provide even heat throughout the griddle.

(9) Uneven browning or abnormal cooking will occur if the temperature setting is incorrect. During a busy breakfast period, controls may be inadvertently set to improper temperatures. Make corrections if necessary. If an unusual heat response continues, report this fact to your instructor or supervisor. Thermostats may need correction or replacement.

(10) Large griddles are usually fitted with controls allowing different temperatures in different sections of the surface. Use whatever settings are necessary for efficient operation during busy and slack periods.

(11) Remember that scraping the griddle during its use is not only necessary for sanitary reasons but to prevent flavor transference from one food to another. A dish of plain scrambled eggs should not convey the flavor of sausage or other food previously cooked on the griddle.

(12) Use a long offset spatula for turning most foods. Wipe the spatula clean after each use. Do not attempt to turn large pieces of food with a small spatula intended for small portions.

(13) Check the accumulated fat in the removable tray beneath the griddle and empty it as often as necessary. It should be cleaned daily.

(14) When a large batch of cold food is placed on a griddle, its temperature will drop precipitously. In a well-constructed griddle the recovery period will be rapid. As the breakfast cook, however, you must anticipate such temperature variations. A griddle which is fully loaded at one time will suffer a greater heat loss than a griddle on which individual orders are placed periodically. Govern the cooking time accordingly.

(15) Foods which tend to run, such as beaten eggs, require more griddle space than compact foods such as whole eggs, bacon, etc. Allow this larger area to prevent different foods from mingling.

(16) Although the surface of a griddle is made of hard metal, it can be dented or impaired with the careless use of utensils. Do not strike it with the side of a spatula. When scraping the griddle, move the spatula with slow even pressure; don't hit the griddle surface. Do not use steel wool or coarse metal scrapers for cleaning.

COOKING BREAKFAST CEREALS

The job of making hot breakfast cereals follows a pattern no matter what brand of cereal is prepared. Raw or partially cooked cereals are cooked in salted water until the water is absorbed, the starch is cooked and the cellulose is softened. Directions for cooking are printed on the package, and include the ingredients, method of cooking and yield. The student, however, should be familiar with the three common methods of cooking no matter what package directions are indicated. The three procedures are as follows:

(1) Raw cereal may be combined with *all* the cold water indicated in the recipe, slowly brought to a boil while stirring, and simmered until done.

(2) Raw cereal may be mixed with *part* of the cold water and set aside. The balance of the water is brought to a boil, at which point the cereal mixture is stirred into it and simmered until done.

(3) *All* of the cold water is brought to a rapid boil; the dry cereal is then slowly stirred into it and simmered until done.

Although methods (1) and (2) avoid lumpiness, method (3) seems to be the one most widely preferred by breakfast cooks. Some cereals are so-called "quick cooking," meaning they have been partially cooked during processing. Those not indicated as quick cooking are preferred by some chefs because of the lighter, smoother texture and mellow flavor that results from long, slow simmering. Although cooking breakfast cereals is considered one of the easiest jobs in the kitchen, it has some hazards for beginner cooks. Five common faults and ways of correcting them are listed.

(1) *Lumpiness:* When raw dry cereal is carelessly added to boiling water without proper stirring, those starch granules in immediate contact with the water form a viscous mass, trapping uncooked particles inside. These uncooked particles (lumps) remain, no matter how long the cooking continues. The remedy is to disperse the starch granules before lumps form. The cook should:

(a) Hold a wire whip at the middle of the pot below the surface of the water

(b) Stir the water with the whip, while very slowly pouring the cereal where the whip is agitating the water, and

(c) Continue to slowly add the cereal while stirring vigorously until all the cereal has been added.

(2) *Stickiness:* This is a major fault with oatmeal. It is usually caused by excessive stirring after the cereal has been thickened. When cereal is first added to water, it settles to the bottom, and a layer of water remains on top. During this brief period, as the cereal is swelling and absorbing water, it should be stirred until the water and cereal form into a thick homogeneous mass. At that point, stirring should be drastically reduced. The cereal should be cooked over a low flame until done, stirring only occasionally to make sure there is no bottom sticking. In some kitchens, after the cereal is thickened, it is transferred to the steam table for slow cooking and a minimum of stirring.

(3) *Excessive thickness:* After the cereal has been completely cooked and has been standing in the steam table for an hour or more, the starch sometimes continues to swell and cause undue thickness, just as certain sauces or soups standing in the steam table become thicker in time. If this occurs, the cereal should be carefully thinned with a small addition of boiling water stirred into the cereal, using only as much water as necessary to restore the cereal to its original consistency.

(4) *Skin:* If hot cereal remains in the steam table for long periods without being served or stirred, it may develop a thick skin on top. To avoid it, keep the steam table pot or inset tightly covered except when serving.

(5) *Burnt flavor:* Scorching will occur if the thickened cereal is kept over a flame which is too high. If a steam-jacketed kettle is used for cooking, reduce the heat drastically as soon as the cereal has been added to the boiling water. Check the bottom of the pot or kettle with a spoon or paddle to make sure cereal is not sticking during cooking. If cereal is sticking, but is not scorched, empty it into a clean pot without scraping bottom.

Ratio of Cereal to Water

Many breakfast cooks prepare cereal without reference to any recipe. The general guidelines which they follow remain constant no matter what brand of cereal is used. Oatmeal normally requires twice as much water as oats by volume, not weight. Thus if the cook fills a gallon measure with rolled oats, he will need two gallons of water to make oatmeal. For making cracked wheat cereals such as Wheatena, a gallon of the cereal will require four gallons of water. For making fine granular cereals such as farina or cornmeal, a gallon of the cereal will require five to six gallons of water. Each cereal requires a tablespoon of salt per gallon of water.

BREAKFAST EGG COOKERY

Although eggs are featured widely on luncheon menus, sometimes in elaborate forms, their simplest preparation is at breakfast. At breakfast, however, both the dining room staff and the kitchen are likely to receive the largest number of customer complaints. Patrons will object if the eggs are delayed, if they are lukewarm instead of hot, if they are too soft, too firm or poor in appearance. Sometimes the complaints are unfounded, but more often they are justified. To handle orders quickly and efficiently, the breakfast cook must set up his station each morning so that all foods, utensils and equipment are ready for immediate action. At least one hour before breakfast, eggs should be removed from the refrigerator so that they can reach room temperature, the best temperature for boiling, poaching, omelets and other egg dishes. The eggs should be in carton separators or in a bowl nearby so that they can be cracked, opened and turned into the proper utensil with a minimum of motion.

Pans for frying eggs or omelets should be seasoned (p 104), wiped clean, and within arm's reach. There should be enough pans for the anticipated breakfast business. A container of clarified butter should be as close to the cooking area as possible. Towels for handling equipment, and clean towels of cloth or paper for wiping excess fat from plates should be available. Flexible as well as firm spatulas, forks and wire whips for beating, slotted spoon, skimmer and knives should be in position. Bacon should be blanched for crisping at the last moment. Broiler, griddle and range top should be preheated. The proper pan should be filled with water for poaching eggs. Quartz heating lamps, if used, should be switched on. Once the routine is learned and set up, it can be easily followed from day to day. Although different egg dishes such as omelets or shirred eggs require different methods of preparation, there are some general procedures which apply to all egg cookery.

12 GUIDES TO BREAKFAST EGG COOKERY

(1) All eggs for breakfast cookery should be fresh not only for the sake of flavor but because stale eggs cause problems in poaching,

boiling or frying. There are a number of ways of judging freshness, but for the busy cook behind the range, the simplest way is to open it onto a dinner plate. When it is fresh, the yolk is high and rounded rather than flat or broken, and the white clings to the yolk in a compact shape; the white should not be watery or run to the rim of the plate.

(2) Since freshness is so important to successful egg cookery, the breakfast cook should immediately inform his supervisor if eggs show signs of staleness or of incipient spoilage such as a strong odor.

(3) Eggs should be removed from the refrigerator at least one hour before the dining room is opened for breakfast to allow the eggs to reach room temperature when they are best for most egg dishes. After the breakfast period, any unused eggs should be returned to the refrigerator or to a cook who needs them at the time. If breakfast is served over a long period (from 7 to 11 A.M.), eggs should be removed from the refrigerator in batches, allowing enough time to reach room temperature.

(4) Learn to thoroughly know the performance characteristics of the range tops, open burners or griddle where egg dishes are prepared. If one part of the range top is consistently hotter than another, be prepared to move pans to the positions which best serve your purpose.

(5) To open eggs, crack them sharply against the side of a dish, the side of a cutting board or any hard surface as close as possible to the utensil or dish in which the eggs are to be dropped. Hitting the eggs too lightly causes difficulty in opening them; hitting them too sharply may break the yolks. Experience will guide you rather quickly.

(6) Eggs may be opened using one or both hands. At one time chefs insisted that all eggs be opened with two hands, using the right thumb to remove any white remaining in the shell. Nowadays, busy breakfast cooks use one hand to open eggs. It is a special knack, but not a difficult one which an instructor or supervisor can demonstrate. To open an egg with one hand, hold the hand over the egg, crack the bottom against a hard surface, move the front of the shell forward with the thumb and first two fingers, move the back of the shell rearward with remaining fingers, and drop the egg into the container or pan. This will take a moderate amount of practice and can best be learned when eggs are being opened in quantity, and when yolks and whites are to be mixed. If yolks and whites are to be separated, both hands should be used to move the yolk back and forth, permitting the white to drop into a container.

(7) When learning to open eggs by hand, or if in doubt about the

freshness of eggs, always open one or two eggs into a dish before adding them to the pan or griddle. Any piece of shell can then be removed. If yolks break, they may be used for another purpose.

(8) The kind of shortening you use for frying will be specified by your supervisor. The best quality shortening, however, for egg frying, omelets, scrambled eggs, etc., is clarified butter (p 98). Butter flavor is desirable for eggs, and the process of clarification raises the smoking point of butter so that it can withstand higher heat without turning black.

(9) When making eggs in quantity, such as scrambled eggs for a large breakfast party, beat the eggs slightly, and let them flow through a china cap. Straining will eliminate any shell particles, hard pieces of white, etc.

(10) Coordinate your work so that breakfast foods that require different lengths of cooking times will be ready simultaneously. If link sausages that take 12 min cooking time are to be served with eggs, they should be partially cooked in advance and kept in a warming unit to be finished when the eggs are ready. If bacon is to be crisped at the last moment, plan to take it off the fire as close as possible to the moment the eggs are finished.

(11) Hot egg dishes should be hot. Plates should be kept in a plate warmer. If plate covers are available, they too should be kept in a plate warmer and used whenever practical.

(12) Listen to orders carefully. A waiter may use slang terms such as "up," "straight up" or "sunnyside up," meaning the eggs are not to be turned; or "over easy," meaning gently fried on both sides; or "soft scrambled" or other terms. If in doubt about an order, ask the waiter precisely what is meant.

Scrambled Eggs   1 Portion, 3 Eggs

Two or three eggs are normally served for a portion although occasionally there may be an order for a single scrambled egg. Usually eggs are not scrambled in the same pans used for omelets or for frying eggs. The reason for this is that in the process of scrambling a small amount of egg residue is often left on the pan, and washing is necessary. When scrambled eggs are prepared on a griddle, any residue is simply scraped off. Unless otherwise ordered, scrambled eggs should be soft but not liquid. No white should be evident. Particles of eggs should be uniformly small and tender. Milk, cream or water may be added in amounts no larger than a tablespoon for three eggs. Water makes the eggs more tender, milk and cream, more firm. Water is neutral in flavor; milk and cream have noticeable flavors. The flame under the pan should be lower than that for fried eggs or omelets in order to prevent formation of large lumps of egg.

Before starting work: Plan to use a cast aluminum pan or pan lined with stainless steel or tin. Pan should have bottom diameter of 6 in. Make sure pan is clean with no film of fat or film caused by fat fumes in kitchen. Keep a bowl or dish on hand in which three eggs can be beaten without spillage. If toast is used as a garnish, plan to prepare it under a broiler or in an automatic toaster so that it is ready when eggs are done.

(1) Assemble the following ingredients:

3 eggs

Clarified butter

Salt

(2) Open eggs into small bowl. Add milk, cream or water (no more than 1 tablespoon) if this is the custom in the place you are working. Do not pour milk, cream or water indiscriminately into eggs, but measure it.

(3) Beat eggs with kitchen fork until whites are no longer visible.

(4) Dip tip of fork in salt box. The wet ends of the fork tines will cause a small amount of salt to adhere. Do not overseason. Pepper is not necessary as a seasoning.

(5) Pour half of a No. 1 ladle (equal to 1 tablespoon) clarified butter into pan. Place pan over low flame.

(6) Swirl butter so that bottom and part of side of pan are covered.

(7) Add eggs. Using fork, stir frequently though not constantly, moving eggs as they coagulate. Some cooks prefer to use a flat or basting spoon for stirring. The same spoon may be used for removing eggs from pan. Cook until eggs are soft scrambled. Do not overcook. Eggs will continue cooking somewhat after being removed from fire.

(8) Remove eggs from pan onto warm plate. Shape eggs in an oval mound in center of plate.

(9) Garnish with toast, if ordered, cut diagonally and placed alongside, not underneath, eggs. If necessary, notify waiter to pick up eggs at once while warm.

Scrambled Eggs, Country Style.—Do not beat eggs before cooking. Add whole eggs to pan with clarified butter. Use a moderate to strong flame. Beat eggs in pan so that whites and yolks are separately visible.

Scrambled Eggs in Quantity.—Scrambled eggs served to large groups are made in advance. Heat butter in saucepan or saucepot set in steam table. Add eggs. Stir frequently with wire whip, scraping bottom and corner of pan, until eggs are soft scrambled. Add milk, cream or water (using no more than 1 tablespoon per 3 eggs) *after scrambling* to keep eggs from coagulating in heavy layers. *Béchamel* sauce (see Chap. 8), made with light cream or half milk and half cream, may be added after scrambling to keep eggs loose rather than bunched. Use 1/2 cup *béchamel* sauce to each 2 doz eggs. Keep eggs warm in a double steam table, that is, the container with eggs should be set in a second container which is in contact with the water in the steam table. Eggs made with *béchamel* sauce do not have the delicate flavor of eggs scrambled to order, but it is the most practical way of handling them for parties where eggs are prepared in advance and must be kept warm until serving time.

Poached Eggs   1 Portion, 2 Eggs

The term poaching, when applied to eggs, means cooking opened eggs in water. There are eating places where eggs are poached in metal rings set in a pan of water, or poached in greased cups used as insets above the water—actually a form of steaming rather than poaching. In better restaurants the traditional way is to poach eggs in such a manner that the whites cover the yolks forming a compact oval shape, leaving the yolks soft and runny. As an aid in poaching eggs in this manner, vinegar is usually added, using 1 tablespoon vinegar per qt of water. The acid of the vinegar hastens the coagulation of the whites, and its flavor is hardly perceptible. In a kitchen where poached eggs are frequently ordered for breakfast, the same saucepan may be used for repeated orders. Keep the saucepan near the flame with the water simmering when not in use. Since freshness is so important in poaching eggs successfully (stale eggs will not hold their shape in the boiling water), it is best to open the first several eggs of a batch into small dishes before adding them to the water in order to check them for freshness. If the eggs seem to be unquestionably fresh, subsequent orders of eggs may be poached by opening the eggs directly into the water, using one or two hands for opening.

Before starting work: Check eggs for freshness. Sometimes there will be several lots of eggs in the storeroom refrigerator. If in doubt reserve less fresh eggs for omelets or scrambled eggs. If possible, obtain fresher eggs for poaching. Keep a clean cloth towel handy so that when eggs are removed from the water, they can be held in a slotted spoon above the towel for draining.

(1) Assemble the following ingredients:

    2 eggs
    White vinegar
    Salt

(2) Into a saucepan at least 4 in. high, pour water to a depth of 2 1/2 to 3 in. The saucepan should be at least 12 in. in diameter, larger if multiple orders are likely to be received. For each quart of water add 1 tablespoon vinegar and 1 teaspoon salt. Stir to dissolve salt.

(3) Bring water to a rapid boil.

(4) Lower eggs into water; do not drop.

Note: Some breakfast cooks stir water with a spoon held perpendicular to the water until a well is formed in water. Eggs lowered into this well form an oval shape. Other cooks open eggs near the side of the pan. If eggs are really fresh, however, and water is rapidly boiling, they will naturally form into a compact mass as they are cooked.

(5) Simmer eggs 2 1/2 to 3 min or until white of egg is firm.

(6) Remove eggs one at a time with a slotted spoon. Hold spoon briefly over clean cloth towel to drain egg completely.

(7) If edge of egg is ragged, it may be trimmed slightly with a knife or scissors.

(8) Place eggs carefully on warm serving plate or on toast. Serve at once.

(9) Remove any egg white debris floating in water. Remove pan from high flame until next order is received.

Poached Eggs Benedict.—For each order, broil or sauté 2 slices ham 1/8 in. thick, each 1 to 1 1/2 oz. Toast an English muffin. Place ham on muffin halves. Place poached eggs on ham. Cover each egg with a 1/4 cup hollandaise sauce (see Chap. 8). Eggs are sometimes garnished with a thin slice of black truffle. Poached eggs Benedict are a popular luncheon item.

Poached Eggs in Quantity.—When poached eggs are served as a garnish with corned beef hash, chicken hash, fresh asparagus or other dishes, they are made in advance and cooked on the soft side only until the whites are set. They are then trimmed of ragged edges and placed in water at room temperature until needed; for serving, they are placed briefly in boiling water and drained as directed above.

Boiled Eggs

Boiled eggs are usually made in an automatic egg boiler, using gas or electric heat. Water is kept simmering, and eggs are lowered in a basket controlled by an automatic timer set for a specific number of minutes. Boilers are built with 1, 2, or 3 units. Normally soft-cooked eggs are simmered 3 to 5 min, medium eggs 6 to 8 min and hard-boiled eggs 10 to 15 min. The job is often handled by a waiter or waitress or by a pantry worker rather than the breakfast cook. As in other egg cookery it is important that the eggs be at room temperture rather than chilled when placed in the egg boiler.

Coddled Eggs

Coddled eggs are eggs in the shell, placed in a container with boiling water. The container is instantly removed from the fire, the container is covered, and the eggs are permitted to remain in the hot water until done, usually 6 to 8 min. Both white and yolk remain tender with an almost creamy consistency.

Fried Eggs   1 Portion, 2 Eggs

Fried eggs are such a simple dish that it would seem pretentious to elaborate on their preparation. But in cooking a dish as easy as fried eggs, the breakfast cook differs from many amateurs mainly in setting up standards or approved models which he aims to achieve. It should be clearly understood that if you follow certain guidelines, you will get definite results. Fried eggs are normally cooked in butter, preferably clarified butter. In some kitchens margarine is used. Bacon or ham fat may be used particularly if ham or bacon and eggs country style are prepared. For frying two eggs, the pan should be 6 in. across the bottom. Fat poured into the pan should be sufficient to coat the bottom and part of the side of the pan. It should not be so great that the eggs swim in fat which later shows up conspicuously on the serving plate. The fat should be hot enough so that within seconds the eggs coagulate on the bottom. It should not be so hot that the eggs brown around the edges and the bottom of the eggs becomes tough. Fried eggs should be round and symmetrical, not torn. The top of the eggs, if not turned over, should show bright yellow yolks and whites that are set rather than milky or raw in appearance.

    Before starting work: If you work in a restaurant where fried eggs are ordered frequently, be sure there are enough seasoned pans on hand for multiple orders. If a griddle is used for frying eggs, it should be preheated to 300° F in the section of the griddle reserved for egg cookery. Preheat the broiler for finishing the tops of the eggs when necessary. Examine breakfast plates to make sure they are clean and have been warmed.

    (1) Assemble the following ingredients:

2 eggs
Clarified butter

(2) Heat 1 tablespoon clarified butter in a pan 6 in. across the bottom. Use a moderate flame. To measure butter, a No. 1 ladle, half full, may be used.

(3) Open eggs into pan. When turning eggs into pan, hold eggs as close as possible to pan bottom to keep yolks from breaking.

Note: Open the first several orders of eggs into a small dish before adding them to the frying pan. If eggs seem consistently fresh with firm unbroken yolks and compact whites, open subsequent orders of eggs directly into pan.

(4) Check heat. If fat seems to be sputtering and eggs are coagulating too quickly, move pan to lower heat. If eggs seem to be setting too slowly, move pan to higher heat.

(5) When eggs are set on bottom but still soft on top, move pan in a rotating motion to make sure eggs are not sticking. Use a thin spatula if necessary to test eggs.

(6) Continue to cook, usually 3 to 4 min, until egg whites are set on top.

Note: To hasten setting egg whites on top, pan may be placed briefly under broiler flame. Do not place pan so close to flame that eggs harden on top. Carefully watch eggs under broiler, and remove the pan the instant the whites are set. Excessive broiling will cause eggs to be rubbery.

(7) Slide eggs from pan onto warm serving plate.

(8) Wipe excess fat from sides of eggs if necessary; use a clean cloth towel or paper toweling.

Fried Eggs Over.—Turn eggs when almost ready to be removed from fire by flipping them in pan or turning them with a wide spatula. Let eggs cook on second side only until set; a white film will form on egg yolks. Serve yolk side up.

Fried Eggs Over Easy.—When eggs are just set on bottom and still raw on top, flip or turn them over for second side to cook only briefly. Eggs are less firm than "fried eggs over."

Ham or Bacon and Eggs, Country Style.—Heat butter as in preparing fried eggs above. Or use rendered ham or bacon fat if this is the custom in the restaurant in which you are working. Place slices of cooked ham or bacon in pan and sauté briefly. Add eggs so that eggs flow over and cover ham or bacon. Cook fried eggs in normal way. When turned onto serving plate, eggs and ham or bacon will be cooked together in a single mass.

Shirred Eggs   **1 Portion, 2 Eggs**

Shirred eggs (*sur le plat* or on the dish) as prepared in most restaurants are simply fried eggs cooked in a shirred egg dish—a ramekin or shallow round dish approximately 6 in. in diameter, made of oven-proof or flame-proof porcelain or of metal, with lips on opposite sides. Formerly, in restaurants and in homes, shirred eggs were baked in the oven. But oven baking is slow, and often uneven; eggs would become well-done on the bottom while almost raw on top. When shirred eggs are cooked on top of the range over a closed flame, their cooking proceeds exactly like that of the previous recipe for fried eggs. If the bottom is completely set and the top is undone, the dish is placed under a broiler flame briefly to finish. The same quality standards that apply to fried eggs should be observed in making shirred eggs. Since the shirred egg dish becomes very hot on the fire, it must be handled with special care to avoid burns. Because the dish retains heat so well, the eggs are always piping hot when they arrive at the table. Also, because of the heat of the dish, the eggs continue to cook somewhat after they are removed from the fire. For this reason slight undercooking is better than overcooking. Shirred eggs frequently appear on luncheon menus garnished with chicken livers, kidneys, asparagus tips, etc.

Before starting work: Examine shirred egg dishes very carefully before adding eggs. Eggs frequently stick to the dish, and the residue may not be removed by routine dishwashing; hand cleaning may be necessary. Be prepared to handle the shirred egg dish with a folded dry towel to avoid burns.

(1) Assemble the following ingredients:
   2 eggs
   Clarified butter
(2) Pour 1 tablespoon clarified butter into clean, dry shirred egg dish. Tilt dish so that bottom and side are coated with butter.
(3) Place dish over closed top flame with moderate heat. Heat dish for about 1/2 min.
(4) Open eggs into dish.
(5) Keep dish over slow to moderate flame.
(6) Cook until bottom of eggs is set and top is almost coagulated.
(7) Using dry towel, very carefully transfer shirred egg dish to broiler to finish cooking.

(8) Keep under broiler flame only until top of whites is set. Avoid overcooking or eggs will be tough.

(9) Again using dry towel, place shirred egg dish on larger plate. Plate is sometimes lined with paper doily to keep shirred dish from sliding.

Shirred Eggs with Bacon, Ham or Sausage.—After heating butter in shirred egg dish, place cooked bacon, ham or sausage in dish. Open eggs into dish, and cook as above.

Shirred Eggs Bercy.—Cook shirred eggs in normal way. After cooking, place 2 broiled or sautéd link sausages in dish, and cover sausages with tomato sauce (puree type, p 220).

Omelet   **1 Portion, 3 Eggs**

When Napoleon tried to make an omelet and failed, he said, "I have attributed to myself talents which I do not possess." Students attempting to make an omelet the first time may feel awkward, but the job is not as challenging as some amateur cooks would have you believe. In some cookbooks the plain omelet below is called a French omelet, distinguishing it from a fluffy omelet in which the egg whites are beaten separately and are combined with the yolks. The recipe below is the standard one followed in almost all commercial eating places. The job does require attention and deftness, but, once learned, is as routine as making scrambled eggs or fried eggs. An omelet should be light, tender, delicately browned on the outside and softly moist inside. Most chefs prefer unmelted butter rather than clarified butter, since the former browns more readily and gives a light brown hue to the finished omelet. The routine is not complicated. Beaten eggs, often mixed with a small amount of water rather than milk to keep the eggs tender, are turned into a hot buttered pan. A quick stir at the beginning is necessary. A layer of egg coagulates on the bottom. Liquid egg on top is allowed to flow to the bottom. When the eggs are almost set, the omelet is folded and turned onto a serving plate. The interior heat of the eggs completes the cooking, leaving the omelet slightly moist inside. It is the practice in some restaurants to let the eggs set on the bottom and complete the top cooking under the broiler. The objection to this procedure is that if the omelet remains only a few seconds too long under the broiler, it will be tough.

Before starting work: If an omelet variation is ordered, such as a western or cheese omelet, be sure the garnish is on hand before the omelet is started. A pan used for omelets may be used for fried eggs but no other dish. Seasoned pans should be available and should be wiped well before cooking. Omelets are started on moderate to high heat and then moved to lower heat to finish. Keep the range top free of other pans so that you can move the omelet pan when necessary.

(1) Assemble the following ingredients:

    3 eggs
    Salt
    1 tablespoon cold water
    1 tablespoon unmelted butter

(2) Open eggs into a small bowl for mixing. Add water.

(3) Beat eggs briefly with a fork.

(4) Dip edge of tines of fork into salt box, and then beat eggs about 1/2 min. Do not overbeat. Overbeating will result in eggs rising high in pan and then later collapsing on serving plate.

(5) Melt butter in pan over moderate to high heat.

(6) As soon as butter begins to sizzle—it should not turn brown—add eggs.

(7) At the first sign that eggs are coagulating on bottom, move pan back and forth with left hand. With right hand stir eggs with bottom of fork 2 or 3 times.

(8) Remove pan to lower heat. If an open flame is used, turn down flame.

(9) In a moment or two, lift eggs without disturbing bottom, to let liquid eggs flow to bottom. A fork or spatula may be used at this step.

(10) As egg continues to cook from bottom to top, a slight layer of uncooked egg will be noted on top. Spread it with flat of the fork to cover base completely rather than permit it to rest in a pool in one spot.

(11) As soon as top no longer shows a pronounced layer of liquid egg but it is still moist looking, lift the pan and tap it to make sure omelet can be moved freely. Use your spatula if necessary to free egg. Carefully slide egg so that middle of omelet rests on far end of pan corner.

(12) If a filling is to be added, such as Spanish sauce, add it to the center of the omelet.

(13) With a flexible spatula fold the far outer edge (one third of the omelet) inward. Hold the folded part momentarily, if necessary, to make it retain its position. Fold the side nearest

you (one third of the omelet) over the top. The omelet is now in three layers.

(14) With the omelet at the edge of the pan, grasp the pan handle with your right hand.

(15) Holding the warm serving plate in the left hand, place the pan so that its edge rests on the edge of the serving plate.

(16) Quickly invert the pan so that the folded side of the omelet rests on the dish.

(17) Using a clean towel, tuck the edges of the omelet inward so that its shape is long and elliptical.

(18) Top of omelet may be brushed with butter if desired. Omelet should be served at once. Use whatever routine is customary to have waiter pick up omelet.

Omelet With Cheese.—Add 1 tablespoon grated Parmesan cheese or 2 tablespoons shredded Swiss cheese to beaten eggs before turning eggs into pan.

Omelet Fines Herbes.—Add 2 teaspoons very finely chopped herbs; usual mixture of herbs is equal parts parsley, chives and chervil.

Spanish Omelet.—Just before folding omelet, add to center of omelet 1/4 cup hot Spanish sauce (see Chap. 8). After omelet is turned onto serving plate, add 1/4 cup hot Spanish sauce at one end of omelet.

Ham Omelet.—Add 1/4 cup diced cooked ham to beaten eggs before turning eggs into pan.

Western Omelet.—To beaten eggs add a mixture of 2 tablespoons diced cooked ham, 1 tablespoon diced sautéd green pepper and 1 tablespoon diced sautéd onion.

BREAKFAST MEATS

Bacon

Normally bacon for breakfast is partially cooked (blanched) in advance and finished to the crisp stage as individual orders arrive in the kitchen. When raw bacon is cold, slices are hard to separate. Sliced bacon should, therefore, be removed from the refrigerator about an hour before the dining room opens for breakfast. About a half hour later, the breakfast cook follows these steps in blanching bacon:

(1) The oven is preheated to 375° F.

(2) Bacon slices are separated to make sure there is no sticking or matting and are rearranged shingle fashion in a shallow baking pan, the lean portion of each slice overlapping the fat portion of another.

(3) The pan is placed in the oven until the bacon is partially cooked, about 10 to 12 min. The bacon will shrink somewhat as the fat melts, and it will lose its raw opaque appearance. Slices are turned over and cooking is continued. Total cooking time is usually 15 to 20 min at which time the bacon is rare.

(4) The partially cooked bacon is removed from the pan. The bacon fat is poured off, and reserved for another use. Special care must be taken to avoid sputtering fat and burns in handling the pan; use a heavy, folded dry towel in each hand.

(5) Bacon slices are then placed over a rack so that fat can drain off. The rack can be improvised. It may be an inverted bowl or platter placed over a larger platter or pan or any other device permitting the bacon to be spread out and drain. Care must again be taken that slices are not sticking to one another.

(6) As orders are received, bacon is cooked to the crisp stage. It may be finished under the broiler, on a pan or griddle or by placing in deep fat preheated to 370° F.

(7) Before serving, the bacon slices are briefly drained on a clean cloth towel or paper toweling and patted dry. Usual portons are 2 or 3 slices.

Ham

Sliced ham for breakfast is served most often as a garnish for egg dishes or griddle cakes. Unlike bacon, which is partially cooked beforehand and finished at the last moment, ham is usually made-to-order since the cooking is brief, usually 3 to 5 min. Much of the ham served for breakfast is the tenderized type, requiring brief cooking, or completely cooked ham. Even the raw Smithfield ham does not require extended cooking when sliced thin for breakfast. Slices of all types of ham are usually 1/8 to 1/4 in. thick. Ham may be cooked in a pan without added fat (pan broiled), on a griddle or under the broiler. If the ham is the tenderized type or ready-to-eat variety, it is cooked only until lightly browned. If it is raw ham (Smithfield or country type), slices will be thinner, about 1/16 in. thick, and cooking time in pan, on griddle or under broiler is again 3 to 5 min. Usual portions are 2 slices weighing 1 to 2 oz each.

Canadian Bacon

Canadian bacon is not bacon as we use the term in this country, but smoked boneless loin of pork. It is cooked in the same manner as ham. See above.

Breakfast Small Link Sausages

Like bacon, link sausages may be partially cooked beforehand and finished when orders are received. The normal cooking time for link sausages of the breakfast type is 10 to 15 min in a pan, in a hot oven or under the broiler. They may be half cooked in 5 to 8 min. To prevent the sausage casings from bursting, they are pierced with a fork before they are put on the fire. Oven cooking is preferred by many breakfast cooks because browning is less spotty. To precook link sausages:

(1) Preheat oven to 400° F.

(2) Separate links by cutting casings between links.

(3) Pierce links with kitchen fork in 2 or 3 places.

(4) Place links in ungreased shallow pan in oven.

(5) Bake, turning once, until browning just starts, 5 to 8 min.

(6) Remove sausages from pan. Discard fat.

(7) Keep sausages in steam table pan or in food warming unit until needed.

(8) When ready to serve, finish browning under broiler, in ungreased pan or on griddle.

Two or three link sausages are the usual portion as an accompaniment to eggs.

OTHER USES OF THE GRIDDLE

Griddle cakes   96 Cakes, 4 – 4 1/2 In. Diameter

When making griddle cakes, the student should keep the work "cake" in mind in aiming for quality standards. Griddle cakes should be as light as a sponge cake, fork tender, with a smooth brown crust which is neither sticky nor rubbery. The shape of the cakes should be uniformly round and of uniform diameter, usually 4 to 4 1/2 in. Toughness or heaviness in griddlecakes—the most common fault—is due to overbaking or overmixing the batter. In many eating places nowadays, a prepared mix is used for griddle cakes. But whether you use a prepared mix or combine your own ingredients, the batter for the anticipated breakfast business is always made beforehand. The temperature of the griddle is all-important. It should range between 375° and 400°F. If the griddle is set at 390°F, the temperature will drop when the batter is poured onto the griddle. If the recovery rate of the griddle is rapid, the temperature will remain within the 375° to 400°F range for the 3- to 4-min baking time required. Griddle-cakes should be turned only once. When the bottom is brown and the edge of the top is dry-looking with bubbles on most of the top surface, the griddle cakes should be turned. When learning to make griddle cakes, it is best to pour the batter for each cake with a ladle. After some experience, the batter is usually poured from a pitcher. One of the main problems in restaurants is leftover batter. If the remainder of the batter is held for the next day's breakfast, there is usually a loss of leavening power, and the batter may also evaporate somewhat. The best practice, when using a leftover batter, is to make a trial griddle cake beforehand. If it is thin or tough, the batter should be discarded. Attempts to modify the batter by adding milk, flour or leavening depend upon guesswork, and the results are often unsatisfactory.

Before starting work: Preheat griddle to 390°F for at least 10 min before making the first griddle cakes. Review 16 guides to cleaning and using the griddle.

(1) Assemble the following ingredients:

4 1/2 lb pastry flour

Note: If pastry flour is unavailable, use 1/2 bread flour and 1/2 cake flour.

5 oz baking powder

1 oz salt

6 oz sugar

12 eggs

3 qt milk

1 1/2 cups cooking oil

Oil for griddle

Note: Some breakfast cooks rub the griddle with larding pork or bacon skin instead of using oil.

(2) Preheat griddle to 390°F.

(3) Pour eggs into bowl of mixing machine.

(4) Beat eggs with wire whip at high speed for 3 min.

(5) Add milk and 1 1/2 cups oil. Beat at medium speed 1 min.

(6) In another bowl or container sift together pastry flour, baking powder, salt and sugar.

(7) Add dry ingredients to bowl of mixing machine.

(8) Beat at low speed only until dry ingredients are moistened. Small lumps in batter will be seen. Batter should not be mixed

smooth. Pour batter into pitchers with spouts. Keep in refrigerator until needed.

(9) Let batter rest 10 min before making griddle cakes.

(10) Brush griddle lightly with oil or rub with larding pork or bacon skin. Grease as much of the griddle as will be needed for the orders you are preparing.

(11) Using a No. 2 ladle (1/4 cup), dip batter from pitcher. Scrape excess batter from outside of ladle if necessary. Work as close to griddle as possible.

(12) Empty the ladle completely for each griddle cake onto griddle, allowing 1/2 in. space between cakes.

(13) When tops of griddle cakes are bubbly and rims dry-looking, turn cakes with spatula. Turn quickly but completely so that unbaked side of cake is in same position on griddle.

(14) When second side is brown, place griddle cakes in a stack on warm serving plates. A portion is usually 3 griddle cakes.

Note: A small scoopful of softened butter or whipped butter is sometimes placed on top of griddle cakes. Chips of butter or additional butter may be served at the table. Maple syrup is served at the table.

Whole Wheat Griddle Cakes.—Use 3 lb pastry flour and 1 1/2 lb whole wheat flour. (If whole wheat flour is coarse, it may not be possible to sieve it. Sieve other dry ingredients, and then mix whole wheat flour with them.)

Blueberry Griddle Cakes.—Add 1 qt raw small ripe blueberries to batter. Increase sugar to 12 oz.

Apple Griddle Cakes.—Add 1 qt finely chopped, peeled, cored raw apples or canned apples to batter. Increase sugar to 12 oz.

Waffles.—Modify recipe by using 24 eggs and 3 cups cooking oil. Bake on preheated waffle iron, following manufacturer's directions.

French Toast   **48 Slices**

What is called French toast in this country is known in France as *pain perdu*, meaning lost or wrecked bread, which is simply the French way of saying stale bread that may be rescued. The bread for French toast should be at least 2 days old so that it can hold its shape when cooked. French toast is bread dipped in a batter of eggs and milk, and then browned on a griddle or in a pan. (In some restaurants the bread is dipped in a cover batter and then deep fried.) Recipes for French toast vary widely. In those eating places where costs must be kept low, there is a minimum of eggs and a maximum of milk. In better restaurants the quantity of the eggs is increased while the milk is decreased. More attractive browning is obtained if French toast is cooked on a griddle rather than in a pan. The amount of the fat on the griddle is somewhat more than that for griddle cakes. The temperature of the griddle, however, should be high (375°F) for fast deep browning. Usual portions are 2 slices of bread per order.

Before starting work: The *garde manger* usually has 2- or 3-day-old white sliced or unsliced sandwich bread which he uses for making bread crumbs. Check with him to obtain bread for French toast. In some restaurants French toast is spread with softened butter just before it is taken to the dining room. If this is the custom in the kitchen where you are working, keep the softened butter on hand as well as the clarified butter used in the recipe.

(1) Assemble the following ingredients:
   48 slices 2-day-old white bread, 1/2 in. thick
   18 eggs
   1 teaspoon salt
   5 oz confectioners' sugar
   2 teaspoons vanilla extract
   2 teaspoons ground cinnamon
   1 pint milk
   Clarified butter (variable)
   Softened butter (variable)
(2) Preheat griddle to 375°F.
(3) Beat eggs in bowl of mixing machine, using wire whip, at medium speed. Beat until whites are no longer visible.
(4) Add salt, confectioners' sugar, vanilla and cinnamon.
(5) Beat at high speed 2 min.
(6) Add milk. Beat 1 min longer at medium speed.
(7) Strain batter through fine china cap into a bowl for dipping.
(8) Grease griddle generously (for the number of slices about to be prepared) with clarified butter.
(9) Dip bread into batter. Hold it only for a few seconds in batter. It will break apart if held too long.
(10) Place bread on griddle. Allow 1/2 in. space between slices.
(11) When bottom is browned (check its color by lifting it with a spatula), turn and brown second side.
(12) Place on warm serving plate. Brush with softened butter. Maple syrup, honey or jam is served at the table.

12

Sandwich Maker

Many of the cookbooks written in the past by professional chefs ignored the subject of sandwiches or gave it an insignificant amount of attention. The whole topic was considered of very minor importance in the field of haute cuisine. It is still a minor department in many kitchens, but in recent years an increasing number of hotel and club restaurants have been featuring sandwiches on their menus, responding to the present-day interest in a brief meal, quickly brought to the table and easily eaten. Sandwiches, in their preparation, range from a simple cold ham sandwich to a hot chicken sandwich with white wine gravy to an open-faced lobster salad sandwich. In busy coffee shops or counter restaurants there are sandwich makers who are also short order cooks or countermen. In large institutional restaurants sandwiches are sometimes made on an assembly line in which hundreds, sometimes thousands, of the same type of sandwich are produced for a single meal.

This chapter deals, however, with the sandwich maker in hotels and club restaurants who serves as assistant to the *garde manger*. As his assistant, the sandwich maker has access to all the cold meats, cheese, dressings, etc., in the *garde manger's* section which serve as fillings for an extensive variety of sandwiches. If meat for sandwiches is to be carved by hand, the *garde manger* may slice the meat or instruct the sandwich maker and supervise him in carving cold meat to order. If meat is to be sliced by machine, the *garde manger* will tell the sandwich maker how thick the slices are to be and how many ounces of meat to use per portion. If there is a special sandwich featured on a certain day such as tartare steak sandwich, and a large quantity of the chopped raw beef mixture is to be made before the meal, either the *garde manger* or the sandwich maker may prepare the chopped meat mixture beforehand. When orders are received, the sandwich maker shapes the meat for each portion, assembles and garnishes the sandwich on the serving plate. During his workday the sandwich maker may assist the *garde manger* in such jobs as peeling shrimp, dicing cooked meat, breading cutlets, etc. But well in advance of the lunch period, he assembles all the breads, sandwich fillings, garnishes, etc., necessary for the station at which he works with its refrigerated table, cutting board, automatic toaster, etc. In some kitchens the sandwich maker also has, as part of his station, a griddle, counter top stove and other equipment necessary for making hot sandwiches such as a western sandwich, hamburg sandwich, etc. In other kitchens hot sandwiches such as hot roast beef or hot corned beef are handled by the cooks behind the range. When certain hot foods are needed, such as fried oysters or grilled bacon for a club sandwich, he may fry the oysters or grill the bacon, or receive these hot foods made to order by other cooks. Although a sandwich maker need not have extensive experience in cooking, he must be a level-headed type of worker who carefully and patiently organizes his station each day so that materials and utensils are all within arm's reach. He must have an accurate memory and be able, during the rush period, to handle a stream of orders efficiently.

JOB SUMMARY

The sandwich maker (1) consults with *garde manger* on special sandwiches featured on a certain day; (2) consults with *garde manger* on all normal daily requirements for routine sandwich making, such as bread, butter, meats, cheese, dressings, etc.; (3) checks leftover sandwich fillings and uses them first or combines them with new batches; (4) fills refrigerated containers at work station and arranges all materials for sandwich making in an orderly way; (5) may mix own dressings such as Russian dressing or use dressings made by the *garde manger*; (6) prepares and refrigerates sandwich garnishes such as sliced tomato, sliced pickles, cole slaw, etc.; (7) fills small paper soufflé cups with sandwich garnishes; (8) prepares sandwich fillings such as chicken salad, tunafish salad, egg salad, etc.; (9) makes sandwiches in advance for quantity service or to order as requested by waiters; (10) assists *garde manger* during nonrush periods.

MANUAL PROCEDURES

He (1) slices bread by hand, with French knife or other knife, or by using automatic slicer; (2) unwraps and stacks sliced bread; (3) may fill bread dispenser; (4) may trim bread of crust, using French knife; (5) softens butter using mixing spoon or paddle, or mixing machine; (6) chops by hand or machine, or dices by hand, meat, poultry, seafood or vegetables; (7) mixes chopped meat, poultry or seafood and vegetables with mayonnaise or other salad dressings; (8) seasons salad fillings for sandwiches and chills them for serving; (9) slices, by machine or hand, cooked meats and poultry; (10) boils eggs; (11) chops or slices hard eggs; (12) peels tomatoes by blanching; (13) trims and slices tomatoes; (14) slices pickles; (15) makes toast in automatic toaster; (16) uses griddle or stove for frying bacon, ham, grilled sandwiches, eggs, etc.; (17) butters bread; (18) places filling of sliced meat, poultry or cheese, or salad mixtures on bread; (19) arranges fillings on bread by hand or with sandwich spreader; (20) places bread on top of fillings; (21) may trim crust of sandwich bread; (22) cuts and arranges sandwiches on plates; (23) garnishes sandwiches with lettuce, tomato, pickle, etc.; (24) fills paper soufflé cups with dressings and garnishes such as cole slaw; (25) during meal wipes equipment including cutting board, counter, utensils, etc.; (26) scrapes and wipes griddle during meal period; (27) after lunch cleans equipment by scrubbing or scraping; (28) cleans, by scouring, other equipment such as automatic meat slicing machine, storage pans, counter areas, etc.

EQUIPMENT AND UTENSILS

In his work he uses (1) French knives, paring knife, ham slicer, roast beef slicer; (2) spatulas, butter spreader, wide sandwich spreaders; (3) mixing spoons; (4) fork; (5) food chopper and food grinder; (6) meat slicer; (7) bread slicer; (8) automatic toaster; (9) sandwich assembly center with large cutting board; (10) refrigerated containers; (11) refrigerator; (12) bowls for fillings and garnishes; (13) scoops; (14) ladles; (15) counter stove; (16) griddle; (17) frying pans.

WORKING CONDITIONS AND HAZARDS

The sandwich maker (1) works at counter station with cold foods arranged for accessibility; (2) works at griddle and counter stove; (3) receives written or verbal orders for sandwiches which must be filled quickly in rotation; (4) is subject to cuts from French knife or carving knife; (5) is subject to cuts from meat slicer or food chopper; (6) may be exposed for long periods to heat and fumes of griddle or other counter equipment.

PLACE IN JOB ORGANIZATION

The sandwich maker may be promoted from dishwasher, pot-washer, counterman or kitchen porter. He may be promoted to *garde manger's* assistant, to *garde manger* or to fry cook.

25 GUIDES TO SANDWICH MAKING

(1) As an apprentice or student in the sandwich section, it is important to keep a written list of all the standard foods and garnishes needed for what the French call *mise en place* or those ingredients prepared in advance of the meal so that, when orders arrive, there will be no delay caused by slicing tomatoes, softening butter, etc. The list will vary from one restaurant to another and should be checked each morning.

(2) Preparation of sliced meats, poultry and cheese as well as sandwich fillings should always be planned for a single day's supply and no more. Meats infrequently used, such as tongue or Smithfield ham, should be carved to order.

(3) Use leftover sandwich fillings first whenever possible. This means extremely careful checking to avoid ingredients with slight or incipient off-odors or off-flavors, or foods that are beginning to stale and have poor texture. Do not mix old and new batches unless you check first with your instructor or supervisor.

(4) Make sure that you understand waiters' orders precisely. Ask them to repeat orders if necessary. In the noise of a busy kitchen, it is easy to misunderstand specific requests for special sandwich preparation.

(5) If you are operating mechanical equipment such as meat or bread slicers, food mixers, etc., be sure you thoroughly know how to start, regulate and clean the equipment.

(6) When using sliced wrapped bread, keep the wrappers on as long as possible, and stack the bread so that slices are exposed to the air as briefly as possible. Break the packages in the center, leaving the paper on, making two stacks so that you can use both hands in reaching for two slices at a time.

(7) If bread is stored in a cabinet at room temperature, be sure the cabinet is clean and well ventilated.

(8) If firmer bread is required, store it in the refrigerator for a day before using it for sandwiches. Bread stales more rapidly in the refrigerator than at room temperature.

(9) Since bread picks up odors of other foods, it is very important

to wash the cutting board well and scrape it, particularly if it has been used for chopping or cutting other foods such as onions. It should also be dried very well before it is used for sandwich making.

(10) During the lunch period wipe the board frequently of all trimmings, and deposit the trimmings in a receptacle nearby.

(11) Keep your French knives sharp and frequently honed. Bread is a soft food, but frequent cutting or timming soon causes the knife edge to become dull.

(12) To make butter sufficiently soft or plastic so that it can be spread easily, it must be worked or creamed beforehand. After creaming, it should be kept in one of the open refrigerated containers at the sandwich station. This is particularly important in very hot weather or in conditions where the butter is likely to melt.

(13) In many sandwich shops, only one slice of the bread is buttered. In finer kitchens both slices are buttered, not only to make the sandwich more moist and rich, but to make the bread adhere to the filling and to keep the bread from becoming soggy when moist fillings are used.

(14) Good bread has a fine smooth texture, firm enough to be buttered without tearing, and moist but not heavy when fresh. Any departure from these norms should be called to the attention of your instructor or supervisor.

(15) When spreading butter, be sure to cover the complete slice to the edges and four corners. Use a continuous sweeping motion with the butter spreader rather than a number of short strokes.

(16) It is the modern practice to use thinly sliced meats rather than thicker slices or a single slab of meat in a sandwich. Thinner slices make the meat more tender, and the sandwich seems more sumptuous.

(17) When placing a meat filling on sandwiches, arrange the meat so that it covers all the bread but does not protrude beyond the margin of the bread. (In some delicatessen sandwich shops, the meat is deliberately placed so that it extends beyond the crust of the bread to given an impression of overflowing abundance.)

(18) In some restaurants it is the practice to fold slices of meat and pile it higher in the center of the sandwich than at the sides. When the sandwich is cut, the high center creates greater eye appeal.

(19) When placing moist filling such as shrimp salad or egg salad on a sandwich, use a scoop measure to control portions.

(20) After placing a scoop filling in the center of a slice of bread, spread the mixture in two directions so that the bread is completely covered. It may be spread so that it is somewhat higher in the center than at the sides.

(21) Lettuce for sandwiches should be crisp, trimmed, washed and well dried.

(22) All materials at the sandwich station should be arranged so various methods of arranging them on the plate are shown in Figs. wiches. The same ingredients should be in the same container position each day.

(23) Keep a long spoon, such as an iced tea spoon, for reaching garnishes in jars such as olives, pickles, etc.

(24) In most restaurants the crust of the bread remains on the sandwich. There are some kitchens, however, in which it is the practice to cut off the crust. When the crust is removed, be sure to use a very sharp French knife so that the crust can be trimmed closely without tearing the bread or disturbing the filling.

(25) Sandwiches are usually cut diagonally before they are placed on the serving plate. There are many other ways of cutting sandwiches for attractive service. Nine ways of cutting sandwiches and various methods of arranging them on the plate are shown in Figs. 12.1 and 12.2.

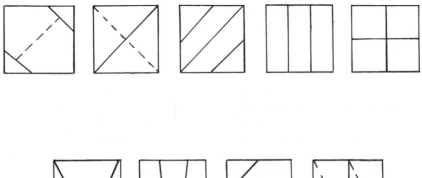

Courtesy American Institute of Baking

FIG. 12.1. CUTTING SANDWICHES

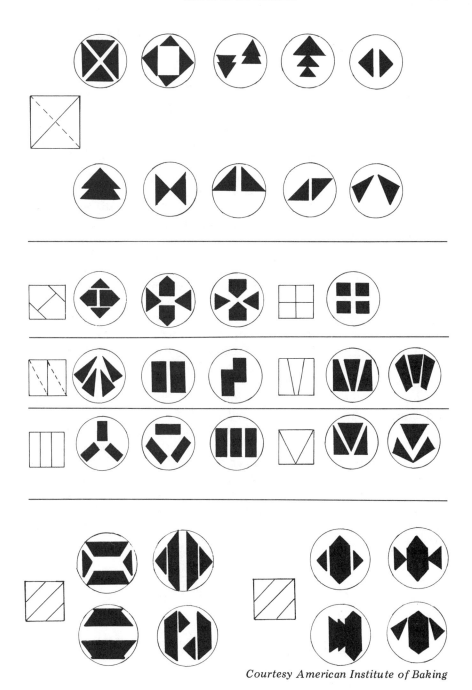

FIG. 12.2. ARRANGEMENT OF SANDWICHES

Chicken Salad Sandwich   12 Portions, Each Sandwich
                                                2 Oz Diced Chicken

The menu price of a sandwich filled with a salad mixture depends
on both the kind and amount of filling. In many sandwich shops,
chicken salad for sandwiches is made with any part of cooked poultry, often including skin, gizzards, and other parts as long as they are
edible. The meat is often put through a meat grinder and in consistency may be closer to a puree than a salad. As long as the fowl is
wholesome and it meets the cost requirements of a particular eating
place, there is nothing wrong with this procedure. But in a restaurant
where standards are expected to be high, and where the ambience,
service and other features mean higher menu prices, a sandwich such
as chicken salad should be prepared with a different end product in
mind. The chicken should be boiled fowl rather than chicken or
turkey roll. If turkey is used, it should be listed on the menu as turkey salad sandwich. There should be no skin, gizzard or heart in the
mixture. The chicken should be cut into small dice, 1/4 in. or less,
rather than chopped. The amount of mayonnaise should be such that
the filling is of medium thick consistency and does not cause the
bread to become soggy. Finally, the amount of salad per sandwich, as
indicated below, should be equal to a No. 10 scoop, which is to say
10 portions to a quart of filling.

Before starting work: Arrange your work schedule so that the skin
and bone of the fowl are removed just before the meat is cut into
dice. If the skin is removed the day before, the meat may become
dry. The meat of the fowl, however, should not be wet when it is
added to the salad. If the fowl have been immersed in chicken broth,
dry them before cutting to keep the salad mixture from becoming
soggy. When cutting the dark meat of the fowl, be sure to remove
all fat and any dark veins. Because of the moist nature of the filling,
day-old white bread is preferred for this type of sandwich; set aside
the bread the day before.

(1) Assemble the following ingredients:
    24 oz (weight after trimming) boiled fowl, white and dark
        meat, cut into dice no larger than 1/4 in.
    6 oz celery, chopped fine
    1 cup mayonnaise
    2 tablespoons lemon juice
    1 teaspoon Worcestershire sauce
    2 teaspoons Dijon mustard
    Salt, pepper
    Softened butter
    24 slices day-old bread

12 medium size leaves of Boston lettuce
1 bunch watercress, washed and dried
12 large stuffed olives

(2) In mixing bowl combine mayonnaise, lemon juice, Worcestershire sauce and Dijon mustard. Mix well with wire whip until completely blended.
(3) Add chicken and celery.
(4) Sprinkle with salt and pepper.
(5) Mix well with wooden spoon. Correct seasoning if necessary. Chill mixture at once.
For each sandwich:
(6) Place 2 slices of bread on work board.
(7) Butter both slices of bread, spreading butter to edge of slice.
(8) Place a No. 10 scoop of salad on 1 slice of bread.
(9) Using wide sandwich spreader, spread filling to edge of bread. If sandwich is to be cut diagonally, the filling may be left somewhat higher in the center than at the edge; otherwise the filling should be spread evenly.
(10) Place second slice of bread on top.
(11) Cut sandwich diagonally or follow any of the suggested ways of cutting on p 368.
(12) Place sandwich on plate, following any of the suggested patterns on p 369.
(13) On each plate place a leaf of Boston lettuce alongside sandwich. Fill the lettuce with watercress and a stuffed olive.

Ham or Tongue Salad Sandwich.—Substitute cooked smoked ham or cooked smoked beef tongue in place of chicken. Use 4 teaspoons Dijon mustard instead of 2. Sliced pickle may be used as a garnish in place of watercress and olive.

Tunafish Salad Sandwich.—Substitute drained canned tunafish for chicken. Tunafish should be chopped rather than diced, but should not be chopped to the puree stage. Omit mustard. One tablespoon grated onion or one tablespoon very finely chopped fresh chives may be added. Sliced tomato, pickle or both may be used as garnish.

Egg Salad Sandwich.—Substitute 12 hard-boiled eggs for chicken. Omit celery. Increase mustard to 4 teaspoons.

Crab Meat, Lobster or Shrimp Salad Sandwich.—Substitute fresh crab lump, boiled diced lobster meat or boiled, diced, peeled and deveined shrimp in place of chicken. Examine crab lump very carefully to make sure there are no pieces of shell. Lobster roe and tomalley may be included with lobster meat. Imported tiny shrimp may be used in place of diced shrimp. Add 2 tablespoons very finely chopped parsley to recipe. Season with salt, celery salt and pepper.

Western Sandwich   **12 Portions, Each Sandwich**
                                        1 Egg, 1 Oz Ham

The western sandwich is served hot and cannot satisfactorily be made in advance. The filling is a mixture of eggs, onions, sweet peppers and ham made into a flat omelet. The sandwich maker must have enough pans to make several orders at a time if necessary. The pans must be seasoned so that food does not stick to them. Special care must be taken to see that the omelet filling is neither too soft nor overdone. In some restaurants a griddle may be used in place of pans. The common "hash house" way of making a western omelet or sandwich is to beat together the egg, chopped raw onion, chopped raw pepper and ham. A much better omelet is produced if the onion and sweet pepper are lightly sautéd before they are added to the eggs, eliminating their raw flavor but still keeping their crispness. When a flat omelet is removed from a pan, the question is how to fit a round omelet on a square slice of bread. The usual technique is to fold the omelet so that it reasonably fits the bread or to cut the omelet into two or three pieces and fit them on the bread.

Before starting work: Choose pans with a bottom diameter no larger than 6 in. Check pans to make sure they are properly seasoned. If a griddle is to be used, scrape it well, particularly if it has been used for hamburgers or other meat items. Keep a cereal dish or small bowl available for beating the egg. Keep the opened salt box nearby for dipping the tines of the fork when seasoning the beaten eggs.

(1) Assemble the following ingredients
   24 slices bread
   12 eggs
   5 oz onion, very small dice
   5 oz sweet green pepper, very small dice
   3/4 lb cooked ham, very small dice
   1 tablespoon parsley, chopped extremely fine
   Salt, pepper
   Softened butter
(2) Melt 2 tablespoons butter in sauté pan. Do not let butter brown.
(3) Add onion and green pepper.

(4) Sauté, stirring almost constantly, until vegetables begin to wilt but are still slightly crisp. Sprinkle with salt and pepper.

(5) Turn vegetables into bowl. Add ham and parsley. Mix well. Set aside within reach.

For each sandwich:

(6) Melt approx 2 teaspoons butter in pan.

(7) While butter is melting, open an egg into a cereal dish or small bowl. Add 1/4 cup (2 oz) ladle of ham mixture. Beat briefly with fork. Dip tines of fork into salt box. Quickly beat egg mixture until yolk and white are blended.

(8) Turn pan so that bottom and part of side are coated with butter.

(9) Add egg mixture.

(10) Stir with fork bottom to distribute ingredients evenly. Sauté until well set on bottom.

(11) Butter 2 slices of bread.

(12) When eggs are set on bottom, flip omelet or turn with spatula to cook second side. Avoid overcooking. Eggs should not be deeply browned.

(13) Turn omelet onto 1 slice of bread. Fold or cut omelet if necessary to fit bread.

(14) Place second slice of bread on top.

(15) Cut sandwich diagonally. Place on serving plate, cut sides out.

Note: Western sandwich may be served ungarnished or may be garnished with sliced tomato and/or dill pickle.

Grilled Reuben Sandwich　　　　12 Portions, Each Sandwich 2 Oz Corned Beef, 1 Oz Swiss Cheese

For the past several decades the Reuben sandwich has grown increasingly popular all over the United States. It may be grilled, as in the recipe below, or not. A grilled sandwich is one that is buttered on the outside and placed on a griddle until it is lightly browned. If there is cheese in the sandwich, the cheese will soften somewhat. After grilling, the components of the sandwich are warm rather than hot. The filling for a Reuben sandwich consists of sliced corned beef, sliced Swiss cheese and sauerkraut. The quality of the ingredients (over which the sandwich maker may have no control) gives the sandwich its distinction. The meat should be prime corned brisket of beef freshly cooked and sliced very thin. This is an instance in which machine slicing is superior to hand carving. The sauerkraut should be the fresh type sold in kegs or barrels rather than the canned. The cheese should be imported Swiss Emmentaler thinly sliced by machine. The bread may be either sour rye or pumpernickel. When rye or pumpernickel bread is grilled, it tends to become hard if left too long on the griddle. It should be grilled only until very lightly browned. Since the pumpernickel is brown to start with, the color change is minimal. In any event the sandwich should not be kept on the grill so long that the cold sauerkraut becomes steamy or the cheese oozes out of the sides of the bread.

Before starting work: Preheat the griddle to 350° F. Make sure the griddle is clean; scrape it if necessary. Check with instructor or supervisor on gauge setting for thickness of meat slices. Before making sandwiches use portion control scale to estimate amount of corned beef, cheese and sauerkraut for each sandwich.

(1) Assemble the following ingredients:
   24 slices round sour rye or pumperknickel bread
   1 1/2 cups Russian dressing
   1 1/2 lb very thinly sliced corned beef brisket
   12 oz thinly sliced Swiss cheese
   1 1/4 lb sauerkraut, well drained
   4 oz onion, chopped extremely fine
   2 tablespoons parsley, chopped extremely fine
   Softened butter
   Note: Clarified butter or melted shortening may be used in place of softened butter.
   12 medium or small dill pickles, either regular or half-sour
(2) In mixing bowl combine sauerkraut, onion and parsley, tossing well.
   For each sandwich:
(3) Place 2 slices of bread on work board.
(4) Spread each slice with Russian dressing.
(5) Place 2 oz corned beef on 1 slice of bread. Fold corned beef if necessary so that it is within the margin of the bread.
(6) Place 1 oz Swiss cheese on corned beef.
(7) Place 2 oz sauerkraut mixture on top of Swiss cheese, spreading it evenly but not allowing it to extend beyond the bread.
(8) Place second slice of bread on top to make sandwich.
(9) Brush griddle with softened or clarified butter, using only enough to brown 1 sandwich.
(10) Using a wide long spatula, quickly place sandwich on griddle before butter browns. Use left hand to keep sandwich intact when transferring to griddle.
(11) Spread top slice of bread with butter.

(12) When bottom of sandwich is lightly browned (the color of pumpernickel will simply deepen rather than become noticeably brown), turn it and brown second side.

(13) Serve at once on warm plates. Sandwich may be cut diagonally or left whole.

(14) Garnish will dill pickle or half-sour dill pickle.

Open Shrimp Salad and	12 Portions, Each Sandwich
Sliced Egg Sandwich	2 Oz Shrimp, 1 Egg

The neatness and appetizing arrangement of any sandwich is important. Obviously it becomes exceptionally important in assembling a cold open-faced sandwich. The recipe below is an example of how the sandwich maker avails himself of the *garde manger's* experience in garnishing a sandwich in order to enhance its eye appeal. The sliced egg, arranged in overlapping rows, is topped with a sprig of watercress and pimiento. The shrimp salad on the second slice of bread is decorated with an S-shaped slice of fluted cucumber. At a hectic lunchtime sandwich counter this kind of careful attention to detail is usually impractical, but in a fine dining room where menu prices allow higher standards, it is the type of sandwich patrons may expect. An open-faced sandwich is eaten with knife and fork, and the portion is larger than that of most closed sandwiches. In preparing the shrimp salad either the normal size domestic shrimp or the tiny imported shrimp may be used. The ingredients of the sandwich are made before the meal period, but each sandwich should be assembled individually to order.

Before starting work: Both the shrimp and the hard egg should be boiled either the day before or at least three hours in advance for proper chilling. Consult with the *garde manger* on the procedure for preparing the cucumber and watercress garnishes. Check also to see if there are any leftover shrimp or hard eggs which may be used.

(1) Assemble the following ingredients:

24 slices of bread

Note: As in all cold sandwiches white, rye, whole wheat or toast may be ordered. Make sure the waiter specifies the bread in an open sandwich.

3 lb raw shrimp, boiled, peeled and deveined (equal to 1 1/2 lb shrimp, edible portion), very small dice

Note: If imported tiny shrimp, boiled and peeled, are being used, they should be left whole. If regular size shrimp are used, make sure they are well drained and dried before cut-

ting. Cut shrimp horizontally into 3 or 4 slices; cut into thin
long strips; cut strips crosswise to make very small dice.
1/2 lb celery, peeled and finely chopped
Salt, celery salt, pepper
2 teaspoons prepared horseradish
1/2 teaspoon Worcestershire sauce
1 tablespoon lemon juice
6 dashes Tabasco sauce
3/4 cup mayonnaise
1 large cucumber
12 hard-boiled eggs, peeled
1 bunch watercress
24 strips pimiento, 2 1/2 – 3 in. long, 1/4 in. wide
Softened butter

(2) Place shrimp in mixing bowl.
(3) Add celery. Sprinkle with salt, celery salt and pepper. Toss
well.
(4) In another small bowl combine mayonnaise, horseradish, Worcestershire sauce, lemon juice and Tabasco sauce. Mix well.
(5) Add mayonnaise mixture to shrimp. Mix well. Correct seasoning if desired.
(6) Place shrimp salad in container and refrigerate until needed.
(7) Wash cucumber and dry. Do not peel.
(8) Using a lemon peel cutter, cut lengthwise incisions 1/4 in.
apart so that the rind is fluted.
(9) Cut 12 slices of cucumber, 1/16 in. thick.
(10) Cut each slice about 3/4 of the way through. Twist cucumber
so that the rind forms an S-shape. Set slices aside and refrigerate.
(11) Cut from 1 – 1 1/2 in. off stem of watercress. Wash watercress.
Drain well. Pat dry with paper toweling. Keep refrigerated.
For each sandwich:
(12) Spread 2 slices of bread with butter. Cut crust off bread if this
is the practice in the restaurant where you work.
(13) Place a No. 10 scoop of shrimp salad on 1 slice of bread. Very
carefully spread salad so that bread is evenly covered.
(14) Carefully place a slice of cucumber on top of salad.
(15) Cut a hard-boiled egg with hard egg slicer; use the type which
cuts the egg into thin rather than a few thick slices.
(16) On second slice of bread arrange overlapping slices of egg,
covering bread completely, keeping yolk and white intact in
each slice.

(17) Take 3 or 4 pieces of watercress and wrap 2 pimiento strips around them.

(18) Place the watercress garnish on the center of the sliced eggs.

(19) Using a large spatula, place each piece of bread on serving plate, being careful not to disturb garnishes.

Hero Sandwiches, Italian Style   12 Portions, Each Sandwich
2 1/2 Oz Meat, 1/2 Oz Cheese

The word hero applies to any sandwich served on long French or Italian bread. The filling can be anything served in a cold or hot sandwich from simple ham or cheese to veal cutlet parmigiana. One of the oldest and still most popular versions is a sandwich made from an assortment of four to six kinds of meat and cheese, garnished with tomatoes and peppers and seasoned with oil and vinegar. Instead of simply using a single type of filling between slices of bread, the maker of an Italian hero sandwich must have a large variety of foods and seasonings ready for rapid service. He must assemble them quickly and be prepared to make changes and deletions if necessary. The sandwich is called Italian style because it features either imported Italian products or products identified with Italian kitchens, such as Genoa salami, provolone cheese, olive oil and oregano. If the sandwich is featured on the menu for a particular day, the sandwich maker should keep all of the ingredients for the filling in one section of his sandwich counter so that they are easily reached. The bread should be a crusty long loaf, wide enough to accommodate the sliced meats, and with enough body so that it does not become soggy with oil and vinegar. If the bread is limp when received from the baker, it may be placed in a moderate oven for five to ten minutes to crisp the crust. Special care should be taken, however, not to char the bread. Sometimes hero rolls are used. Either bread or rolls should be sliced just before the sandwich is made.

Before starting work: Carefully check the recipe so that all ingredients can be assembled in one section of the sandwich counter. The quantity of meat per sandwich is indicated in the recipe. Before mealtime, using the portion control scale, make up a sample portion of filling so that you will be familiar with the amounts and kinds of meats. Sizes of salami may vary from 1 to 4 in. in diameter. A trial run beforehand will enable you to plan the routine more efficiently.

(1) Assemble the following ingredients:

3 loaves long French or Italian bread, each 18 - 20 in. long, 3 - 3 1/2 in. wide.

Note: If loaves are not this size, select equivalent amount of bread necessary.

6 oz zampino (boiled) salami, sliced very thin
6 oz hard Genoa salami, sliced very thin
6 oz prosciutto ham, sliced paper thin
12 oz mortadella bologna, sliced very thin
6 oz provolone cheese, sliced very thin
24 thin slices tomato
6 oz prepared roasted sweet red peppers
24 thin slices onion (optional)
Cruet of olive oil
Cruet of red wine vinegar
Oregano
Dried flaked hot red pepper (optional)

Note: Onion and flaked hot pepper are only used if ordered by customer.

For each sandwich:

(2) Cut a portion of bread approx 4 1/2-5 in. long.
(3) Slice bread in half horizontally.
(4) On bottom half place 1/2 oz zampino salami, 1/2 oz Genoa salami, 1/2 oz prosciutto ham, 1 oz mortadella bologna and 1/2 oz provolone cheese.
(5) Arrange meats and cheese so that slices are evenly distributed and cover bread completely.
(6) Place 2 slices tomato on top.
(7) Cut 1/2 oz roasted sweet pepper into 3 strips; place diagonally on top of tomato.
(8) Rub about 1/4 teaspoon oregano between thumb and forefinger, letting it fall over sandwich filling.
(9) Sprinkle with hot flaked pepper if ordered.
(10) Place 2 slices onion on top if ordered.
(11) Generously sprinkle inside of top slice of bread with oil and vinegar and place top slice over sandwich filling.

Tartare Steak Sandwich   **12 Portions, Each Sandwich**
8 Oz Beef

The word steak means a thick cut of a food, such as beefsteak, lamb steak, salmon steak, etc. Tartare steak, however, is made from finely chopped beef. At one time only the best steaks such as shell steak or filet mignon were used for the dish. The meat is served raw but is seasoned in such a manner that the completed dish is a stimulating, savory mixture with more flavor than many cooked dishes. At one time the meat was literally chopped. When an order was received in the kitchen, the *garde manger* would trim the excess fat from a boneless shell steak and chop the meat with a cleaver or heavy French knife until he had a portion of chopped beefsteak. Nowadays the meat is put through a meat grinder in most restaurants. The meat, however, should be taken from well-marbled beef using either short loin, including the flank, or short hip. Because top quality cuts are used in making it, its menu price is usually high; therefore, careful preparation is essential. The meat should not be ground long in advance of the meal period. In some eating places it is always ground to order. After grinding, the meat is seasoned with egg yolks, salt and pepper and is shaped into a steak from 1/2 to 3/4 in. thick. It is placed on bread and surrounded by the seasonings which the customer or waiter mixes with the meat at the table. Additional bottled seasonings, such as Worcestershire sauce, A-1 sauce, sauce *diable*, sauce *Robert*, etc., are offered to the customer at the table.

Before starting work: Check the meat grinder to make sure it is completely clean; disassemble and wash it if in doubt. Do not use any meat which is sticky, slimy or has an off-odor. If meat is to be ground to order—as is the practice in some restaurants—plan the job with the butcher or *garde manger* so that the meat grinder will be available when needed. There will be leftover egg whites. Turn them over to the soup cook or pastry cook.

(1) Assemble the following ingredients:
      6 lb (trimmed weight) beef shell or sirloin (short hip), completely trimmed of all outside fat and gristle
      2 tablespoons salt
      2 teaspoons freshly ground whole black pepper
      15 eggs
      12 large slices round rye or pumpernickel bread
      Softened butter
      1/2 lb onion, chopped extremely fine
      3/4 cup small capers in vinegar, drained
      1/4 cup parsley, chopped extremely fine
      3/4 cup freshly grated raw horseradish
      36 small leaves Boston lettuce
(2) Cut meat into 1-in. cubes or smaller.
(3) Put meat through grinder using fine blade.
(4) Spread meat out in large bowl or pan separating meat with finger tips.
(5) Separate yolks and whites of 3 eggs. Beat yolks well.
(6) Add salt and pepper to beaten egg yolks, mixing well.
(7) Pour egg yolk mixture over beef. Toss lightly to blend ingre-

dients. Do not squeeze meat or mixture may become too compact.

For each sandwich:

(8) Butter a slice of bread, using rye or pumpernickel. Place it on cold dinner plate or platter.

(9) Lightly shape 1/2 lb meat into a ball. Press ball with palm of hand to flatten into cake 1/2 to 3/4 in. thick. Smooth edge and top of steak with spatula.

(10) Place meat on bread and smooth rim of meat.

(11) With spoon, make an indentation in center of meat to hold egg yolk.

(12) Open egg, separating white and yolk. Place yolk in center of steak. Add white to whites previously separated.

(13) Sprinkle top of meat and egg yolk with parsley.

(14) Place 3 leaves of lettuce around steak. Make sure leaves are small.

(15) Fill first leaf with 1 tablespoon horseradish.

(16) Fill second leaf with 1 tablespoon drained capers.

(17) Fill third leaf with 2 tablespoons chopped onion.

Club Sandwich **12 Portions, Each Sandwich 2 Oz Sliced Chicken, 2 Slices Bacon**

There are many versions of the club sandwich, but the most traditional one is a sandwich of sliced chicken or turkey, bacon, lettuce, tomato and mayonnaise. Although, following kitchen tradition, hot and cold foods are not frequently mixed on the same plate, the club sandwich defies this unwritten law by including cold chicken, cold lettuce, cold tomato and cold mayonnaise with hot crisp bacon and hot toast. Modern practice in most restaurants has replaced sliced chicken with sliced turkey. The sandwich may be assembled, as in the recipe below, with two or three slices of toast per sandwich. Whether the toast is hot when it reaches the customer depends upon the alertness and cooperation of both the waiter and the sandwich maker. Employees should be aware that the longer toast stands after it is made and before it reaches the table, the soggier and more unappetizing it becomes. Bacon, too, is another food of optimum quality the moment it is taken off the fire; the more it approaches room temperature, the less appetizing it becomes. The sandwich maker, therefore, should be especially attentive when club sandwiches are made, and should see that they are served as quickly as possible. Bacon which is partially cooked beforehand is made crisp by finishfing it (a) on the griddle (b) under the broiler or (c) in hot deep fat.

Before starting work: Does the toaster need adjusting so that the bread will be medium brown? Club sandwiches are best served on warm plates. Plan to get the plates from the plate warmer or have the waiter bring them to you just before the sandwiches are ready to be picked up. Make sure that your knife is extremely sharp for cutting the tomatoes.

(1) Assemble the following ingredients:

24 slices white bread

1 1/2 lb thinly sliced boiled fowl or turkey, white meat, trimmed of all skin, gristle or fat

12 large leaves of lettuce, washed and dried

36 thin slices tomato

24 slices bacon, partially cooked, not crisp

Softened butter

> *Note*: Quantities of softened butter and mayonnaise are not indicated in sandwich recipes, since this is a standard item at the sandwich counter; the amount of softened butter to prepare depends upon the total sandwich business anticipated for the meal.

Mayonnaise

Salt, pepper

For each sandwich:

(2) Heat 2 slices bacon to finish to crisp stage.

(3) Place 2 slices bread in toaster.

(4) When bread is toasted, place slices on cutting board.

(5) Spread one slice with butter, coating bread completely to edge.

(6) Spread second slice with mayonnaise, coating bread completely to edge.

(7) Cover buttered slice of bread with 2 oz sliced boiled fowl or turkey, arranging slices so that bread is completely covered. There should be no pieces of fowl or turkey extending beyond margin of bread.

(8) Sprinkle sliced fowl with salt and pepper.

(9) Place 2 slices crisp bacon diagonally on chicken. Fold or cut bacon if necessary to fit within margin of bread.

(10) Place 3 slices of tomato on bacon.

(11) Top bacon with a lettuce leaf.

(12) Place second slice of bread on top.

(13) If crusts are to be trimmed, cut edges of bread neatly with sharp heavy French knife. (If several sandwiches are being prepared, do not stack sandwiches and cut crusts, or filling may become disarranged.)

(14) Cut sandwich diagonally.

(15) Place sandwich on serving plate. Plate is sometimes lined with doily to keep sandwich from sliding. Arrange sandwich so that cut sides of sandwich face outward.

Note: In most restaurants club sandwiches are served ungarnished. If sliced pickle is used as an accompaniment, cut a medium size dill pickle into fan-shaped slices, and place it on a small leaf of Boston lettuce.

Cold Sliced Ham and	50 Portions Each Sandwich
Swiss Cheese Sandwich	2 Ozs Ham, 1 Oz Cheese

If a student were to make 50 sandwiches, such as ham and Swiss cheese, one by one in the normal way, the time and effort expended would be maximum. As a matter of daily routine the sandwich maker doesn't suddenly receive 50 orders for the same kind of sandwich. But if a large number are needed for a meeting, a card party or any similar event, and the order is placed in advance, the sandwiches are prepared in the manner described below. All the components of the sandwich—the bread, butter and sandwich filling—are arranged in a definite work pattern, with the bread in parallel lines on a large work surface (not necessarily the sandwich station). All ingredients and utensils are within arm's reach just as they are at a sandwich station. When sandwiches are made in quantity in this manner, both pieces of bread are buttered so that the bread adheres to the filling. There is always an interval between the time the sandwiches are made and the time they are served. The completed sandwiches, kept in the refrigerator, should be well covered to prevent drying. In setting up the special work lines for a job like this (assuming you are using a work table 30 in. from front to rear), first place the stacks of bread at the rear of the table. Place the sliced cheese and ham in front of the bread, and alongside the ham and cheese place the softened butter and butter spreader. Directly in front of you place four rows of bread, with six slices in each row. This arrangement will enable you to make the sandwiches in batches of 12 each.

Before starting work: If you are using a special table to assemble sandwiches, be sure that it is well scrubbed, scraped with a dough cutter and dried. Bread is not a common cause of food contamination, but sandwiches are. Make sure the containers holding the meat, cheese and butter are well cleaned before they are filled. Check with your instructor or supervisor on the thickness of the ham and cheese slices. Use a portion control scale to determine and verify the amount of filling for sandwiches. Before slicing the ham, trim it of any fat in excess of 1/8 in. If possible, slice whole pieces of ham and cheese with diameters which allow slices to be placed within the margin of the bread.

(1) Assemble the following ingredients:

6 1/2 lb thinly sliced boiled, baked or canned ham
3 1/4 lb thinly sliced Swiss cheese
2 lb (variable) softened butter
100 slices white bread or other bread if ordered
50 large lettuce leaves, washed and dried (optional)
Dill pickles (optional).

Note: If individual dill pickles are to be served with sandwiches, drain and cut them, starting about 1/4 in. from stem end, into parallel slices 1/8 in. thick.

(2) Arrange 4 rows of bread, six slices each, from left to right. When placing bread on work surface, arrange it so that top slices of 1 row, when turned over for closing sandwiches, will match top slices of next row.

(3) Butter each slice of bread using large butter spreader. Move spreader from one corner of bread to another, so that bread is evenly covered with as few strokes as possible.

(4) Place 2 oz ham on bread in alternate rows. Keep meat within edge of bread.

(5) On top of ham, place 1 oz Swiss cheese, keeping cheese within edge of bread.

(6) Place lettuce, if used, on top of Swiss cheese. Lettuce should not extend beyond bread.

(7) Turn buttered slices of bread without the filling over the filled slices so that crusts of bread match.

(8) Place 3 completed sandwiches in a stack on cutting board.

(9) Using the left hand, hold stack with thumb and first finger, forming an arch.

(10) Using sharp French knife, cut sandwiches diagonally.

(11) Transfer cut sandwiches to hotel pan, 12 × 20 in.

(12) Continue to cut and stack sandwiches in this manner.

(13) Again place bread on table in rows, as above, and continue to make sandwiches in this manner until 50 sandwiches are completed.

(14) Cover sandwiches with plastic wrap. On top of plastic wrap place a large moistened towel or cloth to completely cover sandwiches so there is no exposure to air.

Note: An alternate method of covering sandwiches is to fit each pan into a large plastic bag and tie the end of the bag.

(15) Keep sandwiches refrigerated until serving time.

(16) For serving at parties, arrange sandwiches, cut side out, on large serving platters.

(17) Place dill pickles, if used, in separate tray or serving dish at serving table. Provide mustard at serving table or dining tables.

Grilled Cheese Sandwich 50 Portions

In turning out 50 grilled cheese sandwiches for rapid service within a short time, the sandwich maker assembles 50 cold sandwiches beforehand. If the sandwiches are to be speedily assembled, properly grilled and stored for service, the sandwich maker must give this job his total attention. If other sandwiches are ordered at the same time, a co-worker usually handles them. A grilled cheese sandwich should have the light shape of fresh toast rather than the heavy sunken appearance of soggy bread. It should be uniformly brown, and the cheese, while soft, should not ooze out of the sides of the sandwich. To assemble the sandwiches, there must be a large untrammeled table or work area. Cheese should be at room temperature for slicing. After the cold sandwiches are made up, they may be returned to the refrigerator. If the cheese is cold when the sandwiches are placed on the griddle, there is less likelihood of the cheese melting excessively. Sometimes one or two large griddles will be used. Although griddles are thermostatically controlled, the heat distribution is not always uniform; one part of the griddle may be hotter than another and brown the sandwiches faster. The sandwich maker should anticipate this possibility and check the bottom browning by lifting and examining sandwiches from time to time.

Before starting work: In some kitchens where late breakfasts are served, the breakfast cook may still be using the griddle when you need it. Arrange beforehand so that it is free in time. Be sure the griddle is scraped clean and the surface rubbed with a griddle stone if necessary. Remove the cheese from the refrigerator two hours before it is to be sliced. Set the gauge on the slicer so that slices are one oz when tested on the portion control scale.

(1) Assemble the following ingredients:

50 1 1/2-oz slices Cheddar cheese

Note: You will need 4 lb 11 oz cheese. For best handling on the slicer, 5-lb blocks are generally used. Remainder of the block is to be returned to the refrigerator.

100 slices white bread

1 1/2 lb, approx 3 cups, clarified butter, melted margarine or melted shortening

(2) Place 24 slices of bread on a sheet pan.

(3) Place a slice of cheese on each slice of bread; under no circumstances should cheese extend beyond crust of bread.

(4) Top cheese with 2 slices of bread.

(5) Again place a slice of cheese on each slice of bread.

(6) Place a slice of bread on each slice of cheese.

(7) The tray now holds 48 sandwiches. Make 2 additional sandwiches and place them on top.

(8) If sandwiches are not to be made at once, cover them with plastic wrap or wax paper. Cover the wrap with a large moistened cloth or 2 towels if necessary. Bring the cloth around and underneath the pan so that the bread is well sealed against exposure to air. As an alternative method of cover, the entire tray may be placed in a large plastic bag tied at the end.

(9) Store sandwiches in the refrigerator until needed.

(10) At least 15 min before sandwiches are to be made, preheat griddle to 350° F.

(11) Brush the griddle completely with butter.

(12) Using a large spatula place sandwiches in a single layer 2 at a time on griddle.

(13) Brush tops of sandwiches with butter.

(14) When sandwiches are medium brown on bottom (lift several sandwiches in different spots of the griddle to check color), turn sandwiches and brown second side.

(15) Place sandwiches in stacks of 3 and cut in half diagonally.

(16) Place sandwiches in steam table pans. Keep hot in food holding unit set at 140° F or in steam table.

(17) Make balance of sandwiches in above manner and keep warm until served.

Hot Turkey Sandwich, Giblet Gravy   50 Portions, Each
                                                Sandwich 2 Oz Turkey

This job is typical of one that might be assigned either to the sandwich maker or the roast cook. In Chap. 7, there is a recipe for roast turkey and giblet gravy. The recipe is for 50 4-oz portions of turkey. A hot turkey sandwich is essentially the same job with several important exceptions:

(a)   The 4-oz portion of meat is reduced to 2 oz.

(b)   The dressing is omitted.

(c)   The amount of gravy is increased.

When patrons order a hot meat or poultry sandwich with gravy, they expect the bread to be thoroughly covered with gravy. The bread should, therefore, be one or two days old to avoid sogginess. The sandwhich may be served open or closed. In those restaurants where sandwiches are ordered individually over a two- or three-hour meal period, it is possible and desirable to carve the meat to order. If this is the case, the roast cook handles the job. But in other dining rooms where large numbers must be served without delay, the meat is best carved beforehand for rapid continuous service. In such eating establishments, it is the practice to roast the turkey at least one or sometimes two days in advance. The meat is sliced the day before or at least several hours in advance of mealtime and then reheated gently and briefly. For efficient controlled yield, the white meat of the turkey is taken off the carcass and is sliced by machine while the dark meat is carved by hand. In still other places only white meat is used. There are some restaurants where the cold sliced turkey is placed on the bread and covered with gravy sufficiently hot to bring the meat to serving temperature; a second slice of bread is placed on top and again covered with very hot gravy. The student should be aware of these varied practices and be prepared to handle them as directed in any particular kitchen where he is working. The recipe below is planned for using cold turkey sliced by machine and reheated.

Before starting work: Consult your supervisor or instructor at least two days in advance to determine if the job is to be handled at the sandwich station or at the roast cook's station. Meat which has been roasted, chilled, returned to room temperature, carved and again reheated is subject to contamination a number of times. Be sure that if cold meat is carved, it is handled as briefly and expeditiously as possible. Be sure your hands, slicing machine, container pans and work surfaces are as clean as possible. Place the bread in the refrigerator at least one day before it is used.

(1) Assemble the following ingredients:
   1 18-lb roast turkey
   Giblet gravy (p 178), 1 1/2 times the recipe
   100 slices white bread
(2) After turkey is roasted, let it set whole in refrigerator overnight.
(3) Separate leg and second joint from carcass; remove "oysters" from bottom of bird.
(4) With sharp boning knife or knife with pointed end, cut out wish bone; cut off wings.
(5) Run boning knife along keel bone; holding knife close to carcass, carefully separate entire side of breast meat from carcass.
(6) Remove second side in same manner.

(7) Cut each side of breast in half crosswise so there are 4 large chunks of meat.

(8) Remove skin of breast meat.

(9) Slice turkey by machine; check with instructor or supervisor on proper gauge of slicing machine.

(10) Stack white meat in neat overlapping slices in 12 X 20-in. pan.

(11) Using hand and boning knife remove bone of legs and second joints. Skin may be left on or removed.

(12) Slice meat off legs, second joints, "oysters" and wings.

(13) Stack dark meat in pan with white meat.

(14) Cover pan with clean damp towel. Cover towel with aluminum foil, fitting it snugly around edges of pan.

(15) Refrigerate sliced turkey until an hour before mealtime.

(16) Preheat oven to 375° F.

(17) Remove foil and towel from pan. Pour 1 cup hot stock into pan. Again cover with foil (not towel). Be sure foil fits snugly around sides of pan.

(18) Place pan in oven until turkey is hot. Check after 20 min. As soon as turkey is hot, remove pan from oven and place in steam table.

(19) Reheat giblet gravy bringing it to full rolling boil. Place giblet gravy in steam table. Pot with gravy should be in contact with water beneath; water should be bubbling.

(20) Place 2 stacks of white bread within easy reach.

(21) To serve each sandwich, place a slice of bread on serving plate.

(22) Cover bread with 2 oz turkey, dark meat on bottom, white meat on top. Check with instructor or supervisor on ratio of white meat to dark.

(23) Pour 2 oz gravy over meat.

(24) Place second slice of bread on top.

(25) Pour 3 oz gravy over top slice of bread.

Note: Cranberry jelly is sometimes served as a garnish with hot turkey sandwich. If it is indicated on the menu, place 2-oz portions in paper soufflé cups and store in refrigerator until needed. Watercress can also be used as a garnish.

13

Pantry Worker, Salad Maker, Coffee Maker

The worker in the pantry may have any one of the above three job titles, or the duties may be shared by one or two employees. The various foods discussed in this section range from fruit cocktail at the beginning of the meal to desserts and coffee at the end. A comprehensive list of the pantry worker's daily assignments is found in the Job Summary which follows. But, for an overall view of this section, it is best to divide the work into two categories.

First, there are the menu items which the pantry worker prepares by hand at his station. These are:

(a) Salads of greens or raw vegetables (not the cooked meat, poultry or seafood salads of the *garde manger*)

(b) Fresh fruit appetizers such as fruit cocktail, half grapefruit, melon, etc.

(c) Coffee and tea

(d) Special ice cream desserts such as peach melba, certain parfaits, etc.

(e) Fresh fruit juices if squeezed to order or frozen fruit juices needing reconstitution

(f) If there is no breakfast cook, some cooked breakfast items such as griddlecakes, eggs, etc.

The second category includes foods which are merely divided into portions and placed on tableware for serving. These are:

(a) Canned or bottled fruit juices

(b) Desserts such as cakes, pies, stewed or canned fruit, etc.

(c) Cold packaged cereals

(d) Ice cream if served plain

(e) Rolls, bread, muffins, etc.

(f) Cheese as a course at the end of the meal

While the preceding list seems extensive, in actual practice many of the tasks are frequently handled by waiters. For example, the automatic egg boiler may be placed in front of the pantry so that waiters who need eggs simply take them from a bowl, place them in the automatic boiler, set the timer, and pick up the eggs when they are ready. Frequently the waiter rather than the pantry worker puts bread in the automatic toaster, pours tomato juice from a pitcher, dishes portions of ice cream, draws coffee from a coffee urn, etc. Most of the pantry worker's jobs are repetitive. When the routines are properly learned and conscientiously carried out from day to day, the job is a busy but comparatively easy one, not requiring the disciplined daily judgment of cooks behind the range. In many establishments the pantry worker is under the direct supervision of the steward rather than the chef or *garde manger*. Other cooks, however, may come to the pantry for supplies such as milk, cream, bread, etc. Since salad dressings are normally made and stored in the *garde manger*'s section, the saladmaker should get several days' supply of such dressings from the *garde manger*. There are three main areas which call for careful attention and at times exacting judgment. These skills which are outlined and discussed in this chapter are (a) preparation of fruit appetizers, (b) salad making, and (c) coffee making.

Even though the chef in many restaurants does not directly supervise the pantry worker, the menus are written by the chef, and the pantry worker must be aware of advance menus noting special salads, special ice cream desserts, etc., which change from day to day. Any question, therefore, about details of the arrangement of a salad, composition of an ice cream dessert or similar problems should be resolved in consultation with the chef or steward.

JOB SUMMARY

The pantry worker (1) meets with steward and/or chef at beginning of workday to discuss any special menu items for preparation in the pantry; (2) discusses special assignments for private parties such as quantity preparation of fruit cocktail, desserts, coffee, etc.; (3) advises steward of foods to be ordered such as coffee, milk, cream, cheese, ice cream, etc.; (4) requisitions daily needs from storeroom such as cereals, canned fruits, fruit juices, etc.; (5) receives and stores in refrigerator or elsewhere desserts prepared in pastry department; (6) chills fruits, fruit juices, etc.; (7) receives and places in warming units rolls, muffins, etc.; (8) makes available to waiters eggs for boiling, bread for toasting, cold cereals, tea bags, etc.; (9) receives

milk, cream, etc.; (10) fills milk dispenser; (11) brews coffee in urn
or automatic coffee equipment; (12) prepares fruit appetizers; (13)
prepares table d'hôte or a la carte salads not handled by *garde
manger;* (14) prepares special ice cream desserts and divides into
portions desserts such as puddings, pies, cakes, fruit brown betty, etc.

MANUAL PROCEDURES

The pantry worker (1) cuts pies, cakes, tarts, etc., with knife or pie
slicer and places portions on serving dishes; (2) scoops ice cream or
ices and places portions in appropriate dishes; (3) pours dessert
sauces over ice cream or puddings; (4) washes fresh fruits and salad
greens; (5) peels fruits for fruit cocktail; (6) segments fruit with
knife; (7) cuts melons into portions or prepares melons with
parisienne cutter; (8) mixes fruits and fruit juices for fruit cocktail,
fruit compote, etc.; (9) trims, drains and dries salad greens;
chops, slices, dices or tears by hand salad greens and other salad components; (11) tosses salad greens; (12) blanches and peels tomatoes;
(13) slices tomatoes, beets, cucumbers, etc., for salads; (14) places
lettuce cups on plates and fills them with salad components such
as beets, tomatoes, cottage cheese, fruits, etc.; (15) pours dressings
into sauce boats or adds dressings directly to salads; (16) measures
and places ground coffee into urn bag or other filter equipment;
(17) pours boiling water over coffee to brew coffee of specific
strength; (18) fills receptacle with ground coffee for automatic
coffee making equipment; (19) cleans, scours and polishes coffee
equipment with special brushes and cleaning material; (20) pours
brewed coffee into cups or coffee pots; (21) brews tea by pouring
boiling water over loose tea leaves or tea bags; (22) prepares other
beverages such as cocoa by blending hot milk with cocoa or instant
powders.

EQUIPMENT AND UTENSILS

In his duties the pantry worker uses (1) coffee urns, vacuum and
automatic coffee makers and hot water urns; (2) reach-in and walk-in
refrigerators; (3) ice cream freezers; (4) automatic toasters; (5) automatic egg boilers; (6) griddle and waffle bakers (where there is no
breakfast cook); (7) French knives, utility knives and paring knives;
(8) vegetable peeler; (9) parisienne cutter or melon baller; (10) can
opener; (11) citrus juice squeezer; (12) cutting board; (13) mixing

bowls, assorted sizes; (14) ice cream scoops, assorted sizes; (15) colanders, assorted sizes; (16) mixing spoons, perforated spoons, pie cutter, spatulas, ladles and tongs; (17) plastic or aluminum trays; (18) cleaning brushes, assorted sizes.

WORKING CONDITIONS AND HAZARDS

He works in wet areas surrounding sinks used for washing greens, and may work in hot surroundings if griddle is part of equipment. There is a possibility of cuts from French knives or paring knives. His work area is often busy with frequent multiple orders.

PLACE IN JOB ORGANIZATION

The pantry worker may be promoted from dishwasher, glass-washer, silverman or kitchen helper. The next line of promotion is to breakfast cook, *garde manger*'s assistant or steward's assistant.

20 GUIDES TO SALAD MAKING

Salads made in the pantry are usually served as accompaniments to the meal rather than main courses such as those prepared by the *garde manger*. They may be served before, with or after the main course. They may be prepared in bulk quantity, such as tossed green salad assembled in a large kitchen bowl or other container from which the pantryman or waiters serve individual salad plates. They may also be assembled one by one, such as lettuce, tomato and cucumber salads arranged on individual salad plates, and kept chilled until waiters pick them up for service. A choice of dressings may be offered the customer. Dressings may be poured over the salads in the pantry or served on the side in sauce boats. The main quality factors in salads are freshness of materials, crispness of greens, eye appeal, including neatness, and proper ratio of ingredients. The following guides emphasize the main points in successful salad making in the pantry.

(1) When fresh salad materials become dehydrated or lose moisture, they are wilted. To prevent dehydration, do not leave salad greens at room temperature for lengthy periods. Store them in the refrigerator as soon as they arrive. Trim and wash them as quickly as possible, and return them to the refrigerator. After individual

salads are made up, keep them in the refrigerator until they are served.

(2) Salad greens which show signs of rust, rot, excessive wilt, damage from the crate, etc., should be trimmed when received and before they are washed. Such deterioration spreads when greens are stored in the refrigerator.

(3) Use a well-lighted area for the initial trimming of greens as well as for subsequent trimming. The salad maker must consciously remind himself to examine minutely every piece of the salad materials to eliminate bruised, wilted, discolored or otherwise objectionable portions.

(4) All salads from the pantry are served well chilled. Keep all raw materials, finished salads, dressings and salad plates under refrigeration until served. The only salad dressing sometimes kept at room temperature is French dressing made with olive oil.

(5) Keep the dressings in bottles or other containers in refrigerated wells or on cracked ice. If the dressings are temporary emulsions (p 281), keep them in bottles with stoppers that require shaking before dispensing.

(6) Crispness is the quality feature expected in all salad greens. If greens are wilted, crispness can sometimes, but not always, be restored by steeping them in ice-cold water for brief periods of 10 to 15 min. Sometimes the wilt is so extensive that rehydration is impossible, in which case the greens should not be used.

(7) Salad greens must not only be well washed but well dried. If they remain wet, salad dressing will not adhere to them. The dressing will be diluted, and a watery pool will form on the salad plate or bowl.

(8) Greens should be washed in a colander under cold running water. If running water does not rid them of sand, dirt, etc., they should be steeped in a container or clean sink of water, swirled gently, and then lifted from the water. The sand in the bottom of the container is then washed away. This process may have to be repeated 3 to 6 times depending on the amount of soil or dirt on the greens. Certain salads like bibb lettuce or arugula are almost always sandy and have to be washed in 6 cold waters before they are completely clean.

(9) Salad greens are dried by (a) draining in a colander, (b) shaking by hand, (c) continued draining in a colander after shaking (colander should be kept in a refrigerator with good circulation), and (d) patting dry with paper or clean cloth toweling.

(10) Since draining and complete drying of salad greens depend on the time factor, salad greens should be washed, drained and placed

in the refrigerator well in advance of mealtime, from one to two hours.

(11) Although greens must be thoroughly cleaned beforehand, they should be handled as briefly and gently as possible to prevent bruising.

(12) While meat and seafood salads are sometimes marinated for lengthy periods before serving, greens should be combined with their dressing just before they are served to retain crispness.

(13) Some salad greens like Boston lettuce or romaine are easily separated into leaves. Iceberg lettuce, one of the commonest greens, is a compact head with tightly clinging leaves. To separate them, cut out the core and hold the cut-out portion under cold running water. The water will help to gently separate the leaves.

(14) When salad greens are dried, place them in the refrigerator wrapped lightly in wax paper or a clean towel. If they need further drying, place them in the refrigerator with a cloth or paper toweling beneath the greens to absorb water.

(15) When fresh pears, apples, or bananas are cut and exposed to the air, they tend to darken because of oxidation. To prevent discoloration, steep them in an acid solution such as lemon juice and water, orange juice, pineapple juice, etc.

(16) In many restaurants the salad maker is instructed to use a certain size plate for salads served as an accompaniment to the main course. If there is a choice, however, be sure to choose salad plates large enough to contain the salad and leave a margin around the rim of the plate. When bowls are used, the salad should not be piled so high that it cannot be conveniently mixed with the dressing.

(17) Pour only enough dressing over a salad to coat it completely but lightly. There should be no large pool of dressing on the plate.

(18) Many small salads are served on a base of greens. It may be a lettuce cup, a few leaves of romaine, etc. Make sure the base is carefully centered on the plate, and that it is large enough to contain the rest of the salad ingredients.

(19) Salads are frequently garnished with small additions chosen for contrast in color and texture. Such garnishes should be decisive in color such as a diamond-shaped piece of pimiento on a pear, or a sprig of watercress on French endive. Garnishes of this type should not be so small or so lacking in color contrast that they appear to be something accidentally dropped onto the salad plate.

(20) Salad greens are usually torn into bite-size pieces to give them a more natural appearance than if they were cut by knife. In some busy restaurants, however, they are cut by knife as a time-saver. Care should be taken with the kind of knife used. For this purpose

a stainless steel knife which avoids rust is best, since rust is quickly transferred to some salad materials. A stainless steel knife is also best for cutting citrus fruits which are frequently used in salads.

Tossed Green Salad   **50 Portions, Approx 1 Cup Each**

The phrase "tossed green salad" is the term for any salad of leafy greens, with few limitations on the number or choice of greens used. All of the guidelines which emphasize crispness, cleanness, freshness, etc., must be scrupulously followed. The choice of salad greens depends upon the amount of leftover greens in the pantry which are in good condition and the availability of certain greens at specific times of the year. If there is a month, for instance, in which escarole is plentiful, inexpensive and of top quality, the amount of escarole used in the total recipe would be larger than normal. If an item like bibb lettuce or Boston lettuce is running poorly, it might be omitted entirely and another green substituted. Usually each tossed salad is coated with dressing just before it is served. In very busy restaurants, however, a half hour's supply may be tossed in advance, unless, of course, a choice of dressings is offered to the customer. When tossed green salad is served at large banquets, it is all tossed with the dressing just before serving and is then placed on individual salad plates or in individual bowls. Ordinarily large leaves of salad greens like lettuce or romaine are torn. Small leaves like watercress or bibb lettuce are left whole. Very compact leaves like cabbage are cut by knife or on a cole slaw cutter. The term tossed means lifted up lightly in such a way that the greens are mixed but not bruised. Use a light hand, and fluff the greens. Do not flatten or pound them in the bowl.

Before starting work: Make sure you have large clean colanders and large containers like dishpans for holding salad greens after they are trimmed and washed. If salads are to be divided into portions beforehand and placed on salad plates, plan to have sufficient trays to hold the plates in the refrigerator. All salad greens should be trimmed, washed, drained, dried and chilled before they are combined.

(1) Assemble the following ingredients:

Note: Salad greens are indicated by measure or bunches rather than by weight, since their volume rather than weight on the plate determines the size of the portion. The "pieces" below should be approximately 1 in. square or as close to that size as practical.

3 qt iceberg lettuce, pieces

2 qt Boston lettuce, pieces
1 qt bibb lettuce, whole leaves if heads are small
2 qt escarole, pieces
2 qt chicory, pieces
1 qt red or white cabbage, shredded
2 bunches watercress
1 1/2 qt French dressing (variable)

(2) Place all ingredients except dressing in large shallow bowl(s) or stainless steel dishpans.

(3) Toss lightly so that ingredients are combined but not bruised.

(4) If salads are to be served individually, place 1 cup salad in individual bowls or plates. Place bowls or plates on trays and store in refrigerator until ordered.

(5) Just before orders are picked up, sprinkle with French dressing, allowing a generous tablespoon per serving.

(6) If all 50 salads are to be served within a brief period (no longer than a half hour) or are to be served at a banquet at one time, add dressing, toss lightly, and place in individual salad bowls or on plates just before salads are taken to dining room.

Lettuce, Tomato and Cucumber Salad   50 Portions

This is a conventional but perenially popular salad, combining simple color contrasts and differences in texture. Many salads are served on a base or cup of lettuce. The so-called cup may be a single large well-formed leaf or several leaves fitting together. It also may be a slice of iceberg lettuce or iceberg lettuce cut into cubes or shreds on which the other ingredients are placed. The best lettuce for making a cup is Boston, sometimes called "big Boston" or "butterhead," with light green outer leaves and yellow leaves in the center. Tomatoes may be peeled or unpeeled. For easy peeling, dip tomatoes for 20 sec in boiling water, wash under cold water, and remove skin with a paring knife. Tomatoes may be the regular large type, globular in shape, or plum tomatoes. If the latter are used, they should be cut lengthwise in halves or quarters. Tomatoes should be firm but ripe. There are four ways of preparing cucumbers for a salad of this type:

(a) Skin left on

(b) Peeled and sliced crosswise or diagonally

(c) Fluted, that is, cut lengthwise at 1/4-in. intervals with a lemon peel cutter so that long strips of rind remain on cucumber before slicing, or

(d) Peeled and fluted by running the tines of a fork lengthwise over the cucumber.

Salads of this type should be made up on individual plates before mealtime and refrigerated. The dressing may be poured over them just before serving or it may be served separately in a sauce boat.

Before starting work: Examine salad plates under good light to make sure they are all clean. Return any soiled plates to dishwashing section. Examine tomatoes to make sure they are all firm and ripe. If they are bruised, soft or otherwise defective, turn them over to the sauce cook for use in cooked dishes. Check refrigerator shelf space, and rearrange materials if necessary so that trays with salad may be stored in one place.

(1) Assemble the following ingredients:

8 heads Boston lettuce or 4 large heads iceberg lettuce

8 lb fresh tomatoes

6 medium to large cucumbers

Approx 1 1/2 qt French dressing or choice of other salad dressings

(2) If Boston lettuce is used, trim outer leaves if necessary and follow this procedure:

(a) Twist out core of lettuce.

(b) Separate lettuce into leaves.

(c) Wash under cold running water, using colander to hold washed leaves; turn leaves to wash thoroughly.

(d) Gently shake leaves over sink to remove excess water or pat with paper toweling or clean cloth towels; avoid bruising leaves.

(e) Place leaves in colander; place colander in refrigerator at least 1 hour before salads are to be served.

(f) Remove lettuce from refrigerator; examine leaves; if still moist, again pat with paper toweling or clean cloth towels.

(3) If iceberg lettuce is used, trim outer leaves if necessary, and follow this procedure:

(a) Cut out core of lettuce with pointed knife, and hold core end under rapidly running cold water; press head to loosen leaves.

(b) Separate head into leaves.

(c) Shake leaves well over sink to eliminate excess water.

(d) Cut or tear *outer* leaves into pieces approximately 1 in. square.

(e) Separate inner leaves to make cups.

(f) Dry lettuce by shaking and pat dry with paper toweling or clean cloth towels.

(g) Store cups and torn pieces separately in refrigerator; chill at least 1 hour.

(h) If leaves till show signs of wetness, pat dry with toweling.

(4) Cut cucumbers using any one of the suggested methods above.

(5) With sharp pointed knife cut out stem end of tomatoes. Cut peeled or unpeeled tomatoes horizontally into 1/4-in. slices.

(6) Count cucumber and tomato slices, and estimate number of each per portion.

(7) Refrigerate cucumber and tomato slices, if not used at once.

(8) Place 3 rows of 4 salad plates on work table.

(9) Place lettuce, tomatoes and cucumbers within reach.

(10) Line plates with lettuce cups. If iceberg lettuce is used, place whole leaves on bottom and torn lettuce on top.

(11) Place overlapping slices of tomato in center.

(12) On top of tomato slices, place overlapping slices of cucumber.

(13) Place salads on trays, and refrigerate until ordered.

(14) Continue in this manner until 50 salads are made up.

(15) Just before serving, spoon dressing over salad, allowing 1 oz dressing or a No. 1 (1/8 cup) ladle per portion.

Romaine, Endive and Beet Salad   **50 Portions**

Quantities of romaine and French endive in the recipe below are listed by weight rather than by measure as in the previous recipe. Pounds are indicated because variations in the leaf size of both these salad materials are so great that the only reasonably accurate portion control is weight. Romaine is a variety of lettuce sometimes called cos. The leaves are long with a pronounced but delicate flavor. Ideally the salad might be made with just the smaller crisp inner leaves. This can be done if the balance of the romaine is used for tossed green salad. But from the cost standpoint the whole head should be utilized. French or Belgian endive (called by these names because at one time it was imported from Europe in large quantities) is a compact elongated head of white leaves, usually three or four inches long, with a slightly bitter flavor. The leaves are tightly folded and must be separated one by one to keep their shape intact. In many of the finest restaurants, canned beets rather than fresh are used. This is one instance in which the canned product is sometimes the equal of, or superior to, the fresh version. When handling the canned beets, the salad maker should remember that beet juice splattered over other foods in a salad is unattractive. Handle carefully with a fork when arranging them on the plate. The color combination of pale green romaine, white endive and red beets is appetizing only if the salad is neatly assembled.

Before starting work: If you are using a brand of canned beets for the first time, drain the beets and count the slices in order to determine how many slices to allot per portion. This may be a tedious job the first time, but if the same brand of beets is kept in the storeroom, it will not be necessary to repeat the count on subsequent jobs. If beets are whole and are cut into slices, the same count should be made.

(1) Assemble the following ingredients:

5 lb romaine

4 lb French endive

1 No. 10 can sliced or whole beets

Juice of 1 large lemon

Approx 1 1/2 qt French dressing or choice of other salad dressings

(2) Trim romaine of any outer leaves that are rusty, wilted or otherwise objectionable. Some leaves may be wilted or brown only on the top; the balance of the leaves may be useful.

(3) Cut a 1/4-in. slice off bottom of romaine and separate heads into leaves.

(4) Wash romaine well under cold running water, checking both sides of leaves to make sure they are free of soil or dirt.

(5) Drain romaine well. Shake leaves to eliminate water. Pat dry with paper toweling or clean cloth towels. Refrigerate until needed.

(6) Cut a 1/4-in. slice off bottom of endive. Carefully separate into leaves. Cut a larger slice off bottom of endive, if necessary, in order to separate leaves. Try to keep natural shape of leaves intact.

(7) Wash endive well under cold running water.

(8) Drain endive well. Shake leaves to eliminate water. Pat dry with paper toweling or clean cloth towels. Refrigerate until needed.

(9) Drain beets well. After draining, sprinkle with lemon juice. Refrigerate until salads are assembled.

(10) If leaves of romaine are small, they may be used intact. If leaves are large, cut or tear the leaves crosswise into 1-in. pieces or as close to that size as possible.

(11) Place 3 rows of 4 salad plates each on work table. Place romaine, endive and beets within arm's reach.

(12) Line plates with romaine.

(13) Place endive leaves in parallel lines on romaine.

(14) Place appropriate number of beet slices on endive.

(15) When salads are made up, place them on trays and refrigerate until serving time.

(16) Continue in this manner until 50 salads are assembled.

(17) Just before serving, spoon dressing over salads allowing 1 oz dressing or 1 No. 1 (1/8 cup) ladle per portion.

Waldorf Salad   50 Portions

Waldorf salad is a combination of diced apple, diced celery and mayonnaise. It is one of the few salads for which the customer is not offered a choice of dressings. Sometimes, but not always, it is garnished with walnut meat (chopped walnuts). The quality of the salad depends upon the quality of the raw apples as well as the celery, factors over which the salad maker may have no control, but which must guide him in his work. If apples, for instance, show brown or soft spots when cut, these must be carefully removed. If the celery is limp, it should be soaked in ice-cold water in the refrigerator to restore its crispness if possible. Certain varieties of apples quickly turn brown when pared and exposed to the air. To avoid browning, steep the cut apples in an acid fruit juice such as orange juice, pineapple juice or water with lemon juice, allowing 1/4 cup lemon juice per qt of water. The orange juice or pineapple juice need not be discarded. It can be incorporated into fruit cups, pudding sauces, etc. Check with your instructor or supervisor on the possible use of these juices.

Before starting work: If there is a mechanical apple peeler on the premises (one is often used by the pastry chef in making fresh apple desserts), check to see if it may be used in place of paring the apples by hand. If walnut meat is not fresh, place it in a shallow pan in a moderate oven for 8 to 10 min to brown lightly. Pay special attention to browning; walnuts may be scorched if oven is too hot or if left in oven too long.

(1) Assemble the following ingredients:

8 lb fancy table apples such as Delicious, Winesap, etc.

3 lb celery

2 1/2 cups mayonnaise

2 tablespoons lemon juice

2 tablespoons sugar

6 heads Boston lettuce or 3 heads iceberg lettuce

3/4 lb walnut meat

(2) Pare and core apples, using mechanical apple peeler if possible.

(3) As soon as apples are cored and peeled, steep them in a tart fruit juice until cut.

(4) Cut apples from top to bottom into sixths or eighths, depending upon size of apples. Examine core section of apples to make sure there are no sharp pieces of core left in the fruit. Cut them away if they remain in fruit.

(5) Cut apples into 1/2-in. dice or as close to that size as possible. Again return to fruit juice.

(6) Wash celery well on both sides.

(7) Trim celery of all leaves. Pat celery dry with paper toweling or clean cloth towels.

(8) Using vegetable peeler with swivel blade, peel outside of celery removing stringy fibers.

(9) Cut celery into 1/2-in. dice.

(10) Drain apples. Place them on a clean cloth towel or paper toweling to remove excess liquid.

(11) In a large bowl combine apples, celery, mayonnaise, lemon juice and sugar. Stir well and refrigerate until needed.

(12) Wash, drain and dry lettuce leaves. If Boston lettuce is used, keep leaves whole. If iceberg lettuce is used, tear or cut leaves into 1-in. pieces. Iceberg lettuce may also be cut julienne if desired.

(13) Place 3 rows of 4 salad plates each on work table. Place lettuce, apple mixture and walnuts within arm's reach.

(14) Line plates with lettuce.

(15) On top of lettuce, place a No. 12 scoop of apple mixture.

(16) Sprinkle with walnut meat.

(17) Place individual salads on trays and refrigerate until served.

Pear, Cream Cheese and Watercress Salad   **50 Portions**

Although many salads become routine jobs after the saladmaker has performed them several times, this salad is typical of one that requires practical judgment each time it is made. The pears may be either canned or fresh. If fresh pears are used, the peel must be removed by hand. There are many varieties of fresh pears, and peeling must be adjusted to the particular variety chosen. A Bartlett pear is a different shape from a Bosc. The core and stem section are not gouged out by a coring device, but must be carefully removed by a pointed small knife. If canned pears are used, they must be well-drained on paper or cloth toweling to keep the syrup from forming a pool of liquid on the salad plate.

The cream cheese mixture is placed in the hollow of the pear with a pastry bag and tube; this step requires practice and judgment. To make the cream cheese soft enough to be shaped by the pastry bag, it is first softened or worked by hand or in a mixing machine. It is further softened by the addition of cream. If too little cream is used, the mixture will be too firm to handle. Too much cream will make the mixture too plastic to hold its shape. Various factors such as the quality of the cream cheese, its temperature, etc., affect the amount of cream to use, and the salad maker's best guide is to add small quantities at a time until the cream cheese is blended to just the right consistency.

Before starting work: If fresh pears are to be used, check the pears at least a day in advance to determine their stage of ripeness. If further ripening is needed, keep them at room temperature rather than refrigerated. Allow enough time in your work schedule to peel and core the fresh fruit.

(1) Assemble the following ingredients:

50 pear halves, fresh or canned

Note: If fresh pears are used, remove stems, pare with a vegetable peeler with swivel blade, cut in half and very carefully cut out core. If canned pears are used, place them carefully on shallow trays lined with paper toweling or clean towels in order to drain completely.

2 1/2 lb cream cheese

1/2 to 1 cup heavy sweet cream

3 tablespoons chives, chopped extremely fine

6 bunches watercress

Choice of dressings (pp 278-283)

(2) Cut about 1 in. off bottoms of watercress stems.

(3) Wash watercress by steeping in cold water either in large dishpan or in clean sink, swirling leaves, lifting the watercress from water and draining well. Repeat washings if necessary.

(4) Shake watercress to eliminate excess water and drain well in colander. Remove from colander and gently pat dry with paper toweling or clean cloth towels. Refrigerate until needed.

(5) By hand soften cream cheese in mixing bowl working it with mixing spoon or paddle. It may also be softened in a mixing machine with small bowl. A large mixing machine is impractical.

(6) Slowly add cream to cream cheese, working it well until cream cheese is soft enough to be put through a pastry bag and tube and maintain its shape. Check with instructor or supervisor on consistency of cream cheese.

(7) Add chives to cream cheese mixture, blending well.

(8) Place salad plates in row on work table, using only enough plates (usually 3 rows of 4 plates each) to work within arm's reach.

(9) Place watercress, pears and cream cheese mixture near plates.

(10) Place watercress on salad plates.

(11) Place a pear half on top of watercress, hollow side up.

(12) Place cream cheese mixture in pastry bag and star tube. Force a rosette of cream cheese into the hollow of several pears, using steady pressure on bag. Check with instructor or supervisor on size of rosette.

Note: If you are using pastry bag and tube for the first time, it is best to practice with the tube forcing the rosettes onto a clean plate, and then returning the cream cheese mixture to the bag.

(13) Continue to make salads in this manner until 50 portions are prepared. As soon as salads are completed, place them on trays and refrigerate.

(14) Pour dressing over salads just before they are picked up by waiter, or pass dressing separately in a sauce boat.

Avocado, Grapefruit And Pineapple Salad   50 Portions

Fruits with tart accents like grapefruit and pineapple are increasingly popular as salad components. The grapefruit season extends from fall to late spring; those available in the summer are usually of poor quality. Avocados, however, are available all year long. This fruit requires special care: If, when avocados are received, they are not completely ripe, they should be kept at room temperature until the fruit yields to mild hand pressure. The skin of some varieties is thicker than others. The fruit, however, should never be pressed hard or it will bruise. A toothpick or narrow skewer may be inserted into the stem end to test for ripeness.

Segmenting grapefruit is a job that must be done meticulously, and you should plan to allow sufficient time for it. Any white membrane remaining on the segments leaves a bitter unpleasant taste. When grapefruit are segmented, grapefruit juice collects in the bowl, and may be used to prevent browning of the avocado. The number of segments a grapefruit will yield is hard to estimate. It depends upon the variety of grapefruit, size, etc., and the student will have to learn to use judgment in making individual portions of the salad.

Before starting work: Two days before use, check avocados for ripeness if possible. Refrigerate those that are ready. Keep the balance at room temperature. In some markets, suppliers will, upon request, deliver only avocados that are ripe and ready for cutting. Plan to save both the grapefruit juice and the pineapple juice for other uses. Check with your instructor or supervisor. Since grapefruit can only be segmented by hand, be sure to wash your hands well before starting the job.

(1) Assemble the following ingredients:

> 10 large ripe avocados
>
> 100 canned pineapple fingers
>
> *Note*: Check label of canned pineapple. If number of pieces of fruit is indicated, it will be a guide to the number of cans to open.
>
> 8 large grapefruit
>
> 8 heads Boston lettuce or 4 heads iceberg lettuce
>
> 100 strips pimiento, 2 in. long, 1/8 in. thick
>
> Choice of dressings (pp 278–283)

(2) Peel and segment grapefruit, following this procedure:

    (a) Use a sharp medium size French knife, stainless steel if possible, to avoid corrosion. Provide a bowl to collect grapefruit juice and another bowl for segments.

    (b) Holding grapefruit in left hand, cut grapefruit skin in a spiral until all skin and outer white membrane are removed. As an alternative method, place grapefruit on cutting board; cut a slice off top and bottom of fruit; cut balance of skin and white membrane from top to bottom, following shape of fruit with knife. Make sure that no outer white membrane remains on fruit.

    (c) Again holding fruit in left hand, cut between *inner* rows of white membrane to make segments. Let segments drop into bowl. After each grapefruit is segmented, squeeze the fruit over the second bowl to extract as much juice as possible. Some seeds may fall into the juice; it may be strained later.

    (d) Refrigerate bowl with segments until needed.

(3) Trim, wash and dry lettuce. Separate Boston lettuce into cups. If iceberg lettuce is used, tear it into 1-in. pieces or shred by knife. Refrigerate lettuce until needed.

(4) Cut avocado in half lengthwise. Twist lightly, if necessary, to separate halves. Lift out seed, twisting it if necessary.

(5) Holding avocado in left hand, pull skin off, beginning at neck or narrow end. If necessary, use paring knife to remove skin. When avocado is fully ripened, it is not necessary to cut into fruit when paring.

(6) Brush avocado halves on both sides with grapefruit juice.

(7) Cut each avocado half into 5 lengthwise slices. Brush cut slices with grapefruit juice.

(8) Arrange salad plates and salad ingredients on work table as in previous jobs.

(9) Place lettuce cups or torn or shredded lettuce on plates.

(10) On each plate alternately place two slices of avocado, two pineapple fingers and grapefruit segments.

(11) On each salad place two strips of pimiento crosswise or diagonally.

(12) Chill salads, placing plates on trays in refrigerator, until served. Serve with choice of dressings.

Half Grapefruit   50 Portions

A half grapefruit served as an appetizer is typical of a simple job which perhaps because of its simplicity is often performed in a careless or shoddy manner. When properly prepared, a half segmented seedless grapefruit should look as if it were untouched. There are always a few seeds in the so-called seedless grapefruit; they are removed with a fork, while the core in the center remains. Each segment between the inner white membrane is cut one by one with a grapefruit knife and left in place. Too often the pantry worker hastily cuts around the whole edge of the fruit and then hacks the fruit from the core outward into pieces that retain the bitter membrane. Doing the job carefully, it should be pointed out, takes time. Doing it the fast way always impairs quality. The tendency to decorate the half grapefruit with red or green cherries, mint leaves and other garnishes seems to be disappearing. For best eye appeal, the half grapefruit is set in a bowl with very finely cracked ice surrounding the fruit.

Before starting work: Check the shelf space in the pantry refrigerators to make sure there is room for 50 portions. If necessary, rearrange foods on the shelves so that trays of segmented half grapefruit can be placed in the refrigerator when ready. Be sure your cutting board or work table is under strong light so that cutting can be precise. Any nonstainless steel knife with a trace of rust will cause brown marks on the edge of the fruit when cut in half. Wash and dry such knives well before starting the job; wash and dry them during the job after prolonged use.

(1) Assemble the following ingredients:

27 large grapefruit

Note: 2 grapefruit should be set aside for juice to be poured over the prepared fruit just before it is served.

(2) Place 50 dessert dishes, terrapin dishes (small cereal bowls) or other dishes customarily used for half grapefruit on trays, and stack the trays at your work area.

(3) Using a medium size French knife cut enough grapefruit horizontally to fill 1 tray of dishes. Be careful not to cut vertically through the stem end which would prevent the grapefruit from being segmented.

Note: Before cutting each grapefruit in half, place the knife in the center at the point which would separate the grapefruit into equal portions. Grapefruit frequently are not symmetrical, and it is necessary to make adjustments for differences in shape.

(4) With a sharp or serrated grapefruit knife, cut between white membranes to loosen segments. Cut deep enough to reach the bottom of the fruit. Avoid cutting into white membrane around side of fruit. Revolve the fruit clockwise as you are segmenting it. When fruit is completely segmented, gently move the segments, if necessary, to keep them in their original position. Place fruit in dishes on trays.

(5) Place trays of segmented grapefruit on refrigerator shelves in a single layer; do not stack trays directly on top of dishes.

(6) Continue in this manner until 50 portions of grapefruit have been segmented. Refrigerate until serving time.

(7) Cut 2 remaining grapefruit in half, and make fresh grapefruit juice by placing halves on a hand or electric juice squeezer. Pour the grapefruit juice into a small pitcher or liquid dispenser and refrigerate.

(8) If grapefruit are to be surrounded by crushed ice, add ice to dish just before serving. Pour a few teaspoons grapefruit juice over fruit just before serving.

Grapefruit Garnishes.—Any of the following may be used with half grapefruit: maraschino cherry, either half or whole; green tinted cherry, either half or whole; fresh mint sprigs; grenadine syrup; red or black currant syrup; fresh strawberry dipped in beaten red currant jelly. All garnishes are placed in center of fruit.

Fresh Fruit Cocktail   **50 Portions, Approx 6 Oz Each**

What is listed as fresh fruit cocktail on any menu frequently is a mixture of fresh and canned fruits. The canned fruits are used to save labor and food cost. In those restaurants where all the ingredients are literally fresh, the pantry worker's main job is peeling, coring, segmenting, dicing or slicing—procedures much more lengthy than the simple task of placing the fruit in serving dishes. Because the task is so time-consuming the preparation usually occupies the pantry worker during nonrush periods when work can be performed in a less hurried fashion. Previous jobs described the procedures for peeling and dicing apples, peeling and coring pears and segmenting whole grapefruit. The task of segmenting whole oranges is exactly like that of segmenting grapefruit except that the fruit is smaller. In this job the student is introduced to the procedure for slicing fresh pineapple. Its main steps are as follows:

(1) Cut off the crown; leave peel on.

(2) Cut lengthwise into quarters if medium or small fruit is used; cut into sixths if pineapple is large.

(3) Cut off hard core by slicing lengthwise 1/2 to 1 in. from top of wedges.

(4) Slice between fruit and rind to free wedges.

(5) Slice wedges crosswise into 1/2-in. slices.

Before starting work: Review previous jobs for preparation of fresh fruit. Assemble saucer champagne glasses, supreme glasses or whatever glasses are customarily used. Examine them under good light to make sure all glasses are clean with no chipped edges. Return any dirty glasses to glass washing section. Because of the height of some glasses, it may be necessary to allow the space of two refrigerator shelves for 1 tray of filled glasses. Make refrigerator space available beforehand. Check leftover fruit juices before preparing additional juice.

(1) Assemble the following ingredients:

    2 qt fresh grapefruit segments (save juice)
    2 qt fresh orange segments (save juice)
    2 qt apples, 1/2-in. dice
    1 qt pears, 1/2-in. dice
    1 qt sliced fresh pineapple
    1 qt fresh strawberries, 1/4-in. slices
    Canned or frozen pineapple juice
    Orange juice (variable)
    Sugar (variable)

(2) Cover apples and pears as soon as they are cut into dice, with a mixture of pineapple juice, orange juice and grapefruit juice extracted from segmented fruit. (Such juices are normally on hand in the pantry and are supplemented by the juices made when segmenting the grapefruit and oranges. Be sure juices from the fresh fruits are strained to eliminate seeds, pieces of membrane, etc.)

(3) In a large bowl or stainless steel dishpan combine all the fruits. Add sugar to taste, stirring well until sugar is dissolved.

Note: Since fresh fruit cocktail usually is served at the beginning rather than the end of the meal, sweetness should be minimal.

(4) Spoon the mixture into saucer champagne glasses, sherbet glasses, supreme glasses or whatever glassware is customarily used.

(5) Cover each portion with juice from the bowl.

(6) Chill in the refrigerator until served. Normally stemmed glassware is placed on a dessert dish lined with a paper doily to keep the glass from sliding on the plate.

Melon Cocktail   50 Portions, Approx 6 Oz Each

Melon cocktail made from balls of fresh fruit is usually an item of high food and labor cost, the type of fruit appetizer which might be ordered for a banquet. It is frequently served in a supreme glass, a footed piece of tableware which is packed with ice and fitted with a glass insert for holding the fruit. Sometimes melon balls are added to a regular fruit cocktail, but often, as in the recipe below, they make up the complete cocktail. Balls of fruit are made with a hand cutter variously known as the parisienne spoon, parisienne potato cutter, fruit baller or ball cutter. There are three sizes; the medium or large sizes are the ones used for most pantry work. There are 5 principal kinds of melon used for cocktails: cantaloupe, honeydew, cranshaw, Persian and watermelon.

There are times when the pantry worker will have ripe melons, others that are semiripe and some that need several days ripening. Usually those that need extended ripening are kept in a storeroom rather than the busy pantry area. All ripe melons of good quality are heavy for their size. Ripe cantaloupes show a yellow skin beneath the netting and have a discernible aroma. Ripe honeydews are creamy white and have a characteristic ripe fragrance and a barely detectable oily film on the rind. Cranshaw melons and Persian melons should yield at the large end when ripe.

In preparing the melons, cut them in half, remove the seeds, and then with a twisting motion of the cutter make the balls, cutting closely from one end of the fruit to the other. When all the fruit has been cut, the balance of the meat in the melon shells may be scraped or cut away, put through a heavy-duty blender and added to the juice for the cocktail.

Before starting work: If the fry cook is preparing parisienne potatoes, observe him at the job in order to acquire facility in the use of the parisienne potato cutter. As in previous jobs, assemble the serving glasses beforehand making sure they are all clean. If supreme glasses are to be used, count the sections to determine if the 50 glasses are complete. Plan to keep each of the different kinds of melon balls in separate bowls or other containers before combining the fruit. Check with the instructor or supervisor so that crushed ice, if it is to be used, is ready when needed.

(1) Assemble the following ingredients:

Note: Substitutions of one melon for another may be made in order to use available ripe fruit. Watermelon, however, should always be included for its bright color accent. Work very carefully with watermelon to remove all visible seeds.

2 qt watermelon balls

2 qt honeydew balls

2 qt cantaloupe balls

1 qt casaba melon balls

1 qt cranshaw melon balls

3 qt fruit juice (variable)

Sugar (variable)

100 sprigs of fresh mint, washed, patted dry

(2) Remove fruit left in melon shells with grapefruit knife or paring knife. Place in heavy-duty blender. Blend until pureed. Add enough orange juice to pureed fruit to make 3 qt juice. Sweeten with sugar to taste, but do not oversweeten. Melon cocktail is a fruit appetizer and should not have the sugar content of a dessert.

(3) Place 50 inserts for supreme glasses, saucer champagne glasses or sherbet glasses on trays.

(4) If fruit is very ripe and may be bruised by handling, add individual fruits to glasses; otherwise combine fruits and spoon into glasses.

(5) Pour sweetened juice over fruit.

(6) Place 2 sprigs of mint on each portion.

(7) Chill in refrigerator until served.

(8) If supreme glasses are being used, fill them with crushed ice just before melon cocktail is served.

ICE CREAM DESSERTS

The job of storing and dispensing ice cream desserts normally is assigned to the pantry. If the dessert is an unusually elaborate one such as baked Alaska (ice cream covered with meringue baked in the oven), it is usually handled by a cook rather than a pantry worker.

Frequently the ice cream freezer is located in an area adjacent to the pantry so that it is accessible to either the pantry worker or waiters. Orders for plain ice cream or sherbet are filled by waiters who simply scoop ice cream into dessert dishes and sometimes serve them with a cookie, macaroon or small decorated cake known as a petit four. If the ice cream dessert involves a sauce, it will probably be made by the pantry worker rather than the waiter. Thus, if peach melba is ordered, the fruit, ice cream and sauce will be assembled by the pantry worker and then passed to the waiter. It is this latter class of ice cream desserts served with sauces, fruits or other accompaniments with which the student should be familiar. Ice cream sauces or fruit sauces like chocolate sauce or chopped fresh strawberries are prepared in the pastry or dessert section rather than in the pantry. The pantry worker receives them from the pastry section, and stores them in the pantry refrigerator. The care of the ice cream freezer cabinet and its contents is the responsibility of the pantry worker, and the following guidelines should be observed:

(1) Check the temperature of the cabinet each morning to make sure that it is functioning normally. The usual temperature range is 0° to 10°F. In some restaurants softer ice cream is regularly served (on the theory that flavors like vanilla and mocha are more pronounced when the ice cream is softer), and a temperature of approximately 20°F is maintained.

(2) Be sure ice cream scoops are well washed and scalded after each meal period. They are normally kept in a container of water during the meal period or are dipped in water before and after each use. Replace the container with fresh water before each meal or during the meal if necessary.

(3) When fresh ice cream arrives, arrange the containers so that old stock is served first. If necessary, mark dates on the containers to keep stock in proper order.

(4) Waiters tend to scoop ice cream from the center of the containers, leaving a residue on the side. Scrape down the sides of the containers after each meal so that the ice cream is level for the next meal's service.

(5) Note any containers of flavors which are slow selling and from which few if any portions may be taken for several days. Ice cream thus standing, exposed to the air, may pick up off-odors. Report the fact to the instructor or supervisor.

(6) Be sure that ice cream cabinet lids and top of cabinet are kept clean at all times to prevent dirt or foreign matter from falling into the wells of the cabinet.

(7) Make certain that the appropriate size scoop is used for each specific dessert. The scoop for an order of ice cream on a table d'hôte menu is usually smaller than one for an a la carte order.

The following ice cream desserts are some of those featured on restaurant menus. Since quantities of ice cream and ice cream sauces vary widely from place to place, quantities are not indicated. Quantities, however, are controlled by the size of scoops, size of ladles, size of parfait glasses, etc., in the particular restaurant where you are employed or are receiving training.

Peach Melba.—Place half of a cooked fresh or canned peach on bottom of dish. Fill peach with a scoop of vanilla ice cream topped with melba sauce (raspberry puree).

Poire Hélène.—(Rather than "pear Helen," the French terminology seems to be consistently used in most restaurants). Place half of a cooked fresh or canned pear on bottom of dish. Top with a scoop of vanilla ice cream covered with chocolate sauce.

Parfait.—A parfait is traditionally served in a tall, narrow footed glass or silver container. It consists of ice cream and a sauce usually topped with whipped cream; the sauce, such as chocolate or a liqueur, may be on bottom and top of ice cream.

Meringue Glace.—Place a scoop of ice cream in wide dessert dish, then a meringue shell on either side of the ice cream. If desired, serve with a sauce, such as crushed fresh strawberries or chopped marrons (chestnuts in a vanilla syrup), topped with whipped cream.

Frozen Eclair or Frozen Puff.—Eclair shell or cream puff shell is cut in half horizontally; ice cream is added and top of shell returned to place; an ice cream sauce such as butterscotch or chocolate is poured over top.

Coupe.—The popular American ice cream dessert known as the sundae appears on French menus as the *coupe*—ice cream with a sauce or fruit or both in countless combinations of flavors. Pantry worker should consult the chef as to the components of any particular *coupe* listed on the menu.

Bombe.—Several flavors of ice cream and usually one sherbet are packed in a heavy mold which is closed and held in the freezer cabinet until serving time. Bombe is unmolded just before serving and is taken whole to the dining table where it is cut into portions.

COFFEE BREWING

There are some very large kitchens where the term coffee maker is a separate job title on the payroll. One or more persons spend most of the day brewing and serving coffee, and cleaning coffee-making equipment. During off-peak periods they may or may not assist in general pantry work. In moderate size restaurants the job is usually handled by the pantryman. Since making coffee is a routine job, one would think that the standards of quality would be unvarying from day to day. Unhappily this is not the case. Many factors can alter the quality of the coffee and cause customer complaints to multiply, sometimes ceaselessly. First of all there is the blend, quality and age of the coffee beans over which the coffee maker usually has no control. It is the duty, however, of the worker to instantly report any noticeable change in quality to the supervisor whether it be the steward, chef or *sous chef*.

Ideally the best quality coffee is made from beans which are roasted, ground and brewed the same day, as they still are in some European coffee shops. It is impossible to describe coffee quality with a few descriptive words. One can talk about good flavor and good aroma, about acidity, fruitiness, strength, body, etc., but the only way the student can learn judgment is by the experience of drinking several blends of coffee made in the same equipment, and then comparing them for their aroma, flavor, body, aftertaste, color, etc. It is possible, however, from a negative viewpoint, to state certain characteristics which cause any coffee to be low on the quality scale. Coffee should not:

(a) Convey an aroma of staleness; this fault is bound to occur if ground coffee is held too long in the storeroom. Coffee should be ordered from the supplier with as frequent deliveries as possible and should be used as quickly as possible. Staleness will also be evident if coffee is brewed more than an hour before it is served.

(b) Leave an impression in the mouth of off-flavor or rancidity. The common cause is unclean stained coffee brewing equipment.

(c) Present a turbid, so-called muddy appearance. Good coffee should have sufficient brightness and clarity so that a spoon in the cup can be seen about 3/4 the distance to the bottom of the cup. The common causes of this fault are brewing the coffee too far in advance or improper filtering.

(d) Present a watery appearance. If the spoon in the cup is clearly outlined to the bottom of the cup, the coffee is too weak; more coffee grounds are needed per gallon of water, or the coffee may not have been mixed or stirred after it was brewed.

The above observations apply to coffee brewed in the American manner. Exceptions are Turkish coffee, which is extremely thick, and espresso coffee, which is extremely dark.

12 GUIDES TO COFFEE MAKING

(1) Keep packaged coffee in a cool dry place away from any foods with strong odors which coffee can absorb.

(2) Use older stock first. If necessary, write the date of arrival on bags of coffee to keep inventory moving properly.

(3) Use accurate measurements at all times. If 8 oz coffee per gal of water is the formula, follow it exactly whether you are making a half gallon or multiple gallons at one time.

(4) If a stronger brew is prepared for after-dinner coffee, make your revised calculations very carefully. Write them down on paper and check the calculations with your supervisor. Use an accurate scale if fractions of a bag of coffee are used. Check water ratio very carefully.

(5) No other piece of equipment in the kitchen requires more regular top-to-bottom cleaning than a coffee urn. Caffeol, the oil which is developed when coffee beans are roasted, settles in the urn, stains it and decomposes as the urn is used repeatedly, causing off-odors and off-flavors. A regular daily cleaning after each use and at the end of the day as well as a special semiweekly cleaning routine is one of the most important jobs in the pantry. (See "Cleaning a Coffee Urn" below.)

(6) Always bring fresh cold water to a boil. Do not use hot water which has been standing for a prolonged period, and which may be flat tasting.

(7) In areas where water is too hard or too soft, changes in your formula may have to be made. Check with your supervisor.

(8) Brew coffee as close to serving time as possible. The more frequently additional brews are made, the fresher the coffee will be. Check with your supervisor on peak-load periods in the dining room.

(9) Serve coffee in warm cups if possible. Keep cups in warming equipment. If pots of silver or china are used, be sure they are very clean and that they are warm when filled with coffee. Examine interior of pots to make sure there is no coffee stain.

(10) As soon as coffee is brewed, remove the filtering device and the grounds. All the flavor of the coffee grounds has been extracted. Spent grounds left in the equipment can cause bitter substances to spoil the quality of the coffee.

(11) Although boiling water or water slightly below the boiling point is used for brewing coffee, after brewing, the coffee should never be brought to the boiling point. The ideal temperature for serving is 180° to 190°F. Although coffee-making units have thermostatic control to keep coffee in this temperature range, malfunctions can sometimes cause coffee to be too hot or too cool. Report any noticeable difference in serving temperature to your supervisor.

(12) Coffee, once brewed, should not be held longer than 1 hour. Plan work schedule to avoid overproduction for all meals.

In most mass feeding establishments and large restaurants, coffee is brewed in a battery of urns. Each battery usually consists of 3 urns, 1 for boiling water and 2 for brewing. In many establishments where decanters of hot coffee are kept in the dining room or on the serving line, the coffee is brewed in an urn in the pantry or other work area. The principal steps for urn brewing are described below.

Brewing Coffee in an Urn

(1) Fill the hot water urn (not the coffee-brewing urn) with cold water. Set the temperature to boil. The time it will take to reach the boiling point will depend upon the capacity of the urn and the heating unit.

(2) Before a coffee urn is used in the morning, it usually contains water poured routinely into the urn to remain overnight. Empty the urn. Add about a gallon of boiling water and clean the urn with an urn brush. (Use no soap or detergents.) Draw this water off.

(3) Fill the coffee urn bag or the coffee screen filter with the designated amount of coffee. If a bag is used, place the gridded riser in place to support the bag. If filter paper is used, place it carefully in position.

(4) Spread the coffee grounds evenly in the bag or coffee basket. This is extremely important for making a uniform extraction.

(5) Pour boiling water from hot water urn over grounds using exact measurements as shown on gauge; or, if water is poured by hand, use gallon measure in slow circular motion over grounds. Check grounds to see that they are all moistened. Stand on a raised platform, if necessary, to make sure water is being distributed evenly. Place urn cover over urn between pours. Approximately 5 min contact between water and coffee grounds will be required.

Note: If it is awkward to handle a 1-gal measure, 1/2 gal or 3/4 gal may be poured at a time. Be sure to use correct total amount of water. Handling a gallon of boiling water may be hazardous. Hold the container firmly.

(6) As soon as water has dripped through, remove coffee grounds in bag or filter at once.

(7) The brewed coffee at the bottom of the urn will be heavier and darker than at the top. Draw coffee off from bottom—from 1/3 to 1/2 the brew—and pour it back into the urn to mix properly. (Make sure the coffee grounds have been removed.)

(8) Keep brewed coffee at 180° to 190° F.

(9) Plan intervals between brewing so that no batch of coffee is held longer than an hour.

(10) Refill hot water urn, and plan to have it boiling when it is necessary to make a new batch of coffee.

(11) Empty urn bag or filter of used grounds. Rinse well. Keep bag in cold water until needed again.

(12) Replace urn bags whenever they show signs of off-odor or excessive wear.

Note: If glass decanters are used for serving coffee or to keep coffee warm in dining room, be sure such decanters are rinsed well before using and are cleaned twice weekly with a coffee destainer or coffee cleaning compound.

Brewing Coffee in a Vacuum Maker

The vacuum coffee maker is a device with two bowls, the bottom one for boiling water and the top one for brewing coffee. Water boiling in the bottom section expands and rises into the upper bowl containing coffee grounds. When the two bowls are removed from the heat temporarily, a vacuum is created in the lower bowl, and it draws the brewed coffee back. The coffee thus brewed is kept on a thermostatically controlled heating unit for serving.

(1) Rinse top and bottom bowls with hot water. Rinse cloth filter if used. Place clean filter in upper bowl. Set upper bowl aside.

(2) Fill bottom bowl with cold water, following manufacturer's directions.

(3) Place bowl on heating unit to bring water to a boil.

(4) Have measured amount of coffee grounds ready to add to upper bowl.

(5) As soon as water boils, reduce heat or turn off heat.

(6) Add coffee to upper bowl. Fit upper bowl tightly into place. Place combined unit over low heat. Water will rise into upper bowl.

(7) Stir water with coffee grinds 10 to 15 sec.

(8) Remove vacuum maker from heat. Coffee from top section will filter into bottom bowl.

(9) Remove top bowl.

(10) Rinse top bowl and filter with hot water. Set bowl aside for next use. Place cloth filter in cold water until next use.

(11) Place coffee on heating unit set to keep warm at 180° to 190° F.

Brewing Coffee in Half-gallon Automatic Coffee Maker

In many restaurants where small quantities of coffee are made at a time, the vacuum type coffee maker has been replaced by the half-gallon automatic coffee maker. Boiling water is made in a chamber at the top of the equipment and flows over the coffee grounds into a decanter. It is very important that the thermostatic control which brings water to the boiling point be working accurately.

(1) Use a measured amount of coffee, allowing 4 oz per 1/2 gal of water. If coffee is taken from 1-lb packages, weigh each batch carefully.

(2) Turn switch on equipment to produce boiling water.

(3) Place paper filter in filter basket. If cloth filter is used, rinse it well in hot water.

(4) Add measured amount of coffee to filter, spreading it evenly.

(5) Place filter into position for brewing. Place bowl in proper position.

(6) Coffee will flow into bowl; brewing should be completed in approximately 4 min. Any noticeable deviation from this time should be checked.

(7) Remove grounds and filter. If cloth filter is used, rinse it in hot water, and keep it in cold water until next use.

(8) Keep coffee for serving at 180° to 190° F.

Cleaning a Coffee Urn

The following procedure should be followed on a daily basis.

(1) During the day, after the urn is emptied and before its next use, rinse it well with hot water. Add enough water to thoroughly rinse sides of urn. Use a clean, long-handled urn brush. Do not use any cleaning compound.

(2) After the previous step rinse water should run clear. If necessary, fill urn a second time and rinse until water runs clear.

(3) At the end of the day rinse and brush urn at least twice using very hot water. Drain after each rinsing. Rinse until water runs clear.

(4) If faucet valve is removable, disassemble it, and scrub with narrow brush. Scrub pipe leading to urn. If faucet is fitted with removable cap only, detach cap, and scrub faucet and pipe. Rinse well before assembling and putting faucet into place.

(5) Clean urn gauge with narrow gauge brush. Rinse well. Replace urn gauge top.

(6) Rinse urn cover well.

(7) Pour a gallon of fresh water into urn. Place urn cover on top slightly ajar, and leave water until urn is used the next day.

The following procedure should be followed twice weekly or more often in busy restaurants where the normal three-meals-per-day service may also include banquet service or late night suppers.

(1) Clean urn using special urn cleaning compound. Procedure should be carried out during nonrush periods.

(2) Fill urn 3/4 full with hot water. Be sure water in outer jacket matches level of water in urn. Switch temperature control to maximum heat.

(3) Add urn-cleaning compound. Use formula suggested by manufacturer. Mix very well. Brush with urn brush. Brush lid of urn, filtering device and collar. Let solution remain in urn following time period suggested by manufacturer.

(4) Drain urn, saving some of solution for cleaning valve and gauge.

(5) Disassemble faucet, and scrub well with cleaning solution. Rinse well.

(6) Scrub pipe leading to urn, using narrow brush.

(7) Scrub fitting in bottom of urn with narrow brush.

(8) Scrub gauge glasses.

(9) Assemble all parts into normal positions.

(10) Rinse urn and all parts 3 or 4 times with fresh hot water. Make sure that all parts exposed to cleaning solution have been well rinsed.

(11) Make sure no trace of cleaning solution or odor remain in urn or any of the parts.

(12) Detach coffee bag if used, and clean urn ring in above manner.

(13) Fill urn with a gallon of fresh hot water, and let water remain until next use.

Note: Decanters of automatic equipment, vacuum coffee bowls, etc., should also be cleaned twice weekly using the special compound designed for cleaning coffee-brewing equipment.

Coffee Yield—Quantity Production

Normally the pantry worker in charge of brewing coffee is instructed to brew a designated number of gallons for each meal. Instructions will vary during the day. Smaller or larger amounts will be made for weekends, holidays, etc. Special amounts must be brewed for banquets at specific times. The following table shows the yield in cups of 6 1/4 oz each, using 8 oz coffee per gal of water:

Portions	Coffee Grounds	Water
20	8 oz	1 gal
40	1 lb	2 gal
60	1 1/2 lb	3 gal
80	2 lb	4 gal
100	2 1/2 lb	5 gal
200	5 lb	10 gal

14

Dessert Cook

The person in charge of the dessert section in a large kitchen operation usually has the title of pastry chef. Actually, he is responsible not only for the production of pastries but for fruit desserts, custards, puddings, ice cream desserts, etc. It is a specialist job requiring long training and extensive experience. Unlike cooks behind the range who transfer, or are promoted, to other cook's jobs, the pastry chef usually pursues his specialty as a lifelong vocation. He must be deft in handling doughs and be particularly conscious of eye appeal, appetizing color combinations and neat portions. It is extremely important to be able to estimate dessert quantities for a specific day's menus and to be able to multiply or reduce formulas as needed. The dessert cook must cooperate closely with the pantry workers, checking leftover desserts, determining whether leftovers are in good condition, and deciding how much fresh production is needed.

There are some kitchens where certain desserts are purchased from an outside source, and others where desserts may be made on the premises from cake mixes, pie mixes, etc. Despite these trends, all student cooks, no matter what their ultimate job goal may be, should be familiar with the basic skills typified by the recipes in this section. Even if a student's apprenticeship in this area is limited, it is extremely valuable for those entering the food service industry.

JOB SUMMARY

The dessert cook (1) consults with chef or *sous chef* on quantities of desserts to be made for a specific day's menus or for private parties; (2) orders from storeroom staple food items which are kept in the dessert section, such as flour, sugar, shortening, extracts, etc.; (3) orders fresh items for each day's preparation such as butter, cream, eggs, etc.; (4) prepares cakes, pies, cookies, custards, fruit desserts, puddings, gelatin desserts, etc.; (5) checks leftover desserts in pantry, and advises pantry worker as to the disposition of leftovers; (6) may prepare special sauces or fruits for ice cream desserts; (7) supplies certain staple pantry items such as whipped cream, ice cream sauces, etc.; (8) may make certain breakfast items such as stewed prunes or other dried fruits; (9) may make batter for griddlecakes, waffles, etc.

MANUAL PROCEDURES

In his work he (1) weighs ingredients for dessert formulas on balance scale or other scale; (2) preheats ovens; (3) mixes cake batters by combining shortening, sugar, eggs, liquid ingredients, flour and leavening agents; (4) prepares cake pans by greasing and dusting with flour, and pours measured amounts of batter into pans; (5) inserts pans in oven and tests cake for doneness; (6) mixes sugar, syrup, butter and flavorings for frostings; (7) spreads frostings between and over cake layers; (8) peels, cores and slices apples; (9) makes pie fillings from canned fruit by mixing them with sugar and starch and cooking until thick; (10) blends flour and shortening for pie dough; (11) rolls and fits dough into pie pans; (12) fills pie shells; (13) inserts pies in oven, tests for doneness, and removes pies when baked; (14) mixes milk, eggs, sugar and flavor for custards; (15) pours custard mixture into cups and bakes in oven; (16) mixes flour, shortening, sugar and flavoring for cookie doughs; (17) bags dough onto baking sheet; (18) inserts cookies in oven and bakes until brown; (19) mixes flour, eggs and milk for crepe batter; (20) may make crepes in dessert section or turn crepe batter over to cooks at ranges; (21) peels, cores and simmers whole apples in syrup for baked apples; (22) whips cream by beating in machine; (23) cleans pans and other utensils or may have dessert cook's helper perform cleaning jobs.

EQUIPMENT AND UTENSILS

The dessert cook uses the following in his work: (1) electric mixer with beating attachments and bowls; (2) round baker's stove; (3) counter top stove or counter top steam-jacketed kettle; (4) bake ovens, deck type; (5) hand mixing bowls; (6) pastry bags and tubes; (7) bowl knives, spatulas, mixing spoons, French knife and apple corer; (8) balance scale and measuring containers; (9) saucepans; (10) baking sheets, utility pans, pie pans and cake pans.

WORKING CONDITIONS AND HAZARDS

He (1) works near hot deck ovens; (2) frequently works in limited area; (3) stands at work bench for prolonged periods; (4) is subject to burns from handling hot pans.

PLACE IN JOB ORGANIZATION

The dessert cook may be promoted from dessert cook's helper or pantry worker and may eventually be promoted to pastry chef.

Baked Apples   **50 Portions**

The menu term "baked apple" does not accurately describe the cooking procedure below for this dish. There are many restaurants where so-called baked apples are never put into the oven for baking. Instead, the apples are poached in a syrup on top of the range and are then placed under the broiler to be glazed. There are advantages to this modern method: namely, the apples cook uniformly and retain their shape. Apples placed in the oven for baking often lose their shape, partially collapse and turn to a puree. If the oven heat is uneven, some of the apples may be scorched on top while others are incompletely cooked.

The choice of apples is an important consideration. The best apples for baking, retaining shape and developing a mellow flavor are Rome Beauties. These are western apples of extra fancy or fancy grade. A common mistake with baked apples is undercooking. When apples are tested for doneness, it is important to check a number of apples at various spots in the pans. A two-pronged fork should be easily inserted and withdrawn when the apples are completely tender. Any apples which are not completely soft when tested will later turn firm, sometimes hard, after the apples are chilled. Another common fault is the residue of sharp pieces left in the cavity of the apples after they are cored. It may be necessary to insert the apple corer several times in order to gouge out the core thoroughly.

Before starting work: Examine apples for soundness. Do not use any that show signs of excessive softness or discoloration. Be sure apples are washed well to remove any spray residues. Choose baking pans sufficiently deep so that the apples tops will barely reach the tops of the pans.

(1) Assemble the following ingredients:

50 Rome Beauty apples

4 lb granulated sugar (variable)

4 qt water (variable)

Note: The variable quantities of sugar and water will depend upon the size and number of baking pans; sugar and water are made into a syrup, and more or less may be needed to cook the apples.

4 lemons, cut in half for juice

2 lb apricot glaze or apple jelly (variable)

Note: If prepared apricot glaze is not available, it can be made as follows: Put 1 lb canned drained appricots through a sieve; add 1 lb granulated sugar, 3 oz corn syrup, and simmer 5 min.

8 pieces stick cinnamon, each approx 3 in. long

Ground cinnamon

(2) Wash apples well.

(3) Tear off any stems.

(4) Remove cores with apple corer: Insert corer in center of apple (from stem end to blossom end), twisting it to separate core from fruit.

(5) Examine apples by feeling cavity. Reinsert corer, if necessary, to enlarge cavity and remove sharp ends of core.

(6) Using a paring knife, peel apples from stem end one third of the way down. Do not peel beyond the one third line or apples may not hold shape during cooking.

(7) As apples are pared, sprinkle tops with lemon juice. Place apples, pared side down, in baking pans.

(8) Pour water and sugar into a saucepan. Stir well to dissolve sugar. Add stick cinnamon.

(9) Bring to a boil. Simmer 3 min.

(10) Pour syrup into pans with apples. Divide stick cinnamon among pans. (If more syrup is necessary, prepare it, using above ratio of 1 lb sugar to 1 qt water.)

(11) Place pans over medium flame. Simmer slowly until pared end of apple is tender when pierced with two-pronged fork. Test several apples.

(12) With two spoons, turn apples in pan so that pared end is up. Handle apples carefully to keep cooked side intact.

(13) Continue cooking until bottom side is tender. Check tenderness carefully in different parts of pan, using a fork.

(14) Stir apricot glaze if it is chilled. If apple jelly is to be used, beat it with a small whip until it is soft.

(15) Press the top of each apple very carefully with a table fork or two forks until the top is nearly flattened and the cavity almost closed. Do not press so hard that apples collapse.

(16) Spoon apricot glaze or apple jelly over the top of each apple, coating it completely. Again press lightly with fork to mix glaze with apple pulp.
(17) Sprinkle apples lightly with ground cinnamon.
(18) Place pans of apples under broiler, using low flame, keeping pans of apples as far from flame as possible. Handle pans carefully with dry pot holders or heavy dry towels.
(19) Broil until tops of apples are glazed, that is, the surface is shiny. Watch pans carefully, turning when necessary to glaze evenly.
(20) Remove apples from broiler. Cool 1/2 hour at room temperature.
(21) Chill apples in refrigerator. To serve, place apples in deep dessert dishes. Pour syrup over apples.

Cup Custard   48 Portions

Custard is a cooked mixture of milk, eggs and sugar, and is the base for some of the most delicate and at the same time most popular restaurant desserts. Besides the cup custard and caramel custard below, there are custard-based puddings, such as bread and butter pudding, custard sauces and other dessert dishes. Cup custard is the milk, egg, sugar combination poured into oven-proof cups and baked until the mixture forms into a soft, light coagulum. A prominent fault with cup custards is the watery layer which sometimes forms during baking and which becomes apparent as the custard is eaten or if the custard is unmolded. It is due to excessive heat, prolonged baking or insufficient eggs.

Egg yolks, as well as whole eggs, are often added to custard mixtures. The addition of yolks not only provides a firm texture but adds a certain richness which people expect in this dessert. (The French word for custard is *crème* or cream.)

Since overbaking is a cardinal fault with this dessert, the student is advised not to follow home procedures for testing doneness. In many home cookbooks, one is told to insert a knife, and if it comes out clean, the custard is done. The custard may also be overdone, and the knife will still come out clean. A more practical way to test doneness is simply to touch the top of the custard very quickly with the finger tips. When the custard is finished, the top will be firm. Custards should be examined about 5 min before the stated cooking time. Another test is to gently move the pan containing the custards. If they shimmer slightly when moved, further cooking is needed.

Before starting work: Assemble 48 custard cups. Make sure they are all the same size and are clean. Cup custards are baked in pans partly filled with water. Choose baking pans or utility pans deep enough to allow 1 in. of water. The sides of the pans should not be higher than the cups or the custard will not brown.

(1) Assemble the following ingredients:

6 qt milk

24 eggs

24 egg yolks

Note: Egg whites may be turned over to soup cook for clarifying consommé or may be reserved for desserts calling for egg whites.

1 lb 14 oz sugar

2 teaspoons salt

2 tablespoons vanilla extract

Whole nutmeg

1/4 lb softened butter

(2) Preheat oven to 350° F.

(3) Grease custard cups with softened butter. Place cups in baking pans.

(4) Pour milk into saucepan. Heat over slow to moderate flame until milk is scalded, that is, until bubbles begin to appear around edge of saucepan. Do not boil milk.

(5) Place eggs and egg yolks in hand mixing bowl.

(6) Add sugar, salt and vanilla to eggs.

(7) Beat eggs with wire whip until eggs are slightly foamy and sugar is blended with eggs. Scrape bottom of bowl to make sure sugar is blended.

(8) Slowly pour scalded milk into egg mixture while stirring until well blended.

(9) Strain mixture through fine china cap. (Mixture may be strained into pitchers for pouring.)

(10) Pour into greased custard cups in baking pans.

(11) Holding metal grater over cups, grate nutmeg so that each custard is lightly sprayed on top.

(12) Pour hot water to a depth of 1 in. in baking pans.

(13) Very carefully place pans in oven; avoid spilling water while carrying pans.

(14) Bake 25 min, and check custards for doneness. Move pans slightly; if tops of custards are shimmering and seem liquid, continue baking. Lightly touch tops of a few custards. They should feel firm when done. If they are soft, continue baking. Check for doneness in 5 min.

(15) Remove pans from ovens as soon as custards are done. Use a

double or triple thickness of heavy dry towel in each hand or use dry heavy potholders or mitts. Avoid spilling hot water when carrying pans.

(16) Remove custard cups from pan. Use folded, heavy dry towel in hands.

(17) Allow custards to cool at room temperature 15 to 20 min. The custards will continue baking somewhat after being removed from oven, due to interior heat.

(18) Chill custards in refrigerator.

Caramel Custard.—Pour 1 1/2 lb granulated sugar into heavy saucepan. Place over moderate flame. Stir until sugar dissolves and darkens to a caramel color. Pour into greased custard cups, and tilt cups to line bottom and sides. Add custard mixture and bake as above. To serve, run a table knife alongside custard, invert cup and unmold onto dessert dish.

Maple Custard.—Use 3 cups maple syrup in place of sugar. Use 1 tablespoon maple flavoring in place of 2 tablespoons vanilla extract.

Chocolate Custard.—Increase sugar to 3 1/2 lb. Melt 12 oz bitter chocolate over hot water. Pour melted chocolate into scalded milk very slowly, stirring well with wire whip until chocolate is completely blended. Pour mixture over beaten eggs and bake as directed above.

Bread and Butter Pudding, Custard Sauce   48 Portions

Bread and butter pudding is a combination of the previous basic custard and buttered stale bread. It can be made with either bread crumbs or cubes of bread as in the recipe below. The dessert may be served either slightly warm or well chilled. It is important that the bread be at least 3 days old; fresh bread makes the pudding compact and heavy. Like cup custard, it is baked in individual portions although it may be made in large pans if desired. The individual cups are unmolded just before they are served, and make a more attractive dish than the bulk pudding spooned out of a large pan. The custard sauce (called *crème anglaise* in French, or English cream) is a preparation frequently served with a variety of desserts. It is a mixture of milk, sugar, egg yolks and flavoring and should be cooked over low heat to prevent curdling. When removed from the fire, it has the consistency of heavy cream. As it stands in the refrigerator, it becomes slightly thicker.

Before starting work: Examine stale bread to make sure it is clean, free of mold, and has no off-odor. French bread or white sandwich bread may be used. Crusts should be trimmed from bread. Be sure custard cups are all the same size and are clean.

(1) Assemble the following ingredients:

6 qt milk

3 qt bread cubes, 1/2 in. thick, cut from 3-day-old white bread, trimmed of crusts

1/4 lb softened butter

1 lb melted butter

24 eggs

1 1/2 lb granulated sugar

1 tablespoon vanilla extract

1 1/2 teaspoons salt

Ground nutmeg

Ground cinnamon

1 lb raisins

3 qt milk

1 1/2 lb sugar

24 egg yolks

1 tablespoon vanilla extract

1 cup heavy sweet cream

(2) Preheat oven to 350° F.

(3) Grease custard cups with 1/4 lb softened butter.

(4) Cover raisins with boiling water. Let raisins steep in water 10 min. Drain raisins.

(5) Pour 6 qt milk into saucepan. Heat over low flame until milk comes up to the boiling point but does not boil. The milk is scalded.

(6) In mixing bowl beat eggs by hand or machine until whites are no longer visible.

(7) Add 1 1/2 lb sugar, vanilla extract and salt. Beat until well blended.

(8) Slowly add milk to beaten eggs. Stir until well blended. Strain through fine china cap.

(9) In another bowl place bread cubes. Sprinkle with melted butter, tossing bread as butter is slowly added. Sprinkle with nutmeg and cinnamon. Add raisins, tossing all ingredients.

(10) Divide bread among custard cups.

(11) Pour egg mixture over bread in custard cups.

(12) Place cups in baking pans. Pour 1 in. hot water into pans.

(13) Carefully transfer baking pans to oven, avoiding spilling water.

(14) Bake pudding 25 min and test for doneness. Top of pudding should be firm when lightly touched. Remove pans from oven. Remove puddings from pan. Chill in refrigerator.

(15) Scald remaining 3 qt milk.

(16) Place egg yolks, remaining 1 1/2 lb sugar and remaining 1 tablespoon vanilla in heavy saucepan or large steam table inset pan. Blend well with wire whip.

(17) Slowly stir in scalded milk.

(18) Cook over simmering water, stirring constantly, until mixture coats spoon. Container with egg mixture should not touch water. Mixture may also be cooked in steam-jacketed kettle over very low heat, 160° to 170° F. To test mixture for thickness, run finger over spoon. It should leave a furrow which is noticeable for a few seconds before it runs together.

(19) Remove from fire. Stir in heavy cream.

(20) Chill custard sauce in refrigerator.

(21) To serve pudding, run a knife around edge of custard cup. Invert custard cup over dessert dish; shake to unmold pudding.

(22) Pour a 3-oz ladle of custard sauce over each portion of pudding.

Rice Pudding   50 Portions

Cooks are taught that when rice is served as a starch accompaniment with a main dish such as curry of chicken with rice, the grains of rice should be separate, light and on the dry side. But when rice pudding is prepared, the rice is expected to be extremely soft, almost creamy in texture. The main ingredients in rice pudding are rice, milk and sugar. This is the traditional formula, and the one which is often listed on menus as "old-fashioned" or "creamy" rice pudding. There is another type which includes eggs in the recipe and is akin to rice pudding with a custard base. The more simple formula without eggs below seems to be the most popular. Rice should be the long grain type; instant rice should not be used. Rice pudding is cooked in two stages. The ingredients are first simmered very slowly over a top flame until the mixture becomes somewhat thick and most of the milk is absorbed by the rice. In the second stage the pudding is baked in the oven until a delicate brown crust forms on top. If the brown topping is too pale, dessert cooks sometimes spread a thin layer of whipped cream on the pudding, and place it very briefly under the broiler until the browning is distinct.

Before starting work: The rice pudding recipe below calls for the dessert to be served in custard cups. Make sure all the custard cups are of the same size with no chipped edges. The pudding may be served either slightly warm or ice cold. If the dessert is to be served warm for a lunch or dinner, allow at least 2 1/2 hours cooking time before the meal period. If it is to be served cold, the pudding should be completed and placed in the refirgerator at least 3 hours before the meal so that proper chilling may take place.

(1) Assemble the following ingredients:

5 qt milk
2 lb long grain rice
1 teaspoon salt
1 lb sugar
1/2 teaspoon ground nutmeg
1/4 lb butter
2 tablespoons vanilla extract
1 1/2 lb seedless raisins
1 pt light cream
1/4 lb softened butter

(2) Pour milk into heavy saucepan or steam-jacketed kettle. Heat over a moderate flame only until milk is scalded, that is, until bubbles appear around edge of saucepan. Remove from flame or turn off heat.

(3) Stir in rice, salt, sugar, nutmeg, 1/4 lb butter and vanilla extract. Stir until butter melts.

(4) Continue to cook over very low heat, 160° to 170° F, until rice is tender—about 1 1/2 hours. Stir occasionally, making sure that rice does not stick to bottom or side of pan.

(5) Turn raisins into bowl. Pour boiling water over raisins. Let raisins steep in water 10 min. Drain well. Raisins are now blanched.

(6) Add raisins to rice mixture. Stir in light cream.

(7) Preheat oven to 350° F.

(8) Grease 50 custard cups with softened butter.

(9) Turn rice mixture into custard cups. Place custard cups on baking sheet.

(10) Bake 40 to 50 min or until top of pudding is lightly browned.

(11) If browning is insufficient, beat 1 pt heavy cream until thick. Spread cream over rice pudding. Place under low broiler flame until tops are browned. Watch browning constantly to prevent scorching.

Old-fashioned Strawberry Shortcake   50 Portions

The three previous dessert recipes—cup custard, bread and butter pudding and rice pudding—are found on both European and American menus. Old-fashioned strawberry shortcake is American in origin and is as popular in small tea rooms as in elegant hotels. The dessert is a biscuit, split in two, covered with crushed strawberries and topped with whipped cream. One step in the job—making biscuits—calls for special skills and is a good introduction to students who have had no prior baking experience. The ideal biscuit is light in texture, tender inside, golden brown in color and regular in shape. Biscuit dough is a mixture of flour, salt, shortening, liquid and leavening. It is stiff enough to knead lightly and roll. If the dough is handled with a minimum of mixing and rolling, it will be light.

One of the problems is to roll the dough to a uniform thickness. The recommended technique is to always roll lightly from the center of the dough to the edge in different directions as though one were pointing north, south, east and west. Actually, there is no specific pattern for rolling, except as the eye dictates. When you come to the edge of the dough, always lift the rolling pin up to avoid an excessively thin edge.

Before starting work: Note that all ingredients in this recipe and subsequent baking recipes are listed in pounds and ounces rather than in the volume measurements (such as quarts and cups) cooks are accustomed to using. This is the practice in making baked goods where exact quantities are critically important. If you are unfamiliar with the use of a balance scale, your instructor or supervisor will explain how to use it.

(1) Assemble the following ingredients:

Lb	Oz	
2		Bread flour
1		Cake flour
	2 3/4	Baking powder
	8	Granulated sugar
	1/2	Salt
	8	Butter or shortening
	4	Melted butter
2		Milk
10	8	Whole fresh strawberries
1	8	Granulated sugar
2		Water
3		Heavy sweet cream
	4	Confectioners' sugar
	1/2	Vanilla extract

(2) Preheat oven to 425° F.

(3) Sift both kinds of flour, baking powder, 8 oz granulated sugar and salt into hand mixing bowl.

(4) Add 8 oz butter. Cut in butter, that is, use finger tips to break

butter into pieces about 1/4 in. thick; then rub mixture between palms of hands until it looks like coarse meal.

(5) Slowly add milk by sprinkling rather than pouring. Mix ingredients and form dough into one mass. Use only as much milk as necessary to form dough. If dough becomes wet or sticky, dust it with flour.

(6) Turn dough onto well-floured portion of bench.

(7) Allow dough to set 15 min before further handling. (This step permits the gluten in the flour, the elastic substance which can cause toughness in doughs if improperly handled, to relax.)

(8) Roll out dough to 1/2-in. thickness. Start rolling lightly from center to edge of dough. Check evenness and height of dough at eye level several times during rolling.

(9) Allow rolled dough to relax 5 min.

(10) Cut dough with biscuit cutter of 2 1/4-in. diameter. Dip cutter in flour frequently while cutting. Cut as close to next biscuit as possible to minimize leftover dough scraps.

(11) Place biscuits on lightly greased baking sheets.

(12) Gather scraps of dough. Form into a round mass. Roll to 1/2-in. thickness. Allow dough to relax 10 min.

(13) Cut remainder of dough into biscuits. Allow to relax 5 min.

(14) Brush tops of biscuits with melted butter.

(15) Bake 10 to 12 min or until tops are medium brown. The biscuit will double in volume during baking.

(16) Pour water and 1 lb 8 oz granulated sugar into saucepan. Stir to dissolve sugar.

(17) Heat over a moderate flame until syrup comes to a boil. Simmer 2 min. Set aside and cool to room temperature.

(18) Remove stems from strawberries. Cut away any green parts or defective parts of berries.

(19) Wash strawberries in colander.

(20) Place strawberries in a bowl for chopping. Chop strawberries, using a double mincing knife or an empty No. 2 can as a chopping device. Strawberries will be partly chopped, partly mashed. They may also be chopped in a machine with vertical blades. Do not chop strawberries to a puree. Slices should be visible.

(21) Combine strawberries and sugar syrup. Chill in refrigerator.

(22) Pour cream into bowl of small mixing machine. Bowl and wire beater may be prechilled to aid in whipping.

(23) Whip until cream is thick. Watch whipping constantly; as soon as tracks of beater are visible, stop beating.

(24) Add confectioners' sugar and vanilla. Stir only until blended. Chill, in covered container, in refrigerator.

(25) To serve shortcake, split biscuits horizontally by hand or with knife.

(26) Pour strawberries between and over biscuit halves. Use a 4-oz ladle for pouring strawberries.

(27) Top with whipped cream. Use a No. 20 scoop for whipped cream.

Yellow Layer Cake   **8 Layers, 8-in. Diameter**

There are three main types of cakes produced in the baking departments of restaurants. These are:

(a) Batter-type cakes with a relatively large amount of shortening, made from a smooth dense mixture of sugar, shortening, eggs, milk, flour and leavening.

(b) Foam-type cakes, such as angel food and sponge cake, with little or no shortening which depend for their aeration on the leavening action of a large amount of beaten eggs.

(c) Chiffon cakes which are a combination of (a) and (b).

The batter type cake recipe below follows one of the older procedures called the creaming method, and results in tender cakes of smooth texture, good appearance and flavor. There are three principal steps in preparing the batter:

(a) Shortening and sugar are blended until smooth.

(b) Eggs are slowly incorporated into the mixture.

(c) Liquids (milk and flavoring) and dry ingredients (flour and baking powder) are alternately added until the batter is formed.

In making cakes of any type, bakers are governed by what is known as *formula balance*, that is, a certain ratio of the ingredients that make up the total recipe. If you make any notable change in the ratio, the cake may be a failure. Experienced cooks behind the range often feel they can take liberties with recipes, but bakers are reluctant to do so. If 1 lb of shortening makes a batch of good cakes, it does not follow that 2 lb of shortening will makes cakes twice as good. The amounts of ingredients, therefore, should be scrupulously followed, and should be weighed whenever possible rather than measured in cups or quarts.

It is also important for success in cake baking to have all ingredients at room temperature, which means a temperature range of 70° to 78°F. If the baking section of the kitchen becomes very hot in the summer, it may be necessary to cool some ingredients in order to bring them within this temperature range. Oven temperature, too, is a critically important factor and should never deviate more than 25° F plus or minus. Too hot an oven may cause tunnels, a tough or cracked crust or heaviness. Too low an oven temperature may cause the cake to be crumbly, or to have a sticky crust or hollow center. Shelf ovens, also known as deck ovens, especially designed for baking, are normally used in place of the conventional kitchen ranges. If you have had no experience with deck ovens, be sure to familiarize yourself with their operation including preheating time, thermostat setting, signal lights and other controls.

Besides the oven, the main piece of equipment in cake making is the mixing machine. Again, if the equipment is new to you, you should learn the details of its operation including the use of bowls and mixing attachments such as flat beater, whips, cutting blade, etc. Before plugging in a mixing machine, make sure you know how to raise and lower the bowl, attach the beater firmly in place, and adjust the speed. Make sure both bowl and attachment are clean; examine them under good light; scald and wash them if in doubt. Keep all ingredients, after they are properly measured, adjacent to the mixer. Keep a bowl knife handy, and be prepared to scrape the sides and bottom of bowl periodically for uniform mixing. While mixing the batter, do not leave the mixing machine untended. In a matter of minutes the batter may be overcreamed or overmixed, resulting in cakes with peaks, tunnels or heaviness.

One of the common causes of cake failure is the inability to determine when cakes are properly baked. Always check for the following:

(a) Brownness on top

(b) Shrinkage from side of pan

(c) Top firmness so that cake springs back when touched, and no finger imprint is left.

When checking cakes for doneness, be prepared to remove layers at different times if necessary. Uneven heat distribution may cause faster browning in one part of the oven than another.

Before starting work: Review the recipe, and remove ingredients from the refrigerator which must be brought to room temperature. Assemble cake pans, and check them for cleanliness or odor. Wash them if necessary. Avoid pans that are dented or misshapen.

(1) Assemble the following ingredients:

Lb	Oz	
1	8	Granulated sugar
1		Shortening, emulsifying type
	1/4	Salt
	3/4	Vanilla extract

Lb	Oz	
1		Eggs, beaten by hand until whites are not visible
1	4	Milk
2	4	Cake flour
	1 1/2	Baking powder

Note: One pound of water may be used in place of fresh milk. Add 2 oz powdered milk to sugar-shortening mixture below.

(2) Preheat oven to 375° F.

(3) Sift flour and baking powder together. Set aside.

(4) Place sugar, shortening, salt and vanilla in mixing bowl with flat beater attached.

(5) Beat at medium speed until mixture is light and fluffy, 4 to 7 min. Stop machine at least twice and scrape bowl to blend all ingredients.

Note: When scraping bowl, it may be necessary in some cases to scrape bottom to release unblended ingredients.

(6) Add eggs in 4 stages, creaming well after each addition. Scrape down bowl after each addition.

(7) Add flour mixture and milk alternately in thirds, blending smooth after each addition. Again scrape bowl down several times to make blending complete.

(8) Using a pastry brush, grease 8 8-in. layer cake pans. Dust with bread flour. Invert pans and tap to shake off extra flour.

Note: Cake pans may be lined on bottom with greased paper or with silicone-coated paper; side of pan is also greased.

(9) Scale off mix into pans, allowing 14 oz batter to each pan. Tap pan on bench or spin pan to make batter level on top.

(10) Bake 25 to 30 min or until top of cake springs back when lightly touched.

(11) Place pans on rack to cool.

(12) While cakes are still lightly warm but not hot, invert pans and remove cakes. Tap pan bottom if necessary to release cakes without tearing them.

(13) Place cakes on sheet pan or pans lined with paper.

(14) When cakes are completely cool, they may be iced following directions in next unit.

Buttercream Icing   **10 Lb 8 1/4 Oz Icing**

Icings not only enhance the appearance and flavor of cakes, but help to retain their freshness. They are used to fill cake layers and to cover them. Often they provide a pleasing flavor contrast, such as chocolate icing on a vanilla cake. One of the most popular icings is known as buttercream. It may be made with all butter or a mixture of emulsifying shortening and butter. The shortening helps to make the icing more stable and is less expensive than all butter. Ideally a buttercream should be rich but leave no greasy feeling in the mouth; it should be smooth rather than lumpy in texture. The main sweetening ingredient is confectioners' sugar. Confectioners' sugar is graded by an X designation: Thus 4X is the common type; 6X is more finely powdered and results in greater smoothness. In addition to confectioners' sugar, sugar syrup is used to retard the graining of this type of icing. For covering 2 layers, you will need 14 oz of buttercream.

Before starting work: Make sure the cakes to be iced are cool before the icing is applied. Cakes a day old are easier to handle and less likely to crumble than cakes a few hours out of the oven. Both butter and shortening should be at room temperature—70° to 78° F.

(1) Assemble the following ingredients:

Lb	Oz	
2	8	Granulated sugar
1		Water
	1/4	Cream of tartar
1		Butter
2	8	Shortening, emulsifying type
	3	Milk powder
	1	Vanilla extract
2	12	Confectioners' sugar
	8	Eggs, beaten by hand until whites are not visible

(2) Pour granulated sugar, water and cream of tartar into a heavy saucepan. Stir to dissolve sugar.

(3) Place over a moderate flame. Bring to a boil, stirring occasionally. Boil 1 min.

(4) Cool syrup thoroughly in refrigerator.

(5) Place butter, shortening, milk powder, vanilla and confectioners' sugar in bowl of mixing machine.

(6) Beat with a wire whip at medium speed until mixture is light. Stop machine and scrape bowl when necessary.

(7) Add eggs, 4 oz at a time, in 2 stages, beating well after each addition. Scrape bowl after each addition.

(8) Continue to whip mixture, and add sugar syrup in 4 stages, beating well after each addition, until icing is light. Scrape bowl when necessary.

(9) Store buttercream icing in refrigerator when not in use. Keep well covered.

Finishing 8-in. Layer Cakes with Buttercream

Note: If cakes are peaked or uneven, cut with a sharp French knife to make tops level. Allow 14 1/2 oz buttercream for 2 layers. Cakes which are more than 1 in. high may be cut in half and made into 2 layers. Check with your instructor or supervisor on preparation of cakes for icing.

(1) Combine 2 layer cakes or cut 1 layer in half horizontally as instructed.

(2) For cutting cakes in half, use a serrated knife. Hold one hand on top of cake while cutting with other. Be sure slice is of uniform thickness.

(3) Cut a round piece of cardboard to fit cake bottom and serve as liner. Liner should be slightly larger than cake to allow for icing but should not extend noticeably beyond cake.

(4) Place a layer, top crust down, on cardboard. Brush any loose crumbs off cake.

(5) Using a thin spatula or bowl knife spread 4 1/2 oz buttercream on top layer.

(6) Place second layer on top, fitting it so that sides of cake are symmetrical.

(7) Spread top of cake evenly with icing. (Allow 10 oz frosting for top and side of cake.)

(8) Ice sides of cake from top to bottom, spreading icing down and forward in long steady strokes. Gently turn cake in a direction counter to movement of spatula. (Hands or turntable can be used.)

(9) Top and sides of cake may be finished with a pastry comb after icing is applied; rosettes of icing may be applied around top border of cake. (Check with instructor or supervisor on latter details.)

Coffee Buttercream.—In place of 1 lb water, use 1 lb double-strength brewed coffee preferably made from espresso or French roast coffee.

Chocolate Buttercream.—Add 4 oz melted bitter chocolate to finished buttercream.

Lemon Buttercream.—Reduce water to 12 oz. Add 4 oz lemon juice and 1 oz grated lemon rind.

Vanilla Cookies (French Cookies)   Approx 8 Doz, 3/4 Oz Each

In commercial bakeries cookies are an important item of production. In restaurant bake shops, they are usually a minor item, served mainly as an accompaniment to ice cream desserts or with afternoon tea. For learning purposes, they are an excellent lesson in the use of the pastry bag and tube, a piece of hand equipment used not only by the baker but by the *garde manger* and other cooks. There are many formulas for making cookie varieties, but one of the best known and most widely used is the simple vanilla cookie mix. As in making yellow cake by the creaming method, sugar and shortening are creamed as the first step. Creaming must be thorough to ensure a light product. Eggs are added in stages. Finally flour is blended into the mixture, but no milk is included, resulting in a batter stiff enough to put through the pastry bag and to hold its shape after baking.

Before filling the pastry bag make sure it is clean and free of any odor. Hold the bag and tube up to the light to make sure both show no residue from a previous use. Put the star tube into the bag, pushing it down so that part of it is visible at the small opening of the bag. Fold the top of the bag about 3 in. down so that the filling can be easily added without smearing the outside. Hold the bag in the left hand, and add the cookie batter with a bowl knife or spoon, squeezing the batter with the left hand to force it down toward the tube. Bag should not be more than two-thirds full. Fold the top back into position and twist it to form a tight closure on top. With the index finger and thumb of the left hand, pull downward on the bag until your left hand is on top of the mixture. Pull the tube down, if it is not completely extended. Press the bag with the palm of your left hand to extrude the mixture. Use your right hand to guide, turn and lift the tube.

Before starting work: Recipe allows the use of butter or hydrogenated shortening. If butter is used, be sure it is removed from the refrigerator in time to reach room temperature. These cookies are baked on a dry baking sheet or on parchment paper. Check baking sheet to make sure it is clean and dry. If parchment paper is used, cut it to fit the size of the baking sheet.

(1) Assemble the following ingredients:

Lb	Oz	
1	12	Confectioners' sugar
1	12	Butter or hydrogenated shortening
	1/2	Salt

Lb	Oz	
	1	Vanilla extract
	12	Eggs, beaten by hand until whites are not visible
1		Cake flour
2		Bread flour

(2) Preheat oven to 375° F.

(3) Set up small mixing machine with flat beater.

(4) Place sugar, butter, salt and vanilla in bowl of mixing machine.

(5) Blend at medium speed until very light, about 6 min.

(6) Add eggs, 1/3 at a time. Cream well after each addition. Scrape bowl before each addition.

(7) Sift both kinds of flour.

(8) Add flour to batter. Beat only until flour is incorporated into mix.

(9) Scrape bowl. Beat 1/2 min longer. Do not overmix.

(10) Place star tube in pastry bag, and fill bag 2/3 full with cookie mix.

(11) Bag out cookies of 2-in. diameter. Check with your supervisor or instructor on shape and size of cookies. Bag cookies in uniform lines about 1 in. apart. Make sure all cookies are of the same size and shape. If any are misshapen, the batter may be returned to the bag and reshaped.

(12) Bake until cookies are a golden brown, about 8 to 10 min. Move pan in oven if necessary to brown evenly. Check bottom color of cookies before removing them from oven. Bottoms should be medium brown.

(13) Remove cookies from oven. Allow them to remain in pan until completely cool.

(14) Place cookies in clean container for storage.

Pie Dough   **10 9-In. Pies, Top and Bottom Crust**

Although there are only three principal ingredients in pie dough—flour, shortening and water—success in making a tender, flaky crust often eludes beginners. A good crust is flaky and tender with enough body to hold and enhance its filling. It should be deeply browned at the edges and a lighter brown in the center. It should not break when portions are removed from the pie pan to the serving plate. Pie crusts may be made by machine or by hand. For students learning the job, the hand procedure is valuable in getting the "feel" of a tender dough properly manipulated. The best flour to use is unbleached pastry flour. Bread flour alone, because of its high gluten content, is undesirable. When half bread flour and half cake flour are combined, the mixture approximates pastry flour. Vegetable shortening, lard or butter, or combinations of these, may be used. Vegetable shortening is desirable because of its plasticity and because it can be easily stored and handled at room temperature. Lard and butter both have characteristic flavors which are sometimes considered desirable, while vegetable shortening is relatively neutral in flavor. The main steps in preparing a pie dough are:

(a) Weighing and sifting the flour

(b) Cutting the shortening into the flour, that is, reducing the shortening to small particles, and

(c) Adding salted water and mixing the ingredients until a solid mass or dough is formed.

The larger the pieces of shortening, the more flaky the dough will be. If they are too large, the dough will not form. The smaller the pieces of shortening, the more crumbly the dough will be. Bakers usually cut or break the shortening into pieces no larger than 1/4 in. The amount of water is almost always variable since the moisture content of flour is variable; and mixing procedures may vary from one batch to the next. If too little water is used, the dough will not form into a mass that can be rolled, fitted into the pie pan, trimmed and fluted. If too much water is used, the dough will be heavy.

The cardinal faults in making pie dough are overmixing or over-handling in any way. Excessive handling, including mixing, shaping, rolling, etc., causes the gluten in the flour (the toughening component) to develop noticeably, and the crust to become tough. Veteran bakers used to tell beginners to forget that they had fingers when handling pie dough, since the fingers, when used to squeeze or stretch the dough, were always troublemakers. A raw pie dough, properly mixed, will feel soft to the touch. An overworked dough will be compact and not yield easily to slight pressure. If a dough is properly mixed and seems difficult to roll, it may be chilled for an hour or two which will facilitate rolling.

Before starting work: Since mixing dough in the procedure below is a manual operation, the student should be especially mindful of personal cleanliness. Wash hands well before starting to mix. Examine mixing bowl. Make sure it is thoroughly clean and dry. Shortening should be at room temperature.

(1) Assemble the following ingredients:

Lb	Oz	
5		Unbleached pastry flour
2	8	Shortening

Lb	Oz	
	1 1/2	Salt
	3	Sugar
2	4	Milk

Note: A solution of 2 lb 4 oz cold water and 2 oz powdered milk may be used in place of fresh milk.

(2) Sift flour into a wide bowl.

(3) Dissolve sugar and salt in milk.

(4) Add shortening to bowl.

(5) Cut in the shortening by first breaking it with the finger tips and then rubbing the mixture lightly between palms of hands. Pieces of shortening should not exceed 1/4 in. in thickness.

(6) With one hand, slowly add milk in driblets, while tossing ingredients with other hand until dough is formed. All of the milk may not be needed. It may be practical to stop adding milk and toss ingredients with both hands to avoid excessively wet dough. The more the dough is tossed, the more the moist pieces of dough will tend to cling together.

(7) If additional milk is needed, add it sparingly. If the mixture seems too wet, dust it with a small amount of flour.

(8) Place dough on floured pan, and gently shape it into a rectangle about 3 in. thick. Cover dough with towel and refrigerate 1/2 to 1 hour.

Fresh Apple Pie   **10 9-in. Pies**

The dough prepared in the previous unit was left in a rectangle 3 in. thick. In order to make top and bottom crusts for 10 9-in. pies, follow this procedure:

(1) Cut 10 pieces of dough, each weighing 1 lb.

(2) Subdivide each of the 1-lb pieces into 2 pieces, one weighing 9 oz and the second weighing 7 oz. The 9-oz pieces will be used for the bottom crusts, the 7-oz pieces for the top crusts. Keep larger and smaller pieces separated.

(3) Shape each piece of dough into a ball; handle gently.

(4) Press each piece of dough into a flattened round on floured section of bench or on special canvas cloth dusted with bread flour. Pinch together any cracked or split edges.

Note: The canvas cloth and stockinet-covered rolling pin facilitate rolling pie crusts; they prevent dough from sticking to the bench or rolling pin and avoid use of too much flour in rolling.

(5) Roll 9-oz pieces of dough into circles of 10 1/2-in. diameter. Roll from center outward, lifting rolling pin at edge of dough. Push edges of dough in with palms of hands if necessary to keep dough cir-

cular. If edges show signs of breaking or separating, pinch together at once. Lift dough now and then to make sure it is not sticking. Place crusts in pie pans. Fit dough in loosely. Do not stretch dough. Trim overhanging edge to within 1/2 in. of pan.

(6) Roll 7-oz pieces of dough to 9 1/2-in diameter. Set aside. These will be used for top crust.

To aid in keeping top and bottom crusts from separating during baking, and to give the top crust a rich brown sheen, egg wash is used. This is a mixture of 2 eggs and 1/4 cup cold water stirred until blended. Leftover wash may be refrigerated for another use.

Before assembling pies: The preparation of the crusts just described may be delayed until the apple pie filling is prepared. If crusts are made in advance, cover them with a clean cloth or aluminum foil until needed. Examine pie pans. Make sure they are clean with no sign of rust. Plan to keep your workbench uncluttered so that the crusts and fillings can be handled efficiently.

(1) Assemble the following ingredients:

Pie crusts, tops and bottoms

Lb	Oz	
14		Apples such as Rome Beauties, Baldwins or greenings
4		Sugar
	3	Lemon juice
	8	Water
	1/4	Ground cinnamon
	1/8	Ground nutmeg
	8	Water
	3	Cornstarch
	1/2	Salt
1		Butter

(2) Peel and core applies. Cut apples from top to bottom into 12 or 16 wedges, depending upon the size of apples. Keep apples in salted water to prevent discoloration.

(3) After apples are cored and cut into wedges, drain them well.

(4) Place apples, sugar, lemon juice, 8 oz water, cinnamon and nutmeg into heavy saucepan. Toss ingredients with spoon to blend.

(5) Place saucepan over low flame. Cook only until apples are barely tender.

(6) Mix remaining 8 oz water, cornstarch and salt to a smooth paste.

(7) Slowly stir cornstarch mixture into apples.

(8) Cook 2 to 4 min or until syrup in pan is thickened. Avoid overcooking which may cause apples to break or turn to puree. Break butter into small pieces and add to hot mixture. Toss lightly to blend.

(9) Cool apple mixture to room temperature.

(10) Preheat oven to 425° F.

(11) Divide apple mixture among pies, allowing approx 2 lb filling per pan.

(12) Brush rim of bottom crust with egg wash.

(13) Cut a 1-in. hole in center of top crusts or slit center of crusts to permit steam to escape.

(14) Place top crusts over pie filling.

(15) Fold top edge of each crust under lower edge. Press with palm of hand to seal rims. Rims may be left plain, may be marked with tines of fork or may be fluted.

(16) Flute edges of dough if desired by pressing right index finger inside rim, left thumb and index finger on outside of rim.

(17) Brush top crusts with egg wash.

(18) Place pies in oven, spacing them at least 2 in. apart. Move pies during baking, if necessary, to brown uniformly. Check pies near rear or sides of oven for excessive browning. Baking time is usually 40 to 50 min.

(19) Remove pies from oven. Place on rack to cool. Allow to cool at least 1 hour before serving.

Note: In order to see if pies are finished baking, bakers sometimes move them very carefully to see if the pie is loose in the tin, indicating doneness. Students should only use this procedure under guidance of instructor or supervisor.

Apple Pie Filling (Canned Apples).—Pour 2 lb water, 3 lb 8 oz sugar and 1/8 oz salt into heavy saucepan. Stir well. Bring to a boil. Mix 2 lb water, 8 oz corn syrup and 8 oz cornstarch to a smooth paste. Gradually add to boiling liquid. Simmer until syrup is clear, stirring constantly. Remove from fire. Add 8 oz butter, broken into small pieces, 1/4 oz ground cinnamon and 2 oz lemon juice. Stir until butter melts. Add contents of 2 No. 10 cans of apples, carefully blending thickened syrup and apples. Use in place of fresh apples in apple pie recipe.

Suggested Supplementary Reading

AMENDOLA, J. E. 1960. The Baker's Manual for Quantity Baking and Pastry Baking. Ahrens Book Co., New York.

CARNACINA, L. 1968. Great Italian Cooking. Abradale Press, New York.

CROFT, J. H. 1969. Going Metric in Catering. Pergamon Press, Elmsford, New York.

DIAT, L. 1951. Sauces French and Famous. Rinehart and Co., New York.

DIAT, L. 1961. Gourmet's Basic French Cook Book. Gourmet, New York.

ESCOFFIER, A. 1969. The Escoffier Cook Book. Crown Publishers, New York.

FOLSOM, L. A. 1973. The Professional Chef, 4th Edition. Cahners Books, Boston.

GANCEL, J. 1969. Gancel's Culinary Encyclopedia of Modern Cooking. Radio City Book Store, New York.

HAINES, R. G. 1968. Food Preparation for Hotels, Restaurants and Cafeterias. American Technical Society, Chicago.

KOTSCHEVAR, L. H. 1974. Quantity Food Production. Cahners Books, Boston.

LEVIE, A. 1970. The Meat Handbook, 3rd Edition. AVI Publishing Co., Westport, Conn.

MONTAGNE, P. 1961. Larousse Gastronomique. Crown Publishers, New York.

PEPIN, J. 1976. La Technique: The Fundamental Techniques of Cooking. Quandrangle Books, New York.

SAULNIER, L., and BRUNET, E. 1970. Le Repertoire de la Cuisine. Radio City Book Store, New York.

SULTAN, W. J. 1977. Practical Baking, 2nd Edition. AVI Publishing Co., Westport, Conn.

TERRELL, M. E. 1971. Professional Food Preparation. John Wiley and Sons, New York.

Index

Other AVI Books

A GUIDE TO THE SELECTION, COMBINATION AND COOKING OF FOODS
Vol. 1   *Rietz*
Vol. 2   *Rietz and Wanderstock*

BAKERY TECHNOLOGY AND ENGINEERING
2nd Edition   *Matz*

COLD AND FREEZER STORAGE MANUAL
Woolrich and Hallowell

CONVENIENCE AND FAST FOOD HANDBOOK
Thorner

FABRICATED FOODS
Inglett

FOOD AND THE CONSUMER
Kramer

FOOD BEVERAGE SERVICE HANDBOOK
Thorner and Herzberg

FOOD FOR THOUGHT
Labuza

FOOD PROCESSING OPERATIONS
Vols. 1, 2, and 3   *Joslyn and Heid*

FOOD PRODUCTS FORMULARY
Vol. 1   *Komarik, Tressler and Long*
Vol. 2   *Tressler and Sultan*
Vol. 3   *Tressler and Woodroof*

FOOD QUALITY ASSURANCE
Gould

FOOD SANITATION
Guthrie

FOOD SERVICE FACILITIES PLANNING
Kazarian

FOOD SERVICE SCIENCE
Smith and Minor

HANDBOOK OF PACKAGE MATERIALS
Sacharow

ICE CREAM SERVICE HANDBOOK
Arbuckle

IMMUNOLOGICAL ASPECTS OF FOODS
Catsimpoolas

MENU PLANNING
Eckstein

MICROWAVE HEATING
2nd Edition   *Copson*

MODERN PASTRY CHEF
Vols. 1 and 2   *Sultan*

PRACTICAL BAKING
3rd Edition   *Sultan*

PRACTICAL BAKING MANUAL
Sultan

DATE DUE

NOV 2 5 1987			

DEMCO 38-297